Teaching Reading in Today's Elementary Schools

TENTH EDITION

a b c d e f g h i j k l m n o p q r s t u v w x y z

Betty D. Roe
Tennessee Technological University

Sandy H. Smith
Tennessee Technological University

Paul C. Burns
Late of University of Tennessee, Knoxville

WADSWORTH
CENGAGE Learning™

Australia • Brazil • Japan • Korea • Mexico • Singapore • Spain • United Kingdom • United States

WADSWORTH
CENGAGE Learning™

Teaching Reading in Today's Elementary Schools, Tenth Edition
Roe/Smith/Burns

Executive Publisher: Patricia Coryell

Senior Sponsoring Editor: Shani Fisher

Senior Development Editor: Lisa Mafrici

Senior Marketing Manager: Amy Whitaker

Marketing Coordinator: Samantha Abrams

Senior Project Editor: Shelley Dickerson

Art and Design: Jill Haber

Manufacturing Coordinator: Arethea L. Thomas

Production Service: Matrix Productions

Cover Design Manager: Anne S. Katzeff

Senior Photo Editor: Jennifer Meyer Dare

Senior Composition Buyer: Chuck Dutton

Cover Image: © Photodisc/Superstock

Compositor: GGS

"Seeing It in Practice" icon © Stockbyte/Getty Images

For product information and technology assistance, contact us at **Cengage Learning Customer & Sales Support, 1-800-354-9706.**

For permission to use material from this text or product, submit all requests online at **www.cengage.com/permissions.** Further permissions questions can be e-mailed to **permissionrequest@cengage.com.**

Library of Congress Control Number: 2008933324

ISBN-13: 978-0-618-93857-5

ISBN-10: 0-618-93857-5

Wadsworth Cengage Learning
10 Davis Drive
Belmont, CA 94002-3098
USA

Cengage Learning is a leading provider of customized learning solutions with office locations around the globe, including Singapore, the United Kingdom, Australia, Mexico, Brazil, and Japan. Locate your local office at: **www.cengage.com/global.**

Cengage Learning products are represented in Canada by Nelson Education, Ltd.

To learn more about Wadsworth, visit **www.cengage.com/wadsworth**

Purchase any of our products at your local college store or at our preferred online store **www.ichapters.com.**

Printed in Canada
2 3 4 5 6 7 11 10 09

Brief Contents

Contents

6   Meaning Vocabulary   173

7   Comprehension: Part 1   215

8 Comprehension: Part 2   259

9 Major Approaches and Materials for Reading Instruction   307

10 Language and Literature   355

11 Reading/Study Techniques 387

12 Reading in the Content Areas 423

Preface

Teaching reading in today's schools presents teachers with a number of interesting challenges. Teachers are expected to

- prepare all students to do well on mandatory, high-stakes standardized tests based on national, state, and local standards, as well as on those developed by professional associations, such as the International Reading Association and the National Council of Teachers of English.

- choose methods that are research based and represent best practices.

- work with an ever-changing array of technology with which many of the students are more comfortable than they themselves are.

- choose materials that are high quality, including appropriate trade books from the multitude of children's titles that are available.

- deal with an increasingly diverse population of students, including English-language learners and students with a variety of special instructional needs.

Our Mission

In this book, we strive to give aspiring teachers and inservice teachers the tools to meet these challenges in the following ways:

- *We address the skills and strategies that meet important standards* for reading instruction that are covered by the stressful high-risk tests.

- *We present a multitude of techniques* for teaching these skills and strategies that are based on best practice and a sound research base. Updated research is included in each chapter.

- *We embrace a balanced approach to reading instruction* to ensure that students learn not only how to recognize words, but also how to comprehend their reading materials and even enjoy the process. Theoretical background and the research base behind suggestions are included to give prospective teachers or inservice teachers a balanced perspective.

- *We provide cutting-edge information on the technology that is currently being used in schools* and by many of today's students outside of school.

- *We suggest materials that can be used to enhance reading instruction and reading across the curriculum*, including many trade books that add both information and interest value to lessons.

- *We show how teachers can differentiate instruction* to meet the diverse needs of the schools' populations.

We want to empower teachers to become informed decision makers rather than merely followers of plans provided by others. Toward that purpose, we offer information about many methods and materials for reading instruction, along with sound principles to help teachers choose among these options for their specific students and situations.

Our primary aim is to prepare teachers to develop students' abilities in comprehending text and reading fluently. But we are also committed to helping teachers foster their students' enjoyment of reading.

How Do We Accomplish Our Mission?

Here are the specific ways that we accomplish the goals outlined above:

1. By providing practical information through these *new* and *updated* special features:

   - **Seeing It in Practice**   presents vignettes of actual classroom use of the strategies presented, offering a true context for the strategies and materials discussed in the text.

   - **Putting It into Practice**   provides model activities, lesson plans, and teaching suggestions that your students can try in field experiences, student teaching, or in their own classrooms.

   - **New Teaching Tips**   highlight key ideas with quick instructional pointers.

   - **Numerous examples**   offer additional clarification for information in the text

   - **New Video Cases,**   available on the new Student Website, are keyed to pertinent material in the chapters. They allow students to see actual lessons being taught in real classrooms. They vividly show students how the material in the text is put to practice in the real world of teaching.

2. By offering *new* and *updated* aids to learning the concepts and strategies in the text, as follows:

   - **New Anticipation/Reaction Guides** at the beginning of each chapter help students activate their background knowledge, provide purposes for reading the material, and offer opportunities to reinforce the ideas as they return to the guides after reading.

   - **Key Vocabulary**   terms alert students to important concepts presented in the chapter. This vocabulary can be reviewed using the Flashcards available on the Student Website.

   - **Chapter Introductions**   in each chapter help students develop a mental set for reading the chapter and give them a framework into which they can fit the ideas they will read about.

   - **Marginal icons**   indicate the **textual ties** that provide references to topics that are integral to the entire text. The textual ties are

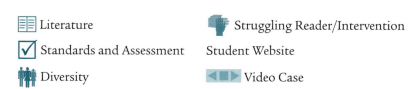

- **Time for Reflection** is a learning aid located at strategic points throughout each chapter to encourage readers to think about the subject matter that has been presented and decide where they stand on debated issues.

- **For Your Journal . . .** presents topics that students can write about in order to further their understanding of the ideas and methods presented in the chapter.

- **. . . And Your Portfolio** presents ideas to include in a portfolio for assessment purposes. Included in this feature are questions that link to Video Cases on the new Student Website.

- A **Glossary** contains meanings of specialized terms used in this book.

- The **Epilogue: Linking It Up** contains a teaching strategies reference guide that cross-references specific instructional needs with appropriate assessments and possible interventions.

3. By redesigning each chapter, including important new material, such as the following:

  - New and revised information on theories and research behind the information

  - New strategies and techniques—while retaining solid, time-tested ideas and procedures—within the practical framework of previous editions

  - New information on current materials and techniques, integrated with valid traditional ideas

  - New focus on English-language learners

  - New focus on struggling readers

  - Cutting-edge technology for education, integrated with more traditional technologies

We Also Provide for the Instructor

We have *expanded* and *improved* the supplemental materials that accompany this text. They include the following:

- **Instructor's Resource Manual** This teaching aid offers instructors chapter outlines, key vocabulary terms and definitions, ideas for instructional media, suggested teaching strategies, and suggested readings. It also has some supplementary content that some instructors may want to add to lectures. The Instructor's Resource Manual is available on the Instructor's Website or in print upon request.

- **Testing CD**   This is a full test bank for instructors in computerized form for ease of use. Assessment items including essay and objective questions are provided for each chapter, as well as ideas for implementing authentic assessment.

- **TeacherPrepSPACE Student and Instructor Websites**   Students and instructors can access valuable content any time via the companion website http://www.cengage.com/education/roe. Some content may be passkey protected. These sites provide additional pedagogical support and resources including self-testing questions, case studies, Video Cases (described fully in the next section), links to technology resources, PowerPoint slides, and more.

- **Video Cases**   Available online (and also in a DVD of all sixty Video Cases to adopters on request) and organized by topic, each "case" is a four- to six-minute module consisting of video and audio files presenting actual classroom scenarios that depict the complex problems and opportunities that teachers face every day. The video and audio clips are accompanied by "artifacts" to provide background information and allow preservice teachers to experience true classroom applications in their multiple dimensions.

- **Eduspace**   For instructors who use a course management system, Eduspace, Cengage Learning's Course Management System, offers a flexible, interactive online platform to help them communicate with students, organize material, evaluate student work, and track results in a powerful gradebook. In addition to the gradebook and other course management tools, Eduspace includes special interactive components such as videos, a discussion board, reflective journal questions, test items, and additional materials to aid students in studying and reflecting on what they have learned.

Audience for the Text

Teaching Reading in Today's Elementary Schools is designed for use in introductory reading education courses for both preservice and inservice elementary school classroom teachers. It also will meet the needs of introductory courses for teachers preparing to become reading specialists and administrators who need to understand reading instruction to serve as instructional leaders in their schools' reading programs.

The large amount of the school day spent on reading instruction in the primary grades makes this content especially important to the primary-grade teacher. In addition, in all grades, but especially in fourth grade and above, students must handle reading assignments in the content areas as well as in reading periods, making our coverage of content-area reading and study skills essential for teachers in these grades. Our book—particularly the chapters on content-area reading and reading/study techniques—contains information that will help teachers implement reading instruction across the curriculum.

A Tour Through *Teaching Reading in Today's Elementary Schools*

Let us take you on a tour through each chapter of this tenth edition of our book. But first, a few general comments.

Those of you who have used earlier editions will recognize that this edition represents a substantial revision. As always, the research base is fully updated. Topics of recent concern, such as standards-based instruction, technology uses in reading instruction (especially Internet applications), effective assessment, high-stakes testing, and ways to help diverse populations (especially English-language learners and struggling readers) learn to read receive special attention. To increase utility to students and instructors, some reorganization of chapters and internal information has also taken place; for example, the area of word recognition, covered in one chapter in last edition, has been divided into two chapters to allow better coverage of this essential area. Material from last edition's chapter on organization for instruction is now integrated into other chapters where the need for the patterns becomes evident.

We have streamlined popular practical features from last edition into two categories: "Seeing It in Practice," for descriptions of actual classroom situations, and "Putting It into Practice," for techniques to try in practicum and field experiences or with regular classroom teaching assignments. These features have been updated with some new situations. We have also added short "Teaching Tips" throughout the text. We provide new references to pertinent lessons on the popular "Read•Write•Think" website and new connections to "Video Cases" on the Student Website that show techniques in action in real classrooms.

Now, have a look at the valuable material in each chapter.

- **Chapter 1: The Reading Act** discusses components of the reading act and theories related to reading to provide a framework for the material to come. It provides additional focus for the reader with fifteen practical, time-tested principles of teaching reading. This edition has increased emphasis on technology and reading and expanded information related to students with special needs, especially English-language learners (ELLs) and struggling readers.

- **Chapter 2: Assessment and Intervention** was moved nearer the beginning of the text to emphasize the importance of basing instruction on assessment. It focuses on assessment of student progress with both standardized tests and informal assessments of reading performance and on assessment of text materials. Some special intervention programs also receive attention. This edition has increased focus on standards of performance and high-stakes testing.

- **Chapter 3: Emergent and Developing Literacy** not only presents information on the stage of emergent literacy, but in this edition also includes the stage of developing literacy. We decided to include developing literacy because students advance through these stages at various developmental rates, and teachers of young children have to be ready to deal with a range of abilities. This edition also has additional suggestions for meeting the needs of young students who are struggling with the reading and writing processes.

- **Chapter 4: Overview of Word-Recognition Approaches** presents an overview of the five major word-recognition techniques and offers in-depth detail about sight words, context clues, structural analysis, and use of the dictionary for word recognition. In this edition, we added new coverage of the incremental rehearsal technique and expanded coverage of the importance of context for learning sight words and methods for helping diverse populations of students learn word-recognition strategies.

- **Chapter 5: Phonics for Word Recognition** offers in-depth coverage of phonics, a problem area for many prospective teachers, and some generalizations related to structural analysis. In this edition, we incorporated material that was previously in a chapter appendix to make it more accessible. We expanded the discussions of onsets and rimes and decodable text. Research on exemplary teachers and the positive effects of invented spelling on phonemic analysis skills also receive attention here. A growing area of concern that we discuss in this edition is the type of problems that ELLs have because of different phonemes in different languages.

- **Chapter 6: Meaning Vocabulary** includes a wealth of updated information about concept development and teaching word meanings. This edition has new examples and new material on needs of ELLs for academic vocabulary, use of cognates to help ELLs with English, the three tiers of vocabulary words encountered in texts, encouragement of word consciousness, and the use of vocabulary cartoons. New literature selections are also suggested. There is new coverage on using the semantic impressions technique and expanded coverage of thesauruses, use of literature selections, and problems faced by ELLs.

Comprehension strategies and skills are covered in two chapters because comprehension is the goal of all good reading instruction. It is far too complex to fit into a single chapter; the chapters are both necessary for a complete understanding of the area. They have only been separated for ease of study.

- **Chapter 7: Comprehension: Part 1** begins with basic background about comprehension instruction. It addresses aspects related to the reader, the reading situation, the text, and the interaction of these three areas. Then it discusses prereading, during-reading, postreading, and general strategies for comprehension instruction. New separate sections look at working with ELLs, working with struggling readers, and considering the physical context for reading.

- **Chapter 8: Comprehension: Part 2** discusses four types of comprehension: literal, interpretive, critical, and creative. It also addresses questioning, a topic of concern for many teachers because of its value in instruction and its difficulty. This edition has expanded sections on critical literacy, visualization, questioning, working with ELLs, and working with struggling readers. It has new information on increasing comprehension through use of visual art, having students design their own activities during a choice time to increase motivation, and the Know-Predict-Wonder technique. It also has several new examples.

- **Chapter 9: Major Approaches and Materials for Reading Instruction** gives students information on basal reading series, literature-based approaches to reading instruction, the language experience approach, programmed reading and computer use, and eclectic approaches. This edition presents new material on modifications of sustained silent reading, use of multigenre picture books, and research on literature-based approaches. It has expanded material on the language experience approach, meeting the needs of struggling readers and ELLs (two new examples), and on guided reading. It has new examples on literature-based instruction and the language experience approach.

- **Chapter 10: Language and Literature** focuses on language development and integration of the language arts. This edition has new material on classroom organization and combining music with literature and language instruction. It also provides additional information on reading aloud, multicultural literature, and a culturally responsive classroom environment.

- **Chapter 11: Reading/Study Techniques** covers study methods, flexibility of reading habits, location of information, organizational techniques, metacognition, and graphic aids. This edition has new suggestions for teaching flexibility of rate, summarization, understanding of graphic aids, and preparation for taking high-stakes tests.

- **Chapter 12: Reading in the Content Areas** compares the difficulty of reading content texts with the difficulty of reading basal readers and discusses the difficulty of supplementary materials, alternatives to the use of content-area texts, general techniques for content-area reading, and specific difficulties of reading in language arts, social studies, mathematics, and science and health materials. This edition has new material on dealing with the structure of content-area texts, importance of frontloading information, dealing with content-area vocabulary, curriculum-based readers' theater, content-area sustained silent reading, use of manipulatives, effective use of appropriate trade books, use of various forms of drama in content classes, and use of picture books in all grades. There are new suggestions for literature to use in teaching content-area subjects. Extensive coverage is given to assisting ELLs and struggling readers with content-area reading.

- **Chapter 13: Use of Technology for Literacy Learning** addresses cutting-edge topics, such as new literacy concepts related to technology use, the role of the teacher in use of technology for literacy learning, and technology as a tool for literacy instruction and learning. This edition has expanded material on WebQuests; visual literacy (viewing and visually representing); assistive technology; production of multimedia products, such as movies and presentations;

concerns with Internet use, such as exposure to inappropriate material and language and plagiarism from Internet resources; and applications for ELLs. It offers new material on blogs, wikis, podcasts, interactive digital whiteboards, concept-mapping software, an approach to writing instruction called "Authoring with Video"; development of multimodal movies; concerns about standards for technology and equal access; and connections of hypertext and postmodern books. It has new references to websites and computer software.

- **The Epilogue: Linking It Up,** which is new to this edition, is located at the end of the book. It provides a follow-up to the assessment chapter. It lists key assessment strategies and links them to the book's discussions of appropriate related instructional techniques. This epilogue will provide a quick, visually accessible guide for teacher education candidates preparing for pedagogy in reading examinations such as the PRAXIS II Series.

All chapters have increased emphasis on key topics that have extensive application across the entire reading curriculum—literature, standards and assessment, diversity, and struggling readers—although the topic of standards and assessment is also represented in detail in Chapter 2 and literature is discussed in Chapters 9 and 10. **Marginal icons** that represent textual ties among these topics are described under "Features of the Text."

Acknowledgments

We are indebted to many people for their assistance in the preparation of this text. In particular, we would like to recognize the contribution that Paul C. Burns made to the first and second editions of this book and the contribution that Elinor P. Ross made to the third through seventh editions of the book.

Although we would like to acknowledge the many teachers and students whose inspiration was instrumental in the development of this book, we cannot name all of them. We offer recognition to the following reviewers:

Vi Cain Alexander, *Stephen F. Austin State University;* Linda J. Armstrong, *University of North Alabama;* Barbara Bartholomew, *California State University, Bakersfield;* Merry Boggs, *Tarleton State University;* Timothy J. Braun, *Loyola Marymount University;* Thomas A. Caron, *East Carolina University;* Julia E. De Carlo, *C.W. Post Campus, Long Island University;* Betty J. Conaway, *Baylor University;* Marie Ann Donovan, *De Paul University;* Laurie Elish-Piper, *Northern Illinois University;* Alice J. Feret, *East Carolina University;* Kathy R. Fox, *University of North Carolina, Wilmington;* Alan M. Frager, *Miami University;* Susan Gapp, *University of South Dakota;* Jennifer K. Geringer, *University of Northern Colorado;* Caroline M. Hagen, *Jamestown College;* Marjorie R. Hancock, *Kansas State University;* Patricia Higgins, *Kentucky State University;* Frances M. Howard, *Georgia State University;* G. Peter Ienatsch, *University of Texas of the Permian Basin;* Nancy E. Jurenka, *Central Washington University;* Cathleen C. March, *D'Youville College;* Kim McDowell, *Wichita State University;* Elisa Michals, *Sacramento State University;* Ann de Onix, *Montana State University;* Beth Rice, *Nova Southeastern University;* Susan M. Rose, *Slippery Rock University of Pennsylvania;*

Judith M. Sherman, *Hood College;* Corlis Snow, *Delta State University;* Ezra L. Stieglitz, *Rhode Island College;* Marion P. Turkish, *William Patterson University;* Janice McCarthy Voss, *Eastern Michigan University;* Beth R. Walizer, *Fort Hays State University;* Elizabeth Harden Willner, *Oklahoma City University;* Nancy L. Wright, *University of Houston Clear Lake;* and Liliana B. Zecker, *DePaul University.*

In addition, we express appreciation to those who have granted permission to use sample materials or citations from their respective works. Credit for these contributions has been given in the source lines.

The invaluable assistance provided by Michael Roe in proofreading is greatly appreciated. Grateful acknowledgment is also given to our editors—Sheralee Connors, Lisa Mafrici, Shani Fisher, Shelley Dickerson, Betty Duncan, and Sara Planck—for their assistance throughout the development and production of the book.

Betty D. Roe
Sandy H. Smith

The Reading Act

Few adults would question the importance of reading to effective functioning in our complex, technological world. Educators have long made reading instruction a priority in the school curriculum, especially in the primary grades. As students enter the middle grades, their exposure to a systematic approach to reading instruction often decreases, although it should not. To develop sufficient reading strategies and higher-order thinking skills, students need instruction in appropriate reading skills and strategies at all levels. Strategies are deliberate actions designed to allow readers to decode and comprehend text. When repetition of good strategies occurs enough to make their application effortless, the reader has acquired a reading skill (Afflerbach, Pearson, and Paris, 2008).

One task that teachers face is to help students see the importance of acquiring reading abilities for performing everyday tasks effectively and the value of reading as a source of information, enjoyment, and recreation. To accomplish this task effectively, teachers need to know something about the reading act, some useful principles of reading instruction, and some of the theories on which instructional practices in reading are based. They should understand the need for a comprehensive, **balanced approach to reading instruction** and the place of reading instruction in the overall language arts curriculum. Teachers must be knowledgeable about many reading approaches and strategies so that they can match approaches and teaching strategies to the needs of students. Research has shown repeatedly that the teacher has more influence on the learning of students in the classroom than any particular method (Blair, Rupley, and Nichols, 2007).

Reading is a complex act that can be viewed as having two parts: the *reading process* and the *reading product*. The reading process has many related aspects—sensory and perceptual, sequential, experiential, thinking, learning, association, affective, and constructive—that combine to produce the reading product. However, the sequences involved in the reading process are not always the same, and different readers do not always perform them in the same way. When these aspects blend and interact harmoniously, good communication takes place between the writer and reader. Good communication is the product of reading and is the result of comprehension of the written message.

This chapter emphasizes the importance of reading and analyzes the reading product and process. The product is discussed first because communication, whether it is to understand a note that was written to oneself or material that has been written by someone else, is the only purpose for reading. The chapter also describes three theories of the reading process and presents some sound principles for reading instruction, with explanatory comments.

ANTICIPATION/REACTION GUIDE

BEFORE
A, **D** or **?**

AFTER
C or **I** (for initial
A or **D** answers)
A or **D**
(for initial **?** answers)

Directions: Before you read this chapter, complete the following anticipation/ reaction guide. In the space before each statement, write **A** if you agree; **D** if you disagree; or **?** if you don't know. After you have read the chapter, complete the guide again to show what you have discovered in the chapter. In the space after each statement, mark whether you were initially correct (with a **C**) or incorrect (with an **I**). Write the letter for the correct answer (**A**) or (**D**) in the space for the statements that you initially marked with a question mark (**?**).

1. Reading is a complex of many skills.

2. The more meaningful that learning is to a child, the more rapidly associative learning takes place.

3. Word calling and reading are synonymous.

4. There is only one correct way to teach reading.

5. Assessing the reading problems of every student in a class is a waste of a teacher's valuable time.

6. Reading and the other language arts are closely interrelated.

7. Teachers should stress reading for enjoyment as well as for information.

8. Current theories about reading account for all aspects of the reading process.

9. Bottom-up processing refers to processing printed text by examining the printed symbols, with little input being required from the reader.

10. According to an interactive model of reading, parallel processing of information from print and from background knowledge takes place.

11. Reading involves constructing the meaning of a written passage.

12. Metacognitive processes are self-monitoring processes.

13. Transactive theories of the reading process take into account the reader, the text, and the context in which the reading takes place.

14. According to current research and theory, children learn better when they can associate new material with prior knowledge.

15. To promote literacy development, teachers should encourage parents of English-language learners to speak only English at home.

16. Today's students need to be proficient in using technology.

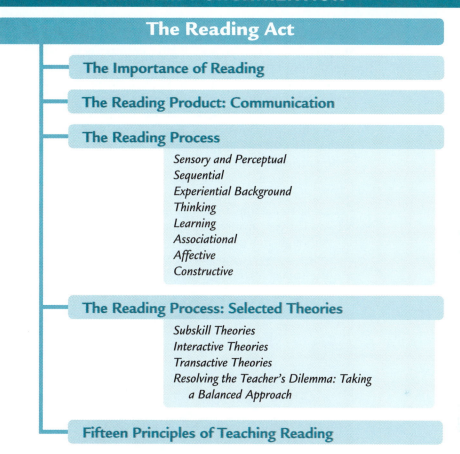

CHAPTER 1 ORGANIZATION

The Reading Act

- **The Importance of Reading**

- **The Reading Product: Communication**

- **The Reading Process**

  Sensory and Perceptual
  Sequential
  Experiential Background
  Thinking
  Learning
  Associational
  Affective
  Constructive

- **The Reading Process: Selected Theories**

  Subskill Theories
  Interactive Theories
  Transactive Theories
  Resolving the Teacher's Dilemma: Taking a Balanced Approach

- **Fifteen Principles of Teaching Reading**

The Importance of Reading

The ability to read is vital to functioning effectively in a literate society. Many children come to school with a sense of the importance of reading in their lives. Unfortunately, not all students arrive at school with this vision, and those who do not need to be helped to acquire it before they will be motivated to learn. Learning to read takes effort, and children who fail to see the value of reading in their personal activities will be less likely to exert this effort than those who do see the benefits.

Fortunately, teachers should have little trouble demonstrating to students that reading is important. Every aspect of life involves reading. Road signs direct travelers to particular destinations, inform drivers of hazards, and alert people to traffic regulations. Other useful items to read include menus in restaurants, labels on cans, printed advertisements, newspapers, and magazines. Reading situations are inescapable. Even very young children can be helped to see the need to read the signs on restrooms, the labels on desks in their classrooms, and the labeled areas for supplies. In fact, these young children are often eager to learn to read and are ready to attack the task enthusiastically.

Reading tasks become increasingly complex as students advance through the grades, and continual attention must be given to these tasks. For example, teachers can introduce middle-grade students to many needs for literacy skills through career-education activities. Students can choose occupations that interest them and analyze the reading skills that each occupation requires. Taking field trips to work environments and listening to resource people speak can help students see how people in different professions use reading in their jobs. Students may also analyze reading demands in a wide variety of recreational (for example, playing football) and functional (for example, ordering items from a catalog) activities. In many cases, the reading activities involve such applications as use of the Internet and e-mail.

Although functional reading is important to everyday living, reading for enjoyment is also an important goal. Teachers must attempt to show students that reading can be interesting to them for reasons other than strictly utilitarian ones.

First- and second-grade students read books during classroom independent reading time.

© Ellen Senisi/The Image Works

Students may read for relaxation, vicarious adventure, or aesthetic pleasure as they immerse themselves in tales of other times and places or those of the here and now. They may also read to obtain information about areas of interest or hobbies to fill their leisure time.

The Reading Product: Communication

The product of the reading act is the communication of thoughts and emotions by the writer to the reader, resulting in the reader's own understanding of ideas that the writer has put into print. Communication results from the reader's construction of meaning through integrating his or her prior knowledge with the information presented in the text.

Today's readers have a wealth of knowledge available to them because they can read material that others wrote in years past. They can read of events and accomplishments that occur in other parts of the globe. Knowledge of great discoveries need not be laboriously passed from person to person by word of mouth; such knowledge is available to all who can read.

Reading is also a means of current communication. A note may tell a child that Mother has gone to the store or inform a baby-sitter about where to call in case of an emergency. A memo from a person's employer can identify the work to be done. An e-mail or text message from a friend may announce an impending visit. Reading can be a way to share another person's insights, joys, sorrows, or creative endeavors. Reading can also enable people to find places that they have never visited before (through maps and directional signs), to take advantage of bargains (through advertisements), or to avert disaster (through warning signs). It is difficult to imagine what life would be like without this vital means of communication.

Communication depends on comprehension, so teachers should teach reading as a thoughtful, critical, and creative process that students can master with appropriate strategies (Santman, 2006). Each aspect of the reading process contributes to the degree of comprehension attained. Word-recognition strategies are essential, but comprehension involves much more than decoding symbols into sounds; the reader must construct meaning while interacting with the printed page. Some people mistakenly view reading as a single skill, that of pronouncing words, rather than a combination of many skills and strategies that lead to the derivation of meaning. Thinking of reading as pronouncing words may have fostered the inappropriate

TEACHING TIP

Reading for Enjoyment

As a teacher, you can take the following steps to help your students see reading as a pleasurable activity:

- Read to your students each day about a variety of themes and topics, from a variety of genres, and from the works of many authors.

- Make many books available for students to look at and read, and set aside time for them to read from self-selected materials.

- Give students opportunities to share information from and reactions to their reading in both oral and written forms.

- Encourage students to relate the things that they are reading to their own experiences.

- Share with students the pleasure that you get from your recreational reading. Let them see you reading something you enjoy during recreational reading periods.

Time for Reflection

What can you add to the list of ways to demonstrate to students the importance of reading?

Can you think of more suggestions about how to show students the enjoyment of reading?

Time for Reflection

Some people believe that just teaching children to pronounce words allows them to achieve communication with the authors of written materials.

What do _you_ think, and why?

practice of using a reading period for extended drill on word calling in which the teacher asks each child to "read" aloud while classmates follow in their books (known as round-robin reading). Some students may be good pronouncers in such a situation but fail to understand anything they have read. Although pronunciation is important, reading involves much more.

Teachers who realize that all aspects of the reading process affect comprehension of written material can more easily identify children's reading strengths and weaknesses and, as a result, offer effective instructional programs based on students' needs. Faulty performance related to any aspect of the reading process may result in reduced comprehension or total lack of comprehension.

The Reading Process

Reading is an extremely complex process. As Frederick McDonald put it, reading is an act that "demands complex sets of responses—some of them cognitive, some attitudinal, and some manipulative (Downing, 1982, p. 535). When they read, students must be able to

- Perceive the symbols set before them and interpret what they see (_sensory and perceptual aspect_).
- Follow the linear, logical, and grammatical patterns of the written words (_sequential aspect_).
- Relate words back to direct experiences to give the words meaning (_experiential aspect_).
- Make inferences from and evaluate the material (_thinking aspect_).
- Remember what they learned in the past and incorporate new ideas and facts (_learning aspect_).
- Recognize the connections between symbols and sounds, between words and what they represent (_association aspect_).
- Deal with personal interests and attitudes that affect the task of reading (_affective aspect_).
- Put everything together to make sense of the material (_constructive aspect_).

Whereas reading can be broken down into subskills, reading takes place only when these subskills are put together into an integrated whole, resulting in fluent reading (reading "smoothly, without hesitation and with comprehension" [Harris and Hodges, 1995, p. 85]). Performing subskills individually is not reading. As Downing (1982) points out, "Practice in integration is supplied only by performing the whole skill ... one learns to read by reading" (p. 537). Therefore, teachers must include time for actual reading for meaning in addition to individual skill instruction.

Technology has affected the teaching of reading and other literacy skills by serving as a vehicle for such instruction. However, it has also added to the literacy

EXAMPLE 1.1 Aspects of the Reading Process

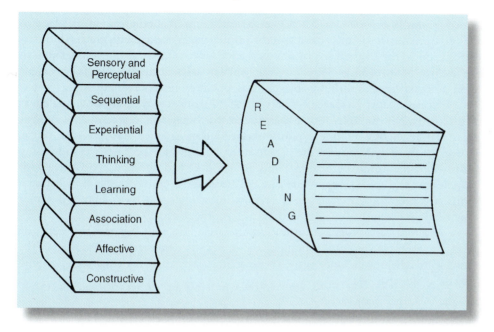

strategies needed for functioning in today's society. Readers must now interpret information in forms other than purely linear printed text and still pictures. They must also deal with sounds, video clips, and animations. They must navigate hypertext and hypermedia environments that allow nonlinear access to presented material through imbedded links. (See Chapter 13 for discussions of hypertext and hypermedia.)

Not only is the reading process complex, but each aspect of the process is also complex. As Example 1.1 shows, the whole process can be likened to a series of books, with each aspect represented by a hefty volume. To completely comprehend the subject matter, a student would have to integrate information from all of the volumes. The series would be more important than any individual volume.

Sensory and Perceptual Aspects of Reading

The reading process begins with a sensory impression, either visual (sight) or tactile (touch). A normal reader perceives the printed symbol visually; a blind reader uses the tactile sense. (Discussion of the blind reader is beyond the scope of this text.) The auditory sense is also very important because a beginning stage in reading is the association of printed symbols with spoken language. A person with poor auditory discrimination may find some reading skills, especially those involved with phonics, difficult to master.

 DIVERSITY

Perception involves interpretation of the sensory impressions that reach the brain. Each person processes and reorganizes sensory data according to his or her background of experiences. When a person is reading, the brain receives visual sensations from the words and phrases on the printed page. Visual perception is the interpretation of these visual sensations as the reader recognizes and gives meaning to these words and phrases. This is accomplished by associating them with the reader's previous experiences with the objects, ideas, or emotions represented.

Because readers' experiences vary, different readers may interpret a single text differently. For example, seeing the printed words *apple pie* can result not only in a visual image of a pie but also in a recollection of its smell and taste. Of course, to make these associations, the person must have prior experience with the thing named by the words. Because different people have had different experiences with apple pies, and apple pies can vary in smell, taste, and appearance, people will attach different meanings to *apple pie*. Therefore, individuals will have slightly different perceptions when they encounter these or any other words.

Auditory perception is also important in reading when readers first turn the visual symbols into sounds (phonic analysis) and then interpret the meanings of the oral words that result. Once again, they use their past experiences to attach meaning to the words they hear.

▶ Vision

The reading act imposes many visual demands on children. Reading requires **visual acuity** (sharpness of vision). Readers must be able to focus their eyes on a page of print that is generally fourteen to twenty inches away, as well as on various signs and visual displays that may be twenty or more feet away. Many first graders have not yet attained 20/20 vision.

DIVERSITY

Children also must learn to move their eyes across a page in a left-to-right progression and to execute a return sweep from the end of one line to the beginning of the next line. This is a difficult, fine-motor movement. Children who have not yet mastered the process will find themselves rereading and skipping lines, both of which impede comprehension. Although teachers often attempt to correct faulty eye movements, sometimes such movements are symptoms of other problems (for example, poor muscle coordination or poor vocabulary) that are the actual causes of the reading difficulties. When the other problems are removed, these symptoms usually disappear.

Some considerations for helping students with visual difficulties follow:

- *Farsightedness.* Farsighted students can see better at a distance than they can up close. These students may learn reading skills more easily by working on charts and whiteboards than by using workbooks and textbooks. Teachers should avoid requiring farsighted students to do a great deal of uninterrupted reading, and they should also use large print for class handouts. Publishers make accommodations for farsightedness in young readers by using large font sizes for their materials.

- *Nearsightedness.* Nearsighted students are able to see better up close than they can at a distance. Although nearsighted students may do well when working

Prescription glasses can correct many eye disorders that may interfere with reading.
© Mug Shots/Corbis

with books, they often cannot see well enough to respond to directions or exercises written on charts or whiteboards.

- *Astigmatism.* Some children may have the eye disorder astigmatism, which results in blurred vision. This problem, as well as nearsightedness and farsightedness, can generally be corrected with glasses.

- *Eye-coordination problems.* If a student's eyes do not work well together, he or she may see two images instead of one. Sometimes when this occurs, the child manages to suppress the image from one eye. If suppression continues over a period of time, he or she may lose sight in that eye entirely. If suppression occurs for only short periods, the child may lose the appropriate place on the page when reading, becoming confused and frustrated.

Visual perception involves identification and interpretation of size, shape, and relative position of letters and words. **Visual discrimination** is the ability to see likenesses and differences in visual forms (for example, between the printed words *big* and *dig*). It is an important part of visual perception because many letters (for example, among *b*, *d*, *p*, and *q*) and words (for example, *big* and *dig*) are very similar in form but very different in pronunciation and meaning. Accurate identification and interpretation of words results from detecting such small variations in form. A child may have good visual acuity (see images clearly) but be unable to discriminate well visually. Teachers can help children develop this skill through carefully planned

DIVERSITY

TEACHING TIP

Visual Accommodations

Refer children to vision specialists if you observe such symptoms as squinting, closing or covering one eye, rubbing eyes frequently, or making frequent errors when copying board work. Before they receive assistance from these specialists, you can make provisions for children who have uncorrected nearsightedness, farsightedness, or astigmatism by adjusting lighting and seating, providing tape-recorded stories and books with large print, and reading orally to the whole class frequently. Encourage students who have trouble tracking print with their eyes to follow along the line of print as you use a pointer when sharing big books or reading material from the board. You can also have students use pointers, highlight tape, or index cards placed below each line of print to help them follow print during individual reading of books.

TEACHING TIP

Auditory Accommodations

Refer students to hearing specialists if you observe such symptoms as inattentiveness in class, requests for repetition of verbal information, frowning when trying to listen, or turning the head so that one ear is always turned toward the speaker. In addition, when providing reading instruction for students with auditory difficulties, speak slowly, clearly, and with adequate volume; seat the child as far as possible from distracting sounds; and supplement reading lessons with visual aids.

activities (discussed in Chapter 3). The final step in visual perception, of course, is attaching meaning to the words by using past experiences as described earlier.

▶ Hearing

Children must be able to hear clearly (have adequate **auditory acuity**) and have adequate **auditory discrimination,** the ability to detect the differences among spoken sounds, in order to learn how to associate **phonemes** (individual speech sounds) with **graphemes** (printed symbols such as letters or letter combinations) for phonics instruction. Students who cannot discriminate among the different sounds represented by graphic symbols (for example, tell the difference in the spoken words *big* and *dig*) will be unable to make the sound-symbol associations necessary for decoding unfamiliar words. (See Chapters 3 and 5 for more on phonemes and sound-symbol associations.)

Students who cannot differentiate among sounds will find the use of phonic analysis frustrating and therefore will need to accommodate by using other word-recognition strategies. Thus, deaf students and students with limited hearing are partially or completely deprived of some methods of word identification. Students whose hearing is temporarily impaired by problems related to colds, allergies, or other physical problems may also experience difficulties.

Sequential Aspects of Reading

Reading is sequential in several ways. Readers must learn to follow the sequence, or order, in which printed material is arranged. English-language material generally appears on a printed page in a left-to-right, top-to-bottom sequence. A person's eyes must follow this sequence to read this

DIVERSITY

material. Learning to follow this sequential pattern can be a new challenge for children who have not been exposed to many printed materials or who have experience with different sequences used in other languages. Readers occasionally regress, or look back to earlier words and phrases, as they read. Although these regressions momentarily interrupt the reading process as the reader checks the accuracy of initial impressions, the reader eventually returns to the left-to-right, top-to-bottom sequence.

Another reason why reading is a sequential process is that oral language is strung together in a sequential pattern of grammar and logic. Because written language is a way of representing speech, it is expressed in the same manner. To understand written language, the reader must be able to follow the grammatical and logical patterns of spoken language.

The sequence of reading text from page to page in a book, front to back, has predominated in years past. Today, hypertext and hypermedia (see Chapter 13) computer materials allow random access to information in an electronic document. This random access presents new challenges to students because they must learn to navigate multiple sequences of nonlinear text and still retain the organizational sense necessary for understanding the topic. (However, on most individual pages of hypertext material, the print is generally still arranged in a left-to-right, top-to-bottom sequence.) Current textbooks also have begun to vary from standard formats somewhat because they have more sidebars. In addition, some children's literature selections, such as *The Magic School Bus* series, have several levels and types of texts presented on the same page.

Experiential Background and Reading

As students have different experiences, they develop clusters of information about things (such as apple pies), places (such as restaurants or airports), or ideas (such as justice or democracy). These information clusters are called **schemata.** Every person has many schemata. Reading comprehension has been described as the act of relating textual information to existing schemata (Pearson et al., 1979). Good readers can skillfully integrate information in the text with prior knowledge about the topic, but poor readers may either overemphasize the symbols in the text or rely too heavily on their prior knowledge of the topic. Poor readers who focus primarily on the text may produce nonsense words that are graphically similar to the ones in the text. This occurs because such readers are not attempting to connect what they read to their experiences or to demand sense from reading. Poor readers who depend too much on prior knowledge may fail to make sufficient use of clues in the text to come close to the intended message (R. C. Anderson, Hiebert, Scott, and Wilkinson, 1985).

Students obtain much of their prior knowledge outside of school from parents and caregivers. Some parents and caregivers provide diverse experiences by conversing freely with children, reading to them, telling them stories, letting them listen to family elders tell stories, traveling with them, showing them pictures, or taking them to movies and on trips. Other parents, for many reasons that are often beyond their control, do not or cannot offer such diverse experiences to their children. By the time they enter school, children with more extensive background experiences have had more chances to develop understanding of the vocabulary and concepts that they encounter in reading than have children with limited experiences. For example, students who have actually been in airports are more likely to be able to attach appropriate meaning to the word *airport* when they encounter it in reading selections than students who have not been to an airport.

Direct experiences with places, things, and processes described in reading materials make understanding of the materials much more likely. We want to emphasize that the children who have had fewer opportunities for early development of experiential background needed for many school activities are not necessarily less able than the others, and provision of needed experiences may result in rapid progress for many. One of the responsibilities for teachers in the early school years is to help these children reach their full potential.

DIVERSITY

Students from other countries often come to the United States with experiential backgrounds that are vastly different from those of the U.S. natives. Students from different countries comprehend and remember best the texts that are most culturally familiar and that have characters who are like them (Drucker, 2003). Students from different parts of the United States or different neighborhoods within the same city may also have vastly different experiences; for example, students from Boston and from New Orleans or students from urban, suburban, and rural areas will come to school with different schemata. Some of these schemata will match the material that is typically used in school, and others will not. The background experiences of all students should be understood by teachers if they are to serve students' educational needs. (Chapters 6 and 7 present more information about schemata.)

Sumida and Meyer (2006) believe that "dominant, mainstream curricula fails to honor students who come to school socialized and prepared with a different, yet equally important set of cultural values and beliefs" (pp. 438–439). Having students share information about their cultures with their classmates can be helpful in honoring the knowledge that these students bring to the class and connecting it to regular class activities (Schwarzer, Haywood, and Lorenzen, 2003). This sharing can be a two-way street and can help the new arrivals develop some background information about the mainstream culture.

Vicarious (indirect) **experiences** also enhance conceptual development. Examples of vicarious experiences that can build concept development are hearing other people tell of or read about a subject; seeing photos or a video of a place, event, or activity; and reading about a topic. Because vicarious experiences involve fewer senses than do direct, concrete experiences, the concepts gained from them may be developed less fully.

Teachers can help broaden all children's concrete experiences through field trips, displays of objects, and class demonstrations. They can also help by providing rich vicarious experiences such as photographs, videos, electronic recordings, computer software, classroom discussions, and storytelling and story-reading sessions.

If reading materials contain vocabulary, concepts, or sentence structures that are unfamiliar to students, teachers must help them develop the background they need to understand the materials. Because students' experiential backgrounds differ, some need more preparation for particular selections than others do, and some may actually need different materials that are more appropriate for them.

English-Language Learners (ELLs)

Some strategies that you can use to assist ELLs include the following:

- Encourage both ELLs and proficient English speakers to engage in classroom conversations that provide the ELLs a chance to develop oral facility with English in preparation for reading instruction.

- Use show-and-tell activities to develop oral proficiency.

- To help in developing word-recognition skills, use planned vocabulary instruction along with shared and repeated reading of predictable texts and systematic instruction in phonics (Lenters, 2004/2005).

- Use language experience stories (accounts developed cooperatively by you and your class members about actual experiences) to help students connect words in their spoken vocabularies with their written equivalents. (See Chapter 9 for information on the language experience approach.)

- Provide translations alongside English texts to support both first- and second-language skills (Lenters, 2004/2005).

- Involve students in creative dramatics activities to provide opportunities for oral and physical interpretations of the text, expanding the ELL's understanding through deeper immersion. Drama activities also offer a chance for public success, resulting in positive experiences for struggling readers (Kraus, 2006) and ELLs for whom the concepts are new.

- Display print materials in the classroom that feature words and alphabets of the languages of students to promote understanding of varying cultures. You can enlist the help of parents or community members in preparing these materials. They may write students' names, common words and phrases, and environmental print in each language represented (Schwarzer, Haywood, and Lorenzen, 2003).

- Along with your students, you can learn selected words in several of the languages spoken by class members, building a sense of community in the classroom (Schwarzer, Haywood, and Lorenzen, 2003).

- Invite parents or other family members to read books to your students in the different languages represented in your class or make recorded versions of such materials available in a listening center (Schwarzer, Haywood, and Lorenzen, 2003).

- Encourage translation projects for family members as purposeful uses of home language (Schwarzer, Haywood, and Lorenzen, 2003).

- Use field trips, demonstrations, visual aids, and modeling to expose students to new words and concepts (Echevarria, Vogt, and Short, 2004; Echevarria and Short, n.d.).

- Have them compose bilingual books and dictate daily news reports that are translated into English (Manyak, 2008).

Many educators believe that you need to give ELLs a chance to develop some oral facility with English before reading instruction begins, but there is some evidence that simultaneous instruction in oral and written English can result in increased oral facility with the language (Dlugosz, 2000). Even if you do not speak a language other than English, you can use culturally responsible reading instruction by making connections between English and students' home languages (Rubinstein-Avila, 2003/2004; Schwarzer, Haywood, and Lorenzen, 2003). Some communications between you and your students and among students can take place with gestures, pointing, or drawing during conversations and discussions. "Putting

It into Practice: English-Language Learners (ELLs)" suggests a number of ways to support ELLs, whose backgrounds of experience frequently differ from those of the majority of students. These practices are also valuable for all students in the class.

The Relationship Between Reading and Thinking

Reading is a thinking process. The act of recognizing words requires interpretation of graphic symbols. To comprehend a reading selection thoroughly, a person must be able to use the information to make inferences and read critically and creatively— to understand the figurative language, determine the author's purpose, evaluate the ideas presented, and apply the ideas to actual situations. All of these skills involve thinking processes.

Teachers can guide students' thinking by asking appropriate questions. Students will be more likely to evaluate the material they are reading if they have been taught to do so. Questions can involve readers in the material and help them make personal connections to it, or they can limit thinking. For example, if students are asked only to locate isolated facts, they may not look for a passage's main idea or consider the author's purpose for writing. *How* and *why* questions are particularly good for stimulating thinking. (See Chapter 8 for extensive coverage of the relationship of reading to thinking and about the use and effects of questioning strategies.)

The Relationship of Reading to Learning

Reading is a complex act that must be learned. It is also a means by which further learning takes place. In other words, a person learns to read and reads to learn.

Learning to read depends on motivation, practice, and reinforcement. Teachers must show students that being able to read is rewarding in many ways. Reading

- Increases success in school.
- Helps in coping with everyday situations outside of school.
- Bestows status.
- Provides recreation.

Students are motivated by the expectation that they will receive these rewards, which then provide reinforcement that encourages students to practice the skills needed for reading.

After students have developed some facility in reading, it becomes a means through which they learn other things. They read to learn about science, mathematics, social studies, literature, and all other subjects, a topic treated in depth in Chapter 12.

We should clarify one additional idea at this time. Teachers sometimes assume the existence of a dichotomy: Students "learn to read" in the primary grades and "read to learn" in the intermediate and upper grades. Although it may be true that teachers devote less attention to the actual process of learning to read at the intermediate level, there is still a need there for attention to reading strategy instruction. In addition, primary students can and do read for information.

Reading as an Associational Process

Learning to read depends on several types of associations. First, children learn to associate objects and ideas with spoken words. Next, they are asked to build up associations between spoken words and written words. In some cases—for instance, when a child encounters an unfamiliar written word paired with a picture of a familiar object—the child makes a direct association between the object or event and the written word without an intermediate connection with the spoken word. In teaching phonics, teachers help learners form associations between graphemes and phonemes. (Chapters 4 and 5 address these associations.)

Practice is important in building associations, but practice in and of itself is not always enough to set up lasting associations. The more meaningful an association is to a student, the more rapidly he or she will learn it.

Positive Reinforcement

When students practice associations through classroom activities, immediate positive reinforcement of correct answers and correction of wrong ones can help establish the associations. Positive reinforcement can include simple verbal or nonverbal feedback about the correctness of an answer or a reward, such as praise or a smile. The sooner that you provide reinforcement after the student makes the response, the more effective the reinforcement is likely to be. For example, you might show a student the word *time* and say, "This printed word is *time*." Then you could show the word again and ask the child to respond with the word *time,* followed by feedback on the correctness of the response. You may offer the student opportunities to repeat this response in a variety of situations, strengthening the association each time that he or she sees that word.

Affective Aspects of the Reading Process

Interests, attitudes, and self-concepts are three **affective** aspects of the reading process. These aspects influence how hard students will work at the reading task. For example, students who are interested in the materials presented to them will put forth much more effort in the reading process than those who have no interest in the available reading materials. (See Chapter 9 for more on developing interests.)

In the same manner, students with positive attitudes toward reading will expend more effort on the reading process than will students who have negative attitudes. Positive attitudes are nurtured in homes where the parents read for themselves and to their children and where reading materials are provided for children's use. In the classroom, teachers who enjoy reading, who seize every opportunity to provide pleasurable reading experiences for their students, and who allow time for recreational reading during school hours are encouraging positive attitudes. Reading aloud to students at all grade levels regularly can help accomplish this objective. In addition, if a student's peers view reading as a positive activity, that student is likely to view reading in the same way, and by reading to the class, you promote positive attitudes among many students at once.

Internal (intrinsic) **motivation** and appreciation of a literature selection can occur when students see themselves as successful problem solvers or find that the selection provides an escape from daily life, evokes an aesthetic response, piques intellectual curiosity, or helps them understand themselves. Any of these

Motivating Students to Read

Laura Young's students are motivated to read by staging an O.S.C.A.R. (Our Students Care About Reading) ceremony. The ceremony is modeled on awards shows, from the red carpet to the after party, but the awards are presented primarily to book characters.

Students read self-selected novels in reading workshop all year. During the school year, students nominate characters from their stories for categories such as Most Outrageous Character, Most Courageous Character, Best Fantasy Character, Best Sci-Fi Character, Best Villain, Best Animal Character, Best Detective, Best Nonfiction Character, Most Changed Character, Best Historical Fiction Character, Best Supporting Character, Best Author (Male), Best Author (Female), Best All Around Female Character, and Best All Around Male Character. Toward the end of the year, the nominations are tallied, and the teacher creates a ballot consisting of three nominees in each category. Students cast their ballots, but they do not find out the results until the big day. Visit the Student Website to see an example of a ballot that Laura used.

Once the three nominees in each category are determined, students sign up to portray them on stage. Other students sign up to portray famous literary characters needed to introduce categories and present awards. Additionally, a host or hostess is selected. Each nominee must write an acceptance speech—from the perspective of the character—in the event that he or she wins. Students also prepare PowerPoint presentations, movie clips, guest readings, and skits that are performed during the ceremony.

Students simulate all the details of an awards show, complete with programs, scenery, and props. The scenery consists of giant (4' × 8') book-cover replicas that students create in groups. Students shape Oscar-like statues from clay. They are kiln-fired and painted gold. Each winner gets a statue to keep. Costumes are created and parties are planned.

The big day begins with red carpet interviews. Then the awards are presented, speeches are read, and books are celebrated. Finally, everybody enjoys an after party. The day is fun for all and certainly celebrates reading.

Analysis of This Activity

Use of self-selected reading was a powerful motivational technique. These students were also motivated by their desire to see a character whom they selected win in a category, to see a character whom they read about portrayed by a classmate, or to portray a character. Writing an acceptance speech provided motivation for students to write. Creating programs, scenery, props, PowerPoint presentations, movie clips, guest readings, or skits was motivational for many otherwise reluctant participants.

Source: Laura Young, Teacher, Algood School, Cookeville, Tennessee, 2007.

Visit the Read·Write·Think website (http://www.readwritethink.org or link from the Student Website) to find lessons designed to motivate students to read. Two examples are "Shaquille O'Neal: Using a Basketball Star to Motivate Readers" and "Sharing Favorite Books Using Interactive Character Trading Cards."

circumstances invite the reader to become involved in the story. External (extrinsic) motivations for reading may include peer pressure, teacher expectations, or the need to meet responsibilities. "Seeing It in Practice: Motivating Students to Read" tells how one teacher highly motivated her students.

Developing reading **fluency** (reading with accuracy, appropriate rate, good expression, and good comprehension [Richards, 2000; Rasinski, 2000; Nathan and Stanovich, 1991; Dowhower, 1991; Zutell and Rasinski, 1991]) is one of the key reading abilities identified by the National Reading Panel (2000), and repeated reading of material is one method that is used to develop fluency. To motivate students to do the needed repeated read-ing, Peebles (2007) uses readers' theater (see Chapters 7 and 12 for discussions of readers' theater) and a strategy called a Rhythm Walk. For a Rhythm Walk, students and teacher pick out a short selection, divide it into appropriate "chunks," and write each chunk on a strip of card stock. The chunks are placed in order in a path around the room, with each strip one step away from the previous one. Students walk from strip to strip, reading the chunks aloud as they go. Students repeat the walk from three to ten times, improving their performance with repetition. Then students read the originally

SEEING IT IN PRACTICE ◀ ■ ▶

Video Case

To see how another teacher builds motivation for learning through contemporary culture and issues, view the Video Case and bonus videos "Classroom Motivation: Strategies for Engaging Today's Students." After viewing the videos, answer in your class journal or in class discussion the questions that are provided with the videos. Pay particular attention to the definition given for motivation. Explain how you would apply the ideas in this case study to a primary grade level.

chosen text independently as it appears in connected form on a page. The teacher follows this with activities to monitor comprehension of the passage. This proce-dure can be varied to fit the needs of particular classes or students. One variation is to pair a struggling reader with a stronger one for the walk. See other motivational strategies used in "Seeing It in Practice: Video Case."

Negative attitudes toward reading may develop in a home environment where parents, for a variety of reasons, do not read. Children from some homes may be given the impression that reading is a waste of time. They may bring this attitude to school. If so, the teacher has the responsibility to help them change it. (See "Seeing It in Practice: Attitude Toward Reading.") Smith and Wilhelm (2004) studied boys' reactions to literacy activities and discovered that outside of school boys pursued literacy activities in which they felt competent but that they rejected literacy activities in school that highlighted their weaknesses. The researchers found that developing competence through successfully sequenced instruction is important before boys are presented with challenging assignments.

When readers are allowed to make decisions about what interests them or what information is important to them in a selection they have just read, they will understand and retain that information better. Discussion of these personal deci-sions gives students opportunities for self-expression, which promote intrinsic motivation. Open-ended tasks motivate students because they allow personal choices, challenges, and control. Social interaction during literacy tasks, book-rich environments, and teachers who model reading also enhance motivation (Gambrell, 1996). To help children learn to read, teachers need to "foster the imagination, facilitate personal identification, and promote social interaction" (Smith, 2003, p. 95).

Students with poor opinions of themselves may be afraid to attempt a reading task because they are sure they will fail. They often find it preferable to avoid the task altogether and try to appear as if they "don't care," rather than risk looking "dumb."

Attitude Toward Reading

James, a sixth grader, grumbled about being asked to participate in any reading activities. One day he told Mr. Hyde, his teacher, "I don't need to be able to read. My dad is a construction worker who drives heavy equipment, and that's what I'm going to be. I won't need to read to do that."

Mr. Hyde responded, "What will you do if you are given written instructions to get to the construction site? Won't you need to read then?"

"I'll ask somebody," James replied.

"What if nobody else is there?" Mr. Hyde persisted.

"I don't think that will happen," James countered.

"Well, what if you can't read the road signs to find the place that you are going? You might even need to read a map to find the place. Or what will you do if you get letters from people? You may not want to ask someone else to read them to you. They could be private. Can't you see some advantages to being able to read, even if you don't have to read a lot at work?"

"I guess so," James mumbled reluctantly.

Mr. Hyde had some arguments that were difficult to refute but probably did not change James's attitude with this one conversation. He needed to be shown repeatedly the benefits that could accrue from reading ability. He also needed to be helped to see that reading can be fun. Mr. Hyde found an informational book containing lots of pictures of heavy equipment and gave James the book to look through whenever he had some time. He did not choose to look at it immediately, but a couple of days later, when the children were having a supervised study time, he took out the book in preference to doing mathematics homework. At first he just thumbed through the pages, but eventually he began to pay closer attention to specific parts of the book. After a day or two, he returned the book and remarked that it was "okay." Mr. Hyde saw a possible avenue to helping James become a reader and pursued it for the rest of the year.

Students with positive **self-concepts,** on the other hand, are generally not afraid to attack a reading task because they believe they are going to succeed.

There are several ways to help students build positive self-concepts. First, in every possible way, the teacher should help them feel accepted. A definite relationship exists between a teacher's attitude toward students, as students perceive it, and students' self-concepts. One of the best ways to make students feel accepted is for the teacher to share their interests, using those interests in planning for reading instruction. Second, the teacher can help students feel successful by providing activities that are simple enough to guarantee satisfactory completion. Third, the teacher should avoid comparing a student to other students. Instead, reading progress should be compared with the student's own previous work. These comparisons can enhance self-concept by providing students with evidence of their growing mastery.

Constructive Aspects of the Reading Process

The reader puts together input from sensory and perceptual channels with experiential background and affective responses and constructs a personal meaning for the text. This meaning is based on the printed word but does not reside completely in it; it is transformed by the information that the reader brings to the text, the reader's feelings about the material, the purposes for the reading, and the context in which the reading takes place. Readers with different backgrounds of experience and different affective reactions will derive different meanings from the same text, as may those with divergent purposes and those reading under varying conditions. A person from the Middle East will understand an article about dissension among Middle Eastern countries differently than will one from the United States. A person reading to find a single fact or a few isolated facts will derive a different meaning from an article than will someone reading to get an overall picture of the topic. A person reading a horror story alone in the house at night may well construct a different understanding of the text than will one reading the same story in broad daylight in a room full of family members.

 DIVERSITY

The Reading Process: Selected Theories

A *theory* is a set of assumptions or principles designed to explain phenomena. The choices that teachers make about types of instruction and emphases in instructional programs are affected by their theoretical positions concerning the reading process. Theories that are based on good research and practical observations can be helpful when planning reading instruction. However, teachers should not forget that current theories do not account for all aspects of this complex process. In addition, theories grow out of *hypotheses*—educated guesses. New information may be discovered that proves part or all of a theory invalid.

It would not be practical to present all the theories related to reading in the introductory chapter of a survey textbook. We discuss three theoretical approaches—**subskill, interactive,** and **transactive theories**—to give you a feeling for the complexities inherent in choosing a theoretical stance.

Subskill Theories

Some educators see reading as a set of subskills that students must master and integrate. They believe that good readers have learned and integrated these subskills so well that they use them automatically. **Automaticity** is "the ability to perform a task with little attention" (Samuels, 2004, p. 1130). It is evident when high-level accuracy is combined with speed; readers who read orally with good expression are exhibiting automaticity in word recognition.

Proponents of subskill theories point out that beginning readers have not yet learned all the subskills and may not integrate well those that they have learned. Beginning readers, therefore, may exhibit slow, choppy reading and perhaps have reduced comprehension because the separate skills of word recognition take so much concentration. Teaching these skills until they become automatic and smoothly integrated is thus the approach that these educators take to reading instruction. A caution comes from Weaver and Shonhoff (1984), who state that

> Although some research suggests that skilled reading is a single, holistic process, there is no research to suggest that children can learn to read and

develop reading skill if they are taught using a method that treats reading as if it were a single process. Therefore, for instructional purposes, it is probably best to think of reading as a set of interrelated subskills. (p. 36)

There is research to support the position that reading is a set of interrelated subskills. For example, one study showed that "roughly 50 percent of the variability in oral reading of connected words is associated with how well one can read these words in isolation" (Samuels and Schachter, 1984, p. 40). Students who are slow in learning to read "often must be given extensive training on each of a variety of tasks, such as letter discrimination, letter-sound training, blending, etc. In this manner a teacher becomes aware of the fact that letter recognition can be considered a skill itself" (LaBerge and Samuels, 1985, p. 713). David LaBerge and S. Jay Samuels developed a hierarchical model of information processing. Their model suggests that students master smaller units before larger ones and integrate them into larger units after mastery (Samuels, 2004). Because fluent readers have mastered each subskill to the point where they use and integrate subskills automatically, they do not clearly see the dividing lines among these skills during their daily reading. "One of the hallmarks of the reader who learned the subskills rapidly is that he was least aware of them at the time, and therefore now has little memory of them as separate subskills" (LaBerge and Samuels, 1985, p. 714).

Other research also supports the importance of integrating subskills. Guthrie (1973) found that reading subskills correlated highly with one another for students who were good readers. The correlations among reading subskills for poor readers were low. These students seemed to be operating at a level of separate rather than integrated skills. Guthrie's findings led to the conclusion that "lack of subskill mastery and lack of integration of these skills into higher order units" were sources of difficulty among less skilled readers (Samuels and Schachter, 1984, p. 39).

Whereas beginning readers first focus on decoding and then switch their attention to comprehension, fluent readers decode automatically and thus can focus attention on comprehension. Beginning readers must switch their attention from decoding to comprehension and back as they read, making comprehension a slow and laborious process, much like the process a person who is learning a foreign language must use. First, the foreign word must be translated before comprehension can occur (Samuels, 2004). This realization may help teachers understand some of the difficulties faced by ELLs in their classes.

 DIVERSITY

Samuels (2004) points out that, although the meanings of familiar words may be automatic for skilled readers,

> The ability to get the meaning of each word in a sentence, however, is not the same as the ability to comprehend a sentence. In comprehending a sentence one must be able to interrelate and combine the separate meanings of each of its words. From this point of view, comprehension is a constructive process of synthesis and putting word meanings together in special ways, much as individual bricks are combined in the construction of a house. (p. 1131)

Those who teach a set of subskills as a means of instructing students in reading generally recognize the importance of practicing the subskills in the context of actual reading and therefore include the use of literature in their instruction to ensure integration. Some teachers, however, neglect this vital phase. They erroneously focus only on the subskills, overlooking the fact that they are the means to an end and not an end in themselves. Researchers such as Samuels (2004) and Adams (2004) point out the need for practice with important subskills. Both agree that practice time must also be spent on reading interesting material that is easy and meaningful. Adams (2004) states, "Deep and ready working knowledge of letters, spelling patterns, and words, and of the phonological translations of all three, is of inescapable importance to both skillful reading and its acquisition—not because it is the be-all or the end-all of the reading process, but because it enables it" (p. 1240). She says that frequent broad reading is important in developing reading proficiency.

Interactive Theories

An interactive theoretical model of the reading process depicts reading as a combination of two types of processing—**top-down processing** (reader based) and **bottom-up processing** (text based)—in continuous interaction. In top-down processing, the act of reading begins with the reader generating hypotheses, or predictions, about the material, using visual cues in the material to test these hypotheses as necessary (Walberg, Hare, and Pulliam, 1981). For instance, the reader of a folktale that begins with the words "Once upon a time, there was a man who had three sons … " forms hypotheses about what will happen next, predicting that there will be a task to perform or a beautiful princess to win over and that the oldest two sons will fail but the youngest will attain his goal. Because of these expectations, the reader may read the material fairly quickly, giving attention primarily to words that confirm the expectations. Close reading occurs only if the hypothesis formed is not confirmed and an atypical plot unfolds. Otherwise, the reader can skip many words while skimming for key words that move the story along. Processing of print obviously cannot be a totally top-down experience because a reader must begin by focusing on the print (Gove, 1983).

In bottom-up processing, reading is initiated by examining the printed symbols. Gove (1983) says, "Bottom-up models assume that the translation process begins with print, i.e., letter or word identification, and proceeds to progressively larger linguistic units, phrases, sentences, etc., ending in meaning" (p. 262). A reader using bottom-up processing might first sound out a word letter by letter and then pronounce it, consider its meaning in relation to the phrase in which it is found, and so on.

An interactive model assumes that students are simultaneously processing information from the print they are reading and information from their background knowledge. Recognition and comprehension of printed words and ideas are the result of using both types of information. David E. Rumelhart's early model indicated that "at least for skilled readers, top-down and bottom-up processing occur simultaneously. … Because comprehension depends on both graphic information and the information in the reader's mind, it may be obstructed when a critical skill or a piece of information is missing" (Harris and Sipay, 1985, p. 10). Rumelhart (2004) represented an interactive model as having graphemic input from which critical features are extracted, and this information is synthesized with a person's syntactical, semantic, orthographic, and lexical knowledge. This model leads to the conclusion that a reader who cannot use clues from the sentences or pictures around an unfamiliar word may fail to grasp the meaning of a word that is central to understanding the passage. Similarly, a reader who has no background knowledge about the topic may be unable to reconstruct the ideas that the author is trying to convey.

Transactive Theories

Rosenblatt (2004) asserts that

> Every reading act is an event, or a transaction involving a particular reader and … a text, and occurring at a particular time in a particular context. … The meaning does not reside ready-made "in" the text or "in" the reader but happens or comes into being during the transaction between reader and text. (p. 1369)

Meaning is constructed during the transaction. Readers employ knowledge gained through past experiences to help them select interpretations, visualize the message, make connections between the new information and what they know, and relate affectively to the material. "Reader and text are involved in a complex, nonlinear, recursive, self-correcting transaction" (Rosenblatt, 2004, p. 1371). The transaction between reader and text is dynamic. No two readings, even ones by the same person at different times, are likely to be identical. The reader often gains personal experience that changes his or her interpretation or adopts a different stance that affects his or her response.

The reader is highly important when reading is viewed as a transaction, and the stance that the reader chooses must be considered. The reader's purpose is reflected in the stance chosen. The reader may take an *efferent stance*, focusing on obtaining information from the text, or an *aesthetic stance*, focusing on the experience lived through during the reading, the feelings and images evoked, and the memories aroused by the text.

Rosenblatt's idea of an efferent–aesthetic continuum helps teachers see that there are both cognitive and affective aspects of all reading activities for both fiction and nonfiction and that the relative importance of each aspect will vary with the text and the reading situation. According to Frager (1993), a wider range of aesthetic responses to content area reading can be encouraged by asking readers what feelings the text aroused in them. Students should both think about the concepts and experience the feelings evoked by the words.

Either stance may be appropriate at a particular time, and it is up to the reader to choose the approach to the reading. Even when reading a single work, readers may shift their stances from more efferent to more aesthetic, or vice versa, but fiction and poetry generally involve a more aesthetic stance (Rosenblatt, 1978, 1991,

1995, 2004). The readers' stances, beliefs, and attitudes affect their responses, as does the context.

Kenneth Goodman (1973) has referred to reading as a psycholinguistic guessing game in which readers "select the fewest, most productive cues necessary to produce guesses which are right the first time" (p. 31). He sees the ability to combine letters to form words as being related to learning to read, but he believes that it has little to do with the process of fluent reading. Fluent readers who are reading for meaning do not always need to identify individual words; they can comprehend a passage without having identified all the words in it. The more experience a reader has had with language and the concepts presented, the fewer **graphophonic clues** (clues from associating sounds with graphemes) from visual configurations he or she will need to determine the meaning of the material. Fluent readers make frequent use of **semantic clues** (meaning) and **syntactic clues** (word-order) within the material as well. Goodman (1973) points out the importance of the reader's ability to anticipate material that he or she has not yet seen. He also stresses that readers bring to their reading all their accumulated experience, language development, and thought in order to anticipate meanings in the printed material.

Acknowledging Rosenblatt's influence, Goodman has moved from a strictly psycholinguistic focus to embrace a transactive focus, acknowledging that through transactions with a text meaning is constructed and the reader's schemata are also changed (K. S. Goodman, 1985). He now asserts that the text a writer constructs has a meaning potential, although the text itself does not have meaning. Readers will use this meaning potential to construct their own meaning (Goodman, 1994; Mills, Stephens, O'Keefe, and Waugh, 2004).

The transactive theory appeals to advocates of a holistic philosophy, or belief system, toward reading. These educators want students to be involved with authentic reading, writing, listening, and speaking activities—that is, activities that are not just contrived to teach particular skills but are designed to communicate. They view the teacher as an initiator and mediator of learning experiences and a curriculum developer who links the curriculum to the learner.

The social context for holistic instruction is a collaborative learner-centered classroom in which all learners are accepted as a part of the community of learners regardless of individual differences. Students make choices, self-evaluate, and take responsibility for their learning. The teacher and other students listen and respond to their spoken and written ideas. The teacher, with student input, is the decision maker. Teachers who embrace this philosophy use whole literature selections in their reading programs; connect writing and reading; and emphasize functional language, reading comprehension, and written expression. These teachers do not rely on a packaged set of materials. They use a variety of methods and materials to fit their instructional needs (Goodman, 1992; Moss and Noden, 1993/1994; Church, 1994; Watson, 1994). Students are motivated to learn when they are given opportunities to express themselves and have choices about their learning.

As we discuss in Chapters 4 and 5, holistic teaching is not devoid of skills instruction. Teachers can blend holistic instructional activities with systematic

Time for Reflection

Some people believe that, for the reader, meaning resides in the text. Others believe that the reader brings meaning to the text. Still others believe that, for the reader to comprehend the meaning fully, reading must involve using both the information in the text and the information that the reader brings to the text in the context in which the reading takes place.

What do *you* think, and why?

direct instruction. Phonics is taught but not separately from reading and writing. Spelling and grammar are viewed as means to an end.

Recently, some scholars have questioned the ability of transactional theory to encompass the cultural issues related to multicultural literature. They believe that it does not provide a stance for critical analysis of this literature. Cai (2008) points out that Rosenblatt sees critical analysis as a part of an efferent stance. Rosenblatt's theory just does not teach a particular critical perspective. Rosenblatt believes that emphasis on the reader's response does not prevent the use of critical approaches in the transactions that take place.

Resolving the Teacher's Dilemma: Taking a Balanced Approach

STANDARDS/
ASSESSMENTS

The current educational situation in many areas can pose a dilemma for teachers. As we discuss later in Chapter 2, teachers and students are held accountable for meeting standards of performance set by their state or school districts. In many cases, performance is monitored by standardized tests. In general, the standardized tests of reading consist of performance of isolated skill activities rather than reading of whole pieces of text and responding to the text in a variety of ways. To prepare their students to score well on standardized tests, teachers may choose to "teach to the test," to ensure that their students are ready for this task, and leave out many activities that address aspects of reading instruction that are not easily measured by standardized tests.

Today, many teachers embrace a balanced approach to reading instruction in which they combine elements of direct skills instruction and elements of holistic instruction in their teaching. They offer authentic literacy activities in the classroom but teach skills directly to help students succeed in those activities. Teachers can incorporate explicit instruction in basic skills as a part of complex projects that demand high-level literacy skill. In this way, they prepare students for real life as well as for annual tests. Strategies may be taught and then practiced using authentic materials rather than just worksheets or other forms of isolated drill (Miller and Duffy, 2006/2007).

Educators from many philosophical backgrounds recognize the need for balance. Students can engage in construction of meaning as part of any teaching approach, and even memorization and rote learning may be useful parts of learning activities under appropriate circumstances. "One's task is to find the right balance between the activities of constructing and receiving knowledge, given that not all aspects of a subject can or should be taught in the same way or be acquired solely through 'hands-on' or student-centered means" (Airasian and Walsh, 1997, p. 447).

Instruction should also maintain a balance between focusing on word recognition and comprehension, with word recognition viewed as a means to enable comprehension, not as a final goal. Comprehension instruction should be emphasized from the very beginning. Students should not have to wait until they can sound out most words to have an emphasis on meaning.

Many teachers who embrace varying theories and philosophies use some of the same techniques to balance instruction. They use the language experience approach (discussed in Chapter 9) and some computer applications to learning (discussed in Chapter 13). They make use of literature with such teaching techniques as thematic literature units, literature circles, some variations of whole-class reading of a core book, and the individualized reading approach, along with associated skill instruction. They use these varied approaches to meet the needs of individual students. Personalized reading, a technique in which students read self-selected books, offers practice needed to develop automaticity, fluency, and motivation. (See more about this in Chapters 9 and 10.)

Still another need for balance is in organization for learning. Teachers should use whole-class, small-group, and individualized instruction to meet specific needs of their students. These types of organization for learning are discussed in Chapters 2 and 10.

 LITERATURE

An example of one type of personalized reading technique is described in the lesson plan "A Daily DEAR Program: Drop Everything, and Read!" found at http://www.readwritethink.org (or link from the Student Website).

Fifteen Principles of Teaching Reading

Principles of teaching reading are generalizations about reading instruction based on research in the field of reading and observation of reading practices. The principles listed here are not all-inclusive; many other useful generalizations about teaching reading have been made in the past and will continue to be made in the future. They are, however, the ones we believe are most useful in guiding teachers in planning reading instruction.

PRINCIPLE 1 **Reading is a complex act with many factors that must be considered.**

The discussion earlier in this chapter of the many aspects of the reading process makes this principle clear. To plan reading instruction wisely, teachers must understand all parts of the reading process.

PRINCIPLE 2 **Reading involves the construction of the meaning represented by the printed symbols.**

A person who fails to derive meaning from a passage has not been reading, even if he has pronounced every word correctly. Chapters 6–8 focus on constructing meaning from reading materials. One conclusion in *Becoming a Nation of Readers* (R.C. Anderson et al., 1985) was that "in addition to obtaining information from the letters and words in a text, reading involves selecting and using knowledge about people, places, and things, and knowledge about texts and their organization" (p. 8).

Obviously, different readers construct meaning in somewhat different ways because of their varied experiential backgrounds. Some readers do not have enough background knowledge to understand a text; others don't use the knowledge they have (R.C. Anderson et al., 1985). For example, suppose a text mentions how mountains can isolate a group of people living in them. Students familiar with

Time for Reflection

Some people think that skills instruction is unnecessary if students are surrounded by print and immersed in a literacy-rich environment. Others think that systematic, direct skills instruction is necessary for a successful reading program. Still others think that both a literacy-rich environment and systematic skills instruction are essential. **What do *you* think, and why?**

 DIVERSITY

◀■▶ **SEEING IT IN PRACTICE**

Video Case
For a look at a classroom with students from another culture, view the Video Case "Diversity: Teaching in a Multiethnic Classroom." The material in this case study also applies to techniques covered in later chapters.

mountainous areas will picture steep grades and rough terrain, which make road building difficult, and will understand the source of the isolation although the text never mentions it. Those unfamiliar with mountains will have more trouble making this inference.

Because students from different cultures may come to school with widely varying backgrounds of experiences, teachers must learn about the cultures from which their students come, to understand students' perspectives. In addition, language and culture are so tightly connected that "nothing comes from separating them because they have no meaning apart from each other" (Gunderson, 2000, p. 694). Affective factors, such as the reader's attitudes toward the subject matter, which may be affected by cultural background, also influence the construction of meaning, as does the context in which the reading takes place.

Student talk is important in constructing meaning. Through use of the Internet, student talk can be extended around the world, and the social aspect of constructing meaning can be taken to extended dimensions. The Internet is also helpful in encouraging construction of meaning because it supports the natural curiosity of students by putting a large source of information within their reach, enhancing their opportunities to discover ideas for themselves (El-Hindi, 1998). Students need to acquire new strategies to use the Internet effectively (Henry, 2006). Chapter 13 discusses this need.

DIVERSITY

One problem with asking students to construct meaning, rather than telling them the "correct" meaning, occurs when this approach to instruction and learning runs counter to parents' beliefs about education and the purpose of schooling. Parents from a variety of cultures may see an emphasis on the process of meaning construction, rather than on the products that demonstrate the acquisition of information, as the teacher's failure to do the "teaching." They may want their children to focus on the accumulation of knowledge that will lead to high test scores and the chance for higher education (Gunderson, 2000), rather than focusing on higher-order thinking and constructing meaning from printed sources and experience.

PRINCIPLE 3 **There is no one correct way to teach reading.**

DIVERSITY

Some methods of teaching reading work better for some students than for others. Each student is an individual who learns in his or her own way. Some students are visual learners, some are auditory learners, and some are **kinesthetic** or **tactile** learners, who learn better through their senses of movement and touch. Some need to be instructed through a combination of **modalities,** or avenues of perception, in order to learn. The teacher should differentiate instruction to fit the diverse needs of students. Of course, some methods also work better for some teachers than they do for others. Teachers need to be acquainted with a variety of methods, including ones that involve technology, so that they can help all of their students. Chapter 9 covers a number of approaches to reading instruction, and Chapter 13 discusses the use of technology in literacy instruction.

PRINCIPLE 4 **Learning to read is a continuing process.**

People learn to read over a long period of time, acquiring more advanced reading skills after they master prerequisite skills. Even after they have been introduced to all reading skills, the process of refinement continues. No matter how old they are or how long they have been out of school, readers continue to refine their reading skills. Reading skills require practice. If readers do not practice, the skills deteriorate; if they do practice, their skills continue to develop.

PRINCIPLE 5 **Students should be taught word-recognition strategies that will allow them to unlock the pronunciations and meanings of unfamiliar words independently.**

Students cannot memorize all the words they will meet in print. Therefore, they need to learn techniques for figuring out unfamiliar words so that they can read when the assistance of a teacher, parent, or friend is not available. Chapters 4 and 5 focus on word-recognition strategies that students need.

PRINCIPLE 6 **The teacher should assess each student's reading ability and use the assessment as a basis for planning instruction.**

Teaching all students the same reading lessons and hoping to deal at one time or another with all the difficulties that students encounter should be avoided. Such an approach wastes the time of those students who have attained the skills currently being emphasized and may never meet some of the desperate needs of other students. Teachers can avoid this approach by using assessment instruments and techniques to pinpoint the strengths and weaknesses of each student in the classroom. Then they can either divide students into needs groups for pertinent instruction or give some students individual instruction. Chapter 2 describes many useful tests and other assessment procedures as well as intervention strategies to use that relate to test results.

 STANDARDS/ ASSESSMENTS

PRINCIPLE 7 **Reading and the other language arts are highly interrelated.**

Reading—the interaction between a reader and written language through which the reader tries to reconstruct the writer's message—is closely related to the other language arts (listening, speaking, writing, **viewing,** and **visually representing**). All of the language arts are necessary to communication, involve thinking, and require construction of meaning. Listening, viewing, and reading are means of receiving or taking in information, whereas speaking, writing, and visually representing are means of expressing information or passing it on to others. The receptive phases complement the expressive phases. For example, people read material that is written; they listen to ideas and speak in response; and they view material that is visually represented. Example 1.2 illustrates the various links among the language arts.

EXAMPLE 1.2 The Interrelationships Among the Language Arts

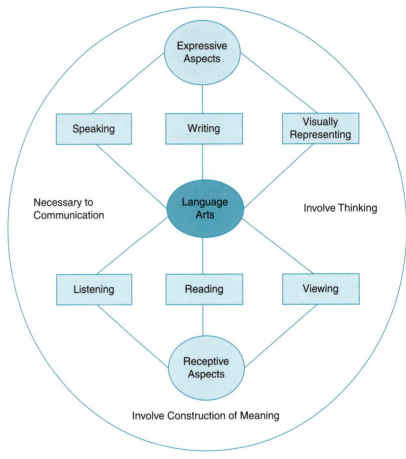

Source: Betty D. Roe and Elinor P. Ross, *Integrating Language Arts Through Literature and Thematic Units* (Boston: Pearson/Allyn & Bacon, 2006), 16.

People learn to speak before they learn to read and write. Learning to read should be treated as an extension of the process of learning spoken language, a process that generally takes place in the home with little difficulty if children are given normal language input and feedback on their efforts to use language. Children's reading vocabularies generally consist largely of words in their oral language (listening and speaking) vocabularies. These are words for which they have previously developed concepts and therefore can comprehend. Some of them have been learned through viewing experiences in which they have heard the words used in the context of a setting that provides referents. This viewing may involve interpreting images, gestures, movement, sounds, and print (Siegel, 2006). Children can more easily learn to read and write words that they have heard and learned to use in their speech correctly. Talking about things they see, hear, touch, smell, taste, and imagine involves exchanging ideas that aid in building concepts (Hill, 2006).

Mastering listening skills is also important because direct association of sound, meaning, and word form must be established in initial reading instruction. The ability to identify sounds heard at the beginnings, middles, and ends of words and the ability to discriminate among sounds are essential to successful phonetic analysis of words. Listening, reading, writing, and viewing are frequently all involved in visually representing, for a presentation may involve producing videos that are scripted and require recording action sequences that involve dialogue—materials that involve the use of visual, auditory, kinesthetic, and tactile modes (Siegel, 2006; Knobel and Lankshear, 2006).

The strategies and skills needed for the language arts are interrelated. For example, the need to develop and expand concepts and vocabulary, which is essential to reading, is evident in the entire language arts curriculum. Concepts and vocabulary terms to express these concepts are basic to listening, speaking, and writing as well as to reading activities. Spoken, written, and visual messages are organized around main ideas and supporting details, and people listen, read, and view to identify the main ideas and supporting details conveyed in the material. Chapter 8 contains many examples of reading skills that have parallel listening skills and related writing and speaking skills, Chapter 10 has more information about all of the language skills, and Chapter 13 presents information on viewing and visually representing.

PRINCIPLE 8 Using complete literature selections in the reading program is important.

Students need to experience the reading of whole stories and books to develop their reading skills. Reading isolated words, sentences, and paragraphs does not give them the opportunity to use their knowledge of language and story structure to the fullest, and reading overly simplified language both reduces the opportunities to use their language expertise and dampens interest in reading the material. Whole pieces of literature can include students' own writing and the writing of other children as well as the works of commercial authors.

 LITERATURE

PRINCIPLE 9 Reading is an integral part of all content area instruction within the educational program.

Teachers must consider the relationship of reading to other subjects within the curriculum of the elementary school. Other curricular areas can provide applications for the skills taught in the reading period. Textbooks in the various content areas are often the main means of conveying content concepts to students. Students also frequently are required to read library materials, magazines, newspapers, and material on web pages. If they cannot read these materials with comprehension, they may fail to master important ideas in science, mathematics, social studies, and other areas of the curriculum. Students who have inadequate reading skills may therefore face failure in other areas of study because of the large amount of reading that these areas often require. In addition, the need to write reports in different content areas can involve many reading and study skills: locating information; organizing information; and using the library and multimedia reference sources, including the Internet. Chapter 13 addresses use of multimedia references and the Internet.

Teachers who give reading and writing instruction only within isolated periods and treat reading and writing as separate from the rest of the curriculum will probably experience frustration rather than achieve student change and growth. Although a definite period scheduled specifically for language instruction may be recommended, this does not mean that teachers should ignore oral and written language skills and strategies when teaching content subjects. The ideal situation at any level is not "reading" and "writing" for separate time periods, followed by "study" of social science or science for the next period. Instead, although the emphasis shifts, language learning and studying should be integrated during all periods at all levels. Chapters 11 and 12 elaborate on these points.

PRINCIPLE 10 **The student needs to see that reading can be an enjoyable pursuit.**

LITERATURE

Schools often produce capable readers who do not read; in fact, today this is a common occurrence. Reading can be entertaining as well as informative. Teachers can help students realize this fact by reading stories and poems to them daily and setting aside a regular time for pleasure reading during which many good books of appropriate levels and from many interest areas are readily available. Teachers can show students that reading is a good recreational pursuit by describing the pleasure that they personally derive from reading in their spare time and by reading for pleasure in the students' presence. When students read recreationally, the teacher should do this also, thereby modeling desired behavior. Pressures of tests and reports should not be a part of recreational reading times. Students in literature-based reading instructional programs that include self-selection of reading materials and group discussion of chosen reading materials are likely to discover the enjoyable aspects of reading for themselves. Chapter 9 discusses such programs.

PRINCIPLE 11 **Sound teaching of all reading skills and strategies is important for all students.**

DIVERSITY

Students need an arsenal of skills and strategies to become independent readers. Some students acquire these skills and strategies quickly and easily and do not need extensive repetition of instruction. Others, however, will need much more detailed instruction with additional repetition. Teachers should be aware of these varying needs and differentiate instruction as appropriate. The task of adjusting instruction to particular students' needs is hard because there is not a ready-made program to use (Mayher, 2006; Smith, 1973). (See Chapter 2 for more about differentiating instruction.)

In some schools, ELLs are given the opportunity to learn skills and strategies through both English and their first languages. In other schools, all instruction takes place in English. Educators have differing opinions about the effectiveness of the different approaches.

Some students in inclusive classrooms have disabilities that can be somewhat alleviated through special approaches and assistive technology. Special equipment is particularly helpful for students with physical challenges.

PRINCIPLE 12 **Reading should be taught in a way that allows each student to experience success.**

The stage of the student's literacy development should be considered for all instructional activities throughout the grades. Not only when reading and writing instruction begins, but also whenever instruction involving any language strategy takes place, at all grade levels, teachers should consider each student's readiness for the instructional activity. If the student's literacy development is not adequate for the task, the teacher should adjust the instruction so that it is congruent with the student's literacy level. This may involve instruction to provide a student with readiness to incorporate the new learning into his or her store of concepts.

Asking students to try to learn to read from materials that are too difficult for them ensures that a large number will fail. Teachers should give students instruction at their own levels of achievement, regardless of grade placement. Success generates success. If students are given a reading task at which they can succeed, they gain the confidence to attack the other reading tasks that they must perform in a positive way. This greatly increases the likelihood of their success at these later tasks. In addition, some studies have shown that if a teacher expects students to be successful readers, they will in fact be successful. As Cambourne (2001) has pointed out,

> We usually achieve what we expect to achieve (or are expected to achieve by others); we fail when we expect to fail (or are expected by others to fail); we are more likely to engage with the demonstrations by those whom we regard as significant and who hold high expectations for us (p. 785).

Therefore, teachers should always provide instruction with the expectation that students will be successful.

Teachers tend to place low-achieving readers in materials that are too hard for them more frequently than they place good readers in such materials. Students who are given such difficult material to read use active, comprehension-seeking behaviors less often than do those who are reading material that they can understand with a teacher's assistance. Placing struggling readers in reading materials on levels that are too high tends to reinforce the inefficient reading strategies that emerge when material is too difficult, making it less likely that these readers will develop more efficient strategies. Although they often do not have high expectations of success under any circumstances, their expectations of success decrease more after failure than do those of good readers (Bristow, 1985).

 **STRUGGLING READER/ INTERVENTION**

SEEING IT IN PRACTICE ◀ ■ ▶

Video Case

View the main and bonus videos in Video Case "Bilingual Education: An Elementary Two-Way Immersion Program" to see one way that teachers approach bilingual education. Answer the provided questions in your journal.

To see how special approaches and assistive technology may be used to enhance learning for challenged learners, view the main and bonus videos in the Video Case "Including Students with Physical Disabilities: Best Practices."

Teachers should give struggling readers material that they can read without undue focus on word recognition. This approach allows them to focus on comprehending the text.

DIVERSITY

Asking students to read from materials that do not relate to their background knowledge can also result in less successful experiences. In view of the wide cultural diversity found in schools today, teachers must be particularly sensitive to this problem and must provide relevant materials for students that offer them a chance for success.

◀▣▶ SEEING IT IN PRACTICE

Video Cases

View the main video and bonus videos in the Video Case "Culturally Responsive Teaching: A Multicultural Lesson for Elementary Students." Answer the provided questions in your journal. What do you think of this way of relating material to the children's backgrounds of experiences? Look back at the material in this chapter on the affective aspects of the reading process. How did the teacher address these issues?

PRINCIPLE 13 Encouraging self-direction and self-monitoring of reading is important.

Good readers direct their own reading, making decisions about how to approach particular passages, what reading speed is appropriate, and why they are reading the passages. They are able to decide when they are having difficulties with understanding and can take steps to remedy their misunderstandings (R.C. Anderson et al., 1985). When they do this, they are using **metacognitive strategies.** Chapters 7 and 11 present more information about the way that good readers read flexibly and monitor their reading.

For an idea of what metacognition involves, visit the Video Case "Metacognition: Helping Students Become Strategic Learners" on the Student Website. This topic will be revisited in connection with other chapter studies as well.

PRINCIPLE 14 A supportive classroom organization can facilitate the teaching of reading.

Classroom organization does not directly involve the reading process or materials, methods, or approaches to teaching reading. It can, however, produce a more conducive atmosphere for learning. Because students come to school with different abilities, experiences, and needs, the teacher should provide organizational patterns that best fit these students. The teacher is the most important variable in the classroom, and a good teacher can be successful with many different organizational patterns. More information on classroom organization is in Chapter 2.

View the Video Case "Elementary Reading Instruction: A Balanced Literacy Program." Answer the provided questions in your journal. How has the teacher used her classroom organization to promote her instructional objectives?

PRINCIPLE 15 Teachers must help students develop facility in using technology to enhance their learning.

Students encounter technology in all aspects of their lives. To operate effectively in today's world, they need to acquire **technological literacy,** the ability to use various technological resources (for example, computers, CDs, and DVDs) for learning and completing various types of projects, such as writing research papers and doing multimedia presentations. More information on technological literacy is presented in Chapter 13.

No matter what teaching approaches are used in a school or what patterns of organization predominate, these principles of teaching reading should apply. All teachers should consider carefully their adherence or lack of adherence to such principles.

SUMMARY

The reading act is composed of two major parts: the reading process and the reading product. The reading process has eight aspects—sensory and perceptual, sequential, experiential, thinking, learning, association, affective, and constructive—that combine to produce the reading product, communication.

Three of the many types of theories about the reading process are subskill theories, interactive theories, and transactive theories. Subskill theories depict reading as a series of subskills that children must master so that the skills become automatic and smoothly integrated. Interactive theories depict reading as the interaction of two types of processing: top down and bottom up. Both types of processing are used to recognize and comprehend words. According to the bottom-up view, reading is initiated by the printed symbols (letters and words) and proceeds to larger linguistic units until the reader discovers meaning. According to the top-down view, reading begins with the reader's generation of hypotheses, or predictions, about the material, with the reader using the visual cues in the material to test these hypotheses as necessary. Therefore, according to interactive theories, both the print and the reader's background are important in the reading process. Transactive theories depict every reading act as a transaction involving a reader and a text at a particular time in a specific context. Readers generate and test hypotheses about the reading material and get feedback from the material. Holistic activities fit well with the transactive theoretical stance because a holistic philosophy embraces the idea of encouraging authentic transactions with text. This philosophy also supports collaborative, learner-centered classroom environments, much reading and writing of whole selections, and student choice. Many teachers blend elements of subskill theory and transactive theories.

Some principles related to reading instruction that may be helpful to teachers include the following:

1. Reading is a complex act with many factors that must be considered.

2. Reading involves the construction of the meaning represented by the printed symbols.

3. There is no one correct way to teach reading.

Time for Reflection

Some people think that reading should be taught only during reading class. Others think that reading instruction should take place, as needed, throughout the entire day.

What do *you* think, and why?

4. Learning to read is a continuing process.

5. Students should be taught word-recognition skills that will allow them to unlock the pronunciations and meanings of unfamiliar words independently.

6. The teacher should assess each student's reading ability and use the assessment as a basis for planning instruction.

7. Reading and the other language arts are highly interrelated.

8. Using complete literature selections in the reading program is important.

9. Reading is an integral part of all content area instruction within the educational program.

10. The student needs to see that reading can be an enjoyable pursuit.

11. Sound teaching of all reading skills and strategies is important for all students.

12. Reading should be taught in a way that allows each student to experience success.

13. Encouraging self-direction and self-monitoring of reading is important.

14. A supportive classroom organization can facilitate the teaching of reading.

15. Teachers must help students develop facility in using technology to enhance their learning.

For your journal ....

1. After studying the principles of reading instruction presented in this chapter, see if you can formulate other principles based on your reading in other sources.

2. What do you know about students from other cultures, students for whom English is a second language, and students who have physical and learning challenges? Did the Video Cases that you viewed give you insight that you needed? If so, what did you learn from them?

.... and your portfolio

1. Write a description of the theoretical stance on reading instruction that makes most sense to you. Give reasons for your position.

2. Conduct your own mini-research project by focusing on a student in your classroom or in one where you are observing. How does this student respond to different types of motivation? What works best and what seems ineffective? Keep an ongoing record and then summarize your findings at the end of your study.

3. Make a list of assistive technology sources for helping students with physical challenges. Go beyond what you find in the video.

Assessment and Intervention

2

KEY VOCABULARY

Pay close attention to these terms when they appear in the chapter.

adequate yearly progress (AYP)

alternative assessment

anecdotal record

assessment

authentic assessment

cloze procedure

criterion-referenced test

curriculum standards

disaggregated data

formal assessment

formative assessment

frustration level

independent reading level

informal reading inventory (IRI)

instructional level

listening comprehension level

miscue

norm-referenced test

performance-based assessment

portfolio

readability

reading miscue inventory (RMI)

Response to Intervention (RTI)

retelling

rubric

running record

standardized test

summative assessment

text leveling

Assessment is the process of collecting and analyzing data for the purpose of identifying and understanding student learning. Assessment is important because it enables teachers to discover each student's strengths and weaknesses, to plan instruction accordingly, to communicate student progress, and to evaluate the effectiveness of teaching strategies. Assessing student learning is essential for effective teaching and should be an integral part of all instructional procedures. Assessment should not simply be equated with testing. It should involve the collection of data from multiple measures—such as day-to-day observation, student conferences and interviews, and analysis of samples of students' work, as well as formal means. Profiles of student learning based on multiple sources of data provide a more valid evaluation of students' capabilities than do single assessments, and they facilitate differentiated instruction for all students (Brimijoin, Marquissee, and Tomlinson, 2003).

In this chapter, we describe current educational trends toward increased assessment of student progress through standardized tests that attempt to measure attainment of knowledge and skills mandated by state and national curriculum standards. We discuss formal assessments, or standardized tests, which are administered only periodically, and a wide variety of informal assessment measures that teachers can use to gather information on a day-to-day basis.

Formative assessments provide information in a timely fashion so as to inform and direct instruction. Formative assessment is continuous and ongoing. It provides relevant feedback for both the learner and the educator (Popham, 2006; Chappuis and Chappuis, 2007/2008). Formative assessments will often provide useful information when working with struggling readers, and should include self-assessments completed by students. Short-term assessments administered at key points provide immediate feedback and allow for a direct focus on specific strategy implementation or skill development. According to Schmoker (2006), they also provide valuable evidence for professional communities of teachers to receive recognition and rewards for their efforts to improve instruction. The connection between assessment and instruction makes it imperative that teachers not only routinely collect assessment data, but also conduct conversations regarding the analysis of the data. These conversations among teachers form the basis for reflection and change.

Summative assessments are administered at the end of an instructional unit or time period. The results summarize the progress of students as they complete their involvement in the learning task. The most powerful summative assessments are

ANTICIPATION/REACTION GUIDE

Directions: Before you read this chapter, complete the following anticipation/reaction guide. In the space before each statement, write **A** if you agree; **D** if you disagree; or **?** if you don't know. After you have read the chapter, complete the guide again to show what you have discovered in the chapter. In the space after each statement, mark whether you were initially correct (with a **C**) or incorrect (with an **I**). Write the letter for the correct answer (**A**) or (**D**) in the space for the statements that you initially marked with a question mark (**?**).

1. Standardized assessments are more helpful to teachers than informal assessments when considering the revision of daily instructional practices.

2. Record keeping is an essential part of observation.

3. Formal assessment is the most appropriate form of assessment for young students.

4. Readability formulas and text leveling both attempt to rank written materials on the basis of characteristics that contribute to text difficulty.

5. A running record is a narrative report of a student's overall progress.

6. A rubric is a performance-based assessment tool that outlines specific scoring criteria.

7. The cloze procedure is an example of a norm-referenced test.

8. Anecdotal records are written accounts of specific classroom incidents.

9. The Response to Intervention (RTI) model involves three tiers or levels of instructional interventions.

10. An informal reading inventory can provide the teacher with valuable assessment information regarding the nature of a student's word-recognition and comprehension skills.

supported by results from a number of formative assessments (Anderson, Grant, and Speck, 2008). **Formal,** or standardized, **assessments** are most often summative.

The gathering of the results of multiple assessments should be a continuous process that forms the basis for designing appropriate intervention plans for all students. Intervention plans address the instructional needs of students, include the conditions of the learning environment, and are implemented through selected techniques. The Response to Intervention (RTI) approach, described later in this chapter, provides a framework for creating a classroom environment where continuous assessment and intervention are merged. A number of appropriate intervention techniques that teachers can use to address instructional needs are described in this chapter and throughout the text.

CHAPTER 2 ORGANIZATION

Assessment and Intervention

- **Current Trends in Assessment**
- **Formal Assessment**
  - *Norm-Referenced Tests*
- **Criterion-Referenced Tests**
- **Alternative and Authentic Assessments**
  - *Observation*
  - *Portfolio Assessment*
  - *Self-Appraisal*
  - *Appraising Literary Interests*
  - *Informal Tests*
  - *Further Considerations About Alternative Assessment*
- **Assessment of Emergent Literacy**
- **Using Assessment to Guide Intervention**
  - *Planning for Intervention*
  - *Response to Interventions (RTI)*
  - *Assessing Text Difficulty*

Current Trends in Assessment

Over the last two decades, schools have responded to concerns regarding the quality of education in the United States. Subject-area specialists, professional organizations, researchers, and government agencies have worked for many years to identify outcome statements for academic learning. These statements have been identified and are currently recognized as **curriculum standards.** Examples of curriculum standards are available from a variety of sources. Some are developed and published by professional organizations that represent specific disciplines, such as the National Council for Teachers of English and International Reading Association (IRA/NCTE, 1996). In addition nearly every state has adopted its own set of

Visit **http://www.reading.org**, **http://www.ncte.org**, or the Student Website to link to the NCTE/IRA standards. You can also link to a compendium of the current K–12 curriculum standards for all content areas, provided by the Mid-continent Regional Educational Laboratory (**http://www.mcrel.org**), along with a variety of standards-based instructional units and lesson plans.

DIVERSITY

DIVERSITY

curriculum standards detailing what students at each grade level should know and be able to do in major subject areas. Local education agencies and individual educators are expected to develop instructional programs that enable students to meet their states' standards. Many of the curriculum standards adopted by individual states or local education agencies are based upon those endorsed by professional organizations associated with the specific content areas or disciplines.

The U.S. government has also invested in standards-based education. The Elementary and Secondary Education Act (ESEA) is a federal law that provides funding for schools serving low-income students. First enacted in 1965, ESEA is periodically renewed by Congress. The most recent version is called the No Child Left Behind (NCLB) Act. The NCLB Act requires that schools receiving funding present evidence of growth toward meeting established learning goals for their students. This measurement of goal success is identified as **adequate yearly progress (AYP).** ESEA also specifies a series of steps that must be enacted by schools that do not demonstrate AYP. Each school must also gather **disaggregated data** and report statistics that show separately the progress of several subgroups of students, including racial/ethnic groups, economically disadvantaged students, students with disabilities, and students with limited English proficiency. These groups have been referred to as "invisible kids" (Haycock, 2006). The long-term goal of the NCLB Act is that all students will demonstrate academic proficiency by the 2013–2014 academic year (Guilfoyle, 2006).

Despite their widespread use, some educators have expressed concerns that curriculum standards are often stated unclearly or are too demanding, presenting a set of ideals that are difficult or impossible to reach in practice (Gallagher, 2005; Rich, 2005). Teachers often struggle with helping students attain the goals of a standards-based curriculum while dealing with the varying needs of a diverse student population that is sometimes a long way from meeting the mandated academic goals.

As schools have implemented standards-based curricula, the need to measure or evaluate the success of these curricula has led to an accountability system that is sharply focused on student achievement. The purpose of the standards movement was to challenge schools to improve. As a result, much emphasis has been placed on standardized measures that compare groups and their performances in academic areas. The NCLB Act requires schools to test students in certain grade levels annually in reading, mathematics, and science.

Many formal assessment procedures—discussed later in this chapter—are used as accountability instruments. Standardized tests, for example, yield scores that school districts use to compare student achievement from year to year and to compare the scores of a district's students with national norms.

TEACHING TIP

Standards

As a teacher, it will be your task to help each of your students reach the goals set by your state's standards as well as possible. You need to become familiar with the standards and devise ways of meeting them within the instruction in the various subjects that you teach. You will also be involved in assessing your students' progress toward those benchmarks. The techniques provided in this chapter can help you meet this goal.

This emphasis on accountability has created an environment of high-stakes testing that has increased pressure for individual teachers and students. Teachers are expected to prepare students to demonstrate progress toward curriculum goals by taking tests mandated by their states and school districts. Some educators feel that the current climate encourages a practice known as "teaching to the test." Jennings and Rentner (2006), for example, raise the concern that mandated testing of reading and math under the NCLB Act has caused districts to reduce time spent on other subjects that are not tested. On the other hand, they state that the act has resulted in more attention to curriculum, teaching methods, and qualifications of teachers.

Other educators express concerns about the disaggregated reporting of test scores required by the NCLB Act. Paul (2004), for example, suggests that the testing under the act puts black and Latino students in imminent educational danger because it can "maintain a system in which the majority of blacks and Latinos never achieve full economic or sociopolitical parity" (p. 648). Sumida and Meyer (2006) are concerned that the act is turning schools with large minority populations and many students of low-socioeconomic status into places that depend on scripted instructional environments that emphasize test preparation.

Educators are concerned about keeping positive aspects of standards-based accountability practices, while eliminating negative ones. Hill (2006), for example, goes so far as to suggest, "presenting test taking as a separate and unique genre, and allowing reasonable but limited amounts of time to well-designed and thoughtful test preparation instruction" (p. 392). Then the rest of the year, teachers can focus on authentic reading and writing activities, keeping testing mandates in perspective.

Other educators also urge keeping testing in perspective by using a variety of assessment methods on an ongoing basis. The International Reading Association stresses that assessment should inform instruction and must be meaningful for those who plan and deliver the instructional program (Lewis and Moorman, 2007). Assessment guides teachers and enables them to individualize instruction. By reflecting on information from multiple sources, teachers can gain an understanding of each student's performance in order to plan long- and short-term instruction, determine lesson content, make instructional decisions, and decide which students need to be engaged in specific learning experiences.

We also believe that assessment should be a continuous process that forms the basis for designing an appropriate intervention plan that scaffolds learning. Teachers collect assessment data by observing students in authentic learning environments, by developing and/or using checklists and rubrics, by collecting and analyzing work samples, and through analysis of artifacts in portfolios, response journals, and retellings. All these techniques are described later in this chapter.

As teachers and administrators work collaboratively in learning communities to implement school improvement plans and develop curricula, the understanding of a variety of assessment data and implications for classroom use is of paramount importance in helping students learn (Guskey, 2007/2008).

Time for Reflection

Some believe that high-stakes testing has resulted in many educators "teaching to the test" and thereby limiting the reading curriculum and students' potential for critical reading. Others believe that these tests ensure accountability for instruction by educators.

What do *you* think, and why?

Formal Assessment

Formal assessment is the use of published **standardized tests** that have been constructed by experts in the field and are administered, scored, and interpreted according to specific criteria. Schools generally administer standardized achievement tests in the spring or fall every year to assess the gains in achievement of groups of students. Most of these tests are batteries, or collections of tests on different subjects, and must be administered under specific conditions and often over the course of several days. Upon their completion, the tests are generally sent to the publisher for scoring, and results are then sent to the school. Because many standardized tests are *computer scored*, they rely heavily on multiple-choice questions or items.

Some educators believe that standardized tests, especially those heavy in multiple-choice items, fail to measure thinking and problem-solving skills and in-depth knowledge of subjects. Critics also suggest that standardized tests do not provide students the most appropriate opportunities to demonstrate what they have learned (Pellegrino, Chudowsky, and Glaser, 2001; Rich, 2005). Despite these concerns, however, standardized tests are used with increasing frequency in current accountability systems. Teachers must therefore be familiar with the construction process and have a working knowledge of the results.

Norm-Referenced Tests

Norm-referenced tests are standardized tests that measure a student's standing in relation to comparable groups of students across the nation or locally. Authors of these tests sample large populations of students to determine the appropriateness of test items. They seek to verify the *validity* and *reliability* of test results so that schools can be confident that the tests measure what they are intended to measure and that results will not vary significantly if students take the same test more than once.

Results of norm-referenced tests are most commonly expressed as standard scores, such as grade equivalents (or grade scores), percentile ranks, or stanines. A *grade equivalent* indicates the grade level, in years and months, for which a given score was the average score in the standardization sample. *Percentile rank* (PR) expresses a score in terms of its position within a set of 100 scores. The PR indicates the percentage of scores in a reference group that is equal to or lower than the given score; therefore, a score ranked at the fortieth percentile is equal to or better than the scores of 40 percent of the people in the reference group. On a *stanine scale*, the scores are divided into nine equal parts, with a stanine of 5 as the mean.

Many standardized achievement tests contain subtests in reading and language that provide useful information for identifying students' general strengths and weaknesses in reading. However, these tests have limitations. To understand the limitations of standardized achievement tests, teachers should consider the following questions:

- *Do tests really reflect what we know about the reading process today?* Some standardized tests do not reflect current thinking about reading comprehension as a strategic process for reasons including the following:

The NCLB Act requires schools to assess students in specific grade levels annually in reading.
© Bob Daemmrich/PhotoEdit

1. The test may check knowledge of vocabulary by asking students to find the one of several words that most closely matches an isolated key word, instead of asking students to identify vocabulary in context, in the manner in which readers nearly always encounter words.

2. The test may assess reading comprehension on the basis of answers to series of short, unrelated paragraphs, instead of asking students to read longer passages as they would in authentic reading situations.

3. The test may present material without regard for students' prior knowledge, instead of considering the way that students' existing schemata interact with the text as students construct meaning.

- *Is the test fair to diverse learners?* Test publishers have been giving increasing attention to the question of the fairness of their tests. They do not want to state questions in a way that will give certain students an unfair advantage or discourage some students so that they will not do their best. Many writers and editors from diverse ethnic backgrounds are involved in test construction, and a number of reviewers edit to correct unintentional, built-in biases. Despite this progress, many observers still question the fairness of tests to some groups, such as English-language learners who haven't acquired a mastery of academic English.

 DIVERSITY

DIVERSITY

- *How are test scores being used?* Results of standardized tests are most beneficial for use at the school, district, state, national, or international levels, rather than for planning instruction for individual students. Standardized test scores should not be used to classify or group students according to achievement levels or to match materials designed for a particular reading level with students who scored at that level. Placements in instructional groups should be the result of ongoing, formative assessments, such as those described later in the chapter (Tyner and Green, 2005).

Some education agencies, such as the state of Tennessee and the Chicago public schools, include longitudinal achievement data as a value-added feature of their formal assessment programs. Whereas many tests attempt to determine evidence of achievement in comparison with a normed sample of the population, value-added scores attempt to profile the academic growth of an individual student. By collecting value-added testing information over a period of time, teachers are better able to profile academic growth, identify learning trends, and note the impact on a student's performance of possible intervening variables, such as the school system, the school, and the individual teacher (Holloway, 2000).

Criterion-Referenced Tests

A **criterion-referenced test** (or objective-referenced test) is designed to yield scores that are interpretable in terms of specific performance standards— for example, to indicate that a student can identify the main idea of a paragraph 90 percent of the time. Criterion-referenced tests are designed to match the standards or expectations of what students should know at successive points, or benchmarks, throughout their school careers. Such tests, which may be commercially prepared or teacher constructed, are intended to be used as guides for developing instructional prescriptions. For example, if a student cannot perform the task of identifying cause-and-effect relationships, the teacher should provide instruction in that area. Such specific applications make these tests useful in day-to-day decisions about instruction. The National Assessment of Educational Progress (NAEP) uses criterion-referenced assessment data to report on what American students in public and private schools know and can do in a number of subject areas (Snow, Burns, and Griffin, 1998; Bell and McCallum, 2008).

Criterion-referenced testing has both advantages and disadvantages. It is an effective way to determine what a student can do or to diagnose a student's knowledge of reading skills. Analyzing the results of a criterion-referenced assessment helps in prescribing appropriate instruction. Another advantage is that students do not compete with other students but only try to achieve mastery of each criterion or objective. A disadvantage of criterion-referenced assessment is that it can make reading appear to be nothing more than a series of skills to be taught and tested. Some teachers may

Visit the Student Website to link to more information about the NAEP testing schedule and the results of these nationally administered standardized tests or find it at http://www.nces .ed.gov/nationsreportcard/.

teach the skills in isolation rather than in combination. Knowledge gained in this way may be difficult for students to apply to actual reading situations.

Another consideration in criterion-referenced assessment is establishing appropriate standards. Establishing standards that are too high results in larger numbers of students who may fail to meet expectations. However, if standards are set too low, many students who are experiencing difficulty in reading will remain unidentified and may not receive appropriate instructional programs with interventions needed for success.

Alternative and Authentic Assessments

Concern about the inadequacies of standardized tests and about the need to look carefully at students' work in order to evaluate student performance has resulted in an increased interest in alternative and authentic assessments. **Alternative** and **authentic assessments** are administered throughout an instructional time frame. They may involve a whole class, small groups, or individuals. Alternative assessments prompt students to construct responses of their own, rather than respond to a prepared prompt (Campbell, 2003). Authentic assessments involve multiple progress indicators, include authentic tasks, and reflect progress in terms of growth over time rather than in terms of a one-time performance. They involve students in creating and self-evaluating their work, thus helping them develop a metacognitive sense of responsibility and ownership (Mueller, 2005).

Observation

During observation the teacher carefully watches the activities of a single student, a group of students, or the whole class in order to collect field notes and, perhaps, draw conclusions regarding a target behavior. The teacher may want to join or participate in a cooperative group activity in an effort to assess and analyze the depth of interaction informally. While observing students, the teacher may ask questions and comment on journal entries in order to stimulate further language and cognitive growth. Often information can be obtained by listening to a student read or discuss or by conducting individual conferences and examining a student's written work. Longer observations often reveal more information regarding students' progress than shorter ones do. Teachers can use their knowledge of learning principles and field notes collected over time to formulate conclusions that can help them develop necessary interventions or determine the progress of their students.

▶ Observation Strategies

Because much student assessment occurs informally, teachers need to interpret their observations with insight and accuracy. "Putting It into Practice: Evaluation Through Observation" shows how this may be accomplished.

Evaluation Through Observation

To successfully evaluate students' literacy development you will need to

- Recognize patterns of behavior and understand how reading and writing processes develop. You might notice, for example, that one student cannot make reasonable predictions or that another uses invented spellings effectively.

- Listen attentively at scheduled conferences, during class activities, and during casual conversations throughout the day.

- Observe in a variety of authentic, literacy-based settings, such as when students are informally writing notes to communicate or are reading to gather or share information.

- Evaluate as you teach, and accept the responsibility for assessing students' needs and responding to them, instead of relying only on standardized test data.

On the basis of observations and reasoning processes, teachers modify instructional strategies, clarify explanations, scaffold learning, use a variety of motivational techniques, adjust classroom management strategies, and provide reinforcement as needed.

Record keeping is an essential part of observation, and it may occur in different ways. Some teachers keep a notebook with a separate page to record field notes for each student; others jot dated comments on sticky notes or on file cards, which they later place in the students' files or portfolios. (See Example 2.1 for a sample observation card.) Use of anecdotal records, checklists, and rating forms can help teachers focus their observations on important areas of literacy learning.

Anecdotal Records. **Anecdotal records** are written accounts of specific incidents in the classroom. The teacher records information about a significant language event: the time and place, the students involved, what caused the incident, what happened, and possibly the implications. Such records may be kept for individual students, groups, or the whole class. Anecdotal records are useful in evaluating progress, planning and individualizing instruction, informing students and others of progress, noting changes in language development, and understanding attitudes and behaviors. Anecdotal records are especially helpful when educators are discussing the progress of students with special needs and English-language learners. Individualized Education Plan (IEP) team members often use anecdotal records to assist in the development of an initial IEP or in the revision of an existing one. Teachers who regularly keep anecdotal records become more sensitive to their students' special interests and needs and develop confidence in making educational decisions when combining multiple sources that include observational data. (See Example 2.2 for a sample anecdotal record.)

DIVERSITY

Checklists and Rating Scales. Some teachers also keep checklists, such as the literacy observation checklist in Example 2.3. Checklists are useful for recording information about student accomplishments and seeing at a glance what has been

EXAMPLE 2.1 Observation Card

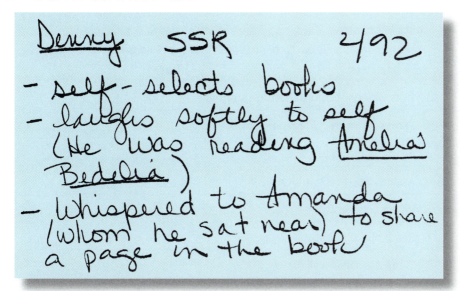

Denny   SSR   2/92

- self-selects books
- laughs softly to self
  (He was reading <u>Amelia Bedelia</u>)
- whispered to Amanda
  (whom he sat near) to share
  a page in the book

Source: Reprinted by permission from Beverly Mackie, Jere Whitson Elementary School, Cookeville, Tennessee

Time for Reflection

Review the descriptions of valid and reliable assessments on page 40. Do you think that data gathered through observations can form the basis for valid and reliable assessment of student progress?

Why or why not?

achieved and what needs further work. Rating scales provide additional information because teachers can assign numbers to each item, perhaps from 1 (lowest) to 5 (highest), according to each student's level of performance or achievement. The teaching tip on page 48 relates to checklists and rating scales.

"Seeing It in Practice: Evaluation of Literature Circles" shows how teacher Natalie Knox used a checklist for evaluation during literature circles (discussed in Chapters 9 and 10) in her sixth-grade class.

EXAMPLE 2.2 Anecdotal Record

It was Lee's first day in our third-grade classroom. He appeared hesitant about joining the other students during our morning activities. I had previously asked another student, Steve, to partner with Lee and help him through the first day. Steve agreed, so I assigned Lee to the desk next to Steve. Steve and Lee ate lunch together, and Steve did help include Lee in a game of kickball during recess. Before independent reading time, another student showed Lee where the classroom library was located, and Steve suggested one of his own favorite books, The Great Kapok Tree. Even though Lee spoke and read little English, Steve partner-read with him, pointing to pictures and words and discussing the story. By the end of the day, Lee was smiling and interacting with small groups of students in the classroom. Before leaving at the end of the day, Steve told me that he thought Lee had had a good day.

EXAMPLE 2.3 Literacy Observation Checklist

Student's name: _____ Teacher's name: _____

Place a check beside each characteristic that the child exhibits.

Characteristics: **Dates:**

1. Uses variety of comprehension strategies. _____ _____ _____

2. Expresses interest in reading and writing. _____ _____ _____

3. Reads voluntarily. _____ _____ _____

4. Applies word-recognition skills. _____ _____ _____

5. Writes coherently. _____ _____ _____

6. Reads aloud fluently. _____ _____ _____

7. Expresses ideas well orally. _____ _____ _____

8. Listens attentively. _____ _____ _____

9. Enjoys listening to stories. _____ _____ _____

10. Asks sensible questions. _____ _____ _____

11. Makes reasonable predictions. _____ _____ _____

12. Evaluates and monitors own work. _____ _____ _____

13. Works well independently. _____ _____ _____

14. Self-corrects errors. _____ _____ _____

15. Shows willingness to take risks. _____ _____ _____

16. Uses clues from visual aids to help with comprehension. _____ _____ _____

▶ Rubrics

A **rubric** is a **performance-based assessment** tool that provides specific criteria used to describe, score, and guide student performance (Campbell, 2003; Saddler and Andrade, 2004). Students receive a number of points that represent minimal to high-quality work, depending on the type of response. A well-constructed rubric lets

Evaluation of Literature Circles

Natalie Knox reminds students of their responsibilities for reading, discussing, writing in their literature logs, and planning for their next session while they are in their groups. She tries to meet with each group as both a participant and an evaluator. As she joins a group that is reading Lois Lowry's *Number the Stars*, she enters the discussion and also keeps a checklist of each student's status. One day's checklist is shown in Example 2.4.

As she visits different groups, Ms. Knox is gaining a great deal of information over a period of time about students' interests and enthusiasm, ability to gain insights about characters and plot development, and skill in group interaction. From her observations, she can make judgments about progress in student responses to literature and social interactions. The informal records of her observations can serve as a basis for parent conferences and entries on report cards. Because this is Ms. Knox's and the children's first time using multiple sets of books from quality literature instead of basal readers, she can also use the checklists to evaluate the success of this instructional approach.

EXAMPLE 2.4 Checklist For Literature-Response Groups

Number the Stars Meeting # 1	Attended	Read to page	Shared # of items	Asked questions for clarification	Made predictions &/or connections with in the book (or other books)	Made connections to real situations	Responded to others in group	Read from response journal
Kristine Zerr	✓	60	✓	- Ellen's family?		- Far away relatives	✓	hesitant
Marie Orly	✓	60	✓✓	- Why star? - Buttons?	- Sister's death?		✓	excellent
Katie Smith	✓	125	✓✓✓✓	- Symbols? - Religion?			✓ Missy Marie	thorough
Missy Guy	✓	65	✓✓✓	- Peter's involvement?		- Family friends religious difference		detailed
Magan Clifton	✓	60	✓✓✓✓✓	- Symbols?	- Fishing? - Mom's ?s	- Aunt's death	✓ Marie	- skipped around - sequence?
Next meeting: 11/19 Read to: p.94								

Rubrics

The following are some guidelines you can use for constructing rubrics:

- Identify the characteristics of the best-quality product or performance.
- Base standards on samples of student work that represent each level of proficiency.
- Use precise language that describes observable behaviors in terms that students understand.
- Avoid negative statements, such as "Cannot make predictions."
- Construct rubrics with 3-, 4-, or 5-point scales, with the highest number representing the most desirable level.
- Limit criteria to a reasonable number.

Checklists and Rating Scales

You can make several copies of a checklist or rating scale for each student and keep them in a folder. By filling out the forms periodically and dating each one, you will create a written record of each student's progress over time. You may also share checklists with students or use them as scoring rubrics or self-assessment tools.

RubiStar (http://www.rubistar .4teachers.org) is a popular website that can help you create rubrics. There is a link to RubiStar at the Student Website.

students know in advance what is expected of them and assists teachers in assessing students' work fairly. Then, when students receive their grades, they are more likely to understand them because they can refer to the criteria. Example 2.5 is a sample rubric.

When constructing rubrics, teachers may want to invite students to suggest criteria to include. Skillings and Ferrell (2000) reported a successful collaborative effort in the development and design of rubrics with second- and third-grade students. After studying teacher-generated rubrics critically, with careful guidance and scaffolding, students were encouraged to generate components of their own. Gradually, students participated in rubric design and development. This process helped students develop critical thinking and meta-cognitive skills.

When used correctly, rubrics are effective instructional and assessment tools (Andrade, 2000). The format of rubrics will vary, but all rubrics share two features: *standards*, which refer to the levels at which students perform tasks, and *criteria*, the specific items or behaviors being evaluated. The Putting It into Practice above offers guidelines for rubrics.

▶ Conferences and Interviews

Another type of informal assessment occurs when teachers have conferences or interviews with students about their attitudes, interests, and progress in reading. Conferences may be scheduled or may occur spontaneously when opportunities arise. The Putting It into Practice on page 49 provides sample questions to use.

Conference or Interview Questions

The following are sample questions that you may ask during a conference or interview:

- Do you like reading? Why or why not?
- Do you think that reading is important? Why or why not?
- What books have you read recently? What did you like/dislike about them? Are you a good reader? Why do you think that?
- What do you do when you have a problem understanding what you are reading?
- What do you do when you come to a word that you don't know?

Through interviews, you can learn how your students make interpretations and construct meaning. You can also gain insights into the reasoning behind students' task performances as students explain their answers. Interviews may be conducted for the purpose of collecting baseline information and then again as exit-type interviews for the purpose of prompting metacognitive reflection.

▶ Retellings

Retelling occurs when a student retells something that she or he has heard or read. Retellings can be done with any genre including all expository and narrative styles of writing. At first, the teacher encourages the student to retell without offering assistance, but when the student appears to have finished, the teacher may prompt by asking open-ended questions, or together they may complete a graphic organizer that can stimulate further retelling. By listening carefully and analyzing documentation, a teacher can learn much about a student's understanding and appreciation of the story. Retellings are effective assessment tools and may be used with either oral or written responses. As an instructional technique, retellings benefit students by improving their comprehension, sense of structure, and use of oral language (Fisette, 1993). (Chapter 7 discusses the instructional use of retellings in greater detail.) A rubric, such as the one in Example 2.5 on page 50, may be used to specify the criteria and standards for the retelling and can serve as documentation for the task.

 LITERATURE

The Student Website lists links to some host websites, such as Homestead (http://www.homestead.com) and TeacherWeb (http://www.teacherweb .com), that provide design templates for students and teachers to create personal or school sites.

Portfolio Assessment

A **portfolio** is a purposeful recording of learning that focuses on the work of the student and involves his or her reflection on that work. Student portfolios may be kept in expandable file folders, three-ring binders, or storage boxes or saved digitally via computer. Some teachers currently take advantage of web-based technologies to maintain a classroom presence and display student portfolio artifacts. Web addresses are assigned and can be accessed easily with an Internet connection. The creation of electronic portfolios integrates technology with performance-based assessment (Wade, Abrami, and Sclater, 2005) and makes viewing and sharing the portfolio easy and convenient. It also facilitates communication between the school and home.

EXAMPLE 2.5 Rubric for Oral or Written Retelling of a Narrative

3	2	1
Characterization		
Accurately recalls both primary and secondary characters.	Accurately recalls only primary or secondary characters, not both.	Incorrectly identifies the characters.
Uses vivid, appropriate descriptive words when discussing the characters.	Provides limited, correct descriptions of the characters.	Provides no descriptions or inaccurate descriptions.
Setting		
Recalls the setting: both place and time.	Recalls only the time or the place, not both.	Provides minimal information or inaccurately describes the setting.
Plot		
Recalls the action or plot in correct sequence as it happens in the story.	Describes some of the events as they occur in the story sequence.	Inaccurately describes events as they happen in the story sequence or describes events out of sequence.
Conflict/Resolution		
Accurately discusses both the conflict and the resolution.	Discusses only the conflict or the resolution, not both.	Discusses fragmented sections of the story with little mention of a conflict or problem with a resulting resolution.

Name of student: _____

Story: _____

Circle type of response:	Written	Oral

Portfolios enable students and teachers to analyze and reflect on student work in order to evaluate progress. Danielson and Abrutyn (1997) believe that it is not the portfolio itself, but the process of portfolio implementation, that helps establish a classroom climate in which both teachers and students recognize that learning is valued. Portfolios should focus on what a student *can* do, unlike tests, which often spotlight areas where students have not yet developed competence.

All artifacts in any type of portfolio should be dated. The specific items chosen by the teacher and/or student will vary according to the purposes for using them and the criteria for selection. Possible inclusions are the following: writing samples (from first draft to published work, to show growth); literacy goals; accounts of classroom experiences; a variety of products that demonstrate purposeful use of language; communications with others; audio and/or video recordings; multimedia presentations; reasons for selecting certain pieces; and reflections and self-evaluations.

Students share their portfolio artifacts with parents during Open House.
© Elizabeth Crews/The Image Works

Portfolios

There is no single way that you should implement portfolios, unless your school or district mandates procedures and inclusions. You will often need to determine what method works best for you and your students. It can be difficult to decide what to include in order to demonstrate, through collected artifacts, the knowledge and skills that students have acquired. You will need to consider how to analyze potential portfolio materials, how to evaluate portfolio contents for grading purposes, and how to guide students' selections of their best work. Questions such as the following can help: Who will see the portfolios? What should a portfolio look like? Who decides what to include? How should information be shared? Depending upon your assessment and instructional purposes, you will also want to consider different types of portfolios. Some different types to consider are as follows:

1. A *working portfolio* is a sampling of student work usually chosen by the student in collaboration with the teacher;

2. A *showcase portfolio* spotlights student-selected samples of best work only and is likely to be shared with family members during conferences;

3. A *record-keeping portfolio* is a collection of records of evaluation and test scores. It is kept by the teacher, often for purposes of accountability.

Portfolios allow for innovative ways to share information that is not always revealed through traditional assessments. Some examples include evidence of community or service learning, culminating performances from an interdisciplinary unit, and creative student products that demonstrate proficiency in a particular subject or skill area.

Although it is important for teachers and students to review portfolios together periodically, such reviews can consume considerable time. Teachers should develop rotating schedules in order to have a conference with each student at least once a month. "Seeing It in Practice: Using Portfolio Assessment" illustrates one teacher's procedure for conferences.

SEEING IT IN PRACTICE

Video Case
View the Video Case "Portfolio Assessment: Elementary Classroom" to observe how teacher Fred Park scaffolds a writing assignment that will later become a portfolio artifact.

Self-Appraisal

Assessment should help students develop the ability to judge their own accomplishments—to set their own goals, decide how to achieve those goals, and evaluate their progress in meeting their goals—in order to experience a sense of ownership in the assessment process (Au, 1990). Teachers can guide their students toward self-assessment by sharing audio or video recordings of oral reading, observation note cards, and checklists and by debriefing after conducting observations. These activities can help students become aware of their strengths and of the ways in which they might improve. Through interviews, teachers can help students focus on their own progress and can model reflection by asking such questions as "How has your

Using Portfolio Assessment

Although this was the first year that Mr. Fernandez had asked his students to prepare portfolios, he was quickly becoming aware of their usefulness. They were very helpful during parent conferences because he could show the parents exactly what their children had done during a six-week period—the progress they had made or, in a few cases, their lack of progress. The parents seemed to understand better what their children were doing by looking at their work than by having him try to explain it.

Mr. Fernandez had also found the samples of students' work useful when it was time to give report card grades. He had always believed that grades should be more than averages of test scores, and now he could use students' work samples to supplement their test score averages. Quite often, an examination of their work told him that his students were capable of better work than their tests indicated. If anyone questioned his judgment about his grades, he could show these samples, along with the test scores, to support his evaluation.

Perhaps best of all, many students liked working on their portfolios. They really enjoyed looking back through their papers, recalling different pieces they had worked on and realizing they were getting better. They also liked being able to choose which pieces to include, although sometimes Mr. Fernandez suggested additional pieces.

Mr. Fernandez moved throughout the room, conferring with students at their desks while they were engaged in an independent reading assignment. Students had their portfolios ready and were prepared for the individual conferences. At the conclusion of the conferences, Mr. Fernandez reflected on how much he had learned about the students' work as they explained their portfolios to him. He learned that he would need to help students make judgments about their work so that they could decide which selections merited inclusion in their portfolios. He would need to spend more time with some students. Some needed help with organizing and completing work. He saw opportunities for peer coaching, integration of special interests, and use of technology and other resources. Mr. Fernandez realized that conducting periodic portfolio reviews was an effective way to get to know his students better, understand their work, and encourage them to think and reflect.

Mr. Fernandez planned to do a few things differently the following year. He had heard of placing an audio recording in each portfolio and recording the children's oral reading periodically. That would be another way to measure their progress. He also needed a better system of weeding out some of their work; their portfolios would be quite bulky by the end of the year. He would try to get some ideas from teachers who were already using portfolios so that he could make the procedure run more smoothly next time.

reading improved in the last month?" and "What goals would you like to set for yourself in reading and writing?"

Students who display metacognition are aware of how they learn and of their personal strengths and weaknesses in relation to specific learning tasks. They ask themselves questions in order to assess the difficulty of an assignment, the learning strategies that they might use, any potential problems, and their likelihood of success. While they are reading or studying, their self-questioning might proceed as follows:

1. Do I understand exactly what I am supposed to do for this assignment?
2. What am I trying to learn?

3. What do I already know about this subject that will help me understand what I read?

4. What is the most efficient way for me to learn this material?

5. What parts of this chapter may give me problems?

6. What can I do so that I will understand the hard parts?

7. Now that I have finished reading, do I understand what I have read?

The self-appraisal form in Example 2.6 is designed primarily for intermediate and middle-level students. It enables students to assess their competency in various reading skills and to recognize areas of strength or weakness. Teachers can use the results to understand students' perceptions of their own needs and to plan appropriate instructional interventions. Another application for self-appraisal is found in Natalie Knox's literature circles, described in "Seeing It in Practice: Literature Circle Self-Evaluation."

EXAMPLE 2.6 Self-Check Exercise

Directions: Read the following sentences and put a number beside each one. Put 1 beside the sentence if it is nearly always true. Put 2 beside the sentence if it is sometimes true. Put 3 beside the sentence if it is hardly ever true.

_____ I understand what I read.

_____ I can find the main idea of a paragraph.

_____ I think about what I read and what it really means to me.

_____ I can "read between the lines" and understand what the author is trying to say.

_____ I think about what I already know about the subject as I read.

_____ I can figure out new words by reading the rest of the sentence.

_____ I can figure out new words by "sounding them out."

_____ I can use a dictionary to figure out how to pronounce new words.

_____ I can use a dictionary to find word meanings.

_____ I know how to find information in the library.

_____ I can locate books I like to read in the library.

_____ I know how to find information on the Internet.

_____ I can read aloud easily and with expression.

_____ I know what is important to learn in my textbooks.

_____ I know how to use the indexes in my books.

_____ I know how to study for a test.

_____ I ask myself questions as I read to make sure I understand.

Literature Circle Self-Evaluation

Students have completed the book for their literature circle, and it is time to fill out the self-evaluations that Natalie has given them. They rate themselves from 0 (not at all) to 3 (above average) on criteria related to their reading, their group responses, and their writing logs. After carefully rating themselves, they give themselves grades and justify their grades with reasons. Some of the students responded as follows:

The grade I think I deserve for this literature group is A because

most of the answers above are number threes. And I love discussing questions and other things about my book.

The grade I think I deserve for this literature group is B because

I think I deserve a B because I sometimes took my vocabulary folder home and left it and then didn't have it.

The grade I think I deserve for this literature group is C because

I think I can do better in keeping up with my journal. Mostly, I keep my voice level down and rarely get called down.

Such self-evaluation encourages students to reflect on their work and to become aware of their strengths and weaknesses. The development of self-assessment and self-appraisal supports the development of a metacognitive independent learner.

Appraising Literary Interests

An observant teacher who takes time to be a sensitive, yet constructively critical, evaluator of student progress is probably the best judge of the quality of their reactions to literature.

An excellent device for showing changes in literary taste over a period of time is a *reading record*, in which students record each book they read, giving the author, title, kind of book, date of report, and a brief statement of how well they liked the book. Reading records are often maintained separately by or for each student. They may classify reading selections by topic, such as poetry, fantasy, adventure, mystery, myths and folklore, animals (or, more specifically, horses and dogs, for example), biography, other lands, and sports. By focusing on their various interests and noting what genres of literature that students read, teachers may encourage them to read about new topics and to expand their reading interests.

 LITERATURE

Time for Reflection

Traditionally, teachers have felt that assessment was their job and that students should have little or nothing to say about their own work.

How might *you* encourage students to appraise their own work?

TEACHING TIP

Evaluating Literary Interests

You may want to ask yourself the following questions in the process of evaluating literary interests:

1. Are students gaining an appreciation of good literature? How do I know?

2. Are students making good use of time in the library and during free reading of books and periodicals?

3. Are students enjoying storytelling, reading aloud, choral reading, and creative drama?

   You can obtain answers to these questions through students' spontaneous remarks ("Do you know any other good books about space travel?"), through directed conversation with the class ("What books would you like to add to our classroom library?"), and during individual conferences, when students have opportunities to describe books they like and dislike.

Informal Tests

In addition to such informal assessments as observations, checklists, rubrics, and portfolios, teachers may administer informal tests for specific diagnostic purposes. They may construct these tests or may find them commercially available electronically or in manuals or books.

‣ Informal Tests of Specific Content or Skills

Sometimes the classroom teacher needs to administer an informal test to determine students' knowledge and understanding of a specific skill or content area. For instance, a teacher might construct a vocabulary test from words that students have studied during a thematic unit. Basal reader programs usually include tests to be used for determining how well students have learned the content of a specific unit of instruction. Workbooks may also contain skill tests to be given periodically. The teacher should use tests for diagnosing students' strengths and weaknesses, deciding if reteaching is needed, and providing direction for future learning experiences.

‣ Cloze Procedure

The **cloze procedure** is an instructional strategy that can also be used as a tool to assess student comprehension. It provides information regarding a student's use of semantics, syntax, and context clues. By filling in words that have been deleted from a textbook selection (as described in "Putting It into Practice: Cloze Test Construction"), the student reveals his or her familiarity with the subject and ability to read the text with understanding. Test results give information about the student's independent, instructional, and frustration levels for both narrative and expository material. Independent, instructional, and frustration levels are discussed further in the "Informal Reading Inventory" section later in this chapter.

‣ Multimedia and Computer Approaches

Multimedia and computers provide motivational alternatives to traditional testing. Photographs of completed projects, audio recordings of students retelling stories or reading orally, and video recordings of student performances and students at work are useful for recording and evaluating students' learning experiences throughout the year. Multimedia computer presentations, prepared by students, show evidence of facility with a number of literacy skills.

Cloze Test Construction

You can construct a cloze test as follows:

1. Select a passage of approximately 250 consecutive words. The passage should be one that students have not read, or tried to read, before.

2. Type the passage, leaving the first and last sentences intact but deleting every fifth word between those sentences. In place of deleted words, substitute blanks of uniform length.

3. Give students the passage and tell them to fill in the blanks. Allow them all the time they need.

4. Score the test by counting as correct only the exact words that were in the original text. Determine each student's percentage of correct answers.

If a student had less than 44 percent of the answers correct, the material is probably at his or her frustration level and is therefore too difficult. You should offer alternative ways of learning the material. If the student had from 44 to 57 percent of the answers correct, the material is probably at that student's instructional level, and he or she will be able to learn from the text if you provide careful guidance for the reading by developing readiness, helping with new concepts and unfamiliar vocabulary, and providing reading purposes to aid comprehension. If the student had more than 57 percent of the answers correct, the material is probably at that student's independent level, and he or she should be able to benefit from the material when reading it independently (Bormuth, 1968).

To use the percentages given here, you must count only exact words as correct because the percentages were derived using only exact words. Synonyms must be counted as incorrect, along with obviously wrong answers and unfilled blanks.

Teachers can use computers for assessment in several additional ways. Online testing allows students to work at computers that have software that analyzes their responses. Sometimes computers are used to scan mark-sensitive answer sheets that students have completed while working with test booklets. The computer scores the tests, thus freeing the teacher from this task. Software is also available to help teachers modify test items and entire tests, perform test and item analysis, collect and analyze test scores and student grades, record grades for various assignments, and compute final grades. *Gradebook Plus* enables teachers to record grades daily and to compute a student's average grade at any time. Web-based technologies also allow teachers and students to create web pages that can be used to display and share portfolio artifacts.

▶ Informal Reading Inventory

Teachers administer **informal reading inventories (IRIs)** to get a general idea of a student's reading levels and strengths and weaknesses in word recognition and comprehension. IRIs can help teachers identify specific types of word-recognition and comprehension difficulties so that they can use this information to plan appropriate instruction. An IRI can indicate a student's

1. **Independent reading level** (level to be read "on his or her own").

2. **Instructional level** (level of the material that the student can read with appropriate scaffolding).

3. **Frustration level** (level of material that thwarts or baffles).

4. **Listening comprehension level** (level of material that the student can comprehend when it is read to him or her).

An IRI typically consists of an analysis of oral and silent reading, as well as listening comprehension. The oral-reading sequence in an IRI should begin on the highest level at which the student achieves 100 percent on a sight word-recognition test. After the oral reading, the teacher asks the student questions about the oral-reading selection; then the student reads a selection at the same level silently and answers questions about that selection.

Material is written at a student's independent reading level when he or she correctly pronounces 99 words out of 100 (99 percent correct) and correctly responds to at least 90 percent of the questions. The material for which the student correctly pronounces 95 percent of the words and correctly answers at least 75 percent of the questions is roughly at the student's instructional level, the level at which teaching may effectively take place.

If a student needs help on more than one word out of ten or responds correctly to fewer than 50 percent of the questions, the material is too advanced and is at the student's frustration level. After the frustration level has been reached, the teacher should read aloud more difficult levels of material until the student reaches the highest reading level for which he or she can correctly answer 75 percent of the comprehension questions. The highest level achieved indicates the student's probable listening comprehension level (potential reading level).

Teachers may make their own IRIs, or they may use commercially prepared inventories. Example 2.7 shows a sample reading selection with comprehension questions and scoring aid from the *Burns/Roe Informal Reading Inventory*.

It is important to remember that the result of an IRI is an estimate of a student's reading levels. The percentages that the student achieves are a significant indication of levels of performance, but the teacher's observations of the student taking the test are equally important.

▸ Miscue Analysis

 STRUGGLING READER/ INTERVENTION

Similar in form and procedures to the IRI, the **reading miscue inventory (RMI)** considers both the quantity and the quality of **miscues,** or unexpected responses. Instead of simply considering the number of errors and giving equal weight to each, the teacher analyzes the RMI for the significance of each miscue. Knowing the type of miscue and what might have caused it provides more information about reading difficulties than knowing only the number of miscues. (Some commercial IRIs, such as the one in Example 2.7, also include a qualitative analysis.)

EXAMPLE 2.7 Reading Selection and Questions from an Informal Reading Inventory

TEACHER 5 ☆

INTRODUCTORY STATEMENT: Read this story to find out about a harbor seal pup that has a special problem.

In the sea, a harbor seal pup learns to catch and eat fish by watching its mother. By the time it is weaned, at the age of four or five weeks, it is able to feed on its own.

Without a mother, and living temporarily in captivity, Pearson had to be taught what a fish was and how to swallow it. Eventually, he would have to learn to catch one himself.

Holly started his training with a small herring—an oily fish which is a favorite with seals. Gently, she opened his mouth and slipped the fish in headfirst. Harbor seals have sharp teeth for catching fish but no teeth for grinding and chewing. They swallow their food whole.

But Pearson didn't seem to understand what he was supposed to do. He bit down on the fish and then spit it out. Holly tried again. This time, Pearson got the idea. He swallowed the herring in one gulp and looked eagerly for more.

Within a week, he was being hand-fed a pound of fish a day in addition to his formula. This new diet made him friskier than ever. He chased the other pups in the outside pen. He plunged into the small wading pool and rolled in the shallow water, splashing both seals and people.

Source: Pearson, A Harbor Seal Pup, by Susan Meyers (New York: E. P. Dutton, 1980), pp. 15–16. [*Note:* Do not count as a miscue mispronunciation of the name Pearson. You may pronounce this name for the student if needed.]

SCORING AID

Word Recognition %—Miscues

99–3
95–11
90–22
85–33

Comprehension %—Errors

100–0
90–1
80–2
70–3
60–4
50–5
40–6
30–7
20–8
10–9
0–10

214 Words (for word recognition)

217 Words (for rate)

WPM

13020

FORM A

5 PASSAGE

COMPREHENSION QUESTIONS

____ main idea	1.	What is this story about? (teaching a harbor seal pup to catch and eat fish; teaching Pearson to catch and eat fish)
____ detail	2.	How does a harbor seal pup learn to catch and eat fish in the sea? (by watching its mother)
____ vocabulary	3.	What does the word "temporarily" mean? (for a short time; not permanently)
____ vocabulary	4.	What does the word "captivity" mean? (the condition of being held as a prisoner or captive; confinement; a condition in which a person or animal is not free)
____ cause and effect/inference	5.	What caused Pearson to need to be taught what a fish was and how to swallow it? (He didn't have a mother to show him.)
____ inference	6.	What is an oily fish that seals like? (herring)
____ cause and effect/inference	7.	What causes harbor seals to swallow their food whole? (They have no teeth for grinding and chewing.)
____ sequence	8.	Name in order the two things that Pearson did the first time Holly put a fish in his mouth. (bit down on the fish and then spit it out)
____ inference	9.	How fast did Pearson learn how to eat a fish? (He learned on the second try.)
____ detail	10.	What made Pearson get friskier? (his new diet of fish and formula; his new diet)

☆

"Putting It into Practice: Miscue Analysis" gives some instructions for analyzing miscues. Miscue analysis helps teachers gain insight into the reading process and helps them analyze students' oral reading (Y. Goodman, 1995). Analysis of the types of miscues that each student makes can help a teacher interpret why the student is having difficulties. To some extent, miscues are the result of the thought and language that the student brings to the reading situation. Therefore, analyzing miscues in terms of the student's background or schemata enables a teacher to understand why some miscues occurred and to provide appropriate instructional strategies that build on the student's strengths.

▶ Running Records

The **running record** is a detailed account of a student's reading behavior. A teacher can use a running record to determine how well that student is reading (Clay, 1979; Harris and Hodges, 1995). The procedure for completing the running record is similar to that used with the IRI or RMI. While a student is reading, the teacher places a check above every word read correctly. When a student makes a miscue, the teacher uses a coding system to mark the type of miscue. After completing the running record, the teacher considers why the student made each miscue by asking, "What made him/her say that?"

Running records are particularly useful for classroom teachers because they can be made quickly and easily in any oral-reading situation in which the teacher can see the text that a student is reading (Lipson and Wixson, 1997). As noted earlier, students' miscues offer insights into how well they use various reading strategies, construct meaning from text, and monitor their own reading (for example, self-correct if something doesn't make sense). As a result, teachers become aware of students' strengths and weaknesses and gain information to guide their instruction (Salinger, 1996).

Further Considerations About Alternative Assessment

Even though alternative assessment gives a great deal of information about how well a student uses reading strategies, it has some limitations that teachers should keep in mind:

- Alternative assessment is subjective; that is, the teacher's personal biases may influence judgments about student performance. Therefore, it is possible for two teachers to assess the same work differently. Also, some teachers may not be knowledgeable about the use of informal strategies or may not have realistic expectations for students at a certain level, so their assessments may not be fair appraisals of student performance.

- Alternative assessment can also take a great deal of time. It takes longer to write frequent narrative reports on student progress than to simply assign numerical or letter grades based on objective test results.

Time for Reflection

When administering running records, some educators believe that counting the total number of miscues a reader makes is sufficient for purposes of evaluation, while others consider it always important to analyze miscues to find the reasons for the unexpected responses.

What do *you* think, and why?

Miscue Analysis

When analyzing miscues, you need to consider whether miscalled words indicate lack of knowledge about phonics or structural analysis, show inability to use context, reveal limited sight word knowledge, result from dialect differences, or suggest some other type of difficulty. Therefore, while listening to a student read, you must evaluate the significance of different miscues. For example, the student who reads "The boys are playing" as "The boys is playing" may be a speaker of a nonstandard dialect and may be using his or her decoding ability to translate the printed text to meaning. This miscue does not interfere with meaning, but many miscues do reflect problems.

In studying the miscues, check for specific items such as the following:

1. Is the miscue a result of the reader's dialect? If the reader says *foe* for *four*, he or she may simply be using a familiar pronunciation that does not affect meaning.

2. Does the miscue change the meaning? If the reader says *dismal* for *dismiss*, the meaning is changed, and the substitution would not make sense.

3. Does the reader self-correct? If the student says a word that does not make sense but self-corrects, he or she is trying to make sense of what he or she is reading.

4. Is the reader using syntactic cues (related to word order in English)? If the student says *run* for *chase*, the student still shows some use of syntactic cues, but if the student says *boy* for *beautiful*, he or she is probably losing the syntactic pattern.

5. Is the student using graphic cues? Comparing the sounds and spellings of miscues and expected words in substitutions will reveal how a reader is using graphic cues. Examples of graphic miscues include *house* for *horse*, *running* for *run*, *is* for *it*, and *dogs* for *dog*.

- Teachers must know how to interpret and apply information from informal records to help children improve their reading strategies.

- It is important to collect alternative assessment data from multiple sources and identify similarities and differences when comparing the outcomes.

Assessment of Emergent Literacy

In 2003 the National Association for the Education of Young Children (NAEYC) presented guidelines for the assessment of young children in a jointly published position statement with the National Association of Early Childhood Specialists in State Departments of Education (NAECS/SDE). The guidelines include recommendations for assessments that are developmentally appropriate and administered in realistic settings and situations that would best reflect the child's actual performance. The position statement also suggests that formal, standardized testing be limited, and if it is used as part of a program accountability system, that only a sampling of children necessary for the study be included, to decrease the burden of testing on the children and to reduce the tendency to make instructional judgments about individual children.

A teacher in an emergent literacy classroom (discussed in detail in Chapter 3) recognizes that most students arrive at school already knowing a great deal about literacy. Many teachers of young students are interested in investigating and documenting not only what a student knows, but also what he or she can apply. Teachers can evaluate children's awareness of the function or purpose of writing by observing their responses to printed labels and messages. By noting children's retellings or answers to questions about stories read to them, teachers can learn about children's comprehension strategies. Children reveal a great deal about their emergent literacy when they pretend to read books, especially by the way they structure stories or use pictures. Their use of invented spellings when they write and their perceptions of the connections between reading and writing as they "read" their writings also indicate their literacy development. Other indications include the ability to dictate coherent stories and to recognize environmental print (words on signs, for example).

Clay's *Concepts About Print* is an assessment tool used by teachers to provide observation data to support the literacy development of young students. *Concepts About Print* is suggested for use during the first two years of literacy instruction and is one component of a more comprehensive tool, *An Observation Survey of Early Literacy Achievement* (Clay, 2006).

Authentic assessment methods are often employed successfully in a natural setting for the purpose of viewing the development of emergent literacy. Teachers can create their own informal checklists of literacy skills and behaviors. Periodically filling out and dating the checklist forms creates a written record of each child's progress. (Example 2.3 provides a sample observation checklist for literacy development.)

Using Assessment to Guide Intervention

STRUGGLING READER/ INTERVENTION

With the current emphasis on accountability and recent changes in legislation, all teachers must understand student performance data, select appropriate formative assessments, identify instructional needs for each student, and be competent in implementing an intervention plan of strategies that will successfully scaffold learning for each student.

Planning for Intervention

DIVERSITY

Once teachers have collected student performance data and identified individual strengths and areas that need development for each student, they must consider the appropriate strategies that will best meet each student's needs. When considering student needs, teachers must refer to all of the performance assessment data, including information about students' interests and learning preferences. Chosen strategies should be evidence based—research studies should support their usefulness—and appropriate for the needs of each student. (Chapters 3–13 describe strategies that may be used in an intervention plan.) Teachers also need to consider classroom elements including what is to be taught, how it is to be taught, and what will provide evidence that the learning occurred.

As intervention plans are constructed, a variety of instructional strategies are considered. Guskey (2007/2008) reminds us selected intervention strategies should be designed to present concepts differently, engage students differently, and support successful learning. Planning should involve some degree of student choice and accommodate student needs and learning preferences. Some effective intervention strategies, described by Guskey, include reteaching, individual tutoring, peer tutoring, cooperative teams, academic games, and learning centers.

The learning environment or climate in the classroom is another important consideration when planning for instruction (Jensen, 2005). When planning for instruction, a teacher should not just consider aspects of the physical environment, such as seating, lighting, and temperature. Good teachers also create a place where students are emotionally safe and feel as if they are respected and valued. Teachers who create this type of classroom spend time establishing relationships, building upon social interactions, and working toward the development of self-efficacy of all students.

Strategies included in an intervention plan may involve whole-group, small-group, or individualized implementation. The grouping of students for instruction is often accomplished by forming flexible small groups. Guided reading (discussed in Chapters 3, 5, and 9) is an example of a model for small-group reading instruction that is growing in acceptance beyond the primary levels (Tyner and Green, 2005). Most teachers implement some form of instructional grouping, although specific grouping patterns often vary according to grade level. Many primary-level teachers are located in self-contained settings with the responsibility for all curriculum areas. Intermediate and middle-level teachers often see larger numbers of students throughout the day and may have few areas of the curriculum assigned to them for instruction. Given the number of students located in any classroom, it is often unrealistic to think that all instruction can be delivered individually, even though it is an extremely successful model.

The concept of a differentiated classroom (Tomlinson, 2003) provides a responsive model for instructional delivery or organization in which teachers modify the content (what is to be learned), the process (how it is to be learned), the product (the demonstration of what is learned), or the learning environment (where the learning occurs). It is through the curriculum that the instructional needs of students are met. According to Tomlinson, the curriculum should be important, focused, engaging, demanding, and scaffolded so that students can succeed.

In responsive, differentiated classrooms, teachers rely on multiple assessments, or informative assessments as described by Tomlinson (2007/2008), to provide the information needed to plan instructional interventions. This allows educators to identify struggling readers early so that modifications of the content, the process, the product, or the environment may be specified appropriately in intervention plans.

 STRUGGLING READER/INTERVENTION

Response to Interventions (RTI)

The **Response to Intervention (RTI)** model provides a framework for a responsive classroom where the learning environment is modified by three tiers of differentiated instruction based upon ongoing formative assessment of student progress.

 DIVERSITY

The federal Individuals with Disabilities Education Act (IDEA) recommends that teachers use a tiered approach to provide instruction to students in an effort to meet all students' instructional needs and to support early identification of students with reading and learning difficulties. Although the number of tiers may vary, typically a three-tier intervention model is used and is described as follows:

- *Primary Instruction.* The first tier involves instruction at the classroom level where the primary instruction is delivered by the classroom teacher. Effective primary instruction requires that classroom teachers be knowledgeable about learning differences. The teacher must know how to screen and collect baseline assessment data, select appropriate strategies for the development of intervention plans to deliver to the whole class and in flexible grouping patterns, and appropriately evaluate progress for all students. The instruction involves a core reading curriculum with formative assessments administered at least three times each year.

 STRUGGLING READER/ INTERVENTION

- *Secondary Intervention.* The second tier, or the secondary intervention, involves instruction delivered to those students who are not making adequate progress in the core curriculum. These students receive additional instruction, typically an additional thirty minutes of a strategic intervention based upon individually assessed needs. The interventionist outlines the strategies and delivers the instruction in small focused groups. Formative assessment data are collected at least twice each month to monitor the progress toward mastery of specific target skills.

 STRUGGLING READER/ INTERVENTION

- *Individual/Small-Group Instruction.* Students who fail to make progress at the tier two level will need to be involved in more individualized or small-group, intensive intervention plans. This is the third tier of instruction. Instruction in tier three is delivered by a specially trained educator or interventionist who has expertise in individualized assessment and instruction (Haager, Klingner, and Vaughn, 2007).

In addition to creating a responsive environment and identifying appropriate strategies based upon students' instructional needs, teachers carefully select instructional materials that support the curriculum and help facilitate learning of the selected strategies. Selecting materials for intervention plans requires teachers to be knowledgeable about curriculum standards. (Many materials that may be used are discussed in Chapters 3–13.) As teachers plan, they must select the resources that will enable them to teach the expected material. Generally, schools adopt curriculum materials such as published basal reading programs or textbooks in the various content areas. Most teachers find, however, that no single resource is sufficient. Many choose to supplement basal readers or textbooks with other appropriate instructional materials. Several factors, including interest, must be considered when selecting instructional resources. One important factor for inclusion in an intervention plan is the appropriateness of the readability level, or difficulty level, of reading materials that are chosen for instruction.

Assessing Text Difficulty

Methods of identifying text difficulty include the use of readability formulas, cloze tests, and text-leveling techniques.

Readability formulas often rank text by numerical values based on syntactic (word order and sentence structure) and semantic (word meaning) difficulty. When teachers have determined the students' reading levels with tests, they can obtain an approximate idea of whether a textbook or literature selection is appropriate by testing it with a standard measure of readability. Among widely used readability formulas, the *Spache Readability Formula* is designed for primary-grade books (Spache, 1966), the *Dale-Chall Readability Formula* is designed for materials from the fourth-grade through college levels (Dale and Chall, 1948), and the *Fry Readability Graph* (Fry, 1977b) can be used on material at all levels.

Because readability formulas are strictly text based, they do not give information related to the interactive nature of reading. For example, they cannot gauge a reader's background knowledge about the topic, motivation to read the material, or interest in the topic, although these are important factors in determining the difficulty of a text for a particular student. In addition, they cannot separate reasonable prose from a series of unconnected words. They cannot measure the effects of an author's writing style or the complexity of concepts presented, and they do not consider the format of the material (typeface and type size, spacing, amount of white space on the page, numbers of illustrations and pictures, and so on). For these reasons, no formula offers more than an approximation of level of difficulty of material. Formulas do, however, generally give reliable information about the relative difficulty levels of textbook passages and other printed materials, and this information can be extremely helpful to teachers. Example 2.8 shows a quick way to estimate readability. Computer programs designed to test readability can also ease the burden of making calculations by hand. Grammar and style checking programs may run several formulas.

Many content-area textbooks are written at much higher readability levels than basal readers for the corresponding grades, and subject-matter textbooks also often vary in difficulty from chapter to chapter. (More on the difficulty of subject-matter textbooks is provided in Chapter 12.) Unfamiliar content vocabulary is a major factor in the higher difficulty levels of many content-area materials.

A cloze procedure is another option for assessing text difficulty and the suitability of a textbook or literature selection for students. Because all the material in a given book is unlikely to be written on the same level, a teacher should choose several samples from different places in the book for a cloze test, to determine the book's suitability for a particular student.

Kathy Schrock's website (http://school .discoveryeducation.com/schrock guide/fry/fry.html) provides general information and a guide for educators, regarding readability resources, including links for the Flesch and Gunning Fox Index. You can link to it from your Student Website.

EXAMPLE 2.8 Fry Readability Formula

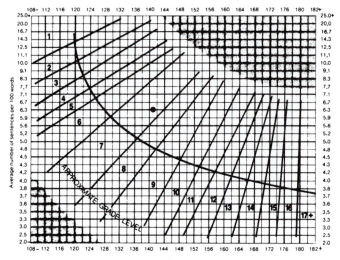

Expanded Directions for Working Readability Graph

1. Randomly select three (3) sample passages and count out exactly 100 words each, beginning with the beginning of a sentence. Do count proper nouns, initializations, and numerals.
2. Count the number of sentences in the hundred words, estimating length of the fraction of the last sentence to the nearest one-tenth.
3. Count the total number of syllables in the 100-word passage. If you don't have a hand counter available, an easy way is to simply put a mark above every syllable over one in each word, then when you get to the end of the passage, count the number of marks and add 100. Small calculators can also be used as counters by pushing numeral 1, then push the + sign for each word or syllable when counting.
4. Enter graph with *average* sentence length and *average* number of syllables; plot dot where the two lines intersect. Area where dot is plotted will give you the approximate grade level.
5. If a great deal of variability is found in syllable count or sentence count, putting more samples into the average is desirable.
6. A word is defined as a group of symbols with a space on either side; thus, *Joe, IRA, 1945,* and *&* are each one word.
7. A syllable is defined as a phonetic syllable. Generally, there are as many syllables as vowel sounds. For example, *stopped* is one syllable and *wanted* is two syllables. When counting syllables for numerals and initializations, count one syllable for each symbol. For example, *1945* is four syllables, *IRA* is three syllables, and *&* is one syllable.

Note: This "extended graph" does not outmode or render the earlier (1968) version inoperative or inaccurate; it is an extension. (REPRODUCTION PERMITTED—NO COPYRIGHT)

Source: "Fry's Readability Graph: Clarifications, Validity, and Extension to Level 17," *Journal of Reading* 21 (December 1977): 249.

Example 2.9 shows a cloze passage for a social studies textbook. This passage contains 283 words. To give the student an opportunity to develop an appropriate mental set for the material that follows, no words have been deleted from the first sentence, and the entire paragraph in which the fiftieth blank occurs has been included to complete the thought that was in progress. A score of fewer than 22 correct responses

EXAMPLE 2.9 Cloze Test

Directions: Read the following passage and fill in each blank with a word that makes sense in the sentence.

The first battle in July 1861 began like a holiday outing. Union supporters packed picnic _____ and followed soldiers
(1)
from _____, D.C., into Virginia. Newspaper _____ also came to get _____ story.
(2)   (3)   (4)
Armies from the _____ and the South met _____ a stream called Bull _____, about 25 miles from
(5)   (6)   (7)
_____, D.C. At first Confederates _____ the Union soldiers back. _____ the Confederates attacked. Fierce
(8)   (9)   (10)
_____ broke out, and the _____ army won the battle.
(11)   (12)
_____ Battle of Bull Run _____ the North that it _____ not win the war _____. Congress passed laws
(13)   (14)   (15)   (16)
calling _____ troops to serve three _____. President Lincoln's generals had _____ plan to save the _____.
(17)   (18)   (19)   (20)
The Union's "anaconda plan" _____ named for the snake _____ squeezes its prey to _____. The Union planned
(21)   (22)   (23)
to _____ the strength out of _____ South by a blockade, _____ closing of southern ocean _____. Union
(24)   (25)   (26)   (28)
ships would stop _____ and keep Southerners from _____ money by selling cotton _____ other countries.
(28)   (29)   (30)
Under the _____ plan, Union ships would _____ control of the Mississippi _____. Confederate states
(31)   (32)   (33)
would then _____ unable to send boats _____ supplies and soldiers to _____ Confederate states. Finally,
(34)   (35)   (36)
Union _____ would try to capture _____, the Confederate capital.
(37)   (38)
The _____ also had plans. One _____ to destroy Union ships. _____ 1862, the South sent _____
(39)   (40)   (41)   (42)
iron-sided steamship, *Merrimack*, up _____ James River. (The South _____ the ship the *Virginia*.) _____
(43)   (44)   (45)
Merrimack was far stronger _____ the Union's wooden ships. _____ Union ships fired at _____, the cannon-
(46)   (47)   (48)
balls could not _____ the ship's sides.
(49)
The _____ day, the Union sent its own iron ship, the *Monitor*, to attack the *Merrimack*. The two ships battled, with no
(50)
clear winner.

Answers: (1) lunches, (2) Washington, (3) reporters, (4) the, (5) North, (6) near, (7) Run, (8) Washington, (9) held, (10) Then,
(11) fighting, (12) Confederate, (13) The, (14) showed, (15) would, (16) easily, (17) for, (18) years, (19) a, (20) Union, (21) was,
(22) that, (23) death, (24) squeeze, (25) the, (26) or, (27) ports, (28) supplies, (29) earning, (30) to, (31) anaconda, (32) take, (33)
River, (34) be, (35) with, (36) other, (37) forces, (38) Richmond, (39) South, (40) was, (41) In, (42) its, (43) the, (44) renamed, (45)
The, (46) than, (47) When, (48) it, (49) pierce, (50) next.

(44 percent correct) indicates that the material is too difficult; a score of 22 to 28 (44 to 56 percent) indicates that the child can manage the material if the teacher gives assistance; and a score of more than 28 (56 percent correct) indicates that the child can read the material independently.

Some authorities prefer cloze tests to informal reading inventories (IRIs) for matching textbooks to students because these tests put the student in direct contact with the author's language without having the teacher as a mediator (through the written questions). Frequently, a reader can understand the text but not the teacher's questions related to it, which can cause the teacher to underestimate the child's comprehension of the material. On the other hand, some children react with frustration to cloze materials; these children would fare better if tested with an IRI. Children should have experience with cloze-type exercises before teachers use this procedure to help match students with textbooks at the appropriate levels.

Text leveling involves organizing texts according to a defined continuum of characteristics so that teachers can match students with appropriate materials (Fountas and Pinnell, 1996; Fry, 2002; Walker, 2008). Whereas readability is determined in an objective manner, leveling of texts occurs more subjectively. In some cases, individual teachers or teams of teachers work collaboratively to level texts and compile a collection of appropriate reading materials. Fountas and Pinnell (1996) offer lists of texts that have been leveled and are suggested for use in the implementation of guided reading, described in Chapters 3 and 9. Characteristics of texts are first identified, and then decisions about the level of difficulty are made. Some characteristics or text factors that are often included in the process of leveling are format, including size and layout of print; content, including concepts and vocabulary; length; illustration support; genre; predictability; and language structure.

Readability may also be considered in the leveling process. The leveling of texts involves observation of students' reading behavior as they interact with the text over a period of time. Running records are maintained and provide information to identify benchmark texts for the various levels. Benchmark texts are those that remain reliable for the level for approximately 90 percent of students. Although the leveling of texts does not rely only on a quantitative formula, it involves consideration of more text factors and is particularly appealing to teachers at the primary levels (Fountas and Pinnell, 1996; Fry, 2002).

SUMMARY

Assessment is a process, not an event. Assessment is ongoing and is an integral part of the instructional program. Assessment procedures are constantly changing as educators seek ways to measure student progress in reading that reflect current views of the reading process. More than ever before, assessment is merging with instruction as teachers continuously observe students, interact with them, and analyze their strengths and weaknesses.

Although teachers use summative results from formal assessment techniques, they are more likely to rely on formative informal assessments to monitor student progress and adjust instruction. As students engage in learning experiences, the teacher collects and analyzes data to determine appropriate intervention plans of instructional strategies that scaffold and support the development of literacy skills.

Formal assessment consists of standardized tests that are administered, scored, and interpreted according to designated procedures. Norm-referenced tests compare students with other students across the nation on the basis of standard scores. Most schools require that achievement tests be administered annually to measure the progress that students have made in overall academic achievement.

The teacher can use criterion-referenced tests to determine how well a student has mastered a specific skill. Skill mastery, however, does not always indicate whether or not the student can generalize, transfer, and apply the skill to actual reading situations.

Alternative assessment can take many forms, and teachers can learn much about their students by developing and utilizing observation strategies. Daily observation is a key to effective assessment, and teachers can record their observations in a variety of ways, including anecdotal records and checklists and rating scales. Rubrics make students aware of expectations by giving specific criteria for scoring their work, and teachers gain insight into students' reading abilities through conferences, interviews, and student retellings. Portfolios are useful for keeping samples of student work, and self-appraisal helps students evaluate their own accomplishments.

Informal tests that cover specific areas, including teacher-made tests on content or skills, provide information about student mastery of specific details. Cloze procedures enable teachers to assess a student's comprehension of material, and multimedia and computers are also used in various ways to assess students' knowledge. The informal reading inventory (IRI), reading miscue inventory (RMI), and running records are similar informal measures that help the teacher identify students' strengths and weaknesses.

The strong connection between assessment and instruction has resulted in the implementation of instructional models such as the Response to Intervention (RTI) framework. The RTI outlines three tiers or layers of instruction that range from general classroom application to customized, individualized instruction for struggling readers. Intervention plans are designed based on assessment data collected at regular intervals. Teachers and others planning interventions are challenged to be knowledgeable about assessment practices and instructional strategies that are scientifically based.

As intervention plans are crafted, it is imperative that teachers and interventionists are informed about the importance of creating the learning environment and are skilled in differentiating the curriculum and selecting the materials used for instruction. From the core curriculum to the customized selection of resources for individual students, teachers must recognize the importance of text difficulty and readability levels and how each should be considered when determining the appropriateness of materials selected for inclusion in an intervention plan.

For your journal . . . .

1. Reflect on the various types of alternative assessment discussed in this chapter. Which of them do you consider most useful? Why?

2. How can the misuse of standardized tests hurt both students and teachers? What can be done to avoid their misuse?

3. What do you think it means to merge instruction and assessment? How can one support the other?

4. View the Video Case "Assessment in the Elementary Grades: Formal and Informal Literary Assessment." In this video, you will see how a second-grade teacher administers multiple assessments. Identify the different assesments in Chris Quinn's second-grade instructional program and outline their purposes. Do you agree with her choice of assessments? How do you plan to incorporate multiple assessments in your classroom?

. . . . and your portfolio

1. Collect samples of student work that you could use as examples for each proficiency level, or standard, of a rubric. Be sure to focus on what you intend to measure.

2. Start an annotated list of recent journal articles that present current views of assessment. Consider how you can apply these views to your classroom.

3. Plan ways to use portfolio assessment in your classroom. Consider your purposes, a desirable format, ways to involve students in the selection and maintenance of portfolio artifacts, and ways to organize and store them.

Emergent and Developing Literacy

3

KEY VOCABULARY

Pay close attention to these terms when they appear in the chapter.

alphabetic principle

big book

cognitive development

creative dramatics

developing literacy

developmentally appropriate
  practice

direct instruction

dramatic play

emergent literacy

environmental print

experience chart

guided reading

invented spelling

phonemic awareness

phonological awareness

predictable book

print conventions

prosody

scaffolding

shared-book experience

sight word

writing workshop

zone of proximal development

Learning to read does not happen all at once when children enter school. We describe in this chapter how children develop gradually as readers and writers in stages, acquiring new understandings about reading and writing as communication. In the early stage of literacy development, children begin to demonstrate an interest in reading. They make personal connections with text. They start to recognize some letter names and a few familiar or high-frequency words. They also begin to scribble and draw in an effort to communicate. These characteristics describe children in the stage of **emergent literacy.** Many children at the preschool and kindergarten levels are described as emergent readers. As children move into and throughout the primary grades, they enter a new stage. Their awareness of the relationships between letters and sounds develops. They increase their sight vocabularies and make generalizations based upon their phonological awareness. They begin to expand connections between themselves and texts. Children at this stage, the **developing literacy** stage, continue to improve their reading and writing skills as they strive for fluency.

What a child learns about language from his or her early environment before coming to school should be the foundation for literacy learning in the classroom. This learning can continue to grow out of the child's natural curiosity about language, functional use of language in authentic situations, and experimentation with ways to use language for effective communication.

In this chapter, we describe how reading and writing develop concurrently, with teacher scaffolding, guidance, and encouragement. This does not mean that instruction in literacy skills is unimportant. On the contrary, children need to develop key skills to become successful readers, writers, speakers, and listeners. The teacher's role is one of creating conditions that enable children to explore language and make discoveries that will lead them to internalize reading and writing skills. The teacher is there both to provide **direct instruction** and to assist learners and intervene when they need help.

Directions: Before you read this chapter, complete the following anticipation/reaction guide. In the space before each statement, write **A** if you agree; **D** if you disagree; or **?** if you don't know. After you have read the chapter, complete the guide again to show what you have discovered in the chapter. In the space after each statement, mark whether you were initially correct (with a **C**) or incorrect (with an **I**). Write the letter for the correct answer (**A**) or (**D**) in the space for the statements that you initially marked with a question mark (**?**).

AFTER
C or **I** (for initial
A or **D** answers)
A or **D**
(for initial **?** answers)

1. Language learning begins at birth and is continuous.

2. A child's phonemic awareness is a good predictor of future reading success.

3. A close relationship exists between cognitive development and the growth of concepts about language.

4. The preferred frequency for teachers to read aloud to children is once a week.

5. According to Piaget, language comes before thought.

6. Many children engage in unconventional forms of reading and writing before they enter school.

7. Young children need direct instruction in how to speak when they first begin talking.

8. Home environment has little or no effect on language learning.

9. Children must learn to read before they can learn to write.

10. The guided reading model involves the assignment of students to fixed groups for instruction during reading.

11. Children use invented or temporary spellings to express the ways they perceive letter-sound associations.

12. Early reading of environmental words helps children realize that print represents meaning.

CHAPTER 3 ORGANIZATION

Emergent and Developing Literacy

Development of Cognition and Language

Cognitive Development
Language Development

Learning to Read and Write

Developing Phonemic Awareness
Preparation for Phonics
Letter Recognition
Print Concepts and Print Conventions
Developmentally Appropriate Practices
Print-Rich Environments
Environmental Print
Reading Aloud
Guided Reading
Self-Selected Reading and Writing
Early Writing Strategies

Development of Oral Language Skills

Listening
Oral Expression
Dramatic Play
Creative Dramatics

Classroom Environment

Diversity in a Literacy-Centered Classroom
Importance of Experiential Background
Importance of Choice

Home and School Connection

Importance of Assessment and Early Intervention

Reading Recovery
Success for All

Development of Cognition and Language

Language acquisition has long held the interest of linguists and psychologists and has most recently given rise to new research in the areas of neuroscience and cognitive psychology (Sousa, 2005). The study of the connection between the way that children learn to use language and the way that they grow in the ability to know and understand concepts or ideas is of great interest to many who hope to learn more about the way that the brain works and how that knowledge can be applied in an educational setting.

Cognitive Development

Jean Piaget and Lev Vygotsky developed two major theories regarding how children's cognition, or thinking, develops. Both offer insights into the development of children's language skills and how teachers can facilitate the development.

▸ Piaget's Theory

Jean Piaget, a Swiss psychologist highly respected for his theory of **cognitive development,** asserted that thought comes before language and that language is a way of representing thought. Piaget divided cognitive development into four periods: sensorimotor, preoperational, concrete-operational, and formal-operational.

Most emerging readers demonstrate characteristics of Piaget's *preoperational period*. They begin to engage in symbolic thought using symbols to stand for spoken words. They realize that writing represents meaning, a concept that is basic to reading comprehension (Waller, 1977).

In this stage, children are rapidly developing concepts but are limited in their ability to use adult logic. They are egocentric; that is, they consider things only from their own points of view. This characteristic prevents children from thinking clearly about the events in a story, except from their own limited perspectives. Although most children at this stage cannot state the rules governing the syntax of their primary language, they do demonstrate syntactic or grammatical awareness in their speech; that is, they can use words in a logical order as they form sentences.

Children at the preoperational level lack many of the concepts needed to understand reading and writing processes, and they are often frustrated when teachers expect them to perform such beginning reading tasks as memorizing rules and deciding which words follow a rule, understanding that a single letter can represent multiple sounds, and changing letters to sounds and back to letters (Harp, 1987). Children at this level would probably be more successful in classrooms with a wide variety of language materials and experiences that would allow them to form their own concepts about print.

Many factors influence when children arrive at the different stages identified by Piaget. Not all children go through Piaget's stages at the same ages; in fact, children may be advanced in some areas, displaying many of the skills characteristic of one stage, while they have not mastered other skills characteristic of that same stage. Such factors as the child's individual traits, the home environment, the type of support given, and the child's sensory-perceptual experiences, cultural context, and emotional involvement account for much of the variability in the ages at which children move from one stage to another (Fortson and Reiff, 1995; Sameroff and McDonough, 1996–1997; Snow, Burns, and Griffin, 1998).

Realizing that children in any classroom are at a variety of levels, the teacher should apply **developmentally appropriate practices,** techniques for working with young children in which the teacher considers each child's competencies and adjusts instruction accordingly (Gestwicki, 1995; Richey and Wheeler, 2000). Knowledge of developmental stages enables the teacher to select appropriate strategies for emerging and developing readers. In May 1998, the International Reading Association and the National Association for the Education of Young Children (IRA/NAEYC) composed a joint position statement that provides guidance for teachers of young children in various settings.

Developmental learning occurs naturally, with minimal instruction, as a child grows up. According to Holdaway (1979) it "is highly individual and noncompetitive; it is short on teaching and long on learning; it is self-regulated rather than adult-regulated; it goes hand in hand with the fulfillment of real life purposes; it emulates the behavior of people who model the skill in natural use" (p. 14). Speech develops in this way, and many educators argue that literacy should develop in a similar manner.

Activities that are developmentally appropriate promote self-esteem because children feel good about themselves when they complete tasks successfully. Self-esteem affects how well a child performs in school, and it should be established early because self-concept becomes more difficult to change as the child grows older (Sameroff and McDonough, 1996–1997). Negative influences on self-esteem include inappropriate learning tasks that may be too difficult or too easy, teaching methods that ignore natural learning styles, and unreasonably high expectations (Gestwicki, 1995). Some teaching procedures cover a range of abilities so that each child can experience success within a whole-class setting. For example, during shared book reading, some children may simply be learning directionality (directional orientation) by following the teacher's pointer from left to right; others may be acquiring letter-sound correspondences; and a few may be matching printed words to spoken words. Because each child participates at some level, each can feel successful.

▸ Vygotsky's Theory

The Russian developmental theorist Lev Vygotsky stated that childhood experiences give rise to two different groups of concepts—spontaneous and scientific (Dixon-Krauss, 1996; Vygotsky, 1986). Vygotsky defines *spontaneous concepts* as those

DIVERSITY

Time for Reflection
Some researchers believe that environmental factors greatly influence a child's language acquisition and cognitive development.

What factors do *you* believe affect language development, and why?

STANDARDS/
ASSESSMENTS

You can link to the IRA/NAEYC position statement from your Student Website or find it at http://www.naeyc.org/.

◀ ■ ▶ **SEEING IT IN PRACTICE**

Video Case

To better understand Vygotsky's zone of proximal development and how it is actualized in the classroom setting, visit the Student Website to link to the Video Case "Vygotsky's Zone of Proximal Development: Increasing Cognition in an Elementary Literacy Lesson." In the bonus videos, you'll see how developmental psychologist, Dr. Francis Hurley, draws upon this theory to support students' abstract thinking in a poetry lesson. You also have access to students' writing samples.

that children learn informally in the course of everyday concrete experiences at home and elsewhere. Verbal interactions with parents and others help children gain meaning from these experiences. Vygotsky defines *scientific concepts* as those that children learn during systematic classroom instruction when teachers present information. In other words, spontaneous concepts result from what children directly see or manipulate, and scientific concepts help children formalize their understandings as the teacher transmits knowledge verbally. Therefore, children need exposure to a wide variety of experiences, combined with structured class activities, in order to advance in cognitive development.

Vygotsky also suggested that children's cognitive development occurs through social experiences with others, especially those who can help children expand their thinking or other skills. Vygotsky's **zone of proximal development** is the span between a child's actual skill level and his or her potential level with assistance, or the difference between what a child can do alone and what the child can do with help (Vygotsky, 1986). The teacher can be most effective by serving as a mediating adult within this zone. As such, the teacher provides **scaffolding,** offering support that is gradually withdrawn as learners become capable of performing independently. With beginning readers, one way that a teacher creates a scaffold is by taking the lead during interactive storybook reading and then gradually turning the responsibility for interaction over to students (Dixon-Krauss, 1996). "Seeing It in Practice: Video Case" offers a view of a teacher working in students' zones of proximal development.

Language Development

A child's literacy development begins at birth. A baby's experiences help define how his or her brain forms the connections, or synapses, between the brain cells in key language centers such as the cortex. During preschool years, a child's ability to understand and use language develops rapidly. Early childhood is a time marked by observable language development and language acquisition. It is a time when children first demonstrate sensitivity to **prosody,** or elements of speech such as rhythm and intonation that convey emotion. During these early years, children are still highly influenced by their experiences, as they begin to imitate language patterns that surround them. During this time, not only do children attempt to use oral language, but they also experiment with communication through writing (Wolfe & Nevills, 2004).

Language development is a continuous, interactive, and purposeful process. Children learn to speak without instruction by imitating speech sounds and observing the interactions of language users. Language learning is more than imitation, however, because each individual constructs language according to personal needs and motivations. The child acquires speech through immersion in a language environment that provides speech models, motivation for speaking, and interactions with other speakers. The beginning speaker engages in trial and error and takes risks to establish communications with others. With the degree of influence from early environmental conditions, it is no wonder that children arrive at school at various levels of literacy development.

A child's early attempts at language are intuitive; that is, the child uses language reasonably well but lacks *metalinguistic awareness*, the ability to think about language and manipulate it objectively. For example, a child may say, "I want some candy," but may be unable to tell how many words were spoken or recognize that this group of words is called a *sentence*. Many children can use language that they cannot describe in linguistic terms, such as *word, sentence, sound,* and *letter* (Hare, 1984; Lightbrown and Spada, 1999). Because many children fail to understand linguistic terminology, they cannot make sense of instruction based on these terms. If a child does not understand the meanings of language-related terms, he or she must experience considerable confusion when a teacher says, "Look at the *middle letter* of this *word*. The *vowel* has its *short sound* because it is followed by a *consonant*."

"Putting It into Practice: Recognition of the Concept of Word" provides a model activity for teachers who wish to develop children's skill in recognizing words as basic elements of speech. It is important to realize that children develop an understanding of the concept of *word* gradually through many experiences. Also, because individual children are at various developmental levels for acquiring this concept, for some the lesson will confirm what they were already beginning to realize, whereas for others, who are less ready, the lesson will have little or no meaning.

Early experiences with written language that may occur during the first year of life, such as playing with alphabet blocks and listening to stories read from books, lay the foundation for a lifelong process of learning to read and write (Teale and Sulzby, 1989; Clay, 1979). Children progress through developmental stages in oral language (from babbling to mature speech) and written language (from scribbling to legible writing), moving toward ever-higher levels of language proficiency. Thus, literacy evolves in a natural, connected way over an extended period of time as the learner discovers new insights about language and how it works.

Emergent literacy is defined as a developing awareness of the interrelatedness of oral and written language (Teale and Sulzby, 1989; Juel 1991). It is based on the assumption that language learning occurs naturally in the home and community as children see print and understand its function in their environment. They learn about literacy from adult models, particularly family members, and they develop knowledge of reading and writing concurrently. Before they understand letter-sound associations, they scribble messages or draw letter-like forms that have meaning for them and then "read" their messages to others. Many kindergarten children understand a great deal about how language works. They make sense out of the writing in their environment by relating words (such as *McDonald's*) to corresponding places

Recognition of the Concept of Word

On a large chart, make two copies of a story based on an experience that children have shared. Run your fingers under the first sentence on one of the charts as you say to the children: "Read this sentence with me." Then use your hands to frame individual words as you say to them: "Look at the groups of letters between the spaces. We call each group of letters a *word*." Ask them:

"How many words are in this sentence?" Do the same thing with the other sentences on the chart. Then cut the sentences into strips and ask several children to cut the strips into words. Give each child a word. Say to the children: "Can you find your word on our other chart? If you can, hold your word next to or under the word on the chart."

(a restaurant). They expect print to be meaningful and to communicate ideas. They understand some characteristics of written language, such as directionality, spacing, sequencing, and form. They have some knowledge of letter names, auditory and visual discrimination, and correspondence between written and spoken words. (Auditory and visual discrimination were introduced in Chapter 1 and are discussed further in this chapter.) They know what books are and how to use them.

LITERATURE

The teacher must build on children's existing knowledge about language by understanding each child and providing developmentally appropriate literacy experiences. According to Wolfe and Nevills (2004), "Linguistic awareness is best developed within the context of the child's work and play" (p. 53). Having children perform isolated drills and memorize rules without understanding their meanings is unlikely to help them learn to read. Emerging readers should have opportunities to build upon language experiences and interact with predictable or repetitive stories. It is the teacher's responsibility to ask questions about language, read to and with the children, provide authentic reading and writing tasks, and encourage and guide children in their developing sense of language through the use of developmentally appropriate activities.

◀■▶ SEEING IT IN PRACTICE

Video Case

To observe how one teacher orchestrates the various elements of a balanced literacy program in her second-grade classroom, view the Video Case "Elementary Reading Instruction: A Balanced Literacy Program." The bonus videos will provide a glimpse of how teacher Sandra Jenoski engages her students in a range of developmentally appropriate independent and purposeful literacy tasks. In an interview, Ms. Jenoski explains in detail how she creates and facilitates the program for her young developing readers.

Learning to Read and Write

The National Reading Panel (2000), in response to a U.S. congressional mandate, identified specific competencies and methodologies important for student achievement in reading. Their report outlined phonemic awareness, phonics, fluency, vocabulary, and text comprehension as five key areas of reading instruction. These five key areas are also key areas of focus in the curriculum standards or assessment benchmarks for many states. The report further suggested that the methodologies used should emphasize explicit instruction and active engagement of students in authentic tasks and the development of metacognitive selection of strategies by students during the reading event (Taylor, Peterson, Pearson, and Rodriguez, 2002). Each of the key areas named by the panel includes many aspects as students develop. Throughout this book, we discuss how teachers can nurture each of these competencies, always stressing developmentally appropriate methodologies.

 STANDARDS/ ASSESSMENTS

Developing Phonemic Awareness

Phonemic awareness, an understanding that spoken language consists of a series of small sound units, or *phonemes*, is a powerful predictor of success in reading (Adams, 1990; Pearson, 1993; Stanovich, 1993/1994; Yopp, 1992; Armbruster, Lehr, and Osborn, 2001). It is both a prerequisite for learning to read and a consequence of the increased awareness of language that comes from learning to read (Yopp, 1992). The National Reading Panel (2000) suggests that phonemic awareness is an important component of a balanced literacy program. Also important is **phonological awareness,** described as the knowledge of speech sound relationships or the ability to identify not just phonemes, but also syllables and individual words. Both abilities enable individuals to make connections between the sound structure of oral language and text (Moats, 2001). When children pay close attention to speech sounds and use their discoveries about letter-sound relationships to guide their writing and reading, they increase their functional and meaningful use of written language (Richgels, Poremba, and McGee, 1996).

Yopp (1995b) says, "Most youngsters enter kindergarten lacking phonemic awareness. Indeed, as we have noted, few are conscious that sentences are made up of individual words, let alone that words can be segmented into phonemes" (p. 20). Phonemic awareness can be taught directly, and training in phonemic awareness has been shown to be effective and to have a positive effect on reading acquisition (Lundberg, Frost, and Peterson, 1988; Yopp, 1992). Use of read-aloud books is a way to integrate phonemic awareness into the instructional program, because many books have rhyme, alliteration, assonance, and other features that allow children to play with the sounds of language (Yopp, 1992, 1995a; Griffith and Olson, 1992).

 LITERATURE

> ### TEACHING TIP
>
> ### Developing Phonemic Awareness
>
> You can help students develop phonemic awareness by having them do the following:
>
> - Identify, from a set of words, those words that begin with the same sound.
> - Identify the initial and final sounds in words.
> - Combine and blend sounds to say a word and segment a word into separate sounds (Armbruster, Lehr, and Osborn, 2001).
> - Use invented spellings so that they become conscious of the sounds that make up words (Pearson, 1993).
>
> Exposing children to literature that plays with the sounds of language (Griffith and Olson, 1992) and involving them in songs and games that draw attention to the sounds of language (Yopp, 1992) are additional strategies for the development of phonemic awareness.

Richgels and his colleagues (1996) suggest a "What Can You Show Us?" activity to develop phonemic awareness in a holistic context. They describe it as a "functional, contextualized, social literacy activity" (p. 641). It accompanies shared reading activities. Before shared reading, a *preparation* step involves selecting reading materials and displaying them appropriately; for example, if the text is copied onto a chart, the features of words that the teacher wants to emphasize can be highlighted in some way. The next step involves the children's *preview* of the text and discussion of what they see. Next, *student demonstrations* of what they know about the text (for example, identifying letters of words) take place. The shared reading (teacher reading, joint reading, and student activities) comes next. During and after this activity, students apply what they know about the text. There may be further student demonstrations.

Preparation for Phonics

To learn to read, children must acquire knowledge of letters and their corresponding sounds. The task of associating sounds with letter names requires students to use auditory and visual discrimination abilities.

▶ Auditory Discrimination

According to Harris and Hodges (1995), *auditory discrimination* "is the ability to hear phonetic likenesses and differences in phonemes and words" (p. 15). Through auditory discrimination and phonemic awareness, students recognize that speech is composed of separate sounds, or phonemes. Students must be able to hear sounds within words, or they will be unable to form mental connections between sounds and letters (Adams, 1990; Adams et al., 1991; Beck and Juel, 1995; Juel, 1988, 1991; Pearson, 1993).

Introducing children to simple rhymes is an effective way to sensitize them to the likenesses and differences among verbal sounds. The teacher can ask children to pick out the words that rhyme and to supply words that rhyme with a given word. This ability is fundamental to the construction of "word families." (Word families are discussed further in Chapter 5.) "Putting It into Practice: Auditory Discrimination" describes another type of activity to help children develop auditory discrimination abilities.

▶ Visual Discrimination

Visual discrimination is the process of visually identifying similarities and differences. Students need practice with simultaneous and successive visual discrimination of letters and words. *Simultaneous discrimination* occurs when children match printed symbols that are alike while they can see both symbols. *Successive discrimination* occurs when children find a duplicate symbol after a stimulus symbol is no longer visible. Activities requiring children to discriminate among letter and word forms are more useful to beginning readers than activities requiring them to identify similarities and

Auditory Discrimination

Name several puppets with double names to stress initial consonant sounds (Molly Mouse, Freddie Frog, Dolly Duck, and Bennie Bear). While holding a puppet, say: "I'd like you to meet Molly Mouse. Molly Mouse only likes things that begin the same way that her name begins. Molly Mouse likes milk, but she doesn't like water. I am going to name some things that Molly Mouse likes or doesn't like. You must listen closely to the way each word begins. Raise your hand if I say something that Molly Mouse likes. Keep your hand down if I say something that Molly Mouse doesn't like. Let's begin. Molly Mouse likes meat." The children should raise their hands. If they don't seem to understand why she likes meat, talk about the beginning sound and give additional examples. Then say: "Molly Mouse likes potatoes." The children should keep their hands down.

differences among geometric forms (Sippola, 1985). "Putting It into Practice: Visual Discrimination" models an activity to help children develop visual discrimination abilities.

Letter Recognition

Children should learn letter names early so that the teacher and the class have a common referent—for example, understanding when the teacher talks about the letter *f* or the letter *n* (Farr and Roser, 1979). Knowledge of letter *names* is important for talking about similarities and differences among printed words, but knowledge of letter *sounds* is more useful in decoding words.

It is critical that that beginning readers understand the **alphabetic principle,** the concept that letters represent speech sounds (Pikulski, 1989). Some children learn this principle intuitively, but most need help. Children who learn both the names and the sounds of letters can read better than children who learn only letter names (R. C. Anderson, Hiebert, Scott, and Wilkinson, 1985). Holdaway (1979) suggests introducing two contrasting letter-sound combinations, such as *m* and *f*, and having children find these letters in familiar stories that the teacher has read with them. After they find many examples, which they can readily identify because of their familiarity with the stories, they work with other letter-sound relationships, including *b*, *g*, *s*, and *t*. Because of the insights they have gained, many children now can learn the remaining initial consonants and consonant blends on their own.

LITERATURE

▶ Development of Sight Vocabulary

Preschool children and children entering kindergarten are rapidly acquiring **sight words,** words they recognize instantly without analyzing them. Teachers can encourage sight word recognition by exposing children to commonly used words, such as names, number and color words, and environmental words.

Sight vocabulary can be learned in a number of meaningful ways. Ashton-Warner (1963) described the use of *organic words*, words that are meaningful or emotionally

Visual Discrimination

Write on the board some letters that are similar in appearance (*b*, *d*, and *p*, for example). Say to the children: "Let's look at these letters. Are any of them alike? How are the first two letters different? What is different about the other letter?"

Then say to them: "Now I am going to give you a copy of a page of the story that we read today. Look at the first letter on the board. [Point to the letter.] Then look at the page from the story. Every time you see this letter in the story, circle it with your green crayon. [Give them time to search for the letter *b* and mark their pages.] Now look at the second letter. [Point to it.] Every time you see this letter in the story, circle it with your red crayon. [Give them time to do this.] Now look at the third letter. [Point to it.] Every time you see this letter in the story, circle it in yellow. [Give them time to do this.]" Then display a large copy of the story and let individuals come up and point to the letters that should have been circled in the different colors, while children check their own papers.

Repeat the activity with a set of words containing these letters, such as *big*, *pet*, and *dog*. Ask the same questions about the words. Then have the children perform a similar activity with the words, using fresh pages from the story so that their previous marks will not confuse them.

charged, such as *ghost*, *kiss*, and *Mother*. Each child chooses a word that has special personal meaning, and the teacher writes that word on a card and gives it to the child. A word card is kept as long as the word is known; when the word is forgotten or no longer meaningful to the child, the card is discarded. Other strategies for teaching sight words include the creation of "word walls" and participation in "word sorts," as described in Chapters 5 and 6, using vocabulary that children find interesting or important.

Print Concepts and Print Conventions

During the emergent literacy stage, children will begin to interact with print, develop an understanding of directionality, identify some letters, and recognize familiar words. Children will learn to move their eyes across the page in a left-to-right progression and execute a return sweep from the end of one line to the beginning of the next. Children will also learn to read from top to bottom and distinguish between drawing and writing. They will begin to scribble, write familiar words, and read what they have written.

Many children, especially those who have been read to often, begin to "talk like a book" at a very young age (Clay, 1979; Cunningham and Allington, 1999). They pretend to read by imitating literary style and content instead of using conversational style. Illustrations and previous readings by adults help children construct the text that they pretend to read even though these children cannot yet read the actual words. Children often practice "pretend reading" to a younger sibling or a grandparent. "Talking like a book" is an important step in learning to read because it shows acquisition of basic literacy concepts, such as realizing that print can be turned into spoken words and that books use a special type of language. These concepts are sometimes called **print conventions**—that is, generally accepted concepts about reading and writing. The reader expects the writer to use certain conventions involving placement of words on a page, directionality, capitalization, and punctuation, and the writer assumes the reader will follow them.

Developmentally Appropriate Practices

The teacher must build on the emerging reader's existing knowledge about language by understanding each child and providing developmentally appropriate literacy experiences. As "Seeing It in Practice: First Day of School" shows, developmentally appropriate experiences can and should begin the very first day of school.

Teachers should encourage children to become aware of purposes for reading and writing. Charts on which teachers record dictations about students' experiences, as well as labels for identifying objects, remind students that print communicates meaning. Attractively displayed books invite children to read, and writing materials at play centers encourage them to write lists and memos (Booth, 1994).

The classroom environment should provide opportunities for language growth that are similar to those provided in a positive home environment (Holdaway, 1979; Cunningham and Allington, 1999). Here are some guidelines based on this concept (Fisher, 1989; Wood and Nurss, 1988; Fortson and Reiff, 1995; Salinger, 1996):

- Provide a wide variety of materials for purposeful writing and reading.
- Place labels and key words around the room at the children's eye level.
- Organize the room so that children can follow the classroom routine and take care of their belongings independently.
- Display children's work so that they can see it and discuss it with others.
- Encourage children to compose stories from wordless picture books and to respond creatively to literature.
- Provide opportunities for expressing ideas, thoughts, and feelings through talk.
- Immerse children in literature and in early drawing, writing, and read-along experiences.
- Organize areas of the classroom into learning centers that contain varied and interesting materials that invite students to become engaged in a particular theme.

Print-Rich Environments

Emerging and developing readers need print-rich environments. Words should be everywhere—on bulletin boards and walls, on children's work and book jackets, and as labels on objects around the room. There should be charts dictated by the children and books on shelves and at centers. Pocket charts are useful instructional tools often found in preschool, kindergarten, and primary classrooms. A large pocket

Time for Reflection

Some teachers believe that they should decorate the classroom with attractive displays so that children enter an intriguing, welcoming room on the first day of school. Other teachers prefer to leave the classroom nearly bare until the children create their own displays and charts; these teachers feel that children will develop a sense of ownership and pride if their contributions are recognized.

What do *you* think, and why?

First Day of School

Early in the day, Oliver Jordan calls the children to the story rug and introduces the big book version of Bill Martin, Jr.'s *Brown Bear, Brown Bear, What Do You See?* Eagerly the children listen as he reads and watch as he turns the brightly colored pages. Soon they are chiming in on some of the words, helped along by the picture clues. When they beg him to read it again, he does so and invites all of them to read it with him. In additional readings throughout the day, children read pages by themselves and with partners. They listen with headphones as they follow along in small book versions, and by the end of the day, they consider themselves to be readers.

Analysis of Scenario

Many children come to school eager to learn to read. In Mr. Jordan's class, the children were excited because they felt that they were really reading. According to Booth (1994), the way that children encounter print at the beginning of school may determine their attitudes toward reading for the rest of their lives.

---

chart is constructed so that the pockets hold letter cards, word cards, or sentence strips. The pockets and strips provide manipulatives for children to place items in order, sequence the events of a story, or place letters in correct order to spell a target word. An example of how a pocket chart may be used is described in "Seeing It in Practice: Reading from a Pocket Chart."

Environmental Print

Many children learn to read **environmental print**—words they frequently see around them—long before they enter school. Teachers can link the home/community environment with that of the classroom by displaying environmental print, including advertisements and promotional materials for familiar products such as toothpaste, cereals, and fruit juices. Another advantage of using environmental print is that it is free and readily available. Often children bring examples to share, read them, and display them for others to read. Using the children's knowledge of environmental words, the teacher can begin teaching letter-sound relationships, as "Seeing It in Practice: Environmental Print" on page 86 shows.

Reading Aloud

LITERATURE

The foundation of emergent literacy development is the reading aloud of well-chosen texts by the teacher. Daily time in the preschool and primary grades dedicated to reading aloud encourages the understanding of story elements and organization of expository texts for students. Reading aloud has long been recognized as an important instructional strategy for the development of literacy in young children (Wolfe and Nevills, 2004).

It is important to note that reading aloud is most effective in the development of language and vocabulary when children are actively involved rather than passively listening. Discussions that are prompted by questions and making

Reading from a Pocket Chart

As part of the morning activities, Tina DeStephen's prefirst graders read their daily schedule from a pocket chart.

Ms. DeStephens discusses the day's schedule with the children and talks about "something special," which may be a visitor, a trip, or an invitation to see another class perform a play. "Self-selection" refers to such options as playing with blocks, doing handwriting, making a puppet show, playing instruments, painting at the easel, using math manipulatives, and playing in the housekeeping center. Before the children work independently, Ms. DeStephens makes sure that each child has decided what to do.

Morning	Afternoon
Attendance / Tally	Lunch
Pledge / Song	Storytime
Calendar / Weather	Quiet self-selected reading
Language workshop	Buddy reading
Author's Chair	Reading conferences
Something Special	Self-selection
Recess	Clean-up
Math	Time to go home

Analysis of Activity

This daily ritual serves many purposes. Ms. DeStephens and the children anticipate the day's events together as they read and discuss the activities. The children are comfortable and secure in this familiar routine, and they consider their choices and make decisions about what they will do. They realize that reading is purposeful, they reread now-familiar words, and they become aware of sequence.

predictions along with teacher modeling of responses or thinking aloud can influence comprehension and language development. It is not simply reading aloud but how read-alouds are conducted that matters. Based upon this premise, McGee and Schickedanz (2007) offer the repeated interactive read-aloud technique as a research-based approach appropriate for preschool and kindergarten. The approach involves crafted questions and interactive dialogue featuring primarily picture books and predictable books. McGee and Schickedanz indicate that teachers with whom they have worked have also successfully used more sophisticated storybooks and nonfiction selections.

Teachers should read aloud to children several times each day because story sharing creates far-reaching benefits for the listener. Stories introduce children to new vocabulary, language patterns, concepts, cultures, and lifestyles. Hearing stories read

Environmental Print

Since Mr. Burke has been encouraging the children to share examples of environmental print, they have responded enthusiastically. Today, as the children present their treasures, Mr. Burke notices a teaching opportunity. He says, "Tina and Jeff, will you please tell us what you brought?" (Tina has a label from a pizza box, and Jeff has an empty popcorn bag.) Then he says, "Who can tell me the name of the letter we see at the beginning of *pizza*? What letter do we see at the beginning of *popcorn*? Now let's say these words and listen to see if they sound alike at the beginning."

When the children have identified the letter and realized that the words begin with the same sound,

he says, "Can you find another word in the room that starts with the same letter?" When Carole finds the word *party* in a chart story about last week's Halloween party, he asks, "Does *party* begin with the same sound we hear at the beginning of *pizza* and *popcorn*?" When the children reply affirmatively, he puts the letter *p* at the top of a chart and writes *pizza*, *popcorn*, and *party* under the letter. Then he says, "Let's read these words again and listen for the sound that *p* makes. When we find other words that begin with the letter *p*, we can add them to our chart."

aloud may bring about an interest in reading and desire to learn to read. Well-chosen stories can be the basis for creative expression such as drama, music, and art.

Big books with enlarged pictures and print that the entire class can read together offer an excellent way for children to learn to read, even on the first day of school (as shown in the earlier "Seeing It in Practice: First Day of School"). **Predictable books** have patterned stories that use repetition, rhythmic language patterns, and familiar concepts. Even during a first reading by the teacher, children join in on the repetitive lines or familiar chants. For example, when the teacher reads, "And the little red hen said—," the children respond, "I'll do it myself!" This procedure enables a child to "confirm the predictability of written language" (Wiseman, 1984, p. 343). Stories such as Bill Martin, Jr.'s *Brown Bear, Brown Bear* and Audrey Wood's *The Napping House* contain familiar sequences of this sort. Children will soon read these books by themselves if the teacher has reread them and pointed out the corresponding words.

As children read and reread stories—by themselves and to one another—and engage in reading and writing activities related to the stories, they are participating in what Holdaway (1979) calls the **shared-book experience.** Teachers may use the following procedure for sharing big books with their children; it is an extension of the bedtime story shared between parent and child (Holdaway, 1979; Strickland, 1988):

- Introduce the story by initiating a discussion that relates students' experiences to the text, presenting the title and author (using these terms), guiding the children to make predictions about the story, and showing eager anticipation for reading the story.

- Read the story with expression. Run a pointer slowly under the words as you read them so that the children can match the spoken words with the print

A teacher's reading aloud to children helps them develop an awareness of story structure, acquaints them with new words, and fosters their interest in reading.

© Ron Chapple/Taxi/Getty Images

and observe the directionality. While reading, think aloud about aspects of the story ("I wonder what will happen now!" or "Little Bear must feel very happy!"). Encourage children to make predictions and read familiar parts with you.

- When the story is over, guide a discussion about major points; then find and reread corresponding parts of the text to confirm the points. Help the children reread the text together until they become fluent and confident.

A number of optional variations and follow-up activities are also useful. To focus on meaning, the teacher may use adhesive notes or flaps to cover meaningful, predictable words and then ask the children to identify the words underneath. The teacher may also select certain phonic or structural elements that are well represented in the story, call the children's attention to them, and lead the children to discover word-recognition strategies for decoding words with these elements. The children may wish to illustrate parts of the text, write their own versions, find other books related to the same topic, or extend the text in some other way. Since many big books have accompanying audiotapes and sets of small books, the children may read a small version to a listener or listen to a tape of the big book while following along in the smaller one.

Guided Reading

Guided reading is another form of support that places the student in a more formal instructional situation (Fountas and Pinnell, 1996). **Guided reading** is a framework or model of instruction that involves explicit modeling of reading strategies by the teacher while students are actively engaged in reading trade books (books marketed to the general public) appropriate for their instructional reading levels and interests. Often students participate in guided reading groups three to five days each week. While in a group, students interact with new books each time. A student's assignment to a group is flexible, and student progress is assessed regularly. Leveled books are often used to meet the individual readability needs of students as they participate in the groups (Walker, 2005). (Text leveling was discussed in Chapter 2.)

The individualized instruction, the use of leveled texts based upon students' reading levels, the type of lesson delivery, and the ongoing assessment are aspects that make guided reading beneficial for all students. However, Avalos, Plasencia, Chavez, and Rascón (2007/2008) describe a modification of the guided reading model that makes it more effective for English-language learners. The modifications include an increase in the instructional cycle, the use of culturally relevant texts, and the selection of specific strategies that target oral reading, phonemic awareness, phonics instruction, and writing.

Self-Selected Reading and Writing

When students are interested in what they are learning, it supports and promotes active engagement and motivation. Making sure that you include some element of student choice also helps ensure that students will view content as relevant and important (Jensen, 2005). Believing that children gain confidence and skill in reading from free selection, Fisher (1991) explains her procedure for daily *choice-time reading*. The children may choose whatever they wish to read: big books or small versions of them, trade books, magazines, books published by other children, poems, or songs written on charts around the room. They may follow along in a book as they listen to a recording of a familiar story, or they may read with the teacher, with a friend, with a visitor, or alone. Sometimes they role-play a shared-reading session, taking turns being the teacher and inviting a small group to respond.

Independent reading, the chance for students to read books on their own, provides further support for the development of skill and confidence. The reading and rereading of familiar texts is a regular event in a literacy-rich classroom. Independent reading also encourages students to read a variety of materials available throughout the classroom (Fountas and Pinnell, 1996).

❱ Learning to Write

We have stressed that many children know a great deal about written language before entering school. Children actually perceive themselves as writers long before they can write conventionally. They experiment with making scribbles, sometimes interspersing pictures and letterlike shapes and believe that their "writing" conveys messages.

When teachers invite children to write in kindergarten, they should follow certain basic guidelines (based on Sulzby, Teale, and Kamberelis, 1989; Sulzby, 1994; Ollila and Mayfield, 1992):

- Accept the form of writing the child can use; it does not have to be adult writing.
- Allow children to share their writing and respond to what other children have written.
- Let children "write" their own names on their work to give them a sense of ownership.
- Encourage children to use writing to communicate with other people.
- Provide a variety of writing materials that are readily available.
- Be a model by letting children see you writing purposefully.
- Provide ample time for children to write.
- Help children realize the importance of writing in their lives.

Early Writing Strategies

For young children, writing is often a social event. Children confer with one another, sharing their skills and searching for resources and examples. They may tentatively compose stories and tell them to their friends before writing them. When children actually get down to the serious business of writing, Donald Graves observed, they talk to themselves, audibly or subaudibly (Walshe, 1986). They verbalize as they physically form letters and words in the process of formulating their stories.

When children begin kindergarten and are given opportunities to write, some are in the prephonetic stage and place letters on paper without regard for the sounds they make. They tell the teacher what they have written, and the teacher records what they dictate while helping them see relationships between spoken and written words. In kindergarten most children continue to scribble, draw, and use nonphonetic strings of letters (Sulzby, Teale, and Kamberelis, 1989; Cunningham and Allington, 1999).

Once children have a sense of letter-sound relationships, they begin to use **invented spellings.** Harris and Hodges (1995) define invented spelling as "an attempt to spell a word whose spelling is not already known, based on a writer's knowledge of the spelling system and how it works" (p. 123). Writing with invented or temporary spellings enables children to apply their knowledge of letter-sound relationships for their own purposes. Example 3.1 shows how a kindergartner reacted to a dinosaur theme by drawing a picture and writing a story with invented spellings. Example 3.2 shows a first grader's use of invented spellings in a message to a friend.

Close observation of children's invented spellings provides insights into their awareness of letter-sound relationships. Because consonant sounds are more distinctive than vowel sounds, children often use them to represent the key sounds in the words they are trying to spell, either omitting or misrepresenting vowel sounds. Sometimes, in fact, beginning spellers use only the initial consonant of the word that they wish to spell. In Example 3.1, Taylor shows considerable knowledge of phonics by systematically sounding through each word and representing each sound with the letter he hears, as in *dinaswrs*. Taylor also mixes some conventional spelling (that is, *of* and *the*) with his spelling inventions. Trudy (Example 3.2) also reveals excellent awareness of letter-sound relationships in the word *dadokaded*.

With both writing samples, we can learn a great deal about children's beginning reading and writing competencies. Continuing with Example 3.3, we observe that Sheila, a kindergartner, writes from left to right, leaves spaces between words, and writes in complete sentences. She has a good sense of sound-letter relationships, although she sometimes omits some sounds (*WH* or *WIt* for *went*). She spells the *-ing* ending correctly. She writes mostly in uppercase letters and does not use any punctuation.

EXAMPLE 3.1 Kindergartner's Use of Invented Spellings

This story reads as follows: The meat eater of the dinosaurs. Will Tyrannosaurus Rex survive?

Source: Taylor Bennett, Sycamore Elementary School, Cookeville, Tennessee. Used with permission.

PUTTING IT INTO PRACTICE

Demonstrating Spelling Processes

Say to the children: "We've been talking about going camping, and today we set up a tent in our room. Some of you may want to write about tents in your journals. Can you help me spell *tent*? Let's say *tent* slowly together and listen for the sounds. What letter makes the sound we hear at the beginning?"

When a correct response is given, say: "Let's say *tent* again and stretch it out. Think about the sound we hear next. What letter makes that sound?"

When a correct response is given, ask: "Is there another sound? Let's say *tent* once more, very slowly." Write the corresponding letter for the correct sounds as the students respond.

To reinforce the sound-letter relationships, ask: "Can you find a word in our room that begins like *tent*?" Ask a child to come to the board and write the correct letters where they should go; then ask the other children if they agree. Then ask the children to say the letters in *tent* and remind them to use these letters if they write about tents.

EXAMPLE 3.2 First Grader's Use of Invented Spellings

This story reads as follows: Roses are red. Violets are blue. These golden flowers remind me of you. Dedicated to Janet.

Source: Trudy Walker, Capshaw Elementary School, Cookeville, Tennessee. Used with permission.

EXAMPLE 3.3 Beginning Writing

The story reads as follows: I went to get a present for my mom. Everybody was shouting hurrah and singing happy birthday.

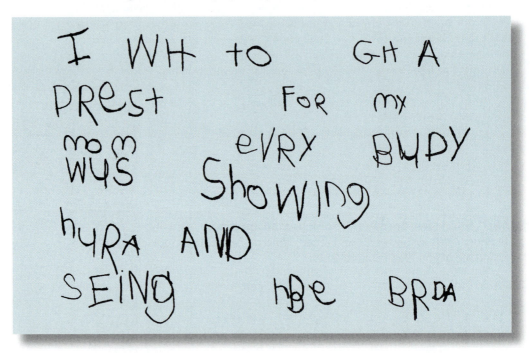

Source: Sheila Vogel, Kingston Elementary School, Kingston, Tennessee. Used with permission.

Knowledge of which letters represent certain sounds within words is useful not only for writing, but also for decoding words in reading. Using invented or temporary spelling helps children develop phonemic awareness and understanding of the alphabetic principle (Adams, 1990). According to Cunningham and Cunningham (1992), research indicates that "invented spelling and decoding are mirror-like processes that make use of the same store of phonological knowledge" (p. 106). Thus, as children learn to associate sounds with letters, they advance their knowledge of both reading and writing. "Putting It into Practice: Demonstrating Spelling Processes" and "Seeing It in Practice: Getting Children Started in Writing" (page 94) demonstrate ways in which teachers can help children begin to write and read.

▶ Purposeful Writing

When children write to communicate meaning, their writing is purposeful. Some classes support postal system/pen-pal programs with individual mailboxes for receiving letters and a central mailbox for sending letters. Many reasons for writing also emerge at dramatic play centers, where children write telephone messages, take orders for food, make shopping lists, and so on. Other purposeful writing activities include sending messages to school personnel, making greeting cards, sending thank-you notes, writing stories, writing letters, and recording information. Journal writing and writing workshops are two other ways to encourage authentic or purposeful writing for emergent and developing writers.

Writing Workshops.   **Writing workshops**

provide a support framework that includes a minilesson designed to improve writing skills, a writing and conference time when students are authentically engaged in composing while the teacher meets individually with each student, and a sharing time when students read or listen to the sharing of a student's written selection. The writing workshop encourages the process of continuous growth with valuable feedback from both the teacher and peers (Fountas and Pinnell, 1996).

Journal Writing.   Journal writing offers a purposeful writing activity and often gives

the teacher insights into the child's understandings and misinterpretations (Fallon and Allen, 1994). The teacher may give each child a booklet, often made of folded, stapled, unlined sheets of paper, to write in during a special time each day. Children may copy, scribble, print, or draw anything they wish in their journals, and the teacher may record in conventional print what the children dictate. "Seeing It in Practice: Getting Children Started in Writing" shows how journal writing may be initiated.

Story Writing.   Story writing can be a logical

extension of either direct or vicarious experiences. If a class writes a story after a field trip, students should first discuss the trip. By asking carefully selected questions, the teacher can encourage them to form valid concepts and use appropriate vocabulary words. Students then dictate sentences for the teacher to write on an **experience chart** like that in Example 3.4. More discussion on the language experience approach, or LEA, is found in Chapter 9.

Perhaps the most important reason for writing dictated experience stories is that it helps children realize that speech can be recorded and that print makes sense. This awareness occurs as the teacher reads the story back to the children in the words they have just dictated. After repeated readings by the teacher, the children may also be able to "read" the story. The teacher can make copies of the story for all the children to take home and share with their families. As a result of their involvement with the story, children may learn to recognize some high-interest words and some words used more than once (such as *we*, *zoo*, and *bus* in Example 3.4 on page 96).

SEEING IT IN PRACTICE ◀ ■ ▶

Video Case

To see how a writer's workshop is implemented in a regular fourth-grade classroom, visit your Student Website to link to the Video Case "Elementary Writing Instruction: Process Writing." In this video, you will see how the classroom teacher and the literacy coordinator collaborate and engage students in various stages of writing through a writer's workshop.

TEACHING TIP

Experience Stories

Stories about an experience may be dictated by a whole class, a group, or a single child. When individual children tell stories, parents, teaching assistants, older children, classroom volunteers, or teachers can act as scribes. These stories should be about things that are important to the children, such as their families, pets, or favorite activities. The children may illustrate them and combine them into booklets that are then shared around the library table and eventually taken home by the authors. Following are some appropriate experiences for story writing:

Taking a field trip	Observing an animal
Watching an experiment	Popping corn
Visiting a science or book fair	Experimenting with paints
Tasting unusual foods	Planting seeds or bulbs
Entertaining a visitor	Building a pretend space ship

Getting Children Started in Writing

Ms. McLoughlin paused a moment as she moved from one kindergartner to another, offering encouragement as they worked in their journals. She thought back to the beginning of the year when only a few of them could even print their names. For the first few weeks, she had to write in their journals a sentence or two that they had dictated to her to help them grasp the concept that what they said could be written down.

When she had first asked the children to write, they told her they didn't know how. She supplied them with paper and a variety of writing tools, however, and encouraged them to draw a picture first and then write something about it. Some did this with scribbles, some with pictures only, and some with a few letters strewn haphazardly on the page. She accepted their work and asked them to read their stories to her, but she knew she would have to help them discover sound-letter relationships so that they could begin using the letters they needed to make words.

Ms. McLoughlin helped her children discover associations between sounds and letters by pointing them out during shared book reading and having the children pay attention to the letters and sounds in the environmental words at play centers. When the children had developed some knowledge of sound-letter relationships, she demonstrated how to spell words. Even though it took time, she shared individually with each of the children every day and noted in their journals if she helped them sound the words.

In a few weeks, some children were still scribble writing or drawing pictures, but a few had begun to string letters together, often using invented spelling to make words. Ms. McLoughlin remembered the day that Tony asked her to spell *duck* and she had said, "What sounds do you hear? Stretch out the word so that you can hear all of its sounds." Slowly, Tony said the word and then wrote *dk*—a real breakthrough for him. As the children discovered sound-letter relationships, they eagerly attempted to spell any word they wanted to use in their stories.

Now, near the end of the school year, Ms. McLoughlin found that most of her students were writing longer and more readable journal entries. They were working on

refining sentence structure, making sure that there were spaces between words, and placing punctuation marks correctly. She looked at Hank's story and asked him to read it to her. He read:

> Once upon a time there was a tree that wanted to be yellow and he could not decide. So he waited for fall . . . . And he turned yellow. The end. By Hank.

Ms. McLoughlin complimented him on the way his story had a beginning, a middle, and an end—something she encouraged her students to consider as they wrote. They often discussed story structure as they read stories together.

Looking over at Judy's paper, Ms. McLoughlin could see that Judy still had not made the breakthrough to understanding the relationship between sounds and letters. She looked frustrated, so Ms. McLoughlin asked Hank to help Judy with the words she needed. Ms. McLoughlin smiled as she heard Hank using her exact words: "Think of the sounds in *dinner*. What letter makes the sound you hear at the beginning of the word?"

Moving on, Ms. McLoughlin overheard two children conferring. Al said, "You know, when we write *running*, all we have to do is think how to spell *run* and add *ing*. That's easy." When Chris asked Karen how to spell a word, Karen reminded him he could copy the word he needed from yesterday's chart. Ms. McLoughlin was pleased to hear that exchange because she always encouraged the children to use the words displayed in the room to get the correct spelling. Tara wanted someone to listen to her story, and Joshua was asking Jeff to help him write his next word. Ms. McLoughlin was glad to see students learning from each other.

When most of the children had finished, Ms. McLoughlin told them she was ready for them to read their journals to her. Martha came first with a two-page story about her big sister's birthday party. After letting Martha stamp the date on her story, Ms. McLoughlin asked her to select a book to read while the others came to her with their journals. Chuck came next with four pages filled with writing. He eagerly read her a long, involved story

Getting Children Started in Writing *(Continued)*

Source: Hank Replogle, Carthage Elementary School, Carthage, Tennessee. Used with permission.

about dinosaurs, but she noted that his words were made of letters that had no relationship to the sounds in them. Chuck was a bright child and knew a great deal about dinosaurs, but he still could not use letter-sound relationships.

Even though Ms. McLoughlin sometimes asked the children to write about special topics related to holidays or themes, she often let them choose their own topics. Free choice worked well for Matt; his last entry had only

been three words, but today he produced a full-page story about his camping trip with his dad.

Finally, all the children had read their journals to her and were comfortably looking at books. Establishing this routine had taken considerable time and effort, but most of the children now understood the schedule and responded well. Even better, many of them were now able to write simple, well-constructed stories with invented spelling.

EXAMPLE 3.4 Experience Chart Story

Our Trip to the Zoo

We rode in the school bus.
Mr. Spring was the bus driver.
The bus took us to the zoo.
We saw many animals.
We ate popcorn and peanuts.
We thanked Mr. Spring.
Our trip was fun.

Time for Reflection

Some educators say that children learn reading and writing naturally, just as they have learned to speak, and that a supportive environment and a wide variety of experiences are all that they need to figure out the writing system on their own. Others, however, say that children need explicit instruction in specific skills.

What do *you* think, and why?

Children learn many literacy concepts through story writing. They watch as the teacher forms letters that make up words. They notice that language consists of separate words that are combined into sentences. They see the teacher begin at the left side and move to the right and go from top to bottom. They become aware that dictated stories have titles in which the first letter of each important word is capitalized. They realize that sentences begin with capital letters and end with punctuation marks. Besides becoming familiar with mechanical writing skills, children develop their thinking skills. The teacher's questions help them develop skill in organizing and summarizing. As the children retell events in the order of occurrence, they begin to understand sequence. As they recall the important points, they begin to form a concept of *main idea*.

Development of Oral Language Skills

There are many ways that teachers can help children develop listening and speaking skills. They include scheduling sharing times, reading aloud, and creating opportunities for dramatic play and creative dramatics.

Listening

In teaching children to listen, the teacher should choose topics that interest them and make use of words and concepts they understand. As members of an audience,

Sharing Time

At the beginning of school, Paula Franck modeled sharing time with her kindergartners, but now they are conducting it themselves. Ms. Franck and the children are sitting on the rug with Kelly, today's leader, on a chair in front of them. Kelly begins by saying: "Who has something to share today?" Jenny's hand goes up, and Kelly invites her to share. Jenny begins: "This is what my dad brought me from Washington." She shows a model of the Washington Monument and continues to talk about it. When Jenny finishes, she calls on the listeners to make comments and ask questions. Ted says: "I really like what you told us. What is it made of?" Jenny answers and then calls on Chris, who says: "That is very interesting. How big is the real one?"

Analysis of Scenario

Children who speak must be prepared to share and then be able to direct the discussion that follows. Basing their responses on careful listening, members of the audience must say something positive and then ask questions or make comments. Ms. Franck intervenes only when no one has a question or comment, which rarely occurs.

children need to learn to concentrate and become good listeners. "Seeing It in Practice: Sharing Time" presents a scenario that is the product of previous instruction on courtesy in both speaking and listening behaviors.

Teachers can help children improve their listening comprehension by reading both storybooks and informational books to them. For English-language learners, comparing literature selections written in English with the same titles written in the child's primary language is an effective listening comprehension activity. When reading books to the class, teachers should relate the children's experiences to the content of the books. They should choose books that are relevant to class activities, such as field trips, and make the books available to children before and after these activities or events.

LITERATURE

DIVERSITY

Dedicated listening centers or areas are often visible in literacy-rich classrooms. These may include dedicated DVD players, CD or tape players, headsets, story recordings, and multiple copies of read-along books. By recording themselves reading stories to the children, teachers can provide a wide variety of recorded books easily and inexpensively. Recordings of nonfiction books introduce children to expository text, and recorded commentaries on field trips help students recall special events with appropriate specialized vocabulary. Other ideas for listening center recordings include jump rope rhymes, riddles and jokes, interviews, tongue twisters, and poems or jingles.

Oral Expression

Children learn about using language through informal conversations, which they may engage in while working together at centers or on class projects. Teachers' recognition of the value of talk reflects Vygotsky's theory, discussed earlier in this chapter, that children develop intellectually as they interact socially with other children and with mediating adults (Fortson and Reiff, 1995).

TEACHING TIP

Opportunities for Oral Expression

The following list offers ideas for class activities that develop oral expression:

- Making the daily schedule
- Choosing a current event to record on the board
- Planning projects, activities, or experiences
- Discussing a new bulletin board display
- Interpreting pictures
- Brainstorming ideas from "What if…" situations (*example:* "What if we had four arms instead of two arms?")
- Acting out stories
- Carrying on pretend telephone conversations with toy telephones
- Reviewing the day's events
- Engaging in dramatic play

DIVERSITY   STRUGGLING READER/
                     INTERVENTION

Teachers should encourage children to use the opportunities for oral expression that occur throughout the day to develop their skills in oral communication. For example, the classroom environment provides many subjects and opportunities for descriptive talk. Children can compare different building blocks and note their relationships (size, weight, color); they can observe several kinds of animals and consider differences in the animals' feet, skin covering, and size; and they can compare a variety of fabrics in terms of texture, weight, and purpose.

Some teachers may wish to set up language centers to combine verbal communication with cognitive development (Hunter-Grundin, 1990). An adult (teacher, parent, or teaching assistant) leads a small group of children in a discussion that enables them to express opinions, justify points of view, challenge the opinions of others, or suggest possible alternatives. Appropriate topics include ideas for books that children will coauthor, solutions to problems, and subjects related to a theme. The discussion is not a question-answer session but an open expression of thoughts and ideas. It should help students, especially struggling readers and English-language learners, gain confidence in their ability to communicate, and it should stimulate them to think deeply about matters that concern them.

Dramatic Play

Dramatic play occurs when children simulate real experiences, such as cooking dinner or being a cashier. It requires both speaking and listening and often incorporates reading and writing as well. It is spontaneous and unrehearsed, and children assume the roles of people whom they have observed in real life. They think, feel, move, react, and speak according to their interpretations of how these people perform their roles. Both Piaget and Vygotsky said that children construct knowledge and develop intellectually through play (Wortham, 1996). "Putting It into Practice: Dramatic Play" describes a model activity in which children can practice language skills as they play the roles of customer, cashier, food preparer, and order taker. They learn to follow directions and recognize the words for menu items. They also develop mathematical skills as they use play money to pay for their orders and make change.

Ideally, themes for dramatic play centers originate from the children's interests and ideas, with the teacher facilitating the development of the centers. A field trip to a grocery store or fire station may be the stimulus for a dramatic play center. Other typical centers are a kitchen, bakery, post office, bank, business office, hospital, beauty salon, travel agency, aquarium, and restaurant (Dailey and Owen, 1994; Fisher, 1991).

Creative dramatics activities help students acquire listening and speaking skills.
© Elizabeth Crews/The Image Works

Children can plan and prepare each center by bringing supplies, arranging the area, and painting cardboard walls or counters. The teacher should see that materials are available to stimulate the use of oral and written language for communication, such as writing tools, note paper, envelopes, junk mail, file folders, newspapers, recipes, coupons, grocery lists and menus. Only a few materials should be available at first, and others may be added as needed. Props should be safe for children to handle and should have an authentic use in dramatic play.

During dramatic play, the teacher acts primarily as an observer but may also participate briefly to model appropriate behaviors and promote interaction. For instance, at a grocery store, the teacher might ask, "Do you have any specials today?" or "May I use my coupon to buy this soap?"

Dramatic play has many benefits. Because children need to carry on conversations, they must use good language skills. Frequently, children use printed words in their play, and these words later become sight words. These words may be found on package labels, order forms, street signs, or ticket booths. Children discover the need to read when they have to recognize words to play the situation. Perceiving this need stimulates their interest in learning to read.

Dramatic Play

After the children have discussed their experiences at various restaurants, say to them: "How could we make a pretend restaurant in our own classroom? Where could we put it? What are some things we would need? How could we get these things?" Have the children come up with answers and develop a plan. Ask some children to bring in cups, napkins, bags, and take-out containers from restaurants and have others paint a sign. You can provide a toy cash register.

Make an illustrated price list to place above an improvised counter. Help the children learn to read the food words and the prices by asking: "What is the first item on the list? How much does it cost?" Keep the list simple at first and add new items later. When the fast-food center is ready, different children can assume the roles of customers and workers.

Creative Dramatics

Spontaneous story reenactments, or **creative dramatics,** heighten children's awareness of story structure and characterization, which in turn helps them comprehend and recall stories (Martinez, 1993). Acting out stories spontaneously builds interest in listening because children love to hear stories and then perform them. As the teacher reads a story, the children need to pay close attention to the sequence of events, the personalities of the characters, the dialogue, and the mood. Before acting out the story, the class reviews what happened and identifies the characters. As they act, the children must use appropriate vocabulary, enunciate distinctly, speak audibly, and express themselves clearly. Children will want to dramatize some stories several times, switching roles each time. The rest of the class forms the audience and must listen carefully. There is little or no need for props, sets, or costumes.

Puppets are also useful in creative dramatics. Some shy children who are unwilling to speak as themselves are willing to talk through puppets. Children develop good language skills as they plan puppet shows and spontaneously speak their lines.

Creative Dramatics

The following are suggested stories appropriate for classroom dramatization in emergent and developing literacy classrooms:

- *Caps for Sale* by Esphyr Slobodkina
- *The Three Billy Goats Gruff* by Janet Stevens
- *Stone Soup* by Marcia Brown
- *The Napping House* by Audrey and Don Wood
- *There Was an Old Lady Who Swallowed a Fly* by Simms Tabaak

Classroom Environment

In addition to planning activities to develop reading, writing, listening and speaking skills, teachers of children in the emergent and developing literacy stages should maintain a classroom environment that promotes the language and literacy growth of every student. The classroom should be a nonthreatening environment in which students can learn and be actively engaged in authentic language activities. According to Strickland and Morrow (1988), several concepts are basic to the understanding of how the growth in reading and writing occurs. The following list outlines core understandings that provide a foundation for creating a literacy-rich environment:

- Children construct their own knowledge of reading and writing through experimentation and discovery. By bringing the knowledge they already have to new situations, they make connections and look for patterns in printed words.

- Growth in oral language, reading, and writing occurs together. Each language art supports the others because of their interrelationships.

- Children learn reading and writing by actively using them for real purposes. A major task for the teacher is to structure the environment so that children can explore language in meaningful ways.

- Teachers need to consider individual differences in children's abilities, interests, and experiences when planning instruction.

- When necessary, teachers intervene in language learning to help children make connections and move ahead.

- Reading and writing activities take place throughout the school day, not just in separate instructional periods.

In "Seeing It in Practice: Kindergarten Literacy Activities," the teacher has provided a classroom environment that involves many emergent and developing literacy skills.

Diversity in a Literacy-Centered Classroom

Teachers in emergent and developing literacy classrooms must learn about and respect students' individual backgrounds, their experiences, their need for freedom of choice, and the relationships between students' experiences at home and at school. DIVERSITY

It is important to remember that every child who enters school is an individual with a unique personality, a specific set of experiences, and special interests. Children vary in their racial, ethnic, cultural, and economic backgrounds, as well as in their physical and mental abilities (Jasmine, 1995). Although most children come to the classroom using oral language, many are likely to have misconceptions and incompletely formed concepts about written language. Some children may be learning oral, as well as written, English for the first time.

Some students are at risk of failing to acquire the skills that they need to achieve success. Circumstances that place them at risk include (1) low teacher expectations; (2) failure to achieve in a competitive school structure, particularly for children with academic, functional, or physical disabilities; (3) family stress or instability;

Kindergarten Literacy Activities

Before the school day officially begins in Linda Edwards's kindergarten, the children are sitting at tables writing journal entries, gathering around the incubator watching newly hatched ducklings, or sharing books at the reading center. When Ms. Edwards calls the children together, they discuss the date and the weather. They mark the calendar, and one child figures out the number of 1s and 10s in May 17. Ms. Edwards then reads them a story from a big book, moving a pointer under the words as she reads. The children sing a song from the big book, with a parent using the pointer while the teacher plays the autoharp. When Ms. Edwards questions the children about their favorite part, they respond enthusiastically. Then they read the story with her as she moves the pointer below the words again.

Analysis of Scenario

The classroom described in this scenario contains many opportunities for observing and discussing, writing purposefully, and reading independently, as well as learning math concepts, singing songs, and making decisions as a class. Reading and writing are not lessons to be taught during specific time periods but, rather, occur in various forms throughout the day.

(4) poverty or low socioeconomic background; and (5) low self-perception regarding school (Bertrand, 1995). According to Goodman (1986), teachers should accept children as natural and curious learners, recognize their special competencies and needs, find ways to serve them, and support them with patience and encouragement.

Importance of Experiential Background

A broad experiential background is essential for success in reading because children must be familiar with the concepts and vocabulary that they will see in written form in order to gain meaning from them. Through their individual experiences, children gain an understanding of concepts and learn words, or labels, for them. As children encounter a variety of experiences, they modify and refine their perceptions until they get a clear picture of each concept that they have acquired. A child may need many experiences to attain a well-rounded impression of a single idea. "School," for example, is a concept that children do not completely understand until they have experienced it in different ways. (More information on concept development is found in Chapters 1, 6 and 7.)

Children generally best remember experiences that entail actual physical involvement, but it may not always be feasible to provide such concrete experiences. Vicarious experiences also provide opportunities to expand concepts when more active experiences are not possible.

A class project like the one described in "Putting It into Practice: Providing a Direct Experience" can promote growth in vocabulary and concept development and can provide the prerequisite involvement for a language experience approach (LEA) to writing, discussed later in Chapter 9.

LITERATURE

Wordless picture books and pictures can provide vicarious experiences. By looking at the pictures in wordless picture books, children can use their own words to describe events and characters, thus building their experiences along with

Providing a Direct Experience

One day early in the week, say to the class: "Tomorrow we will make some vegetable soup. Remember to bring a vegetable to put in the soup. Now we will write a chart story about the ingredients that we will need for our soup."

The next morning, say: "Tell us about your vegetable. What is it called? What color is it? How does it feel? How does it smell?" Give each child a chance to handle and talk about the vegetables. Then ask: "What do we need to do first to make the soup? What must we do to the vegetables before we put them in the pot? What else should we add?" (Answers include getting and heating the water, washing and cutting up the vegetables, and adding seasonings.) You should cut the vegetables.

When the soup is ready to eat, give each child a cupful. As the children eat, ask: "How does your soup taste? Are the colors of the vegetables the same as when we put them into the soup?" After they have finished eating, let the children dictate another chart story about the sequence of making the soup and/or their reactions to eating it, or have the children write their own stories.

Some concepts that you can help children acquire from this experience and related discussions are (1) soup can be made from a variety of vegetables; (2) after they are cooked, the vegetables change in texture and appearance; (3) it takes time to heat water and cook soup; (4) the water absorbs flavor and color from the vegetables; (5) cold water becomes hot when it is placed on a heated surface; (6) certain foods are classified as vegetables.

As a result of the experience, children's vocabularies might now include *boil, dissolve, ingredients, squash, celery, slice, chop, shred, dice, tomatoes, carrots, corn, peas, liquid,* and *flavor.*

---

vocabulary and concepts. Pictures, particularly those that tell a story, are extremely fruitful sources of new ideas and experiences.

A suggested list of appropriate wordless picture books is located on the Student Website.

Importance of Choice

Children value their ability to make choices—what to do, with whom to work, where to work, which books to read, and how best to do chosen tasks (Rasinski, 1988b). Freedom to choose enables children to make decisions and self-direct their learning. From a study involving six-year-olds, Fresch (1995) found that children select books and activities that meet special needs, such as facing a new challenge, talking with friends about reading and writing, and building confidence through familiar reading. Children can even help create curriculum if their teacher considers their interests, concerns, and inquiries when planning instruction (Fallon and Allen, 1994). "Seeing It in Practice: Freedom to Choose" illustrates the value of allowing children to make choices.

Home and School Connection

It is important that parents and caregivers provide a positive environment for their children's emerging literacy. Parents and caregivers need to become aware that they are their children's first teachers and that the language experiences they provide will have a powerful effect on the children's growth in literacy. Teachers can help significant caregivers to understand and execute their critical role in promoting early literacy by encouraging them to respond enthusiastically to the children's curiosity

Freedom to Choose

Following a unit on giants that included a section on whales, a prefirst grader chose to draw pictures of whales during language workshop. Sprawled on the floor in a corner of the room, Danny carefully sketched a different kind of whale in each of six frames of large segmented paper to be used for a roll movie. He marked the distinguishing features of each whale and then labeled each picture by copying the name of the type of whale. For Danny, such sustained attention was unusual, but whales fascinated him.

Analysis of Scenario

When children are free to choose their activities, their concentration and determination enable them to accomplish remarkable tasks.

about print. The continuity—or lack of continuity—between literacy experiences at home and in school strongly affects learning (National Reading Panel, 2000).

Nistler and Maiers (2000) suggest strengthening the connection between home and school through innovative family literacy programs. Consistent interaction between parents and teachers, recognition of the diversity of family backgrounds, and the viewing of the role of parents and teachers as partners are some characteristics of an effective family literacy program. Many educators promote family literacy programs that encourage adult learners to enhance their own literacy skills while promoting the literacy of their children (Morrow and Neuman, 1995). One school-based family literacy program, in which 95 percent of the families are members of minority groups with low-socioeconomic backgrounds, offers support in language and literacy development because it increases parental awareness of the importance of reading books to further their children's education. Specifically, the program involves parents in planning, includes workshops, invites parent volunteers to read or tell stories to children, provides books for children to take home and share with parents, and encourages teachers to communicate with parents regularly and to suggest ideas for them to try at home (Come and Fredericks, 1995).

Because of the importance of story reading with children, teachers might offer parents some specific pointers. Story reading can be a pleasurable experience for both the reader and the child, especially when accompanied by a lively verbal exchange about the story and the illustrations. Research on home storybook reading has supported the following interactive behaviors for their positive effects on literacy: questioning, praising, offering information, directing discussion, relating concepts to life experiences, modeling dialogue and responses, and sharing personal reactions (Strickland and Morrow, 1990). Here are examples of appropriate questions and comments based on *The Three Little Pigs:*

How is this little pig's house different from our house?

Uh-oh, that wolf is going to cause trouble! Can you read this part with me? (*I'll huff, and I'll puff, and I'll blow your house down.*)

DIVERSITY

LITERATURE

TEACHING TIP

Involving Families in Developing Literacy

The following suggestions may be shared with families to help establish and encourage a partnership between home and school in the promotion of literacy development:

1. Read picture books, beginning at infancy, and consider introducing appropriate chapter books as the child's attention span increases. Make

(Continued)

What do you think will happen next?

That's a good idea! Let's read so that we can find out for sure.

Is the third little pig clever? How can you tell?

By sharing books with their children, parents can make them aware of many print conventions. Behaviors such as pointing to words and letters, talking about words with similar sounds, and observing upper- and lower-case letters occur naturally during parent-child reading. Smolkin and Yaden (1992) found that when parents read with their children, the children were learning to use correct linguistic terms (for example, *letter* and *word*) and becoming aware of directionality, letter forms, and sound-letter relationships. In addition, they were learning new word meanings and using prior knowledge to make sense of text.

In school, teachers often encourage emergent and developing readers to draw and write; these students are also encouraged to write without correcting spelling or handwriting. Teachers who are knowledgeable about developmentally appropriate practices recognize the importance of allowing students in the early scribbling stage to share their writing efforts without the demands of revisions (Cunningham and Allington, 1999). Some parents, however, may expect their children to bring home graded worksheets and may be dismayed by child-created stories using invented spelling. The teacher should communicate with parents, perhaps through weekly newsletters or regular parent workshops, to inform them about classroom practices (Enz, 1995).

use of recordings of stories or books. (These are especially helpful for families who do not speak English at home.)

2. Engage in conversations with the child. Respond to questions and explain "why" and "how." Also listen patiently and supportively when the child struggles to express an idea and respond appropriately.

3. Read together cereal boxes, menus, place mats, street signs, coupons, and other forms of print. Share letters that come in the mail so that the child understands that writing can be used to communicate with others. Involve the child in activities around the home, such as cooking, gardening, and paying bills. Point out the usefulness of recipes, instructions on seed packets, and checkbooks.

4. Point out and read familiar signs, such as ones that say "Wal-Mart," "Kroger," and "STOP." Encourage the child to read them too.

5. Provide writing materials (including computers, if possible) and encourage their use for writing messages, creating shopping lists, and composing letters.

6. Model good reading practices by reading books for your own pleasure. Explain why you are enjoying your book. Encourage the child to "talk like a book" when sharing a storybook with you.

7. Share newspapers and magazines. Encourage the child to find familiar words that appear in advertisements.

8. Engage the child in singing songs, doing finger plays, reciting nursery rhymes, and playing guessing games.

9. Take the child with you on visits and trips. Use specific terms when discussing the experience, such as *flight attendant, pilot, gate,* and *baggage area.*

10. Visit the children's section of the library; let the child get a library card and check out books frequently.

Importance of Assessment and Early Intervention

A variety of causes contributes to the number of struggling readers. These causes may include inadequate reading instruction, social and cultural factors, and physical challenges. Early intervention is the key, and it should begin as soon as a student shows signs of difficulty. These signs are often observable during the emergent

STRUGGLING READER/ INTERVENTION

literacy stage; therefore, it is important that all teachers be able to use a variety of assessment methods to evaluate student progress and that teachers have the skills to develop intervention plans using effective strategies for students who are having difficulties. Chapter 2 provided a discussion of assessment of emergent and developing literacy and suggested some intervention strategies. It also discussed information on the Response to Intervention (RTI) model that provides an implementation guide for classroom application.

STRUGGLING READER/ INTERVENTION

Intervention models used for students who are experiencing difficulty in reading at the emergent or developing stages need to emphasize prevention rather than correction. Intensive early intervention followed by long-term, effective instruction appears to bring about lasting and substantial gains in reading achievement. In addition, the National Reading Panel (2000) recommends systematic, explicit instruction for children at risk or struggling. Two early intervention programs that are based on the premise of prevention and explicit instruction are briefly described here: Reading Recovery and Success for All.

Reading Recovery

Reading Recovery, developed in New Zealand by Marie Clay, is a temporary intervention program intended for first graders who are at risk of early reading failure (Clay, 1979; Sensenbaugh, 1995). A specialist works daily with each child for thirty minutes, usually for a period of twelve to sixteen weeks, until the child has developed effective strategies for independent learning and can function adequately in the regular classroom. From a selection of approximately 500 "little books," the tutor selects those that meet a student's particular interests and needs. Each lesson consists of having the child read many little books and compose a brief story or message. Research evidence indicates that Reading Recovery has enabled children to retain initial gains in reading and continue to make progress.

Success for All

Success for All focuses on low-achieving urban populations. This program involves school reorganization to provide excellent instruction from preschool through the primary grades (Slavin, Madden, Karweit, Dolan, and Wasik, 1994). Its three premises are innovative curriculum and instruction in reading, intensive one-on-one tutoring if reading problems emerge, and regrouping by reading level across the grades for ninety-minute reading instructional periods. The tutor reinforces the direct instruction provided by the regular classroom teacher but also seeks to identify problems and find different strategies. In addition, a family support team attempts to involve parents, making them feel welcome in the school and providing special services.

SUMMARY

Literacy development begins at birth. During the early years, children develop skills in both oral and written communication. Cognitive development and language learning occur together. Children learn language naturally by observing and imitating language users and then constructing language to meet their needs. Educators must nurture emergent literacy, a continuum of literacy growth beginning at birth, and must provide developmentally appropriate learning activities throughout the developing literacy stage. Children already possess knowledge about reading and writing before entering school. Teachers should build on and expand children's growing awareness of language as purposeful communication.

It is extremely important to strengthen the connection between home and school. The development of literacy skills relies on the continuity between the experiences encountered at home and at school. Parents and caregivers are considered their child's first teachers, and the experiences in language development provided in the home environment have a powerful effect on emergent and developing readers and writers.

Teachers act as facilitators of learning by creating experiences to meet the children's needs and interests. A print-rich environment with books, charts, labels, environmental print, and centers provides a further stimulus for language development. Realizing the value of a literate home environment, teachers may suggest strategies to parents and caregivers for guiding their children's literacy development.

Many children's listening and speaking skills are well developed when they enter school. At school, teachers provide opportunities for further growth in listening comprehension and oral expression. Through exposure to reading and writing materials and experiences, some of which occur before entering school, children gain knowledge of print conventions and sight words. Children's growth in reading and writing, based on what they already know, occurs concurrently and interrelatedly through experiences with big books, journal writing, and listening to stories. Participation in guided reading groups supports the development of early reading skills. The development of phonemic awareness and phonological awareness and the use of invented or temporary spelling help children to connect letters with sounds, while writing workshops continue to provide scaffolding and support for early writing attempts.

A growing number of intervention programs for struggling readers now emphasize prevention rather than correction. Many of them rely on the observation skills of teachers who work with children in their emerging and developing stages. It is extremely important for teachers to be knowledgeable and recognize students who may potentially struggle. Many intervention programs are structured to implement an intensive intervention plan followed by the maintenance of long-term effective strategic reading instruction for those students who may be at risk.

For your journal . . . .

1. Respond to any practicum experiences with literacy in early childhood education.

2. Reflect on one or more of the following concepts: invented spelling, developmentally appropriate practice, shared book reading, phonemic awareness, phonological awareness, zone of proximal development, and emergent literacy.

3. Observe one child carefully. How could you provide scaffolding that would move this child through the zone of proximal development?

4. Reflect on the Video Case, "Vygotsky's Zone of Proximal Development: Increasing Cognition in an Elementary Literacy Lesson." Dr. Francis describes the development of students' analytic abilities in a step-by-step fashion, always focusing on student understanding. How will you approach actualizing the zone of proximal development when you have your own classroom?

5. Reflect on the Video Case, "Elementary Reading Instruction: A Balanced Literacy Program." Ms. Jenoski suggests that it takes time to develop a balanced literacy program—as long as six to eight weeks. Does this amount of time surprise you? What do you see as the benefits of establishing such a foundation over a long period of time? What might the disadvantages be?

6. Reflect on the Video Case, "Elementary Writing Instruction: Process Writing." What is your response to the emphasis on nonfiction texts during the writers' workshop featured? Do you agree or disagree with those who advocate for a greater emphasis on nonfiction texts in the primary grades? Explain your thinking.

. . . . and your portfolio

1. Start an annotated bibliography of read-aloud, predictable, and repetitive books that you would like to use with your class.

2. Create a file of pictures that might stimulate children to tell or write their own stories.

3. On a continuing basis, observe a child's emergent literacy and suggest developmentally appropriate practices for providing instruction.

4. Compile a list of websites that provide developmentally appropriate instructional strategies and techniques for use with emerging and developing readers.

Overview of Word-Recognition Approaches

4

Recognizing words is an essential prerequisite for skilled reading with comprehension (Samuels, 1988). Many approaches to instruction have helped students to become independent in word recognition. Word-recognition strategies include sight word recognition, context clues, phonics, structural analysis, and dictionary skills. Research indicates that, regardless of the strategies used to introduce students to reading, the ones who progressed most in fast and accurate word identification in the first grade were the ones who scored best on reading comprehension tests in the second grade (R. C. Anderson, Hiebert, Scott, and Wilkinson, 1985).

Good readers differ from struggling readers in two major ways. Good readers tend to have larger sight vocabularies than struggling readers, and this reduces their need to stop and analyze words. Additionally, when they need to analyze words, good readers often are more flexible in their approach than struggling readers are because they generally have been taught more different word-recognition strategies. Good readers have also been encouraged to try a different strategy if the first one that they try fails. Struggling readers frequently know only a single strategy for decoding words. No one strategy is appropriate for all words, however, so these students are at a disadvantage when they encounter words for which their strategy is not useful. Even if they have been taught several strategies, struggling readers may not have been taught a procedure that will enable them to select the most appropriate strategy or strategies for efficiently decoding a particular word in their reading material.

This chapter presents a variety of methods of word recognition and stresses a flexible approach to decoding unfamiliar words, encouraging application of those word recognition strategies that are most helpful at the moment. It also explains ways to show children how to use a number of word recognition strategies in combination to help them decode words.

Because the amount of information that must be conveyed about word recognition is extremely large, this topic has been divided into two chapters. This chapter offers an overview of five methods: sight words, context clues, phonics, structural analysis, and use of the dictionary. It also provides details on all the methods except phonics, the area of word recognition that most often causes concerns for teachers. Because of its importance and its complexity, phonics is covered in detail in Chapter 5. Two areas of structural analysis—syllabication and accent—are so closely related to phonics that much of the detail on these areas is also covered in Chapter 5.

BEFORE
A, D or **?**

Directions: Before you read this chapter, complete the following anticipation/reaction guide. In the space before each statement, write **A** if you agree; **D** if you disagree; or **?** if you don't know. After you have read the chapter, complete the guide again to show what you have discovered in the chapter. In the space after each statement, mark whether you were initially correct (with a **C**) or incorrect (with an **I**). Write the letter for the correct answer (**A**) or (**D**) in the space for the statements that you initially marked with a question mark (**?**).

AFTER
C or **I** (for initial
A or **D** answers)
A or **D**
(for initial **?** answers)

1. All word-recognition strategies are learned with equal ease by all children.

2. Sight words are words that readers recognize immediately without needing to resort to analysis.

3. The English language is noted for the regularity of sound-symbol associations in its written words.

4. Games with complex rules are good ones to use for practice with sight words.

5. Most practice with sight words should involve the words in context.

6. If teachers teach phonics well, they do not need to bother with other word-recognition strategies.

7. The addition of a prefix or suffix to a root word can change the word's meaning.

8. The apostrophe in a contraction indicates possession or ownership.

9. Context clues used by themselves provide only educated guesses about the identities of unfamiliar words.

10. The language experience approach is good for developing sight vocabulary.

11. For students with special needs, instruction often should be more direct and explicit.

CHAPTER 4 ORGANIZATION

Overview of Word-Recognition Approaches

Word-Recognition Strategies

General Guidelines for Teaching Word Recognition
Sight Words
Context Clues
Phonics
Structural Analysis
Dictionary Study

Word-Recognition Procedure

Word-Recognition Strategies

Word-recognition strategies include

- Developing a store of words that can be recognized immediately on sight.
- Making use of context clues surrounding a word.
- Decoding a word through phonics, or sound-symbol associations.
- Structural analysis, or using the parts of the word to provide clues for recognition.
- Looking up words in dictionaries.

The last four strategies are sometimes referred to as *word-attack* strategies or skills. Students need to be able to perform all of the word-recognition strategies because some will be more helpful than others in certain situations. Students also need to learn the situations in which each strategy can be most helpful. The lists of standards developed by professional organizations and by each state include the ability to use word-recognition skills. High-stake tests are generally based on these standards, and, if teachers fail to teach skills covered in the tests, their students will not perform well on these measures.

 STANDARDS/ ASSESSMENTS

Teaching a single approach to word identification is not wise because students may be left without the proper tools for specific situations. In addition, depending on their individual abilities, some students find some word-recognition strategies

 DIVERSITY

To access the reading/language arts standards set forth by the International Reading Association (IRA) and the National Council of Teachers of English (NCTE), go to the organizations' websites (www.reading.org or www.ncte.org). To locate the state standards for your state and other states, visit the Mid-continent Research for Education and Learning site (www.mcrel.org:80/topics/products/78). Links to these sites are available at the Student Website for this textbook.

easier to learn than others. A student who has a hearing loss, for example, may have difficulty using phonics but may learn sight words easily and profit greatly from the use of context clues.

General Guidelines for Teaching Word Recognition

Teachers can follow a number of general guidelines for teaching word recognition strategies that can result in effective learning by students.

▶ Word Recognition Should Lead to Comprehension

Because words in printed materials must be recognized before the content can be comprehended, some teachers have devoted most of their reading instructional time to word recognition. However, instruction in word recognition should not dominate reading time. Instead, students should spend much time reading connected text. Teachers should devote ample attention to comprehension instruction, or their students may become "word callers" who do not understand the material they are given to read.

Based on his extensive research, Samuels (1988) advocates a balanced reading program that incorporates both decoding skills and skills necessary for reading in context. His research has supported the idea that accurate and automatic word recognition is necessary for reading fluency. This automaticity (application without conscious thought) in word recognition is achieved through extended practice. Repeated readings of the same passages can help move students from accuracy to automaticity in word recognition (Samuels, 2004).

Adams (2004) also endorses the need for word-recognition skills along with strategies for acquiring meaning. She states, "Deep and ready working knowledge of letters, spelling patterns, and words, and of the phonological translations of all three, is of inescapable importance to both skillful reading and its acquisition" (p. 1238) because it enables the reading process. However, she denounces drills on isolated skills. She also emphasizes the need for automaticity in decoding to free students' attention for comprehension.

Although automaticity in decoding is important, children must develop motivation to read—motivation that results from participation in purposeful literacy tasks. This development requires time for reading, book choice, and a chance to discuss the reading material with others (Allen, 1998).

▶ Instruction Should Address Students' Individual Needs

STRUGGLING READER/ INTERVENTION

Students who are having difficulties need high-interest materials that they are capable of using successfully. They should not be given material with which they have previously failed. Instruction in word recognition that involves reading material on a student's frustration level can prevent the student from using sound-symbol patterns, word parts, and context clues to aid in word identification.

Teachers must consider the learning styles of all of their students when planning instruction, especially students who have special needs. Auditory learners learn readily with phonics instruction, visual learners learn sight words more easily, and kinesthetic-tactile learners need to use touch and movement in order to learn best. English-language learners require instruction in use of the English language while they receive instruction in reading. They must build vocabulary and knowledge about English-language features before progressing to learning sound-symbol correspondences (*Struggling Readers, Day 1*, 2000).

 DIVERSITY

▶ Direct Instruction Can Help

All students also must be provided with appropriate materials and direct instruction, as needed, for skills that they lack. Direct instruction has the following characteristics:

- Clearly stated goals that students understand
- Carefully sequenced and structured materials
- Detailed explanations and extensive modeling of reading processes [By modeling, teachers can help readers understand the "invisible mental processes which are at the core of reading" (Duffy, Roehler, and Herrmann, 1988, p. 762).]
- Monitoring of student work with immediate feedback

Direct instruction focuses on academics and is teacher directed. Such instruction is not a matter of asking students to complete skill sheets; instead, it is a planned instructional sequence of explaining and modeling. Instruction is generally continued until skill mastery is achieved (Duffy et al., 1988).

Many researchers have found that direct, systematic instruction in skills and strategies benefits students who have difficulty grasping important reading-writing concepts on their own (Mesmer and Griffith, 2005/2006; Adams, 1990; French, Ellsworth, and Amoruso, 1995; Sears, Carpenter, and Burstein, 1994). These students seem to learn best when direct instruction in basic skills is part of their instructional program.

 STRUGGLING READER/ INTERVENTION

Direct instruction is particularly helpful for students who have difficulty acquiring phonics and decoding skills that are essential for learning to read. After reviewing research on phonics skills, Lyon (1991) concluded that systematic, phonics-based instruction produces more positive outcomes than approaches that rely on contextual reading for students who cannot intuitively learn the alphabetic code.

A potential danger with direct instruction of reading skills in isolation, however, is that children may learn to recognize and pronounce words but be unable to comprehend what they read. For that reason, many educators suggest integrating direct instruction into a reading-writing program and providing the direct instruction within the context of authentic reading activities (Sears et al., 1994; Stahl, 1994). Direct instruction in phonics can occur in holistic classrooms within the context

 LITERATURE

of story reading. For example, the teacher reads a big book with the class and, on later readings, calls attention to beginning sounds of words or to rhyming words. Minilessons (direct instruction) drawn from words in the story follow. (See "Seeing It in Practice: Teaching Phonics Through Literature" in Chapter 5 for ways to teach phonics through literature.)

Systematic teaching appears to be the key to successful phonics instruction, but within systematic teaching, teachers can blend explicit and inductive approaches (Mesmer and Griffith, 2005/2006). For example, a teacher may have students try to figure out something from words on their own and then follow the discovery with explicit instruction about the students' conclusions.

▶ Coaching Can Help

One approach to teaching children to use word-recognition skills that effective teachers employ is coaching. *Coaching* is a form of scaffolding students' learning. This technique consists of supplying cues to students who are attempting to decode unfamiliar words. Clark (2004) studied the cues that teachers use during coaching and found that they were of two types: "general cues to prompt thought and more focused cues to prompt specific action" (p. 441). General cues included questions such as "How are you going to figure that out?" (p. 441). More specific cues focused students' attention to "graphophonic knowledge, word-part identification strategies, and contextual supports" (p. 442). They included questions and statements such as "What two sounds can *c* make? The *y* here sounds like short *i*. Which one should you try here?" or "Does that word make sense in this sentence? What word that begins the same way would make sense?" or "Remember that *ph* makes an *f* sound." or "Look at the picture. Do you see something in the picture that starts with the same sound as that word?" or "This is a compound word. What two words can you see in it?"

> ### TEACHING TIP
>
> **Helping Struggling Readers with Word Recognition**
>
> When coaching students in word recognition, offer general statements and questions first and then provide more specific clues if the student still has trouble. Classmates can also learn how to supply cues to students who are having trouble.

▶ Using Literature Can Help

LITERATURE

STRUGGLING READER/ INTERVENTION

When students are taught with materials that emphasize repetitions of spelling patterns, such as predictable books, stories, and poetry, they tend to develop strategies based on alphabetic principles. This is particularly helpful for struggling readers. These students need to be exposed to texts that contain unchanging patterns that they are able to detect. Some students also need assistance in detecting these patterns. Students may eventually write their own pieces using the patterns of stories that they have read (Walker, 2000).

Sight Words

Young readers also need to develop a store of **sight words,** words that are recognized immediately without having to resort to analysis. The larger the store of sight words a reader has, the more rapidly and fluently he or she can read a selection. Comprehension and reading speed suffer if a reader has to pause too often to analyze unfamiliar words. The more mature and experienced a reader becomes, the larger his or her store of sight words becomes. (Most, if not all, of the words used in this textbook, for example, are a part of the sight vocabularies of college students.) Therefore, one goal of reading instruction is to turn all the words that students continuously need to recognize in print into sight words.

Most children know some sight words when they first come to school. They have learned the names of some of their favorite fast-food restaurants and other businesses from signs, the names of some of their favorite foods and drinks from the packages or labels, or both categories of words, as well as others, from television commercials. Children who have been read stories while sitting on their parents' laps may well have picked up vocabulary from favorite stories that were repeatedly shared. Still, the sight vocabularies of beginning students are meager compared with those that mature readers need.

▶ Teaching Sight Words

Before children begin to learn sight words, they must have developed visual discrimination skills; that is, they must be able to see likenesses and differences among printed words. It is also helpful, although not essential, for them to know the names of the letters of the alphabet because this facilitates discussion of likenesses and differences among words. For example, a teacher could point out that, whereas *take* has a *k* before the *e*, *tale* has an *l* in the same position.

Many educators believe in developing a basic stock of sight words first, then teaching of other methods of word recognition. This allows students to reason inductively about sound-symbol associations and other word elements, such as prefixes and suffixes, coming to understand generalizations and rules

Young readers need to develop a store of sight words.

© David Young Wolff/Photo Edit

through experience with specific examples. There are a number of reasons why sight words need to be taught:

1. The English language contains a multitude of irregularly spelled words—that is, words that are not spelled the way they sound. Many of these are among the most frequently used words in our language. The spellings of the following common words include highly irregular sound-symbol associations: *of*, *through*, *two*, *know*, *give*, *come*, and *once*. Rather than trying in vain to sound out these words, children need to learn to recognize them on sight as whole configurations.

2. Learning several sight words at the very beginning of reading instruction gives the child a chance to engage in a successful reading experience very early and consequently promotes a positive attitude toward reading.

3. Words have meaning for children by the time they arrive at school, but single letters have no meaning for them. Therefore, presenting children with whole words at the beginning allows them to associate reading with meaning rather than with meaningless memorization.

4. After children have built up a small store of sight words, the teacher can begin phonics instruction with an analytic approach, which is described in Chapter 5.

▶ Choosing Sight Words

A teacher must carefully choose which words to teach as sight words. Extremely common irregularly spelled words (*come*, *to*, *two*) and frequently used regularly spelled words (*at*, *it*, *and*, *am*, *go*) should be taught as sight words so that children can read connected sentences early in the program. The first sight words should be useful and meaningful. A child's name should be one of those words; days of the week, months of the year, and names of school subjects are other prime candidates. Words that stand for concepts unfamiliar to children are poor choices. Before children learn *democracy* as a sight word, for example, they need to understand what a democracy is; therefore, this is not a good word to teach in the primary grades.

Lists of basic sight words may give teachers an indication of the words that are most frequently used in reading materials and therefore are needed most frequently by students. The Dolch list of the 220 most common words in reading materials (excluding nouns), though first published in the 1930s, has repeatedly been found to be relevant and useful in more recent materials (Palmer, 1985). Another well-known list of basic sight words is Fry's "Instant Words" (Fry, 1977a). This list presents the words most frequently used in reading materials.

Teaching some words that have regular spelling patterns as sight words is consistent with the beliefs of linguists who have become involved in developing reading materials (see Chapter 9 for further details). Words with regular spelling patterns are also a good base for teaching "word families" in phonics; the *an* family, for example, includes *ban*, *can*, *Dan*, *fan*, *man*, *Nan*, *pan*, *ran*, *tan*, and *van*.

Lists of Dolch words and Instant Words are available at several websites, including the National Institute for Literacy site (http://www.nifl.gov/readingprofiles/Dolch_Fry_Pop.htm). Link to this and other sites offering word lists from the Student Website for this textbook.

Creating a Word Wall of terms and phrases found in public places—such as "Wet Paint," "No Trespassing," "Danger," and so on—allows students to learn, through repetition, words that are important to them in daily life. This technique can be helpful to students who have reading difficulties.

▶ Introducing Sight Words

A potential sight word must initially be identified for learners by the teacher. "Putting It into Practice: Introducing Sight Words" offers some suggestions for how this can be done.

 LITERATURE

You can read aloud to children as they follow along in their books or on a chart. This is a way to identify vocabulary for children within a meaningful context.

You can also use labels to help students learn to recognize their own names and the names of some of their classmates. On the first day of school, give each child a name tag and label each child's desk with his or her name. You may also label the area where the child is supposed to hang a coat or to store supplies. Explain to the children that the letters written on their name tags, desks, and storage areas spell their own names and that no one else is supposed to use these areas. Encourage the children to look at the names carefully and to try to remember them when locating their belongings. Although the children may initially use the name tags to match the labels on the desks and storage areas, by the time the name tags are worn out or lost, the children should be able to identify their printed names without assistance.

You can generally accelerate this process by teaching the children how to write their names. Have them first trace the name labels on their desks with their fingers. Next, have them try to copy their names on sheets of paper. At first, you should label all students' work and drawings with the students' names, but as soon as the children are capable of writing their names, they should label their own papers. From the beginning, the children's names should be written in capital and lowercase letters, rather than all capitals, because this is the way names most commonly appear in print.

You can also teach the days of the week as sight words. Each morning, you can write "Today is _____." on the board and fill in the name of the appropriate day. At first you may read the sentence to the children at the beginning of each day, but soon some children will be able to read the sentence successfully without help.

The *language experience approach*, in which students' own language is written down and used as the basis for their reading material, is good for developing sight vocabulary. This approach (described in detail in Chapter 9) provides a meaningful context for learning sight words, and it can be used productively with individuals or groups. The word-bank and word-sort activities associated with this approach are particularly helpful.

Constructing picture dictionaries, in which students illustrate words and file the labeled pictures alphabetically in a notebook, is another good activity for helping younger children develop sight vocabulary. This procedure has been effective in

 DIVERSITY

Introducing Sight Words

Away to introduce sight words is to show students the printed word as you pronounce it, or pair the word with an identifying picture or actual object. If the word names something in the classroom, such as a door, make a label for the door so that students can see the connection. You may want to label chairs, desks, windows, and other parts of the room and its contents. Seeing the association of the word and the object repeatedly will help your students learn the word. You can play a game by writing the names of objects on the board and having students locate the items in the room by finding the matching labels.

STRUGGLING READER/ INTERVENTION

helping children whose primary language is not English learn to read and understand English words.

The *incremental rehearsal technique* "facilitates mastery, builds fluency, and leads to retention of reading words for struggling readers" (Joseph, 2006, p. 803). It involves presenting unknown words along with known words in specific ratios (Joseph, 2006; Burns 2004). Better retention is obtained when the ratio of known to unknown words is greater. For example, the teacher identifies nine words that have been mastered by students (known words) and ten words that are unknown and places them on index cards for the procedure. Then unknown words are taught one at a time. Each one is shown to the student and identified, and then is shown multiple times with ever increasing numbers of the known words (first one, then two, then three, possibly up to nine) until it becomes a known word. At that point, the newly learned word replaces one of the original known words, and the procedure continues with the second unknown word, then the third, and so on until all of the words are known. The procedure may be particularly effective for use with irregular words (those that do not follow standard phonics principles) but is extremely time consuming. It might be good for use by a classroom assistant (paraprofessional, parent, or other volunteer).

Regardless of the method of presentation, one factor is of paramount importance: The children must *look* at the printed word when it is identified in order to associate the letter configuration with the spoken word or picture. If children fail to look at the word when it is pronounced, they have no chance of remembering it when they next encounter it.

Teachers can encourage children to pay attention to the details of the word by asking them to notice ascending letters (such as *b, d, h*), descending letters (such as *p, g, q*), word length, and particular letter combinations (such as double letters). Careful scrutiny of words can greatly aid retention.

Children learn early to recognize some sight words by their visual *configurations*, or shapes. Teachers should not overly stress this technique because many words have similar shapes. But because many children seem to use the technique in the early stages of reading, regardless of the teacher's methods, a teacher can use configuration judiciously to develop early sight words. One way to call attention to shape is to have the children frame the words to be learned:

The limitation of configuration as a sight word–recognition clue is demonstrated by the following words:

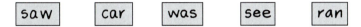

Few words are learned after a single presentation, although Ashton-Warner (1963) claims that children will instantly learn words that are extremely important to them. Generally, a number of repetitions are necessary before a word actually becomes a sight word. (See Chapter 3 for more about Ashton-Warner.)

▶ Practice with Sight Words

Teachers should carefully plan practice with potential sight words. This practice should be interesting because children will more readily learn those things that interest them. Games, such as those we discuss later in this section, are useful if they emphasize the words being learned rather than the rules of the game. Teachers should also plan a variety of ways to practice sight words because no single method works best for every child (Ceprano, 1981).

A review of research shows that children learn sight words better when they receive directed experiences with the words in context, although teaching distinctive word features and using picture clues also facilitate learning. Some research also shows that teaching words in isolation or with pictures does not ensure that children will acquire the ability to read words in context (Ceprano, 1981). Teaching words in context is important because readers cannot pronounce many words out of context with certainty—for example, *read*. The following sentences illustrate the importance of context:

I *read* that book yesterday. I can't *read* without glasses.

Another reason for using context when presenting sight words is that many commonly used words have little meaning when they stand alone. Prime examples are *the*, *a*, and *an*. Context for words may be a sentence (*The* girl ate *a* pear and *an* apple) or short phrases (*the* girl, *a* pear, *an* apple). Context is also useful if a person's pronunciation is less clear than it should be. Children may confuse the word *thing* with *think* unless the teacher has presented context for the word: "I haven't done a useful thing all day."

LITERATURE

A natural approach to sight word instruction is reading to children as they follow along. Teachers may use this approach with groups of students when big books are available; this approach enables all children in the group to see the words. They may also read from books that are available in multiple copies in the classroom, with each child or pair of children following along on individual copies of the story. Books with accompanying audio recordings or electronic books (discussed in Chapter 13) can promote sight vocabulary in a similar way. The value of highly predictable books for beginning readers is widely recognized (McGill-Franzen, 1993; Saccardi, 1996a, 1996b). Peterson (1991) has arranged a continuum of Reading Recovery books from easy to more complex, based partially on the context provided. The books at the easiest levels are highly predictable from the pictures and repetitive sentence patterns.

Encountering words that are in the context of an environment can generate interest in learning sight words. Taking a walk in the students' neighborhoods and attending to the print there may spark interest. Orellana and Hernández (2005) found that inner-city children who were taken for such a walk were not as interested in the signs and other writing that the teachers pointed out but were excited about finding and reading print that was meaningful to them. They looked for the names of the streets where they lived, the places where they shopped, the places where family members worked, and the graffiti on walls, signs, and sidewalks. These children needed to relate personally to the words before they saw the importance of reading them.

Using Basal Readers.   Much teaching of sight word recognition takes place as a part of basal reader lessons:

- The teacher frequently introduces the new words, possibly in one of the ways described here, before reading, discussing meanings at the same time.

- Then students have a guided silent-reading period during which they read material containing the new words in order to answer questions asked by the teacher.

- Purposeful oral-rereading activities offer another chance to use the new words.

- Afterward, teachers generally provide practice activities suggested in the teacher's manual of the basal reading series.

- Follow-up activities may include skill sheets, games, manipulative devices, and special audiovisual materials. Writing new words is helpful for some learners, especially for kinesthetic learners (those who learn through muscle movement).

Learning Function Words.   *Function words*—words, such as *the* and *or*, that have only syntactic meaning rather than concrete content—are often particularly difficult for children to learn because they lack concrete meaning and because many of them are similar in physical features. These words need to be presented in context repeatedly so that the surrounding words can provide meaning. When there are pairs of troublesome words that are likely to be confused (for example, *was* and *saw*), teachers should present them one at a time. Teaching words with more obvious differences in features first, then those with subtler differences, is also a good approach. For example, teach *that* with words like *for* and *was* before presenting it with *this* and *then*. Teachers can also delete the words from passages, leaving blanks for students to fill in with the target words.

Using Practice Aids.   Teachers can use flashcards to foster automaticity in word recognition. Research indicates that "teaching children to read words faster can improve reading comprehension dramatically" (Nicholson, 1998, p. 188).

Another technique is to list sight words on a circular piece of cardboard and have children paper-clip pictures to appropriate words. The teacher can make this activity self-scoring by printing the matching words on the backs of the pictures, as shown below.

Using Games.   Games such as word bingo are useful for practice with sight words. The teacher or a leader calls out a word, and the children who recognize that word on their cards cover it. When a child covers an entire card, he or she says, "Cover," and the teacher or leader checks the card to see if all the covered words were actually called.

Teachers may consider increasing their use of physically active games, such as those in which children stand and act out action verbs. A comparison of the use of physically active games, passive games, and worksheets showed that physically active games were most effective in increasing the sight vocabularies of remedial first

A Read·Write·Think lesson plan called "Bingo! Using Environmental Print to Practice Reading" incorporates an environmental print Bingo game. Another lesson plan from the same source that stresses environmental print is called "I Know That Word! Teaching Reading with Environmental Print." Both are available at http://www.readwritethink.org, or link from the Student Website for this book.

 STRUGGLING READER/ INTERVENTION

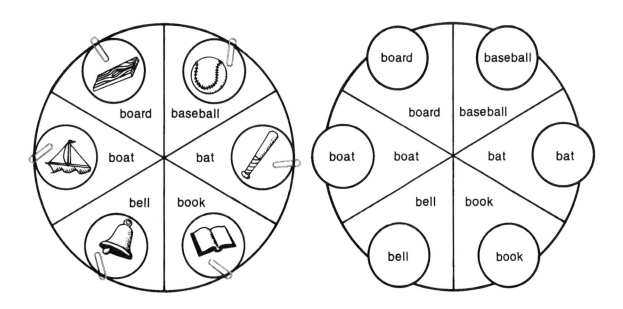

Developing Sight Vocabulary

Mr. Barkley, a first-grade teacher, found that three children were having trouble remembering the action words in the stories they were reading. He called these children over to a corner of the room near the board and wrote these words on the board: *jump, walk, run*. He introduced the words by saying, "We have seen these words in our stories this week, but they have been hard for you to remember, so we are going to practice reading them as we play a game. This word is *jump*. Can you jump for me?" The children jumped. Then he said, "Good. Whenever you read the word *jump* for this game, I want you to jump just like that."

Mr. Barkley introduced *walk* and *run* in the same way. The students readily demonstrated each one.

Then Mr. Barkley brought out a game board with a racetrack oval drawn on it. Each space in the path around the oval had a simple sentence containing either *jump*, *walk*, or *run* written on it. The children took turns spinning a spinner and moving the number of spaces indicated around the racetrack with a personally selected token (one of several different miniature race cars). A child who landed on a space had to read the sentence, tell what it meant, and perform the action in the sentence.

For example, the child might read, "Mary can jump," and then say, "That means Mary can do this." Then the child would stand up and jump. If a child could not read the sentence or tell/show what it meant, another player could "steal his or her play" by reading the sentence and performing the action. The player who got to try this would be determined by having the opponents of the player who missed spin the spinner for a high number.

The first child around the track won the game, but all three children were actively involved with the action words and made progress in reading them correctly as the game continued.

Analysis of Scenario

Mr. Barkley used a physically active game to develop the children's sight vocabularies after more passive reading activities had failed to be effective with these children. He targeted the activity for the children who were having difficulty, rather than forcing repetitive practice on those who had mastered the words. He also presented the words in sentence contexts to encourage children to recognize the words in typical reading situations, rather than as isolated entities.

Time for Reflection

Some people believe that sight words should be taught in context. Others believe that they should be taught in isolation. Still others believe that both methods should be used.

What procedures would *you* use, and why?

graders. Passive games were next, and worksheets were the least effective, although the children who used the worksheets did gain some sight vocabulary (Dickerson, 1982). "Seeing It in Practice: Developing Sight Vocabulary" describes such an activity.

Context Clues

Context clues—the words, phrases, and sentences surrounding the words to be decoded—help readers determine what the unfamiliar words are. Here we will focus on the function of context clues as *word-recognition* aids; Chapter 7 considers the function of context clues as *comprehension* aids.

Because research has shown that syntactic and semantic context influence readers' identification of words, it is important that word-recognition skills be introduced and practiced in context (Jones, 1982). Much of the written material to which primary-level readers are introduced falls well within their comprehension as far as vocabulary and ideas are concerned, but many students cannot always recognize in printed form the words that are familiar in oral form. Context clues can be extremely helpful in this process. Research also shows that context clues help younger and less able readers recognize words more than they help older and better readers (Gough, 1984; Daneman, 1991).

 STRUGGLING READER/INTERVENTION

▶ Picture Clues

Picture clues are generally the earliest context clues that children use. Picture Walks (going through the selection and analyzing the pictures for information) may be used as a strategy before reading a story to help develop concepts and vocabulary. If children are exposed to many pictures of a character, such as one named Julie, in beginning reading materials, they may come to recognize the character instantly. When they are shown a page containing a picture of Julie and a single word, they may naturally assume that the word names the picture and that the word is *Julie*. If they do not relate the picture to the word in this manner, the teacher can ask a question such as "Who is in the picture?" to lead them toward understanding the relationship. If a child responds, "A girl," the teacher might ask, "What kind of letter is at the beginning of the word?" The response "A capital letter" would prompt the question "What kinds of words have we talked about that begin with capital letters?" After eliciting the answer "Names," the teacher can then ask, "What is the name of the girl in the picture?" This question should produce the response "Julie." Finally, the teacher asks, "Now what do you think the word is?" At this point, a correct response is extremely likely. The teacher should use a procedure that encourages the use of picture clues *along with*, rather than apart from, the clues available in the printed word.

Teachers should not overemphasize picture clues. These clues may be useful in the initial stages of instruction, but they become less useful as the child advances to more difficult material, which has a decreasing number of pictures and an increasing proportion of print. Encouraging too much reliance on pictures may result in too little time spent on developing word-analysis skills.

▶ Semantic and Syntactic Cues (Clues)

Both meanings in the surrounding context and the syntax of a sentence can cue the meaning of an unfamiliar word. Semantic and syntactic cues are two important types of context clues. As soon as possible, teachers should encourage first-grade children to use written context as a clue to unknown words. The idea of using context clues can be introduced by oral activities like the one in "Putting It into Practice: Use of Oral Context." The sentences can often be drawn from stories that have just been read or listened to in class.

In the sample sentences in the "Putting It into Practice" activity, children can use both semantic (meaning) and syntactic (grammar) clues in choosing words to fill in the blanks. Children generally use these two types of clues in combination, but to clarify the differences between them, we will consider them separately first.

PUTTING IT INTO PRACTICE

Use of Oral Context

Read sentences such as the following to the children, leaving out words as indicated by the blanks. Sentences can be drawn from books that you plan to share later in class. After reading each sentence, ask the children what word they could use to finish the sentence in a way that would make sense. The children will find that the sentences that have missing words at the end are easier. In some cases, the children may suggest several possibilities, all of which are appropriate. Accept all of these contributions with positive comments.

Sample Sentences

1. Jane went out to walk her _____.
2. John was at home reading a _____.
3. They were fighting like cats and _____.
4. I want toast and _____ for breakfast.
5. Will you _____ football with me?

Semantic cues (clues) are clues derived from the meanings of the words, phrases, and sentences surrounding the unknown word. In the examples in the "Putting It into Practice" activity, children can ask themselves the following questions to decide what words would make sense:

Sentence 1. What are things that can be walked?

Sentence 2. What are things that can be read?

Sentence 3. What expression do I know about fighting that has *like cats and* in it?

Sentence 4. What food might be eaten with toast for breakfast?

Sentence 5. What things can you do with a football?

Syntactic cues (clues) are provided by the grammar or syntax of our language. Certain types of words appear in certain positions in spoken English sentences. Therefore, word order can give readers clues to the identity of an unfamiliar word. Because most children in U.S. schools have been speaking English since they were preschoolers, they have a feeling for the grammar or syntax of the language. Syntactic clues help them discover that the missing words in sentences 1 through 4 in the oral-context model activity are nouns, or naming words, and that the missing word in sentence 5 is a verb, or action word.

Looking at each item, we find various clues. In sentence 1, for example, we expect *her* to be followed by a noun. *A* is usually followed by a singular noun, as in sentence 2. Sentences 3 and 4 both employ *and*, which usually connects words of the same type. In sentence 3, children are likely to insert a plural animal name because of the absence of an article (*a, an, the*) and because the animals already mentioned, *cats*, are plural. Similarly, in sentence 4, *and* will signal insertion of another food. Sentence 5 has the verb marker *will*, which is often found in the sequence "Will you (verb) . . . ?"

DIVERSITY

As we pointed out earlier, semantic and syntactic clues should be used together to unlock unknown words. However, because of differing syntactic patterns found in languages other than English, English-language learners may not be able to make use of syntactic clues in English until their oral language skills in English increase.

❯ Teaching Strategies for Using Context Clues

Early exercises with context clues may resemble the oral-context exercise described on page 124. It is good practice for a teacher to introduce a new word in context and let children try to identify it, rather than simply telling them what the word is. Then children can use any phonics and structural analysis knowledge they have, along with context clues, to help them identify the word. The teacher should use a context in which the only unfamiliar word is the new word; for example, use the sentence "My *umbrella* keeps me from getting wet when it rains" to present the word *umbrella*. The children will thus have successful examples of the value of context clues in identifying unfamiliar words.

When a child encounters an unfamiliar word when reading orally to the teacher, instead of supplying the word, the teacher can encourage the child to skip it for the time being and read on to the end of the sentence (or even the next sentence) to see what word would make sense. Although most of the examples in this section show only a single sentence as the context, children should be encouraged to look for clues in surrounding sentences as well as in the sentence in which the word occurs. Sometimes an entire paragraph will be useful in defining a term.

Using Context Clues with Phonic and Structural Elements.　The teacher can encourage use of the sound of the initial letter or cluster of letters, sounds of other letters in the word, or known structural components, along with context. In a sentence where *hurled* appears as an unknown word in the phrase *hurled the ball*, a student might guess the verb *held* from the context. The teacher could encourage this student to notice the letters *ur* and try a word that contains those sounds and makes sense in the context. Of course, this approach will be effective only if the student knows the meaning of *hurled*. Encouraging the student to read subsequent sentences could also be helpful because these sentences might disclose a situation in which *held* would be inappropriate but *hurled* would fit.

Cloze Activities.　A *cloze passage*, in which words have been systematically deleted and replaced with blanks of uniform length, can be a good way to work on using context clues. For this purpose, the teacher may also use a modified cloze passage, deleting certain types of words (for example, nouns), rather than using regularly spaced deletions. Students should discuss their reasons for choosing the words to be inserted in the blanks, and the teacher should accept synonyms and sometimes non-synonyms for which students have a good rationale. The point of the exercise is to have students think logically about what makes sense in the context. (Other uses for the **cloze procedure** and more details about it are found in Chapters 2 and 7.) An easier task for students is to use a passage in which the deleted words are replaced by words from choices that are provided. This task may work better with younger students and those who are having difficulty with reading tasks.

A modified cloze procedure can be used with a story summary to develop students' skill in decoding in a meaningful context. The first letter of the deleted word is provided, which helps students use their knowledge of sound-symbol relationships in addition to choosing words that make sense in the context (Johnson and Louis, 1987). A student who encountered the following sentence with a blank instead of a word at the end might fill in the blank with either *bat* or *glove*:

> *Frank said, "If I am going to play Little League baseball this year, I need a new ball and* _____."

If the sentence indicated the initial sound of the missing word by presenting the initial letter *g*, the student would know that *glove*, rather than *bat*, was the appropriate word:

> *Frank said, "If I am going to play Little League baseball this year, I need a new ball and* g _____."

Word-part clues can be used in the same way. (See the material on structural analysis later in this chapter and in Chapter 5 for more on word parts that might be used.) In the following sentence, a student might insert such words as *stop* or *keep* in the blank:

> *I wouldn't want to* _____ *you from going on the trip.*

A student who had the help of the familiar prefix *pre-* to guide his or her choice would choose neither. The word *prevent* would obviously be the proper choice:

> *I wouldn't want to pre*_____ *you from going on the trip.*

Suffixes and ending sounds are also very useful in conjunction with context to help in word identification. Sample sentences for practice activities can be drawn from stories that the children are about to read in class.

Using Context Clues to Teach Homographs.

Some words are difficult to pronounce unless they appear in context. Many **homographs**—words that look alike but have different meanings and sometimes different pronunciations, such as *row*, *wind*, *bow*, *read*, *content*, *rebel*, *minute*, *lead*, *record*, and *live*—are prime examples. Here are some sentences that demonstrate how context can clarify the pronunciations of such words:

1. The *wind* is blowing through the trees. Did you *wind* the clock last night?
2. She put a *bow* on the gift. You should *bow* to the audience when you finish your act.
3. Would you *rebel* against that law? I have always thought you were a *rebel*.
4. Did your father *record* his gas mileage? Suzanne broke Jill's *record* for the highest score in one game.

Combining Word-Recognition Techniques.

Context clues are best used with phonics (discussed briefly in this chapter and in depth in Chapter 5) and structural analysis skills (discussed in this chapter and in Chapter 5). Context clues help children identify words more quickly than phonics or structural analysis clues alone, by helping them make educated guesses about the identities of unfamiliar words. But without the confirmation of phonics and structural analysis, context clues provide only guesses. As we mentioned earlier, when a blank is substituted for a word in a sentence, students can often use several possibilities to complete the sentence and still have it make sense. When children encounter unknown words, they should

Basal Reader Vocabulary Instruction

When teaching basal reader lessons, you will need to teach important vocabulary words. You may want to use the following process, recommended by DeSerres (1990):

Present each word on the board in sentence context, having students write the word in another sentence or phrase context on an index card for their word banks, and let them share their sentences. Later, use modified cloze stories in which you have deleted the target vocabulary words. Have students fill in the blanks by choosing from their word cards as the class reads the story together. Then have students fill in the blanks on individual copies of the stories and read the stories to partners. Ask partners to point out any parts that do not make sense. Later, have students produce their own stories, using as many words as they can from their word banks.

make educated guesses based on the context and verify those guesses by using other word-analysis skills.

Phonics

Phonics is the association of speech sounds (*phonemes*) with printed symbols (*graphemes*). In some languages, this sound-symbol association is fairly regular, but not in English. A single letter or combination of letters in our alphabet may stand for many different sounds. For example, the letter *a* has a different sound in each of the following words: *cape, cat, car, father, soda.* The words *live* and *read* have vowels that represent different sounds, depending on the context in which the words are found. On the other hand, a single sound may be represented by more than one letter or combination of letters. The long *e* sound is spelled differently in each of the following words: *me, mien, meal, seed,* and *seize.* To complicate matters further, the English language abounds with words that contain letters that stand for no sound, as in i*s*land, *k*night, *w*rite, lam*b*, *g*nome, *p*salm, and r*h*yme.

The existence of these spelling inconsistencies does not imply that phonics is not useful in helping students decode written English. We discuss inconsistencies to counteract the feeling of some teachers that phonics is an infallible guide to pronouncing words in written materials. In addition, teaching phonics does not constitute a complete reading program. Phonics is a valuable aid to word recognition when used in conjunction with other skills, but it is only *one* useful skill among many. Mastering this skill, and thus gaining the ability to pronounce most unfamiliar words, should not be considered the primary goal of a reading program. Students can pronounce words without understanding them, and deriving *meaning* from the printed page should be the objective of all reading instruction. Still, pertinent empirical research studies show that the more phonics knowledge that students obtain and learn to apply in decoding written words, the better they perform in reading (Groff, 1998). Use of phonics knowledge to decode words is important to readers at all levels. Good readers are automatic at recognizing and using letter sequences and letter and sound redundancies (Mather, Sammons, and Schwartz, 2006).

Time for Reflection

Some people think phonics is all that a student needs for a word-recognition program. Others think that several different word-attack methods are needed.

How would *you* decide which methods should be taught, based on the research presented in this chapter?

Emphasizing the benefits of using phonics in conjunction with context clues, Heilman (2002), points out, "English spelling patterns being what they are, children will sometimes arrive at only a close approximation of the needed sounds. … Fortunately, if they are reading for meaning, they will instantly correct these errors" (p. 1).

Chapter 5 covers phonics terminology, principles, and techniques in detail.

Structural Analysis

Structural analysis is closely related to phonics and has several significant facets:

1. Inflectional endings
2. Prefixes and suffixes
3. Contractions
4. Compound words
5. Syllabication and accent

The first four are related to meaningful word parts, and when they are used to access word meanings, rather than just pronunciation, they are referred to as parts of morphemic analysis, which is discussed in detail in Chapter 6.

Structural analysis strategies and skills enable children to decode unfamiliar words by using units larger than single graphemes. This procedure generally expedites the decoding process.

▶ Inflectional Endings

Inflectional endings are added to nouns to change number, case, or gender; are added to verbs to change tense or person; or are added to adjectives to change degree. They may also change a word's part of speech. Because inflectional endings are letters or groups of letters added to the endings of root words, some people call them *inflectional suffixes*. Table 4.1 shows some examples of words with inflectional endings:

Generally, the first inflectional ending to which children are exposed is *-s*. This ending often appears in early reading materials and should be learned early in the first grade. Other inflectional endings that children are likely to encounter in these early materials are *-ing* and *-ed*. Older students who have not yet mastered inflectional endings also need instruction in these common word elements.

A child can be shown the effect of the addition of an *-s* to a singular noun through use of illustrations of single and multiple objects. An activity such as that shown in "Putting It into Practice: Recognizing Inflectional Ending *-s*" can be used to practice this skill. "Putting It into Practice: Recognizing Inflectional Endings" provides a model activity for several inflectional endings and demonstrates further possibilities for practice with different inflectional endings. "Putting It into Practice: Using *-'s* for the Singular Possessive" shows a lesson for teaching possessive endings. The first example is likely to be most useful with young students and English-language learners who have not been familiar with the possessive endings in

TABLE 4.1 Examples of Words with Inflectional Endings

Root Word	New Word	Change
boy	boys	Singular noun changed to plural noun
host	hostess	Gender of noun changed from masculine to feminine
Karen	Karen's	Proper noun altered to show possession (change of case)
look	looked	Verb changed from present tense to past tense
make	makes	Verb changed from first- or second-person singular to third-person singular
mean	meaner	Simple form of adjective changed to the comparative form
happy	happily	Adjective changed to adverb

English. The second and third examples are likely to be useful with older students as well as younger ones.

▶ Prefixes and Suffixes

Prefixes and suffixes are *affixes*, letters or sequences of letters that are added to root words to change their meanings and/or parts of speech. A *prefix* is placed before a root word, and a *suffix* is placed after a root word.

Students can learn the pronunciations and meanings of some common prefixes and suffixes. Good readers learn to recognize common prefixes and suffixes instantly; this helps them recognize words more rapidly than they could if they had to resort to sounding each word letter by letter. Knowledge of prefixes and suffixes can help readers decipher the meanings as well as the pronunciations of unfamiliar words (discussed in Chapter 6).

The suffixes *-ment, -ous, -tion,* and *-sion* have especially consistent pronunciations and thus are particularly useful to know. The suffixes *-ment* and *-ous* generally have the pronunciations heard in the words *treatment* and *joyous*. The suffixes *-tion* and *-sion* have the sound of *shun,* as heard in the words *education* and *mission*.

Recognizing Inflectional Ending -s

Give this practice sheet to the children. Ask the children to read and follow the directions. Then go over the practice sheet with them orally, asking how each word that shows more than one thing looks different from the word that shows only one thing. They should come to the conclusion that -s at the ends of the words indicates more than one thing.

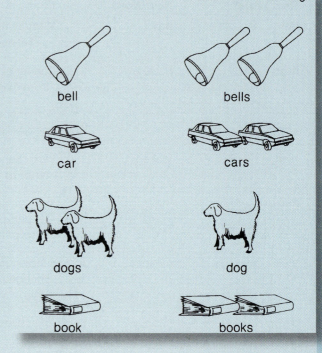

Directions: Circle the word that describes two things.

bell   bells

car   cars

dogs   dog

book   books

Whereas prefixes simply modify the meanings of the root words, suffixes may change the parts of speech as well as modify the meanings. Some examples of the resulting modifications are listed in Table 4.2. Activities like the one in "Putting It into Practice: Recognizing Prefixes and Suffixes" can be useful in working with those word elements.

In the third and fourth grades, students begin to encounter more words that contain prefixes, suffixes, or both (White, Sowell, and Yanagihara, 1989; Nagy and Anderson, 1984). White, Sowell, and Yanagihara (1989) have identified nine prefixes (un-; re-; in-, im-, ir- [meaning not]; dis-; en-, em-; non-; in-, im- [meaning in or into]; over- [meaning too much]; and mis-) that cover 76 percent of the prefixed words in the *Word Frequency Book* (Carroll, Davies, and Richman, 1971). They recommend that these prefixes be taught systematically during grades 3 through 5, beginning with *un-*, which alone accounts for 26 percent of the prefixed words. An analysis of their word counts would lead us to add *sub-, pre-, inter-,* and *fore-* to the recommended list because they occur as frequently as *over-* and *mis-,* thereby covering 88 percent of the prefixed words.

Recognizing Inflectional Endings

Write on the board sentences containing inflectional endings that have already been discussed, taken from a book that has been shared in class. Ask the children to read the sentences silently, looking for the inflectional endings that they have studied in class. After the silent reading, let volunteers go to the board, circle the inflectional endings in the sentences, and tell how each ending affects word meaning or word use.

You may not wish to use all possible examples from the book in this activity. Instead, you can encourage students to go back to the book itself, either individually or in pairs; locate the inflectional endings under consideration; and make a list of the words they find. These words can be discussed later in the whole group or in small groups, with students finding the words in the story and reading the sentences in which they appear.

TABLE 4.2 Some Affixes That Change the Meanings of Root Words

Root Word	Affix	New Word	New Meaning or Change
happy	un-	unhappy	not happy
amuse	-ment	amusement	verb is changed to noun
worth	-less	worthless	meaning is opposite of original meaning

White and his colleagues (1989) have also identified ten suffixes and inflectional endings that are part of 85 percent of the suffixed words in the *Word Frequency Book*: *-s, -es*; *-ed*; *-ing*; *-ly*; *-er, -or* (agentive); *-ion, -tion, -ation, -ition*; *-ible, -able*; *-al, -ial*; *-y*; and *-ness*. The inflectional endings *-s, -es, -ed*, and *-ing* alone account for 65 percent of the incidences of suffixed words in the sample.

▶ Contractions

The apostrophe used in contractions indicates that one or more letters have been left out when two words were combined into one word. Students need to be able to recognize the original words from which the contractions were formed. Example 4.1 shows common contractions, with their meanings, that teachers should present to students.

▶ Compound Words

Compound words consist of two (or occasionally three) words that have been joined together to form a new word. The original pronunciations of the component words are usually maintained, and their meanings are connected to form the meaning of the

> A lesson plan for providing direct instruction in the past tense marker *-ed*—"Word Study with *Henry and Mudge*—can be found at the Read•Write•Think website. Go to http://www.readwritethink.org or link from the Student Website for this textbook.

Using -'s for the Singular Possessive

Tell the children: "When I say, 'This is the book of my brother,' I mean that the book belongs to my brother. Another, shorter way to say the same thing is 'This is my brother's book.' The *apostrophe s* on the end of the word *brother* shows that the noun following *brother* (*book*) belongs to *brother*."

Have the children examine stories they have read recently for examples of the use of -'s. Let them read the sentences they found that contained -'s and tell the meanings of the phrases in which it occurs.

EXAMPLE 4.1 Common Contractions

can't/cannot	I'd/I had or I would	I'll/I will	shouldn't/should not
couldn't/could not	they'd/they had or they would	I'm/I am	we've/we have
didn't/did not	they'll/they will	I've/I have	won't/will not
don't/do not	they're/they are	isn't/is not	wouldn't/would not
hadn't/had not	they've/they have	let's/let us	you'll/you will
hasn't/has not	wasn't/was not	she'd/she would or she had	you're/you are
he'll/he will	we're/we are	she'll/she will	you've/you have
he's/he is or he has	weren't/were not	she's/she is or she has	

TEACHING TIP

Contractions

You may want to teach contractions in related groups—for example, those in which *not* is the reduced part, those in which *have* is the reduced part, and so on. You can ask students to locate these contractions and their uncontracted referents in context and use them in writing to enhance their learning.

new word: *bedroom*, for example, is a room in which there is a bed. Students can be asked to underline or circle component parts of compound words or to put together familiar compound words as practice activities. "Putting It into Practice: Recognizing Parts of Compound Words" shows an exercise for teaching compound words.

▶ Introduction to Syllabication and Accent

A *syllable* is a pronunciation unit. Part of structural analysis is dividing words into syllables, many of

Recognizing Prefixes and Suffixes

After instruction in prefixes and suffixes, give students duplicated sheets containing paragraphs from a story that has just been shared in class. Ask them to circle the prefixes and suffixes that they see in the paragraphs, working independently. Then divide them into small groups and have them compare and discuss their responses. Each group should come to an agreement about the correct answers. Finally, check the group responses in a whole-class discussion, calling on small-group representatives to give each group's responses to various items.

For example, in Alexander's *Nadia the Willful*, the following words appear: *stubbornness, willful, kindness, graciousness, return, emptiness, punishment, remind, uneasily, hardness, coldness, unhappiness, bitterness, inside, recall, recalled, unbidden, happiness, sharpness,* and *forward*. Some of the words occur several times. The paragraphs in which these words appear can be duplicated for this exercise.

Not all of the words need to be used in a single lesson. You may wish to use one prefix or suffix at a time.

which may be taught as common word parts; for example, common prefixes, suffixes, and root words occur in many multisyllabic words. The degree of stress placed on a syllable is referred to as *accent*. Because many phonics generalizations apply not only to one-syllable words but also to syllables within longer words, many people believe that breaking words into syllables can help determine pronunciation. Some research indicates, however, that syllabication is usually done after the reader has recognized the word and that readers use the sounds to determine syllabication rather than syllabication to determine the sounds (Glass, 1967). If children normally attack words using sounds first, then syllabication would seem to be of little use in a word-analysis program. On the other hand, many authorities firmly believe that syllabication is helpful in decoding words. For this reason, a textbook on reading methods would be incomplete without discussions of syllabication and a related topic, stress or accent. Because many syllabication and accent generalizations involve phonic elements, such as vowel and consonant sound variations, a detailed discussion of syllabication and accent is included in Chapter 5.

Readiness for learning syllabication includes the ability to hear syllables as pronunciation units. "Putting It into Practice: Syllabication" is an early exercise on syllabication.

In dictionaries it is the syllable divisions in the phonetic respellings, rather than the ones indicated in the boldface entry words, that are useful to students in pronouncing unfamiliar words. The divisions of the boldface entry words are a guide for hyphenation in writing, not for word pronunciation.

Accentuation generally is not taught until children have a good background in word-attack skills and is often presented in conjunction with dictionary study as a tool for word attack. More will be said on this topic in the next section.

Dictionary Study

Dictionaries are valuable tools that can help in completing many kinds of reading tasks. They can help students determine pronunciations, meanings, derivations, and

Recognizing Parts of Compound Words

Display a page from a big book (or a transparency made from a regular-size book) that contains several compound words. Let students come to the book (or the projected image) and point out the words that are made up of two or more words. [Point out that some of the compound words are two words joined with a hyphen.] For example, Ackerman's *Song and Dance Man* includes the words *Grandpa, Grandma, cardboard, leather-trimmed, inside, half-moon, spotlight, woodpecker, somebody's, bathroom, gold-tipped,* and *stairway.* Write the words on the board. Let volunteers come to the board and circle the separate words that make up each compound word. Have a class discussion about the way to decide how to pronounce compound words.

DIVERSITY

parts of speech for words they encounter in reading activities. They can also help with word spellings if children have some idea of how the words are spelled and need only to confirm the order of letters within the words. Picture dictionaries are used primarily for sight word recognition and spelling assistance. Children can be introduced to picture dictionaries as early as the first grade. They can learn how dictionaries are put together and how they function by making their own picture dictionaries. Picture dictionaries can be especially effective for English-language learners. Intermediate-grade students can develop dictionaries of special terms, such as *My Science Dictionary* or *My Health Dictionary*. From these they can advance to beginning and intermediate dictionaries.

This section deals mainly with the role that the dictionary plays in helping children with word recognition; Chapter 6 discusses the dictionary as an aid to comprehension of word meanings. Study skills related to dictionary use, such as the use of guide words, are covered in Chapter 11.

Although the dictionary is undeniably useful in determining the pronunciation of unfamiliar words, students should turn to it only as a last resort for this purpose. They should consult it only after they have applied phonics and structural analysis clues, along with knowledge of context clues. There are two major reasons for following this procedure. First, applying the appropriate word-recognition skills immediately, without having to take the time to look up the word in the dictionary, is less of a disruption of the reader's train of thought and therefore less of a hindrance to comprehension. Second, a dictionary is not always readily available; thoroughly mastered word-recognition skills, however, will always be there when they are needed. When using other word-attack skills has produced no useful or clear result, children should turn to the dictionary for help. Obviously, before students can use the dictionary for pronunciation, they must be able to locate words in it. This skill is discussed in Chapter 11.

After students have located particular words, they need two more skills to pronounce the words correctly: the ability to interpret phonetic respellings and the ability to interpret accent marks.

Syllabication

You can have children as young as first graders listen to words and clap for every syllable heard. Ask the children to say words aloud and listen for the syllables. Let them clap once for each syllable as it is pronounced. Include both single-syllable and multisyllabic words in the exercise.

Some example words you may use are as follows:

1. rule
2. table
3. meaningful
4. middle
5. disagreement
6. person
7. fingertip
8. name

◗ Interpreting Phonetic Respellings and Accent Marks

The pronunciation key, along with knowledge of sounds ordinarily associated with single consonants, helps in interpreting phonetic respellings in dictionaries. A pronunciation key is present somewhere on every page spread of a good dictionary. Students should not be asked to memorize the diacritical (pronunciation) markings used in a given dictionary because different dictionaries use different markings; learning the markings for one could cause confusion when students use another. The sounds ordinarily associated with relatively unvarying consonants may or may not be included in the pronunciation key. Because they are not always included, it is important that children have some knowledge of phonics (see Chapter 5). The "Putting It into Practice" activities—"Phonetic Respellings," "Pronunciation Key," and "Accent Marks"—can help you teach students to understand these topics.

Some words will have only one accent mark, whereas others will have marks showing different degrees of accent within a single word. Students need to be able to translate the accent marks into proper stress when they speak the words. Activities such as those in "Putting It into Practice: Accent Marks" can help them learn.

Word-Recognition Procedure

It is helpful for all readers to know a procedure for decoding unfamiliar words independently. The following word-recognition procedure provides a set of steps for readers to follow when they encounter unfamiliar words. A reader may discover the word at any point in the following procedure; he or she should then stop the procedure and continue reading. Sometimes it is necessary to try all of the steps.

Step 1. Apply context clues. This may involve reading to the end of the sentence or paragraph in which the word is found to take in enough context to draw a reasonable conclusion about the word.

Step 2. Try the sound of the initial consonant, vowel, or blend, along with context clues.

Phonetic Respellings

Try these three activities related to interpretation of phonetic respellings:

1. Have students locate a given word in their dictionaries (example: *cheat* [*chēt*]). Call attention to the phonetic respelling beside the entry word. Point out the location of the pronunciation key and explain its function. Have the children locate each sound-symbol in the key—*ch, ē, t*. (If necessary, explain why the *t* is not included in the key.) Have the children check the key word for each symbol to confirm its sound value. Then have them blend the three sounds together to form a word. Repeat with other words. (Start with short words and gradually work up to longer ones.)

2. Code an entire paragraph or a joke using phonetic respellings. Provide a pronunciation key. Let groups of children compete to see who can write the selection in the traditional way first. Let each group of students who believe they have done so come to your desk. Check their work. If it is correct, keep it and give it a number indicating the order in which it was finished. If it is incorrect, send students back to work on it some more. Set a time limit for the activity. The activity may be carried out on a competitive or a noncompetitive basis.

3. Give students a pronunciation key and let them encode messages to friends. Check the accuracy of each message before it is passed on to the friends to be decoded.

Step 3. Check for structure clues (prefixes, suffixes, inflectional endings, compound words, or familiar syllables).

Step 4. Begin sounding out the word using known phonics generalizations. (Go only as far as necessary to determine the word.)

Step 5. Consult the dictionary.

STRUGGLING READER/ INTERVENTION

A teacher may explain this five-step strategy in the following way. For students with special needs, the instruction often needs to be more extensive, including much supervised practice for each step.

1. Try to decide what word might reasonably fit in the context in which you found the unfamiliar word. Ask yourself: "Will this word be a naming word? A word that describes? A word that shows action? A word that connects two ideas?" Also ask yourself: "What word will make sense in this place?" Do you have the answer? Are you sure of it? If so, continue to read. If not, go to Step 2.

2. Try the initial sound(s) along with the context clues. Does this help you decide? If you are sure you have the word now, continue reading. If not, go to Step 3.

3. Check to see if there are familiar word parts that will help you. Does the word have a prefix or suffix that you know? If this helps you decide on the word, continue reading. If not, go to Step 4.

PUTTING IT INTO PRACTICE

Pronunciation Key

Write the following hypothetical pronunciation key on the board. Tell students: "Pretend that this list of words is part of the pronunciation key for a dictionary. Choose the key word or words that would help you pronounce each of the words listed below it. Hold up your hand when you have written the number of the appropriate key word on your paper beside the number of each entry word."

You may form the list of words from a book that students are about to read, thereby giving them some advance preparation for the words that they will meet in the book.

When all students have made their choices, call on a volunteer to reply to each one, telling why he or she chose a particular answer.

Pronunciation key: (1) cat, (2) āge, (3) fär, (4) sāfə (5) sit

1. cape (kāp)
2. car (kär)
3. ago (ə/go)
4. aim (ām)
5. fad (fad)
6. race (rās)
7. rack (rak)
8. affix (ə/fiks)

4. Begin sounding out the word, using all of your phonics skills. If you discover the word, stop sounding and go back to your reading. If you have sounded out the whole word and it does not sound like a word you know, go to Step 5.

5. Look up the word in the dictionary. Use the pronunciation key to help you pronounce the word. If the word is one you have not heard before, check the meaning. Be sure to choose the meaning that fits the context.

A reader who is confronted with the unfamiliar word *chamois* might apply the strategy in the following way:

1. "'He used a chamois to dry off the car.' I've never seen the word *c-h-a-m-o-i-s* before. Let's see. … Is it a naming word? … Yes, it is, because *a* comes before it. … What thing would make sense here? … It is something that can be used to dry a car. Could it be *towel*? … No, that doesn't have any of the right sounds. Maybe it is *cloth*? … No, *cloth* starts with *cl*."

2. "*Ch* usually sounds like the beginning of *choice*. … I can't think of anything that starts that way that would fit here. … Sometimes it sounds like *k*. … I can't think of a word that fits that either. … *Ch* even sounds like *sh* sometimes. … The only word I can think of that starts with the *sh* sound and fits in the sentence is *sheet*, and I can tell that none of the other sounds are right."

3. "I don't see a prefix, suffix, or root word that I recognize, either."

Accent Marks

1. Write several familiar multisyllabic words on the board. (*Bottle* and *apartment* are two good choices.) Explain that when words of more than one syllable are spoken, certain syllables are stressed or emphasized by the speaker's breath. Pronounce each of the example words, pointing out which part or parts of each word receive stress. Next, tell the class that the dictionary uses accent marks to indicate which parts of words receive stress. Look up each word in the dictionary and write the dictionary divisions and accent marks for the word on the board. Pronounce each word again, showing how the accent marks indicate the parts of the words that you stress when you pronounce them. Then have students complete "Putting It into Practice: Pronunciation Key."

2. Introduce the concept of accent as described in the previous activity. Then distribute sheets of paper with a list of words such as the following.

   (1)   des′ ti na′ tion
   (2)   con′ sti tu′ tion
   (3)   mys′ ti fy′
   (4)   pen′ nant
   (5)   thun′ der storm′

   Ask volunteers to read the words, applying the accents properly. When they have done so, give them a list of unfamiliar words with both accent marks and diacritical (pronunciation) marks inserted. (Lists will vary according to students' ability. Use words from their classroom reading material rather than random words.) Once again, ask the children to read the words, applying their dictionary skills.

3. Write the following words on the board.

   (1)   truth ful
   (2)   lo co mo tion
   (3)   fric tion
   (4)   at ten tion
   (5)   ad ven ture
   (6)   peo ple
   (7)   gig gle
   (8)   emp ty
   (9)   en e my
   (10) ge og ra phy

   Call on volunteers to pronounce these words and decide where the accent is placed in each one. Have them come to the board and indicate placements of accents by putting accent marks after the syllables where they think the accents belong. Then have all students look up the words in the dictionary and check the placements of the accents. Anyone who finds an incorrectly marked word can come to the board, make the correction, and pronounce the word with the accent correctly placed.

4. "Maybe I can sound it out. *Chămois*. No, that's not a word. *Kāmois*. That's not a word either. *Shămois*. I don't think so. … Maybe the *a* is long. *Chāmois*. No. *Kāmois*. No. *Shāmois*. No."

5. "I guess I'll have to use the dictionary. What? *Shăm′ ē*? Oh, I know what that is. I've seen Dad use one! Why is it spelled so funny? Oh, I see! It came from French."

A crucial point for teachers to remember is that students should not consider use of word-recognition skills important only during reading classes. They should apply these skills whenever they encounter an unfamiliar word, whether it happens during reading class, science class, a free reading period, or in out-of-school situations. Teachers should emphasize to their students that the strategy explained here is applicable to *any* situation in which an unfamiliar word occurs. They should also encourage students to self-correct their reading errors when the words they read do not combine to make sense.

SEEING IT IN PRACTICE ◀ ■ ▶

Video Case
Visit the Video Case "Elementary Reading Instruction: A Balanced Literacy Program." View the main video and decide how word-recognition activities can fit into a balanced reading program. Look at the three bonus videos that deal with word-recognition activities, as well. Can you think of other centers that would be appropriate for helping develop word-recognition skills?

SUMMARY

Word-recognition skills help readers identify words while reading. One skill is sight word recognition, the development of a store of words that a person can recognize immediately on sight. Use of context clues to help in word identification involves using the surrounding words to decode an unfamiliar word. Both semantic and syntactic clues can be helpful. Phonics, the association of speech sounds (phonemes) with printed symbols (graphemes), is very helpful in identifying unfamiliar words, even though the sound-symbol associations in English are not completely consistent. Phonics will be discussed in Chapter 5. Structural analysis skills enable readers to decode unfamiliar words by employing units larger than single graphemes. The process of structural analysis involves recognition of prefixes, suffixes, inflectional endings, contractions, and compound words, as well as syllabication and accent. Some aspects of structural analysis that are closely related to phonics are discussed in Chapter 5. Dictionaries can also be used for word identification. The dictionary respelling that appears in parentheses after the word supplies the word's pronunciation, but the reader has to know how to use the dictionary's pronunciation key to interpret the respellings appropriately.

Students need to learn to use all of the word-recognition skills. Because they will need different skills for different situations, they must also learn to use the skills appropriately.

An overall strategy for decoding unfamiliar words is useful. The following five-step strategy is a good one to teach: (1) use context clues; (2) try the sound of the initial consonant, vowel, or blend, in addition to context clues; (3) check for structure clues; (4) use phonics generalizations to sound out as much of the word as necessary; and (5) consult the dictionary.

For your journal

1. Write a description of how you would teach sight recognition of function words that do not represent concrete images, words such as *for* and *which*.

2. React to the following statement: "I do not believe in teaching children to use context clues. It just produces a group of guessers."

and your portfolio

Plan a lesson to teach one or more word-recognition strategies, using a popular picture book that contains appropriate examples of structural analysis elements.

Phonics for Word Recognition

Phonics involves the association of **phonemes,** or sounds, with written symbols, called **graphemes.** Phonic analysis is one type of word-recognition skill that can help students become independent readers. Unfortunately, many teachers are uncomfortable with phonics instruction, perhaps because they did not have good phonics instruction when they were in elementary school or because they have forgotten much of the phonics instruction after becoming mature readers. Regardless of the reason, teachers need to master this approach to word recognition. Research on exemplary teachers reveals that they use both direct and embedded approaches to phonics instruction (Villaume and Brabham, 2003).

This chapter presents the benefits to students of learning phonics strategies, explains variability of sound-symbol associations in English, and discusses the elements of effective phonics instruction. It also describes major approaches and specific strategies for teaching phonics.

KEY VOCABULARY

Pay close attention to these terms when they appear in the chapter.

analytic approach to phonics instruction

consonant blend

consonant digraph

diphthong

grapheme

onsets

phoneme

phonemic awareness

phonics

rimes

synthetic approach to phonics instruction

vowel digraph

ANTICIPATION/REACTION GUIDE

AFTER
C or **I** (for initial
A or **D** answers)
A or **D**
(for initial **?** answers)

Directions: Before you read this chapter, complete the following anticipation/reaction guide. In the space before each statement, write **A** if you agree; **D** if you disagree; or **?** if you don't know. After you have read the chapter, complete the guide again to show what you have discovered in the chapter. In the space after each statement, mark whether you were initially correct (with a **C**) or incorrect (with an **I**). Write the letter for the correct answer (**A**) or (**D**) in the space for the statements that you initially marked with a question mark (**?**).

1. Phonemic awareness is the awareness that speech is composed of separate sounds.

2. The smallest unit of sound in a language is called a grapheme.

3. A rime is a vowel and the letters following it.

4. Consonant letters are more consistent in the sounds they represent than vowel letters are.

5. Every syllable contains a vowel sound.

6. Open syllables end in consonant sounds.

7. The schwa sound is often found in unaccented syllables.

8. Phonics is all that is needed for a student to become a good reader.

9. It is impossible to teach too many phonics rules, because these rules are extremely valuable in decoding unfamiliar words.

10. It is wise to teach only one phonics generalization at a time.

11. Phonics generalizations often have numerous exceptions.

12. Teaching a small store of sight words can be the first step in implementing a synthetic approach to phonics instruction.

CHAPTER 5 ORGANIZATION

Phonics for Word Recognition

Benefits of Learning Phonics

Terminology

Variability and Phonics

Consonants
Consonant Digraphs
Vowels
Vowel Digraphs
Diphthongs

Elements of Effective Phonics Instruction

Prerequisites for Phonics Instruction
Reinforcement and Context
Phonics Generalizations

Major Approaches to Teaching Phonics

The Synthetic Approach
The Analytic Approach
Combining Approaches: Onsets and Rimes

Specific Teaching Strategies

Key Words
Consonant or Vowel Substitution
Rhymes
Word Walls
Games

Putting Phonics Instruction into Perspective

Benefits of Learning Phonics

Phonics techniques are not intended to be ends in themselves; rather, they are means to the end of successful reading. They help students pair spoken and written words and lay the groundwork for them to develop their own decoding routines. To establish such routines, students must be allowed to do large amounts of reading in appropriate materials.

Although sound-symbol associations in English writing are not as regular as those in some other languages, if beginning readers can attain an approximate pronunciation of a written word by applying phonics generalizations, they can go on to infer the true pronunciation of the word. Groff (1986) found, for example, that "100% of the second graders tested could infer and produce the *o* of *from* as /u/ after first hearing it as /o/. The pronunciation /from/ was close enough to /frum/ for these young pupils to infer its correct pronunciation" (p. 921). He concluded that children need practice in making such inferences. First, they need to apply phonics generalizations to unfamiliar words, producing approximate pronunciations of the words. Then they can infer the real pronunciations of the words by thinking of words they know that are close in sound to the approximations achieved by the generalizations.

Considering the context in which the word occurs is also helpful. This process will be harder for English-language learners (ELLs) who have not acquired large listening and speaking vocabularies of English words. Therefore, ELLs need help in developing extensive vocabularies of English words to allow them to make effective use of phonics generalizations. However, Chiappe and Siegel (2006) found that ELLs can acquire initial literacy skills in English, regardless of oral language limitations.

Skilled readers appear to identify unfamiliar words by finding similarities to known words (R. C. Anderson, Hiebert, Scott, and Wilkinson, 1985). For example, a reader might work out the pronunciation of the unknown word *lore* by comparing it with the known word *sore* and applying the knowledge of the sound of *l* in other known words, such as *lamp*. Such an approach can help students identify polysyllabic words as well as single-syllable words (Cunningham, 1978, 1979; Allen, 1998).

Any approach to reading instruction should have definite transfer effects; that is, the skills and strategies should carry over to use in different reading situations. Carnine (1977) studied the transfer effects of phonics and whole-word approaches to reading instruction. He found superior transfer to new words among students who were taught phonics. The phonics group even had greater transfer to irregular words, although it was not extensive. Research with adults has been interpreted as indicating that teachers should present *several* sound-symbol correspondences for each grapheme, rather than just one-to-one correspondences, thereby providing

TEACHING TIP

Check Your Phonics Knowledge

If you are not familiar with phonics terminology and approaches to teaching phonics and their benefits, you will not be able to help your students learn this important way to decode unfamiliar words. Go to the Student Website for this book and take the multiple-choice phonics test provided. It will give you an idea of your present knowledge of phonics. Take it again after you have finished the chapter, to assess your learning.

DIVERSITY

their students with a mental set that includes recognizing that different sounds can be represented by a particular grapheme in different words. If such a procedure had been used in this study, the phonics approach might have produced more transfer to irregular words. "Seeing It in Practice: Development of Phonics Knowledge" shows one way that students begin to acquire phonics principles.

Terminology

To understand written material about phonics and structural analysis, teachers need to be familiar with the following terms. These terms will be important to understanding the material in this chapter and in subsequent chapters.

Phoneme.   The smallest unit of sound in a language is called a phoneme.

Grapheme.   A written symbol for a phoneme is called a grapheme.

Vowels.   The letters *a, e, i, o,* and *u* represent vowel sounds, and the letters *w* and *y* take on the characteristics of vowels when they appear in the final position in a word or syllable. The letter *y* also has the characteristics of a vowel in the medial (middle) position in a word or syllable.

Consonants.   Letters other than *a, e, i, o,* and *u* generally represent consonant sounds. *W* and *y* have the characteristics of consonants when they appear in the initial position in a word or syllable.

Consonant Blends (or Clusters).   Two or more adjacent consonant letters whose sounds are blended together, with each individual sound retaining its identity, constitute a **consonant blend.** For example, although the first three sounds in the word *strike* are blended smoothly, listeners can detect the separate sounds of *s, t,* and *r* being produced in rapid succession. Other examples are the *fr* in *frame,* the *cl* in *click,* and the *br* in *bread,* to mention only a few. Many teaching materials refer to these letter combinations as consonant clusters rather than consonant blends.

Consonant Digraphs.   Two adjacent consonant letters that represent a single speech sound constitute a **consonant digraph.** For example, *sh* is a consonant digraph in the word *shore* because it represents one sound and not a blend of the sounds of *s* and *h.* Additional examples of consonant digraphs appear on page 147.

Vowel Digraphs.   Two adjacent vowel letters that represent a single speech sound constitute a **vowel digraph.** In the word *foot, oo* is a vowel digraph. Additional examples of vowel digraphs appear on page 148.

Diphthongs.   Vowel sounds that are so closely blended that they can be treated as single vowel units for the purposes of word identification are called **diphthongs.** Unlike vowel digraphs, in which the two vowels produce a single sound, diphthongs are actually vowel blends because the vocal mechanism produces two sounds. An example of a diphthong is the *ou* in *out.* Additional examples of diphthongs appear on page 148.

Development of Phonics Knowledge

Marty, a first grader, was turning the pages of a calendar in his classroom, finding numbers that he recognized on each page. Suddenly he called to his teacher excitedly, "Mrs. Overholt, this is almost like my name!"

Mrs. Overholt joined Marty at his table. "Yes, it is," she replied. "Show me the part that is the same."

Marty pointed to the letters M, a, r, in sequence.

"That's right," Mrs. Overholt said. "Can you tell me what month this is?"

"No," Marty said.

"The month is March," said Mrs. Overholt. "Does it sound a little like your name, too?"

"Yes," Marty almost squealed. "The beginning of it sounds like the beginning of my name."

"You really listened carefully to hear that," Mrs. Overholt said. "Those letters stand for the same sounds in your name and in the word *March*. Keep your eyes open for other words like this. You may be able to figure out what they are by remembering what you found out about letters and sounds."

Analysis of Scenario

Mrs. Overholt used a teachable moment with Marty. He had made a discovery about words that excited him, and his teacher helped him to expand it.

Variability and Phonics

Because the English language contains a great deal of variability, students must use other strategies, in addition to phonics, to confirm the pronunciation guesses that they arrive at by applying phonics generalizations. Teachers and students will need to be aware of many exceptions to generalizations and typical sound-symbol associations, including the following.

Consonants

Although consonant letters are more consistent in the sounds they represent than vowel letters are, they are not perfectly consistent. The following list shows some examples of variations with which a reader must contend.

Consonant	Variations	Consonant	Variations
b	board, lamb	n	never, drink
c	cable, city, scene	p	punt, psalm
d	dog, jumped	q(u)	antique, quit
f	fox, of	s	see, sure, his, pleasure, island
g	go, gem, gnat		
h	hit, hour	t	town, listen

Consonant	Variations	Consonant	Variations
j	just, hallelujah	w	work, wrist
k	kitten, knee	x	fox, anxiety, exit
l	lamp, calf	z	zoo, azure, quartz

Consider the cases in which *y* and *w* take on vowel characteristics. Both letters represent consonant sounds when they are in the initial position in a word or syllable, but they represent vowel sounds when they are in a final or medial position. For example, *y* represents a consonant sound in the word *yard* but a vowel sound in the words *dye*, *myth*, and *baby*. Notice that three different vowel sounds are represented by *y* in these words. *W* represents a consonant sound in the word *watch* but a vowel sound in the word *cow*.

Consonant Digraphs

A consonant digraph is two adjacent consonants that produce a single sound. Several consonant digraphs represent sounds not associated with either of the component parts. These are as follows:

Consonant Digraph	Example	Consonant Digraph	Example
th	then, thick	ph	telephone
ng	sing	gh	rough
sh	shout	ch	chief, chef, chaos

Other consonant digraphs generally represent the usual sound of one of the component parts, as in *wr*ite, *pn*eumonia, and *gn*at. Some sources consider one of the letters in each of these combinations as a "silent" letter and do not refer to these combinations as digraphs.

Vowels

The variability of the sounds represented by vowels has been emphasized before. Some examples of this variability are as follows:

Vowel Letter	Variations
a	ate, cat, want, ball, father, sofa
e	me, red, pretty, kitten, her, sergeant
i	ice, hit, fir, opportunity
o	go, hot, today, women, button, son, work, born
u	use, cut, put, circus, turn

In the examples here, the first variation listed for each vowel is a word in which the long vowel sound, the same as its letter name, is heard. In the second variation, the short sound of the vowel is heard. These are generally the first two sounds taught for each vowel.

DIVERSITY

English-language learners often need extra help with vowels. Helman (2004) believes that students need to be comfortable with the short vowels before they attempt work with long vowels and other vowel patterns. Think-aloud activities by the teacher can help students learn about confusions caused by the differences in sound-symbol associations in English and their first languages and clarify their understanding of English sound-symbol associations.

An extremely common sound that children need to learn is the schwa sound, a very soft "uh" or grunt usually found in unaccented syllables. It is heard in the following words: sof*a*, kitt*e*n, opportun*i*ty, butt*o*n, circ*u*s. As you can see, each of the vowel letters can represent the schwa sound in some words. Three types of markings represent the three types of vowel sounds we have discussed:

Marking	Name of Mark	Designation
ā, ē, ī, ō, ū	macron	long vowel sound
ă, ĕ, ĭ, ŏ, ŭ	breve	short vowel sound
ə	schwa	soft "uh" sound

Many dictionaries place no mark at all over a vowel letter that represents the short sound of the vowel.

Vowel Digraphs

A vowel digraph is two adjacent vowel letters that represent a single speech sound. Some vowel digraphs represent sounds not associated with either of the letters involved. These are as follows:

Vowel Digraph	Example
au	taught
aw	saw
oo	food, look

Other vowel digraphs generally represent the usual sound of one of the component parts, as in br*ea*k, br*ea*d, b*oa*t, s*ee*d, and *ai*m. Some sources treat one of the letters in these combinations as "silent" and do not refer to them as digraphs.

Diphthongs

There are four common diphthongs, or vowel blends:

Diphthong	Example	Diphthong	Example
oi	foil	ou	bound
oy	toy	ow	cow

Notice that the first two diphthongs listed (*oi* and *oy*) stand for identical sounds, as do the last two (*ou* and *ow*). Remember that the letter combinations *ow* and *ou* are *not always diphthongs*. In the words *snow* and *blow*, *ow* is a vowel digraph representing the long *o* sound. In the word *routine*, *ou* represents the $\overline{oo}$ sound, and in the word *shoulder*, *ou* represents the long *o* sound.

These variations do not imply that phonics is not useful in helping children decode written English, but they do indicate that children should learn other word-recognition strategies to use when they cannot be sure of pronunciation from their use of phonics.

Elements of Effective Phonics Instruction

For phonics instruction to be effective, students need to be ready to learn phonics, and teachers need to provide them with a reason to learn phonics. They can do this by providing contexts in which phonics strategies will be useful. Teachers also need to target key phonics generalizations and decide how to communicate them.

Prerequisites for Phonics Instruction

Educators know that children must be able to distinguish one letter from another and one sound from another before they can associate a given letter with a given sound. *Visual discrimination* is the ability to distinguish likenesses and differences among forms, and *auditory discrimination* is the ability to distinguish likenesses and differences among sounds. To achieve these skills, children must first understand the concepts of *like* and *different*. Also, to achieve auditory discrimination, they must have **phonemic awareness,** or the awareness that speech is composed of separate sounds (phonemes). (See Chapter 3 for more on phonemic awareness.) Children must be able to hear sounds within words, or they will be unable to form mental connections between sounds and letters (Beck and Juel, 1995; Griffith and Olson, 1992; Juel, 1988, 1991; Ball and Blachman, 1991; Lundberg, Frost, and Peterson, 1988; Pearson, 1993; Adams, 1990; Gill, 1992). They must also have some understanding of the *alphabetic principle* (the concept that letters are symbols for phonemes, or sounds). (Information on visual and auditory discrimination and the alphabetic principle is found in Chapter 3.)

"Putting It into Practice: Developing Phonics Prerequisites" suggests some activities that you can use to help students develop these important skills.

Reinforcement and Context

A good phonics program provides sufficient reinforcement for a skill that is being taught and offers a variety of reinforcement opportunities. The practice activities in this text offer some ideas for reinforcement opportunities. Although reinforcement in phonics instruction may include practice with single letters and sounds, it must

Developing Phonics Prerequisites

The following activities can help children develop auditory discrimination and phonemic awareness.

Sound Play Activities

- Take nature walks with the children or share tape recordings of everyday sounds. Listen to and identify sounds in the environment.
- Share tongue twisters that feature specific phonemes.

Identifying Sounds

- Give students individual mirrors and tell them to look at the positions of their lips, tongue, and teeth when they are pronouncing certain sounds and words. Use these observations to discuss how certain sounds are produced.
- Create a list of word pairs. Some should have the same number of phonemes, others different numbers. Pronounce the word pairs and ask students to indicate which pairs have the same number of phonemes and which do not.

- Create a list with pairs of words. Some should end with the same phoneme. Pronounce each word pair and ask students to indicate if the members of the pair end with the same sound or with different sounds.
- Prepare a class picture dictionary. Write the upper-case and lowercase letter that represents the initial phoneme of each word you enter. Collect pictures for each of the letter sounds.
- Create a mobile or collage that features words or pictures of words that begin or end with a specific sound (phoneme).
- Play a consonant riddle game by presenting the riddle in the following frame: "I'm thinking of something that rhymes with dish but starts with /f/. What can it be?"
- Use Word Walls to display words that feature specific sounds or patterns.

LITERATURE

include application of the strategy or skill with whole words and longer pieces of discourse, such as sentences and paragraphs. The following sequence is suggested by Spiegel (1990b): "auditory discrimination of the sound of interest, visual discrimination of the letter pattern, and then work with words, sentences, and short paragraphs" (p. 328). We believe that this practice should be expanded to include work with whole selections, such as predictable books that contain the letter-sound association that is being emphasized. In fact, a whole selection, in the form of a big book, may be shared with the children orally, with children chiming in on the highly predictable parts wherever possible. From this beginning, the teacher may have students locate the letter representing the sound under consideration, listen for the sound as he or she reads portions of the story aloud again, and make their own generalizations about the relationship between the sound and the letter that represents it. The children will not state their personal generalizations in the same form as the rules that would be found in a reading text, of course, but they will understand each connection more deeply and retain it better if they have discovered it themselves. When children are taught language skills and strategies in a context that includes use of books and other whole selections, a balanced approach to literacy instruction has been attained.

The teacher reads a literature selection with a specific phonic element to the class.
© Tony Freeman/Photo Edit

When considering the use of predictable books, be aware that Johnston (1998) concluded that "while beginners are more likely to learn words that repeat and are easily decodable, these were not the most common words in the predictable books [she] used" (p. 670). Although predictable text offers context clues, the ease of reading through context may detract from careful processing of print.

Decodable text has simple sentence structures, controlled letter-sound correspondences, controlled spelling patterns, and controlled use of high-frequency irregular sight words. Decodable books may or may not be predictable. The text difficulty of these books increases gradually as the grade level increases (Brown, 1999/2000). Teachers may use decodable texts that contain regular letter-sound relationships (but are not necessarily predictable texts) to provide scaffolding for students who are just moving from partial-alphabetic to full-alphabetic reading. Decodable texts can give students a place to practice the sound-symbol associations that they are learning (Mesmer, 1999).

Check your Student Website for lists of predictable and decodable books and alphabet books that you may want to use.

Reading alphabet books can help children learn some letter-sound associations. These books should be chosen with care to ensure that they represent common sounds for the letters, present multiple words that begin with each letter, have words with which children are familiar, and provide clear illustrations for the words.

DIVERSITY

English-language learners need explicit instruction in phonics, but they often have a disadvantage when trying to learn sound-symbol associations because of the dissimilarity between the sound-symbol associations in English and their home language. Sound-symbol associations should be taught using materials that present them in a systematic and multisensory manner. Such ways include use of visuals, gestures, and facial expressions; providing chances for students to talk; and defining key words in directions that are given (Lenters, 2004/2005; Manyak and Bauer, 2008; Lesaux and Siegel, 2003; Vaughn, Mathes, Linan-Thompson, and Francis, 2005).

The relevance of learning sound-symbol associations is much clearer when students can see the letters and sounds as a part of a meaning-bearing system rather than as isolated bits of meaningless information. English-language learners need to have their instruction in phonics as a part of reading instruction that also includes reading of texts, discussion of stories that are read to them, work on developing vocabulary, and instruction in writing (Manyak and Bauer, 2008; Lesaux and Siegel, 2003; Vaughn et al., 2005).

In *Becoming a Nation of Readers*, Richard Anderson and his colleagues (1985) point out that "a high proportion of the words in the earliest selections children read should conform to the phonics they have already been taught" (p. 47). Because of this fact, many educators make use of decodable texts as a part of their phonics instruction. Decodable texts can facilitate students' learning of important sound-symbol associations and can emphasize the importance of considering all letters in a word, and their order, for the purpose of decoding. Judicious use of decodable text may also provide successful reading experiences needed to motivate struggling readers (Jenkins, Vadasy, Peyton, and Sanders, 2003).

TEACHING TIP

Helping English-Language Learners Benefit from Phonics Instruction

You need to work on the use of oral language with English-language learners before you begin to work on phonics skills with them. Among other things that can help them acquire oral English knowledge is modeling the use of English by reading aloud from picture books as you show the pictures. You can point to details in the pictures as you discuss them later. You can also use many game-like activities to work on the oral language in a nonthreatening atmosphere.

You should learn the commonalities and differences between English and students' first languages and use this information to help students see similarities and differences. For example, although English and Spanish have a number of phonemes in common, each language also contains sounds that are not found in the other language (Helman, 2004). Spanish-speaking students, for example, may progress more rapidly if you give them more work with particular phonemes and combinations of phonemes in English that do not occur in Spanish (August and Shanahan, 2006). Different spellings of the common phonemes can also cause confusion when students begin to learn to read English.

You can help these English-language learners by leading guided practice of pronunciation of English words in a low-stress environment. Some examples of low-stress activities are choral reading (discussed in Chapter 10) and echo reading (discussed in Chapter 3) (Helman, 2004). Having students make bilingual dictionaries is another activity that may be helpful.

Marilyn Adams points out that participating in language experience activities, writing with invented spelling, sharing books, and reading interesting texts can help students internalize the alphabetic principle, which is important to phonics instruction ("A Talk with Marilyn Adams," 1991). The National Reading Panel report showed "that helping children invent spellings is one of the best ways to teach phonemic awareness and phonics" (Yatvin, Weaver, and Garan, 2003, p. 32), and this statement has been confirmed by more recent research as well (Williams and Lundstrom, 2007).

Phonics Generalizations

Some teachers believe that good phonics instruction is merely a matter of the teacher presenting a series of generalizations that children are expected to internalize and use in the process of word identification. Difficulties arise from this conception, however.

First, students tend to internalize a phonics generalization more rapidly and effectively when they can arrive at it inductively. That is, by analyzing words to which a generalization applies and by deriving the generalization themselves from this analysis, children will understand it better and remember it longer than if the teacher provides the generalization.

Second, the irregularity of the English-spelling system results in numerous exceptions to phonics generalizations. Children must be helped to see that generalizations help them to derive *probable* pronunciations rather than infallible results. When applying a generalization does not produce a word that makes sense in the context of the material, readers should try other reasonable sound possibilities. For example, in cases where a long vowel sound is likely according to a generalization, but it results in a nonsense word, the child should be taught to try other sounds, such as the short vowel sound, in his or her search for the correct pronunciation. Some words are so totally irregular in their spellings that even extreme flexibility in phonic analysis will not produce close approximations of the correct pronunciations. In such situations, the child should be taught to turn to the dictionary for help in word recognition, as described in Chapter 4.

Third, students can be so deluged with rules that they cannot memorize them all. An approach of simply presenting students with many generalizations may result in their failure to learn any generalization well. The task of applying phonics generalizations is often even harder for children learning English who have learned different sound-symbol associations in their first language.

Teachers can enhance a phonics program by presenting judiciously chosen phonics generalizations to students, as long as they are taught, not as unvarying rules, but as guides to best guesses. Authorities vary on which generalizations to present (Bailey, 1967; Burmeister, 1968; Clymer, 1996; Emans, 1967), but they agree on some. Considering the findings of phonics studies and past

 DIVERSITY

Time for Reflection

Some people believe children should learn basic skills before they begin reading stories, but others believe they should learn skills as they encounter the need for them within stories.

What do *you* think, and why?

teaching experience, we believe that the following generalizations are among the most useful:

1. When the letters *c* and *g* are followed by *e*, *i*, or *y*, they generally have soft sounds: the *s* sound for the letter *c* and the *j* sound for the letter *g*. (Examples: *cent, city, cycle, gem, ginger, gypsy*.) When *c* and *g* are followed by *o*, *a*, or *u*, they generally have hard sounds: *g* has its own special sound, and *c* has the sound of *k*. (Examples: *cat, cake, cut, go, game, gum*.)

2. When two like consonants are next to each other, only one is sounded. (Examples: *hall, glass*.)

3. *Ch* usually has the sound heard in *church*, although it sometimes sounds like *sh* or *k*. (Examples of usual sound: *child, chill, china*. Examples of *sh* sound: *chef, chevron*. Examples of *k* sound: *chemistry, chord*.)

4. When *kn* are the first two letters in a word, the *k* is not sounded. (Examples: *know, knight*.)

5. When *wr* are the first two letters in a word, the *w* is not sounded. (Examples: *write, wrong*.)

6. When *ck* are the last two letters in a word, the sound of *k* is given. (Examples: *check, brick*.)

7. The sound of a vowel preceding *r* is usually neither long nor short. (Examples: *car, fir, her*.)

8. In the vowel combinations *oa*, *ee*, *ai*, and *ay*, the first vowel is generally long and the second one is not sounded. (Examples: *boat, feet, rain, play*.) This may also apply to other double-vowel combinations.

9. The double vowels *oi*, *oy*, and *ou* usually form diphthongs. The *ow* combination may also form a diphthong, although it frequently stands for the long *o* sound. (Examples: *boil, boy, out, now*.)

10. If a word has only one vowel and that vowel is at the end of the word, the vowel usually represents its long sound. (Examples: *me, go*.)

11. If a word has only one vowel and that vowel is *not* at the end of the word, the vowel usually represents its short sound. (Examples: *set, man, cut, hop, list*.)

12. If a word has two vowels and one is a final *e*, the first vowel is usually long, and the final *e* is not sounded. (Examples: *cape, cute, cove, kite*.)

Teachers can help students learn to decode and spell by teaching them to understand the spelling system used in English, according to Norman and

Calfee (2004): "For example, *dime* is pronounced that way because the final *e* tells the *i* to say its name. ... [T]he system integrates decoding and spelling in a single process" (p. 43).

In their summary of *Beginning to Read: Thinking and Learning About Print* by Adams (1990), Stahl, Osborn, and Lehr (1990) emphasize that rote learning of abstract generalizations will not produce a skillful decoder. They point out the importance of connecting the generalizations with experience. They conclude that phonics generalizations have only temporary value; in fact, "once a child has learned to read the spellings to which they pertain, they are superfluous" (p. 126).

Finally, teachers should keep in mind a caution about the teaching of phonics generalizations that involve the use of such terms as *sound* and *word*. Studies by Reid and Downing indicate that young children (five-year-olds) have trouble understanding terms used to talk about language, such as *word*, *letter*, and *sound* (Downing, 1973), and Meltzer and Herse (1969) found that first-grade children do not always know where printed words begin and end. In addition, one group of second through sixth graders who were studied had difficulty in dealing with abstract phonics terms such as *consonant*, *consonant blend*, *consonant digraph*, *vowel digraph*, *diphthong*, *possessive*, *inflectional ending*, and others. These children, however, had learned sound-symbol associations without being able to define the phonics terms involved (Tovey, 1980).

Rosso and Emans (1981) tried to determine whether knowledge of phonic generalizations helps children decode unrecognized words and whether children have to be able to state the generalizations to use them. They found statistically significant relationships between knowledge of phonic generalizations and reading achievement, but they pointed out that this link does not necessarily indicate a cause-and-effect relationship. They also discovered that "inability to state a phonics rule did not seem to hinder these children's effort to analyze unfamiliar words.... This study supports Piaget's theory that children in the concrete operations stage of development may encounter difficulty in describing verbally those actions they perform physically" (p. 657). Teachers may need to investigate techniques for teaching phonics generalizations that do not require children to verbalize the generalizations.

TEACHING TIP

Linguistic Terminology

Before teaching a lesson using linguistic terms, check to be sure that students grasp such concepts. Deemphasize technical terminology when working with students who have not mastered the terms.

▶ Aspects of Syllabication and Accent Related to Phonics

Many teachers present aspects of syllabication and accent, which are structural analysis skills, as they teach phonics because the sounds of phonic elements are affected by their location in syllables and the amount of stress on the particular syllables. A *syllable* is a letter (or group of letters) that forms a pronunciation unit. Every syllable contains a vowel sound. In fact, a vowel sound may form a syllable by itself (*a/mong*). Only in a syllable that contains a diphthong is there more than one vowel sound. Diphthongs are treated as single units, although they are actually vowel blends. Even though each syllable has only one vowel sound or diphthong, a syllable may have more than one vowel letter. Letters and sounds should not be confused. The word *peeve*, for example, has three vowel letters, but the only vowel sound is the long *e* sound. Therefore, *peeve* contains only one syllable.

There are two types of syllables: open and closed. *Open syllables* end in vowel sounds; *closed syllables* end in consonant sounds. Syllables may in turn be classified as accented (given greater stress) or unaccented (given little stress). Accent has much to do with the vowel sound that we hear in a syllable. Multisyllabic words may have primary (strongest), secondary (second strongest), and even tertiary (third strongest) accents. The vowel sound of an open accented syllable is usually long (*mī'/nus, bā'/sin*); the second syllable of each of these example words is unaccented, and the vowel sound represented is the schwa, often found in unaccented syllables. A single vowel in a closed accented syllable generally has its short sound, unless it is influenced by another sound in that syllable (*căp'/sule, cär'/go*).

Following are several useful generalizations concerning syllabication and accent:

1. Words contain as many syllables as they have vowel sounds (counting diphthongs as a unit). Examples: *se/vere* (final *e* has no sound); *break* (*e* is not sounded); *so/lo* (both vowels are sounded); *oil* (diphthong is treated as a unit).

2. In a word with more than one sounded vowel, when the first vowel is followed by two consonants, the division is generally between the two consonants. Examples: *mar/ry, tim/ber*. If the two consonants are identical, the second one is not sounded.

3. Consonant blends and consonant digraphs are treated as units and are not divided. Examples: *ma/chine, a/bridge*.

4. In a word with more than one sounded vowel, when the first vowel is followed by only one consonant or consonant digraph, the division is generally after the vowel. Examples: *ma/jor, ri/val* (long initial vowel sounds). There are, however, many exceptions to this rule, which make it less useful. Examples: *rob/in, hab/it* (short initial vowel sounds).

5. When a word ends in *-le* preceded by a consonant, the preceding consonant and *-le* together constitute the final syllable of the word. This syllable is never accented, and the vowel sound heard in it is the schwa. Examples: *can/dle, ta/ble*.

6. Prefixes and suffixes generally form separate syllables. Examples: *dis/taste/ful, pre/dic/tion*.

7. A compound word is divided between the two words that form the compound, as well as between syllables within the component words. Examples: *snow/man, head/quar/ters*.

8. Prefixes and suffixes are usually not accented. Example: *dis/grace'/ful*.

9. Words that can be used as both verbs and nouns are accented on the second syllable when used as verbs and on the first syllable when used as nouns. Examples: *pre/sent'*—verb; *pres'/ent*—noun.

10. In two-syllable root words, the first syllable is usually accented, unless the second syllable has two vowel letters. Examples: *rock'/et, pa/rade'*.

11. Words containing three or more syllables are likely to have secondary (and perhaps tertiary) accents, in addition to primary accents. Example: *reg'/i/men/ta'/tion*.

Generalizations about syllabication can be taught by presenting many examples of a particular generalization and leading students to state the generalization.

The syllable divisions in the phonetic respellings (see Chapter 4) in the dictionary, not the ones in the entry words, are aids to pronunciation of unfamiliar words.

Major Approaches to Teaching Phonics

There are two major approaches to phonics instruction: the synthetic and the analytic. A third approach, based on "word families," has been developed to combine features of both approaches.

The Synthetic Approach

In the **synthetic approach to phonics instruction,** the teacher first has children learn the speech sounds that are associated with individual letters. Because letters and sounds have no inherent relationships, this task is generally accomplished by repeated drill on sound-symbol associations. The teacher may hold up a card on which the letter *b* appears and expect the children to respond with the sound ordinarily associated with that letter. The next step is to blend the sounds together to form words. The teacher encourages the children to pronounce the sounds associated with the letters in rapid succession so that they produce a word or an approximate pronunciation of a word, which they can then recognize and pronounce accurately. This blending process generally begins with two- and three-letter words and proceeds to much longer ones. Of course, this procedure tends to cause teachers and students to add vowel sounds when trying to isolate the consonants, thereby distorting the sound of the consonant and making blending more difficult for many students.

In this approach, children are sometimes asked to pronounce nonsense syllables because these syllables will appear later in written materials as word parts. Reading words in context does not generally occur until these steps have been repeatedly carried out and the children have developed a moderate stock of words.

Although blending ability is a key factor in the success of a synthetic phonics approach, many commercial materials for reading instruction give little attention to its development. Research indicates that children must master both segmentation of words into their component sounds and blending before they are able to apply phonics skills to the decoding of unknown words and that the ability to segment is a prerequisite for successful blending. Research also indicates that a teacher cannot assume children will automatically transfer the skills that they have been taught to unknown words. Direct instruction for transfer is needed to ensure that it will occur (Johnson and Baumann, 1984). "Putting It into Practice: Segmenting and Blending Words" presents some activities that you can use to help children learn to segment words and blend sounds.

The Analytic Approach

The **analytic approach to phonics instruction** involves teaching some sight words, followed by teaching the sounds of the letters within those words. Many educators prefer this approach, and it is used in many basal reading series, partly because it avoids the distortion that occurs when consonants are pronounced in isolation. For example, trying to pronounce a *t* in isolation is likely to result in the sounds *tə*. Pronouncing a schwa sound following the consonant can adversely affect the child's blending because the word *tag* must be sounded as *tə-a-gə*. No matter how fast children make those sounds, they are unlikely to come very close to *tag*. With an analytic approach, the teacher would refer to "the sound you hear at the beginning of the word *top*" when cueing the first sound in *tag*. The same process may be used to introduce other consonants, consonant blends, consonant digraphs, vowels, diphthongs, and vowel digraphs in initial, medial, and final positions.

One possible problem with the use of analytic phonics, however, is that children may not be able to extract an individual sound just from hearing it within a word. Therefore, some educators believe that advantages of asking students to produce phonemes in isolation in some circumstances can outweigh the disadvantages.

TEACHING TIP

Working with Consonant Sounds

You can help students avoid the distortion of consonant sounds that results from trying to isolate these sounds when decoding unfamiliar words. First have them isolate the vowel sound and produce it. Then have them blend the initial consonant or consonant cluster with that vowel sound. Finally, have them blend the remaining consonants at the end of the word with the onset-vowel chunk that has already been pronounced.

For example, if *band* is the unfamiliar word, the sound of the letter *b* is not easy to isolate without distortion. Therefore, the student would isolate the vowel sound (*a*) and pronounce it, then blend the initial consonant *b* with the *a* (say *ba*), and finally blend the consonant blend *nd* with the onset-vowel chunk (*ba*) to produce the complete word *band*.

Whole-language teachers often teach phonics with an analytic approach. Phonics is taught in whole-language classrooms, but according to Dahl and Scharer (2000), it is "not a separate curriculum; instead it [is] woven into daily whole language activities" (p. 588). Much of it takes place while children are doing writing activities. It also takes place during independent reading time. Teachers can engage in ongoing informal assessment so that instruction can match the individual student's needs. Trachtenburg (1990) suggests a procedure that is basically an analytic approach in

STANDARDS/ASSESSMENTS ✓

LITERATURE

Segmenting and Blending Words

You can use activities such as the following to help students learn and practice segmenting words into separate phonemes and blending phonemes into words.

Segmenting Words

- Have students use letter tiles or small objects to represent the phonemes in a word.

- Ask students to pronounce a word. Then ask them to repeat the same word without one of the sounds. Begin by having them delete the initial consonant sound, and conclude by having them delete the final consonant sound.

- Using a large rubber band as a visual, stretch it as you slowly pronounce a particular word. Instruct students to pretend to stretch a rubber band when they pronounce words to identify the individual phonemes, or sounds.

- Use magnetic letters, colored chalk, or markers to visually differentiate segments of words by syllables.

Blending Sounds into Words

- Identify the phonemes in a blending riddle that provides a clue to the meaning. One example might be: "I am thinking of a small, furry animal that meows." The sounds are /k/a/t/.

- Assign each student a specific phoneme. Form teams of students to create words from the blending of their assigned sounds. The words can be shared orally or visually by spelling the words on the board or charts.

- Construct a cloze passage from familiar material that has been read to students or that students have read. Delete every fifth word by covering it with a sticky note or select key words with particular sounds or patterns that you want to review. As students read the material, encourage them to "guess" the missing word, using clues that you provide. Start by providing the initial letter, and continue giving letters for them to use by blending their sounds until the word is identified.

which phonics instruction occurs within the context of reading high-quality children's literature. Here the progression is from the whole literature selection to the phonic element within the selection and back to another whole literature selection for application of the new knowledge. This procedure is consistent with the point of view that, "while the process may be broken down to examine individual pieces, before the instruction ends the process should be 'put back together' so that the children see the relationship between the part and the whole" (Harp, 1989, p. 326).

Trachtenburg's method proceeds as follows:

- First, the teacher reads to the class a literature selection that contains many examples of the phonic element in question. Students may discuss or dramatize the story when the teacher has finished.

- The teacher introduces the phonic element that is the target for the lesson (long *a, e, i, o,* or *u*; short *a, e, i, o,* or *u*; or some other element) by explaining that the children are going to learn one of the sounds for a specific letter or letter combination.

- Then the teacher writes a portion of the story that contains the target element on the board or a transparency. The teacher reads this portion of the story aloud, underlining the words containing the target element as he or she reads.

- The teacher identifies the sound involved and asks the children to read the story portion with him or her and listen for the sound. The teacher may suggest a key word that will help them remember the sound in the future.

- The teacher guides practice with the new sound, using a device in which initial consonants can be varied while the medial vowel remains stationary or a similar device in which both initial and final consonants can be varied. An example of such a device is shown in "Putting It into Practice" on page 168. The teacher may also provide practice with a similar device that allows sentence parts to be substituted, which enables children to practice the sound in larger language chunks. For example, adjectives, verbs, or adverbs could be varied, as could prepositional phrases, verb phrases, or any other sentence part.

- Finally, the teacher presents another book that has numerous examples of the phonic element. Children may then be allowed to read this book independently, read it in unison from a big book, or read it with a partner, depending on their individual achievement levels.

LITERATURE

Trachtenburg (1990) recommends many trade books that repeat long- and short-vowel sounds, including Dr. Seuss's *The Cat in the Hat* for short *a*, Molly Bang's *The Paper Crane* for long *a*, Esphyr Slobodkina's *Caps for Sale* for long and short *a*, Marie Hall Ets's *Elephant in a Well* for short *e*, Holly Keller's *Ten Sleepy Sheep* for long *e*, Ezra Jack Keats's *Whistle for Willie* for short *i*, Rita Gelman's *Why Can't I Fly?* for long *i*, Dr. Seuss's *Fox in Socks* for short *o*, Brock Cole's *The Giant's Toe* for long *o*, Janice May Udry's *Thump and Plunk* for short *u*, and Anita Lobel's *The Troll Music* for long *u*. Consonants can also be studied in literature contexts. Kane (1999) suggests Lois Ehlert's *Circus* for the soft and hard *c* sound, for example.

Oleneski (1992) suggests another way to teach sounds in an analytic manner with authentic material. She duplicated the jump-rope rhyme "Teddy Bear," which the children knew well and let them engage in activities such as reading it and sequencing its parts with sentence strips. Next she covered up certain words and had the children figure out what these words were. She then asked them to predict which letters would represent the beginning and ending sounds of the target words. Students continued to use the poem for reading and writing activities to keep the phonics instruction in context. This procedure could be used with other jump rope rhymes or ball-bouncing rhymes.

"Seeing It in Practice: Teaching Phonics Through Literature" tells how a teacher introduced the long *e* sound in story context, thus using an analytic approach to phonics.

Two "Putting It into Practice" features, one on analytic-inductive lessons and one on analytic-deductive lessons, further illustrate the analytic method. In the inductive lesson, students look at a number of specific examples related to a generalization and then derive the generalization. In the deductive lesson, the teacher states a generalization, and then the children apply the generalization in decoding unfamiliar words.

Four Read•Write•Think lesson plans focus on using literature to teach letter sounds. They are called "Phonic Generalizations in *Chrysanthemum*," "Phonics in Context," "Phonics through Literature: Learning about the Letter *M*," and "Using Folk Tales: Vowel Influences on the Letter *G*." Go to http://www.readwritethink.org or use the link at your Student Website.

Teaching Phonics Through Literature

Ms. Mahan started her class by reading the predictable book *Peanut Butter and Jelly* by JoAnne Nelson to her first graders. By the time she got to page 13, the children were chiming in on the repeated line "But peanut butter and jelly is my favorite thing to eat," as she always encouraged the children to do when they discovered the predictable pattern. When the story had been completed, the teacher responded to requests to "read it again" by doing so. This time the children joined in on the repeated line from the beginning.

The children discussed the story, and Ms. Mahan made a list on the board of the children's personal favorite things to eat.

She proceeded to display subsequent pages from the story, asking the children to watch for the *ea* combination in the words and raise their hands when they saw it. When hands were raised, she let the children identify the words with the *ea* combination. Then the children listened for the long *e* sound in each word. The following words from the story fit this pattern: *eat, meat, peanut, cream, wheat, treat, heat,* and *beat.* They also found the word *cereal* and recognized that they heard the long *e* sound. Because they had not yet had instruction on syllabication or schwa sounds, Ms. Mahan simply agreed that there was a long *e* sound after the *r* and went on to the next word. On page 18, they saw a word with the *ea* combination that did not have the long *e* sound: *bread.* The presence of this word allowed Ms. Mahan to point out that letter-sound relationships are not always consistent and that the letter-sound clues only helped the children make "best guesses" about pronunciations, not absolute certainties.

Ms. Mahan then encouraged the children to play with the words that had been located. She wrote *eat* on the board and asked them how to turn it into *meat.* She let Tammy come to the board and add the needed letter. Then she wrote *eat* again and asked who could turn it into *wheat,* then *treat,* then *heat,* and then *beat.* Finally, she branched out from words that were found directly in the story and let the children form *neat* and *seat.* She also let them transform *cream* into *team, seam,* and *dream* by removing the initial blend and replacing it with other letters.

Then Ms. Mahan pointed out that sometimes there are several ways to spell a particular sound. She used the transparencies of the story again, encouraging the children to listen for the long *e* sound in words other than the ones already underlined. They located *sweet, street, beet, even,* and *cheese.* Ms. Mahan asked if they could suggest any other letter patterns that could spell the long *e* sound. They quickly identified the *ee* combination, and eventually Tommy said that the *e* by itself could also spell the sound.

Ms. Mahan then shared the books *Ten Sleepy Sheep* by Holly Keller and *Never Tease a Weasel* by Jean Soule with the children and put them in the reading center, along with *Peanut Butter and Jelly,* for the children to reread independently or with partners.

The children were then given time to write their own stories about favorite foods. Ms. Mahan asked them to notice which words had the long *e* sound as they wrote. She let them share their stories orally with small groups of their peers.

Combining Approaches: Onsets and Rimes

An approach that has some aspects of both the synthetic approach and the analytic approach is the teaching of **onsets** and **rimes.** "Rimes are spelling patterns or 'chunks' such as *-ate, -ile,* and *-ake.* One-syllable words can be divided into onsets and rimes; the onset is the letter or letters before a vowel, while the rime is the vowel(s) and letters following it" (Gill, 2006. p. 191). In this approach, the teacher breaks

Analytic-Inductive Lesson Plan for Initial Consonant

Write on the board the following words, all of which the children have learned previously as sight words:

dog	did
daddy	donkey
do	Dan

Ask students to read each word together as you point to it. Tell them to listen carefully as the words are pronounced. Then ask: "Did any parts of these words sound the same?" If you receive an affirmative reply, ask: "What part sounded the same?" If you do not get an affirmative reply, pronounce the words for them again, putting a slight emphasis on the beginning sound, and ask the question again. This should elicit the answer that the first sound in each word is the same or that the words sound alike at the beginning.

Next, ask students to look carefully at the words written on the board. Ask: "Do you see anything that is the same in all these words?" This should elicit the answer that all of the words have the same first letter or all of the words start with *d*.

Then ask what students can conclude about words that begin with the letter *d*. The expected answer is that words that begin with the letter *d* sound the same at the beginning as the word *dog* (or any other word on their list).

Next, invite students to name other words that have the same beginning sound as *dog*. Write each word on the board. Ask students to observe the words and draw another conclusion. They may say: "Words that sound the same at the beginning as the word *dog* begin with the letter *d*."

Finally, ask students to watch for words in their reading that begin with the letter *d* to check the accuracy of their conclusions.

---

down a syllable into the part of the syllable before the vowel (onset) and the remainder of the syllable (rime) that begins with the vowel (Allen, 1998; Johnston, 1999; Moustafa and Maldonado-Colon, 1999). In the past, these rimes were referred to as *phonograms* or *word families*. (See Example 5.1.)

An advantage to teaching onsets and rimes rather than teaching individual letter sounds is that "onsets and rimes are much more consistent than single letters" (Gill, 2006, pp. 191–192). An approach to teaching onsets and rimes by combining procedures suggested by Johnston (1999) and Gill (2006) is presented in the "Teaching Tip: Onsets and Rimes."

Gunning (1995) has proposed a system for phonics instruction called Word Building that uses onsets and rimes. The class first builds words by adding onsets to rimes and then by adding rimes to onsets. This is followed by reading that allows

A number of lesson plans at the Read • Write • Think site emphasize onsets and rimes and word families. (Go to http://www.readwritethink.org or link from the Student Website for this textbook.) Three of them make use of literature. One called "Click, Clack, Moo: Reading Word Family Words" uses the notes from Farmer Brown and the animals in the book *Click, Clack, Moo: Cows That Type* by Doreen Cronin. Another one that uses hands-on activities is "Getting the *ig* in Pig: Helping Children Discover Onset and Rime." The third one is "Teaching Short Vowel Discrimination Using Dr. Seuss Rhymes." A lesson called "Word Sorts for Beginning and Struggling Readers" uses hands-on word sorts for work with short-vowel word families.

EXAMPLE 5.1 Onsets and Rimes

Word	Onset	Rime
black	bl–	–ack
may	m–	–ay
am	—	am

Analytic-Deductive Lesson Plan for Soft Sound of *c*

Tell the students: "When the letter *c* is followed by *e, i,* or *y,* it generally has its soft sound, which is the sound you have learned for the letter *s*." Write the following examples on the board: *city, cycle,* and *cent.* Point out that in *cycle,* only the *c* that is followed by *y* has the soft sound. Follow this presentation with an activity designed to check students' understanding of the generalization. The activity might involve a worksheet with items like this:

Directions: Place a check beside the words that contain a soft *c* sound.

_____ cell	_____ cider
_____ cape	_____ cord
_____ cedar	_____ cymbal
_____ cut	_____ cod

The soft *c* sound is the sound that we have learned for the letter _____.

practice with the patterns under consideration. Students may also make words with magnetic letters, mix up the letters and reassemble the words, and then observe how each word changes as letters are added and removed (Clay, 1993). Students are then shown how to decode hard words by using phonic elements that they have learned. This approach can be used with multisyllabic words as well as with single-syllable words.

▶ Analogy Approach

In one rime-based instructional program, the Benchmark Word Identification Program, children compare an unknown word to familiar words in order to decode the words by analogy. Then they use context to check their predictions (Allen, 1998; Stahl, 1992; Gaskins, Ehri, Cress, O'Hara, and Donnelly, 1997). Such an approach is called an *analogy approach*, a *phonogram approach*, or a *word family approach*. Students are taught an initial set of key words containing the phonograms or rimes. After comparing the unknown word to a known one and coming up with a tentative decision about the pronunciation of the unknown word, a student would check to see if the new word made sense in the sentence in which it was found. Fry (1998) discovered that 654 different one-syllable words can be formed with just 38 phonograms and added beginning consonants.

Direct instruction can be useful in teaching phonics through the analogy approach. In every lesson, teachers inform students about "*what* they are going to

Onsets and Rimes

At first you should teach a single word family (rime) at a time, blending different onsets with the chosen rime as words that fit the pattern are found in literature selections that contain the repeated rime. Ask your students to spell words with familiar onsets and the target rime and have them read other literature selections containing this word part. Later, you may introduce more than one word family with the same vowel together. Your students can compare and contrast different rimes, such as *-at* and *-an*, after you have presented both of them (Johnston, 1999). You can use shared reading of poems to teach about onsets and rimes to show students how phonics is helpful when real reading is taking place. You can have your students identify the rhyming words, and you can sort them into lists, according to spelling pattern (Gill, 2006). Eventually, students will be ready to contrast word families that have different vowels, such as *-at* and *-ut*. Students need to be able to sort the families by sound and by sight (Johnston, 1999).

teach, *why* it is important, *when* it can be used, and *how* to use it" (Gaskins, Gaskins, and Gaskins, 1991, p. 215). After this explanation, the teacher models the relevant skill and provides group and individual guided practice for students. Every-pupil response activities and teacher feedback are important program features. Key words are introduced through a structured language experience activity, the writing of a group story with the key words just presented. (The language experience approach is discussed in detail in Chapter 9.) Phonemic awareness activities are also included to facilitate the learning of onsets such as the initial consonant *f* and the initial consonant blend *fr*. Students need to be reflective and analytic about words and spelling patterns. They must learn the importance of analyzing all letters in a word and relating the letters to sounds so that they can retrieve the word later. Students do this by matching sounds to letters as they "stretch out" the pronunciation of the words. The teacher encourages self-talk about the procedure (Gaskins, Ehri, Cress, O'Hara, and Donnelly, 1996/1997; Gaskins et al., 1997). The activity suggested in "Putting It into Practice: Analogy or Compare/Contrast Approach" illustrates the use of this approach.

Research by Ehri and Robbins (1992) has shown that students need some knowledge of phoneme-grapheme correspondences in order to be able to use onset-rime units. In addition, Bruck and Treiman (1992) have found that beginning readers can use analogies, but they tend to rely more on individual phoneme-grapheme correspondences to decode new words. These findings suggest that students need instruction on individual phoneme-grapheme correspondences, especially for vowels, rather than just on relationships between groups of phonemes and groups of graphemes—rime instruction is not sufficient by itself.

According to Fox (2003),

> Letter patterns are more generalizable than word family rimes. Our alphabet represents speech at the sound level, and letter patterns give us clues as to how to pronounce sounds. For example, children who understand the VC (Vowel-Consonant) letter pattern sound out *mat, beg, bun, cop,* and *miss* with equal ease. ... They do not need to know five different word families. (p. 97)

Some research indicates that "programs emphasizing a phonics or code approach to word identification produce superior word-calling ability when compared to programs applying an analytic phonics or meaning emphasis" (Johnson and Baumann, 1984, p. 590). However,

> There seem to be distinct differences in the quality of error responses made by children instructed in the two general methodologies—readers' errors tend to be real words, meaningful, and syntactically appropriate when instruction emphasizes meaning, whereas code-emphasis word-identification instruction results in more nonword errors that are graphically and aurally like the mispronounced words. (Johnson and Baumann, 1984, p. 590)

Analogy or Compare/Contrast Approach

Write the key words *be* and *rain* on the board and pronounce them. Then write: "The student hopes to remain in that group." Verbalize the thought pattern needed to decode the word in this way: "If this [pointing to *be*] is *be*, then this is probably *re*. If this (pointing to *rain*) is *rain*, then this is probably *main*." (The sounds of the initial consonants *r* and *m* must have been taught previously.) "The word is *remain*. Does that make sense in the context?" After receiving an affirmative reply, say, "Yes, *remain* means to stay."

Then provide a list of key words that students have already studied and turned into sight words, as well as several paragraphs, preferably from a story that they are about to read, with difficult words underlined. Ask students to decode these underlined words, using the key words and the strategy that has just been modeled. After students have worked at this task independently, call on several students to verbalize their strategies for the difficult words.

Because the goal of reading is comprehension, not word calling, the analytic approach, which uses meaning-emphasis techniques, seems to be the better choice for instruction.

The choice of approach, however, may not matter as much as the fact that the teacher systematically includes phonics in his or her lesson plans (Armbruster, Lehr, and Osborn, 2001). Systematic, explicit instruction can take place through synthetic, analytic, analogy-based, or onset-rime phonics instruction: "A program of systematic phonics instruction clearly identifies a carefully selected and useful set of letter-sound relationships and then organizes the introduction of these relationships into a logical instructional sequence" (Armbruster et al., 2001, p. 16).

Specific Teaching Strategies

A variety of strategies can be used with all of the major approaches to teaching phonics. They include using key words, consonant- and vowel-substitution activities, rhymes, Word Walls, and games.

Key Words

Key words are often used to teach the sounds associated with vowels, consonants, vowel digraphs, consonant digraphs, diphthongs, and consonant blends. Key words are valuable in helping students remember sound-symbol associations that are not inherently meaningful. People remember new things through associations with things they already know. The more associations a person has for an abstract relationship, such as the letter *d* and the sound of *d*, the more quickly that person will learn to link the sound and the symbol. The person's retention of this connection will also be more accurate.

Consonant or Vowel Substitution

Write a known word, such as *pat*, on the board and ask students to pronounce the word. Then write on the board another consonant letter for which the sound has been taught (for example, *m*). If the letter sound can be pronounced in isolation without distortion, ask students to do so; if not, ask for a word beginning with this sound. Then ask students to leave the *p* sound off when they pronounce the word on the board. They will respond with *at*. Next, ask them to put the *m* sound in front of the *at*, and they will produce *mat*. The same process is followed with other sounds, such as *s*, *r*, and *b*.

This procedure is also useful with sounds at the ends of words or in medial positions. Vowel substitution activities, in which you may start with a known word and have students omit the vowel sound and substitute a different one (for example: s*a*t, s*e*t, s*i*t; p*a*t, p*e*t, p*i*t, p*o*t), can also be helpful.

Use of Games in Phonics Instruction

When planning games, remember that, although competitive situations are motivational for some students, others can be adversely affected by being placed in win/lose situations, especially if they have little hope of being winners at least part of the time. Game situations in which children cooperate or in which they compete with *their own previous records* rather than with one another are often more acceptable.

Many authorities encourage the use of key words. Most of them suggest that words with the consonant sounds at the beginning are best to use for consonants and words that contain only a single vowel sound are best to use for vowels. Some teachers use the names of students and their friends as key words.

Consonant or Vowel Substitution

Consonant- or vowel-substitution activities are useful for helping students see how their knowledge of some words helps them to decode other words. "Putting It into Practice: Consonant or Vowel Substitution" shows how it can be done.

Rhymes

Activities with rhyming words can help children learn to identify phonemes and practice onsets and rimes. Rhyming words are words that end with the same phonogram, or rime. "Putting It into Practice: Rhyming Activities" lists several that you can use.

Word Walls

LITERATURE

For students learning sound-symbol associations, a Word Wall may be helpful. Words found in the predictable books that students are reading can be written on construction paper and placed on the Word Wall, clustered with other words with the same beginning sounds, vowel sounds, or other salient features, such as rimes (Wagstaff, 1997/1998).

Rhyming Activities

- Share nursery rhymes, poems, finger plays, and songs that demonstrate rhyming, repetition, and alliteration.

- Display a picture or an object from a story, nursery rhyme, poem, finger play, or song. Have students identify as many words as possible that rhyme with the name of the object.

- Construct a list of rhyming words drawn from reading materials that are familiar to students. Assign a word to each student. Call out two rhyming words and ask students who have those words to act out the two words.

- Construct rhyming couplets. Read the stem and ask students to complete with a rhyming word. An example of a couplet follows:

I went to the circus in town
To see the funny _____ (clown).

- Have students sit in a circle and ask them to imagine going on a class trip. Then give one student a ball. That student begins a rhyming couplet by completing the following frame:

> "We're going on a trip, and I'm taking a _____ (hat)."

The ball is tossed to a second student, who responds, "We're going on a trip, and I'm taking a _____ (bat, mat, etc.)"

The ball is tossed to another student who continues by starting a new couplet with a different ending.

Students practice word recognition skills for early reading using a "word wall."

© Ellen Senisi/The Image Works

Phonics Activities

1. Give each child a sheet of paper that is blank except for a letter at the top. Have the children draw pictures of as many items as they can think of that have names beginning with the sound of the letter at the top of the page. The child with the most correct responses is the winner.

2. Make five decorated boxes and label each box with a short vowel. Have the children locate pictures of objects whose names contain the short-vowel sounds and file them in the appropriate boxes. Each day take out the pictures, ask the children to pronounce the names, and check to see if the appropriate sounds are present. Do the same thing with long-vowel sounds, consonant sounds, consonant blends, digraphs, diphthongs, and rhyming words.

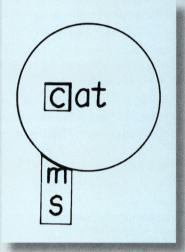

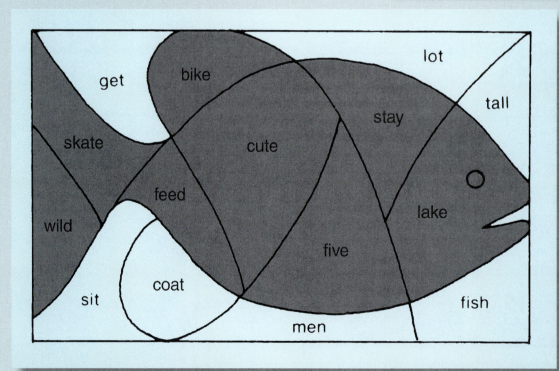

Phonics Activities *(Continued)*

3. Place a familiar word ending on a cardboard disk like the one pictured on page 168. Pull a strip of cardboard with initial consonants on it through an opening cut in the disk. Show the children how to pull the strip through the disk, pronouncing each word that is formed.

4. Divide the class into two groups. Give one group initial consonant, consonant blend, or consonant digraph cards. Give the other group word-ending cards. Instruct students to locate classmates holding word parts that combine with their parts to form real words. Have each pair of students hold up their cards and pronounce the word they have made when they have located a combination. Then let them search for other possible combinations for their word parts.

5. Use riddles. For example: "I have in mind a word that rhymes with *far*. We ride in it. It's called a _____."

6. Let the children find a hidden picture by shading in all the spaces that contain words with long-vowel sounds, as shown on page 168.

7. Have students read sentences made of alliterative words beginning with a sound that you just taught and then write their own alliterative sentences with that sound; for example, Betty Baxter bought big bowls.

8. Have the class make a phonogram tree (*Struggling Readers, Day 1*, 2000), as shown here.

9. Try a spelling-decoding strategy such as the "Making Words" strategy developed by Patricia Cunningham (1991) and described in detail in Aiken and Bayer (2002). Aiken and Bayer say, "Making Words allows each student to manipulate a set of six to eight letters to construct words dictated by the teacher. Each lesson begins with two-letter words and gradually builds to the final word, which uses all of the letters" (p. 68). Subsequently, students sort word cards of the words that they have made by sounds or spelling patterns, and later they discover transfer words that have the same spelling patterns.

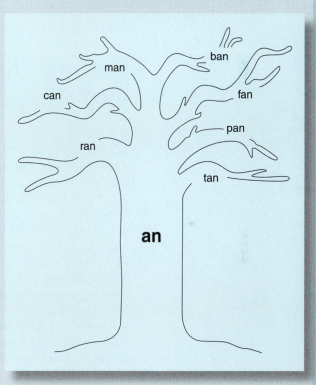

Games

A lesson plan based on Cunningham's "Making Words" procedure—"Word Wizards: Students Making Words"—is available at http://www.readwritethink .org, or you can link to it from your Student Website.

Drill on letter-sound associations need not be dull. Teachers can use many game activities so that more formal activities do not become boring from overuse.

"Putting It into Practice: Phonics Activities" offers some practical examples of both competitive and noncompetitive games.

To be effective, games and other practice exercises should always be preceded by instruction and followed by feedback on results. The absence of prior instruction may cause students to practice the wrong response. Feedback, which should come either directly from the teacher or through a self-correcting procedure (posted answers, for example), will inform students of errors immediately so that they do not learn incorrect responses. When students fail to see reasons for their errors, the teacher will need to provide explanations and reteach the strategy or skill.

Putting Phonics Instruction into Perspective

Regardless of the method used to teach it, teachers must remember that a phonics strategy or skill is a means to an end, not an end in itself, and that phonics is only one method of decoding. Students must learn multiple strategies (Compton-Lilly, 2005). (Other strategies are discussed in Chapter 4.)

Partly because not all English words are decodable through phonics generalizations and partly because other approaches are more efficient, phonics should not be the only strategy taught to students. Readers who can recognize words without resorting to letter-by-letter sounding will recognize them more quickly than those who must sound out the words, and the process will interfere less with their train of thought than sounding out the words would have. When the words to be recognized are seen in context, as in most normal reading activities, the sound of the first letter alone may elicit recognition of the whole word. Context clues can provide a child with an idea about the word's identity, and the initial sound can be used to verify an educated guess. This procedure is efficient and is a good way to identify unfamiliar words quickly.

Of course, the ultimate goal of instruction in phonics and other word identification skills is to turn initially unfamiliar words into automatically recognized sight words. An overall approach to word recognition is provided at the end of Chapter 4 to help students use phonics, along with other word recognition skills, in the most efficient manner.

SUMMARY

Phonics involves the association of phonemes, or speech sounds, with written symbols, called graphemes. The main benefit to students of learning to apply phonics to unfamiliar words is that phonics enables students to decode many unfamiliar words without assistance from other people or a dictionary. Even when students do not obtain an exact pronunciation from applying phonics knowledge, they often obtain a close approximation that, along with the context in which the word is found, will result in proper identification.

Because of the spelling inconsistencies found in the English language, there are many exceptions to phonics principles and generalizations. Students need to realize that phonics generalizations are not infallible aids to pronunciation of all English words, but use of them is one extremely helpful skill among many.

Prerequisites for effective phonics instruction include auditory and visual discrimination. Phonemic awareness and knowledge of the alphabetic principle are also important. When phonics instruction takes place, teachers must provide sufficient reinforcement for skills and strategies that are taught. Some practice activities may involve isolated letters and words, but much practice should also be provided in the context of connected discourse. Students learn phonics generalizations more rapidly and effectively when they arrive at them inductively. Aspects of syllabication and accent are often taught along with phonics because the sounds of phonic elements are affected by their location in syllables and the amount of stress on the particular syllables.

There are two major approaches to phonics instruction: the synthetic approach and the analytic approach. In the synthetic approach, students first learn speech sounds that are associated with individual letters and then learn to blend them together. In the analytic approach, students learn a number of sight words and are taught to recognize the sounds of the letters within those words, to avoid the distortion of consonant sounds that often occurs when they are isolated. An approach that has some aspects of both the synthetic and the analytic approaches is the teaching of onsets and rimes, in which the teacher breaks down a syllable into the part before the vowel and the remainder of the syllable.

Many teaching strategies have been effective in teaching phonics. The most common ones are use of key words, consonant and vowel substitution, rhymes, Word Walls, and games.

Phonics should be viewed as a means to the end of word identification, which is necessary to comprehension, rather than as an end in itself. It should also be viewed as one word-recognition skill that is best used in combination with other skills to discover the pronunciations of unfamiliar words in the most efficient way, rather than as the only skill needed for word identification.

For your journal . . . .

After observing a teacher teaching a synthetic phonics lesson and a teacher teaching an analytic phonics lesson, write an evaluation of the two approaches on the basis of your observations. Be sure to evaluate the methods, not the instructors.

. . . . and your portfolio

Develop a collection of rhymes and poems to use in working with onsets and rimes.

Meaning Vocabulary

6

KEY VOCABULARY

Pay close attention to these terms when they appear in the chapter.

allusion

analogies

antonyms

appositive

categorization

context clues

etymology

euphemism

figurative language

homographs

homonyms

homophones

hyperbole

meaning vocabulary

metaphor

morphemes

personification

schema (pl., schemata)

semantic feature analysis

semantic maps

simile

synonyms

word consciousness

word sort

word webs

In Chapters 4 and 5, we examined the importance of decoding words and developing a sight vocabulary, but these abilities have little value if students do not understand the words. Students' sight vocabularies should be built from words that are a part of their meaning vocabularies. A student's meaning vocabulary is the set of words for which meanings are understood. Because students must understand the concepts that words represent in order to comprehend, meaning vocabulary development is an important component of comprehension (Dixon-Krauss, 2001/2002). There is evidence that students who have limited vocabularies by fourth grade will probably have problems understanding grade-level texts (Kieffer and Lesaux, 2007; Chall and Jacobs, 2003) and the probability is greater for English-language learners (ELLs) (August, Carlo, Dressler, and Snow, 2005).

Many English-language learners can communicate conversationally with their classmates, but have not acquired the academic English vocabulary to understand content-area assignments. Older ELLs who enter school in fourth grade and above with little or no English knowledge have the task of developing their oral English-language skills as well as learning to read in English. If the classroom teacher does not speak their first language and a bilingual teacher or aide is not available to help, much early communication may depend upon English/first-language dictionaries, gestures, and peer or cross-age tutoring from a student who is proficient in an ELL's first language as well as in English. For students who enter school with the ability to read in their first language, but not in English, many concepts related to reading in English will be easier for them to learn. Spanish-speaking ELLs and some speakers of other Romance languages and of Germanic languages may know some of the common root words from their first language that can help them transfer the morphemic analysis strategy to English words (Kieffer and Lesaux, 2007; Nilsen and Nilsen, 2003). More information on teaching ELLs is presented throughout this text.

Research indicates that preteaching new vocabulary terms in a selection can result in significant gains in students' comprehension of that selection (Roser and Juel, 1982; Carney, Anderson, Blackburn, and Blessing, 1984), and that long-term vocabulary instruction, in which words are taught and reinforced over a period of time, enhances comprehension of materials containing those words (McKeown, Beck, Omanson, and Perfetti, 1983; Robinson, Faraone, Hittleman, and Unruh, 1990).

During vocabulary lessons, teachers need to help the students understand that a rich vocabulary helps us to communicate effectively. They must realize that the more words they know and use appropriately, the better they will be able to communicate with others and to understand what others try to communicate to them.

(Continued on page 175)

AFTER
C or **I** (for initial
A or **D** answers)
A or **D**
(for initial **?** answers)

Directions: Before you read this chapter, complete the following anticipation/reaction guide. In the space before each statement, write **A** if you agree; **D** if you disagree; or **?** if you don't know. After you have read the chapter, complete the guide again to show what you have discovered in the chapter. In the space after each statement, mark whether you were initially correct (with a **C**) or incorrect (with an **I**). Write the letter for the correct answer (**A**) or (**D**) in the space for the statements that you initially marked with a question mark (**?**).

1. Context clues are of little help in determining the meanings of unfamiliar words, although they are useful for recognizing familiar ones.

2. Morphemic analysis can help readers determine the meanings of new words that contain familiar prefixes, suffixes, and root words.

3. Homonyms are words that have identical, or almost identical, meanings.

4. The development of vocabulary is essentially a child's development of labels for his or her schemata.

5. Semantic maps show how words are connected to each other in meaning.

6. Instruction in vocabulary that helps students relate new terms to their background knowledge is helpful.

7. Working hard to learn words results in better retention.

8. Both concrete and vicarious experiences can help to build concepts.

9. Vocabulary instruction should not take place during content-area classes.

10. "Think-aloud" strategies can help students see how to use context clues.

11. Semantic feature analysis is the same thing as morphemic analysis.

12. The study of word origins is called etymology.

13. Children instinctively understand figures of speech; therefore, figurative language presents them with no special problems.

14. Wide reading is a prime method of vocabulary building.

15. Being able to recite a dictionary definition means that the students understand the word's meaning.

CHAPTER 6 ORGANIZATION

Meaning Vocabulary

General Principles of Vocabulary Instruction

Vocabulary Development

Complexity of the Task
Choosing Words for Instruction

Instructional Procedures

Building Readers' Schemata
Actively Involving Students
Context Clues
Morphemic Analysis (Structural Analysis)
Categorization
Analogies and Word Lines
Semantic Maps and Word Webs
Semantic Feature Analysis
Use of Dictionaries and Thesauruses
Word Origins and Histories
Figurative Language
Student-Centered Vocabulary-Learning Techniques
Word Play
Combining Strategies

Special Words

Homonyms or Homophones
Homographs
Synonyms
Antonyms
New Words

Most teachers include vocabulary instruction in reading and language arts classes, but they may not realize that students need instruction throughout the day in the specialized or technical words in each content area. Teaching important vocabulary terms or reviewing previously learned terms before reading helps "students activate their background knowledge, relate this knowledge to new concepts, and understand how new words and concepts are related" (Rupley, Logan, and Nichols, 1998/1999). This chapter focuses on developing meaning vocabularies and dealing with the difficulties that certain types of words may present to students. This chapter and Chapter 12 will help teachers plan effectively for vocabulary instruction in various content areas.

General Principles of Vocabulary Instruction

Teachers can approach vocabulary instruction in a variety of ways, but research shows that some vocabulary instructional techniques are more effective than others. The most desirable instructional techniques are those that do the following:

- Help students to integrate new words with their networks of background knowledge, or schemata.
- Assist students in developing elaborated (expanded) word knowledge.
- Actively involve students in learning new words.
- Help students acquire strategies for independent vocabulary development.
- Provide repetition of the words to build ready accessibility of their meanings.
- Have students engage in meaningful use of the words (Graves, 2006; Blachowicz and Fisher, 2000; Nagy, 1988; Blachowicz and Lee, 1991; Beck and McKeown, 1991).

The instructional suggestions throughout this chapter are based upon these principles. Often a single instructional activity addresses several of the principles.

Vocabulary Development

It is difficult to pinpoint the age at which children learn the precise meanings of words. Word learning tends to be incremental. Word knowledge is initially incomplete. It takes place over time as children have more experiences with language (Nagy and Scott, 2000; Clark, 1993). Early in the language development process, they learn to differentiate between antonyms (opposites), making more discriminating responses as they grow older. Sometimes they overgeneralize about word meanings: a very young child who learns the word *car*, for example, may apply it to any motor vehicle, making no discrimination among cars, trucks, vans, and other kinds of vehicles. Some children as old as nine years have trouble distinguishing between the meanings of *ask* and *tell*, and some children as old as ten years have not yet differentiated between the words *brother* and *boy* and the words *sister* and *girl* (McConaughy, 1978). As children mature, they learn more about choosing specific words.

Children increase their vocabularies at a rapid rate during the elementary school years, but they face a complex task. They must not only acquire knowledge of large stores of words, but also depth in their understanding of these words.

The children's vocabularies grow as they have new direct experiences with their environment and listen to and interact with parents, siblings, and others who share these experiences. They also learn through vicarious, or indirect, experiences. Students have vicarious experiences through read-alouds by teachers and other adults and by reading for themselves. These experiences offer them a multitude of words and concepts that are not often found in their daily oral language interactions or experiences. Teachers can read literature aloud to students, explaining the meanings of words they don't know as the reading takes place (Bromley, 2007; Brabham and Villaume, 2002).

Wide reading is a prime method of vocabulary building (Yopp and Yopp, 2007). A number of studies have shown that students' vocabularies expand when they read materials with many new words and when they substantially increase the reading they do (Pressley, 2002; Graves and Watts-Taffe, 2002). Developing enthusiasm for pleasure reading is therefore a worthy goal for teachers. Teachers can also encourage their students' parents and caregivers to model the enjoyment of reading and provide opportunities for pleasurable reading at home.

Complexity of the Task

Vocabulary building involves many kinds of words: words with *multiple meanings*; words with *abstract definitions*; *homonyms*; *homographs*; *synonyms*; and *antonyms*. (These special word types are discussed later in the chapter.) Children must also acquire meanings for a number of relational terms, such as *same/different, more/less, taller/shorter, older/younger, higher/lower*, and so on. In content-area instruction, students must deal with *technical vocabulary* (words whose only meanings are specific to the content areas—for example, *photosynthesis*) and *specialized vocabulary* (words with general meanings as well as specialized meanings that are specific to the content area—for example, *pitch* in the area of music). Content-area materials also abound with special *symbols* and *abbreviations* that children must master in order to read the materials successfully.

Choosing Words for Instruction

Choosing words to teach can be challenging for teachers. One good way is to choose terms from classroom reading materials. The terms should be central to the selections in which they appear. The teacher should activate prior knowledge related to the words before the reading begins and should have students use the new vocabulary in postreading discussion. Words that students still do not understand will need further attention and elaboration. For further experiences, students might use the words in retellings, dramatizations, or writings based on the story or selection (Rupley et al., 1998/1999; Dixon-Krauss, 2001/2002). Beck, McKeown, and Kucan (2002) categorize words into three tiers:

- Tier one—basic words (probably no instruction needed for native speakers of English, although English-language learners may need instruction) DIVERSITY

- Tier two—high-frequency, high-utility words (good focus for general vocabulary instruction)

- Tier three—low-frequency words, often encountered in content textbooks (focus for content-area lessons, as needed)

For application to content-area teaching, teachers should consider which words should be taught to facilitate understanding of each assignment. They should locate any words that are necessary for comprehending the assignment and that should be taught thoroughly, as well as words that are necessary but require only limited instruction (for example, ones that only need a clear definition or ones that are new labels for familiar concepts). Both of these types of words should be dealt with before the students read. Words that are important but are not necessary in order to get the gist of the assignment, that are explicitly defined in the text, and that are high utility and will be encountered in other settings can be addressed during or after reading (Flanigan and Greenwood, 2007).

STRUGGLING READER/ INTERVENTION   DIVERSITY

Many educators believe that teachers should also include "essential" vocabulary words in their instruction. These are words that are important to survival in our complex society. This instruction is particularly important to struggling readers and English-language learners (Davis and McDaniel, 1998). Words that may not be in the students' listening vocabularies include important ones such as *hazardous*, *prohibited*, *expiration*, *evacuate*, *infectious*, and *ventilation*. English-language learners may actually have these concepts but not the English words that represent them.

Because of the capacity limits of working memory, Sousa (2005) encourages the teaching of no more than five words per lesson in elementary school. Similarly, Bromley (2007) suggests that English-language learners and struggling readers should not be taught more than five words at a time, focusing on ones that will be needed again later and ones related to the important concepts in new material. These words should include the most frequently used English words and words used in academic settings and readings (Graves, 2006).

Instructional Procedures

Vocabulary instruction can take place before, during, and/or after reading of assigned material. Although procedures for vocabulary development vary widely, many of them have produced good results, and teachers should be familiar with a variety of approaches. No single approach has been proven to be the best for all students. A number of the programs described here combine several approaches, and good teachers will also use combinations of approaches in their classrooms.

As described earlier in this chapter, wide reading can help students increase their vocabularies. However, research on vocabulary instruction indicates that "direct instruction that engages students in construction of word meaning, using context and prior knowledge, is [also] effective for learning specific vocabulary and for improving comprehension of related materials" (Nelson-Herber, 1986, p. 627).

Language-rich environments at home and at school promote vocabulary acquisition (Anderson and Nagy, 1991; Blachowicz and Fisher, 2000; Brabham, Greene, and Villaume, 2002; Sousa, 2005). Teachers can greatly influence students' vocabulary development simply by being good models of vocabulary use. For example, when teachers read aloud or give explanations to the class, they should discuss any new words used and encourage the students to use them. Teachers should not "talk down" to students but, rather, should use appropriate terminology in describing things to them and participating in discussions with them. In class teachers should use challenging words that are high-frequency words that mature language users employ. They could use words like *commotion* and *timid* for primary students and *adjacent* and *ponder* for middle-grade students (Graves, 2006). Developing students' word consciousness is an important goal in a vocabulary program, and exposure to such words can arouse the students' interest in their meanings. **Word consciousness** is "an awareness of and interest in words and their meanings" (Graves, 2006, p. 7; Graves and Watts-Taffe, 2002).

 LITERATURE

Modeling precise word usage and calling attention to particularly appropriate word choices in literature encourage word consciousness. A teacher may want to have the students read Debra Frasier's *Miss Alaineus: A Vocabulary Disaster* for an entertaining introduction to learning word meanings and possibilities for misunderstanding word meanings. Word play and work with figurative language have also been used to develop word consciousness (Baumann, Ware, and Edwards, 2007).

Learning new vocabulary may just involve acquisition of a new label for a concept that is already known. In this case, the teacher's task is simple. The teacher provides the new term (such as *journey*) and tells the children it means the same thing as a familiar term (such as *trip*) (Armbruster and Nagy, 1992).

Students must also learn to construct word meanings from context, experience, and inferential thinking. (Making inferences is covered extensively in Chapters 7 and 8.) To facilitate retention, teachers should encourage students to use new words in reading, writing, and speaking. The techniques described in this chapter and the ideas presented in Chapter 12 will help teachers plan effectively for vocabulary instruction in various content areas.

 LITERATURE

Manyak (2007) suggests teaching vocabulary related to character traits displayed by characters in the books or stories the students are reading or the teacher is reading to them. He has collected sets of twenty character trait words that he feels are good to teach at each grade level. In his approach, the teacher asks students how they would describe the characters and lists on the board the words that they use. Next the teacher shows students a chart with character names listed vertically on the left side and character traits that he or she has chosen for the characters listed horizontally across the top. The teacher then defines each word and asks if each character listed has each of these traits. For example, "Do you think that Fern (in *Charlotte's Web*) was considerate?" If a student responds, "Yes," the teacher puts an X on the chart under the trait *considerate*. After that, the teacher asks how the term applies to the character. This process is used for each character and each trait. The class also makes a combined chart that lists, by character trait, all the characters from all the texts they have covered. This chart encourages students to compare traits of characters across texts. They review the terms in another context.

Building Readers' Schemata

Vocabulary terms are labels for **schemata,** or the clusters of concepts each person develops through experience. Isabel Beck has stated that *ownership* of a word, or the ability to relate the word to an existing schema, is necessary for meaningful learning (Thelen, 1986). Teachers can help students to connect known words and concepts with new ones and to form concept clusters to show how words are related. Sometimes children cannot understand the terms they encounter in books because they do not know the concepts to which the terms refer. In this case, concept or schemata development involving the use of direct and vicarious experiences is necessary.

A good technique for concept development is to offer as concrete an experience for the concept as possible. The class should then discuss the attributes of the concept. The teacher should give examples and nonexamples of the concept, pointing out the attributes that distinguish examples from nonexamples. Next, students should try to identify other examples and nonexamples that the teacher supplies and give their reasons. Finally, students should suggest additional examples and nonexamples.

For example, to develop the concept of "banjo," the teacher could bring a banjo to class. The teacher would show it to students, play it for them (or get someone else to do so), and let them touch it and pluck or strum the strings. Then they could discuss its attributes, such as a circular body, a long neck, a tightly stretched cover over the body, strings, and the ability to produce music when played. The teacher might show the children pictures or real examples of a variety of banjos, some with five and some with four strings, and some with enclosed backs and some with open backs. Then the teacher might show the children a guitar, pointing out the differences in construction (for example, shape, material forming the front of the instrument, and number of strings). The teacher might also show several other instruments, letting students identify how they are different from and similar to banjos. Students can provide their own examples of banjos by bringing in pictures or actual instruments. They will note that, although there may be some variation in size and appearance, the essential attributes are present. They can also name and bring pictures or actual instruments that are not banjos, such as harps, mandolins, or violins, and explain why these instruments do not fit the concept.

As students progress in school, they are introduced to a growing number of abstract concepts. Concrete experiences for abstract concepts are difficult to provide, but the teacher can use approximations. For example, to develop the concept of "freedom," the teacher can say, "You may work on any of your homework, read a book, or write notes to one another for the next ten minutes, or you may choose not to do anything but rest, draw, or daydream." After ten minutes have passed, the teacher can tell the class that they were given the freedom to choose their activity; that is, they were not kept from doing what they chose to do. The teacher may then offer several examples of freedom, including the freedom to choose friends. Students choose friends on the basis of their own desires. The teacher should also suggest nonexamples, such as players being restricted by a set of rules when playing a game. Next, the teacher should ask the students to give their own examples of freedom and to explain why these examples are appropriate. These may include the freedom we have in this country to say what we think about our leaders. After eliciting several examples, the teacher can ask the students for nonexamples. Students may suggest that people in jail do not have freedom. Finally, the teacher may ask them to be alert for examples and nonexamples of freedom in their everyday activities and to report their findings to the class.

Firsthand experiences, such as field trips and demonstrations, can help students associate words with real situations. Teachers can build student interest and provide a meaningful context for presentation of new vocabulary by using real objects and demonstrations. These approaches should be used before the words are presented in written material that students are assigned to read (Gregg and Sekeres, 2006).

These experiences can be preceded and followed by discussion of the new concepts, and written accounts of the experiences can help students gain control of the new vocabulary. Before a field trip, for example, a teacher may discuss the work that is done at the target location. During the field trip, the teacher or the field trip host can explain each activity to students as they watch it. This explanation should include the proper terms for the processes and personnel involved. After the trip, the students can discuss the experience. They can also manipulate the new terms in several ways that are described more fully later in this chapter. These techniques include making graphic displays of the new terms, classifying them, making comparison charts for the words, or analyzing their structure. Students may write individual summaries of the experience or participate in writing a class summary. They may want to use reference books or the Internet to expand their knowledge about some of the new things they have seen. All of these activities will build both the students' concepts and their vocabularies, thereby enhancing their comprehension of material containing this vocabulary.

Because concrete experiences are not always possible or feasible to use due to time or budget constraints, teachers should also plan vicarious experiences to help students build concepts and vocabulary. Pictures, videos, computer displays, verbal explanations, and virtual field trips are vicarious experiences that can be used to illustrate words that students have encountered in reading and to provide other words for discussion. Books such as thesauruses, student dictionaries, and trade books about words are also useful sources of information about words.

The picture book *Whatley's Quest* by Bruce Whatley and Rosie Smith is an alphabet book that pictures many animals and objects whose names begin with each letter. Discussing each illustration and identifying the words that would label the pictures exposes students to new words and concepts. Students learn from their classmates' comments as well as those of the teacher. Other alphabet books may also work well. Jerry Pallotta's themed alphabet books are especially good for older readers.

SEEING IT IN PRACTICE ◄ ▌ ►

Video Case
View the Video Case "Bilingual Education: An Elementary Two-Way Immersion Program" and observe how the concept of "estimation" and the label for this concept are taught to a group of English-language learners. Does this approach appear to be effective with these students? Why do you think so?

Visit the Student Website to investigate online versions of vocabulary resources for students, such as online thesauruses and dictionaries.

 LITERATURE

LITERATURE

To help first graders learn vocabulary related to content areas, Blachowicz and Obrochta (2005) developed virtual field trips, using books. They structured a series of scaffolded read-aloud experiences to simulate a field trip—focusing on content; engaging the senses; preparing for the experience; offering adult mediation of the experience, including language activities; and following up on the new vocabulary. The teachers chose focal content-area topics for the activity, assembled sets of at least five related texts to be read aloud, chose the target vocabulary, and made posters with thematic pictures to motivate the children to discuss the topics.

The first field trip activity was to discuss what the students knew about the topic and to have them list words that were related to it. Next, the students and teacher engaged in group talk about the motivational poster. The teacher questioned students about the poster and put the words that students used on the poster with sticky notes. As discussion of the poster progressed, the teacher mediated or scaffolded it by asking questions, making explanations, and making suggestions that led to learning about the vocabulary and adding more vocabulary terms. Questions relating the vocabulary to all the appropriate senses were used, eliciting statements about sounds, tastes, touch, and smells. This activity was followed by a read-aloud of one of the target books. Students were asked to listen for key vocabulary and give a "thumbs up" when one of the words was read. More discussion and a writing activity followed. The books were made available for students to read and add to their reading logs.

The same procedure was used for the other books in the set. Students participated in many extension activities such as word games and word sorts throughout the unit. Finally, the students wrote about what they had learned. The lesson plan "3, 2, 1 . . . Blast Off! Vocabulary Instruction Using a Virtual Trip to the Moon" based on this procedure is located at http://www.readwritethink.org.

LITERATURE

Storytelling and story reading are excellent ways to provide vicarious experiences. Research studies have shown that a seven-week program of daily one-hour storytelling/story-reading sessions with language follow-up activities could improve vocabulary skills of kindergarten, first-grade, and second-grade students. Language follow-up activities included creative dramatics, creative writing (or dictation), retelling stories with the flannel board, and illustrating scenes from the stories and describing them to the teacher. When the students who participated in these studies were asked to produce their own stories, those in the experimental groups used more words, more

Direct experiences, such as experiments, demonstrations, or field trips, help students increase their schemata and expand their vocabularies.

© Elizabeth Crews

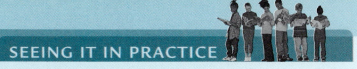

Using Literature Selections to Develop Vocabulary

Dr. Roe, a visiting teacher, was presenting the song "The Old Woman Who Swallowed a Fly" in a first-grade class. After she sang the line "How absurd to swallow a bird," she asked the students, "What does *absurd* mean?" None of them knew.

Dr. Roe told them that *absurd* meant *silly* or *ridiculous*. Then she asked them, "Would it be silly for a woman to swallow a bird?"

The children answered, "Yes," in unison.

"Would it be absurd for me to wear a flowerpot on my head to teach the class?" she then asked.

Again the children answered, "Yes!"

"What are some other absurd things that you can think of?" Dr. Roe finally asked.

Each child gave a reply. If the reply showed understanding of the term, Dr. Roe provided positive reinforcement. If it did not show understanding of the term, her questioning led the child to see why the thing mentioned was not absurd, and the child was given another chance to answer.

Weeks later, when these children encountered the word again in the story *Horton Hatches the Egg,* they remembered its meaning.

Analysis of Scenario

The children encountered a word in the context of a familiar song. The word's meaning was unclear to them, so the teacher supplied both a definition and other examples of the concept that the term named. To ensure that the children really understood the term, the teacher asked them to supply their own examples. This activity helped the children make the word their own through active involvement with it.

different words, and more multisyllabic words in their stories than students in the control groups did (Roe, 1985, 1986; Pigg, 1986). A classroom example of the activities used in these research studies is presented in "Seeing It in Practice: Using Literature Selections to Develop Vocabulary."

According to Thelen (1986), meaningful learning is enhanced by teaching general concepts before specific concepts. Using this approach, the teacher presents the concept of "dog" before the concept of "poodle," for example. In this way, the children have the schemata they need to incorporate new facts that they encounter. For example, they have a prior pool of information about "dogs" to which they can relate the new information about "poodle."

Teachers should be aware of and use their students' experience base when they teach new word meanings, to avoid situations in which students are expected to acquire a store of words for which they have only superficial understanding. When commercial materials are employed, teachers should use discussion to relate word meanings to their students' own experiences. Brainstorming about words and webbing the responses (as described later in this chapter in the section "Semantic Maps and Word Webs") can be a good way to tie vocabulary instruction to background experiences. Students learn new connections as their classmates contribute new related words.

Actively Involving Students

Students learn best through active involvement in learning new words (Blachowicz and Fisher, 2000). The following are several approaches that are particularly focused on active involvement. Many other approaches throughout this chapter also offer active involvement.

▶ Relating Vocabulary to Background Knowledge and Experiences

Many approaches focus on relating vocabulary to background experiences and involve active learning on the part of the students. Spencer and Guillaume (2006) propose teaching vocabulary with a learning cycle that "embeds learning within real-world contexts" (p. 210). The teacher first elicits students' background knowledge and builds a purpose for learning the material by presenting students with a real-world question or topic for focus. The next step is exploration by students (generally including hands-on experiences) of the presented topic. In this step, the instructional goal is developing concepts. In the next step, the teacher's primary objective is to develop the vocabulary that relates to the topic and explo- ration, using a variety of techniques, such as the ones described in this chapter. Some examples are semantic feature analysis, vocabulary maps, analogies, classi- fication activities, dramatization of terms, and study of word histories. Students' misconceptions about word meanings are also addressed. The last step is to have students apply their new word knowledge in another situation, such as in writing assignments, poetry, and presentations.

Another program of vocabulary instruction that emphasizes relating vocabu- lary to students' preexisting word knowledge and experiences was described by Beck and McKeown (1983). In this program, students were actively involved by generating their own context for the terms being taught by answering questions about the words (for example, the teacher might say, "Tell about something you might want to *eavesdrop* on" [p. 624]). The program also helped students to fur- ther their word knowledge by introducing new words in global semantic, or mean- ing, categories, such as *people* or *places*, and by requiring the students to work with the relationships among words. The teacher asked the students to differentiate among critical features of words, to generalize from one word to similar ones, to complete analogies involving the words, and to pantomime words. Thus, students were active participants in the activities described, rather than passive observers. Students were given a number of exposures to each word in a variety of contexts. Finally, rapid responses to words were elicited by using timed activities, some of which were gamelike. These activities kept students actively involved and probably increased their interest as well.

The students involved in Beck and McKeown's program learned the words taught, developed speed and accuracy in making semantic decisions, and demonstrated comprehension of stories containing the target words better than did a control group. They also learned more than the specific words taught, as indicated by the size of their gains on a standardized measure of reading comprehension and vocabulary.

▶ Constructing Definitions

Vocabulary instruction should include both the use of definitions and words in context (ranging from sentences to entire reading selections) to have the maximum effect. Techniques requiring students to think deeply about a term and its relationships to other terms are most effective. Class discussion seems to make students think more deeply about words as they make connections between their prior knowledge and new information.

One procedure uses several techniques for vocabulary instruction. First, the teacher activates what the students know about the target words in the reading selection, using either exclusion brainstorming (in which students exclude unrelated words from a list of possible associated words) or knowledge rating (in which students indicate their degree of familiarity with the words). Then the teacher can elicit predictions about connections between words or between words and the selection's topic, emphasizing connections among words. Next, the students construct tentative definitions of the words, test these definitions against the text as they read, and refine them as needed. Finally, the students use the words in other reading and writing tasks. This approach promotes retention by actively engaging students in predicting and constructing definitions rather than merely memorizing the material presented (Blachowicz, 1986).

▶ Semantic Impressions

Richek (2005) recommends a successful technique called *semantic impressions* in which the teacher lists key words from a story or book chapter in the order they appear in the material, the class discusses each one, and the students compose a group story using the words. After a word is used in the book order, it may be used as needed again later. The teacher writes the story on the board, and students reread it, editing and revising it with supervision. Later, students may compose individual stories. This manipulation of words enhances internalization of the words. A quick practice activity is asking students to include two or more words in single sentences. This encourages students to make cognitive connections among the words.

▶ Illustrating Words

Illustrating words is a procedure that gets students very actively involved in learning the words. Emerging readers and children whose primary language is not English can draw pictures to illustrate new vocabulary words and thereby demonstrate their

 DIVERSITY

understanding. Then the children's illustrations can be shown to a small group of other class members, who try to identify the word being illustrated in each picture and record it on their papers. Finally, each artist tells which word each of his or her pictures represents (Baroni, 1987).

▶ Using Learning Aids

Teaching vocabulary through the use of real objects and demonstrations can build student interest and provide a meaningful context for presentation of the new vocabulary. These approaches should be used before the words are presented in written material that students are assigned to read (Gregg and Sekeres, 2006).

Physical objects that they can handle often help students learn and remember the meanings of new words. *Manipulatives* are especially helpful in explaining or demonstrating meanings of content-area vocabulary. Teachers can use tape measures to show the meanings of certain lengths (*foot*, *yard*, and the like), balance scales to show the meaning of *equilibrium*, cotton balls and water to demonstrate *absorption*, balloons to show the meanings of *inflate* and *expansion*, or rubber bands to demonstrate *elasticity*.

Students can become highly involved in learning vocabulary when they create their own learning aids. They can make concept cards on which they list definitions, synonyms, and examples for the terms. They may even draw pictures to represent the words. Pairs of students can use these cards to discuss word meanings, write short selections containing the words, and quiz one another on the words.

LITERATURE

Richek (2005) had different students make Word Expert Cards for various words to be learned. Then, in pairs, students taught their words to each other. Students also read a novel or textbook material to experience the words in context. Bromley (2007) also suggests having students peer-teach words to each other in small groups, presenting them visually and verbally.

▶ Dramatizing Words

Another active way to clarify word meanings by associating situations with them is dramatization of words. Zumwalt (2003) found that use of a variation of the game charades can motivate students to analyze word meaning carefully. Under some circumstances, dramatization of words has proved more effective than use of context clues, morphemic (structural) analysis, or dictionaries (Duffelmeyer, 1980).

Context Clues

In Chapter 4, we discussed the use of **context clues** to help students recognize words that are familiar in speech but not in print. Context clues can also help students learn the meanings of unfamiliar words. In fact, Graves (2006) states that use of context clues to infer the meanings of unfamiliar words is the most important word-learning strategy.

▶ Locating Context Clues

Several types of context clues are found in written materials. These include

1. *Definition clues*. A word may be directly defined in the context.

   The *dictionary* is a book in which the meanings of words can be found.

2. *Appositive clues*. An appositive may offer a synonym or a description of the word that will cue its meaning. Students need to know that an **appositive** is a word or phrase that restates or identifies the word or expression it follows and that it is usually set off by commas, dashes, or parentheses.

   They are going to *harvest*, or gather in, the season's crops.
   That model is *obsolete* (outdated).
   The *rodents*—rats and mice—in the experiment learned to run a maze.

3. *Comparison clues*. A comparison of the unfamiliar word with a word the child knows may offer a clue. In the examples, the familiar words *sleepy* and *clothes* provide the clues for *drowsy* and *habit*, respectively.

   Like her sleepy brother, Mary felt *drowsy*.
   Like all the clothes she wore, her riding *habit* was very fashionable.

4. *Contrast clues*. A contrast of the unknown word with a familiar one may offer a clue. In the examples, the unfamiliar word *temporary* is contrasted with the familiar word *forever*, and the unfamiliar word *occasionally* is contrasted with the familiar word *regularly*.

   It will not last forever; it is only *temporary*.
   She doesn't visit regularly; she just comes by *occasionally*.

5. *Example clues*. Sometimes examples are given for words that may be unfamiliar in print, and these examples can provide the clues needed for identification.

   Mark was going to talk about *reptiles*—for example, snakes and lizards.
   Andrea wants to play a *percussion* instrument, such as the snare drum or bells.

Although the preceding examples have clues in the sentences in which the new words are found, context can also offer clues in sentences other than the one in which the new words appear, so students should be encouraged to read surrounding sentences for clues to meaning. Sometimes an entire paragraph embodies the explanation of a term, as in the following example:

> I've told you before that the flu is contagious! When Johnny had the flu, Beatrice played with him one afternoon, and soon Beatrice came down with it. Joey caught it from her, and now you tell me you have been to Joey's house. I hope you don't come down with the flu and have to miss the party on Saturday.

LITERATURE

Context clues are available in both text and illustrations in many trade books. *A Gaggle of Geese* by Philippa-Alys Browne, *A Gaggle of Geese* by Eve Merriam, and *A Cache of Jewels and Other Collective Nouns* by Ruth Heller put collective terminology for groups into an interesting context. Teaching children to recognize the context clues in these meaningful settings encourages them to use such clues in their independent reading. Illustrations often provide strong context clues for both beginning readers and English-language learners.

DIVERSITY

Having students find vocabulary words in their environment, write down the context in which they were read or heard, and share their words in context with their classmates has been effective in some classrooms. This technique has worked well with English-language learners (Richek, 2005).

▶ Teaching Students to Use Context Clues

Researchers estimate that average ten- to fourteen-year-old students could acquire from 750 to 8,250 new words each year simply through incidental, rather than directed, contextual learning (Schwartz, 1988; Nagy, Herman, and Anderson, 1985). Directly teaching students to use context more efficiently can even further enhance their levels of vocabulary learning. For example, teachers can show students how to use context in the material by reading the surrounding paragraph, referring to a caption or footnote, or studying illustrations or graphics (Bromley, 2007).

STRUGGLING READER/
INTERVENTION   DIVERSITY

Struggling readers and English-language learners particularly need to learn that context can help them decide on appropriate meanings for multiple-meaning words they encounter. Bromley (2007) points out, "Seventy percent of the most frequently used words have multiple meanings" (p. 531).

Teachers can use a "think-aloud" strategy to help students see how to use context clues. (Think-aloud strategies are valuable in teaching most aspects of reading.) "Putting It into Practice: Intermediate-Level Think-Aloud on Using Context Clues" makes use of this strategy.

After several example think-aloud activities in which the teacher models the use of context clues, the teacher can ask student volunteers to think aloud the context clues for specific words. Students may then work in pairs on a context clues activity and verbalize their context usage strategies to each other. Finally, students should work alone to determine meanings from context clues.

Often context for teaching new words can come from reading selections. Teachers can present in good context difficult words from material about to be assigned for class. The teacher may question students about each word and its context in a way that encourages use of appropriate context clues or other strategies (primarily morphemic analysis or dictionary use) to discover the word's meaning. Class discussion helps students to remember the words presented in this manner.

TEACHING TIP

Creating Contexts for Word Presentation

You can create your own sentences to introduce new words in context. You should use sentences that students can relate to their own experiences and that have only one unfamiliar word each.

Write on the board or display on a transparency the following sentence: "Rather than encountering hostile natives, as they had expected, many settlers found the natives to be amicable." Read the sentence aloud and say: "I wonder what *amicable* means? Let's see; the sentence says, '*Rather than* encountering hostile natives.' That means the natives weren't hostile. *Hostile* means *unfriendly*, so maybe *amicable* means *friendly*."

Many educators recommend explicit instruction to teach use of context clues. The process involves offering verbal explanations for how to use each clue, modeling application of the strategy, and providing guided and independent practice with use of the strategy. For the practice stages, teachers can use magazine articles, trade books, or textbook sections (Baumann et al., 2007; Yopp and Yopp, 2007).

Gipe (1980) used an expanded context method that involved having students read new words in context and apply the words in writing about their own experiences. She compared this method to three others: an association method (in which an unknown word is paired with a familiar synonym), a category method, and a dictionary method (in which students look up the word, write a definition, and use the word in a sentence). The expanded context method was found to be the most effective. The application of the new words may have been the most important aspect of the context method that Gipe used. This type of instruction assists students in integrating the new words with their background knowledge. Readers' theater is another effective way to encourage application and multiple uses of the new vocabulary (Flynn, 2004/2005). Students may also use the new words in writing assignments, poetry, and presentations.

Context clues are useful when the context is explicit about word meaning, but they are less useful when the meaning is left unclear. If the clues are too vague, they may actually be misleading. Furthermore, if the word is not important to understanding the passage, students may not need to process its meaning as deeply as those of more important words, so the explicitness of the context is not important. Teachers should model through think-alouds their decision-making processes about the importance of determining the meaning of the word, the usefulness of the context, and the kinds of clues available there. Students need to realize that the meanings they attribute to the words must make sense in the context.

As mentioned earlier in this chapter, teachers should combine a variety of approaches when teaching vocabulary. If there is not explicit context for important words in a selection, teachers should have students try morphemic analysis clues (described next) or have them look the words up in a dictionary. Students can also use these techniques to help them decide whether or not a meaning suggested by the context is reasonable.

Morphemic Analysis (Structural Analysis)

Like context clues, morphemic analysis, a subset of structural analysis that involves the identification of meaningful word parts, was discussed in Chapters 4 and 5 (this discussion was in the section on structural analysis as a word-recognition skill). It can also be used as an aid in discovering meanings of unknown words. When used to recognize the words for the sake of pronunciation, we used the term *structural analysis* because one of the aspects of structural analysis is syllabication, which does not involve morphemes. All other aspects of the analysis of word structure involve morphemes, so we use the more descriptive term *morphemic analysis* in this context. Graves (2006) says that using word parts to deduce the meanings of words is second to using context clues as an important word-learning strategy.

Children begin to learn about word structure very early. First, they deal with words in their simplest, most basic forms—**morphemes,** the smallest units of meaning in a language. (The word *cat* is one morpheme.) Then they gradually learn to combine morphemes. If an *s* is added to form the plural, *cats*, the final *s* is also a morpheme because it changes the word's meaning. There are two classes of morphemes, distinguished by function: *free morphemes*, which have independent meanings and can be used by themselves (*cat, man, son*), and *bound morphemes*, which must be combined with free morphemes to have meaning. Affixes and inflectional endings are bound morphemes; the *-er* in *singer* is an example.

Knowing meanings of common affixes and combining them with meanings of familiar root words can help students determine the meanings of many new words. For example, if a child knows the meaning of *joy* and knows that the suffix *-ous* means *full of*, he or she can conclude that the word *joyous* means *full of joy*. Some methods of instruction in morphemic analysis that have been used successfully in middle grades, such as disassembling and reassembling words, could be modified to work well in the primary grades (Mountain, 2005; Edwards, Font, Baumann, & Boland, 2004). Teachers can cluster high-frequency prefixes and suffixes into families of word parts that have the same meaning, such as the *not, together, bad*, and *against* prefix families to make them more memorable for students. (For example, the "bad prefix family" includes *mis-* and *mal-*.) Then they can teach the prefixes in families, by having the students disassemble and reassemble words with these prefixes. After a lesson on a particular family, the students can write the prefixes and suffixes, along with their meanings, examples of words that contain them, and sentences that put them in context in "Affixionary" notebooks (Baumann et al., 2007).

Teaching some common Latin and Greek roots can also be helpful. For example, *audi* (hear), *dict* (speak), *port* (carry), *script* (write), and *vis* (see) are common Latin roots; *auto* (self), *bio* (life), *graph* (written or drawn), *hydro* (water), and *ology* (study of) are common Greek roots (Kieffer and Lesaux, 2007).

Prefixes may have more than one meaning. *Un-, re-, in-*, and *dis-*, the four most frequently used prefixes, have at least two meanings each. *Un-* and *dis-* may each mean either *not* or *do the opposite*. *In-* may mean either *not, in*, or *into*. *Re-* may mean either *again* or *back*. Both the word parts and the context of the words should be considered in determining the meanings of prefixed words (White, Sowell, and Yanagihara, 1989).

"Putting It into Practice: The Prefix *un-*" shows an activity using the book *Fortunately*. This activity can help children see how prefixes and suffixes change the meanings of words. *Un-* is the most common English prefix (Carroll, Davies, and Richman, 1971; White et al., 1989).

Teachers can find the lesson plan "Rooting Out Meaning: Morpheme Match-Ups in the Primary Grades" for use in grades 3–5 on determining the meaning of unfamiliar words through understanding morphemes at the Read•Write•Think website (go to http://www.readwritethink.org or link from this book's Student Website). The lesson is based on an article by Mountain (2005) that offers support for teaching morphemic analysis in primary grades. The lesson "You Can't Spell the Word *Prefix* Without a Prefix" on this same site is for grades 6–8. It should be useful with gifted fifth graders as well.

The Prefix *un-*

Have the students read the book *Fortunately* by Remy Charlip. Discuss with them the meanings of *fortunately* and *unfortunately*, using the situations from the book to make the discussion concrete and clear. When they have stated that *unfortunately* means *not fortunately* or *the opposite of fortunately*, have them decide what part of the word means *not*. After they identify the *un-* as the part that means *not*, have them name other words they know that begin with *un-*. Discuss the meanings of these words, pointing out that the prefix means *not* or *the opposite of* in each case in which the remainder of the word forms a root word or a root word and a word ending (as in *unfortunately*), but not when the beginning two letters are not a prefix attached to a root word (such as *under*). Ask them to look in their reading assignments for words starting with *un-* in which *un-* is a prefix added to a root word. Have them use their knowledge of the meaning of *un-* to determine the meaning of each of these words.

"Seeing It in Practice: Use of Morphemic Analysis Skills" shows a more difficult morphemic analysis activity for sixth-grade students. Many meaningful word parts come from Latin and Greek; for example, *helio-* and *geo-* are from Greek, and *-centric* is based on both Latin and Greek forms.

Students can often determine the meanings of compound words by relating the meanings of the component parts to each other (*watchdog* means a *dog* that *watches*). After some practice, they can be led to see that the component parts of a compound word do not always have the same relationships to each other (*bookcase* means a *case* for *books*). "Seeing It in Practice: Compound Words" shows an activity that can offer practice in determining their meanings.

Words with similar spellings and meanings in two languages are called *cognates*. Because Spanish and English have many cognates (for example, *ulterior* is spelled exactly the same; *champion* and *campeón* are similar in spelling), Spanish-speaking English-language learners will benefit from instruction in recognizing these words. Teachers can also help these English-language learners to become aware of the regular relationships between English and Spanish suffixes, such as the relationship between *-idad* (in *originalidad*) in Spanish and *-ity* (in *originality*) in English (Kieffer and Lesaux, 2007; Carlo et al., 2004). Speakers of various languages can be consulted for help with similar comparisons of their languages and English. Some languages, such as those with different alphabets, present more difficult problems.

 DIVERSITY

Categorization

Categorization is the grouping together of things or ideas that have common features. Classifying words into categories can be a good way to learn more about word meanings. An activity such as this is referred to as a **word sort.** Young children can begin learning how to place things into categories by grouping concrete objects according to their traits. Once the children have developed some sight vocabulary, it is a relatively small step for them to begin categorizing the words they see in print according to their meanings. Very early in their instruction, children will be able to

Use of Morphemic Analysis Skills

A sixth-grade science textbook presented two theories of the solar system: a geocentric theory and a helio-centric theory. Two diagrams were provided to help the students visualize the two theories, but the diagrams were not labeled. Mrs. Brown, the teacher, asked the students, "Which diagram is related to each theory?"

Matt's hand quickly went up, and he accurately identified the two diagrams.

"How did you decide which was which?" asked Mrs. Brown.

"You told us that *geo-* means *earth. Centric* looks like it comes from *center*. This diagram has the earth in the center. So I decided it was geocentric. That would mean the other one was heliocentric. Since the sun is in the center in it, I guess *helio-* means *sun*."

Analysis of Scenario

Mrs. Brown had taught an important science word part the first time it occurred in her class. She had encouraged her students to use their knowledge of word parts to figure out unfamiliar words. Matt followed her suggestions and managed to make decisions about key vocabulary on the basis of his knowledge of word parts.

look at the following list and classify the words into such teacher-supplied categories as "people," "things to play with," "things to eat," and "things to do."

Word List

doll	bicycle	ball	run	girl
candy	cookie	boy	baby	sit
toy	dig	sing	mother	banana

The children may discover that they want to put a word in more than one category. This desire will provide an opportunity for discussion about how a word may fit in two or more places for different reasons. The children should give reasons for all of their placements.

Classifying words into categories supplied by the teacher is a *closed-ended sort*. After students become adept doing closed-ended sorts, they are ready for the more difficult task of generating the categories needed for classifying the words presented. The teacher may give them a word list such as the one that follows and ask them to place the words in groups of things that are alike and to name the trait that each set of items has in common. This activity is an *open-ended sort*.

Word List

horse	cow	goose	stallion	foal
gosling	mare	filly	chick	calf
colt	gander	bull	hen	rooster

Children may offer several categories for these words: various families of animals; four-legged and two-legged animals; feathered and furred animals; winged and wingless animals; or male animals, female animals, and animals that might be either sex. They may also come up with a classification that the teacher has not considered.

Compound Words

Mr. Clay based his lesson on the book *The Seal Mother* by Mordicai Gerstein. He introduced the story by saying that it was an old Scottish folktale. He wrote the word *folktale* on the board. Then he asked, "What can you tell me about this word?"

Bobby said, "It is made up of two words: *folk* and *tale*. That makes it a compound word."

"Good, Bobby," Mr. Clay responded. "What does that make you believe this word means?"

"A tale is a story," LaTonya replied.

"That's right," said Mr. Clay. "Can anyone add anything else to what we know about the word's meaning? What does *folk* mean?"

Carl answered tentatively, "A kind of music?"

"There is folk music, just as there are folktales, but we still need a meaning for the word *folk*," Mr. Clay responded.

After he got only shrugs, he explained, "A folktale is a tale, or story, told by the folk, or common people, of a country. Folktales were passed down orally from older people to younger ones over the years. See how both parts of the compound word give something to the meaning?

"Listen as I read this story to you. When I finish, we will try to retell the story by listing the main events."

The children listened intently. When he finished the story, Mr. Clay asked them to list the events in the story in order. As they suggested events, he wrote each one on the board. When he had listed all of the events that they could remember, they discussed how to put some of the events in the proper order. Mr. Clay erased and moved the sentences around until the children were satisfied.

Then Mr. Clay asked the children, "Did you use any compound words to retell the story?"

Hands shot up all over the room. Mr. Clay called on them one by one, and they pointed out *fisherman, sealskin, without, oilcloth, inside, rayfish, everywhere, grandfather,* and *whenever.* The children who mentioned the words were allowed to go to the board and circle them, identify the two words that made up each compound, and try to define each compound word, using the meanings of the two component words. Other students helped in determining the definitions, and sometimes the dictionary was consulted.

Finally, the children were asked to copy the compound words from the board into their vocabulary study notebooks. "I'm putting three copies of *The Seal Mother* in the reading center for the rest of this week," Mr. Clay said. "When you have time, take your vocabulary notebook to the center and read the book to yourself or with a partner. Each time you find one of our compound words, put a checkmark by the word in your notebook. When you find a compound word that we didn't use in our retelling, copy it into your notebook, and write a definition for it, using the meanings of the two words and the context of the sentence in which you found it. We'll discuss the other words that you found on Friday."

On Friday, the children had found a number of words in the book that they hadn't used in their retelling, including *moonlit, moonlight, everything, wide-eyed, tiptoed, another,* and *into.* A discussion of the words and their meanings followed. Mr. Clay asked how the author's use of some of these words added to the children's understanding of the story.

"*Moonlit* and *moonlight* give you a picture in your mind of the scene," Jared said.

"*Wide-eyed* lets us know how his parents' talk made the boy feel," Marissa added.

"*Tiptoed* showed us how he walked quietly," Tyrone said.

"Watch for compound words in other books that you read and use the meanings of the two words in each compound to help you with meanings that you don't already know," Mr. Clay told them as he ended the lesson.

As long as the classification system makes sense and the animals are correctly classified according to the stated system, it should be considered correct. Teachers should encourage students to discover various possibilities for classifications.

There are several benefits to a classification task such as this. Discussion of the different classification systems may help to extend the children's concepts about some of the animals on the list, and it may help some children develop concepts related to some of the animals for the first time. The classification system enables them to relate the new knowledge about some of the animals to the knowledge they already have about these animals or others. If some of the animal terms are new to students, putting these new words into categories can help students remember their meanings. The usefulness of categorization activities is supported by research indicating that presenting words in semantically related clusters can lead to improvement in students' vocabulary knowledge and reading comprehension (Marzano, 1984).

An activity such as the one in "Putting It into Practice: Classification Game" provides an interesting way to work on categorization skills.

The ability to classify is a basic skill that applies to many areas of learning. Many of the other activities described in this chapter, including those for analogies, semantic maps, and semantic feature analysis, depend on categorization.

Analogies and Word Lines

Analogies compare two relationships and thereby provide a basis for building word knowledge. Educators may teach analogies by displaying examples of categories, relationships, and analogies; asking guiding questions about the examples; allowing students to discuss the questions; and applying the ideas that emerge.

Students may need help in grouping items into categories and understanding the relationships among items. For example, the teacher might write *nickel*, *dime*, and *quarter* on the board and ask, "How are these things related? What name could you give the entire group of items?" (Answer: *money*.) Teachers can use pictures instead of words in the primary grades; in either case, they can ask students to apply the skill by naming other things that would fit in the category (*penny* and *dollar*). Or the teacher could write *painter* and *brush* and ask, "What is the relationship between the two items?" (Answer: A *painter* works with a *brush*.) Teachers should remember to simplify their language for discussions with young children, to use examples familiar to English learners, and to have all students give other examples of the relationship (*dentist* and *drill*). After working through many examples such as these, students should be ready for examples of simple analogies, such as "Light is to dark as day is to night," "Glove is to hand as sock is to foot," and "Round is to ball as square is to block." Students can discuss how analogies work: "How are the first two things related? How are the second two things related? How are these relationships alike?" They can then complete incomplete analogies, such as "Teacher is to classroom as pilot is to _____." Younger children should do this orally; older ones can understand the standard shorthand form of *come:go::live:die* if they are taught to read the colon (:) as *is to* and the double colon (::) as *as* (Bellows, 1980).

DIVERSITY

PUTTING IT INTO PRACTICE

Classification Game

Divide the class into groups of three or four and make category sheets like the one shown here for each group. When you give a signal, students start writing as many words as they can think of that fit in each category; when you signal that time is up, a student from each group reads the group's words to the class. Have students compare their lists and discuss why they placed particular words in particular categories.

Appropriate categories in addition to the ones used below are mammals, reptiles, and insects; and liquids, solids, and gases.

Meats	Fruits	Vegetables

Huff-Benkoski and Greenwood (1995) taught second graders how to use analogies. These authors modeled their reasoning processes for the students through think-alouds as they analyzed analogies. They also had students explain their reasoning processes. The children came up with a definition for *analogies*. Classification activities—choosing words that did or did not belong with a given set of words related to a theme study—then received attention. Next, the children were asked to state the relationship between two words and to complete analogies that had one part missing. Finally, students produced their own analogies in groups and individually.

Mapping of analogies, as shown in Example 6.1, is also useful (Dwyer, 1988). Teachers might use analogy maps as part of an instructional sequence such as the one developed by Huff-Benkoski and Greenwood (1995). The map in Example 6.1 provides the relationship involved, a complete example, two incomplete examples for the students to complete, and one space for an example that comes entirely from the students.

EXAMPLE 6.1 Analogy Map

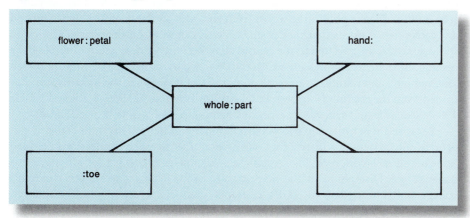

Teachers may use *word lines*, sometimes referred to as *semantic gradients*, to show the shades of meaning of related words, just as they use number lines for numbers (Greenwood and Flanigan, 2007; Blachowicz and Fisher, 2006). They can arrange related words on a graduated line that emphasizes the relationships among the words. Teachers of young children or English-language learners who have not yet mastered certain vocabulary words can use pictures and words for students to match or ask students to locate or produce appropriate pictures. Upper-grade students can be asked to arrange a specified list of words on a word line themselves. Word lines can concretely show antonym, synonym, and degree analogies, as in this example:

DIVERSITY

enormous	large	medium	small	tiny

The teacher can eventually have the students make their own word lines and analogies. Analogies that they could develop based on the word-line example above include "enormous is to large as small is to tiny" (synonym); "enormous is to tiny as large is to small" (antonym); and "large is to medium as medium is to small" (degree).

Semantic Maps and Word Webs

Semantic maps are diagrams that show how words are connected in meaning to each other. They can be used to teach related concepts or to expand or activate students' knowledge about a single concept. To construct a semantic map with a class, the teacher writes, on the board or a chart, a word that represents a concept that is central to the topic under consideration. The teacher asks the students to name other words related to this concept. The teacher can group students' words into broad categories while listing them on the board or chart, or the students can categorize the words after they are all listed. If the teacher does the categorization, the students name the categories. Then the students and the teacher discuss the central concept, the listed words, the categories, and the interrelationships among the words.

The discussion step appears to be the key to the effectiveness of this method because it allows students to be actively involved in the learning. After the class has discussed the semantic map, the teacher can give students an incomplete semantic map and ask them to fill in the words from the map on the board or chart and add any categories or words that they wish. Students can work on their maps as they do the assigned reading related to the central concept. Further discussion can follow the reading, and more categories and words can be added to the maps. The final discussion and mapping allow students to recall and graphically organize the information they gained from the reading (Johnson, Pittelman, and Heimlich, 1986; Stahl and Vancil, 1986). Semantic maps have been especially helpful to students with special needs.

Because a semantic map shows both familiar and new words under labeled categories, the process of constructing one helps students make connections between known and new concepts. The graphic display makes relationships among terms easier to see. Discussion of the map enables the teacher to assess the children's background knowledge, to clarify concepts, and to correct misunderstandings. An example of a semantic map can be found on your Student Website.

Schwartz and Raphael (1985) used a modified approach to semantic mapping to help students develop the concept of "definition." The students learned what types of information are needed for a definition and learned how to use context clues and background knowledge to help them better understand words. Word maps are really graphic representations of definitions. The word maps that Schwartz and Raphael used were like the one in Example 6.2, which defines the concept "snake." The maps contained information about the general class to which the concept belonged, answering the question "What is it?"; the properties of the concept, answering the question "What is it like?"; and examples of the concept.

With the basic information contained in such a map, students have enough information to construct definitions. This procedure for understanding the concept of definition is effective from the fourth-grade level through college. The approach used by Schwartz and Raphael (1985) started with strong teacher involvement, but control was gradually transferred to the students. Students were led to search the context of a sentence in which the word occurred for the elements of definition needed to map a word. Eventually, the teachers provided only partial context for the word, leading the students to go to outside sources, such as dictionaries, for information to complete the maps. Finally, the teachers asked their students to write definitions, including all the features previously mapped, without actually mapping the word on paper.

Word webs are another way to represent the relationships among words graphically. Students construct these diagrams by connecting related words with lines. They do not require classifications of the related words. The words used for the web may be taken from material that students have read in class. Example 6.3 shows examples of word webs that could be used to teach synonyms for commonly used words.

EXAMPLE 6.2 Word Map for Definition

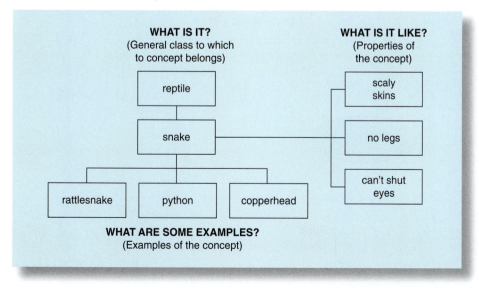

EXAMPLE 6.3 Word Webs to Teach Synonyms for Commonly Used Words

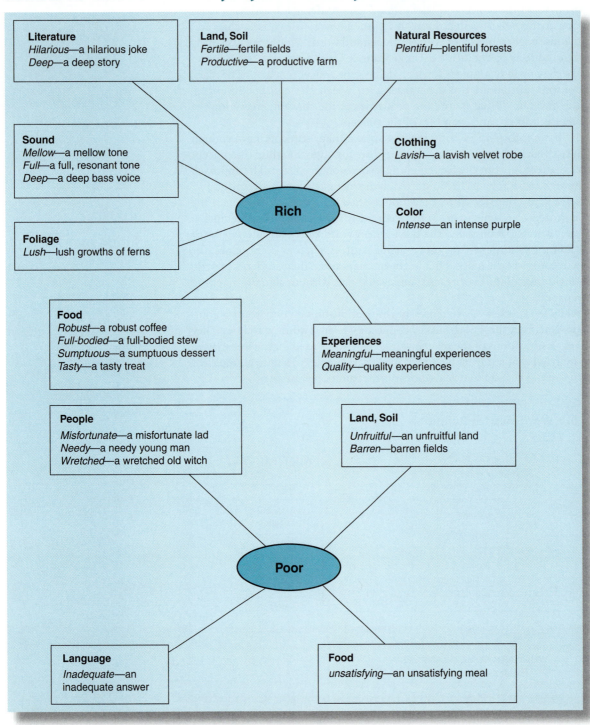

Literature
Hilarious—a hilarious joke
Deep—a deep story

Land, Soil
Fertile—fertile fields
Productive—a productive farm

Natural Resources
Plentiful—plentiful forests

Sound
Mellow—a mellow tone
Full—a full, resonant tone
Deep—a deep bass voice

Clothing
Lavish—a lavish velvet robe

Color
Intense—an intense purple

Foliage
Lush—lush growths of ferns

Rich

Food
Robust—a robust coffee
Full-bodied—a full-bodied stew
Sumptuous—a sumptuous dessert
Tasty—a tasty treat

Experiences
Meaningful—meaningful experiences
Quality—quality experiences

People
Misfortunate—a misfortunate lad
Needy—a needy young man
Wretched—a wretched old witch

Land, Soil
Unfruitful—an unfruitful land
Barren—barren fields

Poor

Language
Inadequate—an
inadequate answer

Food
unsatisfying—an unsatisfying meal

Semantic Feature Analysis

Semantic feature analysis is a technique that can help students understand the uniqueness of a word as well as its relationships to other words (Johnson and Pearson, 1984; Graves, 2006). To perform such an analysis, the teacher lists, in a column on the board or a chart, some known words with common properties. Then the students generate a list of features possessed by the various items in the list. A feature needs to apply to only one item to be listed. The teacher writes these features in a row across the top of the board or chart, and students fill in the cells of the resulting matrix with pluses or minuses to indicate the presence or absence of each feature.

Example 6.4 shows a partial matrix developed by children for various buildings. "Walls" and "doors" were other features the children suggested for the matrix; they were omitted from the example only to save space. Both of these features received a plus for each building, an outcome that emphasized the similarities of the terms *jail*, *garage*, *museum*, and *church*.

The children discussed the terms as they filled in the matrix. In the places where the question marks occur, the children said, "Sometimes it may have that, but not always. It doesn't have to have it." The group discussion brought out much information about each building listed and served to expand the children's existing schemata.

Students can continue to expand such a matrix after initially filling it out by adding words that share some of the listed features. For example, the children added *grocery store* to the list of buildings in Example 6.4 because it shared the walls and doors, and they added other features showing characteristics that differentiate it from the other buildings, such as *food*, *clerks*, and *checkout counters*. After gaining experience with these matrices, children may begin to realize that some words have different degrees of the same feature. At this time, the teacher may want to introduce a numerical system of coding, using 0 for *none*, 1 for *some*, 2 for *much*, and 3 for *all*. Under the feature "fear," for example, *scared* might be coded with a 1, whereas *terrified* might be coded with a 3.

Use of Dictionaries and Thesauruses

The dictionary can be an excellent source for discovering meanings of unfamiliar words, particularly for determining the appropriate meanings of words that have

Visit your Student Website to link to the lesson "Using Word Webs to Teach Synonyms for Commonly Used Words," designed for grades 6–8, or go directly to the Read•Write•Think site at http://www.readwritethink.org.

EXAMPLE 6.4 Semantic Feature Analysis Chart

	barred windows	exhibits	steeple	cross	cars	lift-up doors	guards	oil stains
jail	+	−	−	−	−	−	+	−
garage	?	−	−	−	+	+	−	+
museum	?	+	−	−	?	−	+	−
church	−	−	+	+		−	−	−

TEACHING TIP

Dictionary Use

You should not simply assume that being able to recite a dictionary definition means that students actually understand the word's meaning. You should point out the potential problems with dictionary definitions and should model strategies for determining word meaning.

Students need to know that they should consider the context surrounding a word, read the different dictionary definitions, and choose the definition that makes the most sense in the context. If you don't tell them this, they will have a strong tendency to read only the first dictionary definition and try to force it into the context. You can model the choice of the correct definition for your students so that they can see what the task is. Students will then need to practice the task under your supervision. As Nagy (1988) points out, combining a definitional approach to vocabulary instruction with a contextual approach is more effective than using a definitional approach in isolation. Sentences that illustrate meanings and uses of the defined words can help immensely. Be sure that the students can use the new words in meaningful sentences before deciding that they know the words' meanings.

multiple definitions or specific, technical definitions. Words that have the greatest number of different meanings, such as *run* and *bank*, are frequently very common. Either print or computerized dictionaries can be used. Handheld computerized dictionaries are as portable as print dictionaries.

LITERATURE   Sometimes students learn to recognize words by rote, but do not know their meanings. This situation is found on the first page of Patricia MacLachlan's *More Perfect Than the Moon*, a children's book in which third-grader Cassie says, "I will have to look up the meaning of *ecstatic*. But I can spell it." Teachers could include this book in a read-aloud session to introduce dictionary use.

There are some problems related to dictionary use. Many definitions are short and abstract, with no concrete examples or information repeated in different words (Rhoder and Huerster, 2002). The student may also have to look up other words that are in the definition in order to decipher the meaning expressed in the definition. Teaching word meanings through dictionary use has been widely criticized for these and other reasons. Nevertheless, as research shows, it is a useful technique for vocabulary development if it is applied properly (Graves and Prenn, 1986). Chapter 11 presents information about the mechanics of dictionary use. Chapter 4 discusses using the dictionary for word recognition.

The model activities in the "Putting It into Practice" features, "Appropriate Dictionary Definitions" and "Multiple Meanings of Words," are good to use for practice immediately after instruction in dictionary use and for later independent practice.

Students can also use dictionaries to study **etymology,** the origin and history of words (discussed in more detail next). Dictionaries often give the origin of a word in brackets after the phonetic respelling (although not all dictionaries do this in the same way), and archaic or obsolete definitions are frequently given and labeled so that students can see how words have changed.

A thesaurus is also extremely useful for word study with students in grade 3 and above. A thesaurus provides synonyms and antonyms for words. Thesauruses are available for different levels of students. For example, McGraw-Hill publishes the *Young Learner's Thesaurus with Illustrations* that would be good to introduce use of the thesaurus to young elementary students. It has pictures for many of the words, and it provides example sentences for each synonym's meaning, making it easier for students to choose the appropriate synonym for their needs.

Students need to know that synonyms are grouped by part of speech and different multiple meanings of the target word in thesauruses. Students need to

Appropriate Dictionary Definitions

Write the following sentences on the board. Ask your students to find the dictionary definition of *sharp* that fits each sentence. You may ask them to jot down each definition and have a whole-class or small-group discussion about each one after all meanings have been located, or you may wish to discuss each meaning as it is located. The students may read other definitions for *sharp* in the dictionary and generate sentences for these as well.

1. Katherine's knife was very sharp.
2. There is a sharp curve in the road up ahead.
3. I hope that, when I am seventy, my mind is as sharp as my grandmother's is.
4. We are leaving at two o'clock sharp.

find the ones that fit the use of the target word in a particular context. Some of the listings are words that are only very similar in meaning to the target word. For example, synonyms for *leap* include *hop* and *vault*, but all three would be unlikely to fit into a single context. Some synonyms are for connotations of the word that may be unfamiliar to students and need to be explained.

After initial instruction about the thesaurus, teachers can offer students practice by using games such as Synonym Tic-Tac-Toe, in which students have to find a vertical, horizontal, or diagonal line of synonyms in a tic-tac-toe grid in order to win (Mountain, 2007/2008). Gifted students may work individually and other students in pairs to prepare grids for classmates to use. Students can also develop synonym and antonym word lines, continuums that indicate degrees of meaning. An example of such a word line is found in this chapter under the section "Analogies and Word Lines." Another enjoyable activity is having students complete a crossword puzzle–type grid that requires only filling in synonyms for a key word that is already inserted. Blanks are provided for the synonyms that intersect the key word (Mountain, 2007/2008). Example 6.5 shows a completed synonym crossword.

EXAMPLE 6.5 Synonym Crossword

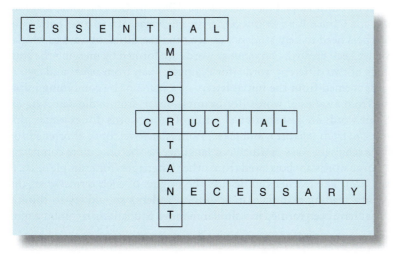

Multiple Meanings of Words

Give your students a list of sentences, drawn from their textbooks, that contain words with specialized meanings for that subject. Have them use the dictionary or the textbook's glossary to discover the specialized meanings that fit the context of the sentences. After your students have completed the task independently, go over the sentences with them and discuss reasons for right and wrong responses.

The material that you give to the students may look something like this:

Directions: Some words mean different things in your textbooks from what they mean in everyday conversation. In each of the following sentences, find the special meanings for the words and write these meanings on the lines provided.

1. Frederick Smith has decided to *run* for mayor.

   _____

2. The park was near the *mouth* of the Little Bear River.

   _____

3. The management of the company was unable to avert a *strike*.

   _____

4. That song is hard to sing because of the high *pitch* of several notes.

   _____

5. That number is written in *base* 2.

   _____

LITERATURE

The teacher may read the book *Thesaurus Rex* by Laya Steinberg to students. Using this book as a model, groups of students can then write similar books using a thesaurus as a source. By the time they finish, they should be comfortable with referring to thesauruses (Mountain, 2007/2008).

Word Origins and Histories

LITERATURE

Students in the intermediate grades can enjoy learning about the histories and origins of words and the kinds of changes that have taken place in the English language. They can learn more about etymology by studying words and definitions that appear in very old dictionaries and by studying differences between American English and British English. Some good references are *Cryptomania! Teleporting into Greek and Latin with the Cryptokids* by Edith Hope Fine, *Slangalicious: Where We Got That Crazy Lingo* by Gillian O'Reilly, and *Curious Word Origins, Sayings and Expressions* by Charles Earle Funk.

Teachers need to help students understand the different ways in which English words have been created. *Portmanteau* words are formed by merging the sounds and meanings of two different words (for example, *smog*, from *smoke* and *fog*). *Acronyms* are words formed from the initial letters of a name or by combining initial letters or parts from a series of words (for example, *radar*, from *ra*dio *d*etecting *a*nd *r*anging). Some words are just shortened forms of other words (for example, *phone*, from *telephone*; *flu*, from *influenza*; and *piano*, from *pianoforte*). Both shortened forms and acronyms represent ways in which our language has become more compact (Richler, 1996). Some words are borrowed from other languages (for example, *lasso*, from the Spanish *lazo*). The teacher can discuss the origins of such terms when they occur in students' reading materials. In addition, students should try to think of other words that have been formed in a similar manner. Students can combine morphemic

Visit Read•Write•Think at http://www.readwritethink.org (or link from the Student Website) to view a lesson plan for middle school students, entitled "Investigating Names to Explore Personal History and Cultural Traditions." This lesson is likely to interest students in word origins because of the personal connections.

analysis and etymology by studying words derived from Latin or Greek word parts, such as *prescription* and *scripture*. They can be encouraged to think of other examples and asked to use the derived words in sentences. The teacher may also wish to contribute other examples from familiar sources.

Iwicki (1992) and her colleagues found that they could enhance vocabulary learning through an activity called Vocabulary Connections. They put the vocabulary terms and definitions on wall charts and then asked students to relate each term to situations in the literature selection they were reading and to situations in previously read books. For example, the word *pandemonium* is used in Marlene Shyler's *Welcome Home, Jelly Bean*. It can later be related to events in Walter Farley's *The Black Stallion*. This activity can be motivational and can encourage use of higher-level thinking skills.

LITERATURE

Figurative Language

Figurative language, or nonliteral language, can be a barrier to understanding written selections. Children tend to interpret literally many expressions that have meanings different from the sums of the meanings of the individual words. For example, the expression "the teeth of the wind" does not mean that the wind actually has teeth, nor does "a blanket of fog" denote a conventional blanket. Context clues indicate the meanings of such phrases in the same ways that they cue the meanings of individual words. English-language learners have special difficulties interpreting figurative language because they lack background exposure to such usage in English (Palmer, Shackelford, Miller, and Leclere, 2006/2007).

DIVERSITY

Adults often assume that students have had exposure to expressions that in fact are unfamiliar to them. Students need substantial help in order to comprehend figurative language. Even basal readers present many of these expressions. Some common types of figurative language that can cause trouble follow.

1. **Simile**—a comparison using *like* or *as*

2. **Metaphor**—a direct comparison without the word *like* or *as*

3. **Personification**—giving the attributes of a person to an inanimate object or abstract idea

4. **Hyperbole**—an extreme exaggeration

5. **Euphemism**—substitution of a less offensive term for an unpleasant term or expression

6. **Allusion**—an indirect reference to a person, place, thing, or event considered to be known to the reader

Teaching students to recognize and understand similes is usually not too difficult because the cue words *like* and *as* signal the presence of a comparison. Metaphors, however, may cause more serious problems. A metaphor is a

SEEING IT IN PRACTICE ◀ ▣ ▶

Video Case

Revisit the Video Case "Vygotsky's Zone of Proximal Development: Increasing Cognition in an Elementary Literacy Lesson" (viewed previously for Chapter 2) to see how one teacher helps her students understand figurative expressions. Notice how she makes sure that even struggling readers understand the expressions. React to her techniques in your journal.

comparison between two unlike things that share an attribute. Sometimes students do not realize that the language in metaphors is figurative; sometimes they do not have sufficient background knowledge about one or both of the things being compared; and sometimes they simply have not learned how to interpret metaphors.

The two things compared in a metaphor may seem to be incompatible, but readers must think of past experiences with each, searching for a match in attributes that could be the basis of comparison. For example, a man might be compared to a mouse on the basis of the characteristic of timidity.

After explaining each type of figurative language, modeling its interpretation, and having students interpret it under supervision, the teacher may provide independent practice activities using material similar to that shown in "Teaching Tip: Similes and Metaphors in Literature."

Teachers can also use an activity like the one in "Putting It into Practice: Figures of Speech" to illustrate the use of a figure of speech.

Student-Centered Vocabulary-Learning Techniques

Some vocabulary-learning techniques focus on students and their individual needs and interests. Explanations of several of these techniques follow.

▶ Self-Selected Vocabulary Activities

Some educators believe that student-selected words should be included in vocabulary instruction (Brabham and Villaume, 2002; Blachowicz and Fisher, 2000). Students can locate unfamiliar words that they would like to learn in their everyday lives (for example, on signs, menus, television, and newspapers) and in their textbooks. On designated days, each student can look up a self-selected word, write its definition, and copy the context in which it was found. In turn, students can present their words, definitions, and contexts and explain why they wanted to learn these particular words. Classmates can then provide additional examples of contexts for the words that they already know. The teacher may also join the discussion and add information. Students learn from their own research and from the others in the class.

Visit the Student Website to find an example of a procedure for teaching metaphorical interpretation that Readence, Baldwin, and Head (1986, 1987) suggest.

TEACHING TIP

Similes and Metaphors in Literature

There are many examples of similes and metaphors in books that children read. For example:

- In Patricia MacLachlan's *More Perfect Than the Moon*, this simile is found on page 43: "Their words wound around us like steam from hot tea."

- David M. Schwartz's *If You Hopped Like a Frog* is a picture book that is filled with similes, such as the one in the title. An added bonus of this book is that it also conveys math and science concepts in an enjoyable manner.

- A historical novel by Ben Mikaelsen, *Red Midnight*, has this statement on page 1: "Those memories are like clouds in my mind." Many more similes are in the book to be discovered and discussed after the book has been read for pleasure or information about conditions in Guatemala in the 1980s.

- In Mark Teague's *Dear Mrs. Larue: Letters from Obedience School*, Ike writes "This is a PRISON, not a school."

- *Maniac Magee* by Jerry Spinelli contains an abundance of both similes and metaphors, such as "The book came flapping like a wounded duck," "He's paralyzed, a mouse in front of the yawning maw of a python," and "The phantom Samaritan . . . hauled him out of there like a sack of flour." All of these are found in the first nineteen pages, and there are many more throughout the book.

PUTTING IT INTO PRACTICE

Figures of Speech

Project the following image or display the cartoon on a transparency.

DENNIS the MENACE

"I hear you been through the mill.....what do they DO there?"

Source: DENNIS THE MENACE® © North America Syndicate.

Lead a discussion about the cartoon, using the following questions as a guide:

1. What does "been through the mill" really mean, as Dennis's mother used it?

2. What does Dennis think it means?

3. How is the woman likely to react to Dennis's question?

4. How does Dennis's mother probably feel about the question?

5. Can misunderstanding figurative language cause trouble at times? Why do you say so?

Have the children suggest other figurative expressions that could produce misunderstandings. Then, as a follow-up activity, let them draw funny scenes in which the misunderstandings occur.

Also have the children look for other examples in newspaper comics. Ask them to cut out the examples and bring them to school for discussion.

Ainslie (2000/2001) uses a similar technique in which she asks her students to act as word detectives who search for unknown words and share them with classmates.

According to Ruddell and Shearer (2002), "Students learn new words not by hearing them explained with other new words, but rather from ongoing and extended transaction with the words, their peers, and their teacher within the context of life and classroom experience" (p. 354). They used the Vocabulary Self-Collection Strategy as a vehicle to help at-risk middle school students to increase word awareness and word-learning strategies. The word study during the week involved such techniques as discussion, semantic mapping, and semantic feature analysis. Students chose many words from their content-area classes, but they also chose words from nonschool sources. The students chose important and challenging words, learned these words, and retained the words over time.

Several lesson plans at Read•Write• Think focus on figurative language. For example, "Figurative Language: Teaching Idioms" is designed for grades 3–5 and "Finding Figurative Language in *The Phantom Tollbooth*" is designed for grades 6–8. Go to http://www.readwritethink .org or link from the Student Website.

Video Cases

View the Video Case "Classroom Motivation: Strategies for Engaging Today's Students." What do you think of the teacher's technique of teaching vocabulary by having the students identify difficult words in the material they are reading? Why did he have them highlight the entire sentence in which the word occurred?

Next, view the main video and bonus videos of the Video Case "Metacognition: Helping Students Become Strategic Learners." What strategies did the teacher have students use to learn vocabulary? How was her approach similar to and different from the techniques used in the classroom motivation Video Case?

Visit Read•Write•Think (at http://www.readwritethink.org or link from the Student Website) to view a middle school lesson plan entitled "Choosing, Chatting, and Collecting: Vocabulary Self-Collection Strategy" that uses a vocabulary self-collection strategy and word maps, as described here.

Video Case

View the Video Case "Using Information Processing Strategies: A Middle School Science Lesson." Notice how the teacher has students keep a vocabulary notebook with the word, the definition, and an example. Also notice how class demonstration is used to make the concept behind the word clearer to the students. Do you think this technique will result in complete understanding of the concepts presented? Why, or why not?

Rosenbaum (2001) asked students to self-select words and used eight techniques for clarifying the meanings of these words for students. She developed a word map for her students to use daily with words they located during independent reading. They included "synonyms, brief descriptions, examples and nonexamples, rephrasing, repetition, associations, and unique expression" (Rosenbaum, 2001, p. 45), techniques that Harmon (1998) had identified to use for this purpose.

Barger (2006) recommends using word jars for which students write words that they find in environmental print on slips of paper and put them in a jar. He uses the book *Donavan's Word Jar* to introduce and illustrate this technique. Students are asked to discuss the meanings of the words they find with their family members. His third graders learned words like *artificial* and *scrumptious* from this activity. These words can be included on bulletin board and Word Walls, to be used as a basis of other activities.

▶ Word Banks or Vocabulary Notebooks

Students can form their own word banks by writing on index cards words that they have learned, the words' definitions, and sentences showing the words in meaningful contexts. They may also want to illustrate the words or include personal associations with or reactions to the words. Students can carry their word banks around and practice the words in spare moments, such as while waiting for the bus or the dentist or at home with their families. In the classroom, the word banks can be used in word games and in classification and other instructional activities.

Vocabulary notebooks are useful for recording new words found in general reading or words heard in conversations or on radio or television. New words may be alphabetized in the notebooks and defined, illustrated, and processed in much the same way as word-bank words. "Seeing It in Practice: Video Case" shows one teacher's use of vocabulary notebooks.

Both word banks and vocabulary notebooks can help students maintain a record of their increasing vocabularies. Generally, word banks are used in primary grades and notebooks in intermediate grades and above, but there are no set limits for either technique.

Word Play

Word play is an enjoyable way to learn more about words. It can provide multiple exposures to words in different contexts that are important to complete word learning. Silly songs and rhymes are among the types of word play that "promote a love of words" (Brabham and Villaume, 2002, p. 265). Word play requires students to examine word parts and context and consider meanings. It results in active learning and meaning construction and encourages practice with words (Graves, 2006; Blachowicz and Fisher, 2004).

Riddles are a very effective form of word play. To use riddles, children must interact verbally with others. To create riddles, they have to organize information and decide on significant details. Riddles can help children move from the literal to the interpretive level of understanding (Gale, 1982). Riddles provide both context clues and high-interest material. Both of these factors promote vocabulary learning (Tyson and Mountain, 1982). Both riddles and puns require an awareness of the multiple meanings of words. Using this awareness to create such word play with others can expand the understanding of both the creator and his or her companions.

Riddles can be classified into several categories: those based on homonyms, on rhyming words, on double meanings, and on figurative/literal meanings, for example. (See the section "Special Words" later in this chapter.) An example of a homonym riddle is presented in "Putting It into Practice: Word Play."

Riddles work best with children who are at least six years old (Gale, 1982), and they continue to be especially effective with children through eleven years of age. After that, interest in this form of word play wanes.

"Putting It into Practice: Word Play" presents some ways to engage students in word play.

The use of comic strips and cartoons to work on meaning vocabulary is motivational to students. The figurative-language activity in the Putting It in Practice on page 205 that makes use of a "Dennis the Menace" comic is one example. Another example is the use of cartoons in *Vocabulary Cartoons: Kids Learn a Word a Minute and Never Forget It*, which presents a word, its pronunciation, its meaning, a sound-alike word to offer a mnemonic device when paired with a cartoon, and examples of the word in context. A page from this book is shown in Example 6.6 on page 209.

Combining Strategies

As we have noted, many teachers and researchers have developed successful programs that combine a number of specific vocabulary instruction strategies.

One technique that has been successfully used to teach important content-area words, as well as general vocabulary, involves having students focus on multiple aspects of the vocabulary words: word meanings; differences in words; the words in context; roots, derivatives, and variants of words; and parts of speech of the words

Time for Reflection

Some teachers think that having students learn the dictionary definitions of weekly teacher-chosen vocabulary words is a good approach to vocabulary instruction. Others believe in more use of student-centered methods to help students acquire meaning vocabulary.

What do *you* think, and why?

Time for Reflection

What forms of word play are particularly effective in enhancing vocabulary development?

Why do *you* believe this is so?

Word Play

Try these word-play activities with your students.

1. Have them write words in ways that express their meanings; for example, they may write *backward* as *drawkcab*, or *up* slanting upward and *down* slanting downward.

2. Ask them silly questions containing new words. Example: "Would you have a terrarium for dinner? Why or why not?"

3. Discuss what puns are and give some examples. Then ask your students to make up or find puns to bring to class. Let them explain the play on words to classmates who do not understand it. Example: "What is black and white and read all over?" Answer: A newspaper (word play on the homonyms *red* and *read*). You may want to use *Let the Fun Begin: Wacky What-Do-You-Get Jokes, Playful Puns, and More (Make Me Laugh!)* by Scott K. Peterson, Rick Walton, Ann Walton, Diane Burns, and Clint Burns or *Punny Places: Jokes to Make You Happy (Make Me Laugh)* by June Swanson as a reference for you and your students.

4. Use Hink Pinks, Hinky Pinkies, and Hinkety Pinketies—give students two-word terms and ask them to supply rhyming definitions composed of word pairs that have one, two, and three rhyming syllables, respectively. Give a definition, tell whether it is a Hink Pink, a Hinky Pinky, or a Hinkety Pinkety, and let the children guess the expression. Then let the students make up their own terms. Several examples follow.

Hink Pink: Unhappy father—Sad dad
Hinky Pinky: Late group of celebrators—Tardy party
Hinkety Pinkety: Yearly handbook—Annual manual

5. Have students go on a scavenger hunt in a reading selection for words that fit word meaning clues, such as means the same as . . . ; *means the opposite of . . . ; looks the same, but means something different from . . .* ; and so forth). Tell students to write the words beside the appropriate clues. You also could have them go on a scavenger hunt for context clues to the meanings of specified words and write the clues beside the words.

6. Use crossword puzzles that highlight new words in your students' textbooks or other instructional materials.

7. Use a game suggested by Mountain (2002) in which students start with four syllables on two poker chips—two prefixes on one and two roots on the other, or two suffixes on one and two roots on the other. The students flip the two chips until they form four different words. They discuss the meanings of the words and then place them in appropriate blanks in a cloze passage. (See Chapter 2 for an explanation of cloze passages.) Later the students can make their own Flip-Chip pairs and cloze passages.

8. You can also use commercial games. Lakeshore Publishers offer several board games that provide good practice activities, including *Multiple Meanings Around the World; Synonym & Antonym Gold Rush; Context Clues: Mystery Mansion; and Prefix/ Suffix Cosmic Conquest.*

(Richek, 2005). A teacher may ask students to discuss and write about similarities and differences in two specified terms (Bromley, 2007). A study by Boulware-Gooden, Carreker, Thornhill, and Joshi (2007) offered support for the importance of emphasizing relationships among words. The study showed that vocabulary instruction involving use of synonyms, antonyms, and related words is more effective in creating better scores on vocabulary measures than simply writing the words and using them in sentences.

EXAMPLE 6.6 Use of Vocabulary Cartoons

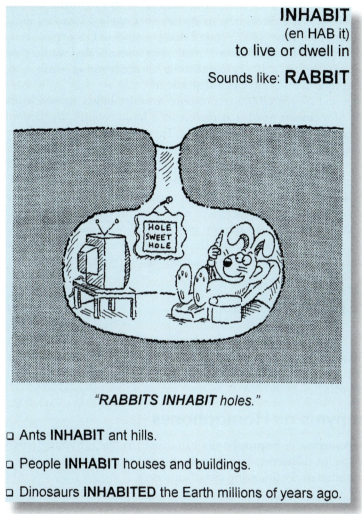

Source: Sam Burchers, Max Burchers, and Bryan Burchers, *Vocabulary Cartoons: Kids Learn a Word a Minute and Never Forget It* (Punta Gorda, Fla.: New Monic Books, 1998), 19.

Graves (2006) has developed a comprehensive vocabulary program with four components: "(1) providing rich and varied language experiences; (2) teaching individual words; (3) teaching word-learning strategies; and (4) fostering word consciousness" (p. 5). Language experiences include taking part in discussions, listening to books being read and stories being told, reading widely, and writing. Individual words can be taught by providing definitional and contextual information and by offering multiple encounters with words. Word-learning strategies include teaching use of context, use of morphemic analysis (recognizing meaningful word parts), and use of the dictionary. In a study that applied Graves's approach, Baumann and his colleagues (2007) found that the students increased their expressive and receptive vocabularies. Students used more sophisticated words, they had more interest in vocabulary and a better attitude toward learning words, and they were able to use vocabulary strategies independently.

Nilsen and Nilsen (2003) recommend a source-based approach that involves the study of a chosen word that represents a basic concept, its dictionary definition, its etymology, and its figurative uses. They show how, when studying cloth, the word *spindle* has many derivative words that have meanings metaphorically related to it. Some of the common ones are *spin* (which has multiple meanings), as well as *spinster, homespun, tailspin*, and *spin-off*. When considering the weaving of cloth, the word *shuttle* can be presented through bringing an actual shuttle to class and letting the students experience the operation. After grasping the literal definition, they can examine such originally metaphoric uses as *shuttlecock, shuttle bus, space shuttle*, and others. This technique can include the webbing of related words in a way that will help students to see the connections and remember word meanings.

Special Words

Many types of words require teachers' careful attention when planning vocabulary instruction. Five special types that we have not discussed in detail earlier are homonyms or homophones, homographs, synonyms, antonyms, and newly coined words.

Homonyms or Homophones

Many **homonyms** or **homophones** can cause trouble for young readers because they are spelled differently but pronounced the same way. Some common homonyms are found in the following sets of sentences.

> I want to *be* a doctor. That *bee* almost stung me.
>
> She has *two* brothers. Will you go *to* the show with me? I have *too* much work to do.
>
> I can *hear* the bird singing. Maurice, you sit over *here*.
>
> Mark has a *red* scarf. Have you *read* that book?
>
> I *ate* all of my supper. We have *eight* dollars to spend.

LITERATURE

Fred Gwynne's *The King Who Rained* and *A Chocolate Moose for Dinner* both have homonyms in their titles, as well as throughout their texts. Pettersen (1988) suggests letting students look for homonyms in all of their reading materials. Students can construct lists of homonym pairs that mean something to them because they discovered at least one of the qualifying words in each pair themselves. If you would like to try this for yourself, the paragraph you are currently reading is a good one to use

Homonym Activities

You can use the following activities to vary your work with homonyms:

1. Have your students play a card game to work on meanings of homonyms. Print homonyms on cards and let the students take turns drawing from each other, as in the game of Old Maid. A student who has a pair of homonyms can put them down if he or she gives a correct sentence using each word. The student who claims the most pairs wins.

2. Have your students web homonyms in the following way:

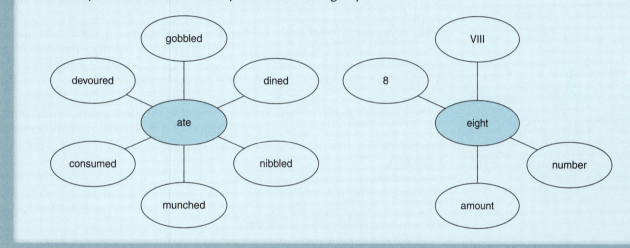

as a starter for such an exercise. (Hint: *all-awl* is one example.) Expanding Pettersen's activity to require the use of each homonym in a meaningful sentence is one way to keep the focus on meaning.

Homographs

Homographs are words that have identical spellings but not the same meanings. Their pronunciations may or may not be the same. Readers must use context clues to identify the correct pronunciations, parts of speech, and meanings of homographs. Examples include

I will *read* my newspaper. (pronounced as though it were *reed*) I have *read* my newspaper. (pronounced like the color *red*)

I have a *contract* signed by the president. (noun: pronounced con′/trakt; means a document) I didn't know it would *contract* as it cooled. (*verb:* pronounced cƏn/trakt′; means to reduce in size)

LITERATURE

The books by Fred Gwynne mentioned in the section on homonyms are also rich sources of homographs.

Synonyms

STANDARDS/
ASSESSMENTS ☑

Synonyms are words that have the same or very similar meanings. Work with synonyms can help expand students' vocabularies. This instruction may be especially important because the vocabulary questions on high-stakes tests often have synonyms for the words in the multiple-choice answers from which they must choose (Mountain, 2007/2008).

Study of the sports page of the newspaper for ways in which writers express the ideas of *win* and *lose* can be a good way to introduce synonyms. The teacher should use this material to show students the way that synonyms can convey different shades of meaning. For example, the headlines "Cats Maul Dogs" and "Cats Squeak by Dogs" both mean that the Cats beat the Dogs, but one indicates a win by a large margin, whereas the other indicates a close game. In addition, some synonyms are on varying levels of formality (for example, *dog* and *pooch*) (Breen, 1989).

LITERATURE

Sylvester and the Magic Pebble by William Steig offers several good opportunities for discussion of synonyms used in describing the rain's cessation, the lion's movement, and the lion's feelings. In *Alexander and the Terrible, Horrible, No Good, Very Bad Day* by Judith Viorst, synonyms are right there in the title, ready for discussion.

A teacher can also provide a stimulus word and have students find as many synonyms as they can. The class can discuss the small differences in meaning of some words suggested as synonyms. For example, the teacher can ask, "Would you rather be called *pretty* or *beautiful*? Why?"

Word webs of synonyms, such as the two webs for *rich* and *poor* in Example 6.3, can be developed by the class or individual students. Class webs may be displayed on charts in the room and added to as students locate new synonyms. In grade 3 and higher grades, students may use thesauruses to locate synonyms. If they do, the fact that there are shades of meaning in various synonyms that are important to usage must be discussed.

Word-processing programs provide a good vehicle for vocabulary instruction. Teachers can give students files containing paragraphs with certain words used repeatedly. The students may use the find-and-replace function to replace all instances of a chosen word with a synonym and then read the paragraph to see if the synonym makes sense in each place it appears. If it does not, the students can delete the synonym in the inappropriate places and either choose more appropriate replacements for the original word or put the original word back into the paragraph. Students can consult the thesaurus feature that comes with many word-processing programs for assistance. Then they can read the file again to see if the words chosen convey the correct meanings and if the variation in word choices makes the paragraph more interesting to read.

A paragraph such as the following one could be a starting place:

Shonda had to run to the store for her mother because, just before the party, her mother got a run in her pantyhose. Shonda had to listen to her mother run on and on about her run of bad luck that day before she was able to leave the house. When she arrived at the store, she saw her uncle, who told her he had decided to run for office, delaying her progress further. She finally bought the last pair of pantyhose in the store. There must have been a run on them earlier in the day.

See Chapter 13 for more information on computer use.

Further material on teaching synonyms can be located in the sections on word webs and on dictionaries and thesauruses in this chapter.

Antonyms

Antonyms are two words that have opposite meanings. Their meanings are not merely different; they are balanced against each other on a particular feature. In the continuum *cold, cool, tepid, warm,* and *hot,* for example, *cold* is the opposite of *hot,* being as close to the extreme in a negative direction as *hot* is in a positive direction. Thus, *cold* and *hot* are antonyms. *Tepid* and *hot* are different, but they are not opposites. *Cool* and *warm* are also antonyms. Similarly, *buy* and *sell* are antonyms, because one is the reverse of the other. But *buy* and *give* are not antonyms because no exchange of money is involved in the giving. The words are different, but they are not opposites. The use of opposition (citing antonyms) in defining terms can help to establish the extremes of a word's meaning and provide its shadings and nuances.

Big Dog … Little Dog: A Bedtime Story by P. D. Eastman provides students with examples of antonyms to discuss in an interesting context. Teachers may wish to locate other trade books that could be used for meaningful exposures to antonyms. LITERATURE

New Words

New words are constantly being coined to meet the changing needs of society and are possible sources of difficulty. Teachers can have their students search for these words in their reading and television viewing and then compile a dictionary of words so new that they are not yet in standard dictionaries. The class may have to discuss these words to derive an accurate definition for each one, considering all the contexts in which the students have heard or seen it. These new words may have been formed from Latin and Greek word elements, from current slang, or by shortening or combining older words.

Some new words are not coined to describe new concepts, but to use language that sets a group apart from others. If these words are used frequently enough over time, they will likely make their way into the dictionary. For insight into how new dictionary entries may originate, you may want to have the students read *Frindle* by Andrew Clements. LITERATURE

SUMMARY

Acquiring a meaning vocabulary involves developing labels for the schemata, or organized knowledge structures, that a person possesses. Because vocabulary is an important component of reading comprehension, direct instruction in vocabulary can enhance reading achievement. Although pinpointing the age at which children learn the precise meanings of words is difficult, children generally make more discriminating responses about word meanings as they grow older, and vocabulary generally grows with increasing age.

There are many ways to approach vocabulary instruction. The best techniques link new terms to the students' background knowledge, help them expand their word knowledge, actively involve them in learning, help them become independent in acquiring vocabulary, provide repetition of the words, and have them use the words meaningfully. Techniques that cause students to work harder to learn words tend to aid retention. Teachers may need to spend time on schema development before working with some vocabulary terms.

Vocabulary development should be emphasized throughout the day, not just in reading and language classes. Students can learn much vocabulary from the teacher's modeling of vocabulary use. Context clues, morphemic analysis, categorization, analogies and word lines, semantic maps and word webs, semantic feature analysis, dictionary use, study of word origins and histories, study of figurative language, a number of student-centered learning techniques, word play, and combinations of these techniques can be helpful in vocabulary instruction.

Some special types of words can cause comprehension problems for children. They include homonyms, homographs, synonyms, antonyms, and newly coined words.

For your journal . . . .

1. Reflect on the value of context clues for vocabulary development.

2. Record your reactions to each of the Video Cases that you viewed as you read this chapter. What did you learn about vocabulary instruction from each one?

. . . . and your portfolio

1. Plan a lesson on dictionary use that requires the students to locate the meaning of a word that fits the context surrounding that word.

2. Plan a lesson designed to teach the concept of "justice" to a group of sixth-grade students.

3. After collecting examples of figurative language from a variety of sources, use them as the basis for a lesson on interpreting figurative language.

Comprehension: Part 1

7

KEY VOCABULARY

Pay close attention to these terms when they appear in the chapter.

anticipation guides

cloze procedure

Investigative Questioning Procedure (InQuest)

K-W-L teaching model

knowledge-based processing

metacognition

multiple intelligences

reciprocal teaching

relative clauses

schema (plural, schemata)

semantic webbing

story grammar

story mapping

text-based processing

think-alouds

The objective of all readers should be comprehension of what they read. Some readers, however, don't understand that reading is not just decoding, but that the material being read should also make sense to them (Cartwright, 2006). Comprehension involves the abilities to explain, interpret, apply, have perspective, empathize, and have self-knowledge (Wiggins and McTighe, 1998). It is an evolving process that often begins before a book is opened, changes as the material is read, and continues to change even after the book is completed. This developmental nature of comprehension is enhanced when the reader interacts with others about aspects of the material after reading it (Shanklin and Rhodes, 1989). Therefore, classroom interaction related to reading materials is important to comprehension development.

As Pearson and Johnson (1978) point out, "Reading comprehension is at once a unitary process and a set of discrete processes" (p. 227). We discuss the individual processes separately, yet teachers must not lose sight of the fact that there are many overlaps and interrelationships among the processes. Strategies are rarely used alone, and the boundaries between strategies are indistinct (Villaume and Brabham, 2002).

Close relationships even exist between comprehension and decoding. Research has shown that good comprehenders are able to decode quickly and accurately ("A Talk with Marilyn Adams," 1991). Thus, developing decoding strategies to the automatic stage is important. Teachers should always keep in mind, however, that use of decoding strategies is merely a means of accessing the meaning of the written material. When good decoders have problems with comprehension, for example, they need help in developing language proficiency and listening comprehension.

Allington (2002) reported studies of effective teachers of reading and writing. These teachers demonstrated for their students strategies used by good readers. They spent much of the school day having their students actually read and write, giving the students a chance to internalize the skills and strategies that they had been taught. Much of the reading was done in materials that the students could read with accuracy, fluency, and understanding. The lowest achievers benefited most from this approach.

Skilled readers are strategic readers. To assist students in becoming strategic readers, Villaume and Brabham (2002) see the need for explicit instruction that is not heavily scripted but is *clear*, involving modeling of strategies, supervised practice of them, and follow-up assistance that clarifies areas where students may encounter problems. Such effective comprehension instruction is presented in a logical and purposeful manner; the interrelated strategies are addressed over time; and learning is monitored, with instruction based on exhibited student needs. Strategy instruction should center on tasks that are of appropriate difficulty for the particular students, and practice with the strategies should be done in the context of real-world tasks. Practice with a strategy should continue until the strategy becomes automatic (Pressley, 1995; Rhoder, 2002).

STRUGGLING READER/ INTERVENTION

To provide tasks that are of appropriate difficulty for particular students, teachers must plan differentiated instruction (see Chapter 2). The level of the content may be varied for different students to provide material that is on their own reading levels; teaching procedures may be modified by spending more time explaining and scaffolding with some students; and assignments may be varied in difficulty to allow students to work at their own levels on the strategy being taught. Scaffolding provides support to students as they perform tasks and nudges them to do things that they might not succeed at or even attempt on their own. Probing questions and teacher prompts are types of scaffolding (McIntyre, 2007). Teachers need to make adaptations for all levels of students, from struggling readers to gifted students. To be successful, some students may need to work with partners or in small groups. High-achieving students need challenging material and assignments. Assignments for gifted students should not simply be longer, but should require higher cognitive processes. The challenge level should fit the students' abilities (McMackin and Witherell, 2005).

Comprehension-strategy instruction should often make use of the students' own textbooks or trade books they are reading. The teacher should tell the students what strategy they are going to learn and how it will help them in their reading. Then the teacher should describe the strategy, model it, provide teacher-guided practice with it, and offer cooperative and independent practice opportunities (Neufeld, 2005/2006). This procedure allows for a gradual transfer of responsibility from the teacher to the student. Baumann, Hooten, and White (1999) recommend that about one-fifth of each reading period should be spent on explicit strategy instruction, and the rest should be spent on reading, responding to, analyzing, and discussing the reading material.

Readers approach a text with much background knowledge concerning their world, and they use this knowledge along with the text to construct the meanings represented by the printed material to meet their purposes for reading. To access the information supplied by the text, they must use decoding, or word-recognition, strategies (covered in Chapters 4 and 5) and comprehension strategies (covered in Chapter 6, this chapter, and Chapter 8).

This chapter discusses the importance of the interaction among the reader, the reading situation, and the text to comprehension. It explores the importance of the reader's prior knowledge, the reader's purposes for reading, the audience for reading, and the characteristics of the text to be read. It also presents strategies to be used before, during, and after reading.

This chapter is a logical continuation of Chapter 6, "Meaning Vocabulary," because vocabulary knowledge is a vital component of comprehension. Therefore, these chapters cannot truly be considered separately and are divided here only for convenience of presentation. The coverage of the types of comprehension in Chapter 8 is also a continuation of the topic, separated only for ease of treatment.

ANTICIPATION/REACTION GUIDE

AFTER
C or **I** (for initial
A or **D** answers)
A or **D**
(for initial **?** answers)

Directions: Before you read this chapter, complete the following anticipation/reaction guide. In the space before each statement, write **A** if you agree; **D** if you disagree; or **?** if you don't know. After you have read the chapter, complete the guide again to show what you have discovered in the chapter. In the space after each statement, mark whether you were initially correct (with a **C**) or incorrect (with an **I**). Write the letter for the correct answer (**A**) or (**D**) in the space for the statements that you initially marked with a question mark (**?**).

1. Each schema that a person has represents what the person knows about a particular concept and the interrelationships among the known pieces of information.

2. Previews for stories that build background related to the stories have a positive effect on comprehension.

3. Character journals are journals filled with character sketches.

4. Comprehension-monitoring techniques are metacognitive strategies.

5. Punctuation marks do not function as clues to sentence meaning.

6. Reading comprehension involves relating textual information to preexisting knowledge structures.

7. Comprehension strategies should be taught in a way that emphasizes their application when students are actually reading connected discourse.

8. Less-able readers may rely too heavily on either text-based or knowledge-based processing.

9. Story grammar activities can increase students' understanding of story structure and serve as a basis for questioning.

10. Relative clauses cause few comprehension problems for readers.

11. Punctuation marks are clues to pauses and pitch changes.

12. Semantic webbing involves systematically deleting words from a printed passage.

13. Think-alouds are useless in teaching metacognitive strategies.

14. The K-W-L teaching model for expository text is strictly a prereading strategy.

CHAPTER 7 ORGANIZATION

Comprehension: Part 1

The Reader

The Reader's Schemata
Other Aspects Related to the Reader

The Reading Situation

Purposes for Reading
Audience
Importance of Task to Student
The Physical Context

The Text

Sentence Comprehension
Organizational Patterns
Types of Text
Helping English-Language Learners Comprehend Text

Interaction of the Reader, the Reading Situation, and the Text

Prereading Strategies and Activities
During-Reading Strategies and Activities
Postreading Strategies and Activities
General Strategies and Activities
Working with Struggling Readers

The Reader

This section discusses factors related to the reader that affect his or her comprehension, including the reader's background knowledge, sensory and perceptual abilities, thinking abilities, word-recognition strategies, and affective aspects, such as attitudes, self-concepts, and interests.

The Reader's Schemata

Educators have long believed that if a reader has not been exposed to a writer's language patterns or to the objects and concepts to which the writer refers, the reader's comprehension will be incomplete. This belief is supported by theories holding that reading comprehension involves relating textual information to preexisting knowledge structures, or schemata (Pearson et al., 1979). **Schemata** are a person's organized clusters of concepts related to objects, places, actions, or events. Each schema represents a person's knowledge about a particular concept and the interrelationships among the known pieces of information. For example, a schema for *car* may include a person's knowledge about the car's construction, its appearance, and its operation, as well as many other facts about it. Two people may have quite different schemata for the same basic concept; for example, a racecar driver's schema for *car* (or, to be more exact, his or her cluster of schemata about cars) will differ from that of a seven-year-old child.

SEEING IT IN PRACTICE ◄■►

Video Case

Revisit the Video Case "Bilingual Education: An Elementary Two-Way Immersion Program" in which concept development is being nurtured in both Spanish and English. How is this particularly helpful for English language learners? What is a major obstacle for these learners that these teachers are addressing? Write your answers in your journal.

▸ Types of Schemata

People may have schemata for objects, events, abstract ideas, story structure, processes, emotions, roles, conventions of writing, and so forth. In fact, "Schemata can represent knowledge at all levels—from ideologies and cultural truths... to knowledge about what patterns of excitations are associated with what letters of the alphabet" (Rumelhart, 1981, p. 13). Each schema that a person has is incomplete, as though it contained empty slots that could be filled with information collected from new experiences. Reading of informational material is aided by the existing schemata and also fills in some of the empty slots in them.

Students need schemata of a variety of types to be successful readers. They must have concepts about the arrangement of print on a page, about the purpose of printed material (to convey ideas), and about the relationship of spoken language to written language. They need to be familiar with vocabulary and sentence patterns not generally found in oral language and with the different writing styles associated with various literary genres.

A *story schema* is a set of expectations about the internal structure of stories. Readers find well-structured stories easier to recall and summarize than unstructured passages. Possession of a story schema appears to have a positive effect on recall, and good readers seem to have a better grasp of text structure than poor readers. Having children retell stories is a good way to discover their grasp of a story schema. (A rubric for analyzing retelling is found in Chapter 2.)

Having many experiences with well-formed stories helps children develop a story schema. Storytelling and story reading are excellent ways to develop children's

STRUGGLING READER/
INTERVENTION

LITERATURE

schemata related to stories. Hearing a variety of stories with standard structures helps students develop a story schema that enables them to anticipate or predict what will happen next. This ability allows readers to become more involved in stories they read so that they are better able to make and confirm or reject predictions—a process that fosters comprehension. The sentence structures in the stories that are told and read to students expose them to patterns that they will encounter when they read literature on their own and will help make these patterns more understandable to them (Rand, 1984; Nessel, 1985; Roe, 1985, 1986). Another way to help develop a student's story schemata is direct teaching of story structure and story grammars, covered later in this chapter in "Story Grammar Activities."

Perhaps the most important concept that students need to have in their "reading schema" is the understanding that reading can be fun and can help them do things. They also need extensive background knowledge about the nature of the reading task and general background knowledge on the topics about which they are reading (Roney, 1984). Often students do not comprehend well because they know very little about the world outside of their immediate environment.

Reading stories to children is an excellent way to develop their schemata related to stories or other materials that they will be expected to read.

© Bill Paxson/Courtesy of Des Moines Public Schools

▶ Research Findings About Schemata

Many research studies have supported schema theory. Anderson and colleagues, for example, discovered that the readers' background knowledge and/or their testing environment affected their recall and comprehension of ambiguous text passages (cited in Pearson et al., 1979). Bransford and Johnson discovered that recall of obscure passages increased if a statement of the passage's topic was provided, resulting in schema activation (cited in Bransford, 2004).

Anything that increases a reader's background knowledge may also enhance reading performance. Increased exposure to social studies, science, art, music, mathematics, and other content areas can therefore improve reading achievement. For example, students at schools with broad curricular scopes have been found to score higher on inferential reading comprehension than students at schools with narrow curricular scopes (Singer, McNeil, and Furse, 1984). Teachers can also encourage family members to involve students in a wide variety of activities outside of school.

Studies have shown that providing background information on a topic before reading is likely to enhance reading comprehension, especially *inferential comprehension*, or reading between the lines (Pearson et al., 1979; Stevens, 1982). These findings indicate that teachers should plan experiences that will provide students with background information to help them understand written material they are expected to read and to help them choose appropriate schemata to apply to the reading.

Readers vary in the relative degree to which they use two processes of comprehension (Spiro, 1979). **Text-based processing** involves the reader primarily trying to extract information from the text. **Knowledge-based processing** involves the reader primarily bringing prior knowledge and experiences to bear on the interpretation of the material. For example, consider this text:

> The children were gathered around a table that held a cake with *Happy Birthday* written on it. Mrs. Jones said, "Now, Maria, make a wish and blow out the candles."

Readers must use a text-based process to answer the question "What was written on the cake?" because the information is directly stated in the material. They must use a knowledge-based process to answer the question "Whose birthday was it?" Prior experience may provide them with the answer, "Maria," because, at parties they have attended, they have consistently seen candles blown out by the child who is celebrating the birthday. Of course, before they use the knowledge-based process, they must use a text-based process to discover that Maria was told to blow out the candles.

Skilled readers may employ one type of process more than **STRUGGLING READER/INTERVENTION** the other when the situation allows them to do this without affecting their comprehension. Less-able readers may tend to rely too heavily on one type of processing in all situations, a habit that results in poorer comprehension (Walker, 2000). Unfortunately, some students have the idea that knowledge-based processing is not an appropriate reading activity, so they fail to use knowledge they have. Reading cannot be exclusively knowledge based: if it were, two people reading the same material would rarely arrive at the same conclusions, and the probability that a person could learn anything from written material would be slight. However, reading is also not exclusively text based: if it were, all people who read a written selection would agree about its meaning. It is far more likely that reading involves both information

TEACHING TIP

Development and Use of Schemata

If your students have trouble using their experiential backgrounds to assist in reading comprehension, you need to find out whether they lack the necessary schemata or whether they possess the needed schemata but cannot use them effectively when reading. If your students lack the schemata, you should plan direct and vicarious experiences to build these schemata, such as having students examine and discuss pictures that reveal information about the subject, introducing new terminology related to the subject, taking field trips, giving demonstrations, or having students read about particular topics in other books. For your struggling readers, you may need to give extensive help with concept development and provide more discussion time before reading than usual. If your students already know about the subject, letting them share their knowledge, preview the material to be read, and predict what might happen can encourage them to draw on their existing schemata.

Make sure that the material that students are asked to read is not too difficult for them. Difficult materials tend to work against use of meaning-seeking activities because they require readers to focus too much on decoding and not enough on comprehension. (Chapter 2 has information on assessing text difficulty.)

EXAMPLE 7.1 Flow of Information During Reading

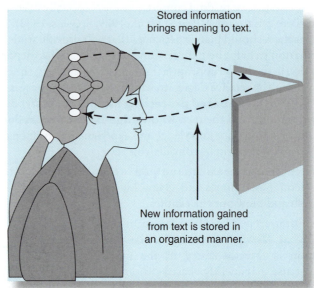

Stored information brings meaning to text.

New information gained from text is stored in an organized manner.

A reader uses information stored in the brain in the form of schemata to help in understanding the message conveyed by the print. The new information gained from the page is then stored in the brain, connected in an organized manner to the schema that it enriched.

supplied by the text and information brought to the text by the reader, which combine with the context of the situation to produce the reader's understanding of the material. (See Chapter 1 for a detailed discussion of this idea.) Example 7.1 illustrates this process.

Other Aspects Related to the Reader

Experiential background is the basis for readers' schemata. The discussion in Chapter 1 of the many aspects of the reading process includes this vital aspect, as well as a number of other aspects related to the reader that affect comprehension. These additional aspects are readers' sensory and perceptual abilities, their thinking abilities, and such affective aspects as self-concepts, attitudes, and interests. Readers' attitudes and interests affect motivation to read, and readers who are not motivated to read are not likely to give the reading task the degree of attention required for high-level comprehension. Facility with word-recognition strategies also enhances comprehension because it releases students' attention from the word-recognition task and allows students to apply this attention to the task of comprehension. Some educators have been concerned that nonstandard dialects could be a major barrier

DIVERSITY

to comprehension. Goodman and Buck (1997) assert that "dialect-involved miscues do not interfere with the reading process or the construction of meaning, since they move to the readers' own language" (p. 459). In other words, students translate the standard English into their more familiar dialects.

Teachers may also find Howard Gardner's theory of **multiple intelligences** of interest. Gardner (1995) says that "an *intelligence* is a biological and psychological potential; that potential is capable of being realized to a greater or lesser extent as a consequence of the experiential, cultural, and motivational factors that affect a person" (p. 202). It is not the same as a learning style; it is applied to a more narrow range of activities. Gardner identifies several distinct areas of potential that readers possess to different degrees (Gardner, 1995; Armstrong, 1994). These areas include *linguistic intelligence*, the ability to use written and spoken words effectively; *logical-mathematical intelligence*, the ability to reason, think deductively, and use numbers effectively; *spatial intelligence*, the capacity to perceive visual-spatial aspects of the world accurately and to create mental images; *bodily-kinesthetic intelligence*, the knowledge of one's body and its physical movements; *musical intelligence*, the recognition of tonal patterns and sensitivity to rhythm; *interpersonal intelligence*, the capacity to understand and relate to other people; *intrapersonal intelligence*, the knowledge of self, including metacognition, spirituality, and self-reflection; and *naturalist intelligence*, the ability to solve problems, observe, classify, and categorize. Lessons that incorporate the use of more than one type of intelligence, or potential, are likely to be appropriate for more students than lessons that involve only one. Several of the techniques described later in this chapter encourage students to use multiple intelligences.

Gardner asserts that there is not one "right way" to use the multiple intelligences theory in education. Furthermore, he says that not every topic can be taught through all intelligences. Trying to teach every topic that way is a waste of time, and some efforts to force attention on particular intelligences are pointless. Playing music in the background while students work in areas other than music does not use musical intelligence, for example. Gardner (1995) does believe that concepts should be taught in a variety of *appropriate* ways so that more students will be reached.

TEACHING TIP

Activating Schemata

You need to help your students activate the background knowledge that they already possess about a selection to be read and help them develop important concepts, related to the reading material, that they do not currently possess. They need to understand that they can use what they already know to help comprehend reading materials.

Consider using a "think-aloud" to show students the process that you use in activating schemata for a passage being read, modeling the mental process so that your students can emulate it. (An example of a think-aloud session appears on pages 239–240.) Some other ways that you can help your students learn this process are to use the prediction strategies in a directed reading-thinking activity (described in Chapters 9 and 12), the preview step of the SQ3R study method (described in Chapter 11), and the purpose questions of the directed reading activity (described in Chapter 9).

Time for Reflection

Gardner does not believe that every topic can be taught through all intelligences, yet some teachers disagree. Gardner, for example, doesn't believe that the mathematical skill of a person who is strong in musical intelligence is enhanced by music being played in the background while the person is doing math problems.

What do *you* think, and why?

The Reading Situation

The reading situation includes purposes for the reading, both self-constructed and teacher directed; the audience for the reading; the importance the reading task has for the individual; and the physical context in which the reading takes place.

Purposes for Reading

All reading that students do should be purposeful, because people who read with a purpose tend to *comprehend* what they read better than those who have no purpose. This may be because these readers are attending to the material, rather than just calling words. For this reason, teachers should set purposes for students by providing them with pertinent objectives for the reading or help them set their own purposes by deciding on their own objectives. Objectives may include reading for enjoyment; to perfect oral-reading performance or use of a particular strategy; to update knowledge about a topic in order to link new information to that already known; to obtain information for an oral or written report; to confirm or reject predictions; to perform an experiment or apply information gained from the text in some other way; to learn about the structure of a text; or to answer specific questions (Blanton, Wood, and Moorman, 1990; Dowhower, 1999; Irwin, 1991).

Teacher-constructed purpose questions can help students focus on important information in the selection and should replace such assignments as "Read Chapter 7 for tomorrow." Providing specific purposes avoids presenting students with the insurmountable task of remembering everything that they read and informs them whether they are reading to determine main ideas, locate details, understand vocabulary terms, or meet some other well-defined goal. As a result, they can apply themselves to a specific, manageable task. However, if teachers always use the same types of purpose questions and do not guide students to set their own purposes, students may not develop the ability to read for a variety of purposes. Purpose-setting activities can help students activate their existing schemata about the topic of the material.

Cunningham and Wall (1994) suggest always setting a purpose for student reading that is either "(a) a clear and precise statement of what the students are to focus on while they read or (b) a clear preview of the task they will be asked to perform after reading" (p. 481). This allows students to use the purpose to help them choose reading strategies. Cunningham and Wall also suggest making purposes more specific for more difficult texts to guide the students to the important and challenging content.

STRUGGLING READER/
INTERVENTION

For maximum effectiveness, Blanton and his colleagues (1990) recommend setting a single purpose for reading, rather than multiple purposes. A single purpose may be especially effective for struggling readers because it can help to avoid cognitive confusion from the overload of multiple purposes. The purpose should be one that is sustained throughout the entire selection, not met after reading only a small portion of the material; in other words, it should be fairly broad in scope. Purposes should be formed carefully because poor ones can actually misdirect students' attention by focusing on information that is not essential to the passage and slighting important information. Purposes should help readers differentiate between relevant and irrelevant information.

Even when teachers set purposes for students initially, responsibility for setting purposes should gradually shift from the teacher to the students. Students are capable of setting their own purposes, and they will be more committed to purposes that they themselves have set than to those set by the teacher. When teachers set purposes for reading, they may then think aloud how the purpose was developed, thus modeling the purpose-setting procedure for later independent use by students. Having students predict what will happen in a story or what information will be presented in an informational selection is a step in helping students set for themselves the purpose of reading to find out if their predictions are accurate. The directed reading-thinking activity, described further in Chapters 9 and 12, encourages such personal purpose setting through predictions on the part of students. Predictions can be more effective than traditional questioning if the predictions are compared with the actual text after reading (Pearson and Fielding, 1991). Therefore, teachers should be sure to follow up on predictions when this type of purpose is used. Actually, all purposes should be discussed immediately after the reading is completed, so that the students will seriously attend to the purposes.

Commercial reading materials tend to offer a variety of types of purpose questions. However, teachers sometimes do not make use of these ready-made questions, or they may paraphrase them. If teachers are going to use self-constructed questions, they should give careful thought to the desired outcomes of the reading and to the types of purpose questions most likely to lead to these outcomes. Teachers should also evaluate any questions provided in the material for relevance to the reading purpose.

Prereading questions should focus on predicting and on relating text to prior knowledge (Neufeld, 2005/2006). Students should be asked about the details that are related to problems, goals, attempts to solve problems, characters' reactions, resolutions, and themes (Pearson, 1985). (More about this type of questioning appears in the section "Story Grammar as a Basis for Questioning" in Chapter 8.)

Even when teachers do not provide purpose questions, students are often guided in the way that they approach their reading assignments by the types of questions that teachers have used in the past on tests. If a teacher tends to ask for factual recall of small details in test questions, students will concentrate on such details and perhaps overlook the main ideas entirely. In class discussion, the teacher may be

Time for Reflection

Some teachers believe that students should always set their own purposes for reading. Others believe that teachers should set the purposes. Still others believe that sometimes it is appropriate for teachers to set purposes, but that much of the time, students should do the purpose setting.

What do *you* think, and why?

Visit Read•Write•Think at http://www .readwritethink.org (or link from the Student Website) for the lesson plan "It Doesn't Have to End That Way: Using Prediction Strategies with Literature" designed for use with students in kindergarten through grade 2.

SEEING IT IN PRACTICE ◀■▶

Video Case

View the Video Case "Multimedia Literacy: Integrating Technology into the Middle School Curriculum." Answer the following questions in your journal: Did the students in the Video Case have a purpose for the reading that they were doing? What was it? Was the purpose effective in motivating the students to read with understanding? Why or why not?

 STANDARDS/ ASSESSMENTS

bewildered by the fact that the students know many things that happened in a story without knowing what the basic theme was. Teachers need to be aware that their testing procedures affect the purposes for which students read content material in their classrooms.

Audience

The audience for the reading may consist of only the reader, reading alone for personal or teacher-directed purposes. In this case, the reader is free to use his or her available reading strategies as needed to meet the purposes. The degree to which the reader has accepted the purposes as valid will affect his or her comprehension of the material.

**STRUGGLING READER/
INTERVENTION**

Sometimes the audience for the reading is the teacher. Teachers have been found to focus more on word-recognition concerns with lower-achieving groups of students and more on meaning with higher-achieving groups (Irwin, 1991), a

Students may read aloud stories that they have written to an audience of their classmates.
© Owen Franken/Corbis

tendency that could be detrimental to the students in lower groups. Anderson, Mason, and Shirey (1983) found that a meaning focus was more effective than a word-recognition focus with both struggling readers and good readers.

Sometimes the audience is other students. In school, a common audience is the reading group. However, some students may comprehend less well when reading to perform in a reading group than when reading independently. They may even react differently to different groups of children—for example, younger students as opposed to students of their own age. Teachers should be aware of this possibility and assess reading comprehension in a variety of settings.

STANDARDS/
ASSESSMENTS

Importance of Task to Student

The degree to which students embrace the purposes for reading the material will affect the attention that they give to the task and the perseverance with which they attempt it. The level of risk involved will also affect the results of the reading. Research has shown that in high-risk situations, such as tests, low-ability and average-ability students tend to simply reproduce the text, whereas high-ability students tend to reproduce and embellish it. In low-risk situations, such as normal classroom lessons, students tend to respond according to their typical verbal interaction patterns with the teacher (Mosenthal and Na, 1980).

STANDARDS/
ASSESSMENTS

The Physical Context

The physical context for the reading includes whether the room is too hot or too cold; the light is too bright, causing glare in students' eyes, or too dark; the seating arrangement is comfortable or uncomfortable; and other people, or specific people, are present. It also involves whether the situation is high risk (for example, taking a test) or low risk (for example, reading for pleasure). Comprehension tends to be better in comfortable, low-risk situations.

The Text

Reading a text involves dealing with its specific characteristics and deriving information from it by using word-recognition and comprehension strategies. Texts are made up of words, sentences, paragraphs, and whole selections. Because vocabulary is one of the most important factors affecting comprehension, Chapter 6 was devoted to vocabulary instruction. Sentence difficulty and organizational patterns are other text characteristics. Although some suggestions in this section focus on comprehension of sentences or paragraphs, comprehension is a unitary act, and eventually all the procedures discussed here must work together for the reader to achieve comprehension of the whole selection.

People who choose texts and supplementary material for students must be aware of the level of difficulty of the material they choose, especially when students will use it independently. The directions provided for students and the instructional language used in such materials should be of high quality. The language of the directions should be clearer than the language of the exercises (Spiegel, 1990a).

Sentence Comprehension

Students may find complicated sentences difficult to understand, so they need to know ways to derive sentence meanings. In intermediate- and middle-school grades, students encounter more of these sentences. Research has shown that systematic instruction in sentence comprehension increases reading comprehension. Teachers should help students learn that sentences can be stated in different ways without changing their meanings. For example, some sentence parts can be moved around without affecting the meaning of the sentence, as in these two sentences:

On a pole in front of the school, the flag was flying.

The flag was flying on a pole in front of the school.

On the other hand, teachers should acknowledge that moving sentence parts *can* affect the meaning. For example, the following two sentences have distinctly different meanings:

Carla helped Teresa.

Teresa helped Carla.

▶ Sentence Difficulty Factors

A number of types of sentences are difficult for children to comprehend. They include sentences with relative clauses and other complex sentences; sentences with missing words; those in the passive voice; and sentences that express negation.

Children understand material better when the syntax is like their oral language patterns, but the text in some primary-grade reading material is syntactically more complex than the students' oral language.

Relative clauses are among the syntactic patterns that do not appear regularly in young children's speech. Relative clauses either restrict the information in the main clause by adding information or simply add extra information. Both types may be troublesome. In the example "The man *who called my name* was my father," the relative clause indicates the specific man to designate as "my father" (Kachuck, 1981).

STANDARDS/
ASSESSMENTS

Teachers should ask questions that assess their students' understanding of particular syntactic patterns in the reading material, and, when misunderstanding is evident, they should point out the clues that can help children discover the correct meanings. Teachers may find it necessary to read aloud sentences from assigned passages and to explain the functions of the relative clauses. Then they may give other examples of sentences with relative clauses and ask the students to explain the meanings of these clauses, offering feedback on correctness or incorrectness and further explanation at this point. Finally, teachers should provide students with independent practice activities to help them set the new skill in memory.

Students who need more work with relative clauses can be asked to turn two-clause sentences into two sentences. Teachers can model this activity also, as in the earlier example: "The man called my name. The man was my father." Supervised student practice with feedback and independent practice can follow, with progressively more difficult sentences. Students can move from this activity into sentence combining, which we will examine next. Finally, they should apply their understanding in reading whole passages (Kachuck, 1981). Until they have used the skill in interpreting connected discourse, it is impossible to be sure they have mastered it.

Sentence combining involves giving students two or more short sentences and asking them to combine the information into a single sentence. (For example, they might be asked to combine these two sentences: "Joe has a bicycle. It is red." Responses might include "Joe has a red bicycle," "Joe has a bicycle, and it is red," "Joe has a bicycle that is red," and "Joe's bicycle is red.")

Discussion of a number of sentence combinations may reveal much about students' syntactic knowledge. Sentence-combining activities also bring out the important fact that there are always multiple ways of expressing an idea in English.

 STANDARDS/ ASSESSMENTS

❯ Punctuation

Punctuation can greatly affect the meaning that a sentence conveys; it represents pauses and pitch changes that would occur if the passage were read aloud with expression. Although punctuation marks represent the inflections in speech imperfectly, they greatly aid in turning written language into oral language. Commas and dashes indicate pauses within sentences. Periods, question marks, and exclamation points all signal pauses between sentences and also alter the meaning:

He's a crook. (Making a statement)

He's a crook? (Asking a question)

He's a crook! (Showing surprise or dismay at the discovery)

Underlining and italics, which are frequently used to indicate that a word or group of words is to be stressed, are also clues to underlying meaning. Here are several stress patterns for a single sentence: *Pat* ate one snail. Pat *ate* one snail. Pat ate *one* snail. Pat ate one *snail*.

In the first pattern, the stress immediately indicates that Pat, and no one else, ate the snail. In the second variation, stressing the word *ate* shows that the act of eating the snail was of great importance. In the third variation, the writer emphasizes that only one snail was eaten. The last variation implies that eating a snail was unusual and that *snail* is more important than the other words in the sentence.

Time for Reflection

Some teachers think that there should be much work with sentence-level comprehension before moving on to whole selections. Others think they should address sentence-level comprehension only within the context of whole selections.

What do *you* think, and why?

Teachers need to be sure that students are aware of the aids to comprehension that punctuation provides and that they practice interpreting punctuation marks. One technique for having students practice using punctuation marks is to have students read stories in parts, as they would a readers' theater or play script, including a narrator for narrative sections.

Organizational Patterns

The internal organization of paragraphs in informational material can have a variety of patterns (for example, listing, chronological order, comparison and contrast, and cause and effect). In addition, paragraphs of each of these types also generally have an underlying organization that consists of the main idea plus supporting details. Whole selections contain these same organizational patterns and others, notably a topical pattern such as the one used in this textbook. Students' comprehension of informational material can be increased if they learn these organizational patterns. The "Putting It into Practice" features, "Chronological-Order Paragraphs" and "Cause-and-Effect Paragraphs," show two examples of procedures for teaching paragraph patterns. Similar exercises may be constructed with longer selections as well, preferably excerpts drawn from books available for the students to read. Teachers can use books like Karla Kuskin's *The Philharmonic Gets Dressed* and Richard Peck's *A Year Down Yonder* for straight chronological order; and time-travel books like Jane Yolen's *The Devil's Arithmetic* to show movement back and forth in time; Judi Barrett's *Animals Should Definitely Not Wear Clothing* and Jean Craighead George's *Who Really Killed Cock Robin* for cause and effect; and Patricia and Frederick McKissack's *Christmas in the Big House, Christmas in the Quarters* for comparison and contrast. Examples of several patterns may be located in a single book, as well. Teachers may introduce complex structures through read-alouds.

Types of Text

Narrative (storylike) selections generally consist of a series of narrative paragraphs that present the unfolding of a plot. They have a number of elements (setting, characters, theme, and so on) that are parts of story grammars (discussed later in this chapter). Although they are usually arranged in chronological order, paragraphs may be flashbacks—that is, narrations of events from an earlier time—to provide readers with the background information that they need to understand the current situation.

Expository (explanatory) selections are composed of a variety of types of paragraphs, usually beginning with one or more introductory paragraphs and composed primarily of a series of topical paragraphs, with transition paragraphs to indicate shifts from one line of thought to another and illustrative paragraphs to provide examples to clarify the ideas. These selections generally conclude with summary paragraphs. Most content-area textbooks are made up primarily of expository text.

LITERATURE

Visit Read•Write•Think (http://www.readwritethink.org or link from the Student Website) to examine the lesson plan "Comparing and Contrasting: Picturing an Organizational Pattern," designed for grades 6–8. This lesson uses picture books as mentor texts for learning strategies for reading text that contains comparisons and contrasts.

Chronological-Order Paragraphs

Write the following paragraph on the board:

Jonah wanted to make a peanut butter sandwich. First, he gathered the necessary materials—peanut butter, bread, and knife. Then he took two slices of bread out of the package and opened the peanut butter jar. Next, he dipped the knife into the peanut butter, scooping up some. Then he spread the peanut butter on one of the slices of bread. Finally, he placed the other slice of bread on the peanut butter he had spread, and he had a sandwich.

Discuss the features of this paragraph, pointing out the functions of the sequence words, such as *first*, *then*, *next*, and *finally*. Make a list on the board, showing the sequence of events, numbering the events appropriately, or numbering them directly above their positions in the paragraph. Next, using another passage of the same type (preferably from a literature or content-area selection that your students have already read), have them determine the sequence under your direction. Sequence words should also receive attention during this discussion. Then have your students detect sequence in other paragraphs from literature or content-area selections that you have duplicated for independent practice. Discuss these independent practice paragraphs in class after the students have completed the exercises. Finally, alert your students to watch for sequence as they do their daily reading.

Teaching students to make use of paragraphs that have specific functions can be beneficial:

- *Introductory paragraphs* usually occur at the beginnings of whole selections or at major subdivisions of lengthy readings to inform the reader about the topics a selection will cover. If students are searching for a discussion of a particular topic, they can check the introductory paragraph(s) of a selection to determine whether or not they need to read the entire selection. (The introductory sections that open each chapter in this book are suitable for use in this manner.) Introductory paragraphs can also help readers establish a proper mental set for the material to follow; they may offer a framework for categorizing the facts that readers will encounter in the selection.

- *Summary paragraphs* occur at the ends of whole selections or major subdivisions. They restate the main points of the selection in a concise manner that omits explanatory material and supporting details. Summary paragraphs offer a tool for rapid review of the material. Teachers can encourage students to use these paragraphs to check their recall of the important points in the selection.

- *Topical paragraphs* within an expository selection are logically arranged in one of the organizational patterns discussed earlier in this chapter. The writer's purpose will dictate the order in which he or she arranges the material—for example, chronologically or in terms of cause and effect. A history textbook

Cause-and-Effect Paragraphs

Write the following paragraph on the board:

Jean lifted the box and started for the door. Because she could not see where her feet were landing, she tripped on her brother's fire truck.

Discuss the cause-and-effect relationship presented in this paragraph by saying: "The effect is the thing that happened, and the cause is the reason for the effect. The thing that happened in this paragraph was that Jean tripped on the fire truck. The cause was that she could not see where her feet were landing. The word *because* helps me to see that cause."

Then lead class discussions related to the cause-and-effect paragraph pattern by using other cause-and-effect paragraphs with different key words (such as *since* or *as a result of*) or with no key words at all. These examples should preferably be chosen from the students' classroom reading materials.

---

may present the causes of the Civil War and lead the reader to see that the war was the effect of these causes.

At times, a writer may use more than one form of organization in a single selection, such as combining chronological order and cause-and-effect organization in history materials.

Writers often use sidebars and boxed material in expository text to provide additional related information or to summarize lists of major points. Pictures with captions are also used for this purpose. Students will need to be alerted to the purposes of these features.

Teachers may take a variety of approaches, but they must give attention to helping students understand text structure. According to Pearson and Fielding (1991), any type of systematic attention to a text's structure facilitates comprehension and retention of the text. Duke (2007) encourages the use of text that is full of information for comprehension instruction, because it gives the students authentic material to comprehend and a reason to comprehend. Attention to text structure is especially important when dealing with content-rich text. Chapter 12 discusses various text patterns in more detail.

Helping English-Language Learners Comprehend Text

 DIVERSITY

English-language learners can have problems with some types of text that they are expected to read for classwork. Lack of cultural familiarity with the text content is an obstacle for many. Using texts with culturally familiar content can help to alleviate this problem. Another helpful technique is sending home books with translations of the material in the students' first languages. Audiotapes of the text in both languages can also be beneficial. Allowing students to respond to the texts in their home languages can give them an opportunity to show more of their capabilities and seems less discouraging for the students than trying to respond in English (Lenters, 2004/2005).

Interaction of the Reader, the Reading Situation, and the Text

Factors related to the reader, the reading situation, and the text all interact as the student reads in instructional settings. To encourage comprehension of whole selections, teachers usually incorporate prereading, during-reading, and postreading activities into lessons. Some techniques are more general and include activities for more than one of these lesson parts. Example 7.2 on page 234 shows some techniques applicable to various parts of a lesson.

Prereading Strategies and Activities

Prereading activities are often intended to activate students' problem-solving behavior and their motivation to examine the material. The making of predictions in the directed reading-thinking activity described in Chapter 9 is a good example of this type of activity. The use of purpose questions as described earlier in this chapter is another example. The following activities can also enhance comprehension of the material by activating schemata related to the subject or type of text to be read, or they can be used to help students expand their schemata by building background for topics covered by the reading material.

▸ Previews

Story previews, which contain information related to story content, can enhance comprehension. Research has shown that having students read story previews designed partially to build background knowledge about the stories increases students' learning from the selections impressively and that story previews can help students make inferences when they read. The previews help students to activate their prior knowledge and to focus their attention before reading (Tierney and Cunningham, 1984). Story previews of trade books are often found on the back cover of the book. For other selections, teachers may have to write short previews.

 LITERATURE

▸ Anticipation Guides

Anticipation guides can be useful prereading devices. Designed to stimulate thinking, they consist of declarative statements related to the material about to be read. Some of the statements are true, and some are not. Before students read the story, they respond to the statements according to their own experiences and discuss them. Merkley (1996/1997) suggests adding an "I'm Not Sure" column to anticipation guides, similar to the "?" option in the guides in this book. She thinks that it causes students who choose this option to attend more carefully to the text to discover the answer. An example of an anticipation guide is on page 235.

EXAMPLE 7.2 Strategies for Use Before, During, and After Reading

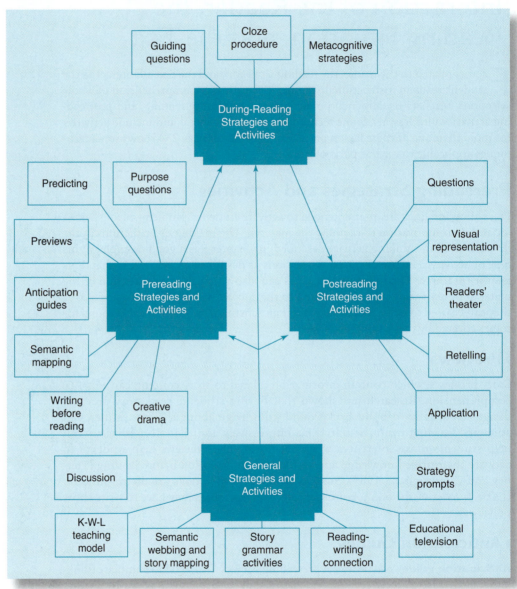

The value of anticipation guides can be extended into the postreading part of the lesson by repeating the process after reading, considering the input from the reading; this results in a combination anticipation/reaction guide. Anticipation/reaction guides appear at the beginning of each chapter in this textbook, and "Seeing It in Practice: Use of Anticipation/Reaction Guides" on pages 236–238 includes another example.

▸ Semantic Mapping

Semantic mapping (discussed in Chapter 6) is a good prereading strategy because it introduces important vocabulary that students will encounter in the passage and activates their schemata related to the topic of the reading assignment. This makes it possible for them to connect new information in the assignment to their prior knowledge. The procedure may also motivate them to read the selection.

▸ Writing Before Reading

Hamann, Schultz, Smith, and White (1991) found that having students write about relevant personal experiences before they read a selection resulted in more on-task behavior, more sophisticated responses to characters, and more positive reactions to the selections. This helped students become more involved with their reading.

▸ Creative Drama

Although creative drama is most often used as a postreading activity, it also may be used *before* a story is read to enhance comprehension. The teacher may describe the situation developed in the story and let the children act out their own solutions. Then they can read the story to see how their solutions compared with the actual story. The teacher can take the parts of various characters to help move the drama along and to pose questions related to setting, characters, emotions, and critical analysis (Flynn and Carr, 1994). Drama may be particularly effective with students who have strong interpersonal skills and are kinesthetic learners.

Use of Anticipation/Reaction Guides

Ms. Bucholtz's sixth-grade class had been studying the many cultures that make up the United States culture. To introduce the Chinese culture to a group of children who had no Chinese-American classmates, she decided to have them read *Child of the Owl* by Laurence Yep, a book for which she had a classroom set. She had prepared an anticipation/reaction guide that was designed to help them banish stereotypes and see the commonalities among all people.

Ms. Bucholtz began the lesson by holding up the book. She said, "Look at the cover of the book I have just given to you. From what you see on the cover, what do you think the book will be about?"

Blake said, "Maybe it will be about a baby owl."

Krystal said, "Oh, don't be silly. The picture is of a Chinese girl and an owl necklace. She's in front of a Chinese store. I think it's about her getting that necklace."

Ms. Bucholtz looked at Krystal and said, "Your prediction is reasonable, but you shouldn't say someone else's is silly. We don't have enough information yet to know if live owls will be in the story."

"I'm sorry, Blake," Krystal said. "Sometimes the cover does fool you, and it almost looks like an owl is flying behind her."

"That looks like a ghost owl. It looks spooky," said DeRon. "Maybe this is a ghost story."

"*Yep* sounds Chinese," Marie said.

"It is," Pete replied. "This guy wrote *Dragonwings* too, and it was great. It was about Chinese who came to America. I guess this one will be too, but the main character will be a girl in this one."

"You'll have to read the book to see if your predictions are right," said Ms. Bucholtz, "but first I want you to turn over that paper I put on your desk."

The children turned over the anticipation/reaction guide shown here.

"Bryan, read the directions for us," Ms. Bucholtz requested.

Bryan read the directions.

Then Ms. Bucholtz said, "Please follow the directions and fill in the *Before* column now. Then break into

your cooperative groups and discuss the reasons for your answers with your classmates. When all of you have discussed your answers, you may begin reading. A few minutes before the period ends today, I'll stop you and let you discuss your predictions with your group and set new ones if your old ones no longer seem likely. You'll be reading this book all week. We'll discuss and revise predictions every day and jot down our new predictions. When you finish reading, fill in the *After* column on your guide. You may want to look back in the book to find evidence for your responses to share later. When your entire group is finished, discuss those responses with your classmates. Then we'll talk about the guide as a whole class. Happy reading!"

The students quickly read and completed the guide, but their small-group discussions were filled with uncertainty about the items that specified Chinese-Americans because none of the children knew any. Statements such as the following were heard: "Of course, a person who looked Chinese would 'fit in' in Chinatown. I'd stick out like a sore thumb, though." "The Chinese in that book I read weren't wealthy, but that was a long time ago." "Sure, they do; they always have chopsticks in Chinese restaurants." "They can speak Chinese, because we can speak American." They were quick to support the answers that they had given for more general categories with statements such as the following: "Mr. Woolly looks mean, but he gives us candy when we are in his store." "But Mr. Lynn looks nice, and he is super." "Guess that means 'Sometimes,' right?" "Yeah, 'Sometimes.'" "My Mom bought me a boom box with her new dress money because she felt sorry for me." "My brother spent *all* of his paycheck to buy flowers for this girl he is crazy about, even though he couldn't go to the ballgame with his friends after he did it."

Predictions were quickly revised *after* the day's reading, and they continued to be revised every day.

On Friday, the students independently filled out the *After* column on the guide, some of them mumbling about how wrong they had been. Their discussions of the responses in their small groups were lively, with reading from the text to support many points. Some of the comments were as follows: "*Casey* couldn't even speak Chinese." "Her Uncle Phil

(Continued)

ANTICIPATION/REACTION GUIDE

Directions: As you read *Child of the Owl* by Laurence Yep, you will find out some things about Chinese and Chinese-American people and some things about people in general. Before you read the book, write Yes, No, or Sometimes in the space before each statement to show what you believe to be true at this time. After you read the book, write Yes, No, or Sometimes in the space after each statement to show what you believe then.

1. Chinese-Americans can speak Chinese.

2. Chinese-Americans can write Chinese.

3. Chinese-Americans live in Chinatowns.

4. Chinese-Americans are very close to family members and take care of them when they need help.

5. Chinese-Americans live just like other Americans.

6. Chinese-Americans are wealthy.

7. All it takes to "fit in" in Chinatown is to look Chinese.

8. Chinese owls are supposed to be evil.

9. Chinese-Americans eat with chopsticks, instead of forks and knives.

10. People can hurt people whom they care about.

11. The way that people look and act on the outside is the way they are inside.

12. Chinese-Americans have feelings that are like other Americans' feelings.

13. People make sacrifices for people whom they love.

14. Chinese-Americans have been treated fairly since they came to this country.

During-Reading Strategies and Activities

Some strategies and activities can be used during reading to promote comprehension.

▶ Metacognitive Strategies

Metacognition refers to a person's knowledge of the intellectual functioning of his or her own mind and that person's conscious efforts to monitor or control this functioning. It involves analyzing the way that thinking takes place. In reading tasks, the reader who displays metacognition selects reading strategies that fit the particular reading task (Babbs and Moe, 1983; Dymock, 2007).

While reading, the metacognitive reader is constantly asking if the material makes sense. When it doesn't, this reader takes steps to remedy the situation by using known strategies to repair the lack of comprehension (Afflerbach, Pearson, and Paris, 2008).

Effective use of metacognitive techniques has a positive effect on both comprehension and study skills. Therefore, some information related to the use of metacognitive skills as an aid to comprehension is included here, and more information on metacognitive techniques as study strategies is located in Chapter 11.

Part of the metacognitive process is deciding what type of task that the reader needs to complete in order to achieve understanding. Readers need to ask themselves whether they are looking for directly stated information or implied information or needing to connect information from their own backgrounds with the material that the author presents. This decision will help them vary their approaches to the reading.

Use of **think-alouds** can enhance students' comprehension monitoring. Think-alouds involve verbalizing the mental processes that readers engage in to construct meaning from written materials (Baumann, Jones, and Seifert-Kessell, 1993). The process of thinking aloud should include using an instructional format in which

Think-Aloud Session

Mr. Barr's fourth-grade class was beginning a unit on elderly people. Mr. Barr had assembled a number of books featuring elderly characters for the unit of study. The books covered a wide range of reading levels, and some presented complex or unfamiliar concepts. Mr. Barr wanted to encourage students to use their metacognitive skills as they read from this collection of books. He decided to use one book, *The Hundred Penny Box* by Sharon Bell Mathis, for which he had a class set, to model his own metacognitive processes when reading texts.

First he read the title, the author's name, and the illustrators' names from the book cover. "I'll bet this will be a good book," he said. "I've read other books by this author, and they were good books. These illustrators are always good too. I loved their illustrations in *Why Mosquitoes Buzz in People's Ears* by Verna Aardema. Let's see what this book is likely to be about. The picture shows a little boy looking into a box and either getting a penny out or putting one in, while an elderly woman sits in a chair in the background. That box must be the one mentioned in the title. I guess it has a hundred pennies in it. I wonder if they belong to the boy or to the woman, and I wonder if the woman is his grandmother. Maybe she has saved the pennies for him. I'll have to read to find out."

Opening the book to the first page of text, Mr. Barr remarked about the facing page: "I liked the picture on the front better than this one. This one looks a little depressing. I wonder if the book is going to be sad."

Then Mr. Barr read the first paragraph of the text aloud and said, "If Michael is sitting on the bed 'that used to be his' in the room with his great-great-aunt, he probably had to let her have his room. She must have moved in with his family. I wonder how he felt about giving up his bed?... Great-great-aunt.... A great-aunt is the sister of a grandparent, so a great-great-aunt must be the sister of a great-grandparent. Aunt Dew must be pretty old."

Mr. Barr read the next paragraph and said, "I guess the hundred penny box is Aunt Dew's, and she lets Michael play with it sometimes.... Sometimes she would forget who Michael was. I had an elderly uncle who forgot who we were sometimes. He called me by my daddy's name. I wonder what the song has to do with forgetting."

After he read the third and fourth paragraphs, he said, "She called him by his daddy's name too. I think it irritated Michael's mother."

Mr. Barr continued to model his thinking for the students for several more pages. Then he said, "So far it seems that Michael's mother is frustrated with trying to take care of Aunt Dew, but Michael likes to get her to play with him with the box. I think that there is going to be trouble between Michael's mother and Aunt Dew, and I think it will have something to do with that box. I'll have to read on if I want to find out."

Then Mr. Barr asked for a volunteer to read and think aloud about the next part. After reading the second paragraph on page 14, Susan said in alarm, "Is Michael stealing the box? He didn't seem like he would steal from his aunt. I don't think that's it. I'll read on to see."

Several paragraphs later, Susan exclaimed, "Oh, no! His mother is going to burn the box!"

After the next paragraph, Susan said, "But Michael won't let her have it. Is he protecting it from her, or does he want it for himself? I think he's protecting it."

After the next paragraph, Susan said with more assurance, "He *is* protecting it. But I can't believe his mother burned someone else's things up. He's been helping Aunt Dew hide some of her other stuff. Maybe he was going to hide the box. But, if he was, why did he go in the kitchen with it? I'm confused. I'll have to read more."

Mr. Barr stopped her there. He asked her to make a prediction about what would happen next, and she replied, "I think he will run away with the box and save it."

Then Mr. Barr told the class to break up into pre-established groups of four and finish reading the book aloud, taking turns reading and thinking aloud about it as they read. At the end of each person's turn (about

(Continued)

Think-Aloud Session *(Continued)*

two pages each time), that person would summarize the situation and make a prediction about what would happen next.

Eager to read on, the students quickly formed their groups and began to read. The book was short enough to be completed that day.

The next day the students were reminded of the questioning, predicting, connecting to prior knowledge, and summarizing that they had done in the think-alouds the day before. Mr. Barr encouraged them to continue to do these things silently as they read their individually chosen selections for that day.

Refer to the Read•Write•Think lesson plan "Building Reading Comprehension Through Think-Alouds" for another example of a think-aloud. Go to http://www.readwritethink.org or link from the Student Website.

teachers tell their students *what* the strategy is, *why* it is important and helpful for them to know, *how* it functions, and *when* it should be used (Baumann and Schmitt, 1986). Baumann and his colleagues (1993) used think-alouds to model for students the asking of questions about the material, accessing prior knowledge about the topic, asking if the selection is making sense, making predictions and verifying them, making inferences, retelling what they have already read, and rereading or reading further to clear up confusion. Then they had the students use think-alouds as they applied the strategies to their own reading. At times, students were divided into small groups or pairs to apply the think-alouds, an activity that was especially helpful. The researchers built student interest by comparing the students as readers to newspaper or television reporters: they interviewed writers as they read, just as reporters interview people. "Seeing It in Practice: Think-Aloud Session" describes a sample think-aloud.

Palincsar and Brown (1986) suggest **reciprocal teaching** as a way to promote comprehension and comprehension monitoring. In this technique, the teacher and the students take turns being the "teacher." The "teacher" leads the discussion of material that students are reading. The participants have four common goals: "predicting, question generating, summarizing, and clarifying" (p. 772). When using reciprocal teaching, the teacher must explain to the students each component strategy and the reason for it:

1. The predictions that students make provide them with a purpose for reading: to test their predictions. Text features such as headings and subheadings help students form predictions.

2. Generating questions provides a basis for self-testing and interaction with others in the group.

3. Summarizing, which can be a joint effort, helps students to integrate the information presented.

4. Clarifying calls attention to reasons why the material may be hard to understand. Students are encouraged to reread or ask for help when their need for clarification becomes obvious.

Instruction in each strategy is important (Dymock, 2007). At first, the teacher leads the discussion, modeling the strategies for the students. Students add their predictions, clarifications, and comments on the teacher's summaries and respond to the teacher's questions. Gradually, the responsibility for the process is transferred from the teacher to the students. The teacher participates but the students take on the "teacher" role, too. The interactive aspect of this procedure is very important. The reciprocal teaching procedure may need to be modified for English-language learners (ELLs). Some of them may be unable to assume the role of "teacher" but may serve different useful functions, such as translator for other ELLs. Some ELLs may need to answer questions by drawing pictures or pointing (Herrell, 2000).

 DIVERSITY

Simply reminding and encouraging students to use metacognitive strategies, such as making connections between different reading selections, can also lead to their increased use. "Seeing It in Practice: Metacognition" on page 242 shows how one student used her metacognitive skills.

Students need to learn several metacognitive strategies and learn how to choose and combine strategies as needed to help them comprehend (Dymock, 2007). Teaching students to combine the two metacognitive strategies of self-questioning and prediction can result in better comprehension scores for middle school students reading below grade level than using only a self-questioning strategy or traditional vocabulary instruction. This may be because the combination strategy causes them to monitor the information more actively as they read to confirm predictions (Nolan, 1991). Englot-Mash (1991) helps students learn to tie strategies together in a usable manner by presenting them with the flow chart in Example 7.3 on page 243. This chart helps students to think about their fix-up strategies in a concrete way.

 STRUGGLING READER/ INTERVENTION

Studies have shown that gifted students tend to be more efficient in the use of strategies, learn new strategies more easily, are more apt to transfer them to new situations, and are better at discussing their understanding of their cognitive processes than average students. There are, however, indications that gifted students, like other students, can benefit from metacognitive instruction (Borkowski and Kurtz, 1987; Cheng, 1993).

Good readers monitor their comprehension constantly and take steps to correct situations when they fail to comprehend. They may reread passages or adjust their reading techniques or rates. Struggling readers, on the other hand, often fail to monitor their understanding of the text. They make fewer spontaneous corrections in oral reading than good readers do and also correct miscues that affect meaning less frequently than do good readers. They seem to regard reading as a decoding process, whereas good readers see it as a comprehension-seeking process.

 STRUGGLING READER/ INTERVENTION

Direct instruction in which teachers model reasoning processes to help students understand how reading works may be particularly effective for helping struggling readers become more strategic. For example, teachers may model using headings in text to make predictions about the material or to demonstrate how to activate prior knowledge before reading new texts (Bishop, Reyes, and Pflaum, 2006). After demonstrating their own metacognitive strategies, teachers may ask their students to

 STRUGGLING READER/ INTERVENTION

Metacognition

As Ina Maxwell works at her desk one January morning, a student comes by to share a discovery about her reading. The girl is currently reading *Dark Hour of Noon*. "*Dark Hour of Noon* reminds me of *Number the Stars*, that book we read last fall," she says. "In *Number the Stars*, the Nazis came and told the Jews to move to camps. They took butter and other foods. The Nazis were killing Jews. Adolf Hitler was in charge of the Germans."

Analysis of Scenario

Ms. Maxwell encourages her students to make connections with life experiences and previous reading material as they read. Her encouragement and openness to students' comments lead students to share these connections with her, even when they are unsolicited.

◀ ▶ **SEEING IT IN PRACTICE**

Video Case
View the main and bonus videos in the Video Case "Metacognition: Helping Students Become Strategic Learners." How effective was the teacher's modeling of metacognitive strategies? Was the metacognitive strategy of marking the text one that you would use? Why or why not? When would using this strategy be inappropriate? Write your reactions in your journal.

explain how they made sense of material they have read and then may provide additional help if the students' responses indicate the need (Herrmann, 1988).

It is not possible, however, to reduce the mental processes associated with strategic reading to a fixed set of steps, because expert readers use different strategies when encountering unknown words in different contexts. Struggling readers often do not grasp the need for variation from situation to situation.

▶ Guiding Questions

During reading, guiding questions are often used to enhance comprehension. Research indicates that questions posed by the teacher when students are reading seem to facilitate comprehension (Tierney and Cunningham, 1984). Some authorities have suggested that extensive use of self-questioning while reading also will facilitate comprehension (Neufeld, 2005/2006). Teachers can enhance students' learning of the factual information by showing them how to turn each factual statement that they need to remember into a *why* question that they then attempt to answer. (For example: "Why did Davy Crockett leave Tennessee to fight at the Alamo?") Better answers to the *why* questions result in better memory for the facts (Menke and Pressley, 1994).

Shoop (1986) describes the **Investigative Questioning Procedure (InQuest),** a comprehension strategy that combines student questioning with creative drama and encourages reader interaction with text. In this technique, the teacher stops the reading at a critical point in the story. One student takes the role of a major character, and other students take the roles of investigative reporters "on the scene."

EXAMPLE 7.3 Strategy Use

Example: A Skilled Reader's Possible "Flow Chart"

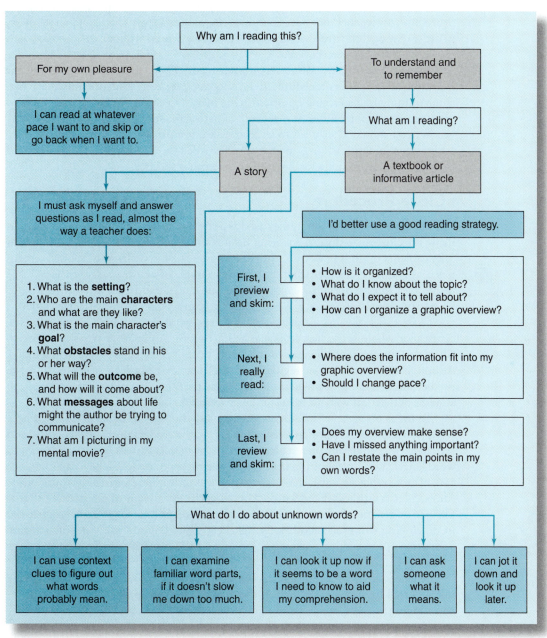

Source: Christine Englot-Mash, "Tying Together Reading Strategies," *Journal of Reading* 35, no. 2 (October 1991): 151.
Reprinted with permission of the International Reading Association.

The reporters ask the character interpretive and evaluative questions about story events. More than one character may be interviewed to delve into different viewpoints. Then the children resume reading, although the teacher may interrupt their reading several more times for other "news conferences." When first introducing the procedure, the teacher may occasionally participate as a story character or a reporter, in order to model the processes involved. The class should evaluate the process when the entire story has been covered.

InQuest lets students monitor comprehension. They actively keep up with "what is known." Before this procedure can be effective, however, students must have had some training in generating questions. One means to accomplish this training is to give students opportunities to view and evaluate actual questioning sessions on television news shows. They need to learn to ask questions that produce information, evaluations, and predictions, and they need to ask a variety of types of questions and to use *why* questions judiciously to elicit in-depth responses.

▶ Cloze Procedure

DIVERSITY

The **cloze procedure** is sometimes used as a strategy for teaching comprehension. In using the cloze procedure, the teacher deletes some information from a passage and asks students to fill it in as they read, drawing on their knowledge of syntax, semantics, and graphic clues. (See Chapter 2 for an example of a cloze passage.) Use of cloze techniques can help English-language learners understand that a reader does not have to be able to read every word of a passage to grasp the meaning (Herrell, 2000).

Cloze tasks can involve deletions of letters, word parts, whole words, phrases, clauses, or whole sentences. In *macrocloze* activities, entire story parts are deleted. The deletions are generally made for specific purposes to focus on particular skills. Although either random or regularly spaced deletions can lead students to make predictions and confirm predictions on the basis of their language knowledge, such systems of deletion will not focus on one particular skill.

To focus on specific skills, teachers can vary the sizes of blanks. When a whole word is deleted and a standard-size blank is left, the readers must use semantic and syntactic clues to decide on a replacement. If the blanks vary in length according to word length, word-recognition skill also can be incorporated. Teachers can make the task of exact replacement easier by providing the additional clue of a short underline for each letter in the deleted words. However, the discussion of alternatives that is likely to be generated when standard-size blanks are used can be extremely beneficial in developing comprehension skills. Teachers should always ask students to state their reasons for making particular choices and should give positive reinforcement for good reasoning.

STRUGGLING READER/
INTERVENTION

Teachers can offer a multiple-choice set of answers for completing each blank, a task referred to as a *maze procedure*. Maze techniques are probably less effective in encouraging learners to use their linguistic resources (Valmont, 1983). However, they may simplify the task for readers who need scaffolding and may prepare students for participating in cloze activities. (See Chapter 2 for more on the cloze procedures.)

Postreading Strategies and Activities

Postreading strategies help students integrate new information into their existing schemata. They also allow students to elaborate on the learning that has taken place. Students should be given an opportunity to decide what further information they would like to have about the topic and where they can find out more. They may read about the topic and share their findings with the class.

▶ Questions

Prereading questions may focus students' learning more than postreading questions do, but research indicates that postreading questions may facilitate learning for all information in the text. There appears to be an advantage to using higher-level, application-type, and structurally important questions, rather than questions that focus on facts or details. Students obtain greater gains from postreading questions if feedback on answers is provided, especially feedback on incorrect answers (Tierney and Cunningham, 1984).

▶ Visual Representation

After reading, students may be asked to sketch or paint what they learned from the text or what it made them think about and then to share their sketches with a group, explaining how the sketches are related to the text. The sharing can extend the comprehension of all participants (Shanklin and Rhodes, 1989).

Quiocho (1997) had students work in groups. One student would read a section of a text aloud while other group members made sketches based on what they were hearing. Group members discussed the accuracy of each sketch, and the sketches were revised on the basis of the discussion.

▶ Readers' Theater and Creative Drama

After students read a story, they can work together, or with the teacher's guidance, to transform the story into a readers' theater script. The act of developing the script from a story involves deciding on important dialogue and narration and thereby increases comprehension (Walker, 2000). Once the script is designed, the students take specific parts and practice reading the script together. Finally, they read the script for an audience.

Kraus (2006) found that having first graders act out a story can improve their comprehension. When they know that they are going to dramatize the story, children are motivated to think about the characters and plot more deeply. Many times the creative drama is impromptu; however, occasionally Kraus has students develop a children's drama presentation for an outside audience. They make sets and costumes and invite parents to the production. Then they have greater reason to learn such techniques as looking at their audience and speaking at the appropriate pace and volume for each situation.

▶ Retelling

Talking about reading material has been shown to have a positive effect on reading comprehension. This talk may help students mentally organize material, a key aspect of active comprehension (Fiene and McMahon, 2007). Therefore, an appropriate comprehension enhancement technique is *retelling* of the important aspects of the material read. To retell a story or selection, the reader must organize the material for the presentation (Walker, 2000). Students are generally paired with partners for this activity. After silent reading of a section from the text, one student retells what has been read, while the other listens. Tellers and listeners alternate. This technique has been used with intermediate-grade students, with whom it resulted in better comprehension than did producing illustrations or answering questions about the text.

Teachers should introduce the retelling technique by explaining that it will help the students see how well they understand the reading selections. The teachers should model good retellings for their students, provide guided practice, and then allow independent practice. When the procedure is first used, short, well-constructed reading selections should be chosen. Prereading and postreading discussions of the story frequently help students improve their retellings. Teachers may wish to record retellings and play them back to allow students to identify their strengths and weaknesses (Morrow, 1989).

Students can retell stories for teachers, classmates, or younger children in the school. Story retellings can be done unaided or with the assistance of the pictures in the book. They can also be done with flannel boards, with props (for example, puppets), or as sound stories in which sound effects are added to the telling of the story. These retellings make children more familiar with the use of "book language" (Morrow, 1989). Teachers can also use retelling to assess student progress (this approach is discussed in Chapter 2).

STANDARDS/
ASSESSMENTS

▶ Application

A good postreading activity for use with content-area selections that explain how to do something (for example, how to work a certain type of math problem or how to perform a science experiment) is to have students perform the task, applying the information that was read. Postreading activities that are often appropriate for social studies reading include constructing time lines of events described in the reading selection and creating maps of areas discussed. Many of the activities described in the "Creative Reading" section of Chapter 8 are good postreading activities that ask students to go beyond the material they have read and create something new based on the reading.

General Strategies and Activities

Some types of strategies are useful throughout the reading process: before, during, and after reading. Several of these are discussed next.

Time for Reflection

How can comprehension strategies be integrated into authentic learning situations across the curriculum?

▶ Discussion

Goldenberg (1992/1993) advocates what he calls "instructional conversations." Basically, these are highly interactive discussions among the teacher and the students. Students focus on a topic chosen by the teacher and are guided by the teacher's questions and probing for elaboration and for text support for their positions, but the discussions are not dominated by the teacher. Students are encouraged to use their background knowledge to contribute to the discussion, and in some cases, the teacher provides needed background information that the students do not have. Sometimes the teacher offers direct teaching of a needed skill or concept.

The discussions generally center on questions for which a number of correct answers may exist. The teacher encourages participation from students but does not determine the order of speaking. Ideas are built on previously shared ones, and the teacher is responsive to students' contributions in order to build a positive climate for students' attempts to construct meaning. It can be helpful for the teacher or students to record on the board, in a list or on a semantic map, the key points that students make during the discussion. Having students write about the topic after the discussion can show what they have learned.

▶ K-W-L Teaching Model

Ogle (1986, 1989) developed what she calls the **K-W-L teaching model** for expository text. The *K* stands for "What I *Know*," the *W* for "What I *Want* to Learn," and the *L* for "What I *Learned*." The *K* and *W* steps take place before reading. In the first step, the teacher and the students discuss what the group already knows about the topic of the reading material. The teacher may ask the students where they learned what they know or how they could verify the information. Students may also be asked to think of categories of information that they expect to find in the material they are about to read. The second step involves class discussion of what the students want to learn. The teacher may point out disagreements about the things that the students think they already know and may call attention to gaps in their knowledge. Then each student writes down personal questions to be answered by the reading. Students then read the material. After they have finished reading, they record what they have learned from the reading. If the reading did not answer all their personal questions, students can be directed to other sources for the answers. (Example 7.4 on page 248 shows a K-W-L study sheet that was filled out by a fourth-grade girl who was working with teacher Gail Hyder.) Weissman (1996) adapts paragraph frames (as described in Chapter 12) to help her first graders complete the "What I Learned" step of the K-W-L, and Sippola (1995) adds a column labeled "What I Still Need to Learn" to the original three columns.

▶ Semantic Webbing and Story Mapping

Semantic webbing is a way of organizing terms into categories and showing their relationships through visual displays that can help students integrate concepts. One

EXAMPLE 7.4 Completed K-W-L Sheet

What I Know	What I Want to Know	What I Learned
a lot of animal live there.	What kind of animal live there.	butter flys, snakes, frogs, bats, fish, bees,
Plant live there.	What kind of plants grow there.	wild pigs, tamarin toucan, herons, 0 celot, lizirds,
A Green house is very hot.	How hot it is in there.	huming birds, sloth.

K - W - L   Welcome to the Green House by: Jane Yolen

flowers
crimson,
orchid
trees, vines
lianas, very hot
A wet house,

Source: Stephanie Hunsucker, fourth grade, Crossville, Tennessee.

type of semantic web consists of a core question, strands, strand supports, and strand ties. The teacher chooses the core question, which becomes the center of the web, to which the entire web is related. The students' answers are web strands; facts and inferences taken from the story and students' experiences are the strand supports; and the relationships of the strands to one another are strand ties (Freedman and Reynolds, 1980).

LITERATURE

Example 7.5 on page 249 shows a semantic web based on *Prince Caspian* by C. S. Lewis, developed by Winter Howard, a sixth grader. Before constructing webs like this one, the students in Winter's class read a portion of the book to a point where the hero found himself in a difficult situation. At this point the teacher, Natalie Knox, asked the students to predict what would happen next. The core question

EXAMPLE 7.5 Semantic Web

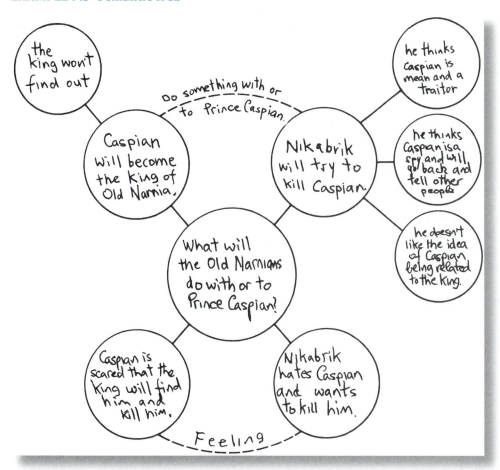

Source: Winter Howard, sixth grade, Central Intermediate School, Harriman, Tennessee.

("What will the Old Narnians do with or to Prince Caspian?") focuses on this prediction. Students answered the question individually, and their answers became web strands (for example, "Nikabrik will try to kill Caspian"). They drew support for strands from the story and from their own experiences. Then the strands were related through strand ties (shown with broken lines in the example). Finally, students used the webs as a basis for reading the end of the story to see what really happened.

Instruction in story structure can benefit reading comprehension. For example, **story mapping** provides mental representations of story structures. A story map is "a graphic representation of all or part of the elements of a story and the relationships between them" (Davis and McPherson, 1989, p. 232). In addition to representing plots, settings, characterizations, and themes of stories visually, these

 LITERATURE

maps (which are sometimes called *literature webs*) can emphasize the authors' writing patterns in predictable books.

Some webs are based on plot structure or story grammar (discussed in the next section), but some are more like structured overviews. One way to construct story maps is to put the theme in the center and arrange main events or settings sequentially in a second level of circles. Circles with characters, events, and actions may be connected to these second-level circles, and each may have additional circles attached to them, arranged in a clockwise order. Teaching readers to fill in story structure components on story maps while they are reading is beneficial to students' comprehension (Davis and McPherson, 1989). Primary-grade students can learn about basic story elements by developing story maps for a single element, such as the characters of a story. Younger students may work at first with pictures and later with written phrases (Felber, 1989; Munson, 1989). Example 7.6 shows one first grader's mapping of just the characters in a story. Bluestein (2002) suggests another type of story map. She asks students to create word webs to describe characters. The map would include a character's words, feelings, and actions that show what he or she is like.

EXAMPLE 7.6 Semantic Mapping of the Characters in a Story

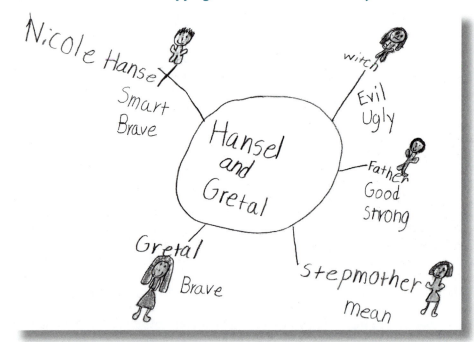

Source: Tiffany Nicole Reagan, Bethany Vincent Frady's first grade, Mary V. Wheeler Elementary School, Pikeville, Tennessee.

Staal (2000) has developed an adaptation of the story-mapping strategy called the Story Face. It is especially useful with grades 1 through 5 because it is easy to construct and remember. The technique is based on the shape of a face, with two circles for the eyes, which contain the setting and the main characters, respectively. Eyelashes (radiating lines) can be added to the eyes for descriptive words about the setting and other characters. The nose is a square in which the problem is written. The mouth is a semicircle of small circles that contain the main events and solution. This semicircle can curve up for a happy story or down for a sad one, and the number of circles for events can vary. This graphic can serve as a visual aid for retelling a story or as a framework for narrative writing. As a framework for narrative writing, the graphic is filled in with the student's own story plan.

Story maps resemble semantic maps or webs (described in Chapter 6 and in this chapter). Story maps help readers perceive the way that their reading material is organized. They can be used to activate schemata for a story that is about to be read, to help students follow the sequence during reading, or as a way to focus postreading discussion. When the story map is used to activate schemata, students may try to predict the contents of the story from it and then read to confirm or reject their predictions. Students may also refer to the map as reading progresses to help them keep their thoughts organized. After reading, students can try to reconstruct the map from memory or can simply discuss it and its relationship to the story events.

> The Read•Write•Think lesson "Graphing Plot and Character in a Novel" works with one type of story map. This lesson focuses on interconnections of the elements of the novel *The Watsons Go to Birmingham*. Go to http://www.readwritethink.org or link to this lesson from the Student Website.

▶ Story Grammar Activities

A *story schema* is a person's mental representation of story structures, the elements that make up a story, and the way they are related. Knowledge of such structures appears to facilitate both comprehension and recall of stories. Students' written stories can serve as a source for understanding their concepts of story, and their retellings of stories also reveal story knowledge (Golden, 1984).

STANDARDS/
ASSESSMENTS

A **story grammar** provides rules that define these story structures (Dymock, 2007). Educational researchers have developed different story grammars. Jean Mandler and Nancy Johnson include six major structures in their story grammar: setting, beginning, reaction, attempt, outcome, and ending (Whaley, 1981). In a simplified version of Perry Thorndike's story grammar, the structures are setting, characters, theme, plot, and resolution (McGee and Tompkins, 1981). Teachers may be able to help students develop a concept of story by using these or other story grammars. They can also help students focus on particular elements of a story grammar, including setting, character, and themes.

Fowler (1982) suggests the use of *story frames* to provide a structure for organizing a reader's understandings about the material. Frames are sequences of blanks linked by transition words that reflect a line of thought. Frames like the ones in Example 7.7 at the bottom of page 252 can be used with a variety of selections. Oja (1996) says, "Using story frames along with basic elements of story grammar directs both students' and teachers' attention to the actual structure of the story and how the content fits that structure" (p. 129).

Developing a Concept of Story

You can use many activities to develop the concept of story. For instance, you can

1. Read stories and talk about their structure in terms that your students understand. Folktales and fairy tales make good choices because they have easily identifiable parts.

2. Have your students retell stories, after you discuss story structure.

3. Have your students read or listen to stories and predict what comes next, followed by discussion of the predicted parts.

4. Give your students stories in which whole sections are left out, indicated by blank lines in place of the material, ask them to supply the missing material, and then have them discuss the appropriateness of their answers.

5. Divide a story into parts and scramble the parts; then ask your students to rearrange the parts to form a good story.

6. Let your students participate in a turn-taking activity for working on the concept of story. Each student starts by writing a setting for a story and then passing his or her paper to a classmate, who adds a beginning and passes the paper along to another classmate. As the papers are passed from student to student, each one contributes a reaction, attempt, outcome, or, finally, an ending. When the stories are complete, the students can read them aloud to the class (Spiegel and Fitzgerald, 1986).

EXAMPLE 7.7 Sample Story Frames

Frame 1: Setting

The setting for the story is _____ _____
　　　　　　　　　　　　　　　　(where)　　　　　　　　　　(when)

I could tell where the story took place because the story said "_____

_____."

I could tell when it took place because the story said "_____

_____."

Frame 2: Characters

The main character in this story is _____
　　　　　　　　　　　　　　　　　　　　　　　　　　　　(name)

I could tell that _____ was _____
　　　　　　　　　(name)　　　　　　　　　　　　(trait)

because the story said "_____."

I could tell that _____ was _____
　　　　　　　　　(name)　　　　　　　　　　　　(trait)

because the story said "_____."

Students can fill out story frames as they read or after reading. The frames can be the basis for the postreading class discussion of a story. Because the frames are open ended, the discussion will include much varied input. The teacher should stress that the information used in subsequent blanks should relate logically to the material that came before it. Students may use frames independently after the process has been modeled and practiced in class, and the class may also discuss the results. This technique is especially useful with primary-grade students and struggling readers (Fowler, 1982).

STRUGGLING READER/
INTERVENTION

Norton (1992b) suggests several ways to help younger students understand plot structures, including acting out stories through creative drama, drawing plot diagrams, identifying the plot structures of wordless books, and writing stories based on wordless books. Acting out nursery rhymes that have logical sequences (for example, "Little Miss Muffett") allows students to identify characters, action, and sequence in a simplified setting. By asking the students to try to act out the events of the story in a different order, the teacher can show them how changing the order of events destroys the story.

LITERATURE

Creative dramatics can help young students comprehend stories. The active reconstruction of a story through drama focuses their minds on the characters, setting, and plot of the story. Students can resolve conflicts among different interpretations through discussion. Stories with a lot of dialogue are good for use with drama. As students read these stories, they must use their knowledge of such print conventions as quotation marks to interpret what each speaker is saying (Bidwell, 1992).

To help students comprehend stories that start and end at the same place, with a series of events in-between, the *circle story* can be effective (Smith and Bean, 1983). The teacher draws a circle on a large sheet of paper and divides it into a number of pie-shaped sections corresponding to the number of events in the story. The teacher reads the story to the students, who then decide which events need to be pictured in each section of the circle. Circle story completion can be done in small groups, with each student responsible for illustrating a different event. If the paper is large enough, all students can work at the same time.

Teachers can improve understanding of story features such as plots, themes, characters, and setting by using movies, a medium in which students generally have high interest. For example, they can list types of plots that movies may have and let the students match movies to plots (Sawyer, 1994). This understanding can then be transferred to stories in books through parallel techniques.

Focus on Settings. Settings may serve simply as backdrops for stories, or they may be integral to the narrative, influencing characters, action, and theme. Use of sensory imagery by the author helps to make the setting clear. Pictures in the book also enhance the effect of the words in the text in clarifying setting (Watson, 1991).

Focus on Characters. To fully comprehend a story, readers must understand the characters. Preadolescents often focus on what is happening in a story rather than on the reasons behind the actions. They may assume that story characters think and feel the same way they do, even if the characters come from very different backgrounds.

Younger children may focus on only part of a story and consider only the perspective of the main character. Story maps that include character perspectives that go with each story event can help students understand stories more fully (Emery, 1996). Having students create a collage of words describing a character's traits, drawn from both text and pictures and superimposed on a drawing of the character, can also be helpful (Golden, Meiners, and Lewis, 1992). Use of character interrogations, in which one student plays the character and other students question him or her, is another valuable way to work on understanding characterization, as is the use of character journals, which is discussed in the next section (Van Horn, 1997).

Awareness of story characters' emotions is particularly helpful in understanding cause-and-effect relationships in the stories. Students need instruction in understanding emotional words and finding clues to characters' emotional states, and they need to realize that story characters may experience several emotions simultaneously (Barton, 1996). Word lines, such as those described in Chapter 6, and word webs can be used to show the relationships among the words. Barton (1996) uses the categories "strong," "moderate," and "mild" to organize related emotion words in word webs. For example, *ecstatic* would be placed under "strong" in a web for the word *happiness*.

Teachers can ask students questions to help them make connections between their own emotions and those of story characters. One question that Barton (1996) suggests is, "Has anyone ever treated you like this character is being treated by the people around him/her? How did it feel?" (p. 25). Teachers can also alert students to clues that authors supply about characters' emotions, such as explicit character statements and actions, explicit plot events, text features, and emotional words. Implicit clues that need attention may come from the setting, the characters' thoughts, the story mood, or the author's style (Barton, 1996).

Focus on Themes.   Students need to be able to identify themes, which "are often implicit and emerge gradually as the story unfolds" (Au, 1992, p. 106). Themes are ideas that extend throughout the whole text. (Some stories may have several themes.) The teacher can offer support through questions and comments as students work at constructing the theme of a story. Gradually, students can take more responsibility for the construction. Students learn from opportunities to discuss themes with peers.

Cautions.   Even though there is much interest among educators in the use of story grammars, questions about this technique remain. Results of studies on the effectiveness of story grammar instruction in increasing reading comprehension have been contradictory (Dreher and Singer, 1980; Greenewald and Rossing, 1986; Sebesta, Calder, and Cleland, 1982; Spiegel and Fitzgerald, 1986). Some have shown positive effects, and others have shown no benefits. It must be remembered that story grammars describe only a limited set of relatively short, simple stories, ones derived from a fairy tale or folktale tradition, and are unable to describe stories that have characters with simultaneously competing goals (Fitzgerald, 1989; Mandler, 1984).

Read•Write•Think offers two lesson plans that let each student take on the persona of a character from a book and use powerful adjectives to describe his or her own character and the other characters. Visit http://www .readwritethink.org or link from the Student Website to view the lessons "Action Is Character: Exploring Character Traits with Adjectives" (for grades 6–8) and "Charlotte Is Wise, Patient, and Caring: Adjectives and Character Traits" (for grades 3–5).

▶ Reading-Writing Connection

Composition and comprehension both involve planning, composing, and revising. Although these steps may seem clear in composition, their equivalents in reading may be less obvious. Teachers may need to think of the prereading activities related to background building, schema activation, and prediction as the planning phase in comprehension; of developing tentative meanings while reading as the composing phase; and of revising the meanings when new information is acquired as the revision phase.

Writing can be involved with reading-comprehension instruction at each phase. In the prereading phase, students can write story predictions based on questioning or prereading word webs. During reading, students can take notes in the form of outlines or series of summary statements. Macrocloze activities related to story grammars and the use of story frames are other ways to use writing to enhance reading. Interpretive reading activities, such as rewriting sentences that contain figurative expressions into literal forms and rewriting sentences that contain pronouns by using their referents instead, are also writing activities.

Creating a *character journal* involves writing diary entries from the viewpoint of a character in a story. Students can be asked to write a diary entry for each chapter in a book. The entries are written in first person. Students are encouraged to write as the character might have written, without concern for mechanics and spelling. Personal comments not in the voice of the character can be allowed, but they should be put in parentheses or brackets to set them apart from regular entries. Teacher responses to the entries can help encourage the students and reassure them about their competence. When students are asked to compose diary entries for characters in the literature they are reading, they become more intensely involved in the reading. To accomplish this, the students must get inside a character's head and experience the events through his or her eyes. Taking a character's perspective in this way can improve comprehension (Hancock, 1993).

Writing in cooperative groups helps students understand the elements of a story. For example, after students have read a selection, the teacher can give each group a character to describe. He or she can instruct the group members first to web the characters' attributes and evidence from the story and then to write character descriptions based on the web (Avery and Avery, 1994).

More on the reading-writing connection appears in Chapters 1, 9, 10, and 12. Many writing activities are also a part of instruction in creative reading, as described in Chapter 8.

▶ Educational Television

Reading Rainbow is a television program that presents books to children. It regularly tries to relate the topics in featured books to children's experiences, a procedure that facilitates comprehension. This modeling of a solid comprehension strategy may help students to apply the strategy in their own subsequent reading. The *Reading Rainbow* website offers information on books, games, and contests.

To learn more about *Reading Rainbow* and *Between the Lions* and get schedule information, go to http://www.pbskids.org, or link from the Student Website.

Between the Lions is another program that focuses on reading. It is aimed at children from four to seven years old. The show features a family of lions and interesting characters, such as "Tiger Words," a sports figure who plays with vowels and consonants. Other characters, with similarly clever names, also promote literacy skills. The lions, the "mane" characters, have a library. In their library, books and story characters come alive. Each episode of the show starts with the lion family reading a story, poem, or other piece of writing together. The show's website includes illustrated stories that are read to the children as chunks of the text are highlighted for the reader; video clips that have words with target sounds highlighted for the children; and literacy games.

DIVERSITY

Parents can encourage their children to watch such sound programming instead of programs that are primarily for entertainment. Watching, as well as visiting the programs' websites, may be particularly helpful for English-language learners (and perhaps for other members of their families).

▶ Strategy Prompts

Physical objects can provide prompts to help readers who are learning new strategies or struggling to use particular strategies in their reading. The physical prompts provide scaffolding to support students as they work on developing and integrating comprehension strategies. Fournier and Graves (2002) found that a scaffolded reading experience throughout prereading, during-reading, and postreading activities increased students' comprehension of short stories.

STRUGGLING READER/ INTERVENTION

Strategy access rods are instructional aids for struggling readers (Worthing and Laster, 2002). Each rod has a one-sentence reading strategy printed on it. The strategies are written in first person. The reader has in front of him or her, for easy reference, a personalized collection of rods that represent different strategies. Comprehension strategies can be color coded to represent before-, during-, and after-reading strategies. An example of a before-reading strategy is "I predict!" (Worthing and Laster, 2002, p. 123). Struggling readers who encounter comprehension difficulties can then choose, from available strategies, ones that are appropriate for the reading event.

Newman (2001/2002) developed comprehension strategy gloves that could serve a similar purpose for beginning and struggling readers, as well as more advanced ones. She had a prereading glove, a narrative structure glove, and an expository structure glove with icons on the gloves to prompt recall of questions that need to be answered by the students.

STRUGGLING READER/ INTERVENTION

Working with Struggling Readers

Struggling readers have the same needs for comprehension strategies that other readers have. Common barriers to their progress, however, are insufficient prior knowledge or inability to determine when it is appropriate to use this knowledge, avoidance techniques, and lack of fluency in reading. Teachers can help struggling readers by adjusting their strategy instruction and carefully choosing the reading materials they use with these readers.

Because of frequent failures at reading tasks, the teacher may need to spend extended amounts of time helping struggling readers learn the strategies in a stress-free environment. Research by Sprenger (2007) emphasizes lowering stress to enhance memory. As discussed earlier in the chapter, these readers also need to have instruction in metacognitive strategies so that they will be able to monitor their own reading and have a choice of strategies to use when their comprehension is poor (Massey, 2007).

Teachers need to take particular care to adjust materials for struggling readers to the students' current reading levels. Series books that have familiar characters and plots may be useful starting places for students trying to bridge the gap between simple text and more complex texts. Choices of appropriate books from multiple genres can be helpful. If students are hesitant to branch out into other genres, teacher read-alouds from other genres can provide a nudge to try other types of books.

Smith (2006) successfully used think-aloud mysteries with struggling readers. These mysteries were selections that provided clues in each sentence to the topic of the article. Students in small groups, guided by the teacher, read the mysteries a sentence at a time and individually made predictions from the information in each sentence. The process required predictions based on the text and on prior knowledge, as well as the ability to adjust predictions as new information that refuted old predictions was discovered. Questioning by the teacher about reasons for predictions encouraged students to use higher-order thinking skills.

SUMMARY

The central factor in reading is comprehension. Because reading is an interactive process that involves the information brought to the text by readers, the information supplied by the text, and the reading situation, good comprehension depends on many factors. Among them are readers' experiential backgrounds, sensory and perceptual abilities, thinking abilities, and word-recognition strategies, as well as their purposes for reading, their audience for the reading, the importance of the reading to them, their facility with various comprehension strategies that will help them unlock the meanings within the text, and the physical environment in which they are reading. Readers' schemata, built through background experiences, aid comprehension of printed material and are themselves modified by input from this material.

Having a purpose for reading enhances comprehension. Teachers should learn how to set good purposes for students' reading assignments and discover how to help them learn to set their own purposes.

The audience for reading affects the reading strategies used. The audience may be the reader himself or herself, the teacher, or other students.

The importance that the reading has for the reader is also a factor. High-risk reading for a test may be done differently from low-risk reading in the classroom setting.

Features of the text itself also affect comprehension. Sentences that are complex, contain relative clauses, are in the passive voice, have missing words, or express negation may need special attention because students may have difficulty comprehending them. The meaning conveyed by punctuation in sentences should receive attention. Students also need help in understanding the functions of paragraphs and the organizational patterns of paragraphs and whole selections.

Prereading, during-reading, and postreading activities can foster children's comprehension of reading selections. Prereading activities such as previews, anticipation guides, semantic mapping, writing before reading, and creative drama can be helpful. Metacognitive strategies, questioning, and the cloze procedure are among the techniques that can be used during reading. Postreading activities usually involve questioning, making visual representations, using readers' theater and creative drama, retelling, and application of concepts. Some activities—such as discussion; the K-W-L procedure; semantic webbing and story mapping; story grammar, story frames, and other story structure activities; writing activities related to reading; educational television; and strategy prompts from physical objects—may be involved in prereading, during-reading, *and* postreading activities at various times.

Struggling readers need to acquire the same comprehension strategies as other students. Teachers need to adjust materials to fit their reading levels, provide additional time on strategies as needed, and help them learn to monitor their own reading.

For your journal . . . .

1. Choose a short selection about an uncommon subject. Question your classmates to find out how complete their schemata on this topic are and give them copies of the selection to read. Later, discuss the difficulties that some of them had because of inadequate prior knowledge. In your journal, write your observations about this activity and indicate what you could have done to develop schemata before the reading took place.

2. Record your reactions to each of the Video Cases that you viewed as you read this chapter. What did you learn about comprehension instruction from each one?

3. Study your own state's standards and record ideas from this chapter that meet particular standards.

. . . . and your portfolio

1. Construct a time line for a chapter in a social studies text that has a chronological-order organizational pattern. Write a description of how you could use the time line with children to teach this organizational pattern.

2. Construct an anticipation guide for a well-known folktale.

3. Construct a story map for a story.

Comprehension: Part 2

8

KEY VOCABULARY

Pay close attention to these terms when they appear in the chapter.

Whereas Chapter 7 emphasized the role of the reader, the text, and the reading situation, as well as some comprehension strategies, this chapter examines two types of comprehension—literal and higher-order—and describes approaches for developing each type. To process ideas that are directly stated is literal comprehension, the most basic type. Higher-order comprehension includes interpretive, critical, and creative comprehension. To read between the lines is interpretive reading; to read for evaluation is critical reading; and to read beyond the lines is creative reading. Regardless of the type of comprehension involved, "Instructional methods that generate high levels of student involvement and engagement during reading can have positive effects on reading comprehension" (Williams, 2002, pp. 253–254).

This chapter also discusses questioning techniques that can be used to guide reading, enhance comprehension and retention, and assess comprehension. Three important activities related to effective questioning are discussed: preparing questions, helping students answer questions, and helping students question. Although Chapters 7 and 8 look at different aspects of comprehension, the material in both chapters is necessary to understanding the overall process.

anaphora

creative reading

critical reading

ellipsis

idiom

interpretive reading

literal comprehension

propaganda techniques

schema

story grammar

topic sentence

visualization

In addition, when you read the section "Recognizing Propaganda Techniques," pay close attention to the terms used there.

Visit the Student Website to see a chart that shows literal and higher-order comprehension and their elements.

ANTICIPATION/REACTION GUIDE

AFTER
C or **I** (for initial
A or **D** answers)
A or **D**
(for initial **?** answers)

Directions: Before you read this chapter, complete the following anticipation/reaction guide. In the space before each statement, write **A** if you agree; **D** if you disagree; or **?** if you don't know. After you have read the chapter, complete the guide again to show what you have discovered in the chapter. In the space after each statement, mark whether you were initially correct (with a **C**) or incorrect (with an **I**). Write the letter for the correct answer (**A**) or (**D**) in the space for the statements that you initially marked with a question mark (**?**).

1. Literal comprehension involves acquiring information that is directly stated in a selection.

2. Students must attend to details when they follow directions.

3. Critical reading is reading for evaluation.

4. Critical reading strategies are easier to teach than literal reading strategies.

5. Critical readers are not interested in copyright dates of material they read.

6. An inference is an idea that is implied in the material, rather than being directly stated.

7. Elementary school students are too young to be able to recognize propaganda techniques.

8. Critical readers read with a questioning attitude.

9. Creative reading involves going beyond the material presented by the author.

10. Teachers should give little class time to creative reading because it is difficult to assess.

11. In composing comprehension questions for testing purposes, teachers should use several types of questions.

12. Listing questions and sequence questions are the same thing.

13. The main idea of a paragraph is always stated in the form of a topic sentence.

14. Readers make inferences that are consistent with their schemata.

CHAPTER 8 ORGANIZATION

Comprehension: Part 2

Literal Comprehension

     Finding Details
     Understanding Sequence
     Following Directions
     Recognizing Cause-and-Effect Relationships

Higher-Order Comprehension

     Interpretive Reading
     Critical Reading
     Creative Reading

Effective Questioning

     Preparing Questions
     Helping Students Answer Questions
     Helping Students Question

Comprehension Challenges for Struggling Readers

Literal Comprehension

Reading for **literal comprehension,** or acquiring information that is directly stated in a selection, is important in and of itself and is also a prerequisite for higher-level comprehension. The specific, explicitly stated details in a paragraph or passage are the basic facts on which main ideas, cause-and-effect relationships, inferences, and so on are built. Literal comprehension involves many skills, including locating details, recognizing sequences, following directions, and recognizing cause-and-effect relationships.

Finding Details

The sentence "John carried a name card so that his cousin would recognize him at the airport" offers two details that readers can note: *John carried a name card*, and *John was at the airport*. Recognizing that the reason for him carrying a name

TEACHING TIP

Helping Students Learn to Locate Details

You can use the following activities to help students learn to locate important details:

1. Give your students a set of directions for a task that they need to complete and have them number the important details (or steps), as has been done in the following example. Go through one or more examples before you ask them to work alone or cooperatively with partners or in small groups.

   To make a good bowl of chili, first (1) sauté the onions for about ten minutes. Then (2) add the ground beef and brown it. (3) Stir the mixture frequently so that it will not burn. Finally, (4) add the tomatoes, tomato sauce, Mexican-style beans, salt, pepper, and chili powder. (5) Cook over low heat for forty-five minutes to one hour.

2. Make some copies of a menu. After modeling for the students how to locate items and prices, ask them to read the menu and answer specific questions such as these:

   a. What is the price of a soft drink?

   b. Can you order a baked potato separately? If so, under what heading is it found?

   c. What else do you get when you order a steak?

The Read•Write•Think lesson plan "Sequencing: A Strategy to Succeed at Reading Comprehension" suggests creating a timeline of events to determine the sequence in a tall tale. Go to http://www.readwritethink .org or link from the Student Website for this book.

card (cause) was to allow his cousin to recognize him (effect) is another detail. To locate details effectively, students may need some guidance as to the types of details signaled by specific questions. For example, a *who* question asks for the name or identification of a person, or sometimes an animal; a *what* question asks for a thing or an event; a *where* question asks for a place; a *when* question asks for a time; a *how* question asks for the way something is or was accomplished; and a *why* question asks for the reason for something. After discussing these question words and their meanings, the teacher can model for students the locations of answers to each type of question in a passage displayed on the board or projected on a screen. Then the students can participate in an activity such as the one in "Putting It into Practice: Locating Details in a Newspaper Story" to practice the skill. Newspaper articles are good for practice of this sort because lead paragraphs tend to include information about *who, what, where, when, why*, and *how*. The teacher should provide feedback on the correctness of responses as soon as possible after the students complete the activity.

Understanding Sequence

Sequence, the order in which events in a paragraph or passage occur, is signaled by time-order words such as *now, before, when, while, yet, after*, and so on. Students must learn to recognize straightforward chronological sequence, as well as flashbacks and other devices that describe events "out of order." Teachers must model the process of finding the correct sequence of events in a passage, pointing out useful time-order words, before expecting students to locate such sequences independently.

Following Directions

The ability to read and follow directions is a prerequisite for virtually all successful schoolwork. It involves understanding details and sequence. (See the Putting It into Practice boxes on pages 263 and 264, and the Teaching Tip on page 265.)

The teacher should take a set of directions for performing a task and model following these directions carefully, reading the directions aloud as each step is

Locating Details in a Newspaper Story

Have your students read the following newspaper article and answer the questions in small groups, making sure that every group member agrees to each answer chosen.

> The Live Wire Singers will be performing in concert at Lowe's Auditorium on First Street at 7:00 p.m. this Friday, to benefit the Children's College Fund. Admission is $20 per person or $30 per couple. This group presents programs of current pop songs and old standards. They have performed in thirty-six states to sell-out crowds during the past year.

1. Who is involved in this event?
2. What is about to take place?
3. Where will it take place?
4. When will it take place?
5. How or why will it take place?

Have a whole-class discussion of the article, with members from the different groups giving their groups' answers and the reasons for their answers.

---

completed and commenting on the meaning of each instruction. Then he or she should follow the directions again, leaving out a vital step. Class discussion about the results of not following directions carefully should then occur. After several modeling episodes, the teacher should consistently refer students to written directions instead of telling them how to do everything orally. Students can be asked to read the directions silently and then repeat them in their own words. There are numerous opportunities for students to practice following directions. They may read and follow directions for working math problems, playing an instrument, or participating in games and crafts.

Recognizing Cause-and-Effect Relationships

Recognizing and understanding a cause-and-effect relationship in a written passage is an important reading skill. It is considered a literal skill when the relationship is explicitly stated ("Bill stayed out because he was ill."); it is considered an interpretive skill if the relationship is implied.

Perhaps because literal comprehension is the easiest to deal with in the classroom, teachers have given it a disproportionate amount of attention; but students also need to achieve higher-order reading comprehension to become thoughtful and effective citizens.

TEACHING TIP

Activities to Practice Sequence

You can use the following activities to help students recognize sequences:

1. Discuss with the students the functions of such key words as *first*, *next*, *last*, and *finally*. Then give them a paragraph containing these words and ask them to underline the words that help show the order of events.

2. Have the students read a selection such as a well-known folktale. Then list the events in the story out of sequence and show students how to reorder them, explaining why the events came in that order.

A lesson plan for teaching cause and effect to students in kindergarten through grade 2 entitled "The Day Jimmy's Boa Taught Cause and Effect" can be found at the Read•Write•Think site. Go to http://www.readwritethink.org or link from the Student Website for this book.

Following Directions

Give your students handouts with the following directions, or similar ones, printed on them. You may want to use more items with intermediate- and upper-grade students.

Directions: Read all the items before you begin to carry out each instruction. Work as quickly as you can; you have five minutes to finish this activity.

1. Write your name at the top of the paper.

2. Write the date below your name.

3. Turn the paper over and add 15 and 25. Write the answer you get on this line: _____.

4. Count the number of times the word *the* appears in these directions. Put the answer on this line: _____.

5. Go to the board and write your name.

6. Count the people in this room. Put the answer on this line: _____.

7. Now that you have read all of the directions, take your paper to the teacher. It should have no marks on it.

After the students have finished the exercise, hold a discussion about why some of them made marks on the paper that they would not have made if they had read all the directions before starting to follow them. Emphasize the importance of reading and following directions carefully to avoid errors.

Higher-Order Comprehension

Higher-order reading comprehension goes beyond literal understanding of a text. It is based on the higher-order thinking processes of interpretation, analysis, and synthesis of information. In this section, we discuss the higher-order comprehension processes of interpretive reading, critical reading, and creative reading.

Good readers employ a variety of higher-order strategies. They interpret and evaluate the material that they read. They adjust the way that they read to the type of text being read. They paraphrase ideas accurately, relate the ideas to their background knowledge, draw conclusions about the ideas, consider the author's purpose, and consider the accuracy of the material. They monitor their understanding as they read and adjust their reading strategies accordingly. In other words, they are very active readers (Pressley, 2002; Duke and Pearson, 2002).

DIVERSITY

Knowledge is necessary to higher-order thinking, but students do not always use the knowledge they possess to think inferentially, critically, and creatively, and they may have misconceptions about certain topics—misconceptions that are more detrimental to comprehension than no background knowledge at all. Students in all groups, regardless of socioeconomic level or ethnic origin, vary in background knowledge, but it is true that "membership in specific cultural groups goes far in determining what a reader knows that can be related to text—and thus goes far in determining a reader's interpretation of text" (Pressley, 2001, p. 8). Limited background knowledge about U.S. language and customs can negatively affect English-language learners' comprehension (Ganske, Monroe, and Strickland, 2003). Semantic mapping (described in Chapter 6) accompanied by group discussion can help students who have little individual knowledge about a topic to pool their information and expand their knowledge.

Believing that young students who come from all kinds of environments want to make sense of their world, Barton, Sawyer, and Swanson (2007) looked for ways to help students through the use of ideas from the field of art. They developed a strategy for helping third graders from families living in a low-income, urban environment to increase their reading comprehension by teaching them to use focused observation, or contemplation, to discover important details in reading. The educators modeled observational strategies to lead the students to focus on story details and think flexibly, as well as to look at a story from different perspectives. They encouraged students to look for symbolic connections and immerse themselves in a story as active participants. Visual art (pictures in books and sculpture) was used to help students expand their thinking about observations that they made. These educators have published detailed descriptions of their strategies and the means of teaching them (Barton et al., 2007).

Working with second graders at a similar school, Paugh, Carey, King-Jackson, and Russell (2007) also found ways to provide their students with higher-order literacy experiences. They turned a "Choice Time" period into a time when students were allowed to design their own activities to help them learn mandated literacy skills. These students had creative ideas, and even some resistant students "bought in" to the enjoyment of learning while they expressed themselves.

Making predictions about reading material is an important and motivational higher-order reading strategy. A hypothesis-testing process can be initiated in which students make predictions and then read to confirm or reject them. If the predictions must be rejected, the students revise them. In all cases, they must be ready to explain why they made the predictions they did and why they believe that the predictions can be accepted or must be rejected.

Students need to realize that any evidence that refutes a prediction is enough to show the prediction is not valid but that even a great deal of supporting evidence in favor of a prediction may not conclusively prove that it is true. They also need to realize that just because a prediction has not been refuted at one point in the reading does not mean that evidence to refute it will not appear later. By refuting unsupportable predictions, students reduce uncertainty about the story's outcome. Teachers should ask students if their predictions have been proved wrong yet and other, similar questions, to encourage them to search for refuting evidence.

TEACHING TIP

Activities to Practice Following Directions

1. Teach your students the meanings of words commonly encountered in written directions, such as *underline*, *circle*, *divide*, *color*, *example*, *left*, *right*, *below*, *over*, and *match*.

2. Write directions for an activity and have the students perform it. Possible activities include construction and cooking projects, as well as science experiments and magic tricks. Discuss the results that occur if the correct sequence is not followed. Directions can be cut apart, scrambled, and reconstructed to give students an opportunity to demonstrate their comprehension of the necessary sequence.

3. Use an activity like one described in "Putting It into Practice: Following Directions" on page 264.

Asking for predictions when the text offers clues about what will happen helps make students aware of the usefulness of text information in making inferences. Asking for predictions when there are no text clues about what will happen encourages creative thinking on the part of the readers. Both types of prediction activities are good to include in lessons over time. Before students are asked to make and verify predictions, the teacher should model the strategy with a variety of materials.

Reading-response activities can also help students develop higher-order comprehension skills. There are many such activities that teachers can use, including literature logs, buddy journals, and essays. Character journals, in particular, can lead to development of empathy with the characters.

> Find suggestions for reading-response activities in Chapters 9 and 10.

Interpretive Reading

Interpretive reading is reading between the lines or making inferences. It is the process of deriving ideas that are implied rather than directly stated. Interpretive reading includes making inferences about the main ideas of passages, cause-and-effect relationships that are not directly stated, referents of pronouns, referents of adverbs, and omitted words. It also includes detecting the mood of a passage, detecting the author's purpose in writing a selection, drawing conclusions, and interpreting figurative language.

No text is ever fully explicit. Some relationships among events, motivations of characters, and other factors are left out, with the expectation that readers will figure them out on their own. Readers must therefore play an active role in constructing the meanings represented by the text. They must infer the implied information by combining the information in the text with their background knowledge of the world. Stories that require more inferences are more difficult to read.

Readers base inferences on their **schemata.** Even very young children can, during their daily activities, make inferences by connecting new information to information they already possess. It is important to realize, however, that children have less prior knowledge than adults do and that, even when they possess the necessary background knowledge, they do not always make inferences spontaneously, without teacher direction.

STRUGGLING READER/
INTERVENTION

Active involvement with the ideas in the material enhances students' abilities to make inferences related to it. Comparing events in students' own lives with events that might occur in stories they are about to read is one way to help students see the thinking processes that they should use when they read. Even struggling readers show the ability to make inferences about the material they are reading when such a procedure is used.

Teachers should explain to students how readers can use important words in a passage to help them make a particular inference about the passage. Then they should have students practice and apply this procedure. Teachers should emphasize the importance of modifying initial hypotheses about implications of the material when additional information shows the hypotheses to be incorrect. If this isn't done, students may distort subsequent information in an attempt to make it conform to their original inferences.

To help students learn to revise their hypotheses when reading, teachers can use a passage that contains a word with multiple meanings, asking students to hypothesize about possible meanings for the word on the basis of the initial sentences in the passage. Then they can have students read further to confirm or disprove these predictions. Another way to help is to have the students read stories written from unusual points of view to see how early inferences based on knowledge of the original book may not work. One good book to use is *The True Story of the 3 Little Pigs*, by Jon Scieszka (Viking Kestrel), which is written from the wolf's point of view and has surprising plot twists.

 LITERATURE

Pearson (1985) succinctly describes a method related to teaching inference skills that was developed by Gordon and Pearson (1983). Students should "(1) ask the inference question, (2) answer it, (3) find clues in the text to support the inference, and (4) tell how to get from the clues to the answer (i.e., give a 'line of reasoning')" (Pearson, 1985, p. 731). First, the teacher models all four steps; then the teacher performs Steps 1 and 2, while requiring the students to complete Steps 3 and 4; then the teacher performs Steps 1 and 3, requiring the students to complete Steps 2 and 4; finally, the teacher asks the question (Step 1) and the students perform all the other steps. The responsibility for the task is thus gradually transferred from teacher to students.

▶ Interpreting Anaphora

Interpreting anaphora is a task that requires students to make inferences. **Anaphora** refers to the use of one word or phrase to replace another one. Examples include using pronouns in place of nouns (*he* for a noun such as *Bill*), using adverbs for nouns or noun phrases (*here* for a phrase such as *in the kitchen*), letting adjectives stand for the nouns that would have followed them (*several* for *several people*), using a superordinate term to stand for a subordinate one (*reptile* for *rattlesnake*), using an inclusive term to stand for an extended section of text (*this* for *a disturbance in the neighborhood* presented in an earlier sentence), and letting referents in another sentence or clause represent deleted items (*I will too*, following *Mom will bake brownies for the sale*. Here *bake brownies for the sale* is "understood").

At some point, teachers will probably need to address in class all forms of anaphora, using similar approaches. Modeling of the thought processes used is important. Because students, especially English-language learners (Herrell, 2000), frequently have trouble identifying the noun to which a pronoun refers, they need practice in deciding to whom or to what pronouns refer. "Seeing It in Practice: Pronoun Referents" on page 269 offers ideas for instruction about and practice with pronouns. Some other forms of anaphora are discussed in subsequent sections.

 DIVERSITY

Pronoun Referents.   Few, if any, pieces of writing explicitly state the connections between pronouns and their referents (anaphoric relationships), so the task of determining the referent is an inferential one. After reading, students recall structures in which the referent is a noun or a noun phrase more easily than they remember structures in which the referent is a clause or a sentence (Barnitz, 1979).

> Mark wanted an ice cream cone but did not have enough money for it. (noun phrase referent)

> Mike plays the guitar for fun, but he does not do it often. (clause referent)

Similarly, readers find it easier to remember structures in which the pronoun follows its referent than structures in which the pronoun comes first (Barnitz, 1979).

> Because it was pretty, Marcia wanted the blouse.

> Marcia wanted the blouse because it was pretty.

Teachers should call students' attention to the structures just described. They should use stories or content selections that their students are currently reading and explain the connections between the pronouns and referents in a number of examples before asking students to determine the relationships themselves. "Seeing It in Practice: Pronoun Referents" on page 269 is an example of such a procedure.

Adverb Referents.   At times, adverbs refer to other words or groups of words without an explicitly stated relationship. Teachers can explain these relationships, using examples such as the following, and then let students practice making the connections independently.

> I'll stay at home, and you come here after you finish. (The adverb *here* refers to *home*.)

> I enjoy the swimming pool, even if you do not like to go there. (The adverb *there* refers to *swimming pool*.)

Omitted Words.   Sometimes words are omitted and said to be "understood," a structure known as **ellipsis.** Ellipsis can cause problems for some students, so again teachers should provide examples, explain the structure, and then give students practice in interpreting sentences.

> Are you going to the library? Yes, I am. (In the second sentence, the words *going to the library* are understood.)

> I have my books. Where are yours? (Here the second sentence is a shortened form of *Where are your books?*)

After this structure has been thoroughly discussed, students may practice by restating the sentences, filling in the deleted words.

▸ Main Ideas

The main idea of a paragraph is the central thought around which the whole paragraph is organized. It is often, but not always, expressed in a **topic sentence** in expository writing; in narrative writing, fewer topic sentences are found.

Pronoun Referents

Mr. Stevens wrote the following sentence on the board: "Joan put the license plate on her bicycle." Then he read it to the class. After reading the sentence, he modeled the process involved in determining the referent in the sentence by saying, "*Her* is a pronoun that stands for a noun." (For younger children, he might have said "a word that stands for a person, place, or thing"). "The noun usually comes before the pronoun that stands for it. The two nouns in this sentence that come before *her* are *Joan* and *plate*. *Her* indicates a woman or a girl. A plate isn't a woman or a girl, so *her* probably stands for *Joan*."

Then he wrote this second sentence on the board: "Since the book was old, it was hard to replace." He asked the students to determine the referent for *it* in this sentence in the way that he had determined the referent for *her* in the other sentence.

Ronnie said, "*It* refers to *book*."

Mr. Stevens asked Ronnie, "How did you know?"

"You told us that *it* refers to a thing, and the book is the only thing mentioned in the sentence," Ronnie responded.

"That's good thinking," Mr. Stevens replied, as he wrote a new sentence on the board for further guided practice. After another student successfully dealt with this sentence, Mr. Stevens gave the students a handout that included several paragraphs from a book they were reading in class. Each paragraph included pronouns and referents. He asked the students to draw an arrow from each pronoun to its referent and be ready to explain their choices later in the day in small-group sessions.

Analysis of Scenario

Mr. Stevens followed a good instructional plan by first modeling the skill of determining pronoun referents, then offering the students guided practice in which they were asked to support their responses with reasons, and finally having students practice independently, using other sentences chosen from material they were currently reading.

To understand written selections fully and to summarize long selections, students must be able to determine the main ideas in their reading materials. Teachers should provide them with opportunities to practice recognizing main ideas and help them to realize the following facts:

1. A topic sentence often states the main idea of the paragraph.

2. The topic sentence is often, though not always, the first sentence in the paragraph.

3. Not all paragraphs have topic sentences.

4. The main idea is supported by all the details in a well-written paragraph.

5. When the main idea is not directly stated, readers can determine it by discovering the topic to which all the stated details are related.

6. The main idea of a whole selection may be determined by examining the main ideas of the individual paragraphs and deciding to what topic they are all related.

The teacher should model the thought process that students need to follow in deciding on the main idea of a selection before asking them to try this task independently. For paragraphs with topic sentences, the teacher can show students that the topic sentence is the main idea and that the other sentences in the paragraph are related to it by taking a paragraph, locating the topic sentence, and showing the relationship of each of the other sentences to the topic sentence. Then the teacher can give the students paragraphs and ask them to underline the topic sentences and tell how each of the other sentences is related to each topic sentence.

TEACHING TIP

Main Ideas and Details

To give students a concrete analogy for main ideas and details, you can use a familiar object such as a bicycle. The whole bicycle can be identified as the main idea; and the handlebars, seat, pedals, gears, wheels, and chain can represent the supporting details that together make up the main idea.

Activities such as those illustrated in "Seeing It in Practice: Finding Main Ideas" (page 271) and described in "Putting It into Practice: Inferring Unstated Main Ideas" (page 272) can give students practice in locating main ideas in paragraphs.

Individual teachers mean different things when they request main ideas from students. When students are asked to give the main idea of a passage, some produce topics, some topic sentences, and some brief summaries. A *topic* merely identifies the subject matter; a *main idea* also includes the type of information given about the topic. For example, a topic of a paragraph or selection might be "football," whereas the main idea might be "There are several different ways to score in football." Clearly describing your request will help you determine if students are able to determine main ideas.

In many selections, readers must infer the main idea from related details. Even in selections in which the main idea is directly stated, readers generally must make inferences about which sentence states the main idea. The teacher can help develop students' readiness to make such inferences by first asking them to locate the main ideas of pictures. Then the teacher can ask them to listen for main ideas as he or she reads to them. Finally, the teacher can have students look for the main ideas of passages they read themselves.

Eventually, students will determine the main ideas of whole texts. Walmsley (2006) refers to these as "big ideas." He says a big idea is

> the main point of a book, magazine article, argument or film; the moral of a story or the underlying theme of a novel; what an author, poet, speaker, or artist is really trying to communicate; and finally, the life lessons and deeper understandings a reader, listener, or viewer takes from a text, a work of art, or a performance. (p. 282)

Showing students how to infer unstated main ideas is more difficult than showing them how to decide which stated sentence represents the main idea. In situations such as the one shown in "Seeing It in Practice: Finding Main Ideas," the teacher could compare each of the possible choices to the details in the selection, rejecting those that failed to encompass the details. As students practice and become more proficient at identifying implied main ideas, the teacher should omit the choices and ask them to construct the main idea themselves. Assignments can

Finding Main Ideas

Mrs. Braswell wrote the following paragraph on the board:

Edward Fong is a good family man. He is well educated, and he keeps his knowledge of governmental processes current. He has served our city well as a mayor for the past two years, exhibiting his outstanding skills as an administrator. Edward Fong has qualities that make him an excellent choice as our party's candidate for governor.

She said, "I am going to try to locate the topic sentence, the one to which all of the other sentences are related. The topic sentence provides one type of main idea for the paragraph.... Now, let's see, is it the first sentence? No. None of the other sentences appears to support his being a good family man.... Is it the second sentence? No. That idea isn't supported by the first sentence.... Is it the third sentence? No. That sentence may be supported by the second sentence, but not by the others.... Is it the fourth sentence? Yes, I think it is. A candidate for governor would do well to be a good family man, to be well educated and knowledgeable about government, and to have experience as a city administrator. All the other sentences support the last one, which is broad enough in its meaning to include the ideas expressed in the other sentences."

After this demonstration, Mrs. Braswell let one student "think aloud" the reasoning behind his or her choice of a topic sentence for another paragraph. Finally, she had students work on this process in pairs, "thinking aloud" to each other.

begin with paragraphs that include directly stated topic sentences and move to paragraphs that do not have directly stated topic sentences. Teachers can also increase passage length as the students gain proficiency, moving gradually from paragraphs to entire selections.

Because of their obvious morals, Aesop's fables are good for teaching implied main ideas. Teachers can give students copies of fables without the morals and ask them to state the morals, then compare the morals given in the book of fables with the ones stated by the students, discuss any variations, and examine reasoning processes. The big ideas in good literature for children and adolescents generally require students to make inferences because they are revealed indirectly (Walmsley, 2006).

 LITERATURE

Finding the main idea in whole selections of nonfiction generally is a categorizing process in which the topic is located and the information given about the topic is then examined. In fiction, however, there is not a "topic" but a central problem, which is rarely stated explicitly. To help students learn to locate a central problem in a fictional work, the teacher should first activate their schemata for problems and solutions, perhaps by talking about background experiences or stories previously read. Then the class may identify and categorize types of problems. Finally, the teacher should model the process of identifying a central story problem, using a familiar, brief story. By pausing during reading to hypothesize about the central problem and to confirm or modify hypotheses, the teacher

PUTTING IT INTO PRACTICE

Inferring Unstated Main Ideas

Model the generation of a main idea for a paragraph from one of the students' textbooks that has an unstated main idea. Be sure to show how each sentence in the paragraph supports the main idea that you generated. Then display a copy of the following paragraph (or a similar one from one of their textbooks) and main idea choices on the board or a transparency.

> The mayor of this town has always conducted his political campaigns as name-calling battles. Never once has he approached the basic issues of a campaign. Nevertheless, he builds himself up as a great statesman, ignoring the irregularities that have been discovered during his terms of office. Do you want a person like this to be reelected?

The main idea of this selection is

1. The current mayor is not a good person to reelect to office.
2. The mayor doesn't say nice things about his opponents.
3. The mayor is a crook.
4. The mayor should be reelected.

Say: "In this selection, the main idea is implied but not directly stated. Choose the correct main idea from the list of possible ones. Try to use a thinking process similar to the one that I used in the example that I gave for you. Be ready to explain the reason for your choice to your classmates."

TEACHING TIP

Main Ideas

Two activities that use newspaper articles can provide enjoyable practice in identifying main ideas:

1. Gather old newspapers and cardboard for mounting. Cut from the newspapers a number of articles that you think will interest your students and separate the text of each article from its headline. Mount each article and each headline on cardboard. The students' task is to read each article and locate the most suitable headline for it. To make the task easier, have them begin by matching captions to pictures, use very short articles, or use articles that are completely different in subject matter. Have your students discuss the reasons for their choices. Make the activity self-checking by coding articles and headlines. To follow up, you might have the students try to match captions to cartoons.

2. Collect newspaper articles and cut off the headlines. Then have students construct titles using the information in the lead paragraph. Show them how to do this before you ask them to work on the task alone. When they finish, have them compare their headlines with the actual ones.

can show the students how to search for the thing that the central character wants, needs, or feels—the thing that provides the story's problem. The teacher should let the students see how the story's events affect the hypotheses they have made. Events of a story may be listed on the board to be analyzed for the needs or desires of the main character (Moldofsky, 1983).

Cause and Effect

Sometimes a reader needs to infer a cause or an effect that has been implied in the material. Cause-and-effect relationships can be taught using cause-and-effect chains drawn from real life and from stories. Brainstorming out loud about causes and effects may help students develop more skill in this area. The teacher can ask, "What could be the effect when a person falls into the lake? What could be the cause of a baby crying?" Then the teacher should elicit the reasoning behind students' answers. "Seeing It in Practice: Inferring Cause-and-Effect Relationships" describes a practice activity for this skill.

Inferring Cause-and-Effect Relationships

Mrs. Taylor stacked three books on the edge of her desk as her students watched. Then she said, "Cover your eyes so that you can't see the books anymore. Don't peek."

When all eyes were covered, Mrs. Taylor knocked the books off the desk. Then she said, "You can open your eyes now."

The students opened their eyes and saw the books on the floor.

"What caused the books to be on the floor?" Mrs. Taylor asked.

Rob immediately responded, "You knocked them off."

"How do you know that I knocked them off?" Mrs. Taylor persisted. "You didn't see me do it."

"Nobody except you was up there," Rob replied.

"How do you know that I didn't just lay them gently on the floor?" the teacher then asked.

"Because they made such a loud noise," Rob answered. "If you had put them down gently, there wouldn't have been much noise."

"Excellent thinking, Rob!" said Mrs. Taylor. "You used clues to figure out something that you didn't actually see. When you read, you can use that skill, too. Sometimes the author leaves clues about what he wants you to know, but he doesn't come right out and say it. You have to use clues that he gives and 'read between the lines' to find out what happened. We're going to try doing that right now."

Mrs. Taylor passed out a handout with the following paragraphs on it. She said, "Read the following paragraphs and answer the question."

Jody refused to go to bed when the baby sitter told her it was time. "This is a special occasion," she said. "Mom and Dad said I could stay up two hours later tonight."

Reluctantly, the baby sitter allowed Jody to sit through two more hour-long TV shows. Jody's eyelids drooped, but she stayed up until the second show ended.

This morning Jody found it hard to get out of bed. All day she had trouble focusing in class. "What is wrong with me?" she wondered.

Question: What caused Jody to feel the way she did today?

When everyone had finished reading and had answered the question independently, Mrs. Taylor had one student answer the question aloud. The other students verified the answer, and several pointed out the clues in the material that helped them to decide on the answer.

Analysis of Scenario

Mrs. Taylor used a concrete experience to show her students how they made inferences about experiences every day. Then she had them try to apply the same kind of thinking to a reading experience. She asked them to analyze their thinking and to point out the clues they used so that classmates who were having trouble with the skill could see how they processed the information.

◗ Detecting Mood

Certain words and ways of using words tend to set a mood for a story, poem, or other literary work. Teachers should have their students discuss how certain words trigger certain moods—for example, *ghostly*, *deserted*, *haunted*, and *howling* convey a scary mood; *lilting*, *sparkling*, *shining*, and *laughing* project a happy mood; *downcast*,

Detecting Mood

Mrs. Vaden read to her class the following excerpt from *Homesick: My Own Story* by Jean Fritz (Dell, 1982, p. 138).

> By the time we were at the bottom of the hill and had parked beside the house, my grandmother, my grandfather, and Aunt Margaret were all outside, looking exactly the way they had in the calendar picture. I ran right into my grandmother's arms as if I'd been doing this every day.
>
> "Welcome home! Oh, welcome home!" my grandmother cried.
>
> I hadn't known it but this was exactly what I'd wanted her to say. I needed to hear it said out loud. I was home.

Mrs. Vaden said, "In this passage, the mood of happiness is effectively developed by describing the girl running into her grandmother's arms, the cries of 'welcome' from her grandmother, and the statement 'I was home.' All these things combine to help us feel the happy mood. Some authors carefully choose words to help readers feel the mood they want to share."

Next, Mrs. Vaden told the students to read a paragraph that she wrote on the board and decide what mood the author wanted to set. Then she asked the students to share the words that helped them decide about the mood and gave them feedback about the correctness of their responses. (See the Student Website for this textbook for the paragraph that she used and the students' reactions.)

sobbing, and *dejected* indicate a sad mood. They should model for the students the process of locating mood words in a paragraph and using these words to determine the mood of the paragraph. Then they can give the students copies of selections in which they have underlined words that set the mood and let them decide what the mood is, judging on the basis of the underlined words. Finally, teachers can give the students a passage such as the one provided in "Seeing It in Practice: Detecting Mood" and tell them to underline the words that set the mood. After the students complete the practice activity, they should discuss the mood that the words established.

▶ Detecting the Author's Purpose

Writers always have a purpose for writing: to inform, to entertain, to persuade, or to accomplish something else. Teachers should encourage their students to ask "Why was this written?" by presenting them with a series of stories, and explaining the purpose of each one, and then giving them other stories and asking them to identify the purposes. The class should discuss reasons for the answers. The activity in "Putting It into Practice: Detecting the Author's Purpose" gives students practice in this skill.

▶ Drawing Conclusions

To draw conclusions, a reader must put together information gathered from several sources or from several places within the same source. Students may develop

Detecting the Author's Purpose

Display the following list of reading selections on the board or display the actual books. Ask students to consider the selections and decide, for each selection, whether the author was trying to inform, entertain, persuade, or accomplish a combination of purposes.

The New Way Things Work by David Macaulay

The Long Road to Gettysburg by Jim Murphy

The Good, the Bad, and the Goofy by Jon Scieszka

Puzzled Penguins: A Maze Adventure by Patrick Merrill

"Put Safety First" (a pamphlet)

After each student has had time to make a decision about each selection, ask volunteers to share their responses and the reasons for each one. Clear up any misconceptions through discussion.

---

readiness for this skill by studying pictures and drawing conclusions from them. Answering questions like the following may also help. The teacher should model the process before having students attempt it.

1. What is taking place here?
2. What happened just before this picture was taken?
3. What are the people in the picture preparing to do?

Cartoons may be used to good advantage in developing this comprehension skill. The teacher can show the students a cartoon like the "Dennis the Menace" cartoon and ask a question that leads them to draw a conclusion, such as "What kind of news does Dennis have for his father?" Putting together the ideas that an event happened today and that Dennis's father needs to be relaxed to hear about it enables students to conclude that Dennis was involved in some mischief or accident that is likely to upset his father. The teacher can model the necessary thinking process by pointing out each clue and relating it to personal knowledge about how parents react. Then students can practice on other cartoons.

In the early grades, riddles such as "I have a face and two hands. I go tick-tock. What am I?" offer good practice in drawing conclusions. Commercial riddle books, used in such a way as to allow readers to answer riddles and explain the reasoning behind their answers, may also be helpful for developing

LITERATURE

DENNIS the MENACE

Ketcham
10-5

"LET ME KNOW WHEN YOU'RE RELAXED ENOUGH TO HEAR ABOUT SOMETHIN' THAT HAPPENED TODAY."

Source: DENNIS THE MENACE® © North America Syndicate.

Drawing Conclusions

Divide the class into small cooperative groups. Give each group a copy of a handout containing the following two paragraphs. Tell the students: "Read each paragraph and answer the question that follows it. After each person in your group has finished, discuss the answers with the members of your group and explain why you answered as you did. Modify your answers if you believe your thinking was wrong originally. Be ready to share your decisions with the rest of the class."

Ray went through the line, piling his plate high with food. He then carried his plate over to a table, where a server was waiting to find out what he wanted to drink. Where was Ray?

_____

_____

Cindy awoke with pleasure, remembering where she was. She hurried to dress so that she could help feed the chickens and watch her uncle milk the cows. Then she would go down to the field, catch Ginger, and take a ride through the woods. Where was Cindy?

_____

_____

Hold a whole-class discussion in which representatives from each small group share their groups' answers.

---

this skill. The activity in "Putting It into Practice: Drawing Conclusions" presents another good way to practice this skill.

To draw conclusions about characters' motives in stories, students must have some knowledge about how people react in social situations. Teachers' questions can encourage inferences by requiring students to consider events from the viewpoints of different characters; to reflect on the characters' probable thoughts, feelings, and motives; and to anticipate the consequences of the actions of various characters.

▶ Interpreting Figurative Language

Interpreting figurative language is an inferential task. Idioms abound in the English language. An **idiom** is a phrase that has a meaning different from its literal meaning. A person who "keeps his eyes peeled," for example, does not actually peel his eyes, but uses them intently. Idioms make language more difficult to comprehend, but they also add color and interest.

 DIVERSITY

Students who are not part of the mainstream culture often lack the backgrounds of experience with that culture to help them interpret idioms. They may be confused over the idea that a word or phrase has different meanings in different contexts, and its meaning in an idiomatic context may be very different from any of its denotative meanings.

It may be helpful to teach idioms by defining and explaining them when they occur in reading materials or in oral activities. Studying the origins of the expressions may also be helpful. After an idiom's meaning has been clarified, students need to use it in class activities. They may rewrite sentences to include newly learned idioms or replace these idioms with more literal language.

One of the best ways to teach figurative language, as well as all interpretive reading strategies and skills, is through think-alouds. "Seeing It in Practice: Figurative Language Instruction" includes excerpts from a think-aloud used by a primary-grade classroom teacher in which she emphasized the figurative language in the selection. It shows how she followed up the think-aloud to focus attention specifically on personification.

Chapter 6 discusses different types of figures of speech and presents more teaching suggestions.

Critical Reading

Critical reading is evaluating written material—comparing the ideas discovered in the material with known standards and drawing conclusions about their accuracy, appropriateness, and timeliness. The critical reader must be an active reader, questioning, searching for facts, and suspending judgment until he or she has considered all the material. Critical reading depends on both literal and interpretive comprehension; grasping implied ideas is especially important.

People must read critically to make intelligent decisions based on the material they read, such as which political candidate to vote for, which products to buy, which charitable organizations to support, which television programs to watch, and so on. Because children face many of these decisions early in life, they should receive early instruction in critical reading.

Teachers can begin promoting critical reading in the first grade, or even kindergarten, by encouraging critical thinking. When reading a story to the class, they can ask, "Do you think this story is real or make-believe? Why do you think so?" If the children have difficulty in answering, questions such as the following can be helpful: "Could the things in this story really have happened? Have you ever heard of any real children who can fly? Have you ever met or heard of anyone who stayed the same age all of the time? Do all people grow up after enough years have passed?"

Critical thinking can also be promoted at an early stage through critical reading of pictures. If children are shown pictures that contain inaccuracies (for example, a car with a square wheel), they can identify the mistakes. Children's magazines often contain activities of this type, and illustrators of books sometimes inadvertently include incorrect content. After the children have read (or have been read) a story containing such a picture, ask them to identify what is wrong in the picture, based on information in the story.

◄▮▮► **SEEING IT IN PRACTICE**

Video Case
View the Video Case "Using Information Processing Strategies: A Middle School Science Lesson." Consider the teacher's comment that the students need information in order to think critically. Did he make that point convincingly? How will this knowledge affect your teaching procedures?

Figurative Language Instruction

Evelyn Forbes was reading aloud from the story "The Big Green Umbrella" by Elizabeth Coatsworth while the students followed along in their books. As she read the paragraph of text that said that "the umbrella seemed to grow tired of keeping the rain off the Thomases on rainy days and standing in the dark corner. . . . It had heard the talk of the winds . . . whispering of raindrops, which had seen all the world. . . . The umbrella acted," she stopped and inserted her thoughts about the text. "Wind can't really talk, and raindrops can't whisper," she mused. "Umbrellas can't grow tired, hear, or act. People do. Why is the author making the umbrella have the characteristics of a person?" At this point she paused and discussed personification with her students, connecting it to previous reading they had done. After the discussion, she drew the accompanying diagram on the board and had the students tell what characteristics given to the umbrella were characteristics of a person. She wrote these characteristics on the raindrops falling from the umbrella.

Reading further, Mrs. Forbes came to the statement that "it soared upward like a kite" and "turned head-over-heels like a child at play." She repeated the similes and said, "These words paint a picture in my head of kites flying in a blue sky while children turn somersaults in the grass. What pictures are in your heads?" Then she called the students' attention to the use of *like* to compare the umbrella with things that she knew about that she could picture.

Later in the paragraph, the umbrella was said to be "dancing and bowing above the river," and the students were able to apply their knowledge of personification once more. Mrs. Forbes stopped reading after a few more paragraphs in which the story characters speculated about the plight of the umbrella. She said, "Mr. Thomas is wrong about the umbrella. What do you think is going to happen?" The students' predictions ended the lesson for that day, leaving them eager for reading time the next day, when they would discover whether or not their predictions were right.

A girl shares with her classmates her evaluation of a book she has just read.

© Chris Ware/ The Image Works

Critical listening instruction and critical reading instruction are appropriate for readers at all levels of proficiency. Such instruction has been effective with students in grades 1 through 6, regardless of whether or not they have already mastered basic decoding skills, and instruction in critical listening has been shown to improve critical reading and general reading comprehension for low-performing readers in grades 4 through 6 (Boodt, 1984).

STRUGGLING READER/ INTERVENTION

Critical reading is closely related to revision in writing. Both activities require critical thinking. Students must evaluate their own writing to improve it, just as they evaluate the writing of others as they read.

Critical literacy instruction is sometimes avoided because it addresses issues that are controversial and potentially disturbing. McDaniel (2004) points out that multiview social issues books for younger children, particularly, are hard to locate. She suggests Anthony Browne's *Voices in the Park* as a book that offers the perspectives of four very different people on the same incident and brings up issues related to prejudice. Foss (2002) said of her work with middle school students that "although our critical conversations make students uncomfortable and push them to think more deeply, those discussions tend to be the ones students remember the most" (p. 402). Teachers, as well as students, may find these discussions uncomfortable, but ultimately valuable, educational experiences.

LITERATURE

To foster critical reading skills in the classroom, teachers can encourage students to read with a questioning attitude and can lead them to ask questions such as the following when they are reading nonfiction:

1. Why did the author write this material?

2. Does the author know what he or she is writing about? Is he or she likely to be biased? Why or why not?

3. Is the information in the material current?

4. Does the information make sense when my background knowledge is considered?

5. Is the author approaching the material logically or emotionally? What emotional words does he or she use?

6. Is the author employing any undesirable propaganda techniques? If so, which ones? How does he or she use them? (Several propaganda techniques are described later in this chapter.)

The editorial cartoon by Charlie Daniel provides a good illustration of a child critically analyzing a situation. Based on her background knowledge, the girl decides

© Charlie Daniel. *It Was Self-Defense…He Drew on Me: Editorial Cartoons by Daniel.* Knoxville News-Sentinel, 1994. 135.

that the notice on the TV may not be ideally located to give the viewers ample warning. (Think about much of the coment on TV today.)

Fiction can also be read critically, but the questions that apply are a little different:

1. Could this story really have happened?

2. Are the characters believable within the setting furnished by the story? Are they consistent in their actions?

3. Is the dialogue realistic?

4. Did the plot hold your interest? What was it that kept your interest?

5. Was the ending reasonable or believable? Why or why not?

6. Was the title well chosen? Why or why not?

 LITERATURE

For both fiction and nonfiction, students may need to ask these questions: "Whose story is this?" "Who benefits from this story?" "Whose voices are not heard?" (Leland, Harste, and Huber, 2005, p. 259). Questions about what caused particular character reactions in the picture book *The Other Side* by Jacqueline Woodson can help students who live in a monocultural setting understand issues that develop in a multicultural setting. Questions such as these make students more aware of social issues. After answering such questions, students may brainstorm ideas for improving relationships among the characters.

Groups of students may discuss their reading material, whether all of them have read the same selection or some of them have read different selections on a common topic or from a common genre. The students prepare for the group meeting by reading material, taking notes about the information, and marking (with strips of paper or sticky notes) passages in the book that support their answers. Then they discuss the material, offering ideas and responding to the comments of the other group members. In this activity, analysis of the material is meaningful to the students. They choose what is significant in the material, and they relate the material to matters of importance to them—for example, how the author's use of language affects the story—rather than relying upon the teacher to direct the activity.

▶ Critical Reading of Literature

 LITERATURE

Many excellent books for young people are filled with themes of honesty and dishonesty, sharing and selfishness, courage and cowardice, and others. Discussion of these themes in the context of the stories' characters, with consideration of alternatives available to them and of the appropriateness or inappropriateness of their actions, can build skill in critical reading (McMillan and Gentile, 1988). Students can be asked to compare the actions of the characters to standards of behavior set by the law, the school, parents, and so forth.

Literature analysis can be a vehicle for teaching critical reading. One activity is to have students evaluate the evidence that Chicken Little had that the sky was falling and decide whether or not the other animals were right to just take her word for it.

Critical thinking is often important to the interpretation of humor. Therefore, humorous literature can be an enjoyable vehicle for teaching critical reading skills. It is especially good for determining the author's purpose (often to entertain, but sometimes also to convince through humor) and for evaluating content (especially distinguishing fact from fantasy and recognizing assumptions).

To analyze characterization in literature selections, students must be able to make inferences about characters, going beyond directly stated information about them. Teachers need to model this process for their students, using clues from material that students have to read to form hypotheses about characters' emotions, beliefs, actions, and desires. The teachers can tell how their prior knowledge and beliefs affected their inferences. Then students can be asked to attempt to make inferences in the same way. Students need to know that authors reveal information about characters through narration; the characters' words, thoughts, and actions; and things other characters say about them. Cynthia Voigt's *Homecoming* and *Dicey's Song* are both good to use for helping students learn to make inferences about characters.

A grid such as the one in Example 8.1, based on the character of Hank Zipzer in Henry Winkler and Lin Oliver's *Hank Zipzer: Help! Somebody Get me Out of Fourth Grade*, leads students to collect evidence about a character, interpret the evidence, and make a generalization about the evidence after all of it has been collected. Looking for commonalities and discrepancies in the data and considering the amount of evidence available for a conclusion that is drawn are important to good critical analysis. When readers draw evidence from the reactions of other characters in the story, they must evaluate the credibility of the sources before accepting that evidence (Commeyras, 1989).

DIVERSITY Careful questioning by the teacher to extend limited and stereotyped depictions of people in reading materials can help students develop expertise in critical reading. Students must be encouraged to relate their personal experiences to the materials. They can examine stereotyped language in relation to stories in which it occurs, and teachers can point out the problems caused by looking at people and ideas in a stereotyped way. For example, some books give the impression that certain nationalities have particular personality characteristics, but it should be easy to demonstrate that not all people of that nationality are alike, just as not all citizens of the United States are alike. Multicultural literature can be a vehicle through which teachers can create awareness of cultural variations and of negative biases that exist toward some groups, allowing progress to be made toward elimination of these biases (Barta and Grindler, 1996).

DIVERSITY Teachers can ask students to compare different versions of folktales by constructing Venn diagrams and comparison charts. Such activities can improve comprehension and show commonalities in stories from different cultures. Example 8.2 shows a comparison of an Appalachian folktale with a Russian one.

Students can also analyze the differences between book and video versions of stories. If the students have adequate schemata for understanding the text, it is better to have them read the text before seeing the video. Sometimes students may be exposed to the story on video, but only a portion of the text version may be used in instruction. Then some students may be motivated to finish the text on

EXAMPLE 8.1 Sample Character Grid on Hank Zipzer

Evidence from Book	What I Think
1. What kinds of statements does this character make?	
A. Wisecracks.	A. Has a sense of humor
B. Insults to sister and her friend.	B. Not always kind.
My summary: Wants classmates to think he's cool.	
2. What kinds of actions does the character take?	
A. Schemes to avoid parent–teacher conference	A. Has lots of ideas to avoid conflict.
B. Sneaks.	B. Risks being caught to find out what he wants to learn.
My summary: Will do things he knows he shouldn't to avoid being embarrassed.	
3. How does the character think?	
A. He schemes.	A. He can think up good plans.
B. He has a low opinion of himself.	B. He knows he's not good in school.
My summary: He's smarter than he thinks, just has trouble with things that don't interest him.	
4. What do others say to the character?	
A. Breathe.	A. Gets "uptight."
B. Stay focused.	B. Hank's mind wanders.
My summary: Hank can't even keep his attention on things that do interest him.	
5. How do others treat the character?	
A. Friends help out.	A. They like him and are loyal.
B. Grandfather is helpful.	B. Grandfather thinks he's a good kid.
My summary: Hank is basically a nice guy although he's not nice to his sister.	
6. How do others describe the character?	
A. Has learning challenges.	A. Needs to study harder.
My summary: Hank's not a bookworm type kid.	
7. Over all, what do I think the character is like?	
Hank is a fun kid who doesn't like school.	

EXAMPLE 8.2 Comparison of Folktales

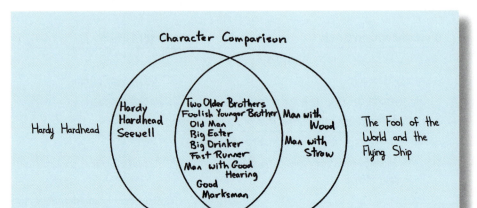

Character Comparison

Hardy Hardhead

Hardy Hardhead Seewell

Two Older Brothers
Foolish Younger Brother
Old Man
Big Eater
Big Drinker
Fast Runner
Man with Good Hearing
Good Marksman

Man with Wood
Man with Straw

The Fool of the World and the Flying Ship

STRUGGLING READER/
INTERVENTION

their own. Most video versions are necessarily abbreviated versions. However, seeing an abbreviated presentation of a story that provides information about its basic structure may offer needed support for struggling readers, giving them the confidence to attempt to read the text (Duncan, 1993). Seeing enjoyable video versions of lengthy books, such as the Harry Potter books, may motivate students to read long, complex books.

Students can use Venn diagrams to show how characters were alike and different in video and text versions of stories. They can also write video reviews, including notes about how true the video was to the book. Some of the books that have video versions available for comparison are *Sarah, Plain and Tall*; *Where the Red Fern Grows*; *The Secret Garden*; *Bridge to Terabithia*; *Tuck Everlasting*; *Holes*; and several Harry Potter books. (See Chapter 13 for an example in which students compared text and video versions of a story.)

▶ Evaluating Factors Related to the Author

Krieger (1990) found that middle school students were not aware of the authors of the material they read and the devices the authors used (flashbacks, foreshadowing, and so forth) for special purposes. She read to these students, modeling her thinking processes concerning why the author included certain details. She asked them to make predictions about what might happen next from clues left by the author. Outside assignments, such as keeping listening journals with their reactions to the stories, allowed for further thinking about the story and/or the author. This listening experience familiarizes students with the ways that authors express ideas, making it more likely that they will be able to read stories with understanding later.

A critical literacy curriculum emphasizes discussion: "Students involved in a critical literacy curriculum read the world and the word, by using dialogue to engage texts and discourses inside and outside the classroom" (Cadiero-Kaplan, 2002, p. 377). Students who take this approach to reading history, for example, see it "as a record told from one perspective that can be examined from other perspectives" (p. 378). Acknowledging the bias that may be present in a particular point of view enables students to draw more valid conclusions from reading than they would if they accepted everything that is in print as true.

The proficient critical reader must consider and evaluate factors related to the person who wrote the material, taking into account the following four categories.

Author's Purpose.   The critical reader will try to determine whether the author wrote the material to inform, to entertain, to persuade, or for some other purpose. This is an interpretive reading skill.

Author's Point of View.   The critical reader will want to know whether the writer belonged to a group, lived in an area, or held a strong view that would tend to bias any of her or his opinions about a subject in one way or another. Two accounts of the American Revolutionary War might be very different if one author was from England and the other was from the United States.

Students can learn more about point of view by writing letters or essays about issues from different points of view. For example, they might imagine that a school dress code is being considered and take the point of view of an elementary school student, then that of a concerned parent, and finally that of a school principal.

Author's Style and Tone.   The author's style is the manner in which he or she uses vocabulary (vividness, precision, inclusion of emotional words, use of figurative language) and sentence structure (the order in which the elements of the sentence appear). Special attention should be given to use of figurative language (see Chapter 6), and to the use of emotional words, which do much to sway the reader toward or away from a point of view or attitude. Note the effects of these two sentences:

Author 1: Next we heard the heart-rending cry of the wounded tiger.

Author 2: When the tiger was shot, it let out a vicious roar.

Teachers should be aware of undesirable aspects of the style or tone of some writers of material for children and adolescents. A condescending tone, for example, is quickly sensed and resented.

Author's Competence.   The reliability of written material is affected by the author's competence to write about the subject in question. If background information shows that a star hockey player has written an article on the nation's foreign policy, intermediate-grade students will have little trouble determining that the reliability of the statements in this article is likely to be lower than the reliability of a similar article written by a person directly involved in making policy.

To determine an author's competence, students should consider his or her education and experience, referring to books such as *Current Biography Yearbook 2006* and *Ninth Book of Junior Authors & Illustrators* or to book jacket flaps to find this information. Teachers can give students a topic and ask them to name people who might write about it. Students can discuss which people might be most qualified, or they can compare two authors of books on the same subject and decide which one is better qualified.

In these days of heavy use of Internet sites, determining the competence of authors is made more difficult. Students should be taught to be wary of material posted on the Internet by unknown authors or on sites that do not screen the material and provide information about the authors.

▶ Evaluating the Material

Besides comprehending the material literally, the critical reader needs to be able to determine and evaluate the following factors.

Timeliness.   The critical reader will wish to check the date that the material was published because the timeliness of an article or a book can make a crucial difference in a rapidly changing world. An outdated social studies book, for example, may show incorrect boundaries for countries or fail to show some countries that now exist; similarly, an outdated science or health book may refer to a disease as incurable when a cure has recently been found.

Accuracy and Adequacy.   Nonfiction material should be approached with this question in mind: "Are the statements presented here true?" The importance of a good background of experiences becomes evident in this situation. A reader who has had previous experience with the material will have a basis of comparison not available to a reader who lacks this experience. A person with even a little knowledge of a particular field can often spot such indications of inadequacy as exaggerated statements, one-sided presentations, and opinion offered as fact. Readers without experience in the subject can always check reference material to see if the statements in the material are supported elsewhere.

Material found on the Internet poses a particular problem. As Owens, Hester, and Teale (2002) point out, "Just because a site is listed in the first set of hits that appear on the search screen does not mean it is a legitimate or useful site" (p. 623). In some cases, companies or organizations pay to ensure that their site turns up at or near the top of specific searches. Students need to be led to see the potential biases that might be associated with

---

TEACHING TIP

Currency of Material

Locate old science or geography books containing statements that are no longer true and use them to show the importance of using current sources. Let students compare old and new books to find the differences (for example, new material included and information that has changed over time) and discuss which types of material are most likely, and which least likely, to depend on recent copyright dates for accuracy.

such sites. Double-checking information in other reference materials is highly advisable when material from Internet sites is used. Brainstorming about the biases that are most likely to appear on specific sites is a good classroom activity. Information about how to evaluate websites is provided in Chapter 13.

Appropriateness. Critical readers must be able to determine whether the material is suitable for their purposes. A book or an article can be completely accurate and yet not be applicable to the problem or topic under consideration. For example, a student looking for information for a paper entitled "Cherokee Ceremonies" needs to realize that an article on the invention of the Cherokee alphabet is irrelevant to the task at hand.

To promote the use of critical reading strategies, teachers can use Inquiry Charts (I-Charts) (Hoffman, 1992). First, the class identifies a topic and formulates the questions that will be the basis of the inquiry. The teacher records these on a large I-Chart. References, such as textbook selections, trade books, encyclopedia articles, magazine articles, and websites that pertain to the topic, are also collected and listed on the I-Chart as they are used.

Next, the teacher questions the students to discover their prior knowledge about the topic and enters their responses on the I-Chart under the identified questions. Information that students have or collect that is not related to the identified questions is recorded under "Other Interesting Facts and Figures." If students have other questions that were not initially identified, these are listed under "New Questions." The students read the source material independently or in a group, or the teacher reads it to them. Students may read the sources that are appropriate for their reading abilities. Each source is discussed, and the class makes decisions about the appropriateness of the information contributed for answering the identified questions. Information pertinent to the questions is recorded in the proper spaces. More "Interesting Facts" and "New Questions" may also be added.

After all sources have been read and information from them recorded, students can write a summary that includes the information from all sources. Then students compare what they had listed as prior knowledge with the newly acquired information and clarify any misconceptions that they previously held. Unanswered "New Questions" are researched further by individuals or small groups, who locate appropriate sources for the information, and report findings to the class. [See Example 8.3 for an example of an I-Chart. The format was modified from the one that Hoffman (1992) developed, which had separate summaries for each heading.]

Differentiating Fact from Opinion. This skill is vital for good critical reading. Readers often unquestioningly accept as fact anything they see in print, even though printed material is frequently composed of statements of opinion. Some authors intermingle facts and opinions, giving little indication that they are presenting anything but pure fact.

EXAMPLE 8.3 I-Chart

Guiding Questions

	Topic: Frederick Douglass	1. Who was Frederick Douglass?	2. How did he help oppose slavery?	3. How did he become a free-man?	4. Other Interesting Facts	5. New Questions
	What We Know	A black man who fought against slavery	Made speeches	Don't know		
S O U R C E S	Frederick Douglass Fights for Freedom. By Margaret Davidson. New York: Scholastic.	He was born a slave; he became a freeman.	He made speeches; he helped the Underground Railroad; he started the first newspaper for blacks.	He escaped and was a fugitive slave, but even then wrote a book and made speeches. He fled to England, where they raised money to buy his freedom.	It was illegal to teach a slave to read and write. He learned from poor white friends who could go to school.	What laws did he influence after the Civil War?
	Narrative of the Life of Frederick Douglass, An American Slave. By Frederick Douglass. New York: Anchor Books.	He was a very proud, brave, and determined man.	His book and his speeches made people more aware of terrible conditions for most slaves.	Even with much planning, his first attempt to escape failed, but a later attempt worked.	He learned shipyard skills and earned high wages but had to turn them over to his master. He taught other slaves to read. He sometimes had harsh masters who beat him until his back bled.	Why did enough people who didn't own slaves favor slavery and allow it to continue and allow the fugitive slave act?

Summary: He was born a slave. He worked hard. He learned to read even though it was illegal to teach slaves to read. At times he had very harsh masters who beat him until his back bled. He escaped and helped fight against slavery. He gave lectures and wrote a book at the risk of being caught and put into slavery again. He told people what slavery was really like. Although it was illegal to teach slaves to read, he learned to read and he taught other slaves. He learned a trade and could earn high wages. He eventually fled to England where people contributed to buy his freedom. He started a newspaper for blacks.

Find out what laws he helped get made. Find out why slavery was allowed.

Some readers have trouble reading critically because they lack a clear idea of what constitutes a fact. *Facts* are statements that can be verified through direct observation, consultation of official records of past events, or scientific experimentation. The statement "General Lee surrendered to General Grant at Appomattox" is a fact that can be verified by checking historical records. For various reasons, opinions cannot be directly verified. For example, the statement "She is the most beautiful girl in the world" is unverifiable and is therefore an opinion. Even if all the girls in the world could be assembled for comparison, people's standards of beauty differ, and a scale of relative beauty would be impossible to construct.

Knowledge of key words that signal opinions—such as *believe, think, seems, may, appears, probably, likely,* and *possibly*—can be extremely helpful to readers. By pointing out these clues and providing practice in discrimination, teachers can help students develop the ability to discriminate between facts and opinions.

Students must also understand that not all opinions are of equal value because some have been based on facts, whereas others are unsupported. Critical readers try to determine the relative merit of opinions as well as to separate the opinions from the facts.

Activities similar to the one in "Putting It into Practice: Fact and Opinion" on page 290 may also be used to help students make this difficult differentiation.

Recognizing Propaganda Techniques.   Students of all ages are constantly deluged with writing that attempts to influence their thinking and actions. Some of these materials may be used for good purposes and some for bad ones. For example, most people would consider propaganda designed to persuade people to protect their health as "good" and propaganda intended to persuade people to do things that are harmful to their health as "bad." Because propaganda techniques are often used to sway people toward or away from a cause or point of view, students should be made aware of these techniques so that they can avoid being unduly influenced by them.

The Institute for Propaganda Awareness has identified seven undesirable **propaganda techniques** that good critical readers should know about:

1. Name calling—using derogatory labels (*reactionary, troublemaker*) to create negative reactions toward a person without providing evidence to support such impressions.

2. Glittering generalities—using vague phrases to influence a point of view without providing necessary specifics.

TEACHING TIP

Fact and Opinion

Use newspaper editorials to provide your students practice in distinguishing fact from opinion, especially in the intermediate grades. Have students underline each sentence in the editorial with colored pencils, one color for facts and another for opinions. Then ask them to discuss which opinions are best supported by facts.

You can also ask students to write editorials about topics of interest. Their editorials should include facts, their own opinions, and their reasons for holding these opinions.

Fact and Opinion

Give students copies of the following paragraph, which opens the book *Homesick: My Own Story* by Jean Fritz (Dell, 1982, p. 9).

> In my father's study there was a large globe with all the countries of the world running around it. I could put my finger on the exact spot where I was and had been ever since I'd been born. And I was on the wrong side of the globe. I was in China in a city named Hankow, a dot on a crooked line that seemed to break the country right in two. The line was really the Yangtse River, but who would know by looking at a map what the Yangtse River really was?

Ask students to read this opening paragraph carefully, underlining any parts that are statements of opinion, based on the definition of opinion that was discussed in class. Ask them to decide what they can tell about the main character from both the facts and the opinions revealed in this opening paragraph. Then have them decide how the opinion or opinions that they have located are likely to affect the story they are about to read.

Let your students share their reactions to this opening passage before they begin to read the book. After they have finished reading the book, have them discuss whether or not their initial reactions were accurate.

3. Transfer technique—associating a respected organization or symbol with a particular person, project, product, or idea, thus transferring that respect to the person or thing being promoted.

4. Plain-folks talk—relating a person (for example, a politician) or a proposed program to the "common people" in order to gain their support.

5. Testimonial technique—having a person, often well-known, endorse a product or proposal.

6. Bandwagon technique—playing on the urge to do what others are doing by giving the impression that everyone else is participating in a particular activity.

7. Card stacking—telling only one side of a story by ignoring information that favors the opposing point of view.

Teachers should describe propaganda techniques to the class and model the process of locating these techniques in printed materials. Then their students should practice this skill. Students can learn to detect propaganda techniques by analyzing newspaper and magazine advertisements, printed political campaign material, and requests for donations to various organizations.

TEACHING TIP

Propaganda

Have a propaganda hunt. For middle-grade students, label boxes with the names of the seven propaganda techniques listed earlier. Then ask students to find examples of these techniques in a variety of sources and to drop their examples into the boxes. Let the class evaluate each example for appropriateness to the category in which it was placed. (You may only want to focus on the bandwagon technique with younger students.)

You may also ask students to write material that will persuade their classmates to do something. Then have them examine the material for the techniques their classmates used.

LITERATURE **Making Value Judgments.** Readers need to be able to determine whether the actions of both fictional and real-life characters

Critical Reading

Activities like the following ones can be used to provide students with practice in critical reading strategies.

1. Have students compare editorials from two newspapers with different viewpoints or from different areas. Have them decide why differences exist and which stand, if either, is more reasonable, based on the facts provided.

2. Ask students to compare two biographies of a well-known person by answering questions such as "How do they differ in their treatment of the subject? Is either of the authors likely to be biased for or against the subject? Are there contradictory statements in the two works? If so, which one seems most likely to be correct? Could the truth be different from both accounts?" (There are appropriate biographies for students in all grades.)

3. Use computer simulation programs for practice in making critical judgments. These programs provide simulated models of real-life experiences with which students can experiment in a risk-free manner.

4. Ask students to examine newspaper articles for typographical errors and to determine whether or not each typographical error changed the message of the article.

5. Have the class interpret political cartoons from various newspapers, referring to news on which they believe the cartoons were based.

6. Ask students to examine the headlines of news stories and decide whether or not the headlines fit the stories.

7. After they study the nutritional aspects of sugar and chemical food additives, have students examine the ingredients lists from popular snacks, asking themselves what food value various snacks have, according to their labels.

8. Use a lesson plan such as the Read•Write•Think lesson, "Investigating Junk Mail: Negotiating Critical Literacy at the Mailbox" to tie critical reading to real life.

are reasonable or unreasonable. To help students develop this ability, teachers may ask questions such as the following:

> Was the Little Red Hen justified in eating all the bread she made, refusing to share with the other animals? Why or why not?

> Was it a good thing for Heidi to save bread from the Sessmans' table to take back to the grandmother? Why or why not?

To complete this type of activity, readers draw on their schemata related to right and wrong actions. Because of their varying schemata, not all students will answer in the same way.

Creative Reading

Creative reading involves going beyond the material presented by the author. Like critical reading, creative reading requires readers to think as they read, and it also requires them to use their imaginations. Such reading results in the production of new ideas.

Teachers must carefully nurture creative reading, trying not to ask only questions that have absolute answers because such questions may discourage the diverse

Link to the Read•Write•Think lesson on investigating junk mail from the Student Website for the book, or go to http:// www.readwritethink.org.

Time for Reflection

Some teachers tell students that they should believe certain things "because it says so in the book." Others tell them, "Don't believe everything that you read."

What would *you* tell them, and why?

processes characteristic of creative reading. To go beyond the material in the text, readers must make use of their background schemata, combining this prior knowledge with ideas from the text to produce a new response based on, but not completely dictated by, the text. Creative readers must be skilled in predicting outcomes, visualizing the things they read about, solving problems, and producing their own creations.

▶ Predicting Outcomes

Predicting outcomes, discussed earlier as a good purpose-setting technique, is a creative reading skill. To predict outcomes, readers must put together available information, note trends, and then project these trends into the future, making decisions about what events might logically follow. A creative reader is constantly predicting what will happen next in a story, reacting to the events that he or she is reading about, and drawing conclusions about their results.

Often the students' creative intuition leads to the generation of one or more high-quality possibilities for what will happen next. Jaeger (2007) says, "Intuitive knowledge is bound by experience; it is embedded in the actions and reactions of our everyday lives; it is located in the emotional, physiological, and cognitive realms; and it balances the more systematic process of rational thought" (p. 442). Every life experience that a student has, in or out of the classroom, enhances the chances for creative intuition (Jaeger, 2007).

 LITERATURE

To help students acquire the skill of reading creatively, teachers should model the thought process involved. After students practice on various texts, the teacher can ask them to explain their reasons for thinking as they did. Some questions that middle school students might answer for Gordon Korman's *Schooled*, for example, are as follows:

> What would have happened if Mrs. Donnelly hadn't lived at Garland Farm when she was young?

> What would have happened if Cap hadn't driven Mr. Rodrigo to the hospital?

> A question for younger students from Kimberly Willis Holt's *Piper Reed: Navy Brat* might be

> What would have happened if Tori hadn't overheard Piper getting Sam ready to pretend to be a gypsy fortune teller?

Jaeger (2007) suggests use of the Know-Predict-Wonder technique. Students look at the cover of a book that they are about to read and brainstorm what they *know* about the book's content, based on the picture and print on the cover. Then they *predict* what they think may be in the book, based on their expectations about things that might happen because of some clue on the cover. Then they tell the things that they *wonder* about the book's content, although the cover offers no clues. The teacher then gives one important bit of information about the book's content and lets the students expand the Know-Predict-Wonder lists, using this new information. (For more activities to work on predicting outcomes, see the Student Website for this textbook.)

◗ Visualization

Visualization is seeing pictures in the mind, and readers draw on their existing schemata to accomplish this. By vividly visualizing the events depicted by the author's words, creative readers allow themselves to become a part of the story; they see the colors, hear the sounds, feel the textures, taste the flavors, and smell the odors that the writer describes. They will find that they are living the story as they read. By doing this, they will enjoy the story more and understand it more deeply.

Parsons (2006) points out that the story becomes more concrete for readers as they are able to elaborate on the images they have created. She says that visualization has three dimensions: picturing (forming mental images in the form of still pictures), watching (feeling as if you are beside the character as an observer of a scene), and seeing (living through the experience as if you are present as a participant).

Students can be encouraged to see pictures in their minds as they read silently, although training in visualization may be less effective with very young children, who may not be able to form images on command, than with third- through sixth-grade students (Tierney and Cunningham, 1984). Such *guided imagery* has been shown to enhance comprehension and can help with later recall of the events that the student has read about. Guided-imagery activities before reading a story can help readers draw on their past experiences to visualize events, places, and things in a story. Creating such images before reading has been shown to result in better literal comprehension than is produced by creating the images after reading (Harp, 1988).

Teachers should model their own mental processes as they visualize objects, prior experiences, and written descriptions to help students develop techniques for visualization. Next, they can lead students to visualize and describe concrete objects after they have closely examined them in the classroom and then to visualize and describe objects or experiences outside the classroom. If students draw the objects they visualize, they can compare their drawings to the actual objects or photographs of them at a later time. Teachers can also read high-imagery stories to their students and have individuals share their mental images with partners or small groups. The students can illustrate the stories or make three-dimensional representations from clay (Onofrey and Theurer, 2007; Fredericks, 1986).

The Read•Write•Think lesson "Guided Comprehension: Visualizing Using the Sketch-to-Stretch Strategy" shows one technique for working on visualization with students in grades 3–5. Another multifaceted lesson found at the same location is "Mind Pictures: Strategies That Enhance Mental Imagery While Reading," designed to be used with grades 6–8. Go to http://www.readwritethink.org or link from the Student Website for this book.

◗ Solving Problems

 LITERATURE

Creative readers relate the things they read to their own personal problems, sometimes applying the solution of a problem they encounter in a story to a different situation. For instance, after reading the chapter in *Tom Sawyer* in which Tom tricks his friends into painting a fence for him, a student may use a similar ruse to persuade a sibling to take over his or her chores or homework.

To help students become problem solvers, teachers need to use books in which different types of problems are solved. After reading aloud or letting their

Visualization

The following activities encourage visualization:

1. Ask open-ended questions to help students visualize objects or experiences. For example, if a student says that she sees a house, you can ask, "What does it look like?" If she replies that it is white with green trim, you may ask, "What is the yard like?"

2. Using a paragraph or statement that contains almost no description, ask students questions about details that they would need to picture the scene in their minds. An example follows:

> The dog ran toward Jane and Susan. Jane held out her hands toward it and smiled.

Questions: What kind of dog was it? How big was it? Why was it running toward the girls? What happened when the dog reached the girls? Where did this action take place? Was the dog on a leash, behind a fence, or running free?

3. Have students dramatize a story that they have read, such as the folktale "Caps for Sale." To dramatize the story well, they must picture the setting and characters, as well as the action that takes place.

4. Compare the characters, action, and scenery in a movie with mental images formed from reading a book or story.

---

students read such a book, the teachers can ask the students questions such as the following:

1. What problem did the character(s) in the story face?

2. How was the problem handled?

3. Was the solution a good one?

4. What other possible solutions can you think of?

5. Would you prefer the solution in the book or one of the others?

Literature selections abound with characters trying to solve problems in efficient and inefficient ways. Students can analyze these problem-solving situations. Problems in a story can be identified as they occur. Discussion of the situation can take place as each problem arises. *Encyclopedia Brown* and *Nate the Great* mysteries offer good problem-solving opportunities for students in intermediate and primary grades, respectively (Flynn, 1989).

▶ Producing New Creations

Art, drama, and dance can be useful in elaborating on what students read. Drawing scenes from a story, acting out scenes from the story, or interpreting the story through movement are all good activities. In addition, by creating a new ending for a story, adding a new character, changing some aspect of a character, or inserting an additional adventure within the framework of the existing story, students approach reading creatively. Analysis of a dramatic interpretation of a story can provide students with a model of creative response to the narrative (Duncan, 1993).

Time for Reflection

Some teachers believe that only literal-level thinking should be expected of young children when these children read. Others believe that the children can and should do higher-order thinking about their reading.

What do *you* think, and why?

Creating New Products

Use activities like the following ones to encourage students to create new products. Most of them involve responding to literature through writing. (More on the reading-writing connection appears in Chapters 10 and 12.)

1. Ask your students to illustrate a story that they have read, using a series of pictures or three-dimensional scenes.

2. Have your students write plays or poems based on works of fiction that they have read or write prose narratives based on poems that they have read.

3. Have students transfer the story of *Heidi* to the Rocky Mountains or to Appalachia.

Effective Questioning

All teachers use both written and oral questions as a part of class activities. They may ask questions as a way of setting purposes for students' reading, of starting discussions, or for assessing knowledge with tests and quizzes. Regardless of when they are used, questions have been found to foster increased comprehension, apparently because readers give more time to the material related to answering them (Durkin, 1981). Students also remember best information about which they have been directly questioned. Additionally, the types of questions that teachers ask about selections affect the type of information that students recall about the selections. Research indicates, for example, that asking more inference questions during and after the reading of stories results in improved inferential comprehension (Pearson, 1985). Because questions have such a strong influence on student learning, teachers need to understand thoroughly the process of preparing questions.

STANDARDS/ASSESSMENTS

Questions can be phrased differently and still address the same content. The phrasing of questions can make them easier or harder to answer. Some require simple answers, and some require complex ones. Eliciting all the information obtainable from one question that requires a complex response may take several questions requiring simple responses.

Wiggins and McTighe (1998) urge teachers "to use provocative and multilayered questions that reveal the richness and complexities of a subject." They call these questions "essential" because they emphasize "the key inquiries and the core ideas of a discipline" (p. 28). These educators recommend using "essential questions" as the central focus of courses, units, and lessons. Introductory questions such as "In what ways is a fairy tale 'true'? In what ways is any documentary 'false'?" (p. 35) are appropriate for comparing such material as myths, novels, biographies, and histories. Wiggins and McTighe (1998) also suggest that teachers use only two to five of these questions for a unit and that they plan concrete activities and inquiries related to each one. Teachers should word essential questions in such a way that students can understand them and should assess their understanding of each question focus at the beginning of a lesson. In addition, teachers should present questions about a central concept in the order of simple to complex. The questions asked early in the unit should always point toward the larger essential questions, and teachers should lead students to ask broader questions prompted by their answers to questions more narrowly focused. Guiding a unit of study by using essential questions can also help address diversity in academic ability in a classroom because essential questions can prompt gifted and talented students to explore the central, significant ideas of a discipline through independent learning and inquiry.

DIVERSITY

Preparing Questions

Teachers often ask questions that are devised on the spur of the moment. This practice no doubt results from the pressure of the many different tasks that a teacher must perform during the day, but it is not good for at least two reasons. First, questions developed hastily, without close attention to the material involved, tend to be detail questions ("What color was the car? Where were they going?") because these

Students remember best information about which they have been directly questioned.

© Jeff Cadge/Getty Images

EXAMPLE 8.4 Options for Questioning

Questions Based on Comprehension Factors

1. Main idea—identify the central theme or idea of the selection.
2. Detail—identify directly stated facts.
3. Vocabulary—define words to fit the context of the selection.
4. Sequence—identify the order of events in the selection.
5. Inference—infer information implied by the author.
6. Evaluation—judge ideas presented, on the basis of a standard.
7. Creative response—go beyond the material and create new ideas based on the material read.

Questions Based on Source of Answers

1. Textually explicit—answers are directly stated in the text.
2. Textually implicit—answers are implied by the text and require inferences on the part of the reader.
3. Scriptually implicit—answers come from the reader's background knowledge.

Questions Based on Story Grammar

1. Setting—when and where the story took place and who was involved.
2. Initiating event—the event that started the story sequence.
3. Reaction—the main character's reaction to the initiating event.
4. Action—the main character's actions caused by the initiating event and subsequent events.
5. Consequence—the result of the main character's actions.

questions are much easier to construct than most other types. But detail questions fail to measure more than simple recall. Second, many hastily constructed questions tend to be poorly worded, vague in intent, and misleading to students. Example 8.4 shows some options on which to base questioning.

▶ Questions Based on Comprehension Factors

One basis for planning questioning strategies is to try to construct specific types of questions to tap different types of comprehension and different factors related to comprehension. Seven major types of questions are generally useful in guiding reading: main idea, detail, vocabulary, sequence, inference, evaluation, and creative-response questions.

◀■▶ **SEEING IT IN PRACTICE**

Video Cases
View the main video and bonus videos in the Video Case "Reading Comprehension Strategies for Elementary School Students." How did the teachers encourage students to answer inferential questions appropriately? Was the technique effective? Would you use it in your teaching? Why or why not? Enter your thoughts into your journal.

Now revisit the Video Case "Vygotsky's Zone of Proximal Development." Notice how the teacher helps the students answer inferential questions by tying the process to their personal experiences. Did this procedure appear to be effective? What makes you think so?

Main Idea Questions. Main idea questions ask the students to identify the central theme of the selection. Possible main idea questions are "What is a sentence that explains what this selection is about?" "Why was the patchwork quilt so important in this story?" Main idea questions help students become aware of the relationships among details.

Detail Questions. Detail questions ask for bits of information stated in the material, such as "Who was coming to play with Maria? What was Betty bringing with her? When did Betty finally arrive? Where had Betty left her bicycle?" Although it is important for students to assimilate the information these questions cover, very little depth of comprehension is necessary to answer them all correctly. Therefore, even though these questions are easy to construct, they should not constitute the bulk of the questions that the teacher asks.

Vocabulary Questions. Vocabulary questions check students' understanding of word meanings, generally as used in a particular selection. For discussion purposes, a teacher might ask students to produce as many meanings of a specific word as they can, but purpose-setting questions and test questions should ask for the meaning of a word as it is used in the selection being read.

Sequence Questions. Sequence questions check the students' knowledge of the order in which events occurred in the story. The question "What did Alex and Robbie do when their parents left the house?" is not a sequence question because students are free to list the events in any order they choose. The question "What were the three problems that Alex and Robbie had, in the order that they happened?" requires students to display their grasp of the sequence of events.

Inference Questions. Inference questions ask for information that is implied but not directly stated in the material. These questions require some reading between the lines. The following is an example:

Margie and Jan were sitting on the couch listening to Jonas Brothers CDs. Their father walked in and announced, "I hear that there is a Jonas Brothers concert at the Municipal Auditorium next week." Both girls jumped up and ran toward their father. "Can we go? Can we go?" they begged.

Question: Do you think Margie and Jan liked to hear the music of the Jonas Brothers? Why or why not?

Evaluation Questions.   Evaluation questions require students to make judgments about the material. Although these judgments are inferences, they depend on more than the information implied or stated by the story; the students must have enough experience related to the situations involved to establish standards for comparison. An example of an evaluation question for Doreen Cronin's picture book *Click, Clack, Moo: Cows That Type* is "Did the cows have reasonable demands? What information in the book and your experience make you believe this?" These questions are excellent for open-ended class discussion but hard to grade as test questions.

Creative-Response Questions.   Creative-response questions ask students to go beyond the material and create new ideas based on the ideas that they have read. Questions requiring creative response are also good for class discussions. As a means of testing comprehension of a passage, however, they are not desirable because almost any response could be considered correct. Examples of creative-response questions include "If the story stopped after Jimmy lost his money, what ending would you write for it?" and "If Meg had not gone to school that day, what do you think might have happened?"

STANDARDS/
ASSESSMENTS

▶ Questions Based on Sources of Answers

Pearson and Johnson (1978) suggest three question types. They label questions as *textually explicit* when the questions have answers that are directly stated in the text, as *textually implicit* when they have implied answers (but the text contains clues for making the necessary inference), and as *scriptually implicit* when the reader must answer them from his or her background knowledge.

The reader's own characteristics interact with the text and the question to determine the actual demands of the question-answering task. A reader's interest, background knowledge, and reading skill affect the difficulty and even the type of question for each reader. The structure of a question may lead a teacher to expect a textually explicit response, whereas the student's background may cause him or her to give a scriptually implicit response (Wixson, 1983). For example, if the text tells readers how to construct a kite, a student who has actually made a kite before reading the material may answer the question on the basis of direct experience, rather than from information presented in the text.

Inability to take the perspective of another person can affect comprehension. Students who can take the perspective of another person do better on scriptually implicit questions than those who cannot (Gardner and Smith, 1987).

▶ Story Grammar as a Basis for Questioning

Another basis for questioning is the use of a story grammar. A story is a series of events that are related to one another in particular ways. As people hear and read many stories, they develop expectations, sometimes called *story schemata*, about the types of things that they will encounter; these help them organize information.

Related story schemata are described by a **story grammar.** Questions based on a story grammar may help students develop story schemata. The questions should be chosen to reflect the logical sequence of events.

David Rumelhart proposed a simple story grammar that "describes a story as consisting of a setting and one or more episodes" (Sadow, 1982, p. 519). The setting includes the main characters and the time and location of the events, and each episode contains an initiating event, the main character's reaction to it, an action of the main character caused by this reaction, and a consequence of that action, which may act as an initiating event for a subsequent episode. (Sometimes some of the elements of an episode are not directly stated.) Sadow suggests the following five generic questions as appropriate types to ask about a story:

1. Where and when did the events in the story take place, and who was involved in them? (setting)

2. What started the chain of events in the story? (initiating event)

3. What was the main character's reaction to this event? (reaction)

4. What did the main character do about it? (action)

5. What happened as a result of what the main character did? (consequence) (Sadow, 1982, p. 520)

Such questions can help students see the underlying order of ideas in a story, but teachers should of course reword them to fit the story and the particular students. For example, Question 1 can be broken into three questions (*where, when, who*), and the teacher can provide appropriate focus by using words or phrases from the story. After students address these story grammar questions, which establish the essential facts, they should answer questions that help them relate the story to their own experiences and knowledge (Sadow, 1982).

▶ Guidelines for Preparation

STANDARDS/
ASSESSMENTS

Some guidelines for preparing questions may be useful to teachers who wish to improve their questioning techniques. The following suggestions may help teachers avoid some pitfalls that other educators have detected:

1. In trying to determine overall comprehension skills, ask a variety of questions designed to reflect different types of comprehension. Avoid overloading the evaluation with a single type of question.

2. Don't ask questions about obscure or insignificant portions of the selection. Such questions may make a test harder, but the students' responses to them are not realistic indicators of comprehension. "Hard" tests and "good" tests are not necessarily the same thing.

3. Avoid ambiguous or tricky questions. If a question has two or more possible interpretations, more than one answer for it has to be acceptable.

4. Avoid useless questions. Questions that a person who has not read the material can answer correctly offer you no valuable information about comprehension.

5. Don't ask questions in language that is more difficult than the language of the selection the question is about. Otherwise, questions may be worded in a way that prevents a student who knows the answer from responding appropriately.

6. Make sure that the answers to sequence questions require knowledge of the order of events. Don't confuse questions that simply ask for lists with sequence questions.

7. Don't ask for unsupported opinions when you are testing for comprehension. Have students give support for their opinions, by asking, "Why do you think that?" or "What in the story made you think that?" If you ask for an unsupported opinion, any answer will be correct.

8. Don't ask for opinions if you want facts. Ask for the type of information that you want to receive.

9. Avoid questions that give away information. Instead of asking "What makes you believe that the boy was angry?" ask, "How do you think the boy felt? Why?" Questions may lead students to the answers by supplying too much information.

10. Use precise terms in phrasing questions related to reading. Ask students to compare or contrast, to predict, or to draw conclusions about the reading (Smith, 1989).

Helping Students Answer Questions

 DIVERSITY

Some students lack familiarity with the question-answer-feedback sequence often used for instructional purposes. They may not have been exposed to this language pattern at home and find it strange and confusing that the teacher is asking for information that he or she already knows. Teachers may need to teach the question-answer-feedback strategy directly so that the students will learn appropriate ways to respond. Teacher modeling of the answers to questions is helpful. In the process, the teacher can explain how to interpret the question, how and where to find the information, and how to construct the answer after the information is located (Armbruster, 1992).

There are other reasons why students have difficulty in answering questions. Some have been asked so many literal questions that they don't realize that it is acceptable to use prior knowledge to answer questions, whereas others try to answer everything from their background knowledge, ignoring information from the text. Some don't have adequate language facility to answer the questions. At times, students simply tell teachers what they think the teachers want to hear. All these types of students and others who have difficulty in answering questions need specific help that focuses on their particular problems (Applegate, Quinn, and Applegate, 2006).

Raphael and Au (2005) believe that teaching question-answer relationships (QARs) can help teachers explain to students the mental processes involved in reading comprehension. QAR instruction encourages students to consider both information in the text and their own background knowledge when answering questions: the material is "In the Book" or "In My Head." The relationship for questions with answers "In the Book" that are directly stated in one sentence in the text is called "Right There." Students look for the words in the question and read the sentence containing those words to locate the answer. The relationship for questions with an answer "In the Book" that require information from multiple sentences or paragraphs is called "Think & Search." If the answers to the questions have to come entirely from the reader's own knowledge, the relationship is called "On My Own." When the answers have to come from a combination of information in the book and in their head, the relationship is called "Author & Me." The key to aiding students in differentiating among the QARs is helping them become aware of the necessary source or sources of the answers to questions. QAR terminology is useful to students in communicating their problems in answering questions. It is also helpful to the teacher in showing students their options for finding answers. After students understand the two major sources of information, the subcategories of each one are taught.

An important part of teaching QARs is modeling the decision about which QARs to use in particular situations and what the correct answers are, based on use of the correct relationship. Supervised practice after the modeling, with immediate feedback on student responses, is also important. The practice can involve gradually increased passage lengths, progressing from simpler to more difficult tasks (Raphael, 1982). Research on the effects of using this strategy has shown that learning the types of QARs can enhance students' success in answering comprehension questions. The training appears to help average- and low-ability students most. Primary-grade children needed more repetition to learn QARs than intermediate-grade children did (Raphael, 1984, 1986; Raphael and Pearson, 1985).

Raphael and Au (2005) recommend the use of QARs "as a framework for comprehension across the grades and school subjects" (p. 213). They believe that it will be especially helpful in serving students with diverse backgrounds, who often have their instruction focused on lower-level skills. All students can be taught comprehension skills through the progression of teaching just the two main categories first, then the two subcategories of "In the Book," and finally the two subcategories of "In My Head." Teachers can show students how particular reading strategies work well with the different subcategories. Some research shows that students can master the subcategories of "Right There" and "Think & Search" by second grade (Raphael and McKinney, 1983) and all subcategories by fourth grade (Raphael and Wonnacott, 1985). Example 8.5 shows the QAR framework.

"On My Own" questions are generally used before reading, encouraging students to think about what they already know and to relate that knowledge to the material that they are going to read. Guided reading questions can be "Think & Search," "Author & Me," and "Right There." Finally, for extension activities, "Author & Me" and "Think & Search" questions work especially well.

STRUGGLING READER/
INTERVENTION

DIVERSITY

The QAR technique is the focus of two Read•Write•Think lesson plans. One lesson entitled "Guided Comprehension: Self-Questioning Using Question-Answer Relationships," uses *The Story of Ruby Bridges* as a focus for the strategy. The other lesson is entitled "Using QARs to Develop Comprehension and Reflective Reading Habits." Access these lessons at http://www.readwritethink.org or link from the Student Website.

EXAMPLE 8.5 Question-Answer Relationships (QARs)

Source: Taffy E. Raphael and Kathryn H. Au, *Group SuperQAR for Testwise Students: Teacher Resource Guide, Guide 6,* 2001, pp. 4 and 5. Used by permission of the publisher, McGraw-Hill/Wright Group.

Helping Students Question

Active readers constantly question the text. As they construct meaning, they ask themselves, "Does this make sense?" Questions about why the material being presented makes sense, also referred to as "elaborative interrogation," can help students remember the texts better, perhaps because these questions cause students to consider their prior knowledge and relate it to the material (Pressley, 2001).

Teaching readers to generate questions throughout the reading process to enhance comprehension has proved to be effective. Students who are taught to ask questions about material being read learn to discriminate good questions from poor ones. A group of students who were taught (through modeling, with gradual phasing out of teacher involvement) to generate their own questions based on a story grammar demonstrated improvements in comprehension (Nolte and Singer, 1985). Interspersing questions in the text to provide a transition from teacher questioning to self-questioning may be helpful.

Time for Reflection

Under what conditions would you encourage students to construct their own questions, and under what conditions would you use teacher-generated questions in your classroom?

What are the reasons for *your* choices?

◀ ▶ **SEEING IT IN PRACTICE**

Video Case
Consider the Video Case "Reading Comprehension Strategies for Elementary School Students: Questioning Techniques" that you viewed when you were considering inferential questions. How did the teacher encourage students to ask questions?

Questioning and sharing responses in small groups can help students improve their critical insights into texts. Student-generated questions can motivate peers to respond and cause the questioner to have more interest in the response. Busching and Slesinger (1995) led students to ask their own questions about what they read. The students wrote, in their reading response journals or notebooks, questions that selections raised. This preserved the questions for ongoing reflection. Busching and Slesinger (1995) discovered that "whether a question is about facts or concepts is less important than whether a question is a part of something significant. The outward form of the question may have little to do with the level, the depth, or the importance of thinking that has occurred" (p. 344). When reading *Rose Blanche*, middle school students first raised factual questions because of their limited backgrounds of experience. Later, more of their questions were on higher levels. Some of their questions became "What if…" questions.

LITERATURE

Comprehension Challenges for Struggling Readers

STRUGGLING READER/
INTERVENTION

DIVERSITY

Struggling readers face many common barriers to comprehension (Massey, 2007). One of these barriers is lack of appropriate prior knowledge. Many struggling readers come from households with low-socioeconomic levels, in which literacy materials—such as books, magazines, newspapers, and writing supplies—are limited. These students also generally have not had extensive experiences related to travel; excursions to plays, concerts, and museums; and such experiences as music lessons or specialized summer camps. English-language learners lack background experience with the language and are often confused by grammatical constructions and figurative language. These students also may lack familiarity with the culture described in the reading and may make inaccurate attempts to track it onto their cultural understandings. For these students, teachers must find ways to build background knowledge through concrete and vicarious experiences.

Other struggling readers have inaccurate information gleaned from unreliable sources, such as other young people, unmonitored websites, and misleading television programs. False background information not only causes confusion for the reader, but can also cause the reader to reject accurate information in reading material. Instruction in critical thinking and reading strategies can help these readers.

Still others have appropriate background knowledge but do not realize that it is permissible to use it. They have the idea that reading is pronouncing the words correctly and getting the information that is directly stated. Therefore, they fail to use their background information to aid in higher-level comprehension tasks. Teachers need to model how background experience and information from the print can be combined to come up with unstated ideas that are appropriate and follow the modeling with guided practice.

When readers are repeatedly unable to comprehend what they read, they often resort to avoidance tactics. They may claim illness just before reading class, come to class without their book or notebook, make irrelevant remarks to redirect the teacher's attention, and use other similar tactics. A student of one of the authors tried to make a joke whenever he was called on to answer a question. The class laughed and was distracted from the fact that he had not understood the reading.

Many of these students have had large doses of phonics skills but have been taught few other strategies for word recognition. They also have often been exposed to mostly literal level comprehension questions, based on the incorrect assumption that they would not be able to do higher-order thinking. All students need a variety of reading strategies to comprehend the different types of text that they encounter, and all students need instruction in higher-order comprehension. Lubliner (2004) found that self-generated, main idea questioning was a successful intervention for a variety of types of struggling readers.

SUMMARY

This chapter examines types of reading comprehension. Literal comprehension results from reading for directly stated ideas. Higher-order comprehension goes beyond literal comprehension to include interpretive, critical, and creative reading. Interpretive reading is reading for implied ideas; critical reading is reading for evaluation; and creative reading is reading beyond the lines. Teachers can generally teach strategies in all these areas most effectively through explanation and modeling, guided student practice, and independent student practice.

Questioning techniques are important to instruction because teachers use questions to provide purposes for reading, to elicit and focus discussion, and to check comprehension of material read. Questions may be based on comprehension factors or story structure. Students may need to be taught how to approach answering questions. Self-questioning by the reader is also a valuable comprehension and comprehension-monitoring technique. Teachers can help students develop the skill of self-questioning.

Struggling readers often lack prior knowledge needed for comprehension. Others have inaccurate information or don't use prior knowledge that they possess. They need to be taught a variety of comprehension strategies to allow them to be successful.

For your journal

1. Using the seven question types based on comprehension factors that are described in this chapter, compose some questions about the content of this chapter or of another chapter in this book. Answer the questions.

2. After you have read a novel written for children, write story grammar–based questions about the story. Answer the questions.

3. Respond to each of the Video Cases that were cited in this chapter.

and your portfolio

1. Make a board or folder game based on a favorite children's book for a grade of your choice.

2. Gather examples of each propaganda technique listed in the chapter, and create a file for each type. Describe instructional uses for your file.

Major Approaches and Materials for Reading Instruction

9

KEY VOCABULARY

Pay close attention to these terms when they appear in the chapter.

dialect

directed reading activity (DRA)

directed reading-thinking activity (DRTA)

eclectic approaches

individualized reading approach

language experience approach (LEA)

linguistics

literature circles

literature-based approaches

minimally contrasting spelling patterns

programmed instruction

thematic literature unit

trade book

word bank

O ver the years, educators have developed many approaches to teaching reading. This chapter discusses some of the more widely accepted approaches. These approaches are not mutually exclusive; many teachers use more than one method simultaneously. They often select the best techniques and materials from a number of approaches to meet the varied needs of individual students in their classrooms. We take the position that no one approach is best for all students or all teachers. Therefore, we attempt to acquaint teachers with the characteristics of different approaches so that they will be able to make an informed choice of which procedures to use in their classrooms. Some approaches are covered in other chapters, for example, Response to Intervention (covered in Chapter 2) and Reading Recovery and Success for All (covered in Chapter 3). Different phonics approaches are covered in Chapter 5. Many teachers, because of the report of the National Reading Panel (2000), look for approaches that facilitate instruction in phonemic awareness, phonics, vocabulary, fluency, and text comprehension. Basal reading series, literature based approaches, and the language experience approach can all be used to accomplish this goal.

AFTER
C or I (for initial
A or D answers)
A or D
(for initial ? answers)

Directions: Before you read this chapter, complete the following anticipation/reaction guide. In the space before each statement, write **A** if you agree; **D** if you disagree; or **?** if you don't know. After you have read the chapter, complete the guide again to show what you have discovered in the chapter. In the space after each statement, mark whether you were initially correct (with a **C**) or incorrect (with an **I**). Write the letter for the correct answer (**A**) or (**D**) in the space for the statements that you initially marked with a question mark (**?**).

1. All basal reading series are alike.

2. Teacher's manuals in basal reading series generally provide detailed lesson plans for teaching each story in a basal reader.

3. Basal reader workbooks are designed to teach reading skills and do not require teacher intervention.

4. The language experience approach (LEA) is only appropriate for the first grade.

5. The language experience approach uses student-created material for reading instruction.

6. A word bank is a collection of words that the teacher believes students should learn.

7. The individualized reading approach uses self-selection and self-pacing.

8. The individualized reading approach involves no direct skills instruction.

9. Close reading of core books, discussion, and writing related to the reading take place in many literature-based classrooms.

10. Thematic literature units involve the reading of a single book by all class members and the writing of a book report on the book.

11. The directed reading-thinking activity is a good alternative to the directed reading activity when the teacher wishes to provide a more student-centered experience.

CHAPTER 9 ORGANIZATION

Major Approaches and Materials for Reading Instruction

Basal Reading Series

Uses and Misuses of Basal Materials
Types of Basal Reading Programs
Instructional Procedures Used with Basal
    Reading Series

Literature-Based Approaches

Whole-Class Reading of a Core Book
Literature Circles
Thematic Literature Units
Individualized Reading Approach
Literature-Based Programs and English-Language
    Learners
Research Supporting Literature-Based Programs

Language Experience Approach

Implementation in Kindergarten
Implementation in the Primary Grades
Implementation in Higher Grades
Use with Students Who Have Special Needs
Some Considerations About the Language
    Experience Approach

Programmed Instruction and Computer Use

Eclectic Approaches

Basal Reading Series

For many years, basal reading series have been the most widely used materials for teaching reading in the elementary schools of the United States. Basal reading series are quite useful for elementary school teachers. They begin with prereading materials and provide materials for development and practice of reading strategies in each grade. Their continuity can aid in curricular planning. When the same basal reading program is used across grades in a school or district, teachers have a good idea of what their students have been taught in past years (Wiggins, 1994).

LITERATURE

Most of today's basal reading series provide anthologies of stories, content-area selections, poems, plays, and other materials that can be the basis for enriching classroom reading activities. They also contain much literature, and many programs present integrated, thematic approaches to reading. Many include whole selections or lengthy excerpts from high-quality literature, often without adaptation. To provide stories with high quality, limited vocabulary, and extensive repetition, many basal readers include unaltered folktales in some of the early readers. They also provide more content-area material than was included in earlier basal readers. Unlike the language in the earlier readers, the language in many of today's basal

DIVERSITY

readers is more natural and conversational. These readers have diversified characters, including people of various racial and ethnic groups, elderly people, and people with disabilities, and depict them in less stereotyped ways than in the past. Women are also portrayed in roles other than the traditional ones.

Publishers of basal readers are continually working to improve them. They welcome feedback from teachers, so teachers should feel free to make their instructional needs known to publishers.

In addition to the student books, basal reading series include teacher's manuals with detailed lesson plans to help teachers use the readers effectively. Teachers who follow these plans use what is called a directed reading activity (DRA), described later in this chapter. Basal reading series also include workbooks and/or duplicating masters of skill sheets that students can use to practice skills and strategies that they have previously learned in class. Many publishing companies offer other supplementary materials to be used in conjunction with basal series,

STANDARDS/ ASSESSMENTS

such as "big books"—chart-sized versions of books that facilitate group instruction; student journals; read-aloud libraries for the teacher; unit tests; puppets to go with some early stories; and computer management, reinforcement, and enrichment activities.

Basal publishers have put many research findings about reading into practice in a context that takes into account the pressures that classroom teachers face. The teacher's manuals offer many valuable suggestions for teaching reading lessons and thus can save much lesson preparation time. Basal readers address considerations from diagnosis to reading appreciation and offer suggestions for both instructional techniques and guided practice. Such suggestions offer positive guidance for teachers, helping them to include all aspects of reading (word recognition, comprehension,

Basal readers are anthologies of stories, content-area selections, poems, and plays.
© Carol Palmer/INDEX-STOCK

oral reading, silent reading, reading for information, and reading for enjoyment) in their reading lessons. Manuals allow for systematic teaching and reteaching of skills and strategies and for systematic review. They provide strategy and skill scope and sequence charts that show what strategies are introduced, taught, and reinforced at different grade levels throughout the series. They also offer ways to monitor the effectiveness of the instruction. Some series have suggestions for differentiating instruction for students who are progressing normally, those who are advanced readers, those who are struggling readers, and those who are English-language learners.

 STANDARDS/
ASSESSMENTS

STRUGGLING READER/
INTERVENTION

DIVERSITY

Uses and Misuses of Basal Materials

Educators who advocate the use of direct instruction in basal reading lessons have suggested a number of recommended practices. They suggest that teachers initially assess the students' knowledge related to each skill to be taught. For students who have not mastered a skill, teachers should (1) explain how to perform the skill; (2) point out when it is needed and why it is important; (3) model the use of the skill for the students, providing them with guided practice with the skill; (4) have students apply the skill in their reading materials; and (5) lead the students in discussion

 STANDARDS/
ASSESSMENTS

Selecting Activities to Fit Your Students

The wealth of material offered in the teacher's manuals allows you to implement the suggestions that fit your needs and discard those that do not. If you try to do everything suggested, however, you may use valuable time for activities that are inappropriate for some groups of students, leaving inadequate time for more suitable activities. You should not try to use every activity provided in basal readers for all students. You should consider the special needs of the students in your classes.

of real-world needs for the skill. These steps may already be included in basal manual instructions. Teachers can add the other steps to create complete skills lessons.

Teachers have a responsibility to plan carefully the use of all materials in their classrooms, including the basal readers, regardless of the presence or absence of guiding suggestions accompanying the materials. Strategy instruction should be planned to fit the needs of their particular classes. They should provide instruction in each strategy or skill before assigning practice materials for that skill, so that students will practice appropriate responses. The teachers should also grade and return completed workbook assignments promptly, because students need to have correct responses reinforced immediately and need to be informed about incorrect responses so that they will not continue to make them. Discussion of the completed pages should follow completion, either before or after checking for accuracy.

If teachers believe that some workbook activities do not give sufficient attention to higher-level comprehension skills, they may want to have students write responses to the selections in reading logs and let students discuss the selections. Many teachers will choose to use a variety of other literature-response activities, such as drama, art, and storytelling, rather than just using the workbook activities, regardless of how well the workbook provides skill activities. Enrichment activities that can be used after reading a basal story to extend the learning experience include asking students to illustrate scenes from the story, write questions to be answered by other class members, write other adventures for story characters, read books by the author of the story or books related to the story, or engage in other activities that encourage active interaction with the content of the selection.

Teachers do not have to follow all suggestions in the manuals—or, indeed, *any* of the suggestions—in order to use basal materials to provide students with a variety of reading materials that would not otherwise be available in many schools. Likewise, they can add their own ideas to the suggestions in the manuals. Basal reading instruction, like other approaches to reading instruction, can be as good, or as poor, as the teachers using it.

Unfortunately, some teachers use basal materials in less than desirable ways. For example, if teachers perceive basals as *total* reading programs, they may fail to provide the variety of experiences that students need for a balanced program. Basals can never provide all of the reading situations a student needs to encounter. Additionally, some teachers assign students to complete pages in basal workbooks or skill sheets to keep some students busy while they meet with other students or do paperwork, or they assign all pages sequentially to all students, regardless of the appropriateness to the individual students' needs. It is important to note that the fault here is with the teachers' procedures and not with the workbooks. Teachers should be aware that the workbooks and skill sheets in basal series are not designed to *teach* the skills and strategies and should not be used for this purpose. They are designed to provide *practice* in skills that have been taught. Teachers should never assign workbook pages for skills that have not yet been taught or for skills that the students have already mastered.

Believing that they can provide all of their students with basal reading materials that are appropriate, some teachers form basal reading groups based on achievement. They place the best readers in the top group, the average readers in a middle group or groups, and the poorest readers in the lowest group. In actuality, however, the match of materials with students is not always good. Forell (1985) has pointed out that good readers are often placed in comfortable reading materials in which word-recognition problems are not frequent and attention can be given to meaning, using context clues to advantage. Poor readers, however, are often placed in "challenging" material that causes frustration and is not conducive to comprehension because so much attention is needed for word recognition—an arrangement that denies them a chance for fluent reading. All readers should be given material that is comfortable enough to allow reasonable application of comprehension skills. However, teachers may be reluctant to place students in materials at as low a level as they need in order to allow this to happen, even though doing so can be beneficial in the long run.

 STRUGGLING READER/ INTERVENTION

Types of Basal Reading Programs

Although the preceding discussion of basal reading programs contained some generalizations about them, our intention is not to imply that all basal reader series are alike. On the contrary, these series differ in basic philosophy, order of presentation of strategies and skills, degree and type of vocabulary control, types of selections, and number and types of practice activities provided. Some supplement workbook/ skill sheet material with student journals that call for more varied responses. Most are eclectic in approach, but some emphasize a single method, such as a linguistic or an intensive phonics approach.

▸ Linguistic Series

Linguistics is the scientific study of human speech. Linguistic scientists (also called *linguists*), such as Leonard Bloomfield, have set forth principles that have affected the development of reading instructional materials. A number of these principles have been applied to many of the basal reading series. Some series have been based specifically on Bloomfield's ideas and have incorporated a number of his beliefs, including the following:

1. Beginning readers should be presented with material that uses only a single sound for a letter at a time. Other sounds for the letter should not be presented until the first association is mastered.

2. Irregularly spelled words should be avoided in beginning reading material, although some (for example, *a* and *the*) must be used to construct sentences that have relatively normal patterns.

Time for Reflection

Would you ask all students to complete all workbook pages, to ensure learning?

Why or why not? If not, what would *you* do?

3. Word-attack skills should be taught by presenting **minimally contrasting spelling patterns,** words that vary by only a single letter. For example, one lesson might contain the words *can, tan, man, ban, fan, ran,* and *pan.* This exposure to minimally contrasting patterns is designed to help the student understand the difference a certain letter makes in the pronunciation of a word.

4. Sounds should not be isolated from words, however, because when sounds are pronounced outside the environment of a word, they are distorted. This is particularly true of isolated consonant sounds; *buh, duh,* and *puh* are sounds incorrectly associated with the letters *b, d,* and *p.*

These materials emphasize reading orally. Reading is viewed as turning writing back into spoken language.

▌Intensive Phonics Series

STANDARDS/
ASSESSMENTS ☑

Series that focus on intensive phonics use a synthetic phonics approach to phonics instruction. (See Chapter 5 for a description of this approach.) The materials often look similar to the ones found in a linguistic series, but the sounds are not isolated from the words in a linguistic approach, whereas they are taught in isolation and then blended into words in a synthetic phonics approach. Instruction is direct and systematic with these materials, and there is a strong emphasis on decoding. Many schools have adopted these materials as a part of their effort to meet the requirements of the federal *No Child Left Behind Act.*

▌Literature-Based and Language-Integrated Series

LITERATURE

Literature-based reading series offer quality literature selections for students to read, often in their entirety and without adaptation. In addition, some series integrate instruction involving all the language arts, including listening, speaking, and writing activities to accompany the literature selections. These activities make the lessons true communication experiences. Having students write in journals and participate in unit studies that tie together selections with similar themes, by the same author, or of the same genre is common in the literature-based and language-integrated series.

These series often stress purpose setting by the students themselves, perhaps through predictions, and much attention is devoted to confirming or rejecting predictions after reading takes place.

Instructional Procedures Used with Basal Reading Series

A number of instructional procedures can be used with basal reading series. Some are built into the manuals included in the series, and some can be easily adapted to use with these materials.

▶ Directed Reading Activity (DRA)

The **directed reading activity (DRA)** is a teaching strategy used to extend and strengthen a student's reading abilities. It can be used with a story from a basal reading series, a selection from content-area materials, or a trade book. A DRA is often built into basal reading series' teacher's manuals. The following five components are frequently included in the DRA.

1. *Motivation and development of background (activating and building schemata).* The teacher attempts to interest students in reading about the topic by helping them associate the subject matter with their own experiences or by using audiovisual aids to arouse interest in unfamiliar areas.

   At this point, the teacher can determine if the students have the backgrounds of experience and language needed for understanding the story, and, if necessary, he or she can develop new concepts and vocabulary before the students read the story.

STANDARDS/
ASSESSMENTS

2. *Directed story reading (silent and oral).* Before students read the story silently, the teacher provides them with purpose questions (or an anticipation guide or study guide) or helps them to set their own purposes (by questioning or predicting) to direct their reading (on a section-by-section basis at lower-grade levels). Following the silent reading, the teacher may ask the students to read aloud their answers to the purpose or study-guide questions, to read aloud to prove or reject their predictions, or to read orally for a new purpose. This section of the lesson is designed to aid students' comprehension and retention of the material.

   Beginning readers may be asked to read the entire story orally, in unison, for practice with the new vocabulary and for practice in reading with expression. Oral reading is not always included in upper-grade lessons.

3. *Strategy- or skill-building activities.* At some point during the lesson, the teacher provides direct instruction in one or more word-recognition or comprehension strategies or skills. Some series provide these activities before story reading and some after.

4. *Follow-up practice.* Students practice strategies and skills that they have already been taught, frequently by doing workbook exercises or playing skill-oriented games.

5. *Enrichment activities.* These activities may connect the story with art, music, or creative writing or may lead the students to read additional material on the same topic or by the same author. Internet research on some aspect of the selection, perhaps the setting for fiction selections or the people and places mentioned for nonfiction can provide enrichment. Creative drama is often included as an enrichment activity that links the reading with speaking and listening. Some educators advocate using some of these activities as prereading activities, rather than using them for extensions of the lessons

after the reading. Used in this way, the activities can help students build and integrate background knowledge.

Although the steps vary from series to series, most basal reading lessons have parts that correspond to this list of components. Directed reading of a story generally involves the teacher asking questions and the students reading to find the answers, or the teacher asking students to make predictions and read to confirm or reject them. Series also usually provide instructions for review of previously taught skills and strategies and reteaching of skills and strategies that have not been mastered.

Comprehension monitoring (metacognitive activities) can become a natural part of a DRA if students use their *predictions*, rather than teacher questions, to set their purposes for reading. The title, pictures, and the students' background information about the general topic that has been activated can be used as a basis for the predictions. Teachers should encourage students to revise their predictions as necessary while they read the material and should also encourage *self-questioning* before and during the reading. Students should be taught to stop reading at logical story breaks and *summarize* the main points of what they have read, as a way to check their comprehension. Summarization of the entire selection can follow completion of the reading. Many basal series incorporate these types of activities into their teacher's manuals.

Example 9.1 shows a page from a reading series that provides an overview of lesson plans for two days. Notice that in addition to reading in the basal text itself, every day there is work on phonics, vocabulary, comprehension, spelling, writing, grammar, and other language skills, as well as reading in leveled books. Many pages of detailed plans are provided for the days covered by this overview. Example 9.2 shows one page from Day 2 of the poetry unit.

▶ Guided Reading

Guided reading has become a popular method of reading instruction. Guided reading involves matching students with books that provide an appropriate level of challenge and familiarity to support the development of each student's reading strategies. It often relies on "leveled books" that are categorized into difficulty levels based on several text factors, such as vocabulary difficulty, predictability, complexity of concepts, illustrations, and size of print (Rog and Burton, 2001/2002). Some books that have been identified as having specific levels of difficulty are available (Fountas and Pinnell, 1996). Because teachers do not always have access to as many "leveled" books as would be needed to carry out the required matching, basal reading anthologies can provide material. The stories in kindergarten through second-grade readers in five basal reading series have been leveled using the text gradient criteria of Fountas and Pinnell (1996, 1999). The basal stories covered levels A through L of the Fountas and Pinnell gradient. Other materials would be needed for levels M through R (Fawson and Reutzel, 2000). Students reading the same material may be placed in groups. The groups for guided reading are flexible, just as we have advocated in this text for all grouping practices.

EXAMPLE 9.1 Overview of Two Days of Daily Lesson Plans for Genre Unit

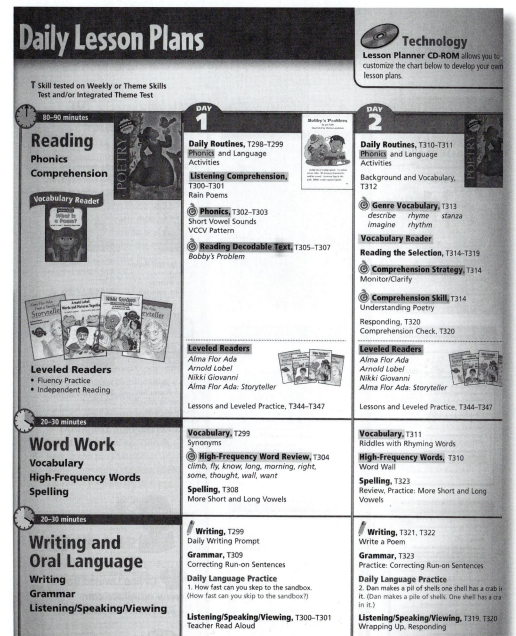

Source: J. David Cooper, John J. Pikulski, et al., "Focus on Genre: Poetry, Theme 2," Teacher's Edition: *Houghton Mifflin Reading: Grade 2.* Copyright © 2008 by Houghton Mifflin Company. Reprinted by permission of Houghton Mifflin Company. All rights reserved.

EXAMPLE 9.2 Pages from Day 2 of Poetry Unit

Background and Vocabulary

Key Concept: Understanding Poetry

Connecting to the Genre Tell children that they are about to read a selection of poems. Have a volunteer read aloud the text on Anthology page 111. Ask children what they think powerful "superwords" might be. (Only a few of these words are needed to say a lot.)

Explain that children will see how a good poem can help readers

- see in their minds what a poet is describing,
- feel what the poem describes.

Ask children to name things or feelings a poem might describe. Then ask them to name poems they already know and to tell about what those poems describe. Record children's responses.

 Journal Have children use their journals to record feelings or things poems might describe. Then have children create a list of things they might wish to describe in poems of their own, for example, friends, animals, adventures, or everyday experiences.

Vocabulary Preview

The Vocabulary Reader can be used to preteach or reinforce the genre vocabulary.

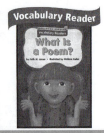

POETRY

Focus on Genre

110

English Language Learners

Language Development

Beginning/Preproduction Choose a poem, such as "People," to read aloud. Write action words, for example *talk, sing, laugh,* and *cry,* and have children pantomime each action.

Early Production and Speech Emergence Have children take turns reading a poem aloud. Have them restate the poem in their own words.

Intermediate and Advanced Fluency Have pairs brainstorm a list of rhyming words related to a theme or topic, such as Feelings or Winter. (sad, glad, mad; snow, blow, go) Have them use the words to create a short poem about the topic.

EXAMPLE 9.2 *(Continued)*

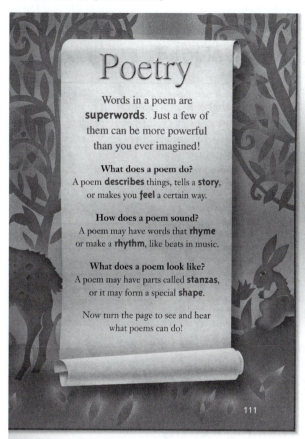

Poetry

Words in a poem are **superwords**. Just a few of them can be more powerful than you ever imagined!

What does a poem do?
A poem **describes** things, tells a **story**, or makes you **feel** a certain way.

How does a poem sound?
A poem may have words that **rhyme** or make a **rhythm**, like beats in music.

What does a poem look like?
A poem may have parts called **stanzas**, or it may form a special **shape**.

Now turn the page to see and hear what poems can do!

111

Introducing Vocabulary

Genre Vocabulary
These words support the Key Concept.

describe to use words to tell about something

imagine to picture in your mind

rhyme having the same ending sound

rhythm a pattern of beats, like music

stanza lines of a poem that go together

Use **Transparency F1–4** to help children develop their understanding of the Genre Vocabulary.

- Read aloud the first item on the transparency.

- Model how to use context clues to find the meaning of the word *stanza* in the second sentence.

- Ask children to use context clues to figure out the meaning of each Genre Vocabulary word in the remaining sentences. Have children explain how they figured out each meaning.

- Ask children to look for these words as they read and to use them as they discuss the poems.

Practice/Homework Assign **Practice Book** page 96.

Transparency F1–4
Poetry Words

rhyme   describe   imagine   rhythm   stanza

1. Sal has a favorite poem about the sea. The first stanza of the poem compares the sea to a huge, running dog. The second part of the poem compares the sea to a sleeping dog.

2. Sal likes poems that rhyme. His favorite poem uses the words *jaws* and *paws*. These two words have the same ending sound.

3. Sal likes poems that describe things. His favorite poem uses special words to tell about the sea, such as *giant, shaking, shaggy,* and *bounding*.

4. When he reads his favorite poem, Sal can imagine a huge dog running onto the beach with a roar. In his mind, he pictures the giant dog shaking and shaking its wet fur.

5. When Sal says the poem aloud, the words sound like the beat of the waves. The rhythm of the poem makes him see the movement of the huge dog as it comes and goes on the beach.

Practice Book page 96

Focus on Poetry
Genre Vocabulary

Name _____

Poetry Words

Circle the word that best completes each sentence.

1. The number of beats in poetry is called the _____.
   (rhythm)(1 point)   rhyme   stanza

2. Words with the same ending sounds are words that _____.
   imagine   (rhyme) (1)   rhythm

3. A group of sentences or lines in a poem is a _____.
   rhythm   (stanza) (1)   describe

4. Poems usually _____ things, such as feelings or places.
   stanza   rhyme   (describe) (1)

5. A good poem can help you _____ what it is talking about.
   describe   rhythm   (imagine) (1)

On another sheet of paper, write three sentences telling what you like or don't like about poetry. Use one of the words you circled in each sentence. (3 points)

Introducing Vocabulary

Source: J. David Cooper, John J. Pikulski, et al., "Focus on Genre: Poetry, Theme 2," Teacher's Edition: *Houghton Mifflin Reading: Grade 2.* Copyright © 2008 by Houghton Mifflin Company. Reprinted by permission of Houghton Mifflin Company. All rights reserved.

Although guided reading is sometimes characterized by teachers as being very different from the use of DRAs, we believe that good teachers generally use DRAs and guided reading in very similar ways. Guided reading lessons begin with an introduction to the story that is focused on concepts important to the story. Just as in a DRA, the purpose is to build background for the material in the story. Teachers set purposes or have students make predictions. They may teach an applicable reading strategy at this time. Teachers need to realize that English-language learners may need more time for concept development than other students. They may also need help with unfamiliar syntax in the selection. Students, especially English-language learners, can benefit from shared reading at this time so that they have a model of fluent reading (Avalos, Plasencia, Chavez, and Rascón, 2007/2008). After this preparation, students read the story silently or aloud softly, while the teacher observes their application of reading strategies and provides support. Thus, students receive instruction that focuses on use of needed reading strategies, to enable them to fully develop a variety of strategies that they can choose from and apply.

DIVERSITY

During the reading, the students' miscues guide the teacher's instructional decisions (Schwartz, 2005). If the teacher observes the student reading a word inaccurately, he or she must make a decision about whether the miscue is a significant one for the particular student and offer instruction in the appropriate strategy, if necessary. (See Chapter 2 for information on miscue analysis.)

After reading, there is discussion of the book, sometimes followed by rereading to find evidence to support answers to the purpose questions or to check predictions. Next, the students may take part in extension activities, such as additional instruction on strategies and vocabulary, dramatizations, writing, and independent reading. These serve the same purpose in guided reading lessons as extension activities do in the DRA. More information on guided reading can be found in Chapter 3.

▶ Directed Reading-Thinking Activity

One alternative to the DRA is the **directed reading-thinking activity (DRTA)**. The DRTA focuses on student control instead of primarily teacher guidance of the reading. The DRTA is a general plan for directing the students' reading of stories in basal reading series, trade books, or content-area selections and for encouraging students to think as they read and to make predictions and check their accuracy. The steps in a DRTA are listed in Example 9.3. Stauffer (1968) offered this background rationale for using the DRTA:

> Children are by nature curious and inquiring, and they will be so in school if they are permitted to inquire. It is possible to direct the reading-thinking process in such a way that children will be encouraged to think when reading—to speculate, to search, to evaluate, and to use. (p. 348)

Teachers can motivate students' effort and concentration by involving them intellectually and encouraging them to formulate questions and hypotheses, to process information, and to evaluate tentative solutions. The DRTA is directed

EXAMPLE 9.3 Steps in a DRTA

Step 1: Making Predictions from Title Clues

Making predictions about what will occur in a text causes students to think about the text's message. To encourage them to do this, write the title of the story or chapter to be studied on the board and have a student read it. Ask the students: "What do you think this story will be about?" Give them time to consider the question thoroughly, and let each student have an opportunity to make predictions. All student predictions should be accepted, regardless of how reasonable or unreasonable they may seem, but the teacher should not make any predictions during this discussion period.

Step 2: Making Predictions from Picture Clues

Have the students open their books to the beginning of the selection. If there is a picture on the first page, ask them to examine it carefully. After they have examined it, ask them to revise the predictions they made earlier, basing their new predictions on the additional information in the picture.

This step provides purposes for reading: trying to confirm one or more predictions from others in the group and to confirm or reject their own. It also encourages students to apply metacognitive skills as they think through their lines of reasoning.

Step 3: Reading the Material

Have the students read a predetermined amount of the story to check the accuracy of their predictions.

Step 4: Assessing the Accuracy of Predictions and Adjusting Predictions

When all students have read the first segment, lead a discussion by asking such questions as "Who correctly predicted what the story was going to be about?" Ask the students who believe they were right to read orally to the class the parts of the paragraph that support their predictions. Students who were wrong can tell why they believe they were wrong. Let them revise their predictions, if necessary, and then ask them to predict what will happen next in the story.

Step 5: Repeating the Procedure Until All Parts of the Lesson Have Been Covered

Have the students read the next predetermined segment of the story to check the accuracy of their predictions. Have them read selected parts orally to justify the predictions that they think were correct and tell why they believe other predictions were incorrect. Have them revise or adjust their predictions on the basis of their reading. Then repeat the making of predictions and the checking of predictions until all predetermined segments of the story have been read.

toward accomplishing these goals. The teacher observes the students as they read in order to assess difficulties and offer help. (See Chapter 2.) Perhaps because students are interacting with the material during reading, the DRTA is extremely useful for improving the students' comprehension of selections. After the reading, skill-building activities take place (Stauffer, 1969). Ambe (2007) found that this approach was successful with middle school students.

Making predictions about what will occur in a text encourages students to think about the text's message. In making predictions, students use their background knowledge about the topic and their knowledge of text organizational patterns. This step provides purposes for reading: trying to confirm one or more predictions from others in the group and to confirm or reject their own. It also encourages students to apply metacognitive skills as they think through their lines of reasoning.

In preparing a DRTA, the teacher should select points at which to pause so that students can make predictions. These points should probably be points of high suspense or ones where the selection has led students to anticipate a coming action. There should be no more than four or five stops in a story. During pauses, the teacher may use one or more open-ended questions to elicit student predictions about the next part of the story.

TEACHING TIP

Making Predictions

When students cannot make predictions as requested, you can model your thinking in making a prediction, using a think-aloud, or you can provide several possible predictions for these students to choose from and ask for the reason that a particular one is chosen. You should accept all predictions and encourage students to reflect on their accuracy later. If your students are new at making predictions, you can use highly predictable materials, such as folktales, to encourage success.

LITERATURE

Literature-Based Approaches

Most educators recognize the value of using good literature as a basis for reading instruction. A **literature-based approach** places emphasis on connecting stories to students' personal background knowledge, on analyzing stories and selections for particular elements, and on monitoring students' understanding of the reading materials.

The foundation of a literature-based program is **trade books**—that is, books not written primarily for instructional purposes. Most teachers make use of trade books for students in their classrooms. They read aloud to the students from these books, urge students to read the books in the classroom reading center or to check them out from the school library for recreational reading, and use them as supplements to basal instruction. In a literature-based program, the teacher uses knowledge of students' backgrounds and attempts to "hook" them on reading selections. The teacher may give book talks designed to interest students in reading particular books; as Shiflett (1998) suggests, they find an engaging book and focus the students' attention on the book by applying techniques that are often used in advertising.

Time for Reflection

Some teachers think a DRA is too prescriptive to use but consider a DRTA acceptable because it gives students some control over their own learning. Other teachers believe that there is a place for each technique.

What do *you* think, and why?

Picture books are useful in all grades, especially because their brevity allows them to be read and discussed in one lesson (Wolk, 2004). They can be used to help students learn to read texts that present stories in multiple genres, such as Aliki's *A Play's the Thing* and Steer's *Pirateology*, which has the different genres included in "fold-out, pop-up, pullout, pull-tab, and glued-in formats" (Kiefer, Price-Dennis, and Ryan, 2006); and Swallow's *Groundhog Gets a Say*. Graphic novels are also popular. Runton's *Owly* Volumes 1–3 is a graphic novel for young children; and Holm's *Babymouse: Our Hero* and Smith's *Bone: Out from Boneville* are both graphic novels for middle graders (Kiefer et al., 2006).

Essential reading skills and strategies can be taught within the context of material that students are actively involved in reading. Baumann, Hooten, and White (1999) found that students understand material better and enjoy reading more when comprehension strategy instruction is incorporated within the context of literature. During reading, the teacher monitors the students' strategy use. After reading, students may participate in activities such as retelling stories with or without flannel boards, writing reactions to books, and conversing about books with the teacher and other students.

Literature-based instruction has been successful with a wide range of students. Zucker (1993) found that use of literature and language instruction with students who had language and learning disabilities resulted in positive gains in listening, speaking, reading, and writing. Stewart, Paradis, Ross, and Lewis (1996) found that literature-based developmental reading programs resulted in improved reading performance by middle school students. They believe that choice was important in developing interest and ownership, which encouraged practice. Practice led to speed and fluency, which resulted in increased comprehension and retention. Time for reading was of course necessary for this model to work.

STRUGGLING READER/ INTERVENTION

On the other hand, Scharer and Detwiler (1992) point out some concerns regarding literature-based instruction. When it is used, teachers find it hard to be sure that all needed strategies and skills are being covered, hard to know how to assess progress, and hard to know how to handle the struggling readers. Certainly, teachers need to be well prepared as language teachers to use the approaches effectively.

STANDARDS/ ASSESSMENTS

STRUGGLING READER/ INTERVENTION

Literature-based programs may be conducted in a number of ways, and combinations of these approaches are common in most literature-based classrooms. Four such approaches are whole-class reading of a core book, use of literature circles with multiple copies of several books, use of thematic literature units, and individualized reading approaches (Zarillo, 1989; Hiebert and Colt, 1989). Each of these approaches will be discussed in turn.

A common adjunct to all of them is *sustained silent reading* (SSR), a form of personalized reading in which students and teachers alike are allowed time to read materials of their own choice without interruption and without evaluation. A number of studies over a long period of time have indicated that students who read most perform better on reading tests (Clausen-Grace and Kelley, 2007). In fact, a study of students in thirty-two countries by the International Association for the Evaluation of Educational Achievement showed that the students scoring highest were ones who "were read to by their teachers daily" and "read the most pages for

STANDARDS/ ASSESSMENTS

pleasure daily" (Fisher 2007, p. 32). Therefore, SSR would appear to be a helpful approach to use.

Numerous educators have emphasized the importance of access to appealing books, an environment conducive to reading, encouragement to read, and modeling of love for books (Kelley and Clausen-Grace, 2006; Clausen-Grace and Kelley, 2007). Self-selection is imperative for SSR, and students must have material available that fits their needs. Cole (1998) found that, during SSR periods, beginner-oriented books—ones similar to primary-level basal stories of earlier years—may be helpful to struggling readers for whom less rigidly constructed texts do not provide enough commonalities in text to facilitate development of decoding and fluency. A number of older trade books have these qualities and should be available, during SSR periods, for students who need these less complex texts with much high-frequency vocabulary.

STRUGGLING READER/ INTERVENTION

In a modification of the SSR approach to include teacher monitoring and student response, a process called "R⁵ (read, relax, reflect, respond, and rap)" was used (Kelley and Clausen-Grace, 2006, p. 151; Clausen-Grace and Kelley, 2007). The teacher conducted read-alouds, shared reading, and book talks to model love for books throughout the day. The read-and-relax phase of their approach was ten to twenty-five minutes of uninterrupted, purposeful reading of a self-selected book after planning (including metacognitive goal setting) and practicing strategy use. During the reflect-and-respond phase, the teacher monitored and supported the students as they read. In addition, one or two one-to-one conferences were held each day. Records were kept on books that students were reading. In the reflect-and-respond phase that followed the reading, students wrote in reading logs about the metacognitive strategies that they had used and the content of the books that they had read. These logs were not used for evaluation, in keeping with the purpose of independent reading. The rap phase included sharing in pairs, followed by whole-class sharing, with each partner reporting on his or her partner's book, and the teacher leading a discussion of reading strategies that were used. The teacher responded to the shared responses with encouragement and amplification. A seven-month study of this approach showed comprehension improvement in "prediction, summarization, literal questioning, interpretation, reflection, and metacognitive awareness" (Kelley and Clausen-Grace, 2006, p. 154).

STANDARDS/ ASSESSMENTS

After successfully using SSR for a number of years, DeBenedictis (2007) gradually modified the approach to embed standards-based learning. She called the modification Sustained Quiet Reading, Writing, Drawing, and Sharing, allocating twenty to twenty-five minutes for reading, writing, and/or drawing about students' chosen reading materials. She followed this with a ten- to twenty-minute discussion period of the reading and writing. Family members were invited to the classroom to model reading and writing with the teacher and to participate in the following discussion. "Students were acquiring vocabulary, using comprehension strategies, problem solving, making predictions, explaining and critiquing different kinds of written materials, and using and applying the writing process" (DeBenedictis, 2007, p. 35).

Some teachers are hesitant to use SSR because of a misinterpretation of the National Reading Panel conclusion that having students read silently with minimal guidance or feedback was "not a sufficient practice when used as the only type of reading instruction to develop fluency and other reading skills" (Clausen-Grace and Kelley, 2007, p. 39). This panel suggested that more research should be done on independent silent reading, not that it should be eliminated, and SSR was never meant to be a complete reading program.

Whole-Class Reading of a Core Book

LITERATURE

Generally, core books used for whole-class reading are acquired in classroom sets so that every student has a personal copy. Teachers select these books for the quality of the material and sometimes because they fit into the overall classroom curriculum by being related to topics under discussion in other curricular areas, such as social studies and science. It is a further advantage if the teacher personally likes the book, for the teacher's attitude is communicated to the students as the reading progresses.

❯ Prereading Activities

Before a book is presented to the class, there may be prereading activities in which the students share personal experiences related to the book's content and activate background information that they possess about the topics or themes covered in it. (See Chapter 7 for information about techniques for schema activation.) The teacher may also present a minilesson on some literary element that is important in the book, such as characterization or flashbacks (Atwell, 1987). Purposes for listening to or reading the material are often set by having students predict what will happen in the story, based on the title and possibly on the picture on the book's cover or the first page of the story. At other times, purposes may be set by having students generate questions about the story that they expect to answer from reading. Occasionally, the teacher may suggest some purpose question that will focus the readers' attention on a key element in the book, such as "How is the setting of the story important to its plot?"

Some students may present the book or a portion of it in a readers' theater as an introduction for other students. Such a presentation can help the other students activate their schemata for the reading to come.

❯ During-Reading Activities

Sometimes the teacher first presents the book to the students by reading aloud part or all of it, depending on the students' reading abilities and the difficulty of the book. A chapter book may be read in installments over a period of days. After the teacher's oral reading, silent reading of the book by the students generally follows. At other times, the students may read the book silently first.

At strategic points in the initial reading or independent rereading, there are usually pauses for small-group or whole-class discussion of the material. If students initially made predictions, these discussions may focus on the predictions, which can be evaluated, retained for the time being, altered slightly, or changed completely, on the basis of the new information. The discussion may also focus on the purpose questions that were generated or on students' personal reactions to the story. To guide these discussions, the teacher may design questions that help the students to relate the story to their own experiences and to think critically and creatively about the material. (See Chapters 7 and 8 for information on critical and creative reading.)

Between reading sessions, students may write reactions to the story in literature logs or journals. The literature logs are responses to each day's reading and may be written just for the individual students, to help them think through what they are reading; or they may be dialogue journals, addressed to the teacher or a buddy who responds to the entries. If the journals are a part of a written dialogue with the teacher, the teacher must respond to each entry with his or her own reaction to the story and/or to the student's reaction. The teacher's comments should be encouraging, thought provoking, and nonjudgmental (Fuhler, 1994). Students should be encouraged to link the reading material with personal experiences. The teacher should model such entries for students by sharing his or her personal journal entries orally. Students should also be encouraged to note phrases and expressions that appealed to them, statements that caused them confusion, and predictions about what will happen next. Many different learning goals may be met through this student-teacher interaction (Flitterman-King, 1988; McWhirter, 1990). An example of one type of literature log is presented in Example 9.4. More information on journals is located in Chapter 10.

▶ Postreading Activities

After the book has been read, follow-up activities should be used to extend the students' understanding and to help them elaborate on the ideas that they gained from the shared book. These activities often involve writing—for example, composing another episode for the characters in the story, another story of the same genre, or a character sketch of a favorite character. Swindall and Cantrell (1999) ask sixth graders to write questions for well-developed characters in the literature selections that they are reading and then to impersonate characters of their choice and answer questions that their classmates, as interviewers, ask them.

Retelling the material in various ways is a good follow-up activity, especially for young children. They may simply retell the story to a partner; they may retell it using a flannel board; or they may act it out through creative dramatics or puppetry. Illustrating the sequence or selected parts of the story or informational book after reading can provide the teacher with insight into the students' degrees of comprehension. Students may also construct group or individual story maps or semantic webs after the reading. The maps or webs can be displayed in the classroom or shared during discussions or oral presentations. Students may apply information learned from the story or an informational book (for example, how to tie knots, make a kite, or do origami), or they may read related materials because their interest in the topic has been aroused.

EXAMPLE 9.4 Literature Log

Name: *Mike*

Date: *November 3*

Title of Book: *Hatchet*

Pages: *page 1 through page 40*

Summary of Passage

Brian is flying north in a small plane to spend the summer with his father in an oil field in Canada. The pilot has a heart attack, and the plane crashes. Brian is stranded in a forest with only his hatchet to use to survive.

Running Comments

p. 1 – Brian gets to ride in the co-pilot's seat. Sounds like fun.

p. 2 – Brian is pretty bummed out because his parents are getting a divorce. He's mad at his mother. She must be the reason for the divorce. I'd be bummed out too.

p. 4 – The pilot lets Brian try using the controls. He actually gets to fly the plane a little. Cool stuff.

p. 8 – Brian's mother gave him a hatchet to take with him. That must be why the book is named Hatchet. Brian isn't very excited to get it.

p. 10 – The pilot has a heart attack. That's real trouble.

p. 14 – Brian has to try to fly the plane to keep it from crashing. But he doesn't know where he is or which way he should go. I think I'd try to turn around and go back toward where we came from.

p. 17 – He's going to try to get help using the radio. Good move.

p. 24 – No help from the radio and he's out of gas. He thinks he's going to die in the crash. I don't think so. I think the rest of the book will be about him surviving in the forest.

p. 28 – Yep. He survived the crash.

p. 30 – Yep. His mother is the cause of the divorce.

p. 32 – He made it through the night without a fire. I'd think he'd get awfully cold that far north. Even in Tennessee it gets pretty cool at night in the early summer.

My Reaction

I want to see what he does to survive and to get help.

▶ Modifications of Whole-Class Reading of a Core Book

Teachers have made many individual modifications of the procedures for close, careful reading of a book by a class. Shaw (1988) had fifth graders keep narrative journals in which they wrote after reading each chapter of their book, taking the perspective of the main character to relate that character's adventures. Through this activity, they learned much about summarizing and the first-person narrative form. Journal writing encourages active reading.

Dugan (1997) uses transactional literature discussions that include "getting ready, reading and thinking aloud, wondering on paper, and looking back" (p. 87). Getting ready includes reviewing and making predictions during the reading—predictions that the students then try to confirm or reject. Teachers need to model the think-aloud process and to encourage students to think aloud as they read. (This step eventually evolves into thinking silently as they read.) As they read, or just after they finish, students write responses to the reading on sticky notes that are placed on the pages to which they refer. These written responses can provide fodder for discussions in which students respond, question, listen to their classmates, and make links between the events in the story, between the story and their personal experiences, or between their ideas and their classmates' ideas. After their talk sessions, the students write in their journals. Finally, they review what they have learned. Teachers offer scaffolding throughout this process, gradually withdrawing the scaffolds as students no longer need them.

Wertheim (1988) created a personal teaching guide for the novels that she had her students read by listing difficult vocabulary at the beginning of each chapter; underlining important vocabulary in the text; writing discussion questions on the pages to which they pertained (coded as literal, inferential, and critical); writing other, more inclusive, questions at ends of chapters; and listing follow-up activities at the end of the book.

"Seeing It in Practice: Whole-Class Reading of a Core Book" describes one way to do close reading of a core book. This example is not a prescribed procedure; many variations are possible.

LITERATURE

Literature Circles

In **literature circles,** the teacher generally chooses several books for which multiple copies are available, introduces each one with a book talk, and lets the students choose which book to read. The structured book choices lead students to try books in a variety of genres and by a variety of authors. It may be necessary to ask students to list their top three choices and to assign a book from among these choices because of the limited number of copies available for each book. Usually there are four or five groups in a class, each consisting of four to six members. Martinez-Roldán and Lopez-Robertson (1999/2000) discovered that English-language learners are capable of participating productively in literature circles in mainstream classrooms, so this

DIVERSITY

Whole-Class Reading of a Core Book

In this lesson, the teacher has chosen the book *Patchwork Quilt* because of the way it shows relationships among the characters. This book is good for use with younger readers; for older readers, teachers would probably choose chapter books, with the discussion times coming at the ends of chapters.

The teacher opens with a minilesson on character development, leading students to see how authors reveal characterization through the things the character says and does, the things other characters say about the character, and the ways they react to him or her.

Next, the teacher asks the students to brainstorm their personal associations for the words *Grandma*, *quilt*, and *masterpiece*. Webs of these associations are written on the board or on a chart.

Then the teacher invites the students to predict what the story will be about. They write down their predictions or share them orally with partners or the whole group. The teacher tells the students that, as they read the story, they should look for clues that will either confirm or disprove their predictions and that they should also look for the characteristics of the characters.

The teacher may ask the class to read just the first two pages of the story and then stop to discuss these questions with others at their tables: What is the relationship between Tanya and her grandmother like? Do you have a relationship like that with some older person?

The class may then read the rest of the story, with the number of pages read each time varying with the students' maturity. The following is a list of some possible stopping points and questions for discussion in the small groups:

> *After two more pages*: Did Tanya's mother understand why Grandma wanted to make the quilt? How did the reaction of Tanya's mother to the quilt make Grandma feel? How could you tell?

> *After five more pages*: What did Grandma mean when she said, "A quilt won't forget. It can tell your life story"? Can a quilt really tell stories? If so, how? Did Mama find out what Grandma meant about the quilt telling stories? How do you know?

> *After four more pages*: When Grandma got sick, why didn't she tell the others at first? How did she feel about leaving her quilt unfinished? How could you tell? Why did each person who worked on the quilt do what he or she did? Would you have wanted to work on the quilt if you had been one of them? Why or why not?

> *After the next page*: Was Tanya right to take squares out of Grandma's old quilt without asking permission? Why did she do it? What will Grandma think of it?

> *After the story is finished*: How did Grandma feel about her quilt pieces going into the quilt? What did she say and do that makes you believe that? Why did they give Tanya the quilt? How will Tanya feel about this quilt when she is older? Do you have anything that you feel that way about?

Follow-up activities after the reading may include some of the following:

1. Find another book that tells about a relationship between a child and a grandparent or another older person. Compare and contrast the stories.

2. Design a get-well card that Tanya might have made for her grandmother when she was sick.

3. Write a diary entry that Tanya might have made about her grandmother on the third day after she saw how sick her grandmother was.

4. Pick a character and describe him or her. List his or her characteristics and why you did or did not like him or her.

5. Make a small patchwork quilt for the classroom. (Students provide material scraps for it. The students design the quilt pattern after looking at books about quilts and pictures of quilts. Then they cut out the pieces, and sew them together.) The quilting may be done by a volunteer parent or group of parents, or a resource person may show quilts and demonstrate quilting.

activity can have groups that are heterogeneous in terms of cultural composition, as well as in terms of reading ability, as long as the students have chosen the same book. The teacher presents the books to the students if they are unable to read them independently first.

Groups generally meet two to five times a week, with each group lasting about two to three weeks. When they meet, students decide how far to read each time in order to finish the reading by the deadline and have enough material for good discussions at each meeting. During group sessions, a student leader can conduct the activities, which may consist of silent reading, writing in and sharing literature logs, asking open-ended questions, discussing what was read, and doing extension activities. In their groups, students initiate and sustain discussion topics, connect literature selections to their lives, compare literature selections and authors with each other, note authors' styles, and consider authors' intents. Discussions are directed by the insights and ideas that the students bring to the group, instead of a list of teacher-supplied questions (Brabham and Villaume, 2000). Students are required to provide substantiation for their contributions to the group. They should be receptive to the interpretations of their classmates, but they should also feel free to disagree (Spiegel, 1996). (See Chapter 2 for a teacher's checklist for literature circles.)

STANDARDS/ ASSESSMENTS ☑

Reading response journals or literature logs allow for the collection of reactions to the reading throughout the reading process, not just at the end, and can be the basis for the small-group discussions. When writing in their literature logs, students record personal interpretations, strategies for constructing meaning, questions that arise, and issues they may want to discuss with others (Popp, 1997). One type of literature log or response journal was shown in Example 9.4 on page 327.

Some teachers have students take different roles during group meetings. Daniels (2002, p. 13) believes that use of assigned roles should be a "temporary support device" until students become familiar with group interactions. (See Chapter 10 for types of roles that students may play.)

As groups finish their books, the teacher can encourage students to create extension projects individually, in pairs, or as a group. Examples include reading a similar book or a book by the same author, creating a drama, and writing an epilogue for the story. The students may then share something about their books with other groups.

STANDARDS/ ASSESSMENTS ☑

From reading the students' literature log entries, teachers not only become aware of ways in which students are reacting to literature, but also gain insight into each student's literacy processes. Supportive comments by the teacher can encourage students to react honestly to the material and to persevere in the reading. Sometimes students may need encouragement to be more specific in their entries (Raphael et al., 1992; Fuhler, 1994). To provide such encouragement, Berger (1996) had her students respond to these questions: "What do you notice? … What do you question? … What do you feel? … What do you relate to?" (p. 381) or "How did that make [the character] feel?" These questions led the students to do more than just summarize the reading.

Art provides another option for responding. Whitin (2002) has her students try to show their ideas about the books through sketching. She says, "It's called sketch-to-stretch because as we sketch and talk about our sketches, our minds are stretched to think in new ways" (p. 445). Students use colors, shapes, lines, or complete pictures to represent their thinking and are asked to give reasons for their representations. They also write brief statements that explain their thoughts in words. Whitin emphasizes that story ideas can be represented in many ways; some students use colors and shapes, some more detailed drawings. Often, the symbolism that is used exhibits deep understanding.

Technology can provide ways for students to discuss their reading. A number of researchers have paired university students in reading methods courses with elementary school students to take part in electronic dialogue journals. The university students are expected to model good discussions of plots, characters, and setting through their entries. The authors of this book conducted a similar project and had a high level of success. The elementary school teachers said that their students benefited, and our university students learned a teaching strategy. Both groups enjoyed the interaction (Roe and Smith, 1997). (See Chapter 13 for more details about the project.)

Thematic Literature Units

Thematic literature units are structured around themes, based on topics such as homes, families, survival, taking care of our earth, wild animals, pets, specific geographic regions (for example, South America), or specific groups of people (for example, Japanese); genres, such as biography, science fiction, or folktales; authors, such as Cynthia Voigt, Judith Viorst, or Maurice Sendak; or single books. Shanahan, Robinson, and Schneider (1995) urge development of units around such themes as "We all should try to make the world a better place," rather than just topics, such as "lupines" (p. 718). Barton and Smith (2000) echo the idea of avoiding the use of simple topics that "organize content and activities together simply because they contain or mention a similar subject—bears, cats, dragons, leaves" (p. 55).

Thematic literature units allow students to delve more deeply into ideas and thus develop deeper understandings and see connections among ideas. A theme offers a *focus* for instruction and activities, making it easier for students to see the reason for classroom activities, acquire an integrated knowledge base, achieve depth and breadth of learning, and connect with real audiences (Bergeron, 1996).

There are other values as well. The reflection involved in studying themes can enhance metacognition, but perhaps the biggest advantage of thematic teaching is the promotion of positive attitudes toward reading and writing. The range of topics covered and the opportunity for self-selection promote student interest and positive attitudes. Another advantage is that time is less fragmented in a classroom in which the teacher uses thematic literature units because the teacher can embed instruction in one subject in study of another one (Lipson, Valencia, Wixon, and Peters, 1993).

Visit Read•Write•Think for a sample multiday unit introducing students to literature circles. The unit "Literature Circles: Getting Started" is appropriate for grades 3–5. You can also view a unit for grades 6–8 entitled "Literature Circle Roles Reframed: Reading as a Film Crew." Go to http://www .readwritethink.org or link from the Student Website for this book.

 LITERATURE

A single book or story can be used as the focus for curricular integration. (Example 9.5 shows a web for a unit based on the book *Number the Stars*.) *Webbing* is a technique that connects a central topic or perhaps a book to related ideas. A web is a framework that can cut across curricular areas. Emphasizing that no two webs are alike, Huck, Hepler, and Hickman (1997) recommend webbing as a plan for literature study that grows out of students' interests and the strengths of the books. During the process of creating a web, teachers become aware of the many directions in which books can lead students. Although the teacher uses the web as an overall plan, students contribute their own ideas as the theme unfolds, so the study becomes learner-centered.

Teachers can also develop thematic literature units using books that share similar characteristics. *Text sets* are books that have the same author, theme, topic, genre, or some other characteristic. They can set the stage for critical thinking by students as they look for connections. Text sets provide a basis for discussion of varied interpretations. A text set on Katherine Paterson's books might include *Bridge to Terabithia*, *Lyddie*, *The Great Gilly Hopkins*, *Jacob Have I Loved*, and *The Sign of the Chrysanthemum*. Use of text sets allows small-group discussion in which students can compare and contrast a variety of related books and write in response journals about the relationships they have discovered. Literature comparison/contrast charts can be used in thematic literature units to facilitate the making of connections among the books.

Middle school teachers can pair adolescent literature selections with classics that are related in some way. The connections made between or among the books can enrich the reading (Gallagher, 1995). For example, Katherine Paterson's *Park's Quest* could lead to the reading of Charles Dickens's *Great Expectations*. Both books are concerned with a young man's search for his own identity. S. E. Hinton's *The Outsiders* could also be paired with *Great Expectations*; Ponyboy even says he feels like Pip. Joan Lowery Nixon's *The Name of the Game Was Murder* could be paired with Agatha Christie's *And Then There Were None* (Pavonetti, 1996). Books may be paired according to theme, setting, mood, or some other element.

DIVERSITY

Evans (1994) describes a bilingual thematic literature unit on understanding fear and overcoming it, composed of scary stories from English and Spanish cultures. Because fear is a universal emotion, its use as a topic allows for cultural comparisons of literary treatments of the topic. Thematic literature units are often opened with pre-reading activities for developing background, such as those mentioned earlier for the core book, in which students discuss what they already know about the focus of the unit. Students may brainstorm terms that they associate with the theme, and these terms may be organized into a semantic web. (See Chapters 6, 7, and 12 for more on semantic webs and literature webs.)

The teacher may read aloud one or more books that fit the focus of the unit before allowing students to form small groups to read from multiple copies of other related books. One fifth-grade teacher read aloud *Lincoln: A Photobiography* at the beginning of a unit based on the genre of biography and let the students form small groups to read such books as *What's the Big Idea, Ben Franklin?*; *Eleanor Roosevelt: First Lady of the World*; *A Weed Is a Flower: The Life of George Washington Carver*; and others

The Read•Write•Think lesson "An Exploration of Text Sets: Supporting All Readers" is an example that shows use of text sets for grades 6–8. See it at http://www.readwritethink.org or link to it from the Student Website for this book.

EXAMPLE 9.5 Literature Web

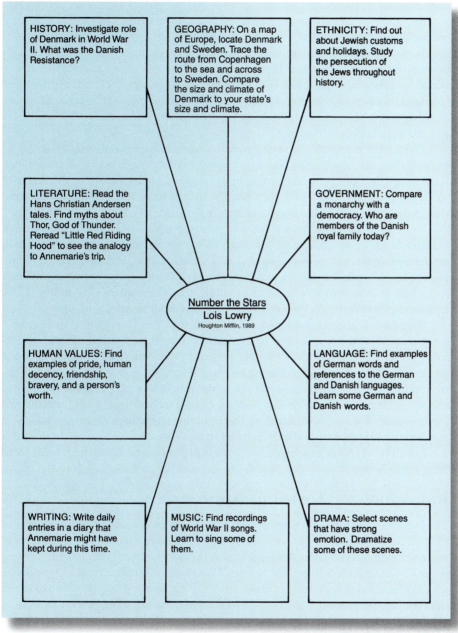

HISTORY: Investigate role of Denmark in World War II. What was the Danish Resistance?

GEOGRAPHY: On a map of Europe, locate Denmark and Sweden. Trace the route from Copenhagen to the sea and across to Sweden. Compare the size and climate of Denmark to your state's size and climate.

ETHNICITY: Find out about Jewish customs and holidays. Study the persecution of the Jews throughout history.

LITERATURE: Read the Hans Christian Andersen tales. Find myths about Thor, God of Thunder. Reread "Little Red Riding Hood" to see the analogy to Annemarie's trip.

GOVERNMENT: Compare a monarchy with a democracy. Who are members of the Danish royal family today?

Number the Stars
Lois Lowry
Houghton Mifflin, 1989

HUMAN VALUES: Find examples of pride, human decency, friendship, bravery, and a person's worth.

LANGUAGE: Find examples of German words and references to the German and Danish languages. Learn some German and Danish words.

WRITING: Write daily entries in a diary that Annemarie might have kept during this time.

MUSIC: Find recordings of World War II songs. Learn to sing some of them.

DRAMA: Select scenes that have strong emotion. Dramatize some of these scenes.

Web based on Lois Lowry, *Number the Stars* (Boston: Houghton Mifflin, 1989).

for which she had secured multiple copies. Single copies of other biographies were also available for independent reading, as were short biographies in basal readers, anthologies, and periodicals (Zarillo, 1989).

Any *genre*, or type of literature, can be a focus for study. Commonly used genres include folktales, poetry, historical fiction, biography, and fantasy, each of which may be divided into subtopics. For instance, the types of fantasy that may be studied include (1) modern literary tales based on folktales, (2) fantastic stories, which are basically realistic but contain elements of fantasy, (3) science fiction, and (4) high fantasy with heroes and heroines who confront evil for the sake of humanity. Chapter 10 has more about genres. Visit the Student Website for this text to see a thematic unit plan for folklore.

The teacher may read aloud to the entire class the selection or selections chosen to open the unit. Some selections may be presented through videos or audiotapes. Each reading should be accompanied by or followed by discussion of the material, writing in literature logs, and other activities, such as those listed for follow-up activities in the section "Whole-Class Reading of a Core Book."

Some unit activities should be designed for whole-group participation (for example, the read-alouds), some for small-group participation (for example, activities related to the multiple-copy books), and some for independent work (for example, literature logs about books read individually). Whole-group activities are likely to include minilessons related to the reading that the students are doing. These minilessons may focus on literary elements or reading strategies.

When small groups meet about the books that they are reading in common, activities such as those described in the section "Literature Circles" can be used. As small-group and independent reading progress, students may continue to build on the webs that they started during the introductory activities. At the end of the unit, culminating activities may include comparing and contrasting the books read and some elements of the books, such as characters, settings, plots, and themes; construction of time lines related to the unit theme; creative dramatics based on readings; writing related to the theme; and so on.

Example 9.6 shows a thematic literature unit plan that is based on a theme focus from a core book.

LITERATURE

Individualized Reading Approach

The **individualized reading approach** encourages each student to move at her or his own pace through self-chosen reading material, rather than requiring students to move through teacher-prescribed material at the same pace as other students placed in the same group for reading instruction. With the individualized reading approach, which is designed to encourage independent reading, each student receives assistance in improving performance when the need for such assistance becomes apparent.

Characteristics of an individualized reading approach include the following:

1. *Self-selection*. Students are allowed to choose material that they are interested in reading. Each student may choose a different book. The teacher may offer

> Visit the Student Website for this book to view a summary of each of the ten days' activities in the thematic literature unit described in Example 9.6.

EXAMPLE 9.6 Thematic Literature Unit Plan

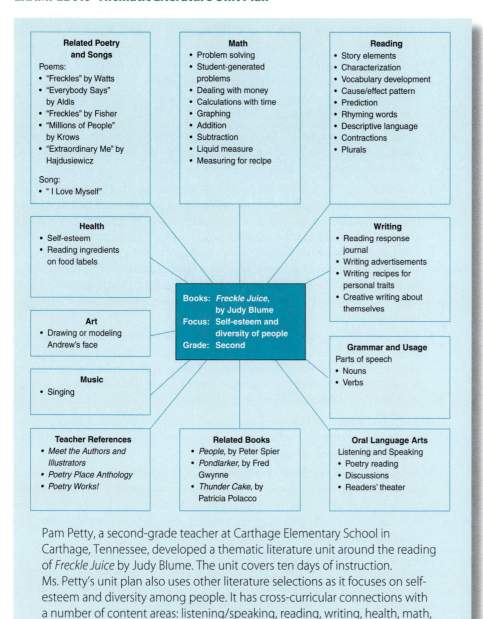

Related Poetry and Songs

Poems:
- "Freckles" by Watts
- "Everybody Says" by Aldis
- "Freckles" by Fisher
- "Millions of People" by Krows
- "Extraordinary Me" by Hajdusiewicz

Song:
- " I Love Myself"

Math
- Problem solving
- Student-generated problems
- Dealing with money
- Calculations with time
- Graphing
- Addition
- Subtraction
- Liquid measure
- Measuring for recipe

Reading
- Story elements
- Characterization
- Vocabulary development
- Cause/effect pattern
- Prediction
- Rhyming words
- Descriptive language
- Contractions
- Plurals

Health
- Self-esteem
- Reading ingredients on food labels

Writing
- Reading response journal
- Writing advertisements
- Writing recipes for personal traits
- Creative writing about themselves

Books: *Freckle Juice*, by Judy Blume
Focus: Self-esteem and diversity of people
Grade: Second

Art
- Drawing or modeling Andrew's face

Grammar and Usage
Parts of speech
- Nouns
- Verbs

Music
- Singing

Teacher References
- *Meet the Authors and Illustrators*
- *Poetry Place Anthology*
- *Poetry Works!*

Related Books
- *People*, by Peter Spier
- *Pondlarker*, by Fred Gwynne
- *Thunder Cake*, by Patricia Polacco

Oral Language Arts
Listening and Speaking
- Poetry reading
- Discussions
- Readers' theater

Pam Petty, a second-grade teacher at Carthage Elementary School in Carthage, Tennessee, developed a thematic literature unit around the reading of *Freckle Juice* by Judy Blume. The unit covers ten days of instruction. Ms. Petty's unit plan also uses other literature selections as it focuses on self-esteem and diversity among people. It has cross-curricular connections with a number of content areas: listening/speaking, reading, writing, health, math, art, and music, as shown in the diagram.

suggestions or give help if it is requested, but the decision ultimately rests with the student. Thus, an individualized reading approach has built-in motivation: students want to read the material because they have chosen it themselves.

**STRUGGLING READER/
INTERVENTION**

2. *Self-pacing.* Each student reads the material at his or her own pace. Struggling readers are not rushed through material in order to keep up with the more proficient ones, and more proficient readers are not held back until others have caught up with them.

3. *Strategy and skill instruction.* The teacher helps students as needed, either on an individual basis or in groups, to develop their word-recognition and comprehension strategies and skills.

**STANDARDS/
ASSESSMENTS**

4. *Recordkeeping.* The teacher keeps records of each student's progress. He or she must know the levels of a student's reading performance to know which books the student can read independently, which are too difficult or frustrating, and which can be read with the teacher's assistance. The teacher must also be aware of each student's reading strengths and weaknesses and should keep a record of the strategies introduced and the skills help given to each one. (See Chapter 2 for methods of assessment.) Each student should keep records of books read, new words encountered, and new strategies learned.

**STANDARDS/
ASSESSMENTS**

5. *Student-teacher conferences.* One or two times a week, the teacher schedules a conference with each student; its length may vary from three to fifteen minutes, depending on the purpose. Teachers act as collaborators in the reading of text, as demonstrators of strategies, and as observers and assessors of reading behaviors during conferences (Gill, 2000).

6. *Sharing activities.* The teacher plans some time each week for students to share books that they have read individually. Students may share with the entire class or with a small group.

**STRUGGLING READER/
INTERVENTION**

DIVERSITY

7. *Independent work.* Students do a great deal of independent work at their seats, rather than spending most of the assigned reading period in a group with the teacher. More proficient readers and older students can benefit more from this approach than can struggling readers, younger students, and English-language learners who need more teacher direction.

Exposure to different types of literature can help students build schemata for these types and can provide them with vicarious experiences that help build other schemata, facilitating comprehension. Encountering words in a variety of meaningful contexts extends the students' vocabulary knowledge.

To set up an individualized reading program, a teacher must have available a large supply of books, magazines, newspapers, and other reading materials, covering a variety of reading levels and many different interest areas. This collection will need to be supplemented continuously after the program begins, for many students will quickly read all the books that are appropriate for them.

Before initiating an individualized program, the teacher can plan routines to follow in the classroom, considering questions such as (1) How are books to be checked out? (2) How will conferences be set up? (3) What should students who are working independently at their desks do when they need assistance? The room arrangement can also be planned in advance to allow for good traffic flow. If books are categorized and located in a number of places instead of bunched together in a single location, students will have less trouble finding them, and the potential noise level in the room will be lower. Letting students participate in organization of the book collection, including categorizing and labeling, makes them aware of available books and of genres and topics of the books (Jones, 2006).

The teacher may find that having a file folder for each student **STANDARDS/ ASSESSMENTS** helps in organizing and record keeping. Each file folder can contain both checklists on which to record that student's strengths and weaknesses in applying particular skills and strategies and a form noting conference dates and instructional help given. Students can keep their own records of books read and strategies learned in file folders that are accessible both to them and to the teacher. These records will vary in content, depending on the maturity of the students. For example, Dryden Young, an advanced fourth-grade reader, chose to read *Harry Potter and the Chamber of Secrets*, a book that has a myriad of characters. He kept a list of the characters that he felt were most significant, along with character traits of each one as he saw them. Because his handwriting is not as advanced as his reading ability, Dryden used the computer to make his list, shown (without corrections) in Example 9.7. Although the teacher was aware that he wanted to read the other Harry Potter Books, she might also suggest that he would enjoy David Colbert's *The Hidden Myths in Harry Potter: Spellbinding Map and Book of Secrets* and his *The Magical Worlds of Harry Potter*, which have explanations of the myths, legends, history, geography, word origins, and word play referred to in the Harry Potter books. This background information may lead to Dryden's interest in reading the myths and classics in the English curriculum, as well as interest in word origins and puns.

TEACHING TIP

Preparing for the Individualized Reading Approach

Before you start an individualized reading approach, you should have read a large number of the books available in the classroom, to facilitate your assessment of the students' comprehension. Start a file of comprehension questions and answers for books being used in the program; these questions will be available year after year and will help refresh your memory of the books. Also compile a file of strategy- and skill-developing activities, covering the entire spectrum of word-recognition and comprehension strategies and skills and a wide range of difficulty levels, to use when reading difficulties are identified.

To choose appropriate books that cover a sufficiently broad range of topics and difficulty levels, you should assess the students' reading levels and interests. Two articles that can be helpful in choosing materials on appropriate levels are "Caldecott Medal Books and Readability Levels: Not Just 'Picture' Books" (Chamberlain and Leal, 1999) and "A Newbery Medal-Winning Combination: High Student Interest Plus Appropriate Readability Levels" (Leal and Chamberlain-Solecki, 1998), both of which provide readability information for excellent book choices. There are many sources that can help you find books appropriate for various cultural backgrounds, such as books featuring Hispanic culture or characters (Smolen and Ortiz-Castro, 2000; Martinez-Roldán and Lopez-Robertson, 1999/2000).

EXAMPLE 9.7 Independently Completed Character Trait List for a Self-Selected Book

Harry Potter and the Chamber of Secrets

Harry Potter	curagous brave smart
Ron Weasley	cowerd relatively smart sometimes brave
Hermione Granger	very smart brave helpful
Draco Malfoy	bad not helpful smart
Crabbe	bad dumb eats a lot
Goyle	bad dumb eats a lot
Professor Snape	evil mean bad teacher
Minerva McGonagall	very smart nice good teacher
Mrs. Sprout	smart nice weird good teacher
Filious Flitwik	smart nice out of the way
Gilderoy Lockhart	dumb brager a liar
Tom Riddle	evil smart mean
Hagrid	nice helpful friendly
Dumbledore	nice helpful good princible

Student-teacher conferences serve a variety of purposes, including the following:

1. *To help with book choices.* Teachers should spend some time showing students how to choose appropriate books. Teachers can encourage them to read one or two pages of the books that they think might appeal to them and to consider the number of unfamiliar words that they encounter. If there are more than five unfamiliar words per page, the book might be too difficult, whereas if there are no unfamiliar words, the child should consider the possibility that he or she could read more difficult material. A teacher can suggest potentially interesting books to students who find it hard to make a choice. Student-written book reviews may be provided for students who are having trouble deciding about books. Students can learn to write good reviews by examining models of written reviews and receiving assistance from the teacher or librarian.

2. *To check comprehension.* Conferences help determine how well students are comprehending the books and other materials that they are reading. Much of the time, the teacher and students may have authentic discussions about issues in the book during the conferences. Sometimes, however, the teacher may ask a student to retell all or part of the story or may ask a variety of types of comprehension questions. (See Chapter 8 for information on question types.)

Read•Write•Think offers the lesson "Is This the Right Book for Me? Strategies for Beginning Readers" that can be used to help students in grades K–2 choose books wisely. Go to http://www .readwritethink.org or link from the Student Website for this book.

STANDARDS/
ASSESSMENTS

3. *To check word-recognition strategies and oral-reading skills.* The teacher can ask a student to read orally, observing his or her methods of attacking unfamiliar words and using oral-reading skills, such as appropriate phrasing and good oral expression.

4. *To give assistance in applying strategies and skills.* If a student is the only one in the room who needs help with a particular strategy or skill, the teacher can help that student on a one-to-one basis during a conference.

5. *To plan for sharing.* Some conferences are designed to help students prepare for sharing their reading experiences with others. If a student wishes to read a portion of a book to the class, the teacher might use a conference to listen to that student practice audience reading and to give help with the presentation.

In an individualized reading program, each student is expected to be involved in independent silent reading a great deal of the time. The teacher should make the rules for the reading time very clear and should indicate acceptable activities, such as taking part in student-teacher conferences, selecting a book, reading silently, giving or receiving specific reading assistance, taking part in a reading group, completing a strategy or skill-development practice activity, and keeping records concerned with reading activity.

An individualized reading program can be introduced gradually by using it only one day a week, while using the basal program the other four days, and then increasing the time spent in the individualized program one day at a time over a period of weeks until all five days of the week are devoted to it. An alternative is to introduce the program to one reading group at a time while the remaining groups continue the basal program. After one group has become familiar with the approach, other groups can be introduced to it, until the entire class is participating in the individualized reading program. Teachers who worked with Harris (1996) thought that using the basal for part of the week and literature-based instruction for the other part of the week would be a good way to start.

"Seeing It in Practice: Individualized Reading Approach" on page 340 portrays one teacher's use of the individualized reading approach.

The advantages of an individualized reading approach are the built-in motivation to read books that students have chosen themselves, the lack of negative comparisons among students because the books are not marked with grade designations, the opportunity for students to read at their own individual rates and achievement levels, the personal contact between the teacher and students during conferences, and the opportunity to experience reading as an enjoyable pursuit.

TEACHING TIP

Grouping for Instruction

You can use group instruction in an individualized reading program, if you have students with similar difficulties who need help. The important thing is to be sure that all students get the instruction they need when they need it and are not forced to sit through instruction they do not need.

Individualized Reading Approach

Mr. Neal is sitting at a table with Paul, a student who has been reading the book *Maniac Magee*. They are having a lively discussion about which characters in the story value reading and how they show that they do. Mr. Neal can tell from this discussion how well Paul has comprehended various aspects of the book, but he is also engaged in a valid discussion of the content about which he has a personal opinion with a boy who has his own opinion, feels free to share it, and knows how to use events from the book to back up his ideas.

In the meantime, most of the other class members are reading from self-selected books at their desks or on the carpeted area of the reading center. When Megan has problems with a word in her book, she quietly leans over and asks for assistance from her assigned buddy, Tracy. When Tracy fails to be of help, Megan lists the word, page, and paragraph and reads on in her book.

Trey, who has a great deal of trouble sustaining independent reading over a period of time, is sitting at the computer, reading from a book on CD that allows him to click on words he doesn't know to obtain both pronunciations and definitions. With this assistance, Trey can remain focused on his reading for the entire period.

Jason and Joshua are sitting close together discussing the mock interview that they plan to use during book-sharing time on Friday. Both have read *Hatchet*, and they have decided to share with the rest of the class by having Jason play a reporter and Joshua play Brian. They are intently listing interview questions and answers to use for this purpose.

As Mr. Neal finishes the conference with Paul, he asks who needs some help. Megan and Mark hold up their hands, and Mr. Neal moves to their desks to offer assistance. Then he returns to the conference table and calls Michael, who is scheduled for the next conference, to come to the table. Michael has been having difficulty with word-recognition skills, and Mr. Neal asks him to read orally from some new material in the book that he is currently reading. This allows Mr. Neal to assess the particular difficulties that Michael is having. Realizing that Michael needs the same skill instruction that two other students need, Mr. Neal makes a note to plan small-group instruction for them.

After Michael's conference, Mr. Neal will meet with a small group of students who need help in making inferences when they read. He will model the process for them and have them engage in some directed practice activities.

Each student in Mr. Neal's class has self-selected material to read when he or she is not involved in a teacher-student conference, a peer-planning session, or a needs-group session. The students know the procedures to use when they have trouble, and they know they can receive individual attention during conferences or at intervals during class time if they follow accepted procedures. The fact that they have chosen their reading material heightens their motivation to read it and makes student engagement more likely.

STANDARDS/ASSESSMENTS

Some difficulties with use of this approach are the need to amass and continually replenish a large quantity of reading material, the need to schedule many individual conferences and small-group meetings in a busy school day, the large amount of record keeping that is necessary, and the lack of a sequential approach to strategy and skill development. This last difficulty is most frequently mentioned with the current emphasis on standardized testing. The teachers who use this approach often use it for only a day or two each week, supplementing it with a more structured approach the rest of the week.

Literature-Based Programs and English-Language Learners

LITERATURE

DIVERSITY

Literature can provide an avenue to familiarizing English-language learners (ELLs) with English pronunciation and grammar. It provides English input in a purposeful and authentic context. Read-alouds, literature circles, book talks, retellings, and other literature-response activities can support these students in learning the language.

Martinez-Roldán (2005) mediated discussions about literature with bilingual students by "making requests for clarification, restating comments, asking questions, and making comments designed to encourage and invite students to expand their ideas or express an opinion" (p. 30). She also listened to the students carefully to make sense of their comments and encouraged them to listen to and question one another. This gave them an opportunity to use their own methods of inquiry about things of genuine concern to them, which was a successful way to transact with text.

In selecting books for ELLs, teachers must consider the students' maturity levels, cultural backgrounds, interests, and current reading abilities. Picture books often are good choices, even for older students, because the illustrations provide scaffolding for grasping meaning, and there are many picture books that have themes appropriate for more mature students than those in the primary grades. Teachers can choose several picture books that have the same theme or topic, but are written at different reading levels. When these books are read sequentially, the repetition of vocabulary and ideas, along with the supporting pictures, scaffold the learning of English and the content in the books.

Fiction books that reflect the students' cultures and that have themes that are common to all students, such as adjusting to a move, being different, and family concerns, are likely to appeal to ELLs. Books that offer survival vocabulary and topics, such as money, school activities, foods, clothes, days of the week and months of the year, are all helpful to ELLs. Simple language, predictable text, and informative illustrations all make the books' content more accessible. Bilingual books and books that embed another language's words in the text are also useful, if they are culturally authentic. Williford's *Rudy the Rude Rooster* has English and Spanish words related to manners paired in the text. Rhyming poetry is helpful in word recognition and provides good material for choral reading. Elya's *Cowboy José* uses both interspersed Spanish words and rhyming text effectively. Huggins-Cooper and Vega's *Alien Invaders/Invasores Extraterrestres* provides an informative story in English and Spanish. Gemmell and Leigh's *Chateau-Mystere Mystery Castle: A French Puzzle Story* is a book that introduces basic vocabulary through the solving of a mystery. Han's *The Rabbit's Judgment* is a Korean folktale in Korean and English. Many other bilingual books are available.

Nonfiction trade books can be useful in scaffolding learning from content textbooks. They may use simpler vocabulary and offer more explanation than is common in a textbook. Teachers need to show ELLs how to use text features in nonfiction books (glossaries, tables of contents, graphic aids, and so on) (Vardell, Hadaway, and Young, 2006). (See Chapter 11 for more on teaching these features.)

LITERATURE

STANDARDS/
ASSESSMENTS

Research Supporting Literature-Based Programs

Many educators are concerned about being able to use literature-based programs and still maintain strong strategy and skill instruction needed for good performance on standardized tests. In response, Arya and colleagues (2005) conducted a study comparing the effectiveness of literature-based reading programs and commercial phonics-based programs in developing phonics, accuracy, and comprehension.

The literature-based programs in the study incorporated shared reading, read-alouds, guided reading, independent reading, literature discussions, strategy discussions, interactive writing, guided writing, and independent writing with an overall focus on constructing meaning as reading is done. To help students construct meaning from texts, the teachers gave them instruction in integrating syntactic, semantic, and graphophonic cues. Skills and strategies were taught in context of connected reading. K-W-L, story maps, and comparison/contrast charts are examples of the strategies used.

The phonics-based programs, in use in different classrooms, were both scripted. They also both taught systematic explicit phonics. In one of them, instructional materials included a reading anthology containing stories with controlled vocabulary and concept development written by the program authors. Background knowledge was developed by the stories. It also included word practice using word lists. The other program had an anthology that was organized around thematic units. It contained both classic and contemporary literature that had been previously published, as well as pre-decodable and decodable books for explicit, systematic decoding skill instruction. It incorporated choral readings and teacher questioning to develop fluency and comprehension. Letter recognition, phonemic awareness, phonics, and vocabulary were addressed, as well as fluency and comprehension.

The researchers found that students in the literature-based classrooms focused on constructing meaning and tended to try strategies to correct their reading when it didn't make sense. They included facts from and inferences about the story in their retellings, and the retellings showed some cohesiveness and personal connections to the text. The students in the phonics-based programs relied on graphophonic and syntactic cues more than other cues, frequently making substitutions that didn't make sense—some weren't even real words—and they did not tend to make corrections. They included facts in their retellings, and the retellings were cohesive, but they made few inferences or connections to the text. The researchers concluded,

> The children in the commercial phonics-based programs are not significantly better than the children in literature-based programs in phonics use, in or out of textual context. Neither are they significantly better on accuracy or on comprehension.... The students in the literature-based programs in our study were adept at using graphophonic cues, but they were also

Time for Reflection

Some teachers believe that literature-based instruction using trade books should completely replace the use of basal reading series that contain anthologies of literature. Others believe that using both results in the best instruction.

What do *you* think, and why?

superior in comprehending and comprehension at higher levels. (Arya et al., 2005, pp. 69–70)

Language Experience Approach

The **language experience approach (LEA)** interrelates the different language arts and uses the students' experiences as the basis for reading materials. Students write or dictate a story about an experience that they have had, and this story is used to teach a variety of skills.

The LEA is consistent with schema theory. Because it uses the child's experiences as the basis for written language, the child has adequate schemata to comprehend the material and can thus develop a schema for reading that includes the idea that written words have meaning (Hacker, 1980). The approach has also been used effectively with students who speak English as a second language because it provides material for reading instruction that they can understand (Moustafa, 1987).

 DIVERSITY

With this approach, students can see the relationships between reading and their oral language. Children can use compound and complex sentences and a wide vocabulary in their stories, and they find their own language patterns much easier to read than those in basal readers, probably because clues in a familiar context are easier to use. In fact, students often pick up the long, unusual words in experience stories faster than many of the short service words, probably because the distinctive configurations of these words contribute to recognition.

The rationale for this approach has been stated very concisely by one of its leading proponents, R. V. Allen: "What I can think about, I can say. What I can say, I can write or someone can write for me. I can read what I have written, or what someone has written for me. I can read what others have written" (Dorr, 2006, p. 139).

A child's background may be limited, but every child has experiences that can be converted into stories. In addition, the teacher can plan interesting firsthand experiences that can result in the creation of reading material that is meaningful for all students. Dorr (2006) recommends this approach for all students, especially high-need students with varied schemata. She points out, "A balanced approach includes direct and explicit instruction, as well as extensive opportunities for reading and writing.... The Language Experience Approach (LEA) then becomes a viable method for a teacher to reconsider and select." (p. 138).

This approach to reading is obviously not new, although its implementation has changed over the years. Today the experience charts used in the approach may be either group or individual compositions; stories about field trips, school activities, or personal experiences outside school; or charts that contain directions, special words, observations, job assignments, questions to be answered, imaginative stories or poems related to an experience, or class rules.

The LEA works well with children who have a variety of learning styles. For instance, learners use the auditory mode when stories are dictated or read aloud, the

 DIVERSITY

During the creation of a language experience chart, children see the transformation from oral language to print taking place.

© Elizabeth Crews

kinesthetic (motor) mode when they write stories, and the visual mode when they read stories.

Implementation in Kindergarten

Chapter 3 describes the use of language experience charts in kindergarten and also provides an example of a language experience chart in Example 3.4. At this level, teachers often use the charts to emphasize that oral language can be recorded and reconstructed, rather than focusing on having the children read the charts. Others, such as Karnowski (1989), involve kindergarten students in activities more like those described for the primary grades in the next section. Karnowski uses the LEA with process writing (discussed in Chapter 10), having the children choose their topics for writing from among their previous experiences. Discussion and sometimes dramatic play and/or drawing precede the writing of the story. The initial dictation of the story is revised and edited according to the children's direction, to show that first drafts are not the only drafts. The teacher reads and rereads charts before the children read them independently. Then the teacher uses the charts to teach vocabulary, decoding, and comprehension skills. Of course, the charts are "published" for reading by the children and their peers.

The LEA offers good opportunities for developing the concepts of *writing*, *word*, and *sentence*. During the language experience process, children see the transformation from oral language to print take place, including directionality, spacing between words, and punctuation and capitalization. Framing the individual language units with the hands helps teachers illustrate their meanings to students. Another benefit is that observations made during the dictation and reading of a language experience story and during the follow-up activities can provide the teacher with diagnostic insights into students' reading difficulties (Waugh, 1993).

STANDARDS/
ASSESSMENTS

Implementation in the Primary Grades

Implementation of the LEA with a group of primary-grade students may take a number of forms, but the following steps are typical:

1. Participating in a shared experience
2. Discussing the experience
3. Cooperative writing of the story on a chart, the board, or a computer
4. Participating in extension activities related to the story

After the children have participated in a shared experience and have talked it over thoroughly, they are ready to compose a group experience story. First, the teacher may ask for suggestions for a title, allowing the students to select their favorite by voting. Then the teacher records the title on the board or a transparency. Each child offers details to add to the story, and the teacher records these details. She or he may write "Joan said" by Joan's contribution or may simply write the sentence, sometimes calling attention to capitalization and punctuation while doing so. After recording each idea, the teacher reads it aloud. When all contributions have been recorded, the teacher reads the entire story to the class, sweeping a hand under each line to emphasize the left-to-right progression. Then the teacher asks the class to join him or her in reading the story aloud. Under cover of the group, no child will stand out for not knowing a particular word.

If the children have had numerous experiences with this type of activity, the teacher may proceed to other activities involving the story. If this is a very early reading experience for the group, the teacher may stop after the oral reading, with the plan to continue the next day. The children may be asked to copy the story from the board. The experience of writing the words can enhance memory of them, and the students will have a copy of the story that they can illustrate and take home to read.

On the second day, the class can be divided into three or four groups with which the teacher can work separately. To begin each group session, the teacher rereads the story to the children, using a master chart made the day before. Then the group rereads it with the teacher. Next, a volunteer may read the story with the teacher, filling in the words that he or she knows while the teacher supplies the rest. After each child in the group has had a chance to read, the teacher asks students to find certain words on the chart. The teacher may also show the children sentence strips (prepared the day before) and have them match these strips with the lines on the chart, either letting volunteers reconstruct the entire chart from the sentence strips or using this as a learning-center activity to be completed individually while other groups are meeting. Group charts can be useful in developing many skills and are commonly used for lessons in word endings, compound words, long and short vowels, rhyming words, initial consonants, capitalization, punctuation, and other areas.

If students have made copies of the story or the teacher has made a copy of the story for each student, the student or teacher can underline, on that copy, the words that the student recognizes while reading the story. The teacher may then make word cards of these words, which serve as the beginnings of the children's **word banks.**

Word banks offer many opportunities for instructional activities. They can be used to practice sight vocabulary, to work on word-recognition skills, and to develop comprehension skills. When children have accumulated a sufficient number of word cards in their word banks, they can use them to compose new stories or to play word-matching or visual and auditory discrimination games. To develop comprehension skills, a teacher can use classification games, asking questions such as "How many of you have a color word? A word that shows action? A word that names a place?" When each student has as many as ten word cards, they can begin to alphabetize the cards by the first letter, which gives them a practical reason to learn alphabetical order. They can also develop picture dictionaries representing the words on their cards. English-language learners may put both the English words and their equivalents in their first languages on the picture pages. Students can also search for their words in newspapers and magazines. After they recognize that their words appear in books, they will realize that they can read the books. The uses for word banks are limited only by the teachers' and students' imaginations.

After they have learned the procedure, students will write most experience stories in small groups, sometimes working on a story together and sometimes producing and sharing individual stories. At times, children may dictate their stories to classroom assistants. Some teachers use audio recorders for dictation. It is important that teachers initially transcribe the children's own language in language experience stories, even if the children's language does not fit the teacher's idea of basic words and sentence patterns for reading. If they do not do so, students may miss the concept that what is spoken can be written down for future retrieval. Teachers may later lead students in editing their "playground language" to be more like "book language."

Class stories do not always have to be in the same format. They may take the form of reports, newspaper articles, descriptive essays, or letters, or they can be creative in content while incorporating a particular writing style to which the students have been exposed.

Computers can be useful in a language experience lesson. The teacher can enter into the computer student-dictated material and modify it as the students direct, using a large monitor or projection device. In this case, the teacher can give students individual printed copies to illustrate or include in reading notebooks. At some

DIVERSITY

point, students may enter their stories into the computer themselves. Students can write small-group stories on the computer also. A group can collectively decide what to say, taking turns entering sentences as they are composed, or some students can be in charge of keyboarding and others in charge of content and mechanics, spelling, and grammar.

Sharing stories, whether orally or in written form, is very important because group members will soon see that certain words occur over and over again and that they can read the stories that their classmates write. The experience stories written by the group as a whole may be gathered into a booklet under a general title chosen by the group, and individuals may also bind their stories into booklets. Children will enjoy reading one another's booklets, and a collection of their own stories provides both a record of their activities and evidence of their growth in reading and writing.

 STANDARDS/
ASSESSMENTS

As the children become more experienced with the approach, they may write experience stories by themselves, asking the teacher or turning to their word banks or dictionaries for help in spelling. Teachers may elicit individual stories by asking the children to write something they want the class to know, a kind of written show-and-tell. Teachers should allow children to use invented spellings when they are writing because they can go back and correct spelling and rewrite the story in a neater form later if others are to read it. Rereading and editing require students to make judgments about syntax, semantics, and the topic and about whether or not others will understand the written account. These activities provide ways to emphasize comprehension when using language experience stories.

TEACHING TIP

Making Books from Language Experience Stories

When your students write language experience stories, they can illustrate them and make them into books. You can place them in a classroom library with library pockets and checkout cards, just as they might have in a regular library. Your students can assume the job of librarian on a rotating basis.

Visit the Student Website for this book to read a description of one teacher's use of the LEA with a first-grade class.

Implementation in the Higher Grades

The LEA has many applications above the primary grades. These applications are often in content-area instruction: writing the results of scientific experiments; comparing and contrasting people, things, or events; writing directions for performing a task; and so forth.

Text structures found in content-area textbooks, such as comparison-and-contrast patterns, can initially be taught through language experience activities. Then students will be more likely to understand these structures when they encounter them in content materials. First, the teacher can present students with two items and ask them how these items are alike. Then the teacher can ask how the items are different. The class can construct a chart of these likenesses and differences during the discussion. After the discussion, the students can dictate a language experience story based on the information listed on their chart. The teacher can encourage them to write first about likenesses and then about differences. Heller (1988) has pointed

The Language Experience Approach with Struggling Readers

During her third-grade practicum, Molly Johnson had been assigned to work with three boys who hated to read and were reading at a first-grade level. After deciding to use a language experience chart with them, Ms. Johnson began by reading Tomie de Paola's *The Quicksand Book*. After a discussion about quicksand, she involved the students in making quicksand in a large tub. The children made several charts related to the experience on such topics as what to do if trapped in quicksand, where quicksand is found, and the steps in conducting the experiment. When the three boys finished their work, Ms. Johnson arranged for them to share their information with the rest of the class.

They stood in the front of the classroom and read their charts to their peers, who were visibly impressed by what these boys had done.

Analysis of Scenario

By choosing an interesting topic and holding high expectations, Ms. Johnson had found a way to motivate these students. They became excited about their special project and looked forward to the reading and writing activities related to their study of quicksand. By reading their charts in front of the room, they gained self-esteem and a measure of respect from their classmates.

STRUGGLING READER/ INTERVENTION

out that such direct teaching of story structure can be helpful during language experience activities that are used with older remedial learners.

Many computer applications lend themselves to upper-grade activities, for they allow students to enter their stories easily and provide ease of revision. A good computer application is the production of a newspaper based on experiences around the school. Programs are available that make the production of a nice-looking newspaper relatively easy for the students. Students can be reporters, who write the stories; editors, who edit stories; and "typesetters," who format the edited material (Mason, 1984).

Use with Students Who Have Special Needs

STRUGGLING READER/ INTERVENTION

The LEA can be used to help students with special needs learn how to read. This approach promotes a good self-concept. It shows students that what they have to say is important enough to write down and that others are interested in it. It also promotes close contact between teachers and students. As the example in "Seeing It in Practice: Language Experience Approach with Struggling Readers" shows, the LEA has been highly successful as a remedial technique, allowing low-achieving readers to read material that interests them rather than lower-grade-level materials that they quickly recognize as being designed for younger children.

STRUGGLING READER/ INTERVENTION

DIVERSITY

Dorr (2006) was faced with teaching a science unit on plants to an extremely diverse group of third graders, many at risk for reading failure, who had no common schemata to relate to the topic. Half of the students were English-language learners, and the unit required vocabulary related to fruits and vegetables. Dorr sought a way to use a common link from the varied backgrounds of the students. Some had lived in a city and only seen fruits and vegetables in a can. Others could remember seeing fruits and vegetables grown in garden plots before they immigrated to the United States, and still others were familiar with ethnic fruits and vegetables that are considered exotic in the United States. The common thread that she found to tap into prior knowledge from all of the students was grocery stores. She used a picture of a grocery store to initiate discussion about the store and comparisons and contrasts of that store with ones with which the students were familiar. She worked on developing related vocabulary, sentence construction using key words (including many names of fruits and vegetables, some new and some familiar), and paragraph construction. Finally, her students took a trip to a local grocery store and then wrote about their experience. A display of the students' stories and photographs taken during the trip boosted the students' self concepts, and the stories could be kept so that the students could revisit the vocabulary of the upcoming unit in meaningful context.

Although the LEA is a good approach to use with English-language learners, students who know very little English need to acquire additional vocabulary and knowledge of oral language before they dictate sentences (Dorr, 2006). To increase students' vocabularies, teachers can ask them to touch, name, label, and talk about concrete objects.

 DIVERSITY

"Seeing It in Practice: Language Experience Approach with English-Language Learners" describes the LEA with a Spanish-speaking English-language learner.

The LEA also offers many advantages as a method for teaching reading to students whose dialect differs considerably from Standard English. A **dialect** is a variation of a language that is sufficiently different from the original to be considered a separate entity but not different enough to be classified as a separate language. Dialectal variations are usually associated with socioeconomic level, geographical region, or national origin. In truth, we all speak a dialect of some sort, and differences exist even within a regional pattern.

 DIVERSITY

Each dialect is a complete and functional language system, and no dialect is superior or inferior to another for purposes of communication. However, for individuals to be readily accepted in some social classes and to attain certain career goals, use of Standard English is desirable. Teachers should accept and respect children's dialects as part of their cultures and environments but should also make them aware of Standard English as an important alternative. Critics point out that the LEA might simply reinforce students' dialects without providing contact with Standard English. Gillet and Gentry (1983) propose a variation of the LEA that values children's language but also provides exposure to Standard English. The teacher transcribes the children's story exactly as dictated. The process continues in the traditional way, but later the teacher writes another version of the dictated chart in Standard English with conventional sentence structure, using the same format and much of the same vocabulary. The teacher presents it as another story, not a better one, and children compare the two versions. The students then revise the original chart, making their sentences longer, more elaborate, and more

Language Experience Approach with English-Language Learners

Lance Jasitt acts as an academic and cultural resource to a family of English-language learners who immigrated to Tennessee from Mexico. As one of his instructional activities, he uses a bilingual LEA in some of their lessons because it capitalizes on their schemata, provides meaningful texts as a basis for minilessons in Standard English sentence structure and mechanics, and creates a bridge between the grammars of two languages. It allows the students to integrate oral and written language, engage socially in a learning activity, and create a printed product for rereading and sharing with others.

Mr. Jasitt asked a ten-year-old learner to think back upon his early days in Mexico and to relate a memorable event that would be transcribed by Mr. Jasitt onto a poster-sized sheet of lined paper. After looking at an old photograph, the student recalled an encounter with a cow. The reminiscence was initially dictated in the family's primary language of Spanish and then translated by the student into English. The anecdote follows:

El Becerro

Cuando fui en el estado de Hidalgo yo recuerdo que estaba rebanando la hierba con mi tió. En ese momento vino el becerro y me empujó con su cabeza. Me caí y empecé llorar porque me asusté. Me fui corriendo a la casa.

The Cow

When I went in the state of Hidalgo I remember that I was cutting the grass with my uncle. In that time it came a small cow, and it push me with its head. I fell, and I started to cry because I was afraid. I went running at my house.

Mr. Jasitt used this story as a basis for subsequent minilessons to help the student learn the mechanics of English. On the day of the LEA dictation, he focused only on the consistent use of the past tense. (*Push* should be *pushed*.) Other lessons focused on prepositions, adverbs, and pronouns.

consistent with Standard English. They then practice echo reading and choral reading with this version until they can read it fluently and have acquired additional sight words.

Some Considerations About the Language Experience Approach

If the LEA is the only reading approach used, development of reading skills in a predetermined sequence is not likely. However, there is no single correct sequence for presenting reading skills, and students learn from a variety of programs that provide different skill sequences.

Using only the LEA would also fail to provide systematic repetition of new words and a lack of vocabulary control in general. Still, structure words, which are important and need to be learned in context, are generally repeated quite often.

With the LEA as the exclusive approach to reading instruction, the limitations of the students' backgrounds of experience might drastically limit reading content, and the materials used in reading would also rarely be of good literary quality. However, because the LEA is generally used along with other approaches, such problems are unlikely to develop.

Time for Reflection

Some teachers think that the LEA is too unstructured in relation to skill development to be useful. Others think it is valuable but only as a supplement to other approaches. Still others think it can serve as an exclusive approach in the beginning stages of reading instruction.

What do *you* think, and why?

Programmed Instruction and Computer Use

Two other related approaches are particularly helpful for individualizing instruction—programmed instruction and computer use. **Programmed instruction** is sometimes used to offer individualized instruction. Programmed materials instruct in small, sequential steps. The student is required to respond to the instruction frequently and is instantly informed of the correctness (or inaccuracy) of his or her response (given immediate reinforcement). Because the instruction is presented to an individual student, rather than to a group, each student moves through the material at his or her own pace, thereby benefiting from some individualization. Branching programs provide an even greater degree of individualization by offering review material to students who respond incorrectly to frames, thereby indicating that they have not mastered the skills being presented.

Programmed instruction can also provide follow-up reinforcement for instruction presented by the teacher, freeing teachers from many drill activities and allowing them more time to spend on complex teaching tasks. The programmed materials are designed to be self-instructional and do not require direct teacher supervision.

Programmed instruction does not, however, lend itself to teaching many complex comprehension skills, such as those involving analysis and interpretation, nor does it promote flexibility of reading rate. Word-analysis and vocabulary-building skills are most prominently treated in programmed materials, so teachers need to use other materials (for example, basal texts) or techniques (for example, semantic webbing) to present and provide practice in the complex comprehension skills.

Today the most common method of delivery of programmed instruction is through computer-assisted instruction (CAI). Because of the interactive characteristics of the computer—it can provide immediate responses to input from student users—teachers find that it is a good tool for individualizing instruction. Because of its ability to repeat instructions patiently without showing irritation or judging students negatively, it is also useful for remedial instruction. More information about computer applications is offered in Chapter 13.

 **STRUGGLING READER/ INTERVENTION**

Eclectic Approaches

Eclectic approaches combine the desirable aspects of a number of different methods, rather than strictly adhering to a single one. Research has not found one method that works for everyone but, rather, has repeatedly pointed to the teacher as the key factor in effective programs. An effective teacher integrates materials and methods as is appropriate to meet students' needs. As Duffy and Hoffman (1999) point out, laws or state, school, or district policies that mandate a single method of reading instruction keep teachers from adjusting instruction for students who would learn better from another approach. Many educators agree that "effective teachers are eclectic" (Duffy and Hoffman, 1999, p. 11; Shanahan and Neuman, 1997; Stahl, 1997); therefore, these mandates circumvent the attempts of educational professionals to adapt methods and materials to fit individual situations. Thoughtful eclecticism is based on experience, professional studies and research, and analysis and reflection, and it requires teachers who are adaptive decision makers (Duffy and Hoffman, 1999).

The following examples are only a few possibilities for combining approaches. Teachers should remember that the only limitations are school resources and their own imaginations.

LITERATURE

1. Language experience stories can be based on characters, events, or ideas in either trade books or stories in a basal reader. The teacher can plan an experience related to the story, lead a discussion of the experience, and record the students' dictated account. If an experience such as this is used prior to reading the book or basal story, it can help activate the students' schemata related to the story. It will also probably involve use of some of the vocabulary found in the story, providing an introduction to this vocabulary in context, similar to the way Dorr (2006) used the approach. The story may be used as a basis for skills instruction suggested in the basal reader, as well (Jones and Nessel, 1985).

LITERATURE

2. In a class in which whole-class reading of a core book is taking place, the teacher can structure an experience based on a situation from the particular book being read. For example, if the core book is *The Cay* by Theodore Taylor, the experience might be to try to weave a mat while blindfolded. The students could write a story about the experience and, in the process, develop a better understanding of the difficulty that Phillip had when Timothy asked him to weave a mat, even though he was blind.

LITERATURE

3. Teachers can use the individualized reading approach for two or three days each week and the basal program for the rest of the week, or they can alternate weeks, using the individualized reading approach one week and the basal program the next. They may supplement either or both with occasional language experience activities, either on or off the computer.

LITERATURE

4. Teachers can use a thematic literature unit approach to reading instruction, including pertinent basal reader stories as they are available and using language experience activities as appropriate to the planned curriculum. They may use database software to store information about the unit on the computer in an organized way, and they may use word-processing software to produce written reports about aspects of the theme.

LITERATURE

5. Walker-Dalhouse, Dalhouse, and Mitchell (1997) conducted a literature-based reading program that employed basal themes with middle school students. Some of the selections were from the Houghton Mifflin literature-based reading program; others were theme-related trade books. Writing, language, oral reading, and independent reading were taught in the program. Writing and

An Eclectic Approach

Ms. Gray, a teacher who embraces an eclectic approach to reading instruction, is working with one reading group in a corner of the room during her scheduled reading time. At the same time, students from another reading group are illustrating a language experience story that they wrote on the previous day. As they finish their illustrations, pairs of students from this group are forming sentences with their word-bank words. Several other students are busy reading self-selected library books at their seats.

Three students have returned to the room from the library and have seated themselves together to discuss some research reading that they have been doing on space

travel. One of them is holding the printout from a database query that she made during the library trip.

In another corner of the room, two girls are reading an interactive text story on a computer, discussing each decision and coming to a consensus about it before clicking on their choices.

Analysis of Scenario

In this classroom, all the students are busy at reading tasks, but the tasks involve many different approaches to reading instruction. The teacher has chosen activities that fit the students' individual instructional needs.

grammar lessons were related to the literature theme, although a grammar textbook was used. Oral-reading groups read a common book and discussed it. Students also chose independent books from a group designated by the teachers, and the teachers developed instructional packets for each group. After finishing the provided activities, students had conferences with their teachers.

Time for Reflection

Some teachers believe that they should stay with a single approach to reading instruction. Others believe that using the best ideas from all approaches is preferable.

What do *you* think, and why?

SUMMARY

Basal reading series are the most widely used materials for teaching reading in elementary schools in this country. Basal readers provide teachers with anthologies of reading materials, detailed teacher's manuals, and many supplementary materials. Some basal series contain large amounts of high-quality literature selections and integrate many types of language activities with the reading. Others embrace linguistic or intensive phonics approaches.

The directed reading activity (DRA) is the teaching strategy presented in many basal manuals. This strategy can be used with other reading materials as well. Comprehension monitoring can be made a natural part of a DRA. An alternative to the DRA is the directed reading-thinking activity (DRTA). Another alternative, guided reading, involves steps similar to those of a DRA but focuses on matching students with reading material in leveled books.

Literature-based reading approaches include whole-class reading of a core book, literature circles of students who read books for which there are multiple copies, thematic literature units, and the individualized reading approach. Whole-class reading of a core book, thematic literature units, and the individualized reading approach all include the use of minilessons. Thematic literature units focus on a theme, a genre, an author, or a book. All of these approaches include various types of responses to literature. The individualized reading approach allows students to move at their own paces through reading material that they have chosen. Student-teacher conferences help the teacher monitor progress and build rapport with students. Sharing activities allow group interaction.

The language experience approach (LEA) interrelates the different language arts and uses the students' experiences as the basis for reading materials. This LEA incorporates the visual, auditory, and kinesthetic modes of learning; promotes a positive self-concept; fosters close contact between teachers and students; and serves as an effective remedial technique in the upper grades. This approach can be introduced in kindergarten, but it continues to have applications for all students in higher grades, especially in conjunction with content area activities. It is especially effective for students with special needs and English-language learners.

Some approaches, such as programmed instruction administered through the computer and the individualized reading approach, are particularly helpful for individualizing instruction. Programmed instruction presents information in small, sequential steps. The student responds at each step and receives immediate feedback about whether her or his response was correct or incorrect. Students are allowed to move through the instructional material at their own paces.

An eclectic approach combines desirable aspects of a number of different methods. The only limitation to possible combinations is the teacher's imagination.

For your journal . . . .

1. Visit an elementary school classroom and then write about the instructional materials used in the reading program.
2. Visit a school and watch an experienced teacher use a directed reading activity (DRA). Write your reactions.

. . . . and your portfolio

1. Develop a directed reading-thinking activity (DRTA) for a trade book.
2. Choose a basal reader for a grade level that you might teach. Examine it for variety of writing types (narrative, expository, poetry). Make a chart showing the frequency of the various types. Note also the frequency of different types of content (language skills, social studies, science, art, mathematics, music, and so on).
3. Plan a thematic literature unit for a grade level of your choice. Think about ways that you can actively involve the students with the books.

Language and Literature

There is a close relationship among all of the language arts (listening, speaking, reading, writing, viewing, and visually representing). Instruction in any of them tends to enhance development of the others, as well. Oral language skills develop first. Although a number of children make the transition from oral language to reading easily through instruction, for others it appears to be much more of a challenge (Sousa, 2005). Oral language development has been identified as a predictor of success in learning to read (Roth, Speece, and Cooper, 2002). It is important for teachers to understand the connection between oral language development and the development of literacy in all content areas.

As students make the transition from primary levels to intermediate and middle grades, the instructional organizational patterns in their classrooms often change. Typically, students in the primary grades receive instruction in self-contained settings. As students move throughout elementary and middle school, they may continue in self-contained settings; however, many move to departmentalized classrooms where teachers are assigned to teach specific subject matter. As a result, reading instruction may be delivered through content areas, generally through an English language arts block (Tyner and Green, 2005).

As the organizational patterns of the classroom change, so do the instructional delivery methods and the materials. Students in the primary grades often participate in basal reading programs where initial reading instruction occurs. As students enter intermediate or middle grades, reading demands are increased. Students are expected to interact with a variety of text structures and types. Literature is an effective tool for making connections throughout the curriculum and integrating the language arts into all content areas. All teachers need to be skilled in selecting appropriate literature for students at various levels and for different interests, as well as for helping students choose books for themselves.

KEY VOCABULARY

Pay close attention to these terms when they appear in the chapter.

Caldecott Award
cumulative tales
fables
fantasy
fiction
genre
journal
legends
myths
Newbery Award
nonfiction
pourquoi tales
readers' theater
reading and writing workshops
traditional literature
writing process

AFTER
C or **I** (for initial
A or **D** answers)
A or **D**
(for initial **?** answers)

Directions: Before you read this chapter, complete the following anticipation/reaction guide. In the space before each statement, write **A** if you agree; **D** if you disagree; or **?** if you don't know. After you have read the chapter, complete the guide again to show what you have discovered in the chapter. In the space after each statement, mark whether you were initially correct (with a **C**) or incorrect (with an **I**). Write the letter for the correct answer (**A**) or (**D**) in the space for the statements that you initially marked with a question mark (**?**).

1. Ideally, language arts instruction should be integrated throughout the curriculum.

2. Journal writing is a good opportunity for teachers to correct students' handwriting, spelling, and grammar.

3. In writing and reading workshops, students complete workbook exercises.

4. Literature can be an effective vehicle for integrating the instruction in language arts across the curriculum.

5. When reading aloud, teachers should speak in natural tones and with expression.

6. The Newbery Award is given for excellence in illustration.

7. Silent reading is more difficult than oral reading.

8. Performers in readers' theater memorize their parts.

9. When writing responses to literature, a student's first priority should be the mechanics of writing.

10. There is no need for teachers to read aloud to children after children learn to read for themselves.

11. The Coretta Scott King Award is given to selections by authors and illustrators of African descent.

CHAPTER 10 ORGANIZATION

Language and Literature

Facilitating Language Development

Integrating the Language Arts

Organizing the Integrated Language Arts Classroom
Valuing Cultural Diversity

The Reading-Writing Connection

A Process-Writing Approach
Reading and Writing with Journals
Reading and Writing Workshops

Literature as a Means for Integrating Language

Creating an Environment for Reading and Writing
Literary Genres
Story Reading and Storytelling
Selecting Literature
Responding to Literature

Facilitating Language Development

Guided by the intent to provide students with the opportunities to develop language skills necessary for the pursuit of their individual life goals, the International Reading Association (IRA) and the National Council of Teachers of English (NCTE) developed the *Standards for the English Language Arts* in 1996 (International Reading Association & National Council of Teachers of English, 1996). Listening, speaking, reading, and writing had long been accepted as the language arts, but developers of the *Standards for the English Language Arts* expanded the concept to include viewing and visually representing: "Being literate in contemporary society means being active, critical, and creative users not only of print and spoken language but also of the visual language of film and television, commercial and political advertising, photography, and more" (*Standards*, 1996, p. 5). As teachers challenge students to integrate visual communication with other language forms, students

STANDARDS/
ASSESSMENTS

are learning to use, interpret, and create illustrations, graphs, charts, videos, and electronic displays.

Teachers should encourage children to use language in authentic, integrated situations. Learning is centered on the child, and the child learns communication skills through verbal interaction with others. The following basic tenets for facilitating language development are congruent with the *Standards for the English Language Arts* (1996).

STANDARDS/
ASSESSMENTS ☑

The *Standards for the English Language Arts* may be found at **http://www.reading.org** or **http://www.ncte.org**, or you can link to them from the Student Website for this book.

- *Learning is integrated.* Students learn more effectively when they can see connections and relationships among ideas and subjects than when they learn bits and pieces of information in isolation.

- *Tasks are authentic.* Authentic activities relate to real-world tasks such as writing letters and reading for information. When students can see the purpose and meaning of the work that they do, they understand why it is important to do it.

- *Learning is social.* The purpose of language is to communicate with others. Students therefore learn to use language by sharing ideas, working cooperatively, and becoming part of a community of learners.

- *Classrooms are learning centered.* To feel a commitment to learning language, students need to be actively involved in the learning process by accepting such responsibilities as making choices, taking part in negotiating decisions regarding procedures and curriculum, and self-evaluation.

- *Learning is holistic.* Reading skills and strategies are learned in meaningful context. Students are actively engaged in tasks that promote understanding and meaning-making. For example, instead of learning phonics by filling out worksheets, children learn phonics by observing letter-sound patterns during shared reading.

LITERATURE

- *Literature is an integral part of the curriculum.* Because a widely accepted premise is that students learn to read by reading, classrooms should offer a wide variety of books and related materials. Good books can be used across the curriculum as sources of information and pleasure and can provide the tools necessary to meet the specific instructional needs of struggling readers.

Integrating the Language Arts

The integration of language arts in the classroom is not a new idea; indeed, curriculum designers have advocated it from time to time for decades. (See Example 1.2 on page 28 for a visual organizer of the interrelationships that exist among the many areas of language arts.) In many classrooms, however, the practice of scheduling a specific amount of time for spelling, handwriting, reading groups, grammar, and so forth has prevailed. If each of these is transmitted as a separate, unrelated item, such segmentation of the language arts can interfere with students' natural, purposeful use of language in real situations, and it may result in their failure to apply what they already know about oral language to reading and writing.

Tyner and Green (2005) suggest ways that teachers can implement a language arts block by creating a classroom organization that includes a combination of small-group differentiated reading instruction, student-directed literature circles, and whole-class instruction. These authors recommend a model that includes components that are appropriate for delivery through whole class, small group, and independent practice. Essential components of the model include time for read-alouds, time for shared reading and writing, explicit instruction delivered in small groups, time for independent reading and writing, and time to observe modeled writing. Another important component includes motivation, involving the use of appropriately selected instructional materials.

Organizing the Integrated Language Arts Classroom

Classrooms may be organized in a self-contained format where one teacher is responsible for teaching all subject areas or they may be departmentalized with teachers designated to teach specific subject areas. Within this structure, the language arts block is typically assigned a specific time frame. In many self-contained classrooms, the language arts block is a two-hour block of time. In many departmentalized settings, it is offered in a ninety-minute time frame. Regardless of the time allocated, Tyner and Green (2005) suggest that organizing students into small instructional groups with access to appropriate material is an effective organizational model for instruction.

Some suggestions for small-group configurations follow:

- *Interest Groups.* Based on shared interests, interest groups are recommended for investigating topics through reading, writing, and literature. Students who are familiar with a topic and have a special interest in it can often read material at a higher level on this topic than they normally read other material.

- *Project or Research Groups.* Another type of grouping is based on projects or research that is usually related to a theme. Students with varying ability levels work together by investigating a topic, pooling their information, and planning a presentation.

- *Skills or Needs Groups.* As assessment data are collected and reveal areas of students' need in their use of reading strategies, the teacher may form skills or needs groups for direct or explicit instruction. Each group includes students

STANDARDS/ASSESSMENTS

TEACHING TIP

Scheduling for the Integrated Language Arts Block

For you as the classroom teacher, integration may mean setting aside a large block of time for language arts. This time period allows for flexible scheduling, flexible groupings, and freedom to develop special projects fully. During this extended time period, your students may engage in a variety of language activities, such as pursuing research projects, responding creatively to stories, preparing a school newspaper, or working at a poetry center. With appropriate guidance from you, your students become aware of the interrelationships among the language arts. They see, for instance, how the stories they read can serve as models for the stories they want to write, how the information they need for writing reports can be found by using research materials, or why good handwriting and correct spelling are important for publishing their own works.

who need help with the same strategy. The teacher can assemble a group on a temporary basis and present minilessons, followed by authentic applications of the strategy.

STRUGGLING READER/
INTERVENTION

- *Student Pairs or Partners.* In this configuration, pairs of students, or partners, work cooperatively to read orally, discuss material read, revise or edit written compositions, correspond through journal writing, or engage in peer tutoring.

- *Peer Tutoring.* Peer tutoring occurs when one student tutors another of the same age. Cross-age tutoring involves students of different chronological ages. When implemented and appropriately facilitated, both peer and cross-age tutoring provide students with valuable social and academic benefits.

Although a time period may be allocated for language arts instruction, integrated language experiences should extend throughout the day into every area of the curriculum. For example, reading, writing, speaking, listening, and viewing are essential for learning about ideas that have changed history and about science concepts that have resulted in new discoveries. "Putting It into Practice: Integrated Language Arts Lesson" shows how teachers can provide an integrated language arts lesson by reading a book and then allowing the students to pursue their natural curiosity. During this lesson, students become involved in listening, speaking, reading, writing, and problem solving.

"Seeing It in Practice: Developing a Literature-Based Thematic Unit That Integrates the Language Arts" on page 362 shows how a single book can become the center for learning in many areas. The teacher may introduce a book that so intrigues students that they assume an active role in developing meaningful related activities. They contribute their own ideas so that their investigation is truly learning centered rather than teacher directed. More on the development of thematic units can be found in Chapters 9 and 12.

Valuing Cultural Diversity

DIVERSITY

Culturally diverse students come from many regional cultures, ethnic groups, and religions. In recent years, the enrollment of culturally diverse students in schools has increased dramatically, and the ethnic and racial composition in classrooms has changed. Classrooms are now composed of students whose values, orientations toward school, and speech patterns may differ greatly. Both the cultural and linguistic divergences influence how children learn and how they should be taught.

Multicultural education involves developing an understanding and appreciation of various cultural groups. However, simply having awareness and good intentions to be just and fair are not enough to achieve the level of changes necessary in today's classrooms. All students should receive instruction with consideration for their cultural heritages, their language backgrounds, and their lifestyles. Teachers need to concentrate on teaching the strategies and content necessary for all students to achieve success and pursue their personal goals. Teachers must build upon what students bring to the classroom, value the diversity of the students, and view all

Time for Reflection

Some teachers believe that they need to teach each language art separately (that is, fifteen minutes for handwriting, twenty minutes for spelling, and so on) each day in order to be sure to cover each subject. Other teachers feel that integration of the language arts is more meaningful and that with planning every subject will be adequately covered.

What do *you* think, and why?

After reading Katherine Paterson's *Park's Quest* to the class, ask: "What do you think the title means? What is a *quest*?" Discuss responses. If the students wish to investigate various aspects of the book in more depth, let them form groups to investigate topics that interest them. These topics may lead to such activities as a debate over the U.S. involvement in the Vietnam War, a student-made book or webpage that connects the quest of King Arthur with that of Park, a diary or blog in which students write from Park's perspective after each day on the farm, a report on the causes of strokes and the effects of a stroke on a person's health, or an annotated bibliography of books about the Vietnam War.

students as capable and contributing members of the classroom or school community. "Putting It into Practice: Creating an Inclusive and Culturally Responsive Classroom" on page 363 lists guidelines for creating such a classroom.

The use of multicultural literature helps students connect with people of different cultures and provides them with information and insights about their own heritages. Because it implicitly acknowledges individuals' rights to be who they are, multicultural literature increases understanding of and respect for differences. Ultimately, literature can help reduce fear and prejudice. Louie (2006) suggests that simply exposing students to multicultural literature does not achieve the goals of understanding, enjoyment, and development of empathy. She offers guiding principles for teaching multicultural literature that include checking for authenticity, using variants of a familiar story to build schemata, having students actively respond through discussion and writing while reading, and engaging students in activities that promote understanding of the character and facilitate making connections with self.

DIVERSITY

The Reading-Writing Connection

Many educators have viewed both reading and writing as composing processes (Butler and Turbill, 1987; Flood and Lapp, 1987). Based on prior knowledge, attitudes, and experiences, the reader constructs meaning from text and the writer composes meaningful text. Both reading and writing require the use of similar thinking skills, such as analyzing, selecting and organizing, making inferences, evaluating, problem solving, and making comparisons.

Instruction in either reading or writing contributes to improvement in both of them, partially because both reading and writing require meaning processing (Olness, 2005). Students learn to read like writers and then write like writers. By offering a model, good literature instructs young authors through example and inspires them to create stories of their own. Students quickly detect patterns in predictable and repetitive books, which they imitate as they write themselves (Lancia, 1997; Donovan and Smolkin, 2002; Serafini and Giorgis, 2003). By carefully observing an author's

Developing a Literature-Based Thematic Unit That Integrates the Language Arts

Ms. Brison introduced Chris Van Allsburg's *The Wretched Stone* to her students by asking them to listen for clues that tell what the stone represents. When she finished reading the story aloud, students raised their hands to tell what they thought the stone really was. Isaac, the class scientist, thought it was malachite, and Katrina said it must be a mirror. Others thought it was an object from outer space.

The students begged Ms. Brison to reread the story, and she agreed to do so if they would listen again for clues. This time Janis solemnly said, "I believe it's a television because that's how television makes some people act." The others agreed as they noted the similarities between a television and the stone in the story.

The students wanted to know more about the story, so Ms. Brison asked them what they would like to do with it. Mike suggested finding other books by Chris Van Allsburg to read, and Beth wanted to learn more about the way that sailors lived and worked long ago. Tim said he could teach a group how to make sailor's knots, and Molly said they could write logs as if they were sailors on the ship.

Ms. Brison recorded the ideas on the board and then placed each idea at the top of a piece of chart paper. She wrote *Other* at the top of one chart to allow her students to come up with other creative responses. She told the students to think about what they would like to do and then sign up to work on a topic. Those responsible for finding other books by Van Allsburg checked the school library, the neighborhood branch library, and the downtown library. They found *The Widow's Broom*, *The Stranger*, and *Two Bad Ants*. They also borrowed books that Ms. Brison checked out at the Teacher Center. Each day the children read a different story until they became quite familiar with Van Allsburg's style. "His books always have something mysterious in them," Jack said. "Yes," Connie continued, "and they start like it's for real, and then something happens that makes you know it has to be fantasy."

Students who signed up to research the lives of sailors years ago collected books about sailing, took notes, and compiled an illustrated informational book that told of the hardships of sea travel—the food that sailors ate, the length of their journeys, weather signs, the consequences of storms at sea, and the stars that they used to chart their courses. Some students found stories and legends about pirates, particularly Blackbeard. Van Allsburg's detailed illustrations intrigued many children, who compared his black-and-white drawings in earlier books with the colored ones in more recent books. Students who had read *Jumanji* decided to make their own board game with penalties and rewards. As their projects neared completion, most groups decided to put their work at a center so that they could see what others were doing. Another group of students showcased its work when they dramatized *The Wretched Stone* for the class next door.

Ms. Brison reflected on the effectiveness of the integrated language arts unit. She noted the thoughtful listening demonstrated as her students tried to identify the elements of mystery, the well-supported points that they made while defending their views about Van Allsburg's use of fantasy, the reading of related storybooks and reference materials, and the informational book that they wrote about the harsh life at sea. The logs that they wrote as sailors impressed Ms. Brison most of all. The students had used such vivid descriptive words to express their feelings as they moved from being lively, active sailors to being entranced viewers of the stone.

Ms. Brison realized that while the students were enjoying investigating Chris Van Allsburg, they were learning a great deal about language and literature. She referred to her curriculum guide and checked off several language skills for her grade level: making inferences, differentiating reality from fantasy, recognizing an author's style, locating information, and using reference materials. Of course, there were other skills as well.

Creating an Inclusive and Culturally Responsive Classroom

The following are some general guidelines for creating a learning environment inclusive of students with diverse cultural backgrounds.

1. *Learn about their cultures.* Find out about your students' language and learn cultural variations in word meanings. Learn about your students' living conditions and what things are important to them. Try to discover cultural traits that affect how students learn. Show that you accept and value their cultures, even though they may differ from your own. Provide written and oral information for the family in the primary language spoken in the home, when possible.

2. *Value their contributions.* Take an interest in what your students bring to share and listen to what they say. Create opportunities for their families to share their cultural heritages through learning experiences in the curriculum. Invite family members to serve as guest speakers in the classroom, when appropriate.

3. *Provide a supportive classroom environment.* Let the environment reflect the various cultures represented in the classroom by displaying multicultural literature and materials and including instruction related to multicultural education. Encourage students to bring items from home for display to reflect the different cultures represented in the classroom. Host regularly scheduled curriculum family nights, such as "math night," or "science night," when parents and caregivers can attend and participate in activities to help with homework and gain a deeper understanding of the curriculum.

4. *Provide opportunities for cooperative learning.* Let students work collaboratively to develop social and academic skills, understand and appreciate the diversity among themselves, and learn strategies to use in their interactions outside of school.

5. *Use multicultural literature.* When possible, choose stories related to your students' cultural backgrounds. Exposure to such stories benefits all students. They gain self-esteem by reading about their own heritage and broaden their concepts of the world and the people in it as they read about other cultures.

use of dialogue while reading a story, a student begins to learn how to create dialogue when writing a story. Or in trying to write a description of the setting for a piece of writing, a student may read and reread the setting from another selection to get ideas.

Educators have explored many ways of using the linkage between reading and writing. A literacy program that integrates direct instruction and holistic approaches emphasizes reading and writing with many regular opportunities for students to be actively engaged in authentic tasks. These tasks motivate students and promote their understanding of reading and writing as meaning-making processes.

Calkins (1994) and Graves (1994) emphasize the importance of real-life experiences in the writing process. Based upon this premise, Moore-Hart (2005/2006) organized a summer writers' camp where both students and teachers were collaboratively engaged in a two-week experience that involved a community study and many purposeful writing activities. Both the students and teachers reported benefits from the experience. While the student participants acquired writing skills, the teacher

Visit Read•Write•Think at http://www.readwritethink.org (or link from the Student Website) to view "All About Our Town: Using Brochures to Teach Informational Writing," a lesson designed for grades 3–5. This lesson engages students in a study of their community through print and nonprint resources and illustrates different purposes for writing, including problem solving and functional applications.

Reading and writing contribute to the success of one another. The writing process helps students learn to make meaning from reading and writing.

© Elizabeth Crews

participants gained in professional knowledge about the process that they were able to take to their respective classrooms.

The functional reading and writing applications given in Example 10.1 are appropriate for any learner but particularly useful for providing scenarios with real-life applications for struggling readers and writers.

Teachers and students can use message boards, or centrally located bulletin boards, for sending and receiving messages, and students can correspond with other students through pen-pal programs. Pen-pal programs are sometimes conducted electronically. These are generally referred to as key-pal programs. Computers make it possible, too, for young authors to share their work on electronic bulletin boards, class websites, and other maintained sites. Electronic or Internet pen-pal (or key-pal) programs can provide students the opportunities to correspond and communicate with students from different cultures all over the world (Charron, 2007). Several types of young authors' programs exist for various purposes, including encouraging students to write illustrated bound books and to share their writing with other authors outside their schools. "Putting It into Practice: The Reading-Writing Connection" on page 366 provides ideas for some class activities for combining writing with reading.

EXAMPLE 10.1 Imaginary Functional Applications of Reading and Writing

Your dog is sick. What number do you call for help? Where could you take your dog?

Choose a magazine that you would like to read regularly. Fill out the subscription form.

Your mother is coming home on the bus, but you forget what time she is supposed to arrive. Look it up in the schedule.

You want to watch a television special, but you can't remember the time or channel. Find it in the newspaper or media guide.

Look through a catalog and choose items that you could purchase for less than $100. Fill out the order blank.

You want to write a lost-and-found ad for the bicycle that you lost. Write the ad and find the address and phone number of the newspaper.

You want to order a game that is advertised on the back of a cereal box. Follow the directions for placing the order.

Look at a menu and order a meal for yourself. Calculate how much it costs.

You want to go to a football game in a nearby town. Find the stadium on a map and be able to give directions.

Struggling readers and writers benefit from personalized reading and writing strategies. An effective strategy for struggling readers is repeated shared readings of predictable and repetitive stories and poetry, a procedure that enables students to sense language patterns. Students may then compose their own pieces based on the now familiar patterns. Repeated readings encourage students to use overall contextual meaning and sentence structure to help increase their word-recognition accuracy (Walker, 2005). Semantic mapping (explained in Chapter 6) is another particularly useful strategy for struggling readers because it helps them visualize relationships among concepts, as well as providing practice in reading and writing.

 **STRUGGLING READER/ INTERVENTION**

A Process-Writing Approach

A *process-writing approach* is an approach to writing in which students create their own pieces of writing based on their choice of topic, their awareness of audience, and their development of ideas from initial stages through revisions to final publication. The process is ongoing and recursive, with writing in some form generally occurring every day and with pieces in various stages of development. Example 10.2 on page 367 shows the first and final drafts of a composition written during process-writing instruction by an English-language learner.

 DIVERSITY

The Reading-Writing Connection

Here are some activities that you may want to use to work with reading and writing:

1. Provide opportunities for students to publish: (a) news stories that are modern adaptations of fairy tales and nursery rhymes, (b) news stories that could have been written at the same time and place as the setting of the book that the teacher is reading to the class, (c) a literary digest of news about books, or (d) advertisements for favorite books.

2. Encourage students to write a radio or television script based on a story that they have read. (First, they should read some plays to become familiar with directions for staging and the appropriate writing style for dialogue.) Students could develop a visual presentation by videotaping the performance of their created script or recording it as a digital movie and sharing it on their class website.

3. Arrange for students to correspond with pen-pals or key-pals from other regions of the country either through regular or electronic mail. As they interact, they are likely to become interested in those geographical areas, so provide resource materials for them to read about their pen-pals' homes.

4. Organize a young authors' conference in which students display and read from books that they have published. The conference could take place among classes within a single school, or it could be district-wide.

5. Encourage students to develop multimedia presentations about their favorite books. The presentations could be shared in class or posted and shared electronically on a class website. This provides another opportunity for practice in visually representing information.

Cross-grade process-writing programs provide opportunities for older students to act as literary advisors and/or attentive audiences for younger students and for younger students to act as audiences for older writers. Roe (1990) conducted such a program involving partnerships between fifth graders and second graders, described in "Seeing It in Practice: Cross-Grade Process Writing" on page 368.

▶ Stages of the Writing Process

The **writing process** consists of the following major stages: prewriting, drafting, revising, editing, and publishing and/or sharing. This process may be used at any grade level, although first graders' writing will of course be very simple, and their bookmaking will require a great deal of guidance from the teacher. In fact, in some cases the teacher may write stories from student dictation. As students progress through the grades, they will be capable of producing more complex and more carefully edited works. The stages of the writing process may be briefly described as follows

- *Prewriting.* The author prepares for writing by talking, drawing, reading, and thinking about the piece and by organizing ideas and developing a plan.

- *Drafting.* The author sets ideas on paper without regard for neatness or mechanics.

EXAMPLE 10.2 Process-Writing Drafts by an English-Language Learner

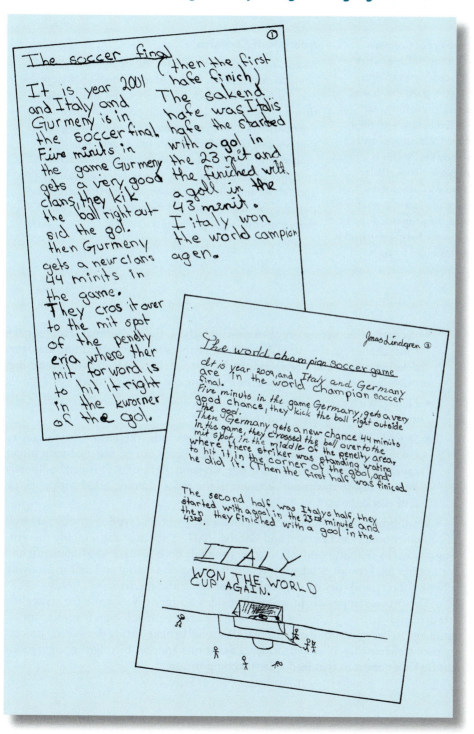

① The soccer final (then the first hafe finich)

It is year 2001 and Italy and Gurmeny is in the soccer final. Five minits in the game Gurmeny gets a very good clans, they kik the ball right out sid the gol. then Gurmeny gets a new clans 44 minits in the game. They cros it over to the mit spot of the penalty eria where ther mit for word is to hit it right in the kworner of the gol.

The sakend hafe was Italis hafe the started with a gol in the 23 mit and the finiched wilt a goll in the 43 menit. Italy won the world campion agen.

③ Jonas Lindgren

The world champion soccer game

It is year 2009, and Italy and Germany are in the world champion soccer final.

Five minuts in the game Germany, gets a very good chance, they kick the ball right outside the god. Then Germany gets a new chance 44 minuts in the game, they crossed the ball over to the mit spot, in the middle of the penalty area, where there striker was standing waiting to hit it, in the corner of the gool, and he did it. (Then the first half was finiced.

The second half, was Italys half, they started with a goal in the 23 rd minute and then they finiched with a goal in the 43 rd.

ITALY WON THE WORLD CUP AGAIN.

Cross-Grade Process Writing

During a cross-grade writing project at Crossville Elementary School, Austin Hamby's fifth graders were preparing to give their completed books to Ann Norris's second graders who were their partners. It was the fifth graders' first attempt at process writing, and most of them were somewhat amazed at how well their stories had developed with input from classmates and teachers during conferences. One boy said, "This is a good story. I'd really like to keep it for myself." Nevertheless, he gave his book to his partner, who was delighted with it and told the story to anyone who would listen. A couple of times fifth graders excitedly showed the program director their writing, saying, "Look what I wrote for my partner! It wasn't part of an assignment; I just wanted to do it."

Analysis of Scenario

Awareness of their audience for the stories caused students to devote much attention to the development process. Students were much more concerned about revising their stories to improve them and copying them neatly for their partners than they had been about polishing stories that were written before the project began. The fifth graders produced whole books for their young partners, complete with title pages, copyright dates, dedications, and "about the author" sections. Writing for authentic purposes obviously made a difference in the quality of these students' writing.

- *Revising.* After getting suggestions from others, the author may wish to make some changes in the initial draft. These changes may include adding dialogue, deleting repetitious parts, adding depth to a character, clarifying meaning, providing needed information, or changing the ending of the story.

- *Editing.* With careful proofreading and the help of peers and the teacher, the author corrects spelling and mechanics.

- *Sharing and Publishing.* After thoughtful revisions, the authors are eager to share finished pieces with real audiences. Pages can be fastened with brads, taped or stapled together, sewn, or professionally bound. Finished books may be kept in the classroom or taken to the school library, fitted with pockets, and checked out.

Word-processing programs can facilitate the scope and type of writing activities in the classroom (Van Leeuwen and Gabriel, 2007). They may also simplify the writing process by enabling students to enter rough drafts quickly, revise frequently, and print their final copies. Students revise by inserting or deleting material and moving chunks of text, and they edit by correcting spelling and mechanics.

STRUGGLING READER/
INTERVENTION

The process approach to writing provides a supportive format for struggling readers and writers. The revision and editing stages provide opportunities for all students to become published authors. Of special benefit during the writing process is peer conferencing, in which students assist one another by offering suggestions and asking questions that lead to better composition.

Reading and Writing with Journals

Students write in **journals** to record their thoughts and ideas, without concern for correctness of form or mechanics. Writers determine the audience, for sometimes journals or designated pages within them are personal, and other times they are meant to be shared. Journals may be spiral notebooks or simply papers stapled together with student-decorated construction-paper covers, or they may be kept in word-processing files or folders. To develop writing fluency, students must have time for journal writing, preferably on a daily basis. Students of any age can do journal writing, with younger children using invented spellings and pictures to express their ideas.

To introduce students to journal writing, the teacher might discuss diary writing and read books written in letter or journal form, such as Joan Blos's *A Gathering of Days: A New England Girl's Journal, 1830–32* or Beverly Cleary's *Dear Mr. Henshaw*. The teacher should write in a journal as the students write, to model the importance of recording thoughts and ideas. Teachers can also encourage parents and family members who write in journals to model their writing habits at home. If students have trouble finding topics, the teacher might offer such suggestions as an important event, a favorite activity, a perplexing problem, or a really good friend. Writers should understand that journals are a place where they can complain, ask questions, or express their true feelings.

 LITERATURE

Journal writing can take many forms:

- *Dialogue journals* are interactive, with the teacher or other reader responding to the student's writing. The responder should never correct the student's writing but can model proper spelling and writing conventions in the response.

- *Reading or literary journals* enable students to write responses to what they have read and receive the teacher's supportive feedback as a guide for further reading.

- In *buddy journals* (Example 10.3), student pairs "converse" in writing on a continuing basis, thus engaging in a meaningful writing and reading exchange.

- A *double-entry journal* enables the student to respond to a passage of particular interest. The student writes what the author says on one side of the page and enters a personal response on the other side. Responses may be drawings, opinions, questions, reflections, or connections to personal experiences (Popp, 1997). In Example 10.4 on page 371, sixth-grader Madyson Burgess responds to *The Westing Game* by Ellen Raskin.

Journal writing is an effective strategy for all learners but especially beneficial for those students acquiring English (Louie, 2006). Teachers should encourage English-language learners to write for authentic purposes even before they are proficient in English. Students may use a combination of symbols, drawings, and invented spellings to communicate their ideas. Dialogue journals enable teachers to move English-language learners toward competency by providing them a nonthreatening, nonstructured medium for exchanging ideas.

 DIVERSITY

EXAMPLE 10.3 Buddy Journal Entries

> Fri, 16, Feb, 1990
>
> Erin,
>   You are a very good reader. You are going to be a better reader if you keep practicing.
>   do you like school? What is your favorite subject? My favorite subject is spelling.
>
>   Your partner,
>   Lesley Ann Richards

> Wed. 21, 1990
>
> Lesley,
>   I do not like school very much.
> My favorite subject is scisce.
>   do you like school?
>
>   Your Partner,
>   Erin Young

Source: Leslie Ann Richards and Erin Young, Crossville Elementary School, Crossville, Tennessee

Visit Read•Write•Think (at http://www.readwritethink.org or link from your Student Website) to view "A Journal for Corduroy: Responding to Literature," a lesson designed to provide a model of reflection and journal writing. The lesson is adaptable for any story that encourages students to interact and write about their adventures shared with the main character in a literature response journal format.

Time for Reflection

What are the advantages and disadvantages of encouraging all students to write freely in journals without regard for mechanical accuracy?

What would *you* do?

Reading and Writing Workshops

Reading and writing workshops provide opportunities for teachers to teach specific strategies directly during brief minilessons and for students to spend most of their time actually reading and writing.

"Writing workshops consist of four steps: a minilesson, a status-of-the-class report, the actual writing workshop, and sharing time" (Atwell, 1998). The

EXAMPLE 10.4 Double-Entry Journal

Quote	My Opinion
"He found Madame Hoo in their rear fourth-floor apartment kneeling before her bamboo trunk, fingering mementoes from her childhood in China".	This in my opinion is saying Madame Hoo is missing her home in China or maybe she is missing her childhood.

Source: Madyson Burgess, Prescott Central Middle School, Cookeville, Tennessee, 1997. Used with permission.

Visit Read•Write•Think (at http://www.readwritethink.org or link from your Student Website) to view two lesson plans for writing workshops. "Writing Workshop: Helping Writers Choose and Focus on a Topic" provides a workshop format and assists students in selecting and planning their topics according to a timeline. The lesson is appropriate for grades 3–5. "Writers' Workshop: The Biographical Sketch" engages the students in research and in establishing criteria for evaluating their products.

minilesson lasts only a few minutes and deals with issues such as following procedures, writing realistic dialogue, and using mechanics correctly. The status-of-the-class check is made as the teacher reviews and records what each student will be doing during the workshop. The writing workshop, when most students write and/or confer, consumes most of the class time. Group sharing occurs during the last few minutes when students share their writing, try out ideas, and respond to one another's writing.

Although formats differ, most reading workshops operate in a similar manner, beginning with a minilesson that might be about comprehension strategies, literary appreciation, or genres. After the teacher records student-selected tasks on the status-of-the-class record sheet, students spend most of their time with self-selected reading and responses. During this time, the teacher may hold conferences with some of the students. Before the end of class, students spend five to ten minutes sharing their activities, books, or projects with one another (Atwell, 1998; Ross, 1996). Such workshops promote inquiry by letting students reflect on literature, interpret it, seek deeper meanings for it, and respond to it in various ways (Heald-Taylor, 1996).

SEEING IT IN PRACTICE ◀ ■ ▶

Video Case

View the Video Case "Elementary Writing Instruction: Process Writing" to observe how a classroom teacher in collaboration with a literacy coordinator guides students through various steps of the writing process and implements a writing workshop with a group of fourth graders.

Time for Reflection

In reading/writing workshops, teachers present skills and strategies during five to ten-minute minilessons, then allow students to read or write during remaining class time. Some teachers spend an entire class period (forty-five minutes or so) teaching skills and strategies, believing that they need this much time to provide instruction.

What do *you* think should be done, and why?

LITERATURE

Literature as a Means for Integrating Language Arts

Literature can be a vehicle for learning to read and write and for developing positive attitudes toward further language learning for all students. Teachers who integrate literature with language arts give students purposes and opportunities for reading and writing throughout the day and across all areas of the curriculum. They read aloud to students daily from various genres of literature and provide a variety of good books for classroom libraries.

Creating an Environment for Reading and Writing

The classroom environment should be supportive of the "whole person" and free from the risks that inhibit honest expression (Jensen, 2005). To help students feel a sense of ownership in their reading, teachers should allow some time for them to choose books or for partner reading or reading aloud to others. Students should also have input into how they are to respond to what they have read and how their own related work is to be displayed or published.

Giles (2005) and Gibson (2004) surveyed thousands of elementary and high school students to determine student preferences for pre- and postreading activities. Students at all levels indicated that they preferred activities that included choice in the selection of books to read as well as the opportunity to own their own books. All students at all levels also indicated that they enjoyed being read to.

Personalized reading allows student choice and does not include a formal assessment. Personalized reading should be implemented at all grade levels and may, for younger students, involve mostly looking at books. This strategy is easily modified for students with special needs. During personalized reading, students are encouraged to choose familiar, predictable, or high-interest books that are easy to read. They may be allowed to read their books orally to partners and discuss them in pairs. Adding personalized writing and encouraging the use of invented spelling can also be effective for struggling readers and writers because it includes the same element of student choice.

STRUGGLING READER/
INTERVENTION

Literary Genres

A teacher's knowledge of literary genres is essential for selecting literature and for establishing an environment that supports both reading and writing. Harris and Hodges (1995) define **genre** as "a category used to classify literary works, usually by form, technique, or content" (p. 94). Example 10.5 lists the characteristics of a number of literary genres or categories.

Understanding different genres assists readers in the recognition of text structure and story elements. Readers who successfully identify common elements can use this knowledge to construct their own stories, strengthening the connection between reading and writing (Buss and Karnowski, 2000; Olness, 2005).

EXAMPLE 10.5 Literary Genres

Literary Genre	Characteristics
Fiction	A broad category of prose that includes imaginative, invented stories written/told for the purpose of entertainment.
Fantasy	A type of prose that requires readers to suspend disbelief. Selections may include time travel, magic, and supernatural characters and events.
Science fiction	A fictional story based upon current or imagined technology or science advancements.
Realistic fiction	Invented or imagined stories that could have happened because they have believable story elements, such as realistic characters and settings.
Mysteries	Prose selections that feature a plot involving a problem that is revealed and must be solved in a series of episodes.
Traditional literature	Prose handed down orally from generation to generation with no identifiable author.
Folktales	A subcategory of traditional literature. Identified by motifs or themes. Characters are often animals or humans. Folktales have universal appeal with many similar variations appearing in multiple cultures.
Cumulative tale	A type of folktale that features a repetitive plot sequence that adds another element with each repetition.
Pourquoi tale	A type of folktale that attempts to explain "why." Many offer explanations for events that occur in nature.
Fable	Brief prose that usually features animals with human characteristics. The ending provides a summary with a moral based upon a lesson learned from the context of the story.

(Continued)

EXAMPLE 10.5 *(Continued)*

Myths	Prose narratives told as truthful accounts that sometimes offer explanations for creation and events that occur in nature. Gods and goddesses are primary characters.
Legends	Prose narratives told as truthful accounts. Characters are human.
Nonfiction	A broad category of prose that provides information supported by authentic facts. Includes biographies and informational books.
Biographies	Nonfiction literature that provides an account or partial account of an actual person's life.
Informational books	Nonfiction literature written to inform and/or instruct.
Poetry	Compositions that include meter and carefully selected words that evoke emotions and images. The content may or may not rhyme.

Story Reading and Storytelling

Reading aloud to students of all ages fulfills many purposes. Oral reading by the teacher serves as a model and allows students to experience literature they might not be able or inclined to read for themselves. It can encourage students to read more on their own because an exciting chapter or section of a book often stimulates students to read the entire book themselves. Besides providing exposure to specific books, reading to students can introduce them to creative and colorful use of language in prose and poetry, present new vocabulary and concepts, and acquaint them with the variety of language patterns found in written communication. Hearing literature read aloud gives English-language learners opportunities to hear the intonation and rhythm of the English language in meaningful contexts and to become familiar with the structure of the language.

DIVERSITY

Research supports the benefits of reading aloud to students. In *Becoming a Nation of Readers*, Anderson, Hiebert, Scott, and Wilkinson (1985) conclude, "The single most important activity for building the knowledge required for eventual success in reading is reading aloud to children" (p. 23). Among the specific benefits of reading aloud are the following:

1. Reading aloud provides a model for fluent oral reading and speaking.

2. Reading aloud provides a chance to practice listening skills.

3. Reading aloud builds background knowledge or schema.

4. Reading aloud expands vocabularies.

5. Reading aloud builds listening comprehension, which facilitates reading comprehension.

6. Reading aloud models structures that can contribute to writing skills.

7. Reading aloud improves syntactic knowledge.

Reading aloud contributes to a variety of skills for emergent and developing readers and provides a rewarding interaction for all students (Lesesne, 2006). Teachers must strive to maximize the academic benefits of reading aloud while emphasizing the enjoyment of the interaction (Beck, McKeown, and Kucan, 2002; Morrow and Gambrell, 2002; Lane and Wright, 2007; Santoro, Chard, Howard, and Baker, 2008).

Teachers approach read-aloud events in different ways. Some limit interactions during story reading and focus on reflective after-reading discussions. Other teachers read stories interactively, encouraging students to respond verbally to their peers, to the text, and to the teacher as they listen. During early interactive read-alouds, teachers and/ or parents can ask questions and engage students in dialogic reading where active reading is guided by the teacher or parent asking "why" and "what" questions followed by responses to answers that encourage and build upon the student's knowledge and skill. The prompts become more specific and open ended as students progress. Interactive strategies, such as dialogic reading, are used to guide students in constructing meaning and making personal responses (Lane and Wright, 2007). Both approaches to read-alouds enable students to connect stories to their lives, explore layers of meaning, develop knowledge about literary elements, and personalize story meanings.

TEACHING TIP

Arranging the Physical Environment

Encourage students to read by arranging portable bulletin boards and dry erase boards, sets of shelves, and other furniture to create nooks and crannies containing chairs, carpets, and cushions for reading. Bookshelves and containers filled with books should be within easy reach. Provide writing materials, including lined and unlined paper, pencils with erasers, colored pens for revising and editing, and folders for completed work. Backs of furniture can become spaces for showing students' work and creating inviting displays about books. Set up writing centers with activities that encourage students to make written responses to books and provide enough time for such reading and writing to take place. Working together, you and your students can design bulletin boards and arrange displays that feature a theme, represent a genre (such as poetry or biography), or focus on books by a popular author.

Create an environment whereby students are given time, a wide selection of books, and encouragement to read. Designate a period of time each day, usually from fifteen to thirty minutes, for silent reading. It is important that you also read to model the value of reading for everyone.

Just before reading a story aloud to the class, the teacher might ask students to listen to how the author uses a lead sentence to create interest in the story or uses dialogue to develop characterization. During the story, the teacher can stop occasionally to point out a literary technique or to ask students to close their eyes and visualize a descriptive passage. Reading from a big book or providing English-language learners with printed copies of the book that is being read aloud can be

 DIVERSITY

helpful. English-language learners benefit from observing English print characteristics and directional patterns, making predictable stories into big books, and developing an awareness and appreciation of literature. During shared big book reading, the teacher can help all students learn to read English by reinforcing reading strategies, modeling good reading, and inviting the students to read along.

After completing the story or chapter, the teacher might ask students what they specifically liked or disliked about the way the author wrote. When they discuss their likes and dislikes with the teacher, students learn to evaluate material, thus making them more critical readers and improving their writing abilities as well. "Seeing It in Practice: Reading Aloud to Students" shows how one teacher reads aloud to her third graders.

In a balanced reading program, teachers read aloud nonfiction as well as fiction. When reading nonfiction, teachers can respond to students' special interests, relate books to thematic units, probe into student-initiated inquiries, read high-interest excerpts selectively, and expand students' knowledge of a variety of topics. As students listen to informational books and discuss ideas from them, they may find it easier and more natural to read expository text for their own pleasure. More middle-school educators have begun to recognize the importance of including nonfiction trade books for self-selection during in-class reading, and as a result students often respond more favorably to reading and demonstrate a greater interest in reading (Moss and Hendershot, 2002).

Storytelling, like story reading, acquaints children with literature and provides good listening experiences. Listeners visualize the story through a "transfer of imagery" (Lipman, 1999). The storyteller uses oral language to prompt the listener to develop his or her own images of the story. Folktales are especially good for telling because they were told and told again long before they were captured in print.

Either teachers or students can tell stories. Students as storytellers can develop fluency and expression in oral language. By preparing and telling stories, they also can develop poise and build self-esteem. As storytellers, students must be aware of pitch, volume, timing, and gesture, as well as the responsiveness of the audience. A logical progression is for students to move from hearing, reading, and telling stories to writing original stories, which are often based on literary patterns that they already know (Roe, Alfred, and Smith, 1998).

Selecting Literature

From the thousands of books published annually for children, teachers and media specialists must select quality literature that students will want to read. Making such decisions is a challenge and a responsibility. Fortunately, there are several sources that teachers can use for reference when they choose literature. A useful source in selecting children's books

TEACHING TIP

Reading Aloud

Read aloud to students in natural tones and with expression, providing time for sharing the illustrations, exploring key words and phrases, and evaluating reactions. The best stories to read aloud are those that students cannot easily read by themselves, that you personally like and are thoroughly familiar with, and that possess the qualities characteristic of the best literature. Trelease's *The Read-Aloud Handbook* (2006) is an excellent source of information about how and what to read aloud to children.

Reading Aloud to Students

Kim Yunker calls her students to a corner of the classroom that has been set up to resemble a room in pioneer days. She asks a student to turn off the lights while she lights a kerosene lamp. Seated in a rocker, she shares a book that relates to the unit theme, "Little House in the Big Woods." She introduces Cynthia Rylant's *When I Was Young in the Mountains* and then begins reading aloud. Occasionally, she interjects questions such as "What is okra?" and "What do you think a johnny house is?" After she finishes the book, she asks questions about life in pioneer days, and her students browse quietly through some of the other books. As the students leave the corner, they return to illustrating spelling words related to the unit (for example, *maple*, *wagon*, and *slate*) or building a model fort from Lincoln Logs.

Analysis of Scenario

In Kim Yunker's class, story reading is integrated with the theme so that students can make connections between the stories and the work that they are doing in other subjects.

is a listing of Newbery and Caldecott Award winners. The John **Newbery Award** is presented annually to the author whose book is selected as the year's most distinguished contribution to American literature for children. Excellence in illustration is the criterion used in granting the annual Randolph **Caldecott Award.**

 LITERATURE

Some educators advocate classics, books that exhibit enduring excellence, as the foundation for reading. Not all classics are popular with students, however, so it is important to choose appropriate works and avoid those that may discourage students from reading. Some favorite classics are *Charlotte's Web*; *The Borrowers*; *Peter Pan*; *The Secret Garden*; *Where the Red Fern Grows*; *The Lion, the Witch, and the Wardrobe*; and *Little House in the Big Woods*.

 DIVERSITY

Another consideration in choosing books is their social significance in relation to human values, cultural pluralism, and aesthetic standards (Norton, 2003). For minority students, multicultural literature based on familiar traditions and values can reflect and validate a student's cultural experiences. For all students, such books can help familiarize students with less familiar cultures. Teachers can ask themselves the following questions to help them choose books that promote cultural pluralism and avoid portraying negative stereotypes:

1. Do the illustrations and text depict the character in the story as a distinct individual or as a stereotype of a particular ethnic group?

2. Is dialect used as a natural part of the story or contrived to reinforce a stereotype?

3. Is the culture treated respectfully or portrayed as inferior?

4. Are the people and the settings described authentically?

One valuable instructional resource when searching for multicultural literature is the *Coretta Scott King Awards* presented annually by the Social Responsibilities Round Table, with support from the American Library Association. Since 1970 this award has recognized African-American authors and illustrators whose books promote peace and world brotherhood (Tunnell and Jacobs, 2008).

Teachers, with the help of librarians or media specialists, should integrate carefully evaluated books into the curriculum. As they tell or read the stories to the class, teachers can promote the development of literacy skills, such as vocabulary, comprehension, and writing skills. Despite adult critics' recommendations, many students prefer to make their own choices. Each year, the International Reading Association–Children's Book Council Joint Committee publishes an annotated list of "Children's Choices," which appears in the October issue of *The Reading Teacher*. Each list is compiled from the efforts of approximately 10,000 children who, working in teams, read new books and vote for their favorites. Because students are the ultimate critics of their literature, teachers and librarians should consider their choices seriously when purchasing and recommending books.

STANDARDS/
ASSESSMENTS

In helping students select books, teachers need to know both the books that are available and their students' needs and interests. Teachers can assess students' personal reading interests by simply asking them to list three things that interest them or by administering an interest inventory. Teachers can guide students' choices by helping them locate books on special topics, sampling new books to pique their interest, allowing time for students to browse in the library, and suggesting titles on occasion. Regardless of this assistance, however, most students will value the freedom to choose their own books.

LITERATURE

Selecting appropriate poetry for students is especially difficult. Suitable poems will amuse, inspire, emotionally move, or intellectually interest children, but poorly chosen poems can prejudice children against poetry. Students prefer poems with rhyme, rhythm, humor, and narration; works by Shel Silverstein (*Where the Sidewalk Ends, Light in the Attic*) and Jack Prelutsky (*The New Kid on the Block, Something Big Has Been Here*) are favorites. The humor they use comes from alliteration, plays on words, or highly exaggerated situations, as in "Sarah Cynthia Sylvia Stout Who Would Not Take the Garbage Out" (from *Where the Sidewalk Ends*). Teachers must sensitively cultivate an interest in poetry by building upon students' preferences for light and humorous verse and gradually moving to the more sophisticated poems written for both children and adults (Kupiter and Wilson, 1993; Tunnell and Jacobs, 2008).

◄ ■ ► **SEEING IT IN PRACTICE**

Video Case
View the Video Case "Elementary School Language Arts: Inquiry Learning" to observe how primary-grade teacher Jenerra Williams structures a lesson that involves the inquiry-learning approach to a study of poetry.

Not to be overlooked are intriguing nonfiction selections, which can supplement textbooks or even substitute for them. So many appealing, well-illustrated informational books on nearly any topic are available that choosing the best books can be difficult.

LITERATURE

STANDARDS/
ASSESSMENTS

Because informational books can be read or viewed at varying levels, most are appropriate for many ages. Young readers can examine illustrations in David Macaulay's *Cathedral* and *Pyramid*, for example, whereas more mature students can read to find out how these structures were built. Worthy (1996) found that nonfiction selections, particularly those dealing with sports, animals, drawing, or cars, are popular with reluctant readers. Joanna Cole's *Magic School Bus* series, a mixture of

Lively responses to literature are likely to occur in classrooms with nurturing environments that provide an abundance of high-quality books, opportunities for library visits, adequate time for selecting and reading, introductions of new books, daily reading aloud, book discussions, and creative experiences with literature.

© Elizabeth Crews/Stock Boston

fact and fiction, appeals to children who enjoy the characters and their escapades, as well as to children seeking information. Fascinating books about animals— books useful for enriching a thematic unit—include *Summer Ice: Life Along the Antarctic Peninsula*, a combination of text and photographs about animal life in Antarctica; *Raptor Rescue: An Eagle Flies Free*, detailing the work of Minnesota's Raptor Center in rehabilitating injured raptors; and *Dolphin Man: Exploring the World of Dolphins*, a photobiography of Randy Wells, an authority on dolphins.

Many teachers prefer paperback books because multiple copies of one book cost the same as a single library edition, allowing teachers to order enough for small groups of children to read and use in follow-up activities and discussions. Paperback books are often available at special reduced rates through numerous book clubs.

TEACHING TIP

Selecting Nonfiction

When selecting nonfiction, teachers should look for the following characteristics (Norton, 2003):

- Content that is accurate and current.
- Content and illustrations that are free of stereotypes.
- Text and illustrations that encourage analytical thinking.
- Text arranged in a logical manner.
- Illustrations that support the text.

Children's magazines and newspapers are available for different reading levels and different areas of interest. These periodicals are excellent classroom resources and offer several benefits for the reading program: (1) the material is current and relevant; (2) the reading range varies in levels of difficulty and content presented; (3) several genres usually appear in a single issue; (4) language activities, such as crossword puzzles, contests, and students' writings, are often included; (5) the illustrations and photographs are excellent and can improve comprehension; (6) their low cost makes them easily accessible; and (7) they are popular with reluctant readers (Worthy, 1996; Tunnell and Jacobs, 2008). Classroom subscriptions to two or three favorites will enrich the reading program.

Responding to Literature

According to reader-response theory, readers are actively constructing meaning as they read. Because each reader differs in terms of background experiences and preformed attitudes, each interprets print and nonprint media somewhat differently. Readers make connections among the texts they read. They also connect what they read in the texts to themselves and make connections to their understanding of the world through *intertextuality* (Keene and Zimmerman, 1997; Tovani, 2000).

As explained in Chapter 1, Rosenblatt (1978, 2005) suggests that readers can approach texts efferently (for information) and/or aesthetically (as a lived-through experience). Usually, readers move back and forth along a continuum between an efferent stance and an aesthetic stance until they settle on a single predominant stance (Cox, 1997). They may be getting information as they read, but they may also be experiencing the emotions of the characters, the mood of the story as the plot unfolds, or a sense of morality toward an episode in history. For example, Lloyd Alexander's *The King's Fountain* gives a historical perspective of village life, but the courageous poor man's efforts to save his village tug at the heart. Both types of responses are important, but teachers tend to ask questions that call for efferent responses (Zarillo and Cox, 1992), even though in some cases aesthetic responses may be more meaningful and more enduring. Students should be allowed to respond in different ways and have adequate time for reflecting on and forming responses to material that they read.

STANDARDS/
ASSESSMENTS

DIVERSITY

Students can express their responses in a variety of ways, including answering teacher questions, participating in literature circles, interpreting literature orally, dramatizing reading selections, writing, or creating art or music. For English-language learners, reader response is especially beneficial because it allows the student to respond to literature uniquely in terms of his or her own cultural background and level of English proficiency. Teachers must establish the environment so that all students feel respected and comfortable enough to share and express their responses (Mohr and Mohr, 2007).

▶ Responding to Questions

Teachers can prepare generic questions to encourage students to respond thoughtfully to literature. These questions may be used during conferences, for written responses, for group activities, or during class discussions. Questions should be open ended, not limited to a single correct answer. Popp (1997) suggests four categories of questions, which are given here with sample prompts for each category.

Evaluation

What did you like or dislike about this book? Why?

Why do you think the main character acted in such a way?

Connection

How did a character make you think of someone you know?

Has anyone you know faced a similar challenge? What was it?

Comprehension

What is a theme of this story?

What does this story mean to you?

Strategy

How did you figure out an unfamiliar word in this story?

What special features helped you understand the story?

Time for Reflection

Some teacher's manuals—and often teachers themselves—identify a single theme or a single correct interpretation for a literary selection. Should teachers accept as correct other themes or interpretations that students discover for themselves? Can more than one answer be acceptable?

What do *you* think, and why?

▶ Literature Circles

An organized procedure for responding to literature is use of *literature circles* (Daniels, 2002). Students form literature circles based on personal choice, group members perform different roles, members engage in the reading of the text, and later they meet in their groups to hold student-led discussions. Throughout, students engage with the text from the perspective of roles that they assume. Examples of the roles include discussion director (creates questions for the group to answer), literary luminary (selects a passage for the group to reread or discuss for a reason and explains why the passage was selected—for example, it was especially interesting or exciting), investigator (researches and shares additional information about the book topic or the author), word wizard (selects vocabulary words that are interesting or difficult and shares the definitions with the group), illustrator (draws or sketches scenes related to the reading), and connector (clarifies connection with text to text, text to self, or text to world). These flexible groups give students opportunities to read and respond to fiction and nonfiction literature, engage in high-level thinking about books, and do extensive and intensive reading. Throughout the process, the teacher serves as a facilitator and does not assume a position in the literature circles.

▶ Oral Interpretation of Literature

Fluent oral reading with intonation and phrasing that accurately reflect the mood and tone of the story or poem is another way to respond to literature. Oral reading is more difficult than silent reading because, in order to convey the author's message to an audience, the reader must pronounce words correctly, phrase appropriately, enunciate distinctly, use proper intonation and prosody, and pace the reading appropriately. To accomplish these goals, the oral reader should have an opportunity to read silently first to become acquainted with the author's style of writing, determine the author's message, and check the correct pronunciation of unfamiliar words. If the passage is particularly difficult, the reader may need to practice it aloud to ensure proper phrasing and intonation.

STANDARDS/
ASSESSMENTS ☑

Oral-reading skills require special attention. The teacher may demonstrate fluent and poor oral reading, let the students analyze these performances, and then help students develop a rubric or draw up a list of standards or guidelines, such as the following:

1. Be sure that you can pronounce each word correctly before you read your selection to an audience. If you are not sure of a pronunciation, check the dictionary or ask for help.

2. Say each word clearly and distinctly. Don't run words together and take care not to leave out word parts or add parts to words.

3. Pause in the right places. Pay attention to punctuation clues.

4. Emphasize important words. Help the audience understand the meaning of the selection by the way that you read it. Read slowly enough to allow for adequate expression and speak loudly enough to be easily heard.

5. Prepare carefully before you read to an audience.

When well-rehearsed oral reading occurs, there should be one or more people with whom the reader is attempting to communicate through reading. Audience members should not have access to the book from which the performer is reading so that they cannot follow the reading with their eyes. Instead, they should listen to the reader to grasp the author's meaning and, if the reader is reading to prove a point, to agree or disagree. The reader must attempt to hold the audience's attention through oral interpretation of the author's words. A stumbling performance will lead to a restless, impatient audience and a poor listening situation.

Some examples of purposes for audience reading include

1. Confirming an answer to a question by reading the portion of the selection in which the answer is found.

2. Sharing a part of a published story, a poem (most poems are written to be read aloud), or an experience story that the reader has enjoyed.

3. Participating in choral reading or readers' theater (discussed in the next section, "Responses Through Drama").

4. Sharing riddles, jokes, and tongue twisters to entertain classmates.

5. Reading stories aloud to students in lower grades.

6. Reading the part of a character in a play or the narration for a play or other dramatic presentation.

LITERATURE 📖

Books by Paul Fleischman contain poems for two voices that invite students or groups of students to collaborate in reading aloud. Sometimes passages are to be read singly and sometimes in unison, but students must read expressively and fluently to achieve the proper effect. *Joyful Noise* contains poems about insects that think and act as humans; *I Am Phoenix* consists of poems that celebrate a variety of birds.

Responses Through Drama

Dramatic interpretations of literature are aesthetic responses that result in individual creative processes and products. Students often feel successful because there are no right or wrong answers. Through drama students can deepen their responses to literature and discover underlying meanings. Drama helps students become aware of different points of view and develops imagination and critical thinking. Through creative drama, English-language learners can interpret the stories they hear, thereby clarifying their understanding of story structure and vocabulary. Role playing enables them to experiment with vocabulary and sentence structure as they explore their feelings.

 DIVERSITY

Drama can take many forms. In *pantomime*, students speak no lines but show what is happening through their gestures and body movements. Simple nursery rhymes and fables are good for pantomiming. *Characterization* focuses on revealing the way that characters feel, act, and relate to other characters in the story; and students attempt to speak, to move, and to modify their facial expressions as they become the story characters. *Creative dramatics* means acting out a story without using a script, and *choral speaking* or *choral reading* is the dramatic interpretation of poetry or other literature with two or more voices. In **readers' theater,** students read aloud in dramatic style from scripts; no sets, costumes, or props are necessary, and the emphasis is on interpretive oral reading. Materials used for readers' theater are most often play scripts but may also be poems or materials from content area texts (Samuels, 2006).

Responses Through Written Expression

Traditional written book reports in which students merely summarize plots of stories have in many cases been replaced by more authentic responses to literature. Students are encouraged to react thoughtfully to what they read by writing in literature logs or critically reviewing books on note cards that are filed for other students to read. In one class, students place minireviews of favorite books that they want to recommend on a bulletin board. Example 10.6 is a sample of a student's recommendation.

Several ideas for activities that combine reading and writing were presented earlier in this chapter. Some additional activities that focus on written responses to literature are included in "Putting It into Practice: Written Responses to Literature."

Responses Through Art and Music

Many students who have difficulty expressing themselves with words prefer to respond to literature in other creative ways, such as through art and music.

Through exposure to well-illustrated picture books, students learn to appreciate the artists' work and may begin to see themselves as illustrators capable of creating their own art. They can interpret stories through many art media, including clay, paint, papier-mâché, fabric pieces, colored pencils and pens, computer drawing programs, and three-dimensional objects. Using such media, they create collages and montages, dioramas and puppet figures, mobiles and stabiles, and illustrations for their own storybooks.

PUTTING IT INTO PRACTICE

Written Responses to Literature

Some activities that you may want to try that involve written responses to literature follow:

1. Ask your students to collect as many Newbery Award books and Honor books (runners-up to Award books) as they can find, read several of them, and ask their friends to read others. After making up and filling out an evaluation checklist for each book, including such criteria as characterization, author's style, authenticity of setting, and plot development, they may add to the checklist comments about the merit of each book.

2. Let each student read a biography of a famous historical figure and write a story about what would happen if that person lived today—for example, how he or she would bring peace to the world, solve medical problems, or protect the environment. The popular *Lincoln: A Photobiography*, by Russell Freedman, would be a good choice.

3. Choose an environmental book, such as Chris Van Allsburg's *Just a Dream*, and have your students discuss the issues that it raises. Ask them each to

choose one issue that especially concerns them and write letters to their congressperson describing the issue and recommending solutions.

4. Read Byrd Baylor's *I'm in Charge of Celebrations* and discuss the meaning of *celebration* as used in this book. Then ask your students to keep journals of their own special celebration days over a period of two or three months. Students may wish to share their celebrations by reading from their journals.

5. Read to your class Mem Fox's *Wilfred Gordon McDonald Partridge* or a similar book about elderly people and discuss both the contributions and special needs of older people. Ask each student to identify an elderly person to whom he or she can write a letter or send a story. Help the students follow through with their plans.

6. After reading several selections of multicultural literature, keep a continuing record on a world map of the settings featured in the selections. Encourage your students to identify the sites of their family origins.

LITERATURE

EXAMPLE 10.6 Book Recommendation

> Hatchet by Gary Paulsen (1988)
>
> A really great survival story! You can almost see inside Brian's mind as he tries to figure out what to do to stay alive. He has so many problems— a bear, a tornado, no food. It's amazing the way he solves his problems. Very exciting!

Students have a natural tendency to respond to the rhythm and melody of music, so combining music with literature and language arts activities can be effective (Kolb, 1996). Music can be used effectively with emergent and developing readers. Younger students can explore sound-symbol relationships through printed copies of familiar songs, while older readers find music helpful in acquiring skills that involve recalling information from long-term memory, such as vocabulary meanings (Tate, 2005).

SUMMARY

Some basic tenets of facilitating language development are that learning is integrated, tasks are authentic, learning is social, classrooms are learning centered, and literature is an integral part of the curriculum. Applications of these principles are found throughout the text.

Instead of separating the language arts into discrete time periods, teachers should integrate instruction in reading, writing, listening, speaking, viewing, and visually representing. When students learn language as an integrated whole, they are likely to view all language arts as meaningful events.

Teachers carefully plan a differentiated curriculum and organize small groups designed to meet the instructional needs of each student. As students make the transition from primary levels to intermediate and middle grades, how reading instruction is delivered will often change. Students are expected to interact successfully with a variety of text structures and types, especially in the content areas. Literature is an effective tool for making connections and integrating the curriculum.

Creating a culturally responsive classroom encourages students to develop respect and understanding for themselves and others. Multicultural literature can provide a resource to assist the teacher in creating a classroom where all students and cultures are accepted and valued.

Many similarities exist between reading and writing. Both are composing processes in which meaning is constructed. Teachers can use this natural connection by guiding students into activities that call for both reading and writing. Process writing consists of five steps: prewriting, drafting, revising, editing, and publishing. Journal writing and reading enable students to record their ideas and, in many cases, read responses from their teacher. Writing and reading workshops provide minilessons and large blocks of time for students to concentrate on actual writing and reading.

Literature is useful for integrating language. Story reading and storytelling provide multiple benefits by enticing students to read and providing them with knowledge. Teachers should be aware of the characteristics of a variety of literary genres, and they should consider both literary merit and the students' interests when helping students choose books. Teachers should also establish environments with an abundance of interesting books and attractive displays that create interest in reading.

Students may respond to literature aesthetically (by making emotional responses) or efferently (by seeking information). Their responses may take place in literature circles or through oral reading, drama, written expression, art, and music.

For your journal   . . . .

1. Read a junior novel, such as *Little House in the Big Woods* or *The Sign of the Beaver*, and respond to it either aesthetically or efferently.

2. If you could choose, how would you prefer to respond to literature—through writing, oral expression, art, music, drama, or in some other way? Why?

3. View the Video Case "Elementary Writing Instruction: Process Writing." What is your response to the way that the teachers focused on nonfiction texts during writers' workshop? Do you agree or disagree with those who advocate for greater emphasis on nonfiction texts in the primary grades? Explain your rationale.

4. View the Video Case "Elementary School Language Arts: Inquiry Learning." Rather than explicitly telling students how to write a sensory poem, the teacher prepares the students and facilitates the process. Can you think of other writing genres that lend themselves to the inquiry approach? If so, which ones and why?

. . . . and your portfolio

1. Begin an annotated list of books that you would like to have in your classroom library and add to the list as you find other selections that you wish to include.

2. When you are visiting schools, jot down literature-related ideas that you see teachers using. These might include bulletin board displays, classroom library corners, theme-related book collections, and students' responses to literature.

3. Organize titles of trade books and websites by categories from different areas of the curriculum. Outline ideas for thematic units and brainstorm ways to connect each resource to the different areas of the curriculum.

Reading/Study Techniques

All students need to develop skills necessary for gathering information, organizing it, and evaluating it in multiple contexts. **Reading/study techniques** are strategies that enhance comprehension and retention of information in print and nonprint sources, and thus help students cope successfully with content-area assignments and with other informational reading. Students need to use study methods to help them retain material that they read, assess their learning, exercise flexibility in reading, locate and organize information, and use metacognitive strategies when studying. They need to learn how to derive information from external and internal organizational text features used by publishers and authors of expository texts. They also need to interpret the information displayed in the numerous graphic aids (maps, graphs, tables, and illustrations) in content-area materials.

All teachers are responsible for teaching study techniques. Primary-level teachers lay the foundation for this instruction, while teachers in higher grades expand it. For example, primary-level teachers can have their students begin to keep assignment books for recording all school assignments, instructions, and due dates. They can teach students to make free-form outlines of stories that they have heard or read. They can occasionally encourage writing of group experience charts in outline form. By modeling the use of indexes and tables of contents of books, teachers can show students how to find needed information. They can explain the use of some parts of books, such as tables of contents and glossaries. They can read aloud information related to content-area study from a variety of reference books and can introduce students to dictionary use with picture dictionaries. Primary teachers can also help their students use the library by showing them the locations of easy-to-read books and explaining the check-in and checkout procedures. Primary-level students can start to learn to read maps (titles, directional indicators, legends), graphs (picture graphs, circle graphs, simple bar graphs), and pictures that often appear in nonfiction material and content-area textbooks.

Teachers may present study techniques during a content class when the need arises or during a reading class, as long as the strategies are applied to content promptly. Students will retain study techniques longer if they apply them to real study tasks in the context in which they will use them. Therefore, it is often effective to designate time during content classes to explain and model study strategies that students need to apply immediately in those classes.

ANTICIPATION/REACTION GUIDE

BEFORE
A, D or **?**

Directions: Before you read this chapter, complete the following anticipation/reaction guide. In the space before each statement, write **A** if you agree; **D** if you disagree; or **?** if you don't know. After you have read the chapter, complete the guide again to show what you have discovered in the chapter. In the space after each statement, mark whether you were initially correct (with a **C**) or incorrect (with an **I**). Write the letter for the correct answer (**A**) or (**D**) in the space for the statements that you initially marked with a question mark (**?**).

AFTER
C or **I** (for initial
A or **D** answers)
A or **D**
(for initial **?** answers)

1. SQ3R stands for Stimulate, Question, Read, Reason, React.

2. Students remember material better if they are given opportunities to discuss it.

3. Study guides are of little help to retention.

4. Massed practice is preferable to distributed practice for encouraging long-term retention.

5. Students should read all materials at the same speed.

6. Many content-area textbooks offer glossaries of technical terms as reading aids.

7. Index practice is most effective when students use their own textbooks rather than a worksheet index that has no obvious function.

8. An effective strategy to scaffold the development of understanding graphs is to assist students in constructing their own meaningful graphs using familiar information.

9. Key words are the words that carry the important information in a sentence.

10. When making a summary, it is important to retain all details in the material.

11. Comprehension monitoring is a skill that can be fully developed in first grade.

12. Graphic organizers are designed to provide visual representations of key concepts or terms.

CHAPTER 11 ORGANIZATION

Reading/Study Techniques

Study Methods

SQ3R
SQRQCQ
Other Techniques to Improve Retention
Test-Taking Strategies

Flexibility of Reading Habits

Adjusting the Approach
Adjusting the Rate

Locating Information

Books
Reference Books
Libraries and Media Centers
Computer Databases

Organizational Techniques

Note Taking
Outlining
Summarizing

Metacognition

Graphic Aids

Maps
Graphs
Tables
Illustrations

Study Methods

Study methods are techniques that help students read, listen to, or view material in a way that enhances comprehension and retention. Study methods are student directed, rather than teacher directed, and should provide students with skills to become independent and strategic learners.

SQ3R

Probably one of the best-known study methods is Robinson's **SQ3R** method: Survey, Question, Read, Recite, Review (Robinson, 1961; Faber, 2006). For this method, the steps can be explained to the students as follows:

- *Survey*. As you approach a reading assignment, notice the chapter title and main headings, read the introductory and summary paragraphs, and inspect any visual aids such as maps, graphs, or illustrations. This initial survey provides a framework for organizing the facts that you later derive from the reading.

- *Question*. Formulate a list of questions that you expect to be answered in the reading. The headings and first sentence of each paragraph may give you some clues.

- *Read*. Read the selection in order to answer the questions that you have formulated. Making brief notes may be helpful in meeting your purposes.

- *Recite*. After reading the selection, try to answer each of the questions that you formulated earlier without looking back at the material.

- *Review*. Reread to verify or correct your recited answers and to make sure that you have the main points of the selection in mind and that you understand the relationships among the various points.

The SQ3R method helps a student remember content-area material better than simply reading the material would. Consequently, it is extremely important for teachers to first model the strategy and then to provide adequate time for students to practice and apply it.

Material chosen for SQ3R instruction should be authentic content material. The teacher can scaffold the survey step by viewing the selection together with students—reading aloud the title and main headings and the introductory and summary paragraphs and discussing the visual aids—in the first practice session.

The step that needs most explanation by the teacher is the Question step. The teacher can model how to take a heading, such as "Brazil's Exports," and turn it into a question: "What are Brazil's exports?" This question should be answered in the section, and trying to find the answer provides a good purpose for reading. A chapter heading, such as "The Westward Movement," may elicit a variety of possible questions: "What is the Westward Movement?" "When did it take place?" "Where did it take place?" "Why did it take place?" "Who was involved?" The teacher can encourage students to generate questions like these in a class discussion during initial practice sessions.

After students have formulated questions, they read to find the answers. The teacher may make brief notes on the board to model behavior that the students should acquire. Then he or she can have students practice the Recite step by asking each one to respond orally to one of the purpose questions, without referring to the printed material. During the Review step, students reread to check all the answers that they have just heard.

In subsequent practice sessions, the teacher can merely alert the students to perform each step and have them all perform the step silently at the same time. It will probably take several practice sessions before the steps are thoroughly set in the students' memories.

SQRQCQ

Another study method, developed for use with mathematics materials, is **SQRQCQ** (Fay, 1965). SQRQCQ stands for Survey, Question, Read, Question, Compute, Question. This approach is beneficial because students often exhibit difficulty reading statement problems in mathematics textbooks. For this method, the steps can be explained to the students as follows:

Reading/study techniques should be taught using the students' textbooks.

© Elizabeth Crews

- *Survey*. Read through the problem quickly to get an idea of its general nature.

- *Question*. Ask, "What is being asked in the problem?"

- *Read*. Read the problem carefully, paying attention to specific details and relationships.

- *Question*. Make a decision about the mathematical operations to be carried out and, in some cases, about the order in which they are to be performed.

- *Compute*. Perform the computations that you decided on in the preceding step.

- *Question*. Decide whether or not the answer seems to be correct, asking, "Is this a reasonable answer? Have I accurately performed the computations?"

As with SQ3R, the teacher should have the whole class practice the SQRQCQ method before expecting students to use it independently. Teaching the SQRQCQ method takes little extra time because it is a good way to manage mathematics instruction. (You may wish to refer to this section again as you read the section in Chapter 12 on mathematics materials.)

Other Techniques to Improve Retention

In addition to providing students with effective study strategies, teachers can improve their students' ability to retain content material by following these suggestions:

1. Conduct discussions about all assigned reading material. Talking about ideas that they have read helps to fix these ideas in students' memories.

2. Encourage students to read assignments critically. Have them constantly evaluate the material that they read. Teachers can avoid giving students the idea that something is true "because the book says so" by encouraging them to challenge any statement in the book if they can find evidence to the contrary. The active involvement with the material that is necessary in critical reading aids retention. (See Chapter 8 for a thorough discussion of critical reading.)

3. Provide time for students to apply the ideas about which they have read in authentic situations. For example, after reading about parliamentary procedure, students can conduct a club meeting; after reading about a simple science experiment, they can actually conduct the experiment. Students learn those things that they have applied in real life better than those they have only read about.

4. Always be certain that students have a purpose for reading before they begin each reading assignment because this increases their ability to retain material. Teachers may supply them with purpose questions or encourage them to state their own purposes. (Information about purpose questions is found in Chapters 7 and 8.)

5. Use audiovisual aids to reinforce concepts presented in the reading material.

6. Activate students' prior knowledge by reading background materials or reviewing information previously introduced to give students a frame of reference to which they can relate the ideas they read.

7. Prepare study guides for content-area assignments. Study guides help students retain their content-area concepts by setting purposes for reading and providing appropriate frameworks for organizing material. (Study guides are discussed extensively in Chapter 12.)

8. Explicitly teach students to look for the author's internal organization of material. Have them outline the material or construct diagrams of the organizational patterns. (Outlining is discussed later in this chapter.)

9. Encourage students to visualize the ideas that the author is describing. This helps them remember information longer. Some students will find it helpful to draw, graph, or chart the ideas that they visualize. Semantic webs are particularly useful. (See Chapter 12 for a description of the use of webs with

content material.) *Inspiration* (Inspiration) and *Kidspiration* (Kidspiration) are software programs that facilitate webbing of ideas.

10. Teach note-taking procedures and encourage note taking. Writing down information often helps students retain it. (Note taking is discussed later in this chapter.)

11. After students have read the material, have them paraphrase and summarize the information in either written or oral form. Moss (2004) suggests the use of retellings as a postreading technique for retaining material in expository texts.

12. Have students participate in distributed practice (a number of short practice sessions extended over a period of time) rather than massed practice (one long practice session) for material that they need to retain for a long time.

13. Encourage *overlearning* (continuing to practice a skill for a while after it has been initially mastered) of material that they need to retain for long periods of time.

14. When appropriate, teach some simple mnemonic devices (short phrases or verses used as memory aids)—for example, "there is *a rat* in the middle of separate." This approach helps students make connections and store information in long-term memory (Chapman and King, 2003).

15. Offer positive reinforcement for correct responses to questions during discussion and review sessions.

16. Encourage students to look for repeated words and concepts because they are likely to be important ones.

17. Encourage students to study more challenging material when they are most alert.

18. Teach students to ask and answer *why* questions about each factual statement in an informational passage (Menke and Pressley, 1994).

Test-Taking Strategies

Although test-taking preparation should not take up a lot of instructional time, students need to retain what they have read in order to do well on assessments. Students who know the material sometimes fail to do as well as they could because they lack adequate test-taking strategies. Students may study in the same way for essay tests and objective tests, for example. Helping students understand how to study for and take different types of tests can improve their performance.

 STANDARDS/ ASSESSMENTS

Teachers can help students prepare for taking essay tests by helping them understand the meanings of specific academic terms, such as *compare*, *contrast*, *describe*, and *explain*, that frequently appear in essay questions. This is especially important for English-language learners and students with special learning needs. The teacher can

 DIVERSITY   STRUGGLING READER/ INTERVENTION

state a potential question that uses one of these terms and then model the answer to the question, explaining what is important to include in the answer. If a contrast is requested, the differences between the two things or ideas should be explained. If a comparison is requested, likenesses should be included. The use of visual/graphic aids such as Venn diagrams can support the concept of comparison/contrast relationships.

To prepare for objective tests, teachers should encourage students to learn important terms and their definitions, study for types of questions that have been asked in the past, and learn to use mnemonic devices to help in memorizing lists.

Providing students focused instruction on taking standardized tests can help them perform better on these tests. Teachers should discuss with students the purpose of the tests and the special rules that apply during testing well before the standardized tests are to be given. They should provide practice in completing test items within specified time limits. A practice test with directions, time limits, and item formats as similar as possible to those of the actual test should be given to familiarize students with the overall testing environment.

It is extremely important that English-language learners and struggling readers understand academic vocabulary often associated with concepts that they are learning. This is important because academic vocabulary may not be vocabulary that they are likely to pick up informally from peers or outside of the school setting. Teachers should dedicate instructional time for the introduction of such vocabulary and provide multiple authentic experiences for application and understanding. In addition, it is also important to provide numerous assessment formats that allow English-language learners and struggling readers to become familiar with different assessment methods, such as essay exams, short-answer questions, and multiple-choice tests. The purpose is not only for test-taking preparation, but also to provide various approaches to increase comprehension (Pilgreen, 2007).

All students must learn to follow the directions for standardized testing exactly, including directions related to recording answers. They should learn to answer first those items that they can answer quickly and to check answers if they have time left. Teachers can also encourage students to consider the words *always*, *never*, and *not* carefully when answering true/false questions because these words have a powerful effect on the meaning. They can make sure that students realize that if any part of a true/false statement is false, the answer must be false. They can also caution students to read and consider all answers to a multiple-choice question before choosing an answer and encourage them to guess rather than leave an answer blank if there is not a severe penalty for guessing.

To help prepare students for high-stakes assessments that they currently encounter in schools, McCabe (2003) suggests that teachers integrate test-like materials formatted similarly to those assessments throughout the curriculum and present them in manageable selections. Students can gain a more confident attitude toward formal assessment as they become familiar with the formatting and experience success with these materials. Distributed practice with such materials will reinforce the modeling of metacognitive strategic thinking and increase the likelihood that students will be able to demonstrate their knowledge during the actual assessment situation. As early scaffolding strategies, teachers can allow students to work collaboratively with peers and use visual aids, such as charts and graphs, to display progress. These strategies help encourage the monitoring of skill building and the development of self-efficacy in preparation for testing.

Flexibility of Reading Habits

Flexible readers adjust their approaches and rates to fit the materials they are reading. Fluent readers continually adjust their reading approaches and rates without being aware of it.

Adjusting the Approach

Flexible readers approach material according to *their purposes for reading* and the *type of material*. For example, they may read poetry aloud to get the full effect of the rhythms and the sound of the words, or they may read novels for relaxation in a leisurely fashion, savoring descriptive passages that evoke visual imagery and taking time to think about the characters and their traits. If they are reading novels simply to be able to converse with friends about the story lines, they may read less carefully, wishing only to discover the novels' main ideas and basic plots.

In order to retain what they need from the material, flexible readers approach informational reading with the goal of separating the important facts from the lesser details and paying careful attention. Rereading is often necessary if the material contains a high density of facts or very difficult concepts and interrelationships. With such material, reading every word may be critically important, whereas it is less important with material that contains few facts or less difficult concepts. Flexible readers approach material for which they have little background with greater concentration than material for which their background is extensive.

Some reading purposes do not demand the reading of every word in a passage. Sometimes **skimming** (reading selectively to pick up main ideas and general impressions about the material) or **scanning** (moving the eyes rapidly over the selection to locate a specific bit of information, such as a name or a date) is sufficient. Skimming is the process used in the Survey step of SQ3R, when students are trying to orient themselves to the organization and general focus of the material. Scanning is useful when searching for names in telephone books or entries in dictionaries or indexes. It is also useful in content-area reading for students as they run their eyes down a page of text to look for numbers, if they need dates, or for capital letters, if they need information about specific people or places.

Teachers, even those at the primary level, should plan explicit instructional time to discuss the internal organizational patterns found in expository text (Dymock, 2005; Sweet and Snow, 2003). These organizational patterns allow the author to convey information through a specific format. For example, much of the information in a social studies textbook may be presented in chronological order. The students' knowledge of how the author conveys information provides clues for locating and deriving information from the material. Knowledge of the structure of expository text can have a positive impact on student comprehension (Pearson and Duke, 2002). More information on internal text organization patterns is located in Chapter 12.

Adjusting the Rate

Students may make the mistake of trying to read everything at the same rate. Some may read short stories as slowly and carefully as they read science experiments, and they may not enjoy recreational reading because they have to work so hard and it takes them so long to read a story. Other students read everything rapidly, often failing to grasp essential details in content-area reading assignments, even though they complete the reading. **Reading rate** should not be considered separate from comprehension. The optimum rate for reading a particular piece is the fastest rate at which the reader maintains an acceptable level of comprehension.

Students will use study time more efficiently if they are taught to vary their rates to fit their reading *purposes* and *materials*. Students should read light fiction for enjoyment much more rapidly than a mathematics problem that must be solved. When reading to find isolated facts such as names and dates, a student will do better to scan a page rapidly for key words than to read every word of the material. When reading to determine the main ideas or organization of a selection, he or she will find skimming more practical than reading each word of the selection.

One way to help students match appropriate rates to materials is to give them various types of materials and purposes, allow them to try different rates, and then encourage them to discuss the effectiveness of different rates for different purposes and materials. This will be particularly helpful if authentic classroom materials are used for the practice.

A technique helpful in guiding intermediate- and middle-grades students in the selection of appropriate reading rates is described by Marcell (2007) as "traffic light reading." A visual representation of a traffic light is constructed and displayed prominently in the classroom. The teacher provides explicit instruction regarding the reading rate appropriate for different purposes (for example, green for recreational reading or skimming). The teacher models using the traffic light to help pick the

The Read·Write·Think lesson plan "Exploring How Section Headings Support Understanding of Expository Texts" provides an example of how intermediate-level teachers can help students understand section headings in expository texts. The three-day lesson plan provides a collaborative opportunity for students to work from a model and construct a written sample to demonstrate understanding. Go to http://www.readwritethink.org or link from the Student Website for this book.

Reading Rate

To help students increase their reading rates, you can

1. Encourage students to try consciously to increase their reading rates. Time their reading for three minutes. At the end of that period, have the students count the total words read, divide by three, and record the resulting numbers as their rates in average words per minute. To ensure that they are focusing on understanding, follow the timed reading with a comprehension check. Students can graph the results of these timed readings over a period of time, along with the comprehension results. Ideally, students will see their rates increase without a decrease in comprehension.

If the students' comprehension does decrease, encourage them to slow down enough to regain an appropriate comprehension level.

2. Help students cut down on unnecessary regressions (going back to reread), by having them use markers to move down the page, covering the lines just read.

3. Help decrease the students' anxiety about comprehension, which could impede their progress, by giving them material written at their independent reading levels for practice in building their reading rates. (Information about independent reading levels is presented in Chapter 2.)

---

right speed. After guided practice, the teacher has students practice independently on multiple texts that are read for different purposes. The traffic-light visual serves as a guide to help students select appropriate strategies and monitor their engagement so that they can read at an appropriate rate.

Emphasis on increasing reading speed is best left until students have well-developed basic word-recognition and comprehension skills. By the time that they reach the intermediate grades, some will be ready for help in increasing their reading rates. It is important to remember that speed without comprehension is useless, so the teacher must be sure that students maintain satisfactory comprehension levels as they keep working to increase their reading rates.

Time for Reflection

Some teachers spend time on development of reading rate but do not address flexibility. Other teachers address flexibility but give little attention to increasing rate. Some teachers work on both aspects. Still others dismiss rate considerations entirely, as inappropriate for elementary school instruction.

What do *you* think, and why?

Locating Information

To engage in many study activities, students need to be able to locate the necessary material. Inquiry learning, for example, requires students to locate applicable information. A review of exemplary elementary classrooms and teachers indicated that in these classes students were encouraged to view themselves as researchers and to approach learning through inquiry (Allington, 2002). Teachers who create inquiry-based classrooms do more than just pose carefully designed questions; they also encourage students to approach learning in an inquisitive manner. They facilitate independent learning and provide opportunities for students to discover knowledge.

The Read•Write•Think lesson plan "Adventures in Nonfiction: A Guided Inquiry Journey" is an example of how primary-level teachers can teach students how to skim, gather information from nonfiction texts, and navigate through an Internet search engine to answer research questions. Find it at http://www.readwritethink.org or link from the Student Website for this book.

STRUGGLING READER/
INTERVENTION   DIVERSITY

Tower (2000) emphasizes the need for students to have experience with nonfiction reading and writing before the inquiry process can be a successful strategy for gathering information. A teacher can help prepare students by pointing out the location aids in textbooks, reference books, web materials, and libraries and by showing them how to access databases.

Books

Most books offer students several features that are helpful for locating needed information, including prefaces, tables of contents, indexes, appendices, glossaries, footnotes, and bibliographies. Although most basal readers have a table of contents and a glossary, they may not contain as many helpful special features as content textbooks; and, although some nonfiction trade books have tables of contents and/or glossaries, not all do. Therefore, teachers should present content textbooks to students carefully. Such instruction is particularly important for struggling readers and English-language learners.

▸ Preface/Introduction

When presenting textbooks to students in the intermediate or middle grades, the teacher can ask them to read the preface or introduction to get an idea of why the book was written and of the manner in which the author or authors plan to present the material.

▸ Table of Contents

All students at the primary and intermediate levels can learn that the table of contents lists the topics the book discusses and the pages on which they appear, making it unnecessary to look through the entire book to find a specific section. The teacher can help students discover information about their new textbooks by asking questions such as the following:

What topics are covered in this book?

What is the first topic discussed?

On what page does the discussion about _____ begin? (This question can be repeated several times with different topics inserted in the blank.)

▸ Indexes

Students in the intermediate and middle grades should become familiar with indexes. They should understand that an index is an alphabetical list of items and names mentioned in a book, along with the pages where these items or names appear, and that some books contain one general index and some contain subject and author indexes, as well as other specialized ones (for example, a first-line index in a music or poetry book). Most indexes contain both main headings and subheadings, and students should be given opportunities to practice using these headings

Using the Index to Locate Information

Several students in Ms. Rand's class needed to find out how to check addition problems that they had completed the previous day, but they had trouble locating the part of the book they wanted and spent too much time on the task. Ms. Rand noticed that none of the students used the index to find the pages. When she questioned a couple of them, she found out that they had only a hazy concept that the index was in the back of the book and that they didn't know how to use it.

The next day, Ms. Rand announced, "Turn to page 315 of your math books and tell me what you find there."

Here is a portion of what the students found:

Addition
    checking, 50–54
    meaning of, 4
    on number line, 10–16, 25–26
    number sentences, 18–19
    regrouping in, 80–91, 103–104
Checking
    addition, 50–54
    subtraction, 120–125
Circle, 204–206
Counting, 2–4
Difference, 111–112
Dollar, 35
Dozen, 42
Graph, 300–306
    bar, 303–306
    picture, 300–303

"It's called the *index*," Tommy replied, as he located the page.

"Right," said Ms. Rand. "The index is a part of the book that can help you find information that you need to locate in the book. It lists the topics in the book in alphabetical order, and after each topic it has the pages on which that topic is discussed in the book. For example, in your index, you can see that information about graphs is found on pages 300 through 306. The dash shows that all the pages in between 300 and 306 are about graphs too. If it had been written this way—300, 306—that would

mean the information would just be on those two pages. Who can tell me which pages have information about circles?"

"Pages 204 and 206," Tamara said.

Ramon broke in: "Page 205 has information about circles, too. You said the dash meant all of the pages between the ones listed."

"Very good," Ms. Rand replied. "Now look under the listing for *Graph*, and notice that there are some words indented there. These are types of graphs, and the particular types are listed with their own page numbers. When there is a list of indented terms under the main term, those terms are related to the main term, but they are there to help you find more specific topics. If I wanted to find out about bar graphs, I could look on pages 303 through 306. I wouldn't have to look at the other pages about graphs because bar graphs wouldn't be discussed there. What if I wanted to read about picture graphs?"

"You would read pages 300 through 303," Penny replied.

"Right! And what if I wanted to find out about regrouping in addition?" Ms. Rand asked.

"Pages 80 through 104," said Morgan.

"All of them?" asked Ms. Rand.

"Well, there are dashes," Morgan replied, "and a comma between the 91 and the 103."

"What do you think that tells you?" Ms. Rand asked.

"I guess that 92 through 102 don't have anything about regrouping on them," Morgan answered hesitantly.

"Good thinking," Ms. Rand replied. "You are getting that punctuation figured out."

Then she told the class, "Now get in your math work groups and see if you can answer the questions on this sheet about the index in your math text." (The sheet asked the students to locate pages on which specific math topics were covered.)

After the small groups had all reached agreement on the answers, the whole class discussed the items to ensure that everyone had been successful in understanding the process.

(Continued)

Using the Index to Locate Information *(Continued)*

At the end of the lesson, Ms. Rand said, "Find the meaning of *addition* and read it to me."

Mark did so.

"Did you look in the index to find the page number?" she asked.

"Yes, I did," Mark said.

"Do you think you found it more quickly by looking in the index than you would have by turning through the book to find it?"

"Yes," Mark replied.

"When you need to look things up in your textbooks, remember that the index can be helpful to you," Ms. Rand reminded the group as the lesson ended.

to locate information within their books. The teacher can lead students to examine the index of a book in order to make inferences about which topics the author considers to be important, judging on the basis of the amount of space devoted to them. "Seeing It in Practice: Using the Index to Locate Information" illustrates how to find information.

In using an index, thinking skills become important when the word being sought is not listed. Readers must then think of synonyms for the word or another form of the word that might be listed. Brainstorming possibilities for alternative listings for a variety of terms could be a helpful class activity to prepare students to be flexible when such situations occur.

▶ Appendices

Students can also be shown that the appendices of books contain supplementary information that may be helpful to them—for example, bibliographies or tabular material.

▶ Glossaries

Primary-level students can be shown that glossaries, which are often included in their textbooks, are similar to dictionaries but include only the important words related to the book in which they are found. Textbooks often contain glossaries of technical terms that can greatly aid students in understanding the books' content. The skills necessary for proper use of a glossary are the same as those needed for using a dictionary. (See Chapters 4 and 6 and later in this chapter for discussions of dictionary use.)

▶ Footnotes and Bibliographies

Footnotes and bibliographies refer students to other sources of information about the subject being discussed in a book, and teachers should encourage students to

Alphabetizing for a Picture Dictionary

Have first graders who are studying a science or social studies topic make a picture dictionary of words they encounter that are related to the topic. For example, if the class is studying animals in science, the students might construct a picture dictionary that includes *bears, deer, lions, tigers, elephants,* and so on. The teacher can list each animal that enters the study on the board, and a student can find a picture of the animal, write the word on a page for the picture dictionary, and illustrate the page. Students can also write or dictate a factual statement about each animal. After a number of pages have been constructed, a small group of students can alphabetize them and place them in a loose-leaf notebook. As more animals are studied, pages can be added for each one. Pages can be constructed by one student and alphabetized in the class picture dictionary by another student. Of course, throughout the study, all students can use the picture dictionary for spelling help or just to browse.

Students also need to learn that the **guide words,** often found at the tops of pages in alphabetically arranged reference books, tell them the first and last words or entries on the page. If students are proficient in using alphabetical order, they should be able to decide if a word will be found on a certain page by checking to see if the word falls alphabetically between the two guide words. "Putting It into Practice: Guide Words" offers a suggestion for practice with guide words.

turn to these sources for clarification, for additional information on a topic for a report, or simply for their own satisfaction.

Reference Books

Elementary school students often need to find information in such reference books as encyclopedias, dictionaries, almanacs, and atlases. Unfortunately, many students reach high school still unable to use such aids effectively. Although some skills related to the use of reference books can be taught in the primary grades (for example, use of picture dictionaries), the bulk of the responsibility for teaching use of reference books rests with the intermediate-grade teacher.

Important skills that students need to effectively use reference books of almost any kind include using alphabetical order, using guide words, and determining key words under which related information can be found. Students begin learning alphabetical order with the first letter of the word and then gradually learn alphabetization by the first two or three letters, discovering that sometimes it is necessary to work through every letter in a word in the process. "Putting It into Practice: Alphabetizing for a Picture Dictionary" offers an idea for developing and strengthening students' knowledge of alphabetical order while introducing them to dictionaries.

Because encyclopedias, almanacs, and atlases are often written at much higher readability levels than other materials used in the classroom, teachers must use caution when assigning work in these reference books. Students are not likely to profit from looking up material in books that are too difficult for them to read. When asked to do so, they tend to copy the material word for word without trying to understand it.

PUTTING IT INTO PRACTICE

Guide Words

Divide the group into two or more teams. Write the word pair *brace—bubble* on the board or a chart. Ask the students to pretend that these words are the guide words for a page of a reference book, such as the dictionary. Explain that you would expect the word *brick* to be on this page because *bri* comes after *bra* and *r* comes before *u*. Then write words, one at a time, from the following list on the board below the word pair. Let each team in turn tell you if the word would be found on the page with the designated guide words. Ask them to tell why they answered as they did. The team gets a point if the members can answer the questions correctly. The next team gets a chance to answer if they cannot. The reason for the answer is the most important part of the response.

1. beaker
2. boil
3. break
4. braid
5. brave
6. border
7. bypass
8. bud

Variation: Write four guide words and the two dictionary pages on which they appear on the board or a chart. For example, you could write

Page 300 *rainbow—rapid*
Page 301 *rapport—raven*

Write the words from the following list below the two sets of guide words, one at a time. Ask each team in turn to indicate on which page the displayed word would be found, or if the word would be found on neither page. Have them tell why they answered as they did. (Of course, you would model the decision-making process for them, as described earlier, before the activity starts.) If the team answers the questions about a word correctly, it is awarded a point. If the team answers incorrectly, the next team gets a chance to answer.

1. rare
2. ramble
3. ranch
4. rabbit
5. rave
6. ratio
7. range
8. raw

However, teachers should keep in mind the difference between *assigning* students to use a particular reference work and scaffolding students' use of interesting reference works that they choose themselves. Readers can handle much more difficult levels of high-interest material than of low-interest material. Therefore, a student who is intensely interested in the subject matter of an encyclopedia article may be able to understand the information, even if his or her usual reading level for academic materials is lower. For this reason, teachers should allow students to try to use material that *may* be too difficult for them. They should, however, never force students to struggle with material that is clearly beyond their range of understanding.

Many skills related to the use of an atlas—including interpreting legends and scales of maps and locating directions on a map—are described in the section on map reading in this chapter. Some factors related to dictionary and encyclopedia use are discussed in the following sections.

Determining the Correct Entry Word

As your students are reading a story that contains many words with affixes, call their attention to the affixed words as they occur in the text. Tell the students that, if they wanted to look up the words in the dictionary, they might not be able to find them listed separately. These words have prefixes, suffixes, and inflectional endings added to root words, so students might need to locate their root words to find them. Choose one word from the text, perhaps *happily*. Point to the word and say: "I recognize the *-ly* ending here. The rest of the word is almost like *happy*. The *y* was changed to *i* when the ending was added. So the root word is *happy*." Repeat this procedure for one or two other words from the text.

Later, as a follow-up activity, write on the board the list of words presented below. Then, for each word, ask your students to find the root word and tell about the other word parts that made the root word hard to find. They may also discuss the spelling changes made in the root word when endings were added.

1. directness
2. commonly
3. opposed
4. undeniable
5. gnarled
6. customs
7. cuter
8. joyfully
9. comradeship
10. concentrating

◗ Dictionaries

Dictionaries can help students find the pronunciation and meanings of words, as discussed in Chapters 4 and 6. Many types of dictionaries are available. Some dictionaries are available on CDs, DVDs, or the Internet. They may provide definitions, spellings, pronunciations, and idioms. Some dictionaries feature interactive multimedia. Users may be able to hear words pronounced when they click on them, hear sound effects related to the words, and play word games. In addition to the standard definitions and pronunciation respellings, there may be color illustrations for many words, sentences using the words, syllabic breakdowns, and plural forms. English-language learners would benefit from instruction in the use of bilingual dictionaries. English speakers, as well, could gain in vocabulary understanding from use of these resources.

 DIVERSITY

Before a student can use a dictionary for any of its major functions, he or she must be able to locate a designated word with some ease. Three important skills are necessary to do this: the general skills of using alphabetical order and guide words, discussed earlier, and the skill of locating variants and derivatives. Variants and derivatives are sometimes entered alphabetically in a dictionary, but more often they either are not listed or are listed in conjunction with their root words. An exercise on determining the correct entry word in the dictionary appears in "Putting It into Practice: Determining the Correct Entry Word." If a word is not listed, the reader must find the pronunciation of the root word and combine the sounds of the added parts with that pronunciation. This procedure requires advanced skills in word analysis and blending.

Encyclopedia Skills

Have your students decide on the volume to use for each of the following topics, without opening the volume:

George Washington
Declaration of Independence
Muskets
British Parliament
Battle of Bunker Hill

Have them check their choices by actually looking up the terms. If they fail to find a term in the volume where they expected to find it, ask them to think of other places to look. Let them check these possibilities also. Continue the process until each term has been located. Here is a possible dialogue between teacher and student:

Teacher: In which volume of the encyclopedia would you find a discussion of George Washington?

Student: In Volume 23.
Teacher: Why did you choose Volume 23?
Student: Because *W* is in Volume 23.
Teacher: Why didn't you choose Volume 7 for the *G*s?
Student: Because people are listed under their last names.
Teacher: Look up the term and check to see if your decision was correct.
Student: It was! I found "George Washington" on page 58.
Teacher: Very good. Now tell me where you would find a description of the Battle of Bunker Hill.
Student: In Volume 2 under "Battle."
Teacher: Check your decision by looking it up.
Student: It's not here. It must be under "Bunker."
Teacher: Good idea.
Student: Here it is. It's under "Bunker Hill, Battle of."

▶ Encyclopedias

Because encyclopedias vary in content and arrangement, students should be exposed to several different sets. Teachers should have them compare the entries from different encyclopedias on a specified list of topics. The activity suggested in "Putting It into Practice: Encyclopedia Skills" can provide students with instruction and practice in the use of the encyclopedia as they work on a thematic unit on the Revolutionary War.

Encyclopedia articles are often difficult for many intermediate-grade readers to comprehend. This makes it harder for them to put the information that they find into their own words. To encourage appropriate encyclopedia use, the teacher can work with the students to construct a list of things that they should look for about their topics, and they can list what they already know about each category of information. Next, the students can examine the graphic aids in the encyclopedia article to gather information. Then they can skim the written material to gather main ideas. Finally, they should read the material carefully and put it into their own words. They should be encouraged to consult other sources to check their facts and obtain additional information.

Electronic encyclopedias have become widely available and are located in many school settings. These encyclopedias are available in a CD or DVD format that is accessed by a computer. There are also encyclopedias on the Internet. Some of these encyclopedias have text, pictures, sound, and animation. They can be searched by using keywords and phrases, alphabetical title searches, and topical searches. They are motivational and easy to use.

▶ Other Reference Materials

Students often need to use materials other than books, such as newspapers, magazines, catalogs, transportation schedules, and pamphlets and brochures, as reference sources. For a thematic unit on pollution, for example, students might search through newspapers, magazines, and government pamphlets for stories and information about pollution and groups that are trying to do something about it, in addition to using trade books related to this problem.

To help students learn to locate information in newspapers, teachers can alert them to the function of headlines and teach them how to use the newspaper's index. Teachers also should devote some class time to explaining journalistic terms, which can help students better understand the material in the newspaper, and to explaining the functions of news stories, editorials, columns, and feature stories. Some of this instruction could be a part of a thematic unit on the newspaper. Students are often intrigued by the procedures involved in publishing a newspaper and the techniques used to design and produce a good newspaper. Activities such as the one in "Putting It into Practice: Using a Newspaper's Index" may be used in such a unit. Whenever possible, teachers should use real newspapers as a basis for activities similar to the one described.

Other instruction could take place as an integral part of other units being used in the classroom. For example, before the students search the newspaper for information on pollution for the unit mentioned earlier, the teacher could introduce activities related to developing the concept of *main idea* (see Chapter 8) to sensitize students to the function of headlines. This could help make their newspaper searches more efficient and meaningful.

In helping students to obtain information from magazines, teachers can call attention to the table of contents and give their students practice in using it, just as they do with textbooks. Distinguishing between informational and fictional materials is important in reading magazines, as is analyzing advertisements to detect propaganda. Chapter 8 contains activities related to these critical reading skills.

To obtain information from many catalogs, students again need to be able to use indexes. Activities suggested in this chapter for using indexes in newspapers and textbooks can be profitably used here as well. The ability to read charts giving information about sizes and about shipping and handling charges may also be important in reading catalogs.

A variety of transportation schedules, pamphlets, and brochures may be used as reference sources in social studies activities. Because their formats vary greatly, teachers will need to provide practice in reading the specific materials that they intend to use in their classes.

Libraries and Media Centers

Libraries or media centers are key locations in schools. Teachers and librarians/media specialists should work together as teams to help students develop the skills that they need to use libraries effectively. (The librarian/media specialist will hereafter be referred to as *librarian* for the sake of easy reference, but the expanded role that this person plays in dealing with multimedia should be kept in mind.)

Librarians can be helpful in many ways. They can show students the locations of books and journals, card catalogs, and reference materials (such as dictionaries, encyclopedias, atlases, and the *Reader's Guide to Periodical Literature*) in the library; explain the procedures for checking books in and out; and describe the expected behavior in the library. Demonstrations of the use of the card catalog (either print or electronic version) and the *Reader's Guide* and explanations of the arrangement of books in libraries are also worthwhile. Prominently displayed posters can remind students to observe checkout procedures and library rules.

LITERATURE

Currently, librarians are more often using library periods not only to help students locate and select books, but also to share literature with them. Librarians may introduce students to book reviews that can guide them in their selection of materials. Students can also be guided to write reviews that they can share with others.

By familiarizing students with reasons for using the library and explaining to them why they may need to use such aids as manual and computerized card catalogs and the *Reader's Guide*, teachers can prepare students for a visit to the library. While they are still in the classroom, students can learn that cards in the manual card catalog are arranged alphabetically and that the card catalog contains subject, author, and title cards. Teachers can display sample cards of each type on posters that are placed

Choosing books of particular interest from the library encourages students to read.

© Comstock Image/Jupiter Images

on the bulletin board. If the school has a computerized card catalog, students will be able to search for books by title, author, and subject, just as they do with the manual card catalog. They can choose the type of search they need, type in the keywords necessary for the search, and view a list of the available books on the monitor.

The librarian or media specialist is a valuable resource for the classroom teacher as thematic units are planned because no unit will be successful if the necessary reading materials are not available in a reasonable supply. Both books and other media are needed for these units, and the books need to be on a variety of levels. Librarians have useful input for teachers and students alike about books that are good for reading aloud, for sustained silent reading, and for reference sources. Cooperative planning between teachers and librarians can ensure that what goes on in the library and what goes on in the classroom are connected. In many schools, students are moving in and out of the library all the time. The library is used as "an extension of the classroom" (Hughes, 1993, p. 294).

TEACHING TIP

Library Skills

You may want to try this activity for practice with library skills: Prepare a scavenger hunt that requires using the library by dividing the class into teams and giving the teams statements to complete or questions to answer. (Example: The author of *The Secret Garden* is . . . .)

"Seeing It in Practice: Locating Information" shows how one class puts their research skills to work.

Locating Information

Students in a fifth-grade classroom are about to begin a study of World War II. They have formed into groups, each of which will research a different topic related to the war. One group is going to research transportation methods for troops.

When the children in Keith's group meet, Keith says, "First we need to know the different types of transportation that were used. I think we can find that in the encyclopedia under 'World War II.' Who would like to check that out?"

"I will," replies Elaine. "I'll look it up on a couple of encyclopedias that we have on CD. That will help us when we divide up jobs later."

"Good," Keith says. "Then we can make a list of the types of transportation, and each one of us can look up one or two of them and get more details. We can use a dictionary for a basic definition and the encyclopedia information for more details on the type of transportation we are looking for, like 'Jeeps.' Where else will we get information?"

"I can check the card catalog," Tammy suggests. "I'll check on the keywords 'World War II' in the subject field first. Then I can try 'Jeeps' and other types of transportation. We may also be able to look for information in books that we find in an Internet search."

"I have a book at home on airplanes," Randy says. "Some of them were from World War II. Can I draw some for our report?"

"Great!" Keith says. "We need some visuals for our report, and you are better at drawing than the rest of us. We'll want some drawings of those planes and tanks and probably some other stuff. We'll all be on the lookout for examples that you can use for models. I'll also ask my Great Uncle Joe about it. He was in the Army in World War II."

Analysis of Scenario

These students have received instruction that made them aware of places to find information for class studies, and they are putting that information to use as they work in their research group. Randy does not immediately have ideas about where to find things in the library, but he recognizes that he has a valuable personal resource and offers it for the study. These students have been taught that there are sources of information other than school materials, and they freely plan to use personal books and even primary sources.

Many students use the library to find books, to read, to write, and to interact with classmates about books. Many also use it to do research on questions they need to answer, and their research is specific and of personal interest. When students need a research skill, librarians now often teach it or direct them to other students who can help with that skill. The library frequently remains open to students all day, allowing access when need exists. Valenza (1996) points out that because multimedia production is a research process, it is an appropriate activity for the school library, where audiovisual and print resources are located, most schools have Internet connections, and librarians are available. (See Chapter 13 for information on multimedia production.)

Computer Databases

In today's schools, students need to be able to locate and retrieve information from computer **databases,** in addition to performing more traditional activities.

Time for Reflection

Some teachers think that the librarian should have the complete responsibility for teaching library skills. Others think the teaching of library skills should be a collaborative effort involving both the librarian and the classroom teacher.

What do *you* think, and why?

A computer database is a collection of related information that has been organized to facilitate retrieval through an electronic search. Each database is somewhat like a filing cabinet or several filing cabinets, with separate file folders for the different articles in the database. The information is categorized and indexed for easy retrieval. Users may create their own databases or use existing ones. Using databases, students pose questions, decide on keywords to access the data, read, follow directions, collect and categorize data, summarize material, and make comparisons and contrasts (Roe, 2000). The electronic encyclopedias discussed earlier are examples of databases that are available in some schools. In addition, many databases can be accessed through the Internet.

> The Read•Write•Think lesson plan "Learning About Research and Writing Using the American Revolution" is an example of how an intermediate-level teacher might guide students through an Internet research project. This series of lessons involves both historical research and poetry composition. Go to http://www.readwritethink.org or link from the Student Website for this book.

Organizational Techniques

When engaging in such activities as writing reports, students need to organize the concepts and information that they encounter in their reading. Teachers at the elementary level must give attention to organizational techniques, such as note taking, outlining, and summarizing.

Note Taking

Teachers may present note-taking techniques in a functional setting when students are preparing written reports on materials that they have read. Students should be taught the following note-taking techniques:

1. Include key words and phrases in the notes that they take.
2. Include enough of the context to make the notes understandable after a period of time has elapsed.
3. Include a bibliographical reference (source) with each note.
4. Copy direct quotations exactly.
5. Indicate carefully which notes are direct quotations and which are reworded.

Key words—the words that carry the important information in a sentence—are generally nouns and verbs, but they may include important modifiers. Example 11.1 shows a sample paragraph and a possible set of notes based on this paragraph. To introduce and scaffold the steps involved in successful note taking, the teacher should project the sample paragraph so the whole class can view it as the steps of the strategy are modeled.

After reading the paragraph shown in Example 11.1, the note taker first thinks, "What kind of information is given here?" The answer, "Problem for restaurant owner or manager—hiring numerous and qualified employees," is the first note. Then the note taker searches for key words to describe the kind of employees needed. For example, cooks who "are able to prepare the food offered by the restaurant" can be described as "qualified cooks"—ten words condensed into two that carry the idea. In the case of the nouns *servers* and *cleaning personnel*, descriptive words related to them

EXAMPLE 11.1 Sample Paragraph and Notes

A restaurant is not as easy a business to run as it may appear to be to some people because the problem of hiring numerous and qualified employees is ever-present. Cooks, servers, and cleaning personnel are necessary. Cooks must be able to prepare the food offered by the restaurant. Servers need to be able to carry out their duties politely and efficiently. Cleaning personnel need to be dependable and thorough. Poorly prepared food, inadequately cleaned dishes, and rude help can be the downfall of a restaurant, so restaurant owners and managers must hire with care.

> Problem for restaurant owner
> or manager—good cooks;
> polite, efficient servers; depend-
> able, thorough cleaning
> personnel. Hire with care.

are added; condensation of phrases is not necessary (although the *ands* between the adjectives may be left out) because the key words needed are found directly in the selection. The last part of the paragraph can be summed up in the warning "Hire with care." It is easy to see that notes based on key words carry the message of the passage in a very condensed or abbreviated form.

A teacher can go through an example like this one with students, telling them what key words to choose and why, and then provide another example, letting the students decide as a group which words to write down and having them give reasons for their choices. Finally, each student can do a selection individually. After completing the individual note taking, the students can compare their notes and discuss the reasons for their choices.

Students can take notes in outline form, in sentences, or in paragraphs. Ivey and Fisher (2006) suggest the use of a two-column note-taking format. This format involves writing key words and main ideas on the left side of the organizer while entering details on the right-hand side and a brief summary at the bottom of the page. Beginners may benefit from taking notes in the form of semantic webs or maps. (See Chapters 6, 7, and 12 for information on these techniques.)

Outlining

Teachers can lead students to understand that outlining is writing down information from the material they read in a way that shows the relationships among the main ideas and the supporting details. To create an outline, students must already know how to recognize main ideas and details. Two types of outlines that are important for students to understand are the *sentence* outline, in which each point is a complete sentence, and the *topic* outline, which is composed of key words and phrases. Because choosing key words and phrases is in itself a difficult task for many students, modeling sentence outlines first is beneficial.

The first step in forming a traditional outline is to extract the main ideas from the material and to list these ideas beside capital Roman numerals in the order in which they occur. Supporting details are listed beside capital letters below the main idea they support and are slightly indented to indicate their subordination. Details that are subordinate to the main details designated by capital letters are indented still further and are preceded by Arabic numerals. The next level of subordination is indicated by lowercase letters, although elementary students will rarely need to make an outline that goes beyond the level of Arabic numerals. A model outline form like the one shown in Example 11.2 may help students understand how outlines are arranged.

The teacher can supply students with partially completed outlines of chapters in their content textbooks and ask them to fill in the missing parts, gradually leaving out more and more details until the students are doing the complete outline alone. To develop students' readiness for outlining, the teacher can use the activity suggested in "Putting It into Practice: Preparation for Outlining."

This activity can be used as a first step in teaching the concept of outlining to primary-level students. The next step might be to have the students make free-form outlines, or story webs, in which they use words, lines, and arrows to arrange key

EXAMPLE 11.2 Sample Outline

```
TITLE
 I. Main idea
    A. Detail supporting I
    B. Detail supporting I
       1. Detail supporting B
       2. Detail supporting B
          a.  Detail supporting 2
          b.  Detail supporting 2
       3. Detail supporting B
    C. Detail supporting I
II. Main idea
    A. Detail supporting II
    B. Detail supporting II
    C. Detail supporting II
```

Preparation for Outlining

1. Provide your students with a set of items to be categorized.

2. Ask them to place the items in categories. More than one arrangement may be possible; let them try several.

3. Provide the students with a blank outline form or template of this type:

4. Have them fill in the outline.

Example:

a. Provide plastic animals: horse, cow, chicken, pig, elephant, lion, sea gull, rooster, tiger.

b. Give the students time to categorize.

c. Provide this outline:

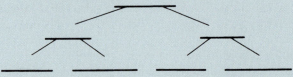

d. Possible solution:

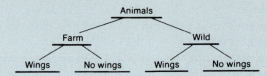

words and phrases from the story in a way that shows their relationships. Using simple, very familiar stories enables students to concentrate on arranging the terms logically rather than on locating the details. Example 11.3 shows a web based on the familiar story "The Three Little Pigs." (See Chapter 7 for more information on webbing or mapping stories.)

EXAMPLE 11.3 Story Web

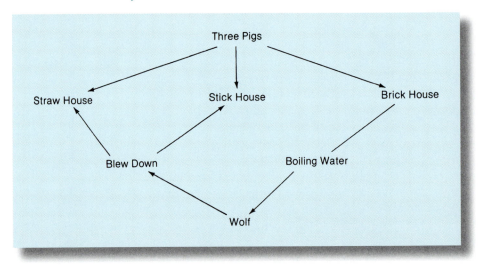

Teacher modeling of web construction should come first. Then one or more story webs may be constructed cooperatively by the whole class. The teacher may need to provide the key words and phrases in early experiences with webbing. The students can then cooperatively develop webs in small groups with help from the teacher's probing questions about connecting lines, directions of arrows, and positions of phrases. They may also ask the teacher questions about their decisions. As the students develop proficiency with the task, the teacher can encourage them to choose key words and phrases themselves, at first with assistance and then independently. Throughout the procedure, scaffolding of student learning is maintained until students can form webs without assistance.

Students can obtain outlining practice by outlining material that the teacher has entered into a computer file. They can move phrases and headings around with a word-processing program and create an outline in relatively painless fashion. Computer programs such as *Kidspiration, Inspiration*, and *PowerPoint* also provide support for the students' creation of outlines of information.

Summarizing

In a summary, a student is expected to restate what the author has said in a more concise form. Main ideas of selections should be preserved, but illustrative materials and statements that merely elaborate on the main ideas should not be included.

Students should be led to see that, when they are making summaries, they should delete trivial and redundant material. Superordinate terms can be used to replace lists of similar items or actions (for example, *people* for *men, women, and children*). Steps in an action may be replaced by a superordinate action (*baked a cake* for *took flour, butter,… and then placed it in an oven*). Each paragraph can be represented with its topic sentence or implied main-idea sentence (Brown and Day, 1983; Brown, Day, and Jones, 1983).

The teacher should model the deletion of nonessential material when constructing summaries and then should have students practice this activity under supervision. Choosing superordinate terms and actions and choosing or constructing topic sentences should also be modeled and practiced. Teachers can use a think-aloud process to demonstrate how to delete redundant, trivial, and supporting information (Allington, 2002). Easy material should be used for beginning instruction, and paragraphs should be summarized before proceeding to longer passages. The think-aloud process is discussed in more detail in Chapter 7.

One way that the teacher can build students' experience with summarizing is to give them a long passage to read and three or four summaries of the passage. The teacher should instruct the students to examine the summaries and decide which one is best and why each of the others is not satisfactory. The teacher should scaffold this exploration process by asking appropriate questions throughout the process. For example, the teacher may ask, "Does this sentence tell something different, or is it just an example?" After the students have been successful in

Time for Reflection
Some teachers believe in teaching only formal outlining. Others think that students can benefit from organizational techniques such as webs.
What do *you* think, and why?

Read•Write•Think offers the lesson plan "Guided Comprehension: Summarizing Using the QuIP Strategy," which provides an example of how an intermediate level teacher can introduce students to the QuIP framework for graphically organizing information and synthesizing the important ideas in written form. Find the lesson at http://www.readwritethink.org or link from the Student Website for this book.

differentiating between the satisfactory and unsatisfactory summaries, the teacher can refer them to a passage in one of their textbooks, along with several possible summaries, and have them choose the best summary and tell why they did not choose each of the others.

Another strategy called 3-2-1 encourages active reading, increases comprehension, and supports development of the summarization process (Zygouris-Coe, Wiggins, and Smith, 2004/2005). The strategy is divided into three components. The student first summarizes three important points discovered during reading. The second step involves the sharing of two new pieces of information learned or the sharing of two insights discovered by the student while reading. As a final step, the student composes one question that he or she still has related to the material.

Metacognition

Metacognition involves knowing what is already known, knowing when understanding of new material has been accomplished, knowing how that understanding was reached, and knowing why something is or is not known (Faber, 2006). Metacognitive strategies are important in reading for meaning and in reading for retention. Students who monitor their own comprehension and use fix-up strategies are more likely to comprehend and retain the information that they read. Recognizing important information and concepts, checking mastery of the information read, and developing effective strategies for study are metacognitive techniques involved in reading for retention (Chapman and King, 2003). Some examples of fix-up strategies include rereading, self-questioning, retelling, predicting and verifying, and reading further while withholding judgment. Schwartz (1997) states that "monitoring strategies involve checking one's attempts to coordinate the variety of cues found in texts" (p. 43). Self-correction, or "fix-it," behaviors are indications that monitoring strategies are occurring.

The RAND Reading Study Group report (Perkins-Gough, 2002) reinforces the importance of metacognitive strategies to comprehension. Students who approach their reading with a purpose, and who actively monitor their understanding as they read, comprehend the material that they are reading better than those who do not. The report suggests that explicit instruction in the use of metacognitive strategies, such as creating and understanding graphic organizers, questioning, and summarizing, can help students develop their abilities to locate, organize, and analyze information. (More information on instruction in metacognitive skills appears in Chapter 7.)

◀■▶ **SEEING IT IN PRACTICE**

Video Case
View the Video Case "Using Information Processing Strategies: A Middle School Science Lesson." Also view the bonus videos. Observe how Mr. Beucler encourages students to locate information and then apply it through a strategy that he identifies as information processing.

Students need to learn to set goals for their reading tasks, to plan how they will meet their goals, to monitor their success in meeting their goals, and to remedy the situation when they do not meet their goals. In order to accomplish learning goals, students need to know certain techniques, such as relating new information to their background knowledge, previewing material to be read, paraphrasing ideas presented, and identifying the organizational pattern or patterns of the text. Students should be taught the value of periodically questioning themselves about the ideas in the material to see if they are meeting their goals (Babbs and Moe, 1983). They need to ask if the information that they have read makes sense. If it does not make sense, they need to learn to ask why it does not make sense. They should decide whether they have a problem with decoding a word, understanding what a word means, understanding what a sentence is saying, understanding how a sentence is related to the rest of the passage, or grasping the focus or purpose of the passage. If they have not met their goals because they did not recognize certain words, students need to use context clues, structural analysis, phonics, and possibly the dictionary. If word meaning is the problem, they can again use any of these techniques (except phonics). If sentence structure or sentence relationships are the problem, they can try identifying key words, breaking down sentences into separate meaning units, locating antecedents for pronouns, and other such techniques.

Teachers often use **graphic organizers** (visual depictions of text material, such as webs) before, during, or after reading to assist students in the comprehension of expository material. Combined with other metacognitive strategies, graphic organizers can help students activate their recall of background information, identify essential information in the reading, and recognize relationships among concepts.

Teachers should teach specific strategies for students to use when they do not comprehend material. To help children develop metacognitive strategies, the teacher must convince them of the need to become active learners. Rhoder (2002) describes a model of metacognitive strategy instruction called "mindful reading," in which students understand, select, and monitor strategies. Rhoder's model includes providing instruction within the students' zone of proximal development (the area of skills that they are capable of learning with the help of an expert), explicit modeling of metacognitive strategies, and then offering opportunities for students to practice strategies and transfer them into new situations.

Moderately difficult material should be used for strategy instruction so that the students will have some actual comprehension problems to confront,

TEACHING TIP

Graphic Organizers

Merkley and Jefferies (2000/2001) suggest the following guidelines for the use of graphic organizers:

1. Conduct a prereading discussion of the relationships illustrated by the graphic organizer.

2. Encourage student input throughout the discussion.

3. Connect to previous learning by correcting errors in understanding and challenging thinking.

4. Reference the upcoming text as a source for additional information.

5. Take advantage of opportunities to reinforce decoding and structural analysis.

Read more about the value of graphic organizers in helping students understand text structures and content material in Chapter 12.

although the material should not be too difficult to be useful. Teachers must scaffold student learning by assisting in activating background knowledge before their students read so that they have the information needed to apply comprehension strategies. Students have to be told what each strategy is and why it is important.

Teacher modeling and student practice of think-alouds can help students learn metacognitive strategies (Walker, 2005). "Think alouds require a reader to stop periodically, reflect on how a text is being processed and understood, and relate orally what reading strategies are being employed" (Baumann, Jones, and Seifert-Kessell, 1993, p. 185). The teacher can model strategies for monitoring comprehension by reading a passage aloud and "thinking aloud" about his or her own monitoring behaviors and hypotheses. Noting things that are currently known and things that are still unknown and modifying these notes as more information is added can be helpful. Students should be drawn into the process in subsequent lessons by practicing the think-aloud strategy with the teacher's guidance at first and then independently. Eventually, they need to apply the monitoring strategy independently (Baumann et al., 1993; Oster, 2001). (A model think-aloud session is included in Chapter 7.)

To check students' monitoring of their own comprehension, teachers can ask students to read difficult passages and then ask questions about them. The students write their answers and indicate their degree of confidence in the answers. Incorrect answers should have low-confidence ratings, and correct answers should have high ratings in order to indicate good comprehension monitoring (Fitzgerald, 1983).

Time for Reflection

Some teachers begin work on comprehension monitoring in the primary grades. Others believe that it is best taught in the middle grades.

What do *you* think, and why?

STANDARDS/
ASSESSMENTS

Graphic Aids

Students' textbooks, especially in the content areas, contain many **graphic aids** to provide information. These aids include maps, graphs, tables, and illustrations, such as pictures, charts, and diagrams.

Mesmer and Hutchins (2002) discovered that a group of fifth-grade students had problems interpreting graphic aids. The educators realized that a complex, multistep process is involved in answering questions from the information in graphic aids. "Students must first read a related question, then read and analyze the graphic, determine the answer, locate the answer within a list of options, and record the selection on an answer sheet" (p. 22). Mesmer and Hutchins had been trying to teach students to use a question-answer relationship (QAR) framework (as described in Chapter 8) to answer questions that require them to consult graphic aids in expository materials. They found that the students tended to treat all questions related to a graphic aid as Right There types, when these questions could be any type, including those that require the use of background knowledge. They also noticed that students did not pay attention to the details on the graphics, such as units of measure and titles. The students often assumed that the graphic's information was going to answer the question directly and failed to pay close attention to the question itself. Learning the characteristics of different kinds of graphic aids was important to helping students answer questions about the aids. After receiving instruction about graphic aids, students were given direct instruction in using the QAR strategy to answer questions about these aids. This proved to be a useful strategy that improved the students' metacognitive and test-taking skills.

Because textbooks contain numerous graphic aids, teachers should explicitly teach how these aids function, model their use for their students, and provide students with supervised practice in extracting information from them. Making their own graphic aids also helps students develop their communication abilities.

Maps

Many maps appear in social studies textbooks, and they are sometimes found in science, mathematics, and literature books. As early as the first grade, students can begin developing skills in map reading, which they will use increasingly as they progress through school, because maps will appear with greater frequency in reading materials.

A first step in map reading is to examine the title (for example, "Annual Rainfall in the United States") to determine what area is being represented and what type of information is being given about the area. The teacher should emphasize the importance of determining what information is conveyed by the title before moving on to a more detailed study of the map. The next step is to teach students how to determine directions by helping them to locate directional indicators on maps and use these indicators to identify the four cardinal directions.

Interpreting the map's **legend** is the next reading task. The legend contains an explanation of each symbol used on the map, and, unless a reader can interpret these symbols, he or she will be unable to understand the information that the map contains.

Learning to apply a map's **scale** is fairly difficult. Because it would be highly impractical to draw a map to the actual size of the area represented (for instance, the United States), maps show areas greatly reduced in size. The scale shows the relationship of a given distance on the map to the same distance on the earth.

Intermediate-level students can be helped to understand about latitude and longitude, the Tropic of Cancer and the Tropic of Capricorn, the North and South

TEACHING TIP

Map-reading skills are best taught when students are asked to read maps for a purpose in one or more of their classes. Map skills should be applied to these authentic materials immediately after instruction takes place. You can

1. Teach your students to apply a map's scale by constructing a map of your classroom to a specified scale. Provide step-by-step guidance.

2. Model the use of a map's legend. Then have your students practice using the map's legend by asking them questions such as the following:

   Where is there a railroad on this map?
   Where is the state capital located?
   Where do you see a symbol for a college?
   Are there any national monuments in this area? If so, where are they?

3. Give students a map of their county or city and let them locate their homes on the map.

4. Give students maps such as the one presented in Example 11.4 and have them answer questions about them.

5. Have English-language learners label parts of maps to become familiar with map terminology.

6. Have students map the locale in a piece of literature that they are reading.

Poles, and the equator. Students should also become acquainted with map terms such as *hemisphere, peninsula, continent, isthmus, gulf, bay,* and many others.

Each time that students look at a map of an area, the teacher should encourage them to relate it to a map of a larger area—for example, to relate a map of Tennessee to a map of the United States. This points out the position of Tennessee within the entire United States.

Students need practice in thinking critically about the information that maps can provide. For example, the teacher may give students a map of the United States in the early 1800s that shows waterways, bodies of water, and population distributions and ask the students to draw conclusions about the population distributions. The effect of the bodies of water should be evident to the students.

Graphs

Graphs often appear in social studies, science, and mathematics books to clarify written explanations. Four basic types of graphs are described as follows and are illustrated in Example 11.5 on page 420.

1. **Picture graphs** express quantities through pictures.

2. **Circle or pie graphs** show relationships of individual parts to the whole.

3. **Bar graphs** use vertical or horizontal bars to compare quantities. (Vertical bar graphs are often easier to read than horizontal ones.)

4. **Line graphs** show changes in amounts.

Students can learn to discover from the graph's title what comparison is being made or what information is being given (for example, time spent in various activities during the day or populations of various counties in a state), to interpret the legend of a picture graph, and to derive needed information accurately from a graph.

An effective strategy to help students learn to read graphs is to have them construct meaningful graphs of their own using familiar information. Following are some examples of graph construction possibilities:

1. A picture graph showing the number of festival tickets sold by each class. One picture of a ticket could equal five tickets.

2. A circle graph showing the percentage of each day that an individual spends sleeping, eating, studying, and playing.

3. A bar graph showing the number of books read by class members each week for six weeks.

4. A line graph showing the weekly arithmetic or spelling test scores of one student over a six-week period.

LITERATURE

5. A picture graph, bar graph, or circle graph of students' predictions about a story (McDonald, 1999).

EXAMPLE 11.4 Sample Map and Questions: Number of American Indians by U.S. Counties, 1970

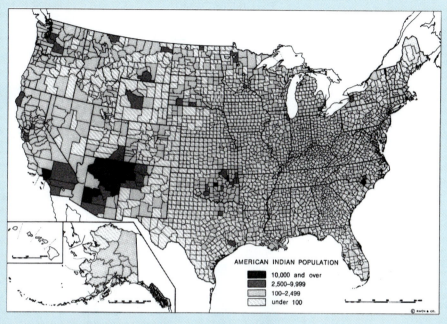

Source: Rand McNally and Company. Reprinted with permission.

Multiple-Choice Questions

1. What is this map about?
   a. American Indian tribes of the United States
   b. Number of American Indians in U.S. counties in 1970
   c. Number of American Indians in U.S. counties today

2. The example shows a main map and two inset maps. What is true about these three maps?
   a. They are all drawn to the same scale.
   b. Two of them are drawn to the same scale.
   c. They are all drawn to different scales.

3. What indicates the densest population?
   a. Solid white
   b. Gray and white stripes
   c. Solid black

4. What was the Indian population in most of Tennessee?
   a. Under 100
   b. 100–2,499
   c. 2,500–9,999

5. The Indian population in Nevada varied from what to what?
   a. 100–2,499
   b. 2,500–10,000
   c. Under 100–10,000 and over

6. In what portion of the United States was there the largest concentration of Indians?
   a. Southwest
   b. Southeast
   c. Northeast

EXAMPLE 11.5 Sample Picture, Pie, Bar, and Line Graphs

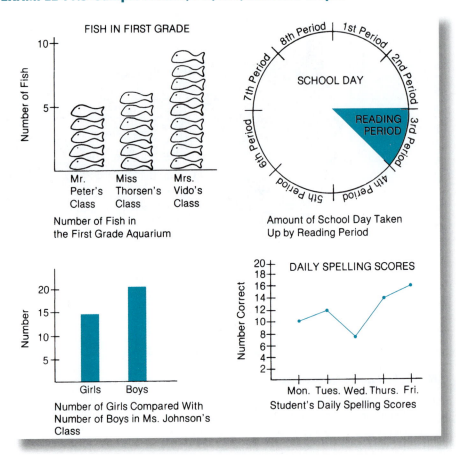

Tables

Tables, which may appear in reading materials of all subject areas, can present a problem because students have trouble extracting specific facts from a large mass of available information. The great amount of information that tables offer in a small amount of space can confuse students unless the teacher provides a procedure for reading tables.

Just as the titles of maps and graphs contain information about their content, so do the titles of tables. In addition, because tables are arranged in columns and rows, the headings can provide information. To discover specific information, students must locate the intersection of an appropriate column with an appropriate row. The teacher should explicitly model reading tables, verbalizing the mental

EXAMPLE 11.6 Sample Table and Questions

Questions

1. What is the product of 5 × 6?
2. What is the product of 9 × 3?
3. Is the product of 5 × 4 the same as the product of 4 × 5?
4. Which number is greater: the product of 3 × 8 or the product of 4 × 7?
5. When a number is multiplied by 1, what will the product always be?
6. Why does 24 appear where the 4 row and the 6 column meet?
7. How do the numbers in the 2 row compare with the numbers in the 4 row?

Multiplication Table

	1	2	3	4	5	6	7	8	9
1	1	2	3	4	5	6	7	8	9
2	2	4	6	8	10	12	14	16	18
3	3	6	9	12	15	18	21	24	27
4	4	8	12	16	20	24	28	32	36
5	5	10	15	20	25	30	35	40	45
6	6	12	18	24	30	36	42	48	54
7	7	14	21	28	35	42	49	56	63
8	8	16	24	32	40	48	56	64	72
9	9	18	27	36	45	54	63	72	81

processes involved in locating the information. Then the students should be instructed to read a table, such as the multiplication table shown in Example 11.6, and answer related questions. Some sample questions are provided.

Illustrations

Various types of illustrations, ranging from photographs to schematic diagrams, are found in textbooks. Illustrations are excellent sources of information. A picture of a jungle, for example, may add considerably to a reader's understanding of that term; a picture of an Arabian nomad may illuminate the term *Bedouin* in a history class. Diagrams of bones within the body can depict the information that cannot readily be observed firsthand. Having English-language learners and students with special needs label illustrations is particularly helpful to their comprehension of content material.

 DIVERSITY   STRUGGLING READER/ INTERVENTION

SUMMARY

Reading/study techniques enhance students' comprehension and retention of printed material. Study methods, such as SQ3R and SQRQCQ, can help students comprehend and retain material that they read. A number of other techniques can also help students with organization and retention.

Developing test-taking strategies can allow students to show more accurately what they have learned. Students need strategies for demonstrating knowledge in a variety of formats such as objective and essay tests. In addition, they need special strategies for participating in standardized testing situations.

Flexible reading habits can help students study more effectively. Students need to be able to adjust their approaches to the reading and to adjust their reading rates.

Students need to learn strategies for locating information in trade books and textbooks. They must be able to use the external features of books to successfully navigate through the material. Students must also be able to locate and extract information from a variety of sources, including the graphic aids found in textbooks. Maps, graphs, tables, and illustrations depict much important information in textbooks and nonfiction trade books.

Ultimately, teachers must provide students with explicit instruction and numerous opportunities to develop skills and strategies for organizing information, designing and using graphic organizers, and for metacognitively monitoring their own comprehension and retention of the material to be learned.

For your journal

1. Choose a textbook from a subject area and grade level of your choice. Examine closely the material on twenty consecutive pages and list the study skills needed to obtain information from these pages effectively.

2. View the Video Case "Using Information Processing Strategies: A Middle School Science Lesson." How does middle school teacher E. J. Beucler define information processing? What do you see as the strength of this lesson? How does Mr. Beucler's strategy compare with your own experiences in building content-area vocabulary?

and your portfolio

1. Using materials of widely varying types, develop and document a procedure to help elementary school students learn to be flexible in their rates of reading.

2. Choose a content-area textbook at the elementary level and plan procedures to familiarize students with the external and internal organization of the book and the reading aids that the book offers.

3. Collect materials that students can use as supplementary reference sources such as newspapers, magazines, catalogs, and brochures and develop several minilessons to help students learn to read these materials effectively.

4. Make a variety of types of graphs into a display that you could use in a unit on reading graphs. Photograph the display.

5. Collect pictures and diagrams that present information. Ask several students to study these pictures and extract as much information from them as possible. Provide a written summary of your analysis.

Reading in the Content Areas

Reading in **content-area textbooks,** such as those for social studies, science, mathematics, and other curricular areas, and in supplementary materials used in content classes is often difficult for students. These textbooks and other informational materials contain **expository** (explanatory) text that can be more difficult for students to read than **narrative** (story) text. These materials also contain many new concepts. Different text features and structures found in informational text pose different problems from those found in narrative text, and the ability to read narrative text is no guarantee that students can read informational text with the same competence (Yopp and Yopp, 2000).

To read well in content-area textbooks, students first need good general reading strategies, including word-recognition, comprehension, and reading/study strategies. (These are discussed in Chapters 3–11.) If they cannot recognize the words that they encounter, they will be unable to take in the information from the material. Without good literal, interpretive, critical, and creative reading-comprehension strategies, as described in Chapter 8, they will not understand the textbook's message. It is especially important to read content-area material critically (Palmer and Stewart, 2005). Good reading/study strategies are also needed to help students comprehend and retain the material.

Special help with content-area reading, at the time when students are expected to do such reading, is important because this is when the students most effectively learn how to apply the strategies and techniques. For example, because of the different organizational patterns of expository text—including topical arrangements and liberal use of meaningful headings, as well as the presence of aids such as tables of contents, indexes, and glossaries—students can find specific facts that they need about a topic without having to read the material from cover to cover. Learning to skim and scan can also help with this process (Palmer and Stewart, 2005). Classrooms in which the teachers integrate learning activities across the curriculum, rather than scheduling separate periods for language, science, social studies, and so on, offer opportunities throughout the day to help students read and comprehend the expository texts generally used in content areas.

LITERATURE

Rather than relying solely on textbooks, teachers may choose nonfiction trade books (library books), newspapers, brochures, and other factual materials to supplement the curriculum in some classes and as the core of the curriculum in others. Students often need to apply the same strategies to reading many of these informational materials as they do to reading content-area textbooks.

Because of the special challenges posed by reading in content-area textbooks, content-area teachers need to know a variety of techniques for helping students understand their reading assignments. A useful technique for all areas is *frontloading*, determining and developing prior knowledge needed to understand the content through prereading activities and creating motivation and purpose for reading the material (Freedman and Carver, 2007). Kristo and Bamford (2004) suggest that teachers use a comprehensive framework to teach nonfiction that is much like the one suggested earlier for general reading skills. It consists of a sequence of instruction that gradually releases responsibility for the reading from the teacher to the student. They suggest beginning with teacher modeling of strategies and moving through shared reading, guided reading, collaborative and independent work, and independent practice.

To teach new concepts, teachers often use concrete items (such as seeds and plants, levers, and rocks and minerals) or manipulatives (such as jigsaw puzzle maps and pictures to match with words) to develop concepts. They also often provide narratives on the topic of study and use material on videotapes, CDs, DVDs, and the Internet to aid comprehension.

STANDARDS/
ASSESSMENTS

Teachers may require retellings or have students summarize the material to check understanding of text material. Summarizing is an extremely helpful comprehension strategy for nonfiction material. Semantic mapping of the main topic, use of the K-W-L procedure, and use of expository paragraph frames are other good techniques. This chapter concludes with an examination of several content areas—language arts, social studies, mathematics, and science and health—along with the specific difficulties that can confront students in reading in these areas, as well as activities to promote readiness and good comprehension. In addition, it presents general content-area reading strategies to use in conjunction with the many strategies already described in Chapters 7 and 8 as comprehension aids in reading content-area material and offers information about specific ways to help English-language learners and struggling readers.

ANTICIPATION/REACTION GUIDE

AFTER
C or **I** (for initial
A or **D** answers)
A or **D**
(for initial **?** answers)

Directions: Before you read this chapter, complete the following anticipation/reaction guide. In the space before each statement, write **A** if you agree; **D** if you disagree; or **?** if you don't know. After you have read the chapter, complete the guide again to show what you have discovered in the chapter. In the space after each statement, mark whether you were initially correct (with a **C**) or incorrect (with an **I**). Write the letter for the correct answer (**A**) or (**D**) in the space for the statements that you initially marked with a question mark (**?**).

1. Content-area textbooks are carefully graded in terms of difficulty and are generally appropriate to the grade levels for which they are designed.

2. One difficulty encountered in all content areas is specialized vocabulary, especially common words that have additional, specialized meanings.

3. All students in the fifth grade can benefit from the use of a single science textbook designated for the fifth grade.

4. Students often must acquire concepts and vocabulary that are introduced early in content textbooks before they can understand later content passages.

5. Offering students instruction in basal readers is sufficient to teach reading skills needed in content-area textbooks.

6. Story problems in mathematics are generally extremely easy to read.

7. Mathematics materials require a student to learn a new symbol system.

8. Science materials need not be read critically because they are written by experts in the field.

9. An expository style of writing is very precise and highly compact.

10. The cause-and-effect pattern of organization is found in many social studies and science and health materials.

11. Study guides may set purposes for reading.

12. Expository text structure can be taught through the language experience approach.

13. Children's literature can be used to teach social studies and science concepts.

14. Expository paragraph frames can scaffold students' attempts to write about content-area topics.

15. Use of picture books should be avoided above the third grade.

CHAPTER 12 ORGANIZATION

Reading in the Content Areas

Content Texts Compared with Basal Reading Series

Difficulty of Texts and Supplementary Materials

Alternatives to Exclusive Use of Content Texts

General Techniques for Content-Area Reading

Motivating Students to Read
Learning Text Structure
Study Guides
Press Conference
Every-Pupil-Response Activities
Readers' Theater
Sustained Silent Reading for Expository Materials
Computer Approaches
Writing Techniques
Using Content Material with Reading of Fiction and
    Writing
Manipulative Materials
Integrating Strategies
Creating Instructional Units

Specific Content Areas

Language Arts
Social Studies
Mathematics
Science and Health

Helping English-Language Learners Develop Content Literacy

Helping Struggling Readers Develop Content Literacy

Content Texts Compared with Basal Reading Series

Reading strategies are often initially acquired in reading class, using basal reading programs. Because content-area books and supplementary materials present special reading problems, however, teachers should be aware that simply offering their students instruction in basal readers, even though today's readers contain more content-oriented text, is not sufficient if the students are to read well in content-area texts and other nonfiction materials.

Much material in basal reading series is written in a narrative style that describes the actions of people in particular situations. These materials do not have the density of ideas typical of content textbooks, which are generally written in an expository style, with heavy concentrations of facts. Students find narrative material easier to read than expository material. Narrative selections often have entertaining plots that students can read for enjoyment. Content selections rarely offer this enticement.

Many students are unfamiliar with the organizational structures of expository texts. Therefore, these students are left without a predictable structure to use when they are asked to read such materials. Students must give attention to each sentence in a content book, because nearly every one will carry important information that they must acquire before they can understand later passages. In basal readers, however, each selection is generally a discrete entity.

Whereas basal readers may have planned repetition of key words to encourage their acquisition, content-area texts present many new concepts and vocabulary terms with little planned repetition. Content-area textbooks are likely to define new terms at their first appearance and then to assume that students will remember their meanings.

All of the content areas have specialized and technical vocabularies that students must acquire. Generally, basal readers contain little specialized or technical vocabulary. Students need multiple high-quality encounters with the specialized and technical vocabulary in their content materials (Flynt and Brozo, 2008; Kamil, 2004; Pearson, Hiebert, and Kamil, 2007). (See Chapter 6 for a discussion of specialized and technical vocabulary.)

Content textbooks contain a large number of graphic aids that students must interpret, whereas basal readers contain fewer of these aids. The illustrations in reading textbooks above first-grade level are often included primarily for interest value, but those in content books are designed to help clarify concepts and need to be studied carefully.

Whereas content-area textbooks have abundant headings that signal the organization of the selections, few such headings are used in basal readers, and the ones that are used may be less informative than those in the content books. As they begin to read content books, students should be helped to see that sometimes the headings outline the material for them, indicating main ideas and supporting details. Content textbooks also often contain sidebars, inset pictures, or diagrams and have picture captions that add important information not included in the text.

Even young students encounter many of these elements. Publishers are responding to this situation. For example, Lakeshore has a Read & Learn nonfiction big book on reading photos, captions, and diagrams.

Teachers' manuals for basal reading series generally include extensive suggestions for teaching comprehension skills, but content-area textbooks often do not. Upon examination of the teachers' manuals of three science and three social studies textbooks for the primary grades, Kragler, Walker, and Martin (2005) found that the manuals tended to focus on assessing and monitoring student understanding, rather than on modeling and scaffolding of comprehension strategies. There was no teacher modeling in the science textbooks, although teachers were asked to "assess prior knowledge before the text is read, build background knowledge for the text, explain various terms in the text, guide the discussions, and ask questions of the students" (p. 255). The social studies texts had some attempts at modeling. One did this in the form of having teachers begin a lesson by giving directions for completing a comprehension task, but the directions included asking students to perform other comprehension tasks for which they were not given instruction. In the other two books, a useful strategy was pointed out to students in the introduction to a unit, but no scaffolding or guided practice was provided. Both series leaned heavily on the use of graphic organizers, but they did not offer instruction on why and when to use these aids. Teachers will have to develop their own strategy lessons for content texts, emphasizing modeling of the strategies.

Go to Read•Write•Think at http://www .readwritething.org or link from the Student Website for this textbook for the lesson "Exploring How Section Headings Support Understanding of Expository Texts" that you can use to emphasize the function of headings in content books.

Difficulty of Texts and Supplementary Materials

STANDARDS/ ASSESSMENTS

The teacher's first step in helping students to read content material is to be aware of the level of difficulty of the textbook and other reading assignments that he or she makes. Teachers must adjust their expectations for each student according to that student's reading ability so that no student is assigned work in material on his or her *frustration level*. Trying to read from material that is too hard for them can prevent students from learning the content. If students are forced to try to read a book or other material at this difficulty level, they may develop negative attitudes toward the subject, toward the teacher, and even toward school in general. Students will probably learn best from printed material that is written on their *independent levels*. They can also learn from textbooks written on their *instructional levels*. (See Chapter 2 for a discussion of independent, instructional, and frustration levels and of techniques for determining readability.) "Putting It into Practice: Differentiating Instruction" discusses how to use information about difficulty levels of textbooks to differentiate instruction.

A good way to decrease the difficulty of content passages for students is to teach the content vocabulary thoroughly before the material containing that vocabulary is assigned to be read. Unfamiliar content vocabulary is a major factor in the higher difficulty levels of many content-area materials. Embedding vocabulary instruction in

Differentiating Instruction

After determining each student's ability to benefit from the class textbook and chosen supplementary materials, you have the information needed to make decisions about differentiating instruction to fit the students. The content-area reading assignments will be on the independent level of some students in the class. These students will be able to read the assignments and prepare for class discussion independently, and they will often be able to set their own purpose questions to direct their reading. The same material will be at the instructional level of other students. For these students, you will need to introduce material carefully, build concepts and vocabulary gradually, and either assign purpose questions or help them set their own purposes. For still other students, the material will be at their frustration level. You will need to introduce these students to the subject and give them some materials with a lower readability level than that of the text or

supplementary material being used with their classmates, to help them better comprehend the concepts for the lesson.

All students can then participate in discussing the material, and you can record significant contributions on the board in the same way as in recording a language experience story. (A detailed discussion of the language experience approach is presented in Chapter 9.) When you ask students to read the contributions from the board at the end of the discussion period, even struggling readers may be able to read fairly difficult contributions because they have heard the sentences being dictated and have seen them being written down. Before the next class, you can duplicate the class summary for each student to use in reviewing for tests. During study periods, you can help the students who are at their frustration levels to reread the notes, emphasizing the new words and concepts.

relevant contexts, which lets students build new concepts (through both concrete and vicarious experiences) before attaching labels to the concepts, is a good practice. It can also be helpful to students for teachers to present the content-area vocabulary terms in the context of sentences or to have students determine the meanings of the terms on their own, through structural analysis, use of context clues, or use of the dictionary. As Spencer and Guillaume (2006) point out, "In science and other content areas, terms are often building blocks for further understanding and need to be remembered" (p. 207). Teachers should monitor discussions and other learning activities and address any misconceptions that come to light. Students should encounter and use the words in multiple oral and written contexts as they work toward mastery of the concepts and integration of the concepts into their schemata. Possible applications are in readers' theater activities, writing books or poems using the vocabulary, and making oral and multimedia presentations with it. This approach is effective with English-language learners, as well as other students (Spencer and Guillaume, 2006).

 DIVERSITY

Alternatives to Exclusive Use of Content Texts

Some students find textbooks difficult to read or are unmotivated to read them because of the density and difficulty of ideas presented. For such students, supplementary trade books offer one viable option for learning content-area

 STRUGGLING READER/
INTERVENTION

 LITERATURE

material. Many students experience their first serious difficulties with reading as they begin reading content-area textbooks, but the continued use of high-interest trade books along with textbooks may ease the transition. Background knowledge and motivation can be built through use of these trade books. Trade books with narrative structures can be easier for reluctant readers to understand and can prepare them to approach the same subject matter in textbooks with more confidence (Ambe, 2007).

LITERATURE

A major consideration when using nonfiction trade books is the accuracy of the information. The facts presented in such books should be accurate and be presented in a manner that clarifies the material without oversimplifying it. For example, Gail Gibbons, author and illustrator of many nonfiction children's books, gathers resource material about her topic, writes her text, and checks with experts in the field to make sure that her material is accurate. She also takes care to see that her illustrations are accurate. She thinks that her illustrations can be more effective than photographs because she can illustrate things in a way that eliminates irrelevant details and focuses on the main topic. She places captions in the illustrations for further clarity (Smolkin and Donovan, 2005). Gibbons and other authors and illustrators of children's books with scientific content use the same communication style as scientists, who integrate verbal text with "quantitative graphs, information tables, abstract diagrams, maps, drawings, photographs, and a host of unique specialized

A teacher helps students locate high-interest supplementary trade books to read along with their content area textbook.

© Bob Daemmrich/The Image Works

visual genres" (Lemke, 1998, p. 88, quoted in Smolkin and Donovan, 2005, p. 57). Smolkin and Donovan (2005) suggest that teachers encourage students to get as much information from the illustrations in the nonfiction text as they can, and they suggest developing a chart called, "In the Pictures but Not the Text" for students to use to accomplish this task.

Regardless of whether or not the students have trouble reading the textbooks, teachers can use trade books to enhance the study of textbook topics and help students learn more about the content. Trade books can be chosen to coincide with students' reading levels, easing one typical problem. These books can be visually appealing to students and therefore can arouse their interest. They can also cover a topic in greater depth than the length limits of a textbook would allow. Newer books provide access to timely information.

Some nonfiction books make use of a narrative format, which students are often more familiar with than they are with nonfiction organizational patterns, although others will have topical, comparison-contrast, problem-solution, cause-and-effect, or other expository patterns. Students need to learn that many nonfiction books do not need to be read in their entirety but can be used to locate information on specific topics within the text without accessing others.

When using trade books, teachers generally identify concepts in the textbooks that need further elaboration and locate trade books that help clarify these concepts. Depending on the **readability** levels of the books, teachers may read them aloud to students or make copies available for the students to read prior to textbook assignments. Teachers may also use trade books after reading of the text to enhance concept acquisition.

Camp (2000) suggests use of "Twin Texts" of fiction and nonfiction to present content. Such trade books are available on a wide variety of topics—for example, the fiction selection *Stellaluna* by Janell Cannon could be paired with the nonfiction *Bats* by Celia Bland, or the fiction selection *Hiroshima* by Laurence Yep could be paired with the nonfiction *Sadako and the Thousand Paper Cranes* by Eleanor Coerr. Each book presents pertinent information that helps students build a framework for understanding content lessons. The fiction selection has factual material woven into a fictional setting and narrative format, and many fiction selections are less packed with new concepts and vocabulary than are nonfiction books. Teachers must be aware, however, as Guillaume (1998) cautions, that the fiction selected should help students understand the topics and should not perpetuate faulty concepts. Publishers have responded to the need for such materials. In their *Language, Literacy & Vocabulary* materials, National Geographic offers dependable leveled science, math, and social studies concept books paired with fiction selections that are thematically linked, along with instruction in language skills in its *Windows on Literacy* materials for grades K–3. This material offers development in academic vocabulary that English-language learners need. Houghton Mifflin's *Soar to Success* intervention series offers some fiction and nonfiction paired books for young students, and the Wright Group's *Take-Twos* are paired fiction and nonfiction books on the same topic for grades 1–4.

 LITERATURE

 DIVERSITY

Use of Twin Texts before the textbook material is read will lead to better understanding of the material because students will have activated or expanded their schemata before reading the textbook and because the Twin Texts provide elaboration on the topic. Teachers may wish to use Venn diagrams (see Chapter 8 for an example) to compare and contrast the fiction and nonfiction selections on the same topic. The K-W-L technique (see Chapter 7) could also be used when students read the Twin Texts. A directed reading-thinking activity (DRTA; discussed in Chapter 9) could be employed in guiding the reading of the trade books. Writing about the central topic and webbing key vocabulary in the books are good follow-up activities (Camp, 2000).

Information from Internet sites can also supplement the textbook information. Teachers may wish to bookmark appropriate sites and provide guidance for the students in how to use them. Videotapes, CDs, and DVDs, too, can provide supplementary information. Teachers may want to suggest appropriate media titles for the school librarian or media specialist to purchase. (See Chapter 13 for more on use of the Internet.)

General Techniques for Content-Area Reading

When working with students who are reading in the content areas, teachers should do many of the things suggested in earlier chapters for directing the reading of any material, such as developing vocabulary knowledge, activating background knowledge about the topic, and providing purposes for reading. They should also teach or remind students to use an appropriate study method, such as SQ3R or another appropriate method; encourage note taking; and offer suggestions to promote retention of the material. Prior knowledge can be accessed and/or developed through such techniques as provision of firsthand experiences, discussion, brainstorming, mapping, and the K-W-L procedure. (Information about these activities appears in Chapters 6, 7, 8, and 11.) Teachers may also use a number of other techniques, such as the DRTA and the language experience approach, both discussed in Chapter 9, and the ones described in this section, to help their students read in content areas more effectively.

The teacher should make reading materials available at a variety of difficulty levels so that all students can participate in acquiring information from print sources. To expose students to nonfiction material, organizational patterns, and authors, teachers should also systematically include nonfiction selections in their daily read-aloud sessions. These read-alouds activate students' current knowledge about a topic, motivate them to read about the topic, and introduce them to content, vocabulary, and organization of informational text (Palmer and Stewart, 2005). Dreher (1998/1999) suggests keeping a log of read-aloud selections to help in balancing types of material read.

Motivating Students to Read

Teachers can stimulate interest in reading content-area materials in a number of ways in addition to use of read-alouds. Two effective strategies are using analogies to help give new ideas familiar connections and telling personal anecdotes that can help personalize reading material. For example, study of arteries and veins in a sixth-grade class could be motivated by drawing an analogy to roads leading into the downtown area; or, in a study of a particular climate, the teacher might share a personal anecdote about a camping trip in such a climate. Teachers should examine each reading assignment for possibilities for motivational introductions (Mathison, 1989; Glynn, 1996).

Stories can help students see the connections that exist among people across time and from different places because of the needs that all people have in common. Participation in storytelling sessions allows students to share experiences that create bonds among classmates that can help them reach content-area goals.

▶ Using the Newspaper to Teach Content Subjects

One type of motivational material that a teacher can use in teaching content areas is the newspaper. Newspapers are considered "grown up" reading material and may appeal particularly to reluctant readers. For science, health, and social studies, in particular, newspapers offer current information that students are learning about from television news and the Internet. The newspaper is a living textbook for social studies, through which students learn about tomorrow's history as it is happening today.

Most major U.S. newspapers offer Newspaper in the Classroom (or Newspaper in Education) programs to help teachers show students effective use of the newspaper for learning in content areas. Participating newspapers provide newspapers and curriculum materials to classes at minimal or no cost. There is material for all areas from reading to social studies to math and science. Teachers may also use special student newspapers in class.

Many newspapers have special pages or whole sections for elementary-level readers. For the youngest students, newspapers supply much material that can be used for interpreting pictures, locating sight words, finding words that fit phonics skills that are being taught, matching pictures in grocery ads with words and prices, and making up stories to go with wordless comic strips. Teachers can also subscribe to news magazines that have been adapted for different grade levels. *Weekly Reader*, for example, has such magazines aligned with several sets of National Standards. They also have two Spanish/English editions (K–1 and grades 2 and up).

STANDARDS/
ASSESSMENTS

DIVERSITY

Newspapers can be used to develop vocabulary and comprehension skills for most elementary school students. Different parts of the newspaper require different reading skills, as noted here:

1. *News and sports stories*—identifying main ideas and supporting details (*who, what, where, when, why*, and *how*), determining sequence, recognizing cause-and-effect relationships, making inferences, drawing conclusions, finding synonyms and antonyms, and detecting bias

2. *Editorials*—discriminating between fact and opinion, discovering the author's point of view, detecting author bias and propaganda techniques, making inferences, and drawing conclusions

3. *Comics*—interpreting figurative language and idiomatic expressions, recognizing sequences of events, making inferences, detecting cause-and-effect relationships, drawing conclusions, and making predictions

4. *Advertisements*—detecting propaganda, making inferences, drawing conclusions, and distinguishing between fact and opinion

5. *Entertainment section*—reading charts, such as the TV schedule, and evaluating material presented

6. *Weather*—reading maps

Each of these skills is discussed in detail in either Chapter 8 or Chapter 11.

The following activities offer practice in reading newspapers for content-area objectives:

1. Have students locate the *who, what, where, when, why,* and *how* in news stories related to content-area topics.

2. Give students copies of news stories or editorials about the same political event, environmentalist rally, or other content-related topic from two different newspapers. Then ask them to point out and discuss similarities and differences.

3. Discuss the symbolism and the message conveyed by each of several editorial cartoons. Then ask students to draw their own editorial cartoons related to issues that they are studying.

4. Have students compare an editorial and a news story on the same topic. Discuss differences in approach.

5. Have students compare human-interest features with straight news stories to discover which type of writing is more objective, which has more descriptive terms, and so on.

6. Ask students to search grocery advertisements from several stores for the best buy on a specified item.

7. Have students study the classified advertisements to decide what job they would most like to have and why. Then have them investigate the qualifications for the job or ask them to write their own classified ads, looking for work in a particular area.

Learning Text Structure

Many students do not use text structure to help them comprehend and retain information from content-area textbooks, but systematic attention to clues about the organizational structure of a text and creation of visual representations of the relationships among ideas aid both comprehension and retention (Pearson and

Fielding, 1991). Six of the more common expository text structures are cause and effect, comparison-contrast, problem-solution, sequence, description, and collection. Description and collection (a series of descriptions about a topic presented together) are more common in elementary-level texts than are the other three types. Getting students to draw pictures depicting sequential text after they read, but before they write about, the material; having them transform the information in the text into a graphic form (for example, a chart or a map); or having them rewrite material in another genre (such as a job advertisement) can help them comprehend text structure.

▶ Using Graphic Organizers

Using completed graphic organizers (such as the webs found in previous chapters) for several passages with the same text structure, teachers can show how passages with the same text structure can have different content. Then they can prepare a graphic organizer for each structure to be taught. Focusing on one structure at a time, they can present students with the graphic organizer for a passage and have them construct a passage based on this organizer (see the section "Webs Plus Writing" in this chapter). After writing their passages, students can compare them with the passage on which the graphic organizer was based.

Construction of time lines and flow charts can help students visualize sequences, and Venn diagrams can help students see common elements of concepts and visualize similarities and differences in order to make comparisons and contrasts.

Maps of the content may be used before, during, and/or after students read it. (See Chapter 7 for a discussion and some examples of semantic mapping.) Sometimes the teacher can construct the maps, and at other times students can do so. The teacher should also ask appropriate questions before, during, and after the reading. (See Chapter 8 for a discussion of questioning techniques.)

> Examples for graphic organizers for some text structures are located at http://www .eduplace.com/kids/hme/k_5/graphorg/. Go to your Student Website for this book for other sites that have examples.

▶ Using Paragraph Frames

Another way to work on students' knowledge of text structure is through the use of expository paragraph frames. *Expository paragraph frames* are similar to the story frames described in Chapter 7. They provide sentence starters that include signal words or phrases to fit the paragraph organization. The sequential pattern appears to be an easy one for young children to recognize and use. The teacher can write a sequential paragraph that uses the cue words for sequence: *first, next, then, finally*. The sentences can be copied on sentence strips, the sequential nature of the material can be discussed in the group, and the students can be asked to arrange the sentences in sequential order in a pocket chart. The students can read the arranged sentences together. Then they can arrange the sentences individually and copy them on their papers in paragraph form. Finally, they can illustrate the information. The teacher can show the students a frame with the signal words and can model filling in the frame with responses elicited from them. At this point, the meanings of signal words can be clarified.

Any expository structure can be used with appropriate frames. Sequential, enumeration, comparison, contrast, and reaction frames all can work well (Lewis, Wray, and Rospigliosi, 1994). One type of frame leads students to tie prior knowledge to new information. Here is an example:

Before I started reading about trucks, I knew _____.

In the book I read, I learned that _____.

I also learned that _____.

The thing that surprised me most was _____.

Study Guides

Study guides are prepared by the teacher to guide expository reading in content fields. They can set purposes for reading, as well as provide aids for interpreting material through suggestions about how to apply reading strategies. These guides also serve as vehicles for group discussions and cooperative learning activities. Discussion of the questions or points from the study guide after reading the material is very important to the learning process.

Teachers sometimes think of study guides as being for older students, but Palmer and Stewart (2005; 2003) report that study guides can be effectively used to help primary-grade students focus on and organize information. There are many kinds of study guides, and the nature of the material and the reason for reading it can help teachers determine which kind to use. *Anticipation guides* and *anticipation/reaction guides* are discussed in Chapter 7. Chapter 7 also has an example of each of these types. Each chapter in this textbook also has an example of an anticipation/reaction guide.

▶ Content-Process Guides

Content-process guides, as shown in Example 12.1, focus on both the content and process aspects of reading. The study guide in Example 12.1 directs students' reading in the following way. First, the overview question offers an overall purpose for the reading, helping students read the material with the appropriate mental set. Each question is designed to lead students to the important *content*, or information, in the section. Following several of the questions are statements with asterisks (*). These statements give students prompts to the reading processes needed to answer the questions. Notice that literal-, interpretive-, and critical-level questions and vocabulary questions are included.

EXAMPLE 12.1 Sample Selection and Content-Process Study Guide

KEY CONCEPT

Matter exists in different physical states.

◀ **BEFORE, you learned**

- Matter has mass
- Matter is made of atoms
- Atoms and molecules in matter are always moving

▶ **NOW, you will learn**

- About the different states of matter
- How the different states of matter behave

VOCABULARY

states of matter p. 27
solid p. 28
liquid p. 28
gas p. 28

EXPLORE Solids and Liquids

How do solids and liquids compare?

PROCEDURE

1. Observe the water, ice, and marble. Pick them up and feel them. Can you change their shape? their volume?

2. Record your observations. Compare and contrast each object with the other two.

MATERIALS

- water in a cup
- ice cube
- marble
- pie tin

WHAT DO YOU THINK?

- How are the ice and the water in the cup similar? How are they different?
- How are the ice and the marble similar? How are they different?

Particle arrangement and motion determine the state of matter.

When you put water in a freezer, the water freezes into a solid (ice). When you place an ice cube on a warm plate, the ice melts into liquid water again. If you leave the plate in the sun, the water becomes water vapor. Ice, water, and water vapor are made of exactly the same type of molecule—a molecule of two hydrogen atoms and one oxygen atom. What, then, makes them different?

Ice, water, and water vapor are different states of water. **States of matter** are the different forms in which matter can exist. The three familiar states are solid, liquid, and gas. When a substance changes from one state to another, the molecules in the substance do not change. However, the arrangement of the molecules does change, giving each state of matter its own characteristics.

Chapter 1: **Introduction to Matter 27** **B**

(Continued)

EXAMPLE 12.1 (*Continued*)

Solid, liquid, and gas are common states of matter.

MAIN IDEA AND DETAILS
Remember to organize your notes in a two-column chart as you read.

A substance can exist as a solid, a liquid, or a gas. The state of a substance depends on the space between its particles and on the way in which the particles move. The illustration on page 29 shows how particles are arranged in the three different states.

❶ A **solid** is a substance that has a fixed volume and a fixed shape. In a solid, the particles are close together and usually form a regular pattern. Particles in a solid can vibrate but are fixed in one place. Because each particle is attached to several others, individual particles cannot move from one location to another, and the solid is rigid.

❷ A **liquid** has a fixed volume but does not have a fixed shape. Liquids take on the shape of the container they are in. The particles in a liquid are attracted to one another and are close together. However, particles in a liquid are not fixed in place and can move from one place to another.

❸ A **gas** has no fixed volume or shape. A gas can take on both the shape and the volume of a container. Gas particles are not close to one another and can move easily in any direction. There is much more space between gas particles than there is between particles in a liquid or a solid. The space between gas particles can increase or decrease with changes in temperature and pressure.

CHECK YOUR READING Describe two differences between a solid and a gas.

The particles in a solid are usually closer together than the particles in a liquid. For example, the particles in solid steel are closer together than the particles in molten—or melted—steel. However, water is an important exception. The molecules that make up ice actually have more space between them than the molecules in liquid water do.

The fact that the molecules in ice are farther apart than the molecules in liquid water has important consequences for life on Earth. Because there is more space between its molecules, ice floats on liquid water. By contrast, a piece of solid steel would not float in molten steel but would sink to the bottom.

Because ice floats, it remains on the surface of rivers and lakes when they freeze. The ice layer helps insulate the water and slow down the freezing process. Animals living in rivers and lakes can survive in the liquid water layer below the ice layer.

Source: From *McDougal Littell Science: Integrated Course 1*, © 2005 by McDougal Littell, a division of Houghton Mifflin Company. Reprinted by permission of Houghton Mifflin Company. All rights reserved.

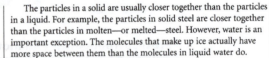

Study Guide

Overview Question: What are the three states of matter, and how are they different?
1. Read page 27 and 28 in your textbook. What is this section about?
2. What is the meaning of the word *matter* in this context?
   *If you can't remember, review page 6 in your textbook to find the definition.

(*Continued*)

EXAMPLE 12.1 (*Continued*)

3. What are the three states of matter? What is each one like?
   *Remember that you can use the boldface words to find important vocabulary.
4. After you do the experiment, record your findings. Answer the two "What do you think?" questions.
5. In what way are the three states of matter alike? How are they different?
6. What does the state of a substance depend on?
7. What causes ice to float?
   *Don't forget to look for clue words.
8. Can you see a gas? How did you know?
   *Put together the information in your head and the information in the textbook to decide on the answer.
9. How does the fact that ice floats benefit life on earth?
   *The clues are there in the book, but you have to put them together.

▶ Pattern Guides

Pattern guides are study guides that stress the relationship among the organizational patterns (text structures), which determine the reading-thinking skills needed for comprehension, and the important concepts in the material. The first step in constructing such a guide is to identify the important concepts in the material. Then information about each concept must be located within the selection, and the author's organizational pattern must be identified. The teacher then integrates the identified concepts, the writing pattern, and the skills necessary for reading the material with understanding in a guide that offers as much direction as specific students need—whether it is the section of text in which the information is located; the page number; or the page, paragraph, and line numbers. Example 12.2 is a completed comparison-contrast guide that is designed for students who need

EXAMPLE 12.2 Comparison-Contrast Guide for States of Matter

	Gas	Liquid	Solid
Volume	Not Fixed	Fixed	Fixed
Shape	Not Fixed	Not Fixed	Fixed
Distance between molecules (particles)	Greatest	Middle (Except for water and ice)	Least (Except for water and ice)
Motion of particles	Highest	Middle	Lowest

EXAMPLE 12.3 Combination Cause-and-Effect and Comparison-Contrast Pattern Guide

| | Effects | | |
Causes	On British	On Indians	On Colonists
Proclamation of 1763	Drew colonists' anger	Land west of Appalachians saved for them	Denied right to settle on land west of Appa-lachians
Seven Years' War	Needed money to pay back loans Had to pay larger numbers of soldiers	Loss of power Not enough British soldiers to keep set-tlers off their lands	Widows and orphans who needed help to buy food

only the section of text designated. The guide is based on the textbook selection in Example 12.1.

Example 12.3 shows a completed complex combination cause-and-effect and comparison-contrast pattern guide based on a section about the Seven Years' War in a social studies text. The guide originally listed the two causes for the students, and they had to fill in the multiple effects.

Press Conference

Press conference is a strategy in which some students take the parts of characters in material that has been read (literature, science, social studies, and current events) and others take the parts of reporters interviewing the characters. The interviews must have carefully planned questions, and the interviewers must take detailed notes from which they compose news stories about the interviewees and/or the events in which they have been involved. These stories are taken through a process-writing approach, and the final versions are published in a class newspaper (Dever, 1992).

Every-Pupil-Response Activities

Every-pupil-response activities, such as engaging in written responses to text, can facilitate participation in discussion about the text. Partner and/or whole-class discussions can follow the writing.

Teachers should remind the students to support their positions with evidence from the text. Students may also use these activities with real-life problems to which they could apply information from the text. Then they can talk about the strategies that would best fit the solution of particular problems, why these strategies should help, when they should be used, and how to use them. Teachers must model strategy use for their students before asking them to participate in practice activities (Gaskins, Satlow, Hyson, Ostertag, and Six, 1994).

Readers' Theater

Having students perform *readers' theater* (a rehearsed dramatic reading of a text in parts by two or more readers) based on the classes' content instruction can be a useful technique. Flynn (2004/2005) calls it Curriculum-Based Readers' Theater (CBRT). Although there are commercially available scripts for some curricular areas, Flynn proposes having students and teachers prepare scripts that allow every member of the groups producing the scripts to have speaking parts.

STANDARDS/
ASSESSMENTS

The activity of constructing readers' theater scripts can satisfy the requirement in many school systems that reading and writing activities must be included in all content areas. It partially addresses two National Standards for English/Language Arts because it involves use of different writing process elements for communication with audiences of peers for an informational purpose and the use of spoken and written language to accomplish the students' purposes. Depending upon the content area involved, it could also meet national standards for other content areas. Flynn (2004/2005) says that use of CBRT involves "students in demonstrating comprehension, paraphrasing, summarizing, synthesizing information, and communicating ideas and information orally" (p. 361).

LITERATURE

Readers' theater with nonfiction trade books can increase active involvement with the material and add to enjoyment of it. Books with dialogue are especially easy to adapt to readers' theater scripts. Some other types of text may be rewritten as dialogue, or multiple narrators may be assigned. Students learn by participating in production of the scripts, as well as by performing in them. Suggestions of books to use for readers' theater include David M. Schwartz's *How Much Is a Million?* for math; Joanna Cole's *The Magic School Bus* series for science; and Russell Freedman's *Buffalo Hunt* and Jean Fritz's *And Then What Happened, Paul Revere?* for social studies.

Sustained Silent Reading for Expository Materials

Sustained silent reading (SSR) is a form of personalized reading that can be highly motivational. General sustained silent reading periods were discussed in Chapter 9. Teachers of content-area subjects may want to have a guided SSR period for the particular content area. Having many nonfiction titles easily accessible to students in the classroom, school library, or media center is necessary for this approach to work well. It can help students become familiar with many expository text structures, without the pressure that accompanies assigned reading. When they have opportunities to interact with informational text, young children increase their facility with it (Yopp and Yopp, 2000). In a school in which different teachers teach different subjects or subject blocks, a teacher of a specific subject area can make available a wide choice of books on different reading difficulty levels on the important topics that must be covered. Then ten to twenty minutes may be set aside each week for structured SSR time. Students would have free choice of material to read from your selected collection, rather than unrestricted free choice.

LITERATURE

Computer Approaches

Teachers can incorporate computer technology with other strategies for helping students with their content reading. Some computer programs allow students to write working outlines for papers; others allow them to write drafts, revise them, and edit them; and still others have templates to facilitate the production of content-area newsletters or magazines.

Computer software can also be used with thematic units. Programs are available for all areas of the curriculum. There are also many appropriate Internet sites for the different areas. Internet projects that pertain to various content areas are discussed in Chapter 13.

Writing Techniques

A number of writing techniques may be used to advantage in helping students learn to read effectively in the content areas. Probably the best known is the language experience approach, which is covered in Chapter 9. Others include semantic feature analysis plus writing, webs plus writing, and keeping learning logs.

▶ Semantic Feature Analysis Plus Writing

The teacher can present the students with a semantic feature analysis matrix like the one in Example 12.4 for material that they are about to read and display the matrix to the class. The students fill in the matrix in the same way that the semantic feature analysis chart in Chapter 6 was completed, leaving blanks when they are unsure about a feature. Then the students read the assigned material to confirm or revise their original markings and to fill in any empty spaces. After the reading, the students and the teacher discuss the matrix and come to an agreement about its completion. If there is disagreement, students return to the text to find support for their positions. Some points may require library or Internet research.

EXAMPLE 12.4 Semantic Feature Matrix for Geometric Shapes

	Straight Lines	Curved Lines	Four Sides	Three Sides	All Sides Must Be Equal in Length
Triangle					
Rectangle					
Circle					
Square					

The information on the feature matrix can then be used as a basis for writing about the reading material. For instance, in Example 12.4, the teacher can choose one geometric shape and can model the writing of a paragraph about it. The students and the teacher can then cooperatively write another paragraph about another shape. Then each student or small group of students may choose other shapes to write about. (Note that the matrix can be expanded to include many more shapes and features.) Using the information from a feature matrix for paragraph writing promotes retention of information covered in the matrix.

▶ Webs Plus Writing

Webs are useful organizers in the content areas. Before the students read the content material, the teacher records the information that the students think they know about the topic of the chapter in the form of a web like the one shown in Example 12.5.

The students may make individual webs, containing only the points that they think are correct. Then they read the material, checking the information on the web and adding the new information they find. In class discussion that follows the reading, the class web is revised, and disagreements are settled by consulting the text. The class can write paragraphs about different strands of the web—for example, about famous leaders from Tennessee.

EXAMPLE 12.5 Web for Content Material

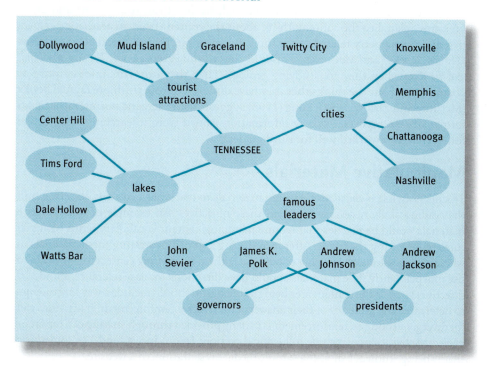

▶ Keeping Learning Logs

Using *learning logs*, or journals, to promote content-area learning is a very effective technique. Students can follow the reading or discussion of a content topic by writing summaries, comments, or questions related to the reading or class discussion. The content teacher can read the comments and adjust future lessons in response to the degree of understanding or confusion reflected in the logs. In social studies and science classes, students can be encouraged to observe things around them, record their observations (in pictures or writing), and associate what they observe with their past experiences and prior knowledge.

Using Content Material with Reading of Fiction and Writing

LITERATURE

Ollmann (1991) suggests using factual content material as part of the prereading phase to prepare students for reading literature that involves content concepts. Encyclopedia articles, travel magazines and brochures, *National Geographic*, or other material can often provide background information related to settings or to scientific concepts involved in stories. When the prereading material is being examined, the teacher can emphasize strategies needed for reading content material, such as skimming, scanning, and use of alphabetical order and guide words in a realistic setting.

Besides reading factual content material, students can read poems and other literature related to the content, think about the content from an aesthetic perspective, and write poetry related to the topic. For example, they can read poems such as Heide's "Rocks" and McCord's "This Is My Rock" and Peters's book *The Sun, the Wind, and the Rain* when they are studying geology. Then they can write in descriptive or poetic form about the things that they have discovered from the more factual books (McClure and Zitlow, 1991). Long (1993) suggests using acrostic poems, rather than formal written reports, to share information gained from researching a topic. She found that they worked well for third graders.

Manipulative Materials

Teachers can use *manipulative* learning materials to teach both content objectives and the reading skills necessary to attain these objectives. An example of manipulative materials would be puzzles that require matching content vocabulary terms with pictures representing the terms. After introducing and demonstrating these materials in whole-class sessions, the teacher should place them in learning centers for students to use independently. The materials should have directions for easy reference, should be directly related to the content area being studied, and should include a way for students to determine the accuracy of their answers or to receive reinforcement. If activities call for divergent thought, reinforcement is usually provided through sharing of a report or project. Activities may include following directions to produce a model of something that is being studied, a diorama, a multimedia presentation, or a website.

Manipulatives are especially helpful with young children and struggling readers. They can help these students to visualize information. When inaccessible objects (such as wild animals) or processes that are not readily observable (such as the water cycle) need to be conceptualized, approximations of real objects (such as stuffed animals, pictures, or sculptures) or demonstrations of processes by the teacher can be helpful (Gregg and Sekeres, 2006). Comparisons of the sizes of animals to animals or objects that the students are familiar with can add to the schemata that the students are developing.

STRUGGLING READER/ INTERVENTION

Integrating Strategies

Because no single technique will enable all students to deal with the many demands of content material, a teacher must know many strategies, teach them directly, and let students know why they help. Students need to be able to pick out an appropriate strategy for a particular assignment.

Creating Instructional Units

Two types of instructional units that are often used in conjunction with content instruction are (1) those in which the theme is a concept or a topic and the activities are related to a single discipline and (2) literature-based units across the curriculum that are interdisciplinary units in which literature selections are the central focus. They include activities that span the curriculum, all based on one or more literature selections. Literature should be an integral part of both types because it puts the content into context and perspective, but many thematic content units have more activities that are not literature related. Reading aloud, independent silent reading, and reading followed by class discussion enhance any unit.

LITERATURE

▶ Thematic Content Units

The use of thematic units was discussed as one approach to literature-based reading instruction in Chapter 9. The same concept can apply to teaching content units. *Thematic content units* involve linking the reading of fiction and nonfiction about a

 LITERATURE

TEACHING TIP

Integrating Strategies

You can use a procedure similar to the directed reading activity to provide a structure for integrating strategies to use in your content instruction.

- *Before Reading.* Present activities to motivate your students to read the material and build their background for reading it, including teaching vocabulary through context clues or by relating the words to words that they already know. You may want to read a nonfiction book on the same topic as the textbook material to build background for students who have limited backgrounds related to the topic. Your students may discuss what they already know about the topic, web this information, and survey the material to be read. After the survey, you can ask them to predict what information will be in the selection. You can provide a study guide to guide the reading, focusing attention on important concepts and/or appropriate reading processes. You may ask your students to read to answer *who*, *what*, *when*, *where*, *how*, and *why* questions; to verify hypotheses; or to discover important material to add to information they have already collected about a topic.

- *During Reading.* Ask your students to refer to and fill in the study guide that you have provided or ask them to take notes on the selection.

- *After Reading.* Conduct activities that lead your students to organize and synthesize information. For example, have them write content-based language experience stories on the material or make graphic representations of the content (graphs, charts, and diagrams). For some material, such as math problems or science projects, your students may be able to *apply* the concepts presented.

Thematic Content Unit on Survival

The students in Ms. Parker's sixth-grade class had been reading books related to the theme of *survival*. Several of them were seated around a table, beginning to discuss how their books were related to the theme.

"In *Julie of the Wolves*, Miyax has to survive by herself on the Alaskan tundra," Tonya began.

"In *Hatchet*, Brian has to survive by himself after his plane crashes in the Canadian wilderness," David said.

"Karana was left alone on an island off the coast of California," Zack said, referring to the main character in *Island of the Blue Dolphins*.

"Well, Phillip wasn't all alone on the Caribbean island in *The Cay* at first, but he did need help because he was blind after the blow to his head," David said. "Timothy, the black man, was really the one who made sure Phillip would survive. He used a lot of survival techniques."

"Let's list the survival techniques the characters used," Bruce said. "We could web them like Ms. Parker had us do with settings last month. We could use headings like 'Food' and 'Clothing.'"

"That's a good idea!" Tonya chimed in. "How about 'Shelter' for another heading?"

"Karana ate abalones and scallops from the sea," Zack said, "and she made herself a fenced-in house and a shelter in a cave."

"That's a good start," said Tonya. "Let's get that down on paper before we go on." She went to the storage shelf and returned with a piece of drawing paper and a black marker. She handed the materials to Bruce, the group member with the best handwriting skills. "Put your ideas and Zack's down before we forget them," she said. "Then we'll add more things from other people."

As Bruce began to write on the drawing paper, several other students began to take notes on their own papers about contributions that they wanted to make.

Analysis of Scenario

The students in Ms. Parker's class had worked in discussion groups many times and were ready to participate when they came to the table. Tonya acted the part of a good leader by getting the discussion started and by collecting materials for the webbing and delegating the task of actually constructing the web to another student. Ms. Parker had taught a valuable skill, webbing, in earlier lessons, and these students remembered it and put it to use.

---

content topic in order to help students get a more comprehensive picture of the topic, as well as completing other nonreading tasks. Facts are often embedded in works of fiction, and narrative structures can be used to convey facts presented in nonfiction. Therefore, both types of books are useful, and students need to be able to read both types. Text sets of books on the content topic are useful in unit instruction. After students read the related texts, they can share and extend their understanding of each text in a different way than would have been possible if they had read only one text. Nonfiction trade books need to be available on a number of difficulty levels, and teachers need to show students how to locate them and use them to find information. Students may also be expected to incorporate information found on the Internet in their discussions and presentations for the unit. "Seeing It in Practice: Thematic Content Unit on Survival" shows students working in a small group within a science class.

LITERATURE

Teachers should not overlook the possible value of picture books in content units for the upper grades. These books are often relegated to the primary grades, but many are appropriate for older students, and they add motivation and variety to lessons. Eve Bunting has written a number of books that would be appropriate for these students, although they can be used with younger students, too. They include *Terrible Things* and *The Wall*. Thematically focused alphabet books by Jerry Pallotta and others are also good. For example, many of Pallotta's books have science and social studies themes. Children's magazines, such as *National Geographic Kids, Cobblestone, Appleseeds, Odyssey,* and *Ranger Rick*, are also useful. Nonfiction offers information in many forms, including text, pictures, and maps.

Some thematic units are related to a single discipline, and some are interdisciplinary, linking content and skills from different disciplines through authentic tasks. (Students may collaborate with the teacher in theme selection, or the content may be chosen by the teacher or mandated by the school district.) Good themes can focus on such wide-ranging areas as horrors of the Holocaust or life long ago contrasted with life today. Teachers can begin by making a web for the content topic with fiction and nonfiction selections, textbooks, magazines, newspapers, videos, software, and Internet sites for use with each subtopic.

STANDARDS/
ASSESSMENTS

After resources have been located and organized, the teacher can plan the classroom activities to be used in the unit, with a web of resources as a helpful reference. Such a web is not a complete plan. Teachers still must decide on goals and objectives for their units because not all concepts presented in all the sources can possibly be used. The standards for the specific content area (or areas) and grade level provide a guide for choosing goals and objectives. After goals and objectives are chosen, the teacher must choose instructional procedures and related activities to meet these goals, gather related materials, schedule unit activities, and decide how to assess the outcomes. Shanahan (1997) points out that the teacher needs to have a clear idea of the desired learning outcomes because thematic unit instruction does not automatically result in learning. He also cautions that instruction in the separate fields, accompanied by drill and practice, is still needed when integration is implemented, because "a common problem in integrated instruction can be that the focus is so much on relevance that students never practice anything enough to get good at it" (p. 18).

To set reading purposes, students can brainstorm questions about a topic. Sometimes the questions to be answered are specified by the teacher. In either situation, students learn to read selectively to answer the questions. They can sort questions into categories, discovering that by doing so they can find answers to more than one question at a time by locating the proper sections of books and becoming aware of the organization of nonfiction. When they share information with the class, they may refer to the text to prove points (Hess, 1991).

A modification of the K-W-L procedure—KWLQ— can help students form questions for inquiry during thematic units (Schmidt, 1999). The first three steps are the same as K-W-L (which is described in

TEACHING TIP

Thematic Units

Because thematic units can connect information from language arts, science, social studies, math art, music, and drama, be sure to give sufficient attention to each discipline involved in the unit. Be aware that some disciplines may not fit into a particular thematic study. You may have to teach a discipline such as math separately from the thematic unit to give it appropriate attention. During thematic studies, give attention to the ways that text is used in the different disciplines. Scientists, mathematicians, historians, and practitioners in other fields think and write differently, so students need to be aware of these different forms (Shanahan, 1997).

Chapter 7). The Q step asks for more questions, to show that learning is continuous. Students are not likely to be successful with inquiry procedures if they are not explicitly taught the steps in such procedures and if they have not seen how the procedures work. They may first need much exposure to nonfiction writing and to the differences in the ways in which fiction and nonfiction are organized and used (Tower, 2000).

Example 12.6 is a summary of a series of lessons for a unit on the Holocaust developed by Debbie Newman, a sixth grade teacher. It involves reading, writing, and art related to the Holocaust.

EXAMPLE 12.6 Summary of Lessons for Holocaust Unit

Topic: Definition Poetry

Curriculum Framing Questions

- **Essential Question:** How do you define the Holocaust?
- **Lesson Plan Question:** How can writing help you to express your individual feelings about the Holocaust?
- **Sample Content Questions**
  1. How do we express our feelings or emotions through writing a definition poem?
  2. What is the purpose of expressing our feelings using poetry?

Standards

- DODEA Curriculum Content Standards for Sixth Grade: English/Language Arts: E1a, E1b1, E1b5, E2a, E2a.1–7, E2b.1–6, E3a, E3b.1–4, E3b.8, E3c.1–6, E4a, E4a.1–6
- ISTE National Educational Technology Standards for Students (NETS:S)—Grades 6–8
  4. Use content-specific tools, software, and simulations to support learning and research.
  5. Design, develop, publish, and present products using technology resources that demonstrate and communicate curriculum concepts to audiences inside and outside the classroom.

Summary

Students will be introduced to a writing assignment entitled "Definition Poetry." For this writing activity, students will complete each stage in the writing process: prewriting, drafting, revising, proofreading, editing, and publishing. The writing assignment will include a four-stanza (paragraph) poem to express feelings that define what the Holocaust means to each student as an individual. First, each student will use his or her individual class novel, reference books, picture books, and Internet sites pertaining to the Holocaust to

(Continued)

assist in creating a first draft of a definition poem. Next, students will prepare their first drafts on the computer. Individual student/peer/teacher conferencing will be conducted during the revision stage of writing. Peer conferences will be used for editing/proofreading. Each student will either draw a sketch for his or her novel or draw or download a picture pertaining to the Holocaust from the Internet. Publishing will occur as the students use software to create and print their individual poems and illustrations as posters entitled *The Holocaust Was*…. Students will save their work electronically in individual writing folders. Each student will share his or her poster by reading it during an evening performance with parents. Posters will be displayed outside the classroom.

Materials/Resources

Handouts [Not included here for space considerations]
1. The Holocaust Was (directions for writing the poem)
2. Rubric for poem, poster, and illustration
3. Reflection on the benefits of this writing assignment and project

Technology
- Software: Microsoft Word
- Hardware: desktop computers with Internet access, school server, scanner, printer

Prerequisite Skills
Students should have familiarity with
- Necessary keyboarding and computer skills
- Multimedia software: Microsoft Word

Learning Activity Modifications for Differentiated Instruction
- **Modifications for Struggling Learners**
  Make modifications as dictated in the student's individual education plan (IEP).
  Supply visual guides. Break activities into manageable sections, and record tasks on a calendar.
- **Modifications for Gifted Learners**
  Encourage students to create their own supplemental assignments or extensions.
  Provide technologies that offer opportunities to use advanced skills and/or programs.
- **Modifications for English-Language Learners (ELLs)**
  Enlist support from native English speakers.
  Provide extra time to complete assignments.

(*Continued*)

EXAMPLE 12.6 Summary of Lessons for Holocaust Unit (*Continued*)

Enlist the help of parents, instructional aides, or ELL teacher to create graphic organizer to guide work.

Assessments

Assessments will include written and informal observations, rubrics, and checklists to evaluate
- Writing assignment: definition poem
- Poster

Reflection

Each student will write a brief paragraph explaining the benefit(s) of this writing assignment.

Source: Debbie Newman, Ed.S., Sixth-Grade Language Arts and Reading, Mahaffey Middle School, Ft. Campbell, Kentucky.

▶ Literature-Based Units Across the Curriculum

LITERATURE

A single piece of literature can be the basis of a unit that will include activities from many curricular areas. Related science, social studies, math, art, and drama content may be taught with the piece of literature as the focal point. Language learning can take place along with reading, discussion, and writing done in relation to the literature selection. Example 12.7 shows one such unit.

Specific Content Areas

STANDARDS/
ASSESSMENTS ☑

To find lists of both national and state standards for language arts and the other content areas that you may be expected to teach, go to the Education World homepage, http://www .education-world.com or link from the Student Website for this book. Look under the heading "More Resources" and click on "State/Nat'l Standards."

Special reading challenges are associated with each of the content areas. It is best to teach skills for handling these challenges at a time when students need the skills in order to read their assignments.

Teachers are expected to make sure that their students meet state and national standards in many content areas, so they may often feel that they should spend all of their time on content rather than instruction in language skills. Upon examination of standards, however, they may find many standards from other content areas depend heavily upon language skills. For example, the National Science Standard NS.K–4.1 Science as Inquiry says that students must develop "abilities necessary to do scientific inquiry." This standard obviously could not be met without language skills.

Language Arts

The **language arts** block of the elementary school curriculum involves instruction in listening, speaking, reading, writing, viewing, and visually presenting. It includes the subjects of reading, literature, and English. Because basal readers that

EXAMPLE 12.7 Literature-Based Unit Across the Curriculum

African-American Folklore
Listen to stories about African-Americans. What is special about these stories? (Virginia Hamilton's *The People Could Fly* is a good source.)

Creative Expression
As a class make a story about what your class did this year. Each of you choose one part of the story. Draw a picture on a square of fabric. Put all the squares together to make a story quilt.

Vocabulary
Learn some new words: *skyscraper, tar beach, union, factory, steel girders, cables,* and *floodlight* from this book. Use the words in a story about city life.

Art
Look at the pictures in this book. What kinds of colors and designs are these? Compare these illustrations with those in other picture storybooks.

Science
Find out about the George Washington Bridge. What are some other types of bridges? What do they look like? How are they built?

Tar Beach,
Faith Ringgold
Crown, 1991

Nutrition/Math
Learn about the food pyramid. Have a picnic with your class. Plan a healthful menu, figure the cost, prepare the food, and send invitations.

Social Studies
Learn about living in a big city. Where do children play? Where do people work? Look at some books about cities to find the answers.

Creative Writing
If you could fly over something to make it your own. what would it be? Draw a picture and write a story about it.

History
What does it mean to be free? Who is not free? Discuss freedom in class and listen to stories about how people became free.

Web based on *Tar Beach* by Faith Ringgold (New York: Crown, 1991).

may be used during reading class were discussed in other chapters of this textbook, they will not be considered here. Although literature is treated briefly in this chapter, more thorough coverage is found in Chapter 10.

▶ Literature

 LITERATURE

Ideally, a literature program should encourage students to learn about their literary heritages and the heritages of others, to expand their imaginations, to develop reading preferences, to evaluate literature, to increase their awareness of language, and to grow socially, emotionally, and intellectually. These goals can be reached through a well-planned program in which the teacher reads aloud to students daily and provides them with opportunities to read and respond to literature. Teachers may teach literary skills directly through a unit on poetry or a novel, or they may integrate these skills with basal reader and language arts lessons.

Teaching Literature Skills.   When developing literature programs, teachers can organize instruction by genres (forms or categories), literary elements, or topics in order to vary students' experiences, and they should introduce students to the specialized vocabulary and skills that they need to develop an appreciation of literature.

In literature classes, students are asked to read and understand many literary forms, including short stories, novels, plays, poetry, biographies, and autobiographies. (See Chapter 10 for more information about genres.) One characteristic of all these forms is the frequent occurrence of **figurative language,** or nonliteral language. Figurative language is sometimes a barrier to understanding because children tend to interpret such language literally. Chapter 6 covers teaching students to deal with figurative expressions.

Literary Elements.   To understand literary passages, students need to be able to recognize and analyze plots, themes, characterization, settings, and authors' styles. The *plot* is the overall plan for the story; the *theme* is the main idea the writer wishes to convey; and *characterization* is the way in which the writer makes the reader aware of the characteristics and motives of each person in the story. The *setting* consists of time and place, and the *style* is the writer's mode of expressing thoughts. Teacher-directed questioning can make students aware of these literary elements and help students understand the interrelationships among them. Following are some points related to major story elements:

1. *Setting.* Teachers should point out how time and place affect the plot, characterization, and mood of a story. Stories must be true to their settings; characters behave differently today from the way they behaved a hundred years ago, and city life involves situations different from those that occur in country life. All of these facts make understanding the setting of a story important. *Bud, Not Buddy* by Christopher Paul Curtis and *Madeline* by Ludwig Bemelmans are good books to use in helping students see the importance of setting.

2. *Characterization.* Students who examine literature with strong characterization find that writers develop their characters through dialogue, actions, interactions with others, and insights into their thoughts and feelings, as well as through description. Students can also take note of how characters grow and change as the story progresses. The characterizations in Cynthia Voigt's *Dicey's Song* make good discussion material. Younger students can

read *Miss Nelson Is Missing* by Harry Allard and James Marshall and compare and contrast the two identities of Miss Nelson.

3. *Plot.* Students may analyze short, simple stories to see how writers introduce their stories, develop them through a series of incidents, create interest and suspense, and reach satisfying conclusions. Awareness of the ways in which plots are developed can increase understanding of narratives. Picture books with predictable plots are good places to start. Mem Fox's *Hattie and the Fox* is a good choice for picture-book plot analysis (Galda, Carr, and Cox, 1989).

4. *Style.* Students should examine written material to analyze the authors' choices of words, sentence patterns, and manners of expression. Teachers and students can discuss and compare the styles of writing in Maurice Sendak's *Chicken Soup with Rice*, Cynthia Rylant's *When I Was Young in the Mountains*, and Patricia MacLachlan's *Sarah, Plain and Tall*.

5. *Theme.* The concept of "theme" is abstract. To help students see how the same theme can be developed in different ways, teachers can select two stories that have the same theme but differ in setting, plot, and other elements. Cynthia Voigt's *Dicey's Song* and Jerry Spinelli's *Maniac Magee* both have themes of wanting to belong and wanting a home, but the setting and plot are extremely different.

One way that teachers may work on these elements is having students do journal writing. (See Chapters 9 and 10 for more on journal writing.) Students may be asked to respond to a story by selecting a character from the story and writing a journal entry as though that character were writing it. The entries can be dated according to the time in which the book takes place. This activity encourages attention to characterization, point of view, and mood.

Webbing literary elements related to a story can help students clarify their concepts of these elements. The teacher can read the story and have the students listen for the elements that need to be added to the web. (See Chapter 7 for two examples of webs made by students.)

Literary Forms. Children's literature consists of a variety of genres, or literary forms, including historical and realistic fiction, biographies, poetry, plays, informational books, and fantasy and folklore. Historical fiction, biographies, and informational books are all useful for integrating with content areas, whereas good realistic fiction serves as a model for helping students to understand others and solve problems in their own lives. Nonfiction selections give students a way to investigate and understand the world, offering a wide range of subjects and ideas to explore (Harvey, 2002). Poetry encourages readers to explore their emotions, and plays offer the pleasure of acting out favorite stories. Both modern fantasy and folklore allow readers to escape into worlds of imaginary characters and events. Teachers should use all of these forms in their literature programs, and they can enhance students' understanding of them by reading literature of all forms aloud and pointing out the characteristics of each genre. (More information on literary genres appears in Chapter 10.)

▶ English

English textbooks cover the areas of listening, speaking, writing, and vocabulary. They generally consist of a series of sections of instructional material followed by practice exercises. The technical vocabulary includes such terms as *noun*, *pronoun*, *homonyms*, *antonyms*, *alliteration*, *intonation*, *revision*, and *parliamentary procedure*. The concepts presented in the informational sections are densely packed; each sentence is usually important for understanding, and examples are abundant. Students need to be encouraged to study the examples, because they help to clarify the information presented in the narrative portion of the textbook. A series of CATegorical™ books by Brian P. Cleary offer entertaining content to help students learn about nouns, adverbs, adjectives, pronouns, verbs and prepositions.

TEACHING TIP

Oral Language Instruction

Plan oral in-class activities to accompany the listening and speaking portions of the English textbook because such practice allows your students to apply the concepts immediately and helps them retain the material. Similarly, to enhance retention, ask your students to apply the concepts encountered in the writing section as soon as possible in relevant situations.

Writing instruction can form the basis for reading activities. Students read to obtain information to include in their compositions, and they read to learn different styles of writing. For example, they read poems to absorb the style of writing before attempting to write poetry, and they read informational books for ideas about the structure that they will need to use to write their own books. Students can also read their own material in order to revise it to enhance accuracy, improve clarity, or ensure correct use of language conventions. They may read it aloud to peers for constructive criticism, or their peers may read it themselves.

LITERATURE

Much of a student's formal vocabulary instruction takes place in English classes. Trade books can often be the basis for vocabulary lessons. Fred Gwynne's *The King Who Rained* and *A Chocolate Moose for Dinner* offer good examples of figurative expressions, homonyms, and words with multiple meanings that can be used to interest students in word study. In the Amelia Bedelia books by Peggy Parish, Amelia takes everything literally, with disastrous results; for example, she makes a sponge cake with real sponges. Brian Cleary's *Pitch and Throw, Grasp and Know: What Is a Synonym?* and Arlene Alda's *Did You Say Pears?* can be used for work on synonyms and homonyms, respectively (Livingston and Kurkjian, 2007).

Newspapers can also be useful sources for vocabulary activities. One obvious activity is to have students try to solve crossword puzzles. They may use their dictionary skills as they work on the puzzles. Struggling readers may work on puzzles in pairs.

STRUGGLING READER/
INTERVENTION

Many comics depend on word play for their humor. Teachers can give students some of these comics and ask them to explain why these comics are funny.

Even the entertainment and sports sections can support vocabulary applications. Teachers can have students study the entertainment section and decide which movies or plays would be most interesting to them, pointing out the descriptive words that attracted them.

Social Studies

Social studies textbooks are generally written in a very precise and highly compact expository style in which many ideas are expressed in a few lines of print. Authors may discuss a hundred-year span in a single page or even a single paragraph; they may cover complex issues in a few paragraphs, even though whole books could be devoted to these issues. Study guides are recommended for helping students read social studies materials with understanding and purpose. These materials can also be supplemented by information in newspapers, magazines, and pamphlets and on the Internet.

Social studies materials are organized in a variety of ways, including cause-and-effect relationships, chronological order, comparisons and/or contrasts, and topical order (for example, by regions, such as Asia and North America, or by concepts, such as transportation and communication). Knowing the organizational pattern of the selection enables students to approach the reading with an appropriate mental set, which aids greatly in comprehension of the material. Chapter 8 presents information for helping students deal with cause-and-effect and chronological order arrangements. Drawing time lines is one good way to work with chronological order, and pattern guides, such as the one in Example 12.3 on page 440, are ways to work on comparison-contrast or cause-and-effect relationships.

Social studies materials also present students with maps, charts, and graphs to read. Ways of teaching the use of such reading aids are suggested in Chapter 11. Social studies materials must be read critically. Students should be taught to check copyright dates to determine timeliness and to be alert for such problems as outdated geography materials that show incorrect boundaries or place names.

In social studies reading, students encounter such technical terms as *democracy*, *tropics*, *hemisphere*, *decade*, and *century*, as well as many words with meanings that differ from their meanings in general conversation. When students first hear that a candidate is going to *run* for office, they may picture a foot race—an illusion that is furthered if they read that a candidate has decided to enter the *race* for governor. If the term *race* is applied to people in their texts, the students may become even more confused. Students who know that you *strike* a match or make a *strike* when bowling may not understand a labor union *strike*. Discussions about the *mouth* of a river could bring unusual pictures to the minds of students. The cartoon on page 456 presents another example. The teacher is responsible for seeing that the students understand the concepts that these terms represent.

Harmon and Hedrick (2000) have developed a technique to enhance vocabulary and conceptual learning in social studies. The procedure that they recommend begins with students brainstorming about the concept, while the teacher lists their

One possibility for finding helpful information on geography is the How Stuff Works website (http://www.howstuffworks.com or link from the Student Website for this book). Click on the "Travel" link. Under "Travel" look for the heading "Destinations" and click on a link of interest. Study of Egypt, for example, could be enhanced by clicking on the link for "The Pyramids of Giza and the Great Sphinx."

Read·Write·Think offers the lesson plan "Using Timeline Games and Mexican History to Improve Comprehension" for teaching students about reading and constructing time lines while studying Mexican history. This lesson could be adapted for use with any historical period or culture. Go to http://www.readwritethink.org or link from the Student Website for this book.

© Jim Adams, Milwaukie, *OR*

ideas. Then the students read to find out more about the concept and confirm the brainstormed ideas, making notes as they read. The students discuss the topic, identifying the most and least important facts about the concept, after the teacher models this process. The discussion also involves concepts or people and places that are similar to, related to, or unrelated to the target concept. At the end of the discussion, the students summarize information about the concept in a single statement. The material collected can be arranged into a web that provides a visual display of the information.

Understanding social studies concepts becomes easier for students when they can relate events and facts to their own lives and events around them. Writing about issues can also enhance understanding. In Example 12.8, a sixth-grade teacher, Debbie Newman, tells in her own words how she incorporated this technique into her classroom and the rewarding result.

▶ Using Literature in Social Studies

Social studies materials are frequently written in a very impersonal style and may be concerned with unfamiliar people or events that are remote in time or place. Students may also lack interest in the subject. For these reasons, teachers should use many interesting trade books to personalize the content and to expand on topics that are covered very briefly in the textbook.

Trade books offer opportunities to meet curricular objectives for both reading and social studies simultaneously. For example, maps in trade books can be used to teach map-reading skills, to locate the places being studied, and to identify the features of the land in these places. When students are using such books, brainstorming about prior knowledge and forming semantic maps can be helpful. Students can list their individual questions about the material, their ideas about how these questions could be answered, and the answers provided by the text. Students may eventually produce their own question-and-answer books about the topic (Guzzetti, Kowalinski, and McGowan, 1992).

EXAMPLE 12.8 Relating Study to Students' Experiences and Current Events

As teachers, we rarely learn of the impact we have on the lives of our students and their parents. Recently, I received the rare gift of discovering how we touch lives as teachers.

At the beginning of the Iraq war, my students and I wanted to show our support for their parents as they were called to war. We decided writing poetry and creating quilts would be our vehicle for offering our support and encouragement while they were so far away from home. Each student created a poem describing what America meant to him or her. Their poems and digital pictures were printed onto fabric, then joined together to create a class quilt and sent to Iraq.

As a new school year began two years later, my rare gift was delivered. My computer's background display was a photo of past students quilting their squares on the quilt. My present students wanted to know about the quilt, so we discussed it. Several days later, one of my students told the class that her father had seen the quilt in Iraq. He told her that the quilt had been hung at the entrance of the medical emergency room. Soldiers were able to read the poems while waiting for assistance. On one particular night with a full ER and no extra blankets, a soldier lay shivering and restless. The quilt was removed from the wall and placed over the soldier. It not only gave him warmth, but comfort as each poem was read aloud to him. The following morning the quilt was returned to the wall.

This is why I teach.

Source: Debbie Newman, Ed.S. Sixth-Grade Language Arts and Reading, Mahaffey Middle School, Ft. Campbell, Kentucky.

The five fundamental themes in geography are location (where a story takes place and why); place (what the place is like); relationships within places (including relationships between humans and the environment); movement of people, materials, and ideas (descriptions and consequences); and regions (including how they change) (Norton, 1993). Norton (1993) shows how the books *People of the Breaking Day* by Marcia Sewell, *Christopher Columbus: Voyager to the Unknown* by Nancy Smiler Levinson, *Encounter* by Jane Yolen, and *The Other Fourteen Ninety-Two: Jewish Settlement in the New World* by Norman H. Funkelstein can help students learn about these five themes in the context of literature rather than textbook discussions. This treatment, supplemented with other books about the period, offers diverse perspectives on the geographical concepts being studied.

 DIVERSITY

Picture books can be valuable for presenting many social studies concepts to older students, as well as primary-level students, because they elaborate on topics that would otherwise get limited attention. Sensitive issues that are ignored in textbooks can often be treated effectively in fictional accounts. Carpenter (2004) suggests

 LITERATURE

children's books that focus on the meaning of citizenship. Among them are Floyd Cooper's *Mandela: From the Life of the South African Statesman*, Kathleen Krull's *Harvesting Hope: The Story of Cesar Chavez*, and Elinor Sisulu's *The Day Gogo Went to Vote*.

Fictionalized biographies and diaries used for social studies instruction are excellent for teaching students to evaluate the accuracy and authenticity of material because authors have invented dialogue and thoughts for the characters to make the material seem more realistic. In the process of verifying information, students should look for any bias that the author might have. A bibliography of sources used in writing the story may be included. If so, students can see how extensive the author's research was. They also may check some of the sources to see how well the material was represented in the story. Students should check reference books for accuracy of dates, places, and names to determine any inaccurate parts. Sometimes, reading an author's foreword or postscript will offer clues to the fictional aspects of a story; for example, at times only the historical events mentioned are true. Students should also be aware that when authors use first-person narrative accounts about historical events, they are adding another fictional aspect to the story. In addition, first-person accounts offer limited perspectives, because any person present at an event cannot know everything that all the people in the story do or everything that is happening at one time. Therefore, understanding point of view is important.

Another approach to reading biographical material is to have students choose a famous person; read that person's biography; do additional research on the person, using multiple sources; make time lines of events in the person's life; and take on the role of that person in role-playing sessions. Because reading research strategies should be taught in context, this procedure provides fertile ground for such teaching. Such studies can also naturally link social studies with science and language.

Reading biographies can help students think about social issues and individuals' involvement with them, assessing the importance of events and understanding the objective and subjective dimensions of the events. This can lead to lessons on determining fact and opinion (Miller, Clegg, and Vanderhoff, 1992). Biographies of famous people who lived during different historical periods add spice to textbook accounts, and using literature about different cultures is one way to approach multicultural issues.

Students can also be drawn into historical periods and issues through historical fiction. Historical fiction transforms a series of events into an interpretation of these events, providing humanizing details. It can help students understand the times in which historical events occurred. Students can become emotionally involved with people from the past. As they identify with the actual historical characters in the books that they read, they encounter multiple perspectives and face conflicting viewpoints that require them to do critical thinking.

As students study these materials, teachers can read related materials to them to build background. Then the students can do activities such as making time lines based on their readings, marking maps to show where events in the reading occurred, classifying characters in terms of their beliefs or allegiances, producing

Read·Write·Think offers two lesson plans for helping third- through fifth-grade students learn about slavery and the Underground Railroad. One lesson, "Critical Perspectives: Reading and Writing About Slavery," uses Deborah Hopkinson's *Sweet Clara and the Freedom Quilt* and Internet sites to develop topical concepts, as well as helping students learn and apply map skills. The other one, "Historical Fiction: Using Literature to Learn About the Civil War," uses *Meet Addy*, a historical fiction book from the American Girls Collection, and a think-aloud questioning strategy to help students learn to make inferences and visualize events. Go to http://www.readwritethink.org or link from the Student Website for this book.

DIVERSITY

mock newspapers from the times, illustrating events and places described, writing diaries for characters in the reading, or writing letters to characters to offer comments and advice (Johnson and Ebert, 1992).

Kornfeld and Leyden (2005) used drama in a first-grade class in a unit on African-American history and literature. They gathered picture books on the topic and presented six of them to the students, who chose three to dramatize. The teachers let students request particular characters to play and then assigned parts. Students were asked what their characters would say and do, with the students who were not in a particular play participating by making suggestions. Some students used words from the books, and others chose their own words. The students practiced each play multiple times, and the dialogue and action evolved with each practice. Students decided on the needed costumes, props, sound effects, music, and scene backdrops. They researched in reference books to decide what animals, plants, landscapes, or city scenes to include in backdrops for the three plays and painted the backdrops. In the process, the students read, wrote, and drew about the topic. They learned about story grammar, logical sequence, and cause-and-effect relationships and developed empathy for others as they learned about history. These students performed their plays for other students in the school and for their parents. Although the teachers didn't base their plans on standards, the result was that the "students met at least 41 of the 57 English language arts standards (California State Board of Education, 2004) for their grade level, as well as many content standards in other subject areas" (Kornfeld and Leyden, 2005, p. 237).

Award-winning trade books can be found for nearly every period of history. Elizabeth Speare's *The Bronze Bow* is a novel about a boy who encounters Jesus in Rome; Marguerite De Angeli's *The Door in the Wall* treats the situation of a boy with a physical disability in fourteenth-century England; *The Courage of Sarah Noble*, by Alice Dalgliesh, describes a young girl who must face the difficulties of living in Connecticut in early pioneer days; *The Sign of the Beaver*, by Elizabeth Speare, is the story of a boy's struggle to survive in the Maine wilderness in the 1700s; Paula Fox's *The Slave Dancer* tells about a boy who becomes involved in the slave trade with Africa during pre–Civil War days; and Patricia MacLachlan's *Sarah, Plain and Tall* unites a woman from the eastern United States with a motherless family on a prairie farm during pioneer days.

Mathematics

Mathematics material is very concise and abstract in nature and involves complex relationships. A high density of ideas per page characterizes this kind of material, and understanding each word is very important, for one word may be the key to understanding an entire section. Yet elementary school teachers too often approach a math lesson in terms of developing only computational skill, overlooking the fact that reading skills can be advanced during arithmetic lessons and that arithmetic statement problems would be more comprehensible if attention were given to reading skills.

Reading in mathematics poses a number of special difficulties. First is the technical and specialized vocabulary. Young children have to learn terms like *plus*, *minus*, *sum*, and *subtraction*, whereas older ones encounter such terms as *perimeter*, *diameter*, *percent*, and *fractions*. Words with multiple meanings also appear frequently. Discussions about *planes*, *figures*, finding the *difference*, or raising a number to the third *power* can confuse students who know other, more common meanings for these words. Many mathematics terms have root words, prefixes, or suffixes that students can use in determining their meanings. (For example, *triangle* means "three angles.") Nevertheless, Whitin and Whitin (1997) encourage teachers to postpone the use of technical mathematics vocabulary until students have had a chance to explain significant concepts in their own words.

TEACHING TIP

Mathematics Symbols

Symbols are often particularly troublesome to readers, perhaps partly because some symbols mean other things in other contexts; for example, - means *minus* in math but is a hyphen in regular print. You can provide matching exercises in which students match mathematical symbols with their meanings to help them learn these symbols.

Difficulties with words are not the only problems students have with math textbooks. They are also required to understand a different symbol system and to read numerals as well as words, which involves understanding place value. Students must be able to interpret such symbols as plus and minus signs, multiplication and division signs, equal signs and signs indicating inequalities, percent signs, and many others, as well as abbreviations such as *ft.*, *lb.*, *in.*, *qt.*, *mm*, and *cm*.

To read numbers, students must understand place value. They must note, for example, that the number 312.8 has three places to the left of the decimal point (which they must discriminate from a period) and that this positioning of the decimal point means that the leftmost numeral indicates a particular number of hundreds, the next numeral tells how many tens, and the next numeral tells how many ones (in this case, three hundreds, one ten, and two ones, or three hundred twelve). To determine the value to the right of the decimal, they must realize that the first place is tenths, the second place is hundredths, and so forth. In this example, there are eight tenths; therefore, the entire number is three hundred twelve and eight-tenths. This is obviously a complex procedure, involving not merely reading from left to right but also reading back and forth.

Mathematical sentences also present reading problems. Students must recognize numbers and symbols and translate them into verbal sentences, reading $9 \div 3 = 3$, for example, as "nine divided by three equals three."

Teachers need to help students read and analyze word (or story) problems, as well. They should arrange such problems according to difficulty and should avoid assigning too many at one time. Story problems can present special comprehension difficulties. They require all of the basic comprehension skills (determining main ideas and details, seeing relationships among details, making inferences, drawing conclusions, analyzing critically, and following directions). Chapter 11 contains a description of the SQRQCQ study method for mathematics, which takes these requirements into account.

Sometimes students find it useful to draw a picture of the situation that a problem describes or to manipulate actual objects, and teachers should encourage such approaches to problem solving when they are appropriate. Teachers should watch their students solve word problems and decide where they need the most help: with computation, with problem interpretation (understanding of problems that they are not required to read for themselves), with reading, or with integration of the three skills in order to reach a solution. Small groups of students who need help in different areas of problem solving can be formed.

Many students are unfamiliar with the text structure of story problems, which usually provide important details at the beginning and place the topic sentence near the end. Braselton and Decker (1994) suggest that teachers have students think of word problems as short stories that they can comprehend by using their prior knowledge.

An effective method for teaching mathematics includes presenting mathematics content in ways that simulate real-life uses, such as problems related to students' everyday experiences. Such problems could be written by teachers and students, perhaps through a group language experience story. Language and mathematics strategy lessons would be interwoven as students performed such tasks as shopping for groceries within a budget, figuring the tax on purchases, conducting surveys, and constructing graphs. A research study showed that students who made up their own math story problems to solve performed better on tests of application skills than did those who practiced solving textbook word problems (Hadaway and Young, 1994). Fortescue (1994) points out that "in writing about math problems or activities, students become familiar with analytical writing while gaining and displaying a deeper understanding of the math concept" (p. 576). Students can also benefit from solving problems written by their peers. "Seeing It in Practice: Video Case" shows one real-life context for mathematics.

Graphs, maps, charts, and tables, which often occur in mathematics materials, were discussed in Chapter 11. Students need help with these graphic aids in order to perform well on many mathematics assignments.

> Students in the primary grades will need help in learning how to read story problems. The Read•Write•Think lesson plan "Giant Story Problems: Reading Comprehension Through Math Problem Solving" is designed to provide this assistance. Go to http://www.readwritethink.org or link from the Student Website for this book.

SEEING IT IN PRACTICE ◄■►

Video Case

View the Video Case "Motivating Adolescent Learners: Curriculum Based on Real Life" and the bonus videos to see how a sixth-grade teacher teaches math concepts like percents, fractions, and decimals in a real life situation. Be sure to look at the list of "Classroom Artifacts." In your journal, list the literacy skills that this teacher has taught and the students are actively practicing.

▶ Using Literature in Mathematics

 LITERATURE

Teachers can use literature to help them teach mathematical material. Counting books, for example, can provide material for teaching addition and subtraction. Mitsumasa Anno's *Anno's Mysterious Multiplying Jar* is good not only for counting, but also for multiplication. It does a good job of presenting the concept of factorials. Rozanne Lanczak Williams's *The Coin Counting Book* offers a venue for teaching how to count money. Through the humorous situations in Rod Clement's *Counting on Frank*, readers can begin to think like mathematicians—experimenting, calculating, and estimating. Two excellent books for developing concepts of large numbers are David M. Schwartz's *How Much Is a Million?* and Andrew Clements's *A Million Dots*, which complements Schwartz's book. A good book for encouraging students to work with division is Pat Hutchins's *The Doorbell Rang*. "Seeing It in Practice: Mathematics Lesson Based on Literature" shows how this book can also be used for addition with younger children. Demi's *One Grain of Rice* is a good book to use for study of how numbers that are doubled grow rapidly (Carr, Buchanan, Wentz, Weiss, and Brant, 2001). Children's literature can also help students learn to tell time. Jules Older's *Telling Time: How to Tell Time on Digital and Analog Clocks!* is useful for this purpose. Hazel Hutchins's *A Second Is a Hiccup: A Child's Book About Time* contains explanations of units of time in everyday terms.

Science and Health

Scientific literacy involves asking and finding answers to questions about experiences and being able to describe and explain natural phenomena. "Observing, questioning, predicting, describing, explaining, and investigating" are scientific practices that are related to literacy (Ebbers, 2002, p. 40). Ebbers points out that students are often encouraged to participate in real scientific activities. El-Hindi (2003) stresses the importance of getting students to reason out loud about scientific concepts during inquiry-learning activities. This process will promote instructional conversations that develop both understanding of the science concepts and their linguistic competence. Writing about scientific concepts, such as keeping logs of observations, can also be helpful.

Science and health textbooks are so dense with information that many students find them difficult to read. Because science textbooks are often written at higher difficulty levels than the basal readers for the same grade level, some students will need alternative materials for science instruction. Trade books are available on all levels of difficulty to meet this need.

Information in science areas is also frequently changing because of new discoveries. Teachers may want to supplement the use of these textbooks with related trade books, magazine articles, and information from the Internet in order to provide more readable and/or more current material.

Extremely heavy use of technical vocabulary is typical in science and health textbooks, in which students will encounter such terms as *lever, extinct, rodent, pollen, stamen, bacteria, inoculation,* and *electron.* Again, some of the words that have technical

---

◀ ▶ **SEEING IT IN PRACTICE**

Video Case

View the Video Case "Middle School Science Instruction: Inquiry Learning." Be sure to watch the bonus videos and examine the classroom artifacts. After viewing, answer in your journal questions 1 and 3 from the video. Also indicate in your journal the ways in which literacy was used in this science inquiry lesson and write your reaction to the teacher's approach to ensuring retention of important chemistry concepts. If you were teaching a lesson in this subject, would you use this approach? Why, or why not?

LITERATURE

An Internet site that could be helpful for science and health instruction is How Stuff Works (Go to http://www .howstuffworks.com or link from the Student Website for this book). The site offers many possibilities for supplementary materials in these areas. "How Bats Work" could be used in some science classes, for example, and "How Vision Works" could be useful in health classes.

Mathematics Lesson Based on Literature

Ms. Barnes opened the class by displaying the book *The Doorbell Rang* by Pat Hutchins. "From the picture on the cover of this book and the title *The Doorbell Rang,* what do you think it will be about?" she asked the students.

"There are lots of people in the picture," Sammy said. "I think a lot of people have come to visit. The doorbell rings every time somebody comes. We have a doorbell that people ring when they come."

"What else does the picture make you think?" Ms. Barnes asked.

"They've tracked up the kitchen," said Monica. "The mom is going to have to clean it up. She'll send them all out."

"Does anybody else have something to add?" Ms. Barnes asked.

"The children don't look happy. Maybe she is running them out," Tasha suggested.

"They are looking out the slot in the door. Maybe the person that just rang the bell is someone they don't like," Jimmy said.

"Or maybe the kids don't want anyone else to come," Don added.

"Listen carefully as I read the story to see if your predictions were right," Ms. Barnes said. "Also listen to see what this book has to do with math."

Ms. Barnes read the story. When she finished, she asked, "Were your predictions right?"

"I was right that lots of people came, and the bell rang every time," Sammy said.

"Mom didn't send them out of the kitchen, so Tasha and I were wrong," Monica said.

"I was wrong," Jimmy said. "They acted like they liked the people who came."

"But I'll bet they really didn't want all of those people to come and share the cookies. I think I was right, even though they don't act bad about it," Don said.

"How does all of this fit into a math problem?" asked Ms. Barnes.

"They have to decide how many cookies to give each person," Don replied.

"That's right. Now we are going to see how they figured it all out," Ms. Barnes said as she handed out stacks of plastic chips to each set of math partners in the room.

"Now," she said, "listen carefully and use your chips to answer my questions as I go back through the story."

She read the first two pages. "How many children were there?" she asked.

"Two," the students chorused.

"How many cookies did each one get?" she asked.

"Six," answered the students.

"We need to know how many cookies there were in all," she said. "What do we do to get this answer?"

"We add them," answered Joey.

"Who can write out an addition problem on the board that we have to solve?" she asked.

Benny went to the board and wrote "6 + 6 = ".

"Now solve the problem," she told them.

The students, who had used the chips to solve problems before, worked with their partners to form two rows of six chips each and count them. Soon hands were up all over the room. When all were finished, Ms. Barnes called on Billy, who proudly answered, "Twelve."

"Did anyone get any other answer?" she asked. A sea of shaking heads answered her. "Good job," she said. She let Sean go to the board and write the answer to the problem after the equal sign. Then she read further in the book.

"How many children were there after Tom and Hannah came?" she asked. Hands went up immediately, without use of the chips.

Ms. Barnes let Sammy give the answer, "Four," and go to the board and write the entire problem and answer: "2 + 2 = 4."

"Show with your chips how Sam and Victoria knew that each one would get three cookies," Ms. Barnes

(Continued)

Mathematics Lesson Based on Literature (*Continued*)

directed. The students arranged their chips into four rows of three chips each.

"Now write an addition problem to show how putting these cookies back on the plate would give us the twelve we started with," she told them. Students wrote on their own papers and consulted with their partners before holding up their hands. Ms. Barnes let Laticia write "3 + 3 + 3 + 3 = 12" on the board. She asked if everyone agreed, and they did.

She repeated the above procedure for the entrance of Peter and his brother and again for the entrance of Joy and Simon and their four cousins, with the added step of asking how many people were at the door when Joy and Simon came. The students quickly did the addition of two plus four without the aid of chips.

At the end of the lesson, the students counted the cookies on the tray that Grandma brought, added that number to twelve by combining the chips from several sets of partners, and put the total number of chips into twelve rows to see how many each one would have before they let in that last person at the door.

---

meanings also have more common meanings—for example, *shot, matter, solution,* and *pitch.* In these classes, as in all content-area classes, the teacher is responsible for seeing that students understand the concepts represented by the technical and specialized terms in their subjects. For example, a science teacher might bring in a flower to explain what *stamens* are and where they are located. Although diagrams are also useful, diagrams are still a step removed from the actual objects, and the more concrete an experience that students have with a concept, the more likely it is that they will develop a complete understanding of the concept.

To obtain valid scientific information, students need to learn how to read a wide variety of scientific materials. These materials may include newspapers, magazines, pamphlets, and reference books, in addition to textbooks. Good scientists and good readers need many of the same skills.

Comprehension strategies, such as recognizing main ideas and details, making inferences, drawing conclusions, recognizing cause-and-effect relationships, classifying items, recognizing sequence, and following directions, are important in reading science and health materials, as are critical reading strategies. The scientist's inquiring attitude is exactly the same as that of the critical reader. Students must determine the author's purpose for writing, must assess the completeness and timeliness of the information presented, and must check the accuracy of the material. Because material can rapidly become outdated, it is very important that students be aware of the copyright dates of these materials.

Casteel and Isom (1994) explain the relationship of literacy processes to understanding of scientific material through the use of a tree analogy. The literacy processes of purpose setting, predicting, organizing, constructing, composing, evaluating, and revising form the root system. These "roots" support the trunk, which consists of the language skills of reading, writing, speaking, listening, and thinking. The trunk supports branches that represent the parts of the scientific method (analyzing results, questioning, hypothesizing, gathering and organizing data, drawing conclusions, and reporting). The branches in turn support the scientific facts, concepts, laws, and theories of science.

Science and health materials must be read slowly and deliberately, and rereading may be necessary to fully grasp the information presented. These materials, like social studies materials, are written in a highly compact, expository style that often involves classification, explanations, and cause-and-effect relationships. The suggestions in Chapter 11 for teaching outlining skills can be especially useful in working with classification, which involves arranging information under main headings and subheadings. The suggestions given in Chapter 8 for recognizing cause-and-effect relationships will help students handle this type of arrangement when it occurs in science textbooks.

The ability to use such reading aids as maps, tables, charts, and graphs is also necessary. Explanations in science and health materials often describe processes, such as the pasteurization of milk, that may be illustrated by pictures, charts, or diagrams designed to clarify the textual material. Teachers might apply the material in Chapter 11 on reading diagrams and illustrations or the material in Chapter 8 on detecting sequence, because a process is generally explained in sequence.

Science textbooks often contain instructions for performing experiments. Readers must be able to comprehend the purpose of an experiment, read the list of materials to determine what must be assembled before the experiment is performed, and determine the order in which the steps must be followed. The suggestions in Chapter 8 on locating main ideas and details, on recognizing sequential order, and on learning to follow directions should be useful when teaching students to read material of this nature. Before they perform an experiment, students should attempt to predict the outcome on the basis of their prior knowledge. Afterward they should compare their predicted results with the actual results and investigate the reasons for any differences. Did they perform each step correctly? Can they check special references to find out what actually should have happened?

Keeping a science log, or journal, is a traditional practice for scientists and makes a natural connection to language instruction. Students can enter a short science-related passage in a journal each day. The passage can vary from a single sentence about a nature observation to a complete explanation of an experiment and its results. Students can also write reports on science projects, detailing the procedures and the findings.

Science activities that involve direct experiences, such as using manipulative materials, doing experiments, or making observations of phenomena, can be used as the basis for language experience stories or charts that will provide reading material in science. This approach is described in Chapter 9. Reading of related concept books, such as the ones mentioned later in this chapter, may provide students with material to use in expanding their stories.

Students work collaboratively on a science and social studies project, locating and marking locations of natural disasters on a map.

© Ellen Senisi/The Image Works

▶ Using Literature in Science and Health

Both fiction and nonfiction selections can help teachers clarify scientific informa-tion (El-Hindi, 2003). Ebbers (2002) identifies seven nonfiction genres that can help students learn about science: reference books, explanation books, field guides, how-to books, narrative expository books (ones that give information through a story format), biographies, and journals. *The Magic School Bus* series by Joanna Cole, *Ground-hog Gets a Say* by Pamela Curtis Swallow, and *Come Back, Salmon* by M. Cone use mul-tiple genres to pass along information in an enjoyable manner. *Come Back, Salmon* contains material that is appropriate for life science, and it emphasizes science as inquiry. More recent books tend to use more different visual features, such as side-bars, time lines, labels, and maps (Broemmel and Rearden, 2006). Discussion of the books offers students a chance to ask questions, share their opinions and back-ground knowledge, make predictions, and engage in inferential and critical think-ing. Literature circles and book club discussions that focus on books about scientific topics could be very effective (El-Hindi, 2003).

Teachers should make a wealth of science trade books available for independent reading, whether it is done in sustained silent reading (SSR) or Drop Everything and Read (DEAR) periods or at home with books that have been checked out of the classroom libraries. That makes it possible for students to discover the books for themselves. Some books that have been useful for particular scientific concepts and topics are Aliki's *Fossils Tell of Long Ago* (fossils), Gail Gibbons's *Planet Earth/Inside Out* (formation, layers, climate, land forms, and more), Stephen Kramer's *Hidden Worlds: Looking Through a Scientist's Microscope* (microscience), Ann Love and Jane Drake's *The Kids' Book of the Night Sky* (astronomy), Robin Page and Steve Jenkins's *What Do You Do With a Tail Like This?* (animal life), David Macaulay's *The New Way Things Work* (digital equipment, mechanics, sound waves, electricity, magnetism, and more), Laurence Pringle's *An Extraordinary Life: The Story of a Monarch Butterfly* (animal life), Eric Schlosser and Charles Wilson's *Chew on This: Everything You Don't Want To Know About Fast Food* (health), Seymour Simon's *Weather* (meteorology), and C. B. Weatherford's *The Sound That Jazz Makes* (sound).

The color photographs and realistic illustrations found in many science books enhance a student's enjoyment and understanding. Science informational books, such as Laurence Pringle's *Into the Woods: Exploring the Forest Ecosystem*, Lynne Cherry's beautifully illustrated *A River Ran Wild: An Environmental History*, and *Around One Cactus: Owls, Bats and Leaping Rats* by A. D. Fredericks provide vivid pictures to help students understand the science concepts. Jeannie Baker's thought-provoking environmental book *Window* shows how a wilderness evolves into a crowded city. Teachers need to analyze books about ecology in order to choose books that show realistic problems, address possible solutions, have positive tones, avoid stereotypes, and are appropriate for the intended audience.

Teachers can use the National Science Education Standards to help them decide if a trade book is suitable for use with their students. Broemmel and Rearden (2006) analyzed seventy-four Teachers' Choices books (identified each year through a joint effort of the International Reading Association and the Children's Book Council) for the suitability of their science content for use in classes at various levels. Overall, Broemmel and Rearden concluded that the Teachers' Choices books with science content had high literary quality and accurate scientific content. Some of the books, however, contained both science content and some aspects of fantasy. For example, in Lynne Cherry's *The Great Kapok Tree*, the animals of a Brazilian rain forest convince a man not to cut down their home. Teachers must use these books in a manner to help students distinguish between the factual parts and the fictional parts.

The Read•Write•Think lesson "Integrating Literacy into the Study of the Earth's Surface" includes teacher read-alouds and student reading of science trade books. Students keep dialogue journals and compose and perform readers' theater scripts about the bodies of water they study. Find it at http://www.readwritethink.org or link from the Student Website for this book.

 STANDARDS/ ASSESSMENTS

You can link to the National Science Education Standards from the Student Website for this book or go directly to http://www.education-world.com/standards/national/index.shtml.

Helping English-Language Learners Develop Content Literacy

Proficiency in the language of content textbooks is often lacking in students who are in the process of learning general English-language usage. Carrier and Tatum (2006) suggest use of both word walls and sentence walls. *Word walls* contain words that students need in their sight and meaning vocabularies, whereas *sentence walls* present the content-area words in the context of well-formed phrases and

 DIVERSITY

sentences that English-language learners (ELLs) can use to express the ideas being discussed. The value of sentence walls to ELLs is that they scaffold the learning of the grammatical structures of English. Sentence walls can also offer sentence frames, to aid in generating questions and sentences about the topic under consideration. Examples offered by Carrier and Tatum (2006) include "What causes _____ to _____?" and "When water condenses, it _____" (p. 286). Frames can be provided for describing, explaining, and analyzing science content. Students can use key vocabulary on the word wall to help complete the sentence frames on the sentence wall. Teachers need to demonstrate use of the word and sentence walls in the context of instruction before students can be expected to use them for scaffolds. Modeling of the use of the two walls provides both a demonstration of the technique and a model of appropriate pronunciation and intonation.

Manyak (2008) suggests a promising technique for working with primary-grade ELLs: composing bilingual books by having students translate stories written in one language into the other. This could be done with expository text, as well.

 ◀ ■ ▶ SEEING IT IN PRACTICE

Video Case

Revisit the main and bonus videos in the Video Case "Bilingual Education: An Elementary Two-Way Immersion Program" to review how one school approaches teaching in a bilingual situation. In your journal, write your opinion of this approach, mentioning its values and some obstacles to using it. Also give your opinion of the use of manipulatives in this lesson.

STRUGGLING READER/
INTERVENTION

Helping Struggling Readers Develop Content Literacy

 LITERATURE

Teachers can help struggling readers access the language of their content textbooks by presenting content words in the context of illustrations and sentences before their students read related passages. Picture books may be especially effective in helping students to visualize the meanings of the printed materials. These students may need initial instruction in using various types of context clues. (See Chapters 4 and 6 for information on teaching use of context clues.) Therefore, use of word walls and sentence walls, as described in the last section, can also be helpful for these readers, especially those who speak nonstandard dialects. Using trade books that cover the topic before reading the textbook can also facilitate development of needed background knowledge and content vocabulary (Carrier and Tatum, 2006; Ambe, 2007).

Struggling readers often need more scaffolding to learn from their content classes. The Read·Write·Think lesson "Let It Grow: An Inquiry-Based Organic Gardening Research Project" involves these readers in hands-on research. Students use books and the Internet and produce written and oral presentations to complete the research project. Find it at http://www.readwritethink.org or link from the Student Website for this book.

Ambe (2007) recommends the use of the DRTA (described in Chapter 9) for improving the comprehension skills of struggling readers. Teaching students to predict and verify ideas in the materials is a strategy that they can subsequently use independently.

Readers' theater is another strategy that offers scaffolding for struggling readers. The repeated readings of the material in rehearsals give them practice on fluency, pronunciation, and expression in a purposeful activity. The repetition also improves retention of the material (Flynn, 2004/2005).

SUMMARY

Teachers must be aware that basal reading instruction alone is not likely to prepare students thoroughly to read in the content areas. Students need to learn reading skills that are appropriate to specific subject areas, as well as general techniques that are helpful in reading expository text. Content texts present more reading difficulties than do basal reader materials. They have a greater density of ideas presented, and they lack the narrative style that is most familiar to the children. They may also contain many graphic aids that have to be interpreted. Teachers need to be aware of the readability levels of the materials that they give students to read, and they must adjust their expectations and reading assignments on the basis of students' reading levels in relation to the readability of available instructional materials.

Students need motivation to read content materials. Use of literature in teaching content and use of the newspaper are teaching approaches that help with motivation in all subject areas.

Many techniques can be used to help students read content-area materials more effectively. Among them are the directed reading-thinking activity, the language experience approach, Press Conference, feature analysis plus writing, use of learning logs, webbing, every-pupil-response activities, readers' theater, use of study guides, use of manipulative materials, computer approaches, integrated approaches, thematic content units, and literature-based units across the curriculum.

Each content area presents special reading challenges, such as specialized vocabulary. Reading in literature involves comprehending many literary forms, including short stories, novels, plays, poetry, biographies, and autobiographies. English textbooks cover the areas of listening, speaking, and writing. The techniques presented in these areas need to be practiced through authentic oral and written experiences. Social studies materials abound with graphic aids to be interpreted and require much application of critical reading skills. Mathematics has a special symbol system to be learned, but perhaps the greatest difficulty in this content area is the reading of story problems. Students need to learn a procedure for approaching the reading of such problems. Science and health materials contain many graphic aids. They also often include instructions for performing experiments, which must be read carefully to ensure accurate results.

Using literature selections to work with content-area concepts is effective in every content area. In addition, including real-life activities and connections to the students' backgrounds of experiences enhances learning and motivation.

Struggling readers and English-language learners generally need special, but often different, types of help in comprehending content-area reading texts. Teachers should be aware of these needs and differentiate instruction as appropriate.

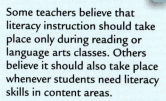

Time for Reflection

Some teachers believe that literacy instruction should take place only during reading or language arts classes. Others believe it should also take place whenever students need literacy skills in content areas.

What do *you* think and why?

For your journal . . . .

1. Write about the usefulness of newspaper reading in your particular content area.

2. Describe how you can make use of trade books in a particular content area.

3. Be sure that you have included in your journal your responses to the Video Cases that you viewed while studying this chapter.

. . . . **and your portfolio**

1. Develop a lesson for teaching students the multiple meanings of words encountered in science and health, social studies, mathematics, or literature. Try out the lesson in an elementary school classroom and write an evaluation of its effectiveness.

2. Select a passage from a social studies or science textbook. Prepare a study guide for students to use in reading and studying the passage.

3. Develop a bibliography of trade books that could be used by students who cannot read a particular content-area textbook.

4. Prepare a comparison-contrast chart for some topic in your content area.

Use of Technology for Literacy Learning

Today's classrooms are likely to be filled with technology that can enhance instruction in all subjects, including literacy instruction. Some of this technology has become familiar over the years, and most teachers are comfortable using it. Some emergent technology is so complex and unfamiliar that it intimidates many teachers—yet teachers should realize that all of the now-familiar technologies were once new and strange to some educators.

Teachers must learn what technological tools exist to help them with their literacy instruction, what strengths and weaknesses each of these tools has, and how best to integrate their use into the literacy curriculum. No application should be chosen just because it is novel, popular, or simply available. Each one must serve a legitimate purpose in the classroom. Used properly, technological tools can offer students instruction in a range of literacy activities, from low-level drill-and-practice to the higher-order thinking activities involved in producing reports and responding to simulations. They can serve as vehicles for presenting material in class, for providing instruction, for producing written material by students, and for recording class activities for the purpose of evaluation. They can also be used to individualize instruction.

Technological applications in classrooms involve use of all language arts skills: listening, speaking, reading, writing, viewing, and visually presenting. They also can enhance learning in any content area.

KEY VOCABULARY

Pay close attention to these terms when they appear in the chapter.

blogs

computer-assisted instruction (CAI)

computer-managed instruction (CMI)

desktop publishing

digital literacy

electronic bulletin boards

electronic discussion groups

electronic mailing list

e-mail (electronic mail)

hypermedia

hypertext

Internet

media literacy

multimedia

podcasts

technological literacy

videoconferencing

visual literacy

WebQuests

wikis

word-processing software

World Wide Web (WWW)

ANTICIPATION/REACTION GUIDE

AFTER
C or **I** (for initial
A or **D** answers)
A or **D**
(for initial **?** answers)

Directions: Before you read this chapter, complete the following anticipation/reaction guide. In the space before each statement, write **A** if you agree; **D** if you disagree; or **?** if you don't know. After you have read the chapter, complete the guide again to show what you have discovered in the chapter. In the space after each statement, mark whether you were initially correct (with a **C**) or incorrect (with an **I**). Write the letter for the correct answer (**A**) or (**D**) in the space for the statements that you initially marked with a question mark (**?**).

1. Teachers should try out software before purchasing it.

2. Only one student at a time can work effectively at a single classroom computer.

3. There are no television programs that fit comfortably into literacy instruction.

4. Comparing a print version of a children's literature selection with a video version of the same story can be a good literacy experience for students.

5. Hypertext and hypermedia usage may lead to "navigational problems" for users.

6. Computer-managed instruction can help teachers keep track of students' performances on learning activities.

7. The accuracy of material that is posted to electronic bulletin boards or placed on webpages is carefully monitored and can be accepted as accurate without the students doing further checking.

8. World Wide Web homepages and blogs are too complicated for elementary school teachers and students to develop and maintain.

9. E-mail projects can allow students to discuss literature selections with authors and other students all over the world.

10. Drill-and-practice programs offer initial instruction in skills.

11. Simulation programs set up situations that work like real-life adventures.

12. Multimedia means an overabundance of media.

13. The ability of computers to read texts aloud enhances their utility for young children and readers with visual disabilities.

14. If a student can make a consistent movement of some kind, he or she can use a computer.

CHAPTER 13 ORGANIZATION

Use of Technology for Literacy Learning

Important New Literacy Concerns

Newly Defined Literacies
Changes in Text Processing
Using Technology to Meet Needs of Diverse Student Populations

The Role of the Teacher

Understanding the Range and Possible Uses of Available Technology
Evaluating Technological Applications
Integrating Technology into the Classroom

Technology as a Tool for Literacy Instruction

Computer Applications
Instructional Transparencies
Television Programs
Audio Recordings
Video Recordings

Important New Literacy Concerns

Integrating technology into education to improve student achievement and make students technologically literate is a national concern. Soon after The No Child Left Behind Act was signed, "U.S. Secretary of Education Rod Paige announced the new 'Enhancing Education Through Technology' (ED Tech) initiative" to emphasize these technology goals (Forcier and Descy, 2008, pp. 101, 103). The emphasis on standards-based instruction has resulted in the development of the International Society for Technology in Education's National Educational Standards (ISTE NETS). The ISTE NETS for Teachers are standards for teacher educators. To ensure that their students will be able to handle the technological challenges that they face,

STANDARDS/
ASSESSMENTS

You can link to ISTE's standards for teachers and students from the Student Website or go directly to http://www .iste.org.

teachers at all levels should be able to meet these standards. The ISTE website also has identified standards that students should meet to avoid the digital divide, "the barrier that individuals must overcome if they do not have access to or understand how to use computers and the Internet" (Forcier and Descy, 2008, p. 47).

Newly Defined Literacies

Technology can be used to help students learn traditional literacy skills and other language skills, but increased use of technology has also expanded the traditional definitions of literacy to include new skills.

▶ Technological Literacy

The U.S. Department of Education (1997) defines **technological literacy** as "the ability to use computers and other technology to improve learning, productivity, and performance."

▶ Visual Literacy

The definition of technological literacy takes in concerns with **visual literacy** because students are bombarded with visual images in movies and on CDs, DVDs, computer games, and Internet sites. Visual literacy is the ability to derive meaning from still pictures, animations, and images in the context of video presentations, as well as the ability to visually present meaning through them (Forcier and Descy, 2008; Lohr, 2008).

LITERATURE

Instruction in visual literacy helps students gain more from their content reading. Most visuals in content books add to the ideas expressed in the text. Such instruction helps students who read picture books, graphic novels (for example, Colfer and Donkin's *Artemis Fowl: The Graphic Novel*) and graphic biographies (for example, Sturm's *Satchel Paige: Striking Out Jim Crow*) to interpret the story. Cartoons and comic strips are useful in teaching visual literacy skills, such as how lines are used to show movements, sounds, and feelings (Roe and Ross, 2005).

This instruction also helps students learn to "read" people's expressions, gestures, and other actions, even when they are not part of media presentations (Williams, 2007). Some examples of non-media use of visual literacy that may motivate young athletes to understand its importance are situations in which quarterbacks "read" the defenses to choose which play to run and defenses "read" the quarterbacks' eyes to determine where the ball will be thrown. Coaches of different sports draw diagrams for plays that must be understood, and students may draw their own plays when they are playing football or basketball for fun with friends.

▶ Media Literacy

Media literacy includes understanding and evaluating information that is viewed and read (Grabe and Grabe, 2007; Forcier and Descy, 2008). Critical reading is hardly a new concept, and some attention has been given in the past to critical viewing of television, but critical viewing has recently become a more prominent concern. The area of media literacy incorporates consideration of how to create and distribute media and how they can affect attitudes and behavior. Because students "spend an average of six-and-a-half hours per day with all media, including computers, video games, radio, and CD players" (Scharrer, 2002/2003, p. 357), concern with media literacy is certainly well founded.

The term **multimedia** refers to the mixing of different media. Multimedia computer programs often have interactive capabilities. For example, when reading an entry from a multimedia encyclopedia, a student may click on a word or symbol to view a picture, see a definition, watch a video clip, or hear an audio clip related to the topic. Evaluating multimedia programs involves not only considering visual and auditory content of the program, but also the kinesthetic, tactile, and cognitive considerations for using the program: for example, methods of interaction and level of thinking required.

▸ Digital Literacy

Digital literacy is a subset of media literacy. Digital literacy involves both "active interpretation of nonverbal symbolic systems" found in electronic messages and "construction of sounds, images, graphics, photos, videos, animations, and movements to add nonverbal components to electronic messages" (Valmont, 2003, p. 92). Therefore, it includes skills in viewing and visually presenting. It takes in analysis of illustrations, lighting, color, and movement as they contribute to the meaning of a digital presentation.

Digitally literate students can learn authentic production tasks that will prepare them for today's workplace. Students in a middle school web-design course were presented with authentic tasks and software tools to learn about web design. The students worked in small groups to make decisions about how to complete real-world tasks—including planning, creating, and publishing on the web an electronic tour of their school. They used digital cameras, computers with web-authoring software, and school blueprints. Students acquired technological skills as well as improving other language skills through activities such as speaking and listening in groups, reading blueprints, viewing, visually presenting, and writing (Basden, 2001). This project definitely required the use of technological literacy.

Changes in Text Processing

Computer applications may be made basically linear or highly interactive. Linear applications provide essentially the same order of presentation of content as most print materials previously used in classrooms. Interactive applications, however, present a much different task that involves accessing information in a nonlinear fashion, controlled by the reader. **Hypertext** is text that can be viewed in an order chosen by the reader. With **hypermedia,** a variety of media—including text, full motion video, sound clips, graphics, and still images—can be viewed and/or heard in an order chosen by the user, making the material highly interactive (Grabe and Grabe, 2007; Kauchak and Eggen, 2008).

Hypertext and hypermedia applications can help students with comprehension; for example, a student can click on boldfaced words, phrases, or icons in the material. Clicking on a word may cause the program to display text that defines the word, a picture, and/or an audio presentation of the word. In this sense, hypertext and hypermedia are similar to footnotes in showing relationships between texts and media (Klein and Olson, 2001). (Reading material on the Internet and some of the books on CD and DVD discussed later in this chapter are examples of hypertext and hypermedia applications.) Hypertext applications may also provide graphic organizers. They may offer options for taking notes as the reading progresses and later printing out notes for review or as a basis for developing essays.

Hypertext and hypermedia materials present new reading challenges, such as problems in navigation in locating information. Readers may continue to click on keywords that lead them further away from the original text and have trouble returning to their original webpages. Obviously, hyperlinks and hypermedia found in electronic texts complicate the process of comprehending text material for those who are accustomed to reading traditional print, which is linear in nature.

LITERATURE

Use of postmodern children's books can be a bridge to helping students understand how to navigate hypermedia. Postmodern books have characteristics that are similar to those of hypermedia, and they require use of similar thinking processes. They may be nonlinear, require much use of inferential skills to connect the text parts, and offer unusual perspectives in their illustrations. They require students to decide in what sequence to view the words and illustrations on a page. They may have multiple storylines and multiple voices and perspectives. Teachers can read such books aloud and allow students time to think about the text and examine the illustrations to decipher the meanings (Goldstone, 2006).

Research on the online reading comprehension strategies that are needed for reading informational text on the Internet has been done with skilled sixth-grade readers as subjects (Coiro and Dobler, 2007). The researchers concluded that "reading Internet text prompts a process of self-directed text construction that may explain the additional complexities of online reading comprehension" (p. 215). Many of the needed strategies, such as use of prior knowledge, inferential reasoning and predicting, and metacognition, are ones that are used in reading printed informational text. Readers of Internet text, however, must also deal with intrusive outside advertisements, links that have address changes, broken links, the possibility of following a link that is totally unrelated to the topic, and the necessity of added physical actions (for example, typing, clicking, and scrolling) as comprehension skills are used. They also need prior knowledge of informational website structure and of web-based search engines. The skills needed to process online text are also ones that cause the most problems for weak readers, possibly indicating that the gap between proficient and weak readers will widen when Internet reading becomes more prevalent (Coiro and Dobler, 2007).

STRUGGLING READER/
INTERVENTION

Using Technology to Meet Needs of Diverse Student Populations

DIVERSITY

STRUGGLING READER/ INTERVENTION

There is ongoing concern in education about meeting the needs of diverse populations. Technology can be used to help address the diverse needs of students in a classroom. Many computer applications, for example, can be used by students working at a variety of reading levels. Gifted and talented students can pursue independent inquiry through Internet research or creating their own websites—activities that often require both divergent and convergent thinking skills. Supportive technology can also help students overcome some reading problems. For example, audio recordings can be paired with printed text to build sight vocabulary and reading fluency. Computer-supported instruction can help scaffold learning for struggling readers. English-language learners may benefit from use of computer programs such as *English for Kids* or *Usborne's Animated First Thousand Words* (Forcier and Descy, 2008).

Some programs allow computers to read texts aloud. This enhances the utility of computer programs for young children, second-language learners, readers with visual disabilities, and struggling readers. A talking word-processing program that has a spelling checker is *Write: OutLoud*. Computers can also provide larger print for visually impaired readers, and the color and typeface of print shown on the monitor can be changed.

LITERATURE

With some programs that present established children's books on CD, students can record sentences in their own voices, enter the sentences into the computer, have the computer read what has been entered back to them, and replay their recorded speech at any point for comparison. This capability makes it possible for students to self-monitor their writing—a feature that is useful for younger children, struggling readers, and English-language learners. These students may also benefit from using CDs, such as *Little Monster at School* (Broderbund), which can be read in English or Spanish. For English-language learners who have Spanish as their first language, the book may be read or listened to in Spanish and then English (Labbo, 2005).

Other computer technologies are available for students who have physical problems. There are special pads that serve as input devices for young children who have not yet developed the fine-motor control necessary for keyboarding, and the same devices can be helpful for students with physical disabilities that affect motor control. Voice-recognition programs are becoming more widely available and more effective, allowing speech input for students who lack motor control (Silver-Pacuilla and Fleischman, 2006).

Computer keyboards with Braille overlays on the keys, used in conjunction with a word-processing program with speech feedback, can enable blind students to type and monitor their writing. Programs are available to translate Braille into words and words into Braille and to allow printouts on Braille printers (Kauchak and Eggen, 2008). Devices that increase text size are available, and the Zoom function available in both Mac and Windows operating systems will allow students to magnify the text on the screen.

◀ ■ ▶ **SEEING IT IN PRACTICE**

Video Case
View the Video Case "Assistive Technology in the Inclusive Classroom: Best Practices" and the bonus videos accompanying it. Also examine the "Classroom Artifacts." In your journal, describe the types of assistive technology used with Jamie. Tell how effective each one appeared to be. Mention any other assistive technology devices that you believe could be beneficial for Jamie. Then describe how comfortable you would be using these devices or others that have been mentioned in the text or in your class lectures.

An application referred to as *word prediction* allows students who have fine-motor difficulties to begin typing words, and the program "predicts the completion of partial words that are input" (Forcier and Descy, 2008, p. 83) as they type, making it unnecessary for students to type the words in their entirety. AlphaSmart uses this word-prediction strategy. Another application, called *abbreviation expansion*, allows whole messages to be encoded and retrieved with a given combination of keystrokes. Touch screens, headsticks, mouthsticks, customized handheld pointers, and remote-control devices that can control equipment with muscle actions, such as head nods, are also available for students with physical problems (Heward, 2006; J. Hopkins, 2006). If a student can make a consistent movement of some kind, the computer can be used. "Seeing It in Practice: Video Case" shows some assistive technology in use.

STRUGGLING READER/
INTERVENTION

Because all curricular applications of technology have to include some instruction in how to use the technology itself, a technique suggested by Leu, Castek, Henry, Coiro, and McMullan (2004) could be of help to struggling readers. They suggest teaching a new technology skill or technological literacy skill first to a student who has struggled with foundational literacies. Then that student can teach the new skill to classmates.

The Role of the Teacher

The teacher has a critical role to play in the application of technology to literacy instruction. He or she is the decision maker about the technological tools that will be used, but a teacher cannot make valid decisions about the best technological applications for classroom use without knowing how to use various types of available technology, what advantages each one has for instruction, and how to plan appropriate uses of technology in their curricula.

Understanding the Range and Possible Uses of Available Technology

Overhead projectors, televisions, and videotape recorders are so commonly available in classrooms that sometimes they are overlooked and sit unused when they would actually be ideal for particular teaching applications. CD and DVD recorders, CD and DVD players, and computers are also available in many classrooms. In some situations, they have to be checked out of the media center, and some schools require that students go to scheduled labs to use computer equipment. The situation is improving yearly, but many classrooms still do not have all of this equipment. Teachers need to know what is available in their schools, not only in the way of hardware, but also the materials to use with it. Computer software, for example, must be available for the particular type of computer (PC or Macintosh, for example) that is in the classroom and also must be compatible with the computer's operating system (for instance, the correct version of Windows, Linux, or the Macintosh operating system).

After teachers discover what is available, they must determine possible uses for the equipment and materials. Teachers should be aware of the many possibilities of using combinations of media. Using videos related to a book before students begin reading the book seems to increase understanding of and aesthetic responses to the material. Other media have also had positive effects on understanding. Students may view videos along with readings, produce videos based on readings, and use information from CDs, DVDs, and the Internet to enhance understanding (Roe, 2000). Students are often presented with or asked to create text documents that have been embellished with other media, such as audio and video elements (Grabe and Grabe, 2007).

As a part of a literacy and technology program called Digital Underground Storytelling for Youth (DUSTY), nine-year-old students told stories and made multimodal movies. One student, Inma, became familiar with the computer technology quickly and became a peer tutor for other students, using teaching techniques that she had seen her teachers use. Inma created a well-developed story with a lot of detail. When she made her movie, she chose images carefully, manipulating them with PhotoShop to suit the story. She also worked to record her voice with good intonation and emotion, and she made good use of music in the presentation (Ware, 2006).

In another example, a group of ethnically and socioeconomically diverse fifth graders investigated the topics of child slavery, racial profiling, and racial prejudice through reading books and newspapers, viewing movies, hearing related songs, examining websites, and conducting surveys. As a result of this study, the students produced a CD entitled *Exploring Freedom*, which contained digital video clips of student presentations of skits, reports, dance, collages, and poetry on the subject. As they rehearsed and filmed their material, they considered the visual, aural, and gestural qualities of the presentations (Damico and Riddle, 2006). DIVERSITY

A third example also involves fifth graders. These students have been taught to summarize with technology by making magazine covers that reflect the contents of a chapter of study. They had to find the main ideas and details in the chapter, differentiating between the more important and less important ideas presented. The process connected with authentic materials familiar to the students. The teachers helped the readers to synthesize the material and create covers that integrated visual images and graphics with important phrases and titles from the chapters.

The teachers first modeled the process of summarizing through think-alouds, identifying key ideas and words from the text, and using clip-art drawings or photo-copied illustrations to represent the printed words. (See Chapter 11 for more information about summarizing.) Students practiced the process of summarizing and then explored magazine covers and the use of images on them to represent ideas. Finally, they designed their own covers for a section of text, choosing text, fonts, colors, and layouts. They shared, evaluated, and revised their completed products (Assaf and Garza, 2007).

Evaluating Technological Applications

All applications of technology in the classroom need to be evaluated for appropriateness and effectiveness, just as other materials should be. Example 13.1 shows some questions that a teacher may wish to ask about any potential application of technology in the curriculum.

Teachers have been evaluating the use of projected transparencies, television programs, audiotapes, and videotapes for a long time. There are, however, some more specific concerns in evaluating computer software, such as the ones listed in Example 13.2. Some of the considerations in Example 13.2 are appropriate only for software that would be considered computer-assisted instructional software, but most of them apply to any software.

TEACHING TIP

Evaluating Software

You should try out software before purchasing it, if possible, because some pedagogically unsound, user-*unfriendly*, and inflexible software is available, along with the many good programs. Reviews in professional periodicals such as *The Reading Teacher* can help you decide, but consulting them is less revealing than actually using the programs.

EXAMPLE 13.1 Evaluation of Technological Applications

To evaluate technological applications for your classroom, answer the following questions:

1. Does the application address content that is needed in this curriculum?
2. Does the application motivate students to learn the content?
3. Does the application clarify the concept for the student in some way?
4. Does the application lend itself to use in your classroom structure?
5. Is the application easy to implement?
6. Is the application instructionally sound?
7. Is the application cost effective?
8. Is the application more effective than other possible approaches to the task?

EXAMPLE 13.2 Evaluating Computer Software

When evaluating computer software, ask the following questions:

1. Is the program compatible with the available hardware and operating system? (Consider the version of the operating system, memory requirements, network possibilities, storage needs, need for CD or DVD players, and so on.)

2. Does the program meet a curricular need better than another approach would?

3. Is the program well documented?

   a. Are the objectives of the program clear?
   b. Are the steps involved in running the program clearly indicated?
   c. Are time requirements for program use described, and are they reasonable for classroom use? (If a program can be saved at any time and re-entered at the same place, some of the problems with time are alleviated.)

4. Is the program user friendly?

5. Is there a management system that keeps up with a student's performance on the program, if that would be appropriate?

6. Are the screens well designed and readable?

7. Is the program essentially crash proof?

8. Is feedback about performance offered to the students? Is the feedback appropriate for them?

9. Do the students have control over the speed of the program presentation, the level of difficulty of the program, the degree of prompting offered by the program (including seeing instructions for use), and the sequence of presentation of material?

10. Is the program highly interactive, requiring more of the student than just page turning?

11. Is sound used appropriately, if at all? Can the sound be turned off without destroying the effectiveness of the program?

12. Is color used effectively, if at all?

13. Is the program adaptable for a variety of levels of students? Are your students within this range?

14. Is the material free of stereotypes and bias?

15. Is there a way that the teacher can modify the program for a particular class, set of data, or student? Is this procedure protected against student tampering?

16. Is the information presented in the program accurate and presented clearly and in grammatically correct form?

Integrating Technology into the Classroom

STANDARDS/
ASSESSMENTS ☑

Any application of technology used for instruction should present, reinforce, or teach a concept; offer tools for recording, collecting, and retrieving data (for example, database and spreadsheet programs); motivate students in their study; or provide assessment opportunities (for example, electronic portfolios). The content should be appropriate to the subject area, grade level, and maturity level of the students. The presentation format should fit into the classroom organizational structure, and the use should be adaptable to the time available. Teachers must decide which applications fit these criteria and which do not. The evaluation questions found in Examples 13.1 and 13.2, along with their knowledge of the students and the curriculum, can help teachers with this decision making.

TEACHING TIP

Using Appropriate Grouping to Fit Different Applications

Various technological applications are ideal for use with individual students, small groups, or whole classes. Some people think that working at a computer has to be a solitary activity; but, on the contrary, students' social interactions while working on some types of computer projects can be highly beneficial because they can pool their knowledge and skills to solve problems.

Integration can take place across the curriculum. Smolin and Lawless (2003) describe activities in a second-grade bilingual classroom. The teacher asked students to interview bilingual business owners near their school about what it means to be bilingual. The activity was designed to meet "standards in language arts, social studies, and technology" (p. 570). To accomplish the task, students used computers, digital cameras, video recorders, and tape recorders. Instruction in the use of each of these tools focused on how they could be used to facilitate the process of interviewing and synthesizing the resulting information into an electronic slide show, which was shared with other students through e-mail. This process also enhanced students' visual literacy skills—understanding and producing visual messages (Smolin and Lawless, 2003; International Visual Literacy Association, 1998). Students gathered information from the Internet, using websites that the teacher chose for age appropriateness and sites located by using search engines designed for children, such as Yahooligans and Ask Jeeves for Kids (Smolin and Lawless, 2003).

DIVERSITY

Technology as a Tool for Literacy Instruction

This chapter is concerned primarily with the application of technology as a tool for literacy instruction, rather than for instruction in general. The following are ways in which many types and applications of technology can be used for this purpose. This discussion will first focus on some newer technologies and conclude with reminders about usefulness of older technologies.

Computer Applications

Computer applications pervade today's schools and, actually, every aspect of students' lives. Unfortunately, computers are not available in large enough quantities to offer every elementary school student substantial computer time each day. Even though not all classrooms have computers, most classes have access, either through resident computers, computers on carts that can be checked out from a central location, or a computer lab that has scheduled times for use by various classes. Because computer skills are necessary for effective functioning in today's society, valid uses of computers in literacy instruction is essential.

Even when only one computer is available in the classroom, there are many possible applications. With a projection device, the computer can be used for recording and displaying language experience stories (see Chapter 9) or any cooperative writing, including creative writing and report writing. These writing efforts can be printed for use by individual students or small groups. The computer can be used to display simulation programs, with children making joint decisions about required choices and a designated student entering data. It can be used to record in databases project information that can be printed out for class use. Or students can work in small groups to prepare sections of a multimedia presentation, which are then combined for sharing with the whole class and other classes.

In whatever way that computers are used in instruction, teachers must ensure that all students have equal access and opportunities to use them. Many educators are concerned that girls may use computers less than boys, putting them at a disadvantage in a world that is increasingly digital. However, some research indicates that girls are adept at using computers for literacy activities outside of school. They create webpages, write blogs, and chat online, and they often participate in some popular role-playing games. The Digital Girls Project (2005) is one program for exploring pre-teen and teenage-girls' knowledge of digital technology (Williams, 2007). Teachers should be aware of some cultural biases that limit expectations for girls in use of technology and encourage development of expertise in both boys and girls.

▶ Interactive Digital Whiteboards

Interactive digital whiteboards (produced under a number of names by different companies) can enhance much instruction that was previously done on dry-erase boards, overhead projectors, or slide projectors. They are essentially electronic dry-erase boards (Lever-Duffy and McDonald, 2008). When they are connected to computers that have special software, they can act as the computers' monitors and input

 DIVERSITY

Time for Reflection

Some teachers believe that little can be accomplished when only one computer is available for a whole class.

What useful applications for a single computer can *you* generate?

One Internet site for locating lesson plans for using digital whiteboards is "Using Electronic Whiteboards in Your Classroom: Profiles, Ideas, Lesson Plans and Web Sites" at http://www.waukesha.k12.wi.us/ WIT/SmartBoard/specificapps.htm. Lessons are included for the language arts and many other curricular areas.

devices. Some of them are wall mounted, and others are on portable stands. They are written on with dry-erase markers, styluses, virtual pens, or even fingers that act as markers. Colors and line widths can be changed, and errors can be deleted with virtual erasers. Pictures and text that are entered into the computer, PowerPoint presentations, or web materials can be displayed on the whiteboard; and the markers can be used to correct, label, rearrange, or annotate them. The board can also function as a touch pad for navigation through computer programs or Internet material, replacing a mouse click. Work can be printed or saved on the computer, making it possible to return to it later for more work (Solvie, 2004; Wendt and Beach, 2007).

DIVERSITY

The digital whiteboard can be valuable at any grade level. One teacher used it with first graders to "highlight letter combinations, inflectional endings, and graphemic components of the words" that were being studied (Solvie, 2004, p. 485). She allowed students to highlight and circle words, erase print, and navigate to web links with their fingers. These activities were good for kinesthetic learners and were motivational for all the students (Solvie, 2004). The digital whiteboard is also good for saving lessons to use with students who are absent.

▶ Word Processing and Desktop Publishing

One of the most obvious applications of computers to literacy instruction is the use of **word-processing software** for both creative writing and writing of a functional nature, such as the writing of research reports. This software takes much labor out of editing and revising written products, making mechanical aspects of writing—such as printing, spelling, and copying—easier. Because words, sentences, and longer passages can be moved around with a few clicks or keystrokes, students are less reluctant to reconsider the content, organization, and mechanical aspects of their papers and to make needed changes. Freedom from recopying an entire document is a definite plus, especially for younger students who may still be laboring to perfect their handwriting and older ones with learning and physical disabilities (Klein and Olson, 2001; Kara-Soteriou, Zawilinski, and Henry, 2007).

DIVERSITY

Word-processing programs have become easier to use over the years. Nevertheless, a group of researchers found that first-grade students generally produced longer writing pieces with paper and pencil than with word-processing programs on the computer. On the other hand, student interaction was greater when the students were using the computers, and they helped each other with spelling and computer use. In agreement with earlier studies, students reported that making revisions with the computer was easier. They complained about their hands getting tired when they wrote with pencil and paper, and most indicated that they preferred writing on the computer. Keyboarding skills were a problem for some students, and the teacher needed to break up the keyboarding time for them. The quality of the writing was about the same with both methods (Van Leeuwen and Gabriel, 2007).

There are word-processing programs on many different levels of difficulty, so it is possible to find tools easy enough for primary students and tools powerful enough to meet the needs of older ones. Maximum advantage of word-processing activities cannot be attained until students become proficient in the use of the program and the hardware. Peer assistance with computer tasks can help alleviate problems. Teachers can capitalize on students' expertise by assigning peer tutors, particularly when lower-achieving students get the chance to be the experts.

STRUGGLING READER/ INTERVENTION

When word-processing software is used, students' written products can be printed in a neat, legible form to be read by class members. This feature may make students take more pride in their work.

Use of spelling checkers and grammar checkers alerts students to words that *may* be misspelled or constructions that *may* need modification, but the checkers do not make the decisions about what will actually be done. Students have to look at each comment and decide upon its merits. This is a critical reading activity that is a natural part of the writing process.

Many word-processing programs include dictionaries and thesauruses, which students can use to help them make decisions about their word choices. The dictionary can be used in deciding if a word has the correct meaning for the context; the thesaurus can be used in choosing a synonym when a word has been overused in a selection or in finding a word that fits the situation exactly.

Students in a fourth-grade writing workshop were more willing to revise and do multiple drafts of research papers when they were allowed to use word processing than they had been previously. In addition, use of the spelling checker helped weak spellers find and correct spelling errors, with the aid of a conventional dictionary. With the aid of the word processors, many students began to write enthusiastically for the first time (Edinger, 1994).

STRUGGLING READER/ INTERVENTION

Teachers also benefit personally from use of word-processing programs to revise and edit their own written products (such as handouts, tests, and communications with parents). Additionally, they can use projection devices to allow an entire group to see the material they have written on the computer, instead of writing on a chart or on the board.

In the past, most teachers used a **desktop-publishing** program to integrate text and graphics in a document, to flow text around graphics, to format text into columns, and to use a number of styles and sizes of type, but now many word-processing programs perform these functions. Students can write stories and research papers and can produce class newspapers and magazines with either word-processing software or desktop-publishing software. Multimedia programs (discussed in the next section) can also be used.

Desktop-publishing programs and multimedia programs are often used to set up special formats for such applications as banners and greeting cards. The programs may have clip art (ready-made images that can be used for illustrations), and students may be able to create their own illustrations or modify the available clip art. *The Print Shop Deluxe* (Broderbund) enables students to produce signs, posters, and banners, as well as to combine text and graphics to customize reports. *Classroom Publisher* (Staz Software) is another easy-to-use desktop-publishing program suitable for grades 3 and up. Broderbund's *Print Shop Web Design* can be used in developing webpages. Lee (2000) found that using desktop-publishing software helped fifth graders feel like "real writers" and that book reports posted on the World Wide Web caused sixth graders to care about the grammar, accuracy, and tone of their writing.

When students have access to the Internet and to word-processing software on their computers, there is a danger that their research reports may consist of material cut and pasted from information that they have found on the Internet, without any real mental manipulation of the material to produce a coherent presentation (Guinee and Eagleton, 2006). Another hazard is that they may find sites that offer papers on their topic that they can use without even having to look up the topic in various sources. Teachers must warn students of the seriousness of plagiarism and presenting other people's material as their own. They can attempt to give assignments that do not lend themselves to direct copying. Some assign reports to be written from unusual viewpoints (for example, a Tory's description of and reaction to the Boston Tea Party). Others require that the reports be written in supervised class periods or that students turn in evidence of each step they took in the process approach to writing the report (brainstorming, location of sources, note taking, and multiple drafts, for example).

▶ Multimedia Publishing

DIVERSITY

Multimedia-publishing software enables students to prepare projects that include text, color, original drawings, imported pictures and clip art, animation, and sound effects such as music and spoken words. Such options make high-interest projects possible. With today's multimedia programs, students can input text with the keyboard, draw onscreen (or draw on paper and scan the material into the computer), use predrawn pictures and backgrounds, record sounds to include in documents, or select sounds from prerecorded ones. This variety accommodates students with different learning styles. Students and teachers can develop multimedia presentations with a variety of special software, including Microsoft's *PowerPoint*, Apple's *Keynote*, and *HyperStudio* (Roger Wagner). Use of programs like *PowerPoint* for presentations may cause students to think more critically about their material (Saltpeter, 2005). "Seeing It in Practice: Multimedia Presentations" describes how two middle school classes completed such a presentation.

STANDARDS/
ASSESSMENTS

Teachers face a challenge in evaluating students' multimedia projects. They need to consider the planning (storyboarding); the variety, appropriateness, and documentation of sources; the organization and design; the clarity of navigation signals; and the choice and integration of media (Brunner, 1996). Slick presentation cannot be allowed to overshadow accuracy and organization.

▶ Databases and Electronic Reference Works

Databases are organized collections of data that have the information filed in such a way that it can be retrieved by category. Databases are usually created and searched by special *database programs*. Students can create their own databases, or they may refer to a variety of databases prepared by others, including electronic encyclopedias and dictionaries. Databases may be found on the Internet or purchased on CDs

A good resource for teachers is the Media Channel's Media Literacy Classroom. It focuses on pedagogy designed to help teachers use media and multimodal literacies for instructional purposes (Orellana and Morrell, 2006). Although the site may not be stable because of funding issues, at the time of publication you could find it at http://www.mediachannel.org/classroom or link there from your Student Website.

Multimedia Presentations

The two middle school classes that are discussed in two other "Seeing It in Practice" features in this chapter, "Conversations About Literature" and "Using Video Recordings," developed a multimedia presentation on each of the books that they read along with their university e-mail partners, and the university partners viewed the presentations just before the end-of-semester meetings.

The middle school classroom teachers organized their classes into cooperative groups to work on specific portions of the multimedia presentation and developed a schedule for the group assignments. Each group produced a rough draft to show what it planned to do. Then each group used the computer to create its portion of the presentation. To do this, the students had to decide what important incidents to include, what sequence to follow, what visual and sound features to incorporate, and what transitions to use. They developed a series of carefully designed and sequenced slides that represented main events and characters in the books. They incorporated student-produced drawings, photographs, and music to develop powerful presentations of content. The university students were impressed by the professional appearance and the thoroughness of the presentations. Such productions required a depth of understanding of the material that went far beyond the ability to describe the stories in words.

or DVDs. Some libraries now have their holdings listed in computer databases that can be searched by author, title, and subject.

Database programs are valuable research tools and can be used to help students organize data for writing reports. Database programs make possible the categorization, storage, and orderly retrieval of data collected during research reading (Kauchak and Eggen, 2008). When using databases, students perform such tasks as reading and following directions, taking notes, gathering and categorizing data, summarizing, posing questions, predicting outcomes, making comparisons and contrasts using collected information, analyzing and synthesizing data, using reference materials, identifying keywords for efficient data access, and testing hypotheses. All these activities require them to be active, purposeful readers.

Electronic reference works, such as dictionaries, thesauruses, and encyclopedias, are elaborate databases that are searchable by keywords and categories. Such reference works take some of the manual labor out of library research, but they still require the same cognitive skills for location of information. Electronic reference works are available at different levels of difficulty. Teachers need to check the intended age groups for these tools when purchases are made or assignments are given. These electronic references offer text articles, video clips, sound or music clips, photos, and web links. Some reference sites provide online access to material that is continually updated (Grabe and Grabe, 2007).

SEEING IT IN PRACTICE ◀■▶

Video Case

View the Video Case "Multimedia Literacy: Integrating Technology into the Middle School Curriculum" and the bonus videos. Also examine the "Classroom Artifacts." In your journal, write your evaluation of how effective use of the multimedia presentations was with this lesson. Can you see applications for this technique in your own classes? Also discuss the way that the teacher gave this assignment and scaffolded the processes involved.

Many encyclopedias and dictionaries are available in electronic format. Some, like the *Britannica*, have both paid and free versions. *Britannica*'s free version is a concise encyclopedia, however. Online encyclopedias have the advantage of being constantly updated. Encyclopedias on CD and DVD, unlike print versions, are very affordable for schools, and often include a dictionary as well. Both general and specialty encyclopedias and dictionaries are available.

 DIVERSITY

Electronic dictionaries for English-language learners, such as the *Longman Interactive English Dictionary* (*LIED*), provide special aids that print dictionaries cannot offer (Butler-Pascoe and Wiburg, 2003). The *LIED* allows students to "compile and save pictures, audio, and video excerpts to contextualize the meanings of words and concepts" (Butler-Pascoe and Wiburg, 2003, p. 126). Help features include audio pronunciation, phonetic transcription, a grammar guide, verb formation, and many others.

▶ Electronic Books (E-Books)

Among the computer applications available are e-books, both fiction and nonfiction. Usually accessed from CDs, e-books vary greatly in features. Some simply show the book pages on the screen, and the user "turns pages" with mouse clicks or keystrokes. These programs have little to recommend them over books, which are more portable and do not require hardware. For some students, they may increase motivation to read, but others find reading from the screen more of a strain and less satisfying than reading from a printed page. Many books on CD today take better advantage of the capabilities of computers by offering more interactive features.

 DIVERSITY

In general, the pages of talking books contain text and illustrations, just as are found in printed books, but many offer the reader a variety of options. Some allow the reader to choose to have the story read in a different language, a definite plus for some English-language learners who have home languages other than English. Most allow the students to read the story independently or have the computer read it aloud. Words or phrases can be highlighted in some books as they are read. This can help to build word recognition.

STANDARDS/ ASSESSMENTS ☑

With some of the books, students can click on words to get pronunciations, meanings, syllable divisions and more detailed explanations. Sometimes the words that students click on for more information are saved in recall lists that the teacher can check. In addition, if readers click on objects in the pictures, some of the picture elements may become animated and sometimes even produce sound effects. Students can often click on the pictures to see labels and hear pronunciations and meanings. This interactivity makes the books highly motivational, but students may be distracted from actual reading by some of the special effects (Labbo, 2000; Lefever-Davis and Pearman, 2005).

LeapFrog School has produced a pocket-sized handheld device called the Tag School Reader, which is part of the Tag School Reading System designed to be used with Tag School Reading System books. This reader allows the user to participate in skill-building activities (Nagel, 2008).

Some readers use the digital pronunciations of single words to confirm the accuracy of their reading, and some try to decode the words before clicking for help. In addition, some readers have the computer read lines first and use this reading as a model to follow as they read the lines, helping them develop good intonation and fluency. Used in this manner, e-books can provide needed scaffolding for many readers (Rhodes and Milby, 2007).

More proficient readers may be irritated by some of the automatic animations and the time that it takes for pages to turn. Having them answer a question on paper after reading each page may help to diminish this reaction. Some readers may become more like spectators than readers when they are fascinated by clicking on all of the links in the graphics and pay more attention to this activity than to reading the text. The digital pronunciations also can allow some students to cease to use their decoding skills, simply relying on the computer to prompt them (Lefever-Davis and Pearman, 2005).

Activity guides accompany some e-book CDs, to give teachers ideas for story preparation, story connections, and story extensions. Teachers should model the use of the books' features so that the students will get the maximum benefit from them. Students may first listen to the story and then, in subsequent readings, read along with it or perhaps echo-read it. Some students will probably need teachers, paraprofessionals, or student assistants to offer some help with the software, especially when it is initially used.

Labbo (2000) suggests many other approaches for using these materials, from word-level activities, such as selecting rhyming words, to metacognitive- and story-response activities, including comparing the digital version of the story to the book version. Teachers must use their own creativity and knowledge of their students to guide the use of e-books. To guide selection, Shamir and Korat (2006) offer a set of criteria for evaluating the developmental appropriateness of books intended for young children. These criteria include appropriateness of story structure, written register, font size, and amount of text on each screen. The criteria also address the degree of child control, the clarity of instructions, and other considerations for young children.

Use of the language experience approach can provide stories that can be transformed into e-books. Teachers can produce e-books that directly connect to their curricula by using a program, such as *PowerPoint*, to develop slide shows. On each slide, the teacher can insert student-generated language, import clip art or photos to illustrate the text (possibly ones taken by the students), add transitions from one slide to another, and add narration or other sound effects (Rhodes and Milby, 2007).

STRUGGLING READER/ INTERVENTION

TEACHING TIP

E-Books

English-language learners benefit from the pictures and animation that interactive books provide. According to Butler-Pascoe and Wiburg (2003), *Just Grandma and Me* and *Arthur's Teacher Trouble* from the Broderbund Living Books Series work well as reading materials for young English-language learners.

▶ Concept-Mapping Software

Some software is designed to help students organize their material for developing reports or projects. Concept-mapping software like *Inspiration* (for older students) is a popular and easy-to-use program for helping students organize their ideas in graphic or outline mode. The students can attach notes to the ideas, and these notes can be either displayed or hidden. Images that represent the ideas may also be inserted into the webs and labeled in graphic mode. *Kidspiration* offers mapping with words and graphic images and outlining for younger students.

Teachers of older elementary school students have used *Kidspiration* to map meaningful word parts (Gill, 2007). For example, if the word *biodiversity* appears in a class unit or a read-aloud story, teachers could model looking up the word parts and sharing their definitions. A discussion of how well the meanings fit into the context could ensue. Then the teachers could share other words with the word part *bio-*, such as *biology* and *biography*, and have their students first guess at the meanings from the word parts, next look up the parts and decide if they were correct, and then look up the complete words to check their conclusions. Finally, they can use *Kidspiration* to map these related words, with the root *bio-* and its definition in the center with clip art to represent life (perhaps a picture with a child looking at a flower), and the other words connected to it in a web with their definitions and appropriate clip art. Later, when they are reading material for their unit on pollution and encounter *biodegradable*, that word can be discussed and added to the web. The software allows easy additions to saved webs.

> **TEACHING TIP**
>
> ### Concept-Mapping Software
>
> You can download free trial versions of *Inspiration* and *Kidspiration* to evaluate for thirty days from the Inspiration Software website (Go directly to http://www.inspiration.com or link from the Student Website for this textbook). Trying software is the best way to know if it will work for your purposes.

▶ The Internet

The **Internet** is a "network of networks" encompassing a multitude of computers throughout the world. Each of thousands of server computers supplies different information or services. Research by the National School Boards Association showed that 50 percent of nine- to seventeen-year-olds who engage in online activities spend some time discussing homework and participating in creative activities, although they spend much time with social networking. Many teachers assign homework that involves Internet use, and some teachers use webpages for informational and instructional purposes (Nagel, 2007).

The **World Wide Web (WWW)** is part of the Internet. The web offers access to billions of pages (Thornburg, 2002). Hypermedia (discussed earlier in this chapter) is "the platform of the World Wide Web" (Wilhelm, 2000, p. 4).

Internet use causes teachers to look at literacy in new ways. The constructivist position that instruction should be organized around primary concepts is supported by the Internet, where a search may turn up hundreds of sites related to the topic of study, and the students can see how multifaceted the topic actually is. Current information on topics is also available, enhancing the students' ability to see the relevance of some studies. Inquiry learning is facilitated by the students' ability to do extensive searches to answer questions that they have generated (El-Hindi, 1998).

Locating Information on the Internet.   Choosing a link (a highlighted word, phrase, or icon) with a mouse click or keystroke can automatically connect a user to a related web location. Locating information on research topics in this way is much easier than having to know and enter each address for the locations of interest.

Students can also conduct keyword searches of the Internet, using special browsers (for example, *Microsoft Internet Explorer*) and search engines (for example, Yahooligans, Google, and Dogpile) to locate information to use for reports or unit studies. This information may be in the form of text, sound clips, video clips, and/or graphics.

Students will need instruction in the use of browsers and search engines. They will probably also need practice in generating keywords to use with the search engines. They must be taught that not all search engines look for information in the same ways. Students must also be warned that some search engines have commercial sites shown because the site owners have paid a fee to have sites included in search results (Henry, 2006). These sites are often listed on the first page of results, either as the first entries or on the side of the page. Some will be labeled as sponsored links, and others may not. An enjoyable way to practice searching for information on school topics is to participate in an Internet scavenger hunt for information specified by the teacher. "Seeing It in Practice: Locating Information on the Internet" shows how one pair of fifth graders conducted an electronic author's study.

> ### TEACHING TIP
>
> ### Choosing a Search Engine
>
> You and your students can find comparisons of and information about search engines at Internet sites such as Choose the Best Search for Your Information Needs (http://www.noodletools.com/debbie/literacies/information/5locate/adviceengine.html). Visit it directly or link from the Student Website for this textbook.

Facilitating Comprehension of Internet Material.   Teachers should not assume that students who can locate class information on the Internet can automatically understand the material that they find. Students need to be taught to approach the material as they would expository material in print sources, looking for organization of information and key concepts. They must also be cautioned to read critically—questioning the accuracy of the information, considering the reliability of the source, and looking for possible bias and misrepresentation of information. Information on the sites should be considered in light of students' background knowledge to help them decide if the information is likely to be incorrect. They must have the purposes of their searches firmly in mind and avoid going off on tangents presented in links embedded in material that is located. They must use skimming and scanning skills, making use of headings and highlighted words to help them determine the value of the site's information for their purpose.

> Students need to be shown how to document Internet information that they use in the reports. A free online citation service is Landmarks Citation Machine. It was developed and has been updated by David Warlick in 2006, and it shows citations in Modern Language Association and American Psychological Association formats. Link to it from the Student Website for this textbook or go directly to http://www.citationmachine.net.

Locating Information on the Internet

Michael and Juan had chosen to do a report on the author Jerry Spinelli for their author study unit. They decided to begin by checking the Internet.

"Let's use Dogpile to find some sites that will have information," Juan suggested. "I can search on his name. I use dogpile.com a lot."

"I use Google because it has a search window on my Internet Explorer homepage," Michael said. "I always get a lot of hits."

"Maybe so, but Dogpile searches lots of engines, including Google," Juan said.

"Really? Cool. You do that search, and I'll go check some of Spinelli's books out of the library," Michael replied.

"I'm on it," Juan said as he headed for the computer. When Michael got back, the boys compared notes.

"I was only able to check out five of his books. They have some others, but they are already checked out. Do you think this is enough?" Michael asked.

"Probably. Some of this stuff from the Internet will probably tell some about his other books. It will give us publisher and customer reviews, too. Here's what I did. I searched for 'Jerry Spinelli' and printed the first twenty of seventy-one hits. Dogpile reports the most relevant ones first. I scanned the page reading the blurbs, like

Ms. Landis said, and found that five of the hits were sponsored. That's another thing about Dogpile that I like. It tells you who paid to be listed. But Dogpile doesn't list them if they don't match your search. I looked at those five and saw that they were trying to sell the stuff about him, so I marked them out. I read the blurbs on the other ones and saw that another one seemed to just be lesson plans. Some looked like they were just about his books. Six seemed to have the kind of stuff we needed, so I thought we would split them up and check them out for information and then put our stuff together. Want to do that?"

"Yeah," Michael said. "We can do that tonight at home and put it together tomorrow and see if we need more."

Analysis of Scenario

Michael and Juan both had computers at home and had done searches before. Their teacher had also given them some good advice about how to decide which hits are most likely to be helpful without visiting the sites. That left them with a manageable number of sites to check first. The boys also appeared to have worked with partners before, and they divided the work to be done fairly evenly. They are likely to end up with a good report.

They need to understand the value of hypertext links in Internet material that may help them discover the meanings or pronunciations of unknown words. Pertinent material may be printed, bookmarked, or cut and pasted into a word-processing document in lieu of taking notes during initial reading.

Students may, however, need to overcome some of the challenges of using hypermedia, described earlier in the chapter, in order to develop the digital literacy needed to construct information from Internet sources. "Web-based texts are typically nonlinear, interactive, and inclusive of multiple media forms" (Coiro, 2003, p. 459). For example, on NASA's website for children, which is called StarChild: A Learning Center for Young Astronomers (http://starchild.gsfc.nasa.gov/docs/StarChild/StarChild.html), a hyperlink in a passage about one topic may lead to a definition of the linked word, to a new passage on a related topic, to activities for the topic, or to a page for an e-mail message to the webmaster. Students need to decide whether or not to use the available links in their quest for information. If students try these links, they must be able to navigate back to the original location. In addition, web-based texts have many interactive aspects. For example, students may be asked to post comments on the material electronically and read the postings of others.

Web-based texts frequently combine text with pictures, sounds, animations, and other representations. Sometimes video and audio clips must be deliberately downloaded before they are available for examination. Therefore, students are faced with accessing, as well as comprehending, these features.

Teachers can use a think-aloud strategy to help students master comprehension of online materials. The procedure should be modeled by the teachers first, preferably by using projection devices to make the computer screens visible to their students as the teachers move through the information. As the teachers locate specific information on the Internet, they detail their thinking processes orally as their students watch. After the information is found, the teachers explain how they make sense of it—using such aids as embedded links to word meanings, pictures, or further explanations on the Internet, as well as already taught comprehension strategies for reading text. Teachers may also model making mistakes, such as clicking on incorrect links, and recovering from their mistakes in order to get back on track. Students can then attempt searches, thinking aloud their reasons for the actions that they take. This process can allow teachers to see which strategies students are failing to use and to review those strategies before further searches are attempted. Students can share their strategies for reading online with one another, another step in passing responsibility for strategy implementation from the teachers to the students (Kymes, 2005).

Manzo, Manzo, and Albee (2002) suggest the use of the iREAP study system for improving reading, writing, and higher-order thinking. It is based on the REAP (Read, Encode, Annotate, Ponder) system for text responses. The *i* in iREAP indicates the addition of the use of the Internet. Students read material, put it into their own words, respond in writing to the material with a variety of types of annotations, and finally think about the material and share reactions with others. The nature of the approach makes it appropriate to use with students "across a broad spectrum of student abilities, needs, and cognitive styles" (Manzo et al., 2002, p. 45), such as are found in inclusion classrooms. Writing a variety of types of annotations makes it more likely that students will attain new insights.

Outstanding annotations may be posted on a webpage with the author cited and will thus become available to students from differing cultures and backgrounds. Annotations from a variety of students about a single selection may be stored electronically in order to form a collection for use by future students.

Teachers must show students how to read websites critically. Example 13.3 offers suggestions for evaluating websites.

The Read•Write•Think lesson plan "Wading Through the Web: Teaching Internet Research Strategies" makes use of a *PowerPoint* presentation to facilitate teaching web research skills. Find it at http://www.readwritethink.org or link from the Student Website for this book.

 STRUGGLING READER/ INTERVENTION

 DIVERSITY

EXAMPLE 13.3 Website Evaluation Questions

Evaluating Websites

When you are evaluating websites, you must consider the reliability of the sources of the material, the accuracy of the content, the clarity of the material presented, and the purposes of the sites. Ask yourself the following questions when judging a website:

1. Can you determine who has developed the site? (If not, you may not want to place undue confidence in its contents.) If so, is the developer a reliable source for the information that you are seeking? (A noted authority on the topic or an agency of the government would be considered reliable. Someone you have not heard of before may need to be investigated.)

2. Is there enough information given on the site developer that qualifications can be checked? (If not, be cautious.)

3. Are sources provided for information displayed on the site, so that the user can cross-check information? (If they are, this is a definite plus.)

4. Does any of the information conflict with reliable sources that you have consulted? (If some of the information is in question, all of it is suspect.)

5. Is the layout of the site busy and confusing, making information difficult to evaluate? (Disorganization, particularly, is a bad sign.)

6. Is site navigation easy? (Sloppy navigational methods sometimes indicate a lack of attention to detail.)

7. Is the presented material grammatically correct, and is it free from errors in spelling and mechanics? (If it is not, the clarity is badly affected.)

8. Is the site free of advertising? (If not, look for possible bias of information presented, based on the advertising present.)

9. If currency of information is important, can you tell when the page was developed and last updated? (If not, be careful in accepting the information. If currency is not a factor—for example, for a Civil War site on which the material is not likely to become dated—this will not be a major concern.)

Source: Betty D. Roe, "Using Technology for Content Area Literacy," in *Linking Literacy and Technology: A Guide for K–8 Classrooms*, edited by Shelley B. Wepner, William J. Valmont, and Richard Thurlow (Newark, Del.: International Reading Association, 2000), 133–155.

Adapting to the Challenges of Internet Use.   Learning to learn is central to acquiring new literacy skills in our rapidly changing technological environment. Students must learn new skills required by the new technologies of literacy. These technologies are continually emerging and will continue to require new skills in the future (Leu, 2002; Castek, Bevans-Mangelson, and Goldstone, 2006). To advance use of new Internet literacy skills, teachers may use Internet Workshop, which involves locating and bookmarking an Internet site related to a unit of study, designing an activity that requires students to use the site to reach unit goals (or letting advanced computer users develop their own inquiry projects), having students carry out the activity, and arranging for students to share results and reactions with classmates in a workshop session. This procedure is appropriate for all grade levels (Leu, 2002; Leu, Castek, et al., 2004). Leu (2002) and a classroom teacher developed an Internet Workshop on the *Titanic* that is located at http://sp.uconn.edu/~djleu/titanic.html.

Educators have a realistic concern about finding developmentally appropriate sites for their students. Publications such as *The Reading Teacher* often offer excellent suggestions for teachers. One site that is useful for kindergarten students learning their alphabet and letter sounds is Starfall.com (http://www.starfall.com/n/level-k/index/play.htm?f) (Labbo, 2006). Educational publications also may suggest books for students for which there are complementary titles. For example, the site entitled The Artist's Toolkit (http://www.artsconnected.org/toolkit) is a good site to visit when Beaumont's *I Ain't Gonna Paint No More!* is read, and Markle's *A Mother's*

 LITERATURE

Second-grade students look at children's Internet safety program on library computers.
© Bob Daemmrich/The Image Works

Internet Research for Making Books

Read several informational alphabet books to your class. (See Chapter 12 to find authors of thematic alphabet books.) Discuss the characteristics of these alphabet books.

Next, choose a topic, such as "Mammals," that you are studying in a particular content area. Discuss what has already been discovered about this topic.

Then divide the class into small groups, assigning one or more letters to each group. Let group members search the Internet for mammals that would fit the assigned letters. Have each group choose, from the mammals that they locate, the ones to use for their book pages. Then have them write and print book pages for their assigned letters, using desktop-publishing software or word-processing software. Put the pages together to form a class book. Print multiple copies to use in the classroom, to share with other classes, and to send home to promote home-school communication. Finally, read the book to the class and let the group members responsible for each page tell about their search strategies.

Other online tools may be helpful to students. In the Read•Write•Think lesson plan "Dear Librarian: Writing a Persuasive Letter," Lisa Fink has her students use online materials, such as a Persuasion Map, a Letter Generator, and possibly a Timeline Tool, that are available through links in the lesson plan. View the lesson at http://www.readwritethink.org or link from the Student Website for this book.

Journey has a natural tie-in with both the movie *March of the Penguins* and the website connected with that movie (http://wip.warnerbros.com/marchofthepenguins) (Livingston and Kurkjian, 2006). When students are reading poetry books, teachers may ask them to write poetry of their own. For work with rhyming poetry, they may want to visit Write Express (http://www.rhymer.com) for ideas (Kara-Soteriou, Zawilinski, and Henry, 2007). Another way to link books with use of the Internet is described in "Putting It into Practice: Internet Research for Making Books."

When students conduct Internet research, teachers and students face some other challenges. One problem with letting students use the Internet for research is that the accuracy of material that is posted to electronic bulletin boards or discussion groups or placed on webpages is not monitored. Anyone can publish material on the Internet, and much inaccurate information appears there, along with the useful material. Students should be encouraged to cross-check information that they find on the Internet in printed reference books, whenever possible. They need to see if the material is documented and to treat both undocumented and anonymous material as questionable. Sites supported by government agencies, educational institutions, and professional organizations are generally the most reliable for use in developing curricula (Roe, 2000).

Teachers may want to show students sites that contain incorrect information, such as the Pacific Northwest Tree Octopus site (http://www.zapatopi.net/treeoctopus.html), a site about an animal that is nonexistent (Henry, 2006), so that they will be more aware of the need for evaluation.

Another problem with letting students use the Internet for research purposes is that many sites

TEACHING TIP

Fitting Websites into Your Curriculum

You may want to supply your students with a list of reliable sites that contain information related to the current topic of study and use this material for class assignments. The material can be made to fit your specific course needs and your group of students. See the Student Website for this textbook for a list of reliable websites for class use.

A hazard of this practice, however, is that many sites are not stable. The World Wide Web is changing daily, and a site that you find today may not be there tomorrow. This situation can be frustrating for searchers. Even sites provided in this and other books may change. Embedded links within sites are particularly prone to change. Remember to update your lists of recommended sites frequently.

contain material that is not appropriate for them to read. To avoid having students access undesirable sites, either accidentally or intentionally, many schools have installed filter software. Visit the Public Library Association website (http://www.pla.org/ala/pla/plapubs/technotes/internetfiltering.cfm) for information about several filtering products. Forbes (2004) suggests using bookmarking to facilitate the use of the Internet in K–8 classrooms. She uses iKeepBookmarks.com (http://www.iKeepBookmarks.com) to bookmark sites that she has chosen to use in instruction. It allows her to present students with only appropriate links, thereby increasing the safety of using the Internet in the classroom. She says it only takes ten seconds to bookmark each site, and she uses it "to teach students how to use the mouse, keyboard, and browser toolbars" (Forbes, 2004, p. 150). She can use icons to give color and visual clues and can annotate each site. The bookmarks help students use computer time more efficiently. This technique is particularly good for young students and students with special needs. English-language learners also should benefit. Although Forbes acknowledges that there are other bookmarking services on the Internet—including Backflip (http://www.backflip.com), Blink (http://www.blinkpro.com), and MyBookmarks (http://www.mybookmarks.com)—she finds that iKeepBookmarks.com works best for her purposes.

 DIVERSITY

TrackStar (http://trackstar.4teachers.org/) is a site that allows teachers to organize and annotate website links. Existing tracks on TrackStar include links to sites that contain the full texts of some children's literature selections. This availability could make possible class activities that would ordinarily require multiple copies of the texts. The selections available are generally classics in the public domain, so they can be used without violating copyright laws.

WebQuests.

WebQuests are inquiry projects that also make use of links to online resources. They can be used to facilitate thematic interdisciplinary teaching. The WebQuest model was developed by Bernie Dodge. Teachers can create WebQuests if they know how to create a document with hyperlinks in Word, Powerpoint, or some similar software. There are online authoring systems that support the development of WebQuests. Some, like Filamentality, InstantWebquest, and PHP Webquest, are free. Others such as QuestGarden (developed by Dodge) and TeacherWeb (especially good for younger students) are available for a small fee (Dodge, 2007).

WebQuests have well-defined purposes and lead students to try out new roles, such as scientist, as they solve realistic problems and conduct research. WebQuests have introductions, tasks, resource lists, process descriptions, evaluation rubrics, and conclusions. Although WebQuests are primarily dependent on web resources, books and other media may be used in addition to the web. WebQuests can encourage multiple ways of representing information (writing, speaking, and visually representing using multiple media). They give students the opportunity to develop multiple perspectives, as they take on the roles of different people, such as consumers, merchants, manufacturers, and so on. In effective WebQuests, students are not just visiting a series of websites or summarizing the material from several websites. Instead, they are collecting and evaluating information, making connections between concepts, and integrating information from various sources (Dodge, 2007; Ikpeze and Boyd, 2007; Coiro, 2003).

Links to many WebQuests can be found at http://www.webquest.org/index .php. A rubric for evaluating WebQuests is found at http://webquest.sdsu .edu/webquestrubric.html.

In one fifth grade, students focused on environmental protection in a WebQuest that their teachers had modified from an existing one to fit the class's purposes. They visited and evaluated various websites, some of which were interactive; listened to, read, and wrote poems about environmental protection; role-played; discussed findings; wrote and performed a reader's theater script; and wrote reports. The teachers provided minilessons and scaffolding throughout the process. Students learned to use Internet resources by navigating, searching, and retrieving information while reading hypertext and multimedia material (Ikpeze and Boyd, 2007).

Developing Positive Dispositions Toward Internet Use.   Developing positive dispositions (tendencies to approach a subject with a particular mindset) toward Internet use through enjoyable and meaningful experiences online is important to turning students into effective learners with this medium. Students are more likely to develop positive dispositions toward Internet use if they have many experiences with it and instruction in its use because students avoid tasks that they have not mastered (Castek et al., 2006).

Enjoyable experiences can include accessing online read-alouds, such as the ones found at BookPALS Storyline (http://www.storylineonline.net), or participating in interactive read-along stories, such as the ones found at TumbleBook Library (http://www.tumblebooks.com), Mythic Journeys (http://www.mythicjourneys.org/ bigmyth/), and RIF Reading Planet (http://www.rif.org/readingplanet/content/ read_aloud_stories.mspx). At the International Children's Digital Library site (http:// www.icdlbooks.org), free digital texts are available in different languages.

DIVERSITY

STRUGGLING READER/ INTERVENTION

There are e-books that can be downloaded from the Internet and read on wireless handheld devices. Researchers from Ball State, led by Richard Bellaver, initiated a multi-year study designed to test this technique as a motivational tool for third and fourth graders. They discovered that the students, including reluctant readers, were more enthusiastic about reading with the e-books than with regular books (Devaney, 2007).

Time for Reflection

Some people think that the motivational effect of using technology—particularly computers—will decline because of regular opportunities for such use. Others think the varied possibilities for using technological tools—especially computers—provide a constant stream of fresh motivation for using technology.

What do *you* think, and why?

▸ Electronic Communications

There are a number of types of electronic communications that are useful for literacy instruction. E-mail (electronic mail), electronic mailing lists (listservs), electronic bulletin boards and discussion groups, podcasts, and videoconferencing all have possible applications.

E-Mail.   Writing can be exchanged among classrooms when **e-mail (electronic mail)** systems are available. Use of such experiences has resulted in more lengthy writing and improved attitudes toward and performance in reading and writing for elementary and middle school students (Moore, 1991).

LITERATURE

An Internet site designed to help children discuss literature with other children is Book Raps at http://www.oz-teachernet.edu.au/projects/br (oz-Teachernet, 2007). Students may also e-mail experts in different subjects about their areas of specialization to obtain information needed for study topics. In a number of programs, college classes and public school students have had e-mail exchanges about books (Roe and

Conversations About Literature

During each of two semesters, students from Livingston Middle School, a rural public school, were paired with teacher education students enrolled in Betty Roe's reading and language arts methods classes at Tennessee Technological University to discuss literature selections that both groups were reading. In the fall semester, both groups read *Bridge to Terabithia*, and in the spring semester both groups read *Tuck Everlasting*. The books were read on a predetermined schedule, and the partners communicated about their reading each week for seven weeks. During the fall semester, the university students also posted comments about literary features of the book to a newsgroup that was limited to the university students in the project. After both groups viewed a videotape of the book that had been read, they communicated with partners by e-mail, comparing and contrasting the book and the video. (See "Seeing It in Practice: Using Video Recordings" (page 514) for more information about this facet of the project.) The middle school students also prepared a multimedia presentation about each book at the conclusion of the reading. (See "Seeing It in Practice: Multimedia Presentations" (page 487) for more information on this part of the program.)

Evaluations of the program by public school and university teachers and students were positive. The public school teachers felt that receiving e-mail motivated their students and enhanced the students' self-esteem. They felt that interacting with college students gave their students a sense of status and of doing high-level work. Some of the middle school students had never read a novel before, but they read these books in order to communicate with their partners. Of course, they got additional reading practice when they read the e-mail correspondence from their partners in order to respond. These students had rarely done much writing, and the teachers saw the writing skills of many increase during the project. The university students had been encouraged to model good writing for their partners in their e-mail exchanges, and most did. Some partners continued to correspond after the semesters had ended. The e-mail communications reflected thinking on all levels of Bloom's taxonomy, and the university students were sometimes surprised at the higher-order thinking displayed by their partners.

The university students also gave the project high evaluations. One wrote, "This particular project not only introduced students to a good piece of literature; it introduced them to interactive technology, which is a skill that will be useful and probably necessary to their futures. It provided feedback that was fun and involving. I would definitely use this technique again" (Roe and Smith, 1997, p. 372).

Smith, 1997; Sullivan, 1998; McKeon, 1999; Niday and Campbell, 2000; Wade and Fauske, 2004; Teale and Gambrell, 2007), instruction, or general conversation. Stivers (1996) paired college methods students with middle school students with special needs, for e-mail conversation and writing instruction. The public school students responded well, and the college students showed enhanced self-esteem as a result of the program. One e-mail project is described in "Seeing It in Practice: Conversations About Literature" (Roe and Smith, 1997).

Another application of e-mail exchanges about books is part of an approach called In2Books (I2B), developed by Nina Zolt (2005) to help historically underachieving students in urban areas. With this approach, teachers present students with grade-level books in five different genres. Teachers who tried I2B in a study by Teale and Gambrell (2007) had the grade-level books, related read-aloud books, and a curriculum guide that helped them plan units that focused on the individual books and genres.

DIVERSITY   STRUGGLING READER/ INTERVENTION

The students in I2B classrooms read the books several times, each time for a different purpose. Students were given adult pen pals from their area, who read the same books and used ideas from a related website to help them compose letters to students about the books, making connections to themselves, the world, and other books. They were also encouraged to ask open-ended questions about the books. They submitted their letters electronically, sometimes enhancing them with graphics. Students received hard copies of the letters, read them, and composed answering letters. The students in second- through fifth-grade classes in the District of Columbia Public Schools in which the I2B method was used "outperformed students in comparison classrooms on a nationally normed, standardized assessment of reading achievement" (Teale and Gambrell, 2007, p. 731).

STANDARDS/ ASSESSMENTS

E-mail dialogues (sometimes referred to as computer-mediated discussions) can take place between students from different schools, states, or countries. Students can discuss the locales in which they live, customs in their countries, current events, topics being studied in school, and literature they are reading. Gambrell (2004) points out, "Computer-mediated discussions differ significantly from teacher-led and peer-led discussions because they are print based, have permanence, and take more time to produce" (p. 212). Because all students can exchange ideas with all other students, marginalized students may be more empowered by these discussions (Gambrell, 2004).

DIVERSITY

One researcher took advantage of the EPals website (http://www.epals.com) to match fourth-grade students from New England classrooms with fourth-grade classrooms in Australia for e-mail exchanges on general topics. The students learned about differences in language usage, culture, animals, and other areas of interest between the two countries. Interviews showed that general-education students, second-language learners, and special-needs students all liked writing to real people and took care in conversing with their partners through e-mail (Charron, 2007).

DIVERSITY

Electronic Mailing Lists.   **Electronic mailing lists** distribute messages to a group of readers who have "subscribed" to the list because of an interest in the topic. All "subscribers" receive all messages sent to the list until they "unsubscribe." The flow of mail to subscribers on these mailing lists is often exceedingly heavy, and the mail must be read and deleted frequently (usually every day).

A class may want to subscribe to a mailing list that is related to a topic of study while that study is going on and then cancel the subscription after the topic is covered in class. Jayne Everitt, for example, wanted her first graders to use the Internet to learn about effects of severe weather. She asked subscribers to the Kidsphere mailing list to send personal accounts of such effects. Students read the responses and charted the locations of the correspondents (Serim and Koch, 1996). Teachers should be careful to monitor the contents of mailing list communications, however, because some outside participants may send inappropriate comments and use objectionable language.

Electronic Bulletin Boards and Discussion Groups.   **Electronic bulletin boards** and **electronic discussion groups** differ from electronic mailing lists in that messages are posted to a network location, and readers who are interested in the topic can read the messages electronically by going to the Internet address. These messages may be posted and read by people from all over the world, and readers can also post to discussion groups for the entire world to see. Once again, teachers should monitor the content of bulletin boards and discussion groups that students in class access, because inappropriate material may be posted. In addition, teachers should monitor their students' posts. Some schools set up limited-access bulletin boards and discussion groups to meet the needs of students who are studying a topic. These groups are less risky to use with elementary school students.

A student in one fifth-grade class used his literacy center time to go to a virtual book club website where students worldwide discuss books. He went to the site's discussion board and read the new posts on *Harry Potter and the Half-Blood Prince*. Then he posted his reactions to the book, remembering that he was writing for people across the globe. His teacher monitored his use of the discussion board. His teacher views such uses of the Internet as building motivation to read, write, and use important literacy skills, such as critical thinking (Castek et al., 2006). LITERATURE

Electronic threaded discussions can take place through the bulletin boards or discussion groups. *Threads* are chains of postings on single topics (Grisham and Wolsey, 2006). One advantage of using threaded discussions is that participants can post and respond at different times, giving the responder a chance to compose a post after having time to give consideration to the topic and the wording. These discussions also allow participants to post and respond in detail, without interruption, and they can be limited to a particular class.

Grisham and Wolsey (2006) tried using these online discussions for literature discussions, a technique suggested by Bintz and Shelton (2004), much as others had used e-mail. The middle school students read Deborah Ellis's *The Breadwinner*, a book about an Afghan girl faced with living under the Taliban's rule, using both electronic threaded discussions, paper journals, and face-to-face discussions. LITERATURE

The teachers monitored the online discussions and modeled responses that were appropriate, as well as *netiquette*, or online etiquette. The researchers discovered that teacher participation in the discussions increased the complexity of their students' responses.

The researchers perceived the face-to-face discussions to be less thoughtful and more routine turn-taking than were the electronic discussions, but after time the face-to-face discussions became less rigid as students made reference to the online posts. Part of the time, the students also kept paper journals, which the researchers found to result in lower-quality responses than those in the online discussions (Grisham and Wolsey, 2006).

SEEING IT IN PRACTICE ◄ ■ ►

Video Case
View the Video Case "Middle School Reading Instruction: Integrating Technology" and the bonus video "Mr. Lawrence Sets Up the Lesson." Also examine the "Classroom Artifacts." In your journal, write your evaluation of how effective use of the online forum was with this lesson. Can you see applications for this technique in your own classes? Did Mr. Lawrence bring any other types of technology into his lesson? If so, how did he do this?

Podcasts. "A **podcast** is essentially an audiofile on the Internet, like a radio program" (Deubel, 2007, n.p.) that can be listened to with your computer or downloaded to a device that can play MP3 files. Podcasts are not interactive. Tags or keywords are used in many podcasts to make searching for content of interest easier. "When you subscribe to a tag ... you automatically receive new podcasts that contain the tag of interest. Thus, content finds you, not the other way around" (Deubel, 2007, n.p.). Fairly inexpensive digital audio recorders are available to move audio clips to the computer for school multimedia projects or to create "radio broadcasts" on the Internet. This approach can also be used for audio blogging or to add audio commentary to a class website (Grabe and Grabe, 2007).

Some elementary and middle school students have developed podcasts, an activity that can cause them to use higher-order thinking skills, writing skills, and the ability to communicate orally, as well as build motivation to participate in the learning activities. In a Nebraska elementary school, students produced a podcast series for kids, including one podcast developed by third graders about the ear and sound. Fifth graders in a California elementary school have produced podcasts about the United States, weather, the human body, the solar system, and other topics. Middle school students in Wisconsin "write storyboards, conference about the content, edit, perform, analyze the raw footage" (Deubel, 2007, n.p.) and perform other learning tasks as they develop podcasts.

STANDARDS/ ASSESSMENTS ☑

Dlott (2007) says that teachers could use a think-aloud strategy to teach the skills needed to develop podcasts before students are asked to create them. Then they should show the students the rubric that will be used to evaluate their products.

Videoconferencing.   At present, most classrooms do not have the equipment needed for **videoconferencing,** but this is an application for literacy instruction that may increase. In videoconferences, individuals hold conferences over the Internet with others whom they can see on their computer monitors and hear

LITERATURE 📖

through their speakers. The advantages of this method for bringing such people as authors of children's books, scientists, and historians into contact with elementary school students are obvious. Students could be responsible for researching the person, literature, or topic of conversation ahead of time, writing interview questions, conducting a controlled interview, taking notes on the discussion, and writing reports on the results—all valid literacy activities. This type of interaction could also take place between two groups of elementary students from different parts of the world (Kauchak and Eggen, 2008).

Virtual school courses, which gained popularity for secondary schools, are now becoming available for elementary and middle schools as well (Galley, 2004). The programs may provide instruction from specialists in some areas of the curriculum, but they should not be relied on excessively because lack of social interaction may limit effectiveness (Maeroff, 2003; Monke, 2005/2006).

▸ Developing Web Material

In many classrooms, teachers encourage students to develop actual websites of various types. This activity helps students develop writing and visually representing skills.

Homepages.   Teachers may want to guide their classes in developing their own web homepages. This is a common practice, and students have posted items such as creative writing, research reports, and the results of scientific experiments. Students in all grade levels find it motivational to have their work published on the Internet. Class newspapers or magazines may also be published on these webpages. It is possible to include text, graphics, photographs, and animations. Because webpages can be accessed from all over the world, the motivation for accuracy and clarity of information presented is great. Students may therefore be more inclined to revise and edit material.

Blogs.   Recently, blogs have proliferated on the Internet. A **blog** is a web log, or web-based journal that allows the author to add audio or video clips and links to other websites. It can invite comments from readers. Students do not need much technical skill to create a blog. It is easier to create a blog than to create a website, so students have easier access to an online medium (Littrell, 2005). Teachers may want to have their students post to a class blog. It is best if students use password-protected blogs. Teachers will have to forbid the posting of personal data if the blog is public. Another option that may be used is having a school host its own blog, allowing greater control of the reading and posting of material (Grabe and Grabe, 2007). "Seeing It in Practice: Use of Blogs" shows how blogs were used with one group of middle school girls.

Julia Siporin created a class blog for her third graders with a character, Jefferson Bear, as host. Her students blog back to Jefferson when he writes to them asking about class activities and content. The teacher provides websites that the students can check for information about Jefferson's questions. The students read the sites to obtain information for their answers (Boling, 2008).

Betty Collum has a class blog that allows her students to participate in online literature discussions. Her fourth graders worked in groups, reading short literature pieces in literature circles (see Chapters 9 and 11). Then each one added a comment about something that stood out in the selection and a question that it elicited. These blogged comments were shared with students who lived in a distant city (Boling, 2008).

Anne Davis, who was a classroom teacher for a long time and now is an instructional technology specialist, says that she believes that blogs can be used in school to help students become better thinkers and writers. However, she cautions that teachers must talk to the students about the postings to their blogs to make this approach effective ("Best of Blogs," 2005).

Wikis.   **Wikis** are websites that let users edit content, generally—but not always—without requiring registration. They do not require the use of HTML, making them accessible to the general public. Because anyone can add, remove, or change information, there is the problem that wiki content may be inaccurate, either intentionally or unintentionally.

The additions or changes to wikis are generally not reviewed before they appear on the website. However, most wikis are easy to edit to correct misinformation. Users often can consult pages that list recent changes or revision histories, so that it is

Free blog-hosting services are available at sites such as http://www.blogger.com, but teachers will have to be aware that commercial sites may not allow the viewers to limit access, and they may display ads.

 LITERATURE

Using Blogs

Annette Littrell (2005) compared the use of blogs and traditional literature response journals by a group of middle school girls. She started by interviewing the girls about their existing uses of technology and paper-and-pen journaling.

The girls read two books by Joan Bauer during an eight-week period. The students changed their response method from traditional journaling to blogging, or vice versa, every two weeks. Mrs. Littrell monitored the frequency with which they made entries and the average length of the entries with each procedure.

The girls were interviewed again at the end of the eight weeks. Mrs. Littrell asked them to elaborate on their journaling activities. Ninety percent of the girls preferred using a blog to using a traditional journal. Some indicated that the blog was more current, easy, and fun. They enjoyed personalizing their blogs and publishing their work for an audience.

Mrs. Littrell found that use of blogs motivated the girls to do more total writing: they wrote 50 percent more often and wrote 30 percent longer entries in the blogs than in the paper-and-pencil journals. This increase of output alone may make the blog approach attractive to teachers.

easy to restore previous text when incorrect information has been added or valid information has been removed. Some wikis are monitored for quality; and some are private, password-protected sites.

Some wikis have a full-text search feature; most others have at least a title search. A widely used wiki is Wikipedia, an online encyclopedia (Wikipedia, 2006). Students need to understand how such an encyclopedia differs from a commercially produced version that cannot be changed by the users.

▶ Interactive Internet Projects

There are many interactive Internet projects that enable students to work with other students from around the United States and even worldwide. These projects can be wonderful learning experiences.

DIVERSITY

Patti Weeg, a Title I technology integration professional developer, reported on global projects in Maryland that used handheld computers (http://www.globalclassroom .org/new.html). Students in two fifth-grade classes were involved. Ms. Sibanda's class sent letters to students in American Samoa on these computers. Miss Hastings' class wrote to students in South Africa and planned to follow that by using Skype for voice communication with their new friends (Weeg, 2006). Skype (http://www.skype .com) is a commercial telephone-over-Internet service.

Internet projects may involve student-to-student or class-to-class interaction. They may involve collection of data for a content-area study or simply exchanging information about different people and places in the world. A good place to go to check out such projects is http://www.schoolworld.asn.au/projects, but there are a variety of other sites that can be used.

Kidlink at http://www.kidlink.org is a site for an organization focused on enhancing global communication among children up through secondary school. There are even Internet sites where young writers can find resources to expand their writing abilities, such as http://www.inkspot.com/young.

Kevin Hodgson, a sixth-grade writing teacher, developed a Youth Radio blog that is the center for an Internet project that encourages students to connect with news stories about their communities, their school studies, and their interests. Classes worldwide have joined his blog, some reporting results of other interactive Internet projects. Classes can prepare podcasts and send them to him to post on the blog, along with an introductory bit of text. Users can click on the audio icons to hear the podcasts.

In Betty Collum's fifth-grade creative writing class, students read novels in literature circles and then wrote poems related to the selections, revising them using an online collaborative writing site (Google Doc at http://www.google.com/google-d-s/intl/en/tour1.html). Students audio-recorded themselves reading their poems, and the teacher sent the audio files to the Youth Radio blog with accompanying text to be posted on the Youth Radio blog. Sometimes a picture is posted on the blog to accompany the audiocast (Boling, 2008).

Another Internet project included a fifth-grade class and a fourth- and fifth-grade combination class in California, working with two online reading-comprehension researchers. Their project was designed to meet language arts and social studies standards, while engaging the students in using online sources and creating a wiki. The students all worked together to research U.S. national parks and create a wiki page about each one. Not only did collaboration occur between classrooms, but also within each class. At least one struggling reader in this project had the Internet know-how to help others do such things as post pictures on the wiki, building his self-esteem and engagement with the literacy skills involved (Castek, Zawilinski, Barton, and Nierlich, 2008).

STANDARDS/ASSESSMENTS

STRUGGLING READER/INTERVENTION

▶ Computer-Assisted Instruction

Computer-assisted instruction (CAI) refers to use of computers to promote learning. Many of the criticisms that have been leveled against CAI really have targeted low-quality programs. CAI can be useful to teachers in providing simulations of real-life situations in order to present new information, promote student attention, and activate schemata (Forcier and Descy, 2008).

Computer software is available for developing many different literacy skills, including alphabet knowledge (*The Alphabet*), phonemic awareness (*Leap into Phonics*), and grammar (*Focus on Grammar Series*). These are all areas of special need for English-language learners (Butler-Pascoe and Wiburg, 2003). Other software is good to work on problem solving (*Arthur's 1st Grade* or *Yoda's Challenge*) and can be used, not only at the target grade level, but also adapted and used at higher grade levels for students with special needs. Organizational software, such as *Inspiration* and *Kidspiration*, can also help with problem-solving tasks (Forcier and Descy, 2008). CAI is also available on some Internet sites.

The heart of a CAI system is the software, the programs that actually provide the instruction or practice. CAI programs can vary widely in quality. To be instructionally sound, the program should present accurate information in a reasonable sequence with an appropriate amount of student interaction. It should not reward

To locate some ongoing and future collaborative projects with schools in the United States and other countries, go to Global SchoolNet Foundation at http://www.globalschoolnet.org/gsnprojects/. Projects for different age groups are added periodically (for example, "Online Book Club" for ages 9–13; "U.S. Postcard Exchange" for ages 5–15; "A Webkinz Exchange!!" for ages 5–13; "MySchool Project Center" for ages 5–14; "Seasonal Changes Through Our Eyes and Yours" for ages 7–10; "Online Literature Circles" for grades 3–12; and "Postcard Geography" for ages 5–19).

DIVERSITY

STRUGGLING READER/INTERVENTION

incorrect answers with clever messages or graphics, while offering bland messages of approval for correct answers. It should be easy to use, providing clear instructions about what to do (1) to advance material on the screen, (2) to respond to questions, and (3) to receive help when needed. Erroneous keystrokes should not "dump" a student out of the program; the program should allow him or her to recover in a clear and easy way.

The four most common types of CAI are drill-and-practice programs, tutorial programs, simulation programs, and educational game programs. Most programs include elements of more than one category of program, although each one may fit primarily in one of the categories (Forcier and Descy, 2008). CAI programs often have a component that takes care of such tasks as record keeping, diagnosis, and prescription of individualized assignments. Such a component is a computer-managed system, and many packages of instructional materials contain both an instructional and a management component.

Drill-and-Practice Programs.   These programs consist of practice lessons on skills that students have previously been taught (Kauchak and Eggen, 2008). They are the simplest types of computer applications and the ones most commonly found in classrooms. They generally focus on increasing retention of factual information. Some drill-and-practice programs allow students more than one opportunity to respond to an item before telling them the correct answer.

Practice is important for developing accuracy in, and automaticity of, reading skills. Computer drill-and-practice programs help students do this by providing repetition without using the teacher's instructional time. When the goal is developing accuracy, the computer can be used to present a few exercises accompanied by clear, immediate feedback, particularly for incorrect answers. After students have attained accuracy, the teacher can have them practice using computer programs with larger numbers of exercises, sometimes emphasizing speed, that are accompanied by less extensive feedback. Some drill-and-practice programs recirculate missed items for further practice, without requiring the teacher to plan or execute such repetition. These programs can take the place of worksheets, which are designed for the same purpose but lack the motivational advantage or interactive nature of computer use and the capability to give immediate reinforcement or planned repetition. Computer drills can also provide such things as graphics, animations, and sound that increase the appeal of the activities.

Tutorial Programs.   With these programs, the computer actually presents instruction in a programmed sequence of small, sequential steps and then follows it with practice activities. These programs also respond to student errors with immediate feedback. Some provide this instruction in the same sequence to all users, simply allowing different students to choose to move through the material at different rates. Branching programs, which are more versatile, can provide remedial instructional sequences when incorrect answers are given. Depending on the correct and incorrect responses that a student makes as the program progresses, he or she may be branched to a remedial sequence of instruction, taken back through the initial instruction, directed through the typical sequence for the instruction, or skipped ahead in the program to avoid unnecessary practice. With some programs, students can also request review, remedial help, or additional practice. Obviously, these branching programs allow for more individualization (Roblyer, 2006).

Some programs are self-paced on a page-by-page basis. Other programs are designed to allow the student to choose a pace for the entire program when the study session starts, and the computer maintains this pace. Starfall (http://www.starfall .com) is a website that offers tutorials in basic reading skills for young children. It is self-paced on a page-by-page basis. The audio, video, and animations make using the tutorials fun for children. It does use a synthetic phonics presentation initially (see Chapter 5), but it immediately presents the sounds in word, phrase, and sentence contexts. Tutorial programs are available at a number of difficulty levels, and some provide a wide range of choices of difficulty level in one package, making them more versatile tools in a diverse classroom. They are particularly helpful for offering instruction to students who are far above or far below the instructional levels of the others in the class. They also can offer makeup instruction for students who have missed that instruction in class, while leaving the teacher free for other tasks (Kauchak and Eggen, 2008; Forcier and Descy, 2008).

 **STRUGGLING READER/ INTERVENTION**

A first-grade teacher, Lisa Hoover, used HyperStudio to develop an interactive multimedia tutorial program on making change for her mathematics class. This tutorial offers scenarios that give students opportunities for practice in making change. The students get continual help as they work to master the skill (Kauchak and Eggen, 2008).

Simulation Programs.   These programs set up situations that simulate real-life activities, such as running a business or traveling west in a wagon train, that cannot be offered in other ways in the curriculum because of limited time, changed conditions (when the past is being simulated), or limited financial and physical resources. They can reinforce material that the teacher has presented or provide a vehicle for discovery learning. Educational simulations such as *The Oregon Trail* and *SimCity* have been used for this purpose for many years. The *SimCity* program, for example, involves planning and record keeping. Now there are whole series of *SimCity*-related games and many versions of *The Oregon Trail* game. The popular *Where in the World Is Carmen Sandiego* program requires students to act as detectives and apprehend a criminal by following geographic clues. This program spawned a whole series of Carmen Sandiego programs and a television series (Grabe and Grabe, 2007; Forcier and Descy, 2008).

Simulation programs can act as virtual field trips (Kauchak and Eggen, 2008). These programs give students the opportunity to use higher-order thinking skills. Students use interpretive and critical reading skills as they examine the current situation, consider their options, and make decisions about how to proceed. The computer responds to students' decisions and presents different outcomes, depending on these decisions. This practice in evaluating options and drawing conclusions often seems more like play than study to students.

Virtual reality programs immerse the user in an environment that appears to be real (Forcier and Descy, 2008). Students can use special equipment, such as goggles and gloves, that allow them to interact with the environment as if they were actually there.

Some videodisc-based simulations present videos of people facing real-world problems that they must solve. After viewing the videos, students can break into groups, identify the problem, determine what information is relevant for solving it, and work out solutions, which can then be presented to the class, analyzed, and discussed (Kauchak and Eggen, 2008). Using these programs requires teacher monitoring, scaffolding, and encouragement.

Simulation programs are often time consuming to use, but if the programs' status can be saved and the programs can be re-entered from the same place in a later session, students will be likely to stay with them until a conclusion is reached. Motivation for using these programs is often high.

Students enjoy joint work with simulation programs (with discussion about each needed decision and collaborative decision making). Discussion becomes animated and thoughtful, and logic is applied in arguments framed in an effort to sway others toward a particular decision.

LITERATURE

Interactive fiction programs present stories that offer readers options for actions, as though they were characters in the story. The story lines are affected by the decisions of the students, so a story may unfold differently each time it is read. These simulation programs show the consequences of decisions based on critical reading. These programs are generally highly motivational, and because they can be used many times by each student, their use is cost effective. Pairs of students may work with these programs together, making decisions collaboratively.

Educational Game Programs.   These programs offer a variety of formats, with some resembling arcade games and others setting up virtual worlds. They are distinguished from other computer games in that they give students experiences related to educational goals, as well as providing a degree of entertainment. Computer graphics and sound effects make it possible to present informational material in a gamelike format; for example, the user might be asked to "shoot down" balloons containing words with long-vowel sounds. Educational games can offer a type of drill and practice, allowing students to work repetitively on fast, accurate responses, gaining automaticity (Kauchak and Eggen, 2008), but they are available in all CAI categories. Many of the games can be played on different levels of difficulty based upon the students' abilities (Forcier and Descy, 2008).

Using some adventure games requires reading instructions, reading for clues, and many critical literacy and visual literacy skills. When Ranker (2006) conducted an informal writing group, he studied an

TEACHING TIP

Using Electronic Games

Use electronic games to reinforce skills that have been taught. Don't just use them as a reward to students who finish their work early; otherwise, students who need the practice most will be the ones least likely to get it. Instead, assign games that are found to be instructionally sound as a regular part of the curriculum to students who are likely to benefit from the practice. You may also want to use them as an option for free time for students who are not in particular need of practice but simply enjoy the games.

eight-year-old boy as he used the video game *Gauntlet Legends* as the basis for his writing. This game has some aspects of adventure games, role-playing games, and arcade-style shooting games. The boy liked drawing better than writing. During writing conferences, the boy was allowed to tell about his detailed drawings that depicted some of the worlds in the video game, and he could impart detailed information from his drawings. When Ranker asked the boy to write about the levels in his game, he said he would, but it would require him to make more drawings. The special complexities of the game, with mazes on each level, could be seen from his drawings.

After the boy had depicted a level to his satisfaction, he wrote about the actions of characters on that level. He illustrated the characters and was persuaded to write about the characters in his illustrations. He described their powers and explained how a player has to make strategic choices about the one he controls (his avatar), his path through each level, and his approach to using his powers. Ranker (2006) thinks that the boy might be motivated to read such books as Lewis's *The Chronicles of Narnia* in school, because of his interest in high fantasy worlds.

 LITERATURE

▶ Computer-Managed Instruction

 STANDARDS/ ASSESSMENTS

Computer-managed instruction (CMI) can help teachers keep track of students' performance and guide their learning activities. CMI systems vary greatly in complexity. CMI systems may provide computer-scored tests on specific objectives and then match each student's deficiencies to available instructional materials, suggest instructional sequences for the teacher to use, or assign material directly to the student. Some systems produce reports for parents and other caregivers on the objectives that their children have mastered. The computer may also perform tasks such as averaging grades on a series of tests, thereby relieving the teacher of quite a bit of burdensome record keeping. Many electronic gradebook programs are available, and they offer numerous options. Some even have family and student access possibilities, through which caregivers and students can dial in to the school computer and, using an identification number, access an individual student's grades and teacher comments. Electronic portfolios enable students to save their work in a variety of formats, such as text, graphics, audio, and video; and they provide a plan for organizing the portfolios. Complete CMI systems are expensive, and they should be evaluated carefully.

Some individual CAI programs have built-in management components. These components allow the teacher to see how well students perform, and sometimes they indicate which items were answered incorrectly. The management components in some programs tell students when to move on to more difficult levels of the program and when to drop back to easier ones. Some of these management components, however, do not save results from session to session.

The Accelerated Reader (AR) Program, a type of reading management software, is widely used across the United States and beyond. The program is intended to motivate students to read more books. The producers of the program emphasize that it is not a complete reading program, should not be used to take the place of instruction because it does not provide reading instruction, and does not assess general reading ability (Renaissance Learning, 2006). The books on which the program is based are ranked by reading difficulty level.

The AR program contains multiple-choice quizzes for thousands of books. Reading practice quizzes are given to students after they have read books for which quizzes are available. Points are awarded based on performance on the quizzes. The quizzes basically test literal comprehension in order to ensure that the student has read the book and to provide motivation to students to read (through incentives, such as accumulation of points, achievement scores, and recognition by others) (Renaissance Learning, 2006). For struggling readers, non-readers, and English-emergent readers, the AR program has Spanish quizzes and recorded voice quizzes (Stiggins, 2005).

STRUGGLING READER/
INTERVENTION

DIVERSITY

The AR program also offers literacy skills quizzes, vocabulary practice quizzes, and textbook quizzes. The literacy skills quizzes test such skills as "inferential reasoning, main idea, cause and effect, characterization, and recognizing plot" (Renaissance Learning, 2006, p. 13). However, they are not available for most books in the system and are not used by all teachers who use the AR program. The textbook quizzes typically contain literal comprehension questions.

Some concerns about use of the program include that teachers may not hold discussions of books to prevent students from learning answers to quizzes from discussion instead of reading; that some parents and teachers may limit the available books to AR books, reducing the students' opportunity to read more widely in books they like; that students may tell each other test answers, especially when AR points affect grades; and that some books on a particular reading level may not have appropriate material for some children who read at that level, and teachers may not know all the titles well enough to supply guidance. Renaissance Learning (2006), the publisher of the AR program, counters that the program emphasizes the importance of adequate *teacher-guided* independent reading and the use of information from AR tests to guide instruction.

Reports of misuse of the program indicate that some teachers are using it for the entire reading program and/or for grading. These practices are not appropriate and will not result in the desired effect of motivation to read more. Pavonetti, Brimmer, and Cipielewski (2002/2003) conducted a study to determine whether the AR program turns children into lifelong readers. Their results were mixed but did not support such claims.

▶ Combining Computer Applications

LITERATURE

Many teachers regularly use combinations of computer applications, along with other media, in their lessons. For example, Mr. Xavier, a fifth-grade teacher, uses the computer program *Reading Galaxy* to introduce two survival novels, *Hatchet* and *Julie of the Wolves*. His students read these two novels as part of a combined language arts/social studies unit. The computer program, designed to stimulate interest in reading, uses a game-show format. It focuses on "character, setting, initial conflicts, and author backgrounds" (Wepner and Ray, 2000, p. 77) for these and other middle school novels. The teacher also uses Internet maps and maps on CD in the unit, as well as Internet sites to check on facts about Alaska. In addition, he sets up Alaskan keypals for his students (Wepner and Ray, 2000).

Students could also read books on CD and then use *Kidspiration* to web the stories just read and use word-processing software to write sequels to the books. They could post their webs and sequels on a class webpage or a blog. Applications are limited only by the imaginations of creative teachers.

❯ Cooperative Learning with Computers

Computer applications work well with cooperative learning. When pairs of students are allowed to work together at the computer, the language interactions are rich, whether the students are reading an electronic book, using a simulation program, or writing a story together. The computer offers opportunities for reading their own writing and that of other students and enables teams of students to share in the preparation of presentations, each bringing personal strengths to the process, which can include searching for information, organizing information, designing a presentation, and implementing the planned design.

SEEING IT IN PRACTICE ◀ ■ ▶

Video Case
View the Video Case "Expanding the Definition of Literacy: Meaningful Ways to Use Technology" and the bonus videos to see how several teachers at elementary, middle school, and high school work with technology for instruction. Be sure to look at the "Classroom Artifacts." In your journal, write your reactions to the technological applications. Mention whether or not you think that the activity shown for the high school could be adapted to use with elementary students. Give your reasons. Also note the ideas that the high school teacher presented that are applicable to all levels.

Instructional Transparencies

Using transparencies displayed on overhead projectors allows teachers who are not artistically inclined to present various types of material in an attractive way. Instructional transparencies may be produced manually, developed on a computer, or obtained from a commercial source.

Writing on blank transparencies as they present new material enables teachers to provide visual clarification or presentation of ideas without turning their backs to their classes, a plus for communication and for maintaining control. This use of transparencies is effective for recording brainstorming sessions, semantic webs of prior knowledge about a topic, or entries for K-W-L charts. (See Chapter 7 for more about these charts, including an example of one such chart.)

When using the process-writing approach (described in Chapter 10), current student work can be displayed on transparencies, and students can discuss possible needs for revision, if the permission of the creators is obtained; or anonymous student work from previous classes may be used for this purpose.

Time for Reflection

Some educators believe that extensive use of computers in classroom instruction will cause children to develop into social isolates, as they sit and interact with a computer screen instead of people. Others say that computers can be used by two or more students in collaborative ways that result in even more positive social interactions than are ordinarily found in a traditional classroom.

Describe situations in which *you* think social interactions are likely to occur or tell why *you* think they are unlikely.

Television Programs

STANDARDS/ASSESSMENTS Televisions in classrooms make possible the incorporation of educational programming into instruction. International Reading Association and The National Council of Teachers of English Standards for the English Language Arts (1996) refer to television programs as visual texts appropriate to study in K–12 classrooms.

Some shows, such as *Reading Rainbow*, fit naturally into the literacy curriculum. In *Reading Rainbow* programs, books are read, illustrations are shared, and related activities are incorporated into the program to make the book presentations more

DIVERSITY meaningful. For many programs, online guides for teachers are available. Some have additional teachers' guides for use in science, social studies, and math and for English-language learners. In addition, any show that covers content currently being studied in a thematic unit could provide background information that would make reading and writing about that topic easier for students. If scheduling to fit the unit's prescribed time slot is a problem, it may be possible to record the program for later use, but teachers must be careful to adhere to copyright laws. Visit the Student Website for this textbook for links to sites that explain copyright laws.

Cable television connections are available in many schools. Special programming and teacher's guides are provided by some cable operators.

Taking notes on television programs for reports or thematic unit projects is also a good way for students to apply literacy skills. Movies that have pertinent con-

LITERATURE tent may be viewed, and students may then write reviews related to their accuracy and effectiveness. Movies based on children's books can serve as an introduction or follow-up to the reading of those books. Some books that have related movies are *Sarah, Plain and Tall; Holes; Bridge to Terabithia,* and *Harriet, the Spy.* Movies can also be discussed along with accompanying texts with similar themes. This can help students hone their critical reading skills as they compare and contrast the books and films.

Audio Recordings

Sometimes a teacher may use audio recordings (on tape, CD, or digital files) that provide information about a subject being studied in class. (This may be done by using listening stations at which several children can listen to the same recording at the same time.) Prerecorded books for read-alongs or prerecorded music that

STRUGGLING READER/INTERVENTION goes along with poetry that is being read may also be used. Students who are having difficulty reading the material and English-language learners can listen to the

DIVERSITY recording as they read, building sight vocabulary as they hear a fluent reader's correct phrasing and pronunciation. Teachers may record the read-alouds that they do for the class and make them available to students who missed the reading or who wish to read along with the recordings. Teachers can also record class activities. Recordings of group discussions or class presentations can be used for later evaluation of the activities. Recordings of a student reading orally over a period of time can be used as portfolio items for evaluation, since they provide convincing evidence of progress.

STANDARDS/
ASSESSMENTS

Students may record themselves reading aloud or practicing an oral presentation and then listen to the recordings to decide if they are ready to perform for the class. They may also record class lectures and discussions to review before tests or to use for note taking in a less stressful situation, with the time pressure removed.

Video Recordings

Many classrooms have videotape recorders, and others have them available for checkout from the media center. Most schools now also have the equipment to do video recording on CD, DVD, or flash memory devices.

Video recordings are available on most topics that are included in the school curriculum, and they are good for introducing new topics for discussion, making new concepts seem more concrete as they are presented in the context of real-life situations, and providing a focus for follow-up discussion at the end of a unit of study.

Video recordings are particularly useful in illustrating text materials for less proficient readers or students with limited experiential backgrounds. They may help to bring a literary selection to life for students or help them understand a process that is described in a content-area textbook.

STRUGGLING READER/
INTERVENTION

DIVERSITY

LITERATURE

As noted earlier in the chapter, movies based on children's books are often available on video recordings (tapes, CDs, or DVDs), or they may be recorded from television for use in the classroom. If the students have already read the book, they may compare and contrast the book and the movie. If they have not already read the book, they may view the movie first; then, students who choose to do so as an individual project may read the book and do the comparison. (See "Seeing It in Practice: Use of Video Recordings.") In some cases, there are several movies based on the same book. *Heidi* is an example of such a book. The students can determine which of the movies portrayed the book most accurately, if video recordings of multiple versions are available.

A good application of video recorders is having students make their own recordings of class presentations or field trips. They can write scripts for skits or plays, do the casting, rehearse for the performances, record the productions, and edit the recordings until they have polished products. Creative drama and readers' theater performances can also be recorded. Simulated newscasts can be written, dramatized, and recorded, with editing as a final step. These activities involve many technological and higher-order thinking skills.

Using Video Recordings

Two classes of middle school students read the book *Bridge to Terabithia* and then viewed a video based on the book. They compared and contrasted the book and the video, coming out firmly in favor of the book. The students felt that the movie at times differed from the book "for no reason at all," although they saw that some changes had been made because of time constraints. They commented, too, that many important details had been left out of the movie, making the character portrayals weaker.

These classes later read the book *Tuck Everlasting* and then viewed a video based on it. Once again they compared and contrasted the movie and the book, with similar results. They found many changes to be unnecessary and inexplicable and even decided that the impact of the plot, as it unfolded, was lessened because the movie contained some foreshadowing that was not in the book (Roe and Smith, 1997).

Visit http://ncam.wgbh.org/awv/resources.html **(or link from the Student Website for this book) for directions for downloading and for using MAGpie software.**

Time for Reflection

Some people think that only "cutting-edge" technology should be used in today's classrooms. They would discard applications that have been around a long time, referring to them as "antiquated."

In what ways do *you* think that older technology can accomplish curricular goals more effectively than newer applications?

Strassman and O'Connell (2007/2008) recommend Authoring with Video (AWV) as a way to motivate student writing, encourage revision of writing, and produce material to share with their classmates and perhaps post to a website or blog. With AWV, the teacher gives students short video clips without audio and asks them to write a narration script to accompany the video. Students can use *MAGpie*, which is free software, to enter their narration script as captions for the video. They can be helped to see how their narration can clarify and amplify the images on the screen. They have incentive to revise to add needed detail as they evaluate the effect of the video on viewers. The resulting videos can be made an instructional resource for a unit of study. It is also possible for students to film their own content. The length of the video production can vary from about three minutes for younger students to thirty minutes for older students.

SUMMARY

As concerns about needs to teach students to deal with technology mount, new literacy concepts have emerged. Technological literacy—which involves visual literacy, media literacy, and digital literacy—for students has become a nationwide goal. Meeting this goal requires students to be able to use technology, including computers, to enhance learning and productivity. Using computers with hypertext and hypermedia requires students to learn to process text in new ways.

The emphasis on technology has focused attention on many applications that can be used to meet the needs of diverse populations in our schools. Synthetic speech and large print on computer screens and printouts, as well as special input devices and output systems, are some of the useful applications.

Teachers are faced with a bewildering array of possible technological applications for their literacy classrooms. They need to understand the range of technology available, how to evaluate the different applications, and how to make technology an integral part of core learning. The International Society for Technology in Education's National Educational Technology Standards (ISTE NETS) for teachers and students can provide guidance in preparing to teach in today's schools.

Among the many technological tools that can be applied to literacy instruction are instructional transparencies, television programs, audio recordings, video recordings, and numerous computer applications. Various combinations of technological tools are also used for multimedia applications. These tools can be used to present information and to enable students to do research and create presentations and written products.

Computers are used in literacy instruction for linking with electronic whiteboards; for word processing, desktop publishing, and multimedia publishing; to access databases, e-books, electronic reference works, and the Internet; for electronic communications such as e-mail, electronic mailing lists, electronic bulletin boards and discussion groups, podcasts, and videoconferencing; for constructing webpages, blogs, and wikis; for computer-assisted instruction, including drill-and-practice, tutorial, simulation, and educational game programs; and for computer-managed instruction.

Teachers still have to deal with more traditional technologies, such as instructional transparencies, television programs, audio recordings, and video recordings. They must integrate all of the technological applications smoothly into their instructional programs.

For your journal ....

1. Keep a section in your journal for reviews of pertinent video and audio recordings and computer programs that you might wish to use in your literacy program. If you can, try each one with students and write an assessment of its effectiveness in your journal. You may want to include your reviews in your portfolio.

2. Don't forget to put your reactions to the Video Cases that you viewed for this chapter in your journal, as directed.

.... and your portfolio

1. Develop a multimedia presentation on a literacy topic of your choice for a grade level of your choice and include a copy of it on CD or other medium in your portfolio.

2. Produce a computer-driven slide presentation, using a program such as *PowerPoint*, to help explain a literacy topic, such as "Propaganda Devices in Advertising." Use the slide show with a group of students to teach a lesson. Evaluate the results in your journal. Put a printout of your slide show in your portfolio, along with the lesson plan that you taught.

Linking It Up

Epilogue

This special section of the book is a handy teaching strategies reference guide. We call it "Linking It Up" because we hope that it will help you to link together and use information located throughout the book, to address your students' specific instructional needs.

There are several ways to use this guide. If you are planning instruction to meet specific standards, begin with the first column. For example, to address vocabulary development standards, you can use an assessment such as an informal reading inventory to determine students' current performance levels. Based on the results, you can provide differentiated instruction, using a variety of intervention strategies listed, to help different students learn the specific vocabulary and skills that they need. At other times, you may begin with the assessment column. If a student's retelling of a text reveals, for example, that the student can decode the words, but has problems understanding the text, you can use the strategies listed to provide intervention to help that student improve comprehension. The far-right column of the guide refers you to the chapters in which you can find full descriptions and advice for implementing the intervention techniques listed.

Be sure to review Chapter 2, "Assessment and Intervention," for full descriptions and advice for implementing the assessment methods.

Instructional Need	Assessment Strategy	Intervention Strategy	Text References
Phonemic awareness	• Observation • Checklists and rating scales • Informal Reading Inventory (IRI) • *Concepts About Print* by M. Clay	• Language activities that emphasize rhyming patterns, songs, poems, and chants • Word sorts • Word Walls • Shared-book experience • Reading aloud	Chapter 2: Assessment and Intervention Chapter 3: Emergent and Developing Literacy Chapter 5: Phonics for Word Recognition

(Continued)

517

Instructional Need	Assessment Strategy	Intervention Strategy	Text References
Sight words	• Observation • Informal Reading Inventory (IRI) • Published sight word list, for example, *Dolch* word list • Retellings • Cloze procedure • Running record • *Concepts About Print* by M. Clay	• Word Walls • Word sorts • Journal writing • Reading aloud • Picture clues • Labeling items in room	Chapter 2: Assessment and Intervention Chapter 3: Emergent and Developing Literacy Chapter 4: Overview of Word-Recognition Approaches Chapter 13: Use of Technology for Literacy Learning
Vocabulary development	• Observation • Retellings • Cloze procedure • Informal Reading Inventory (IRI) • Running record • *Concepts About Print* by M. Clay	• Environmental print activities • Word Walls • Displaying key vocabulary in pocket charts • Word sorts • Wide reading • Direct experiences • Creative dramatics • Graphic organizers, for example, semantic maps • Figurative language • Categorization • Analogies • Context clues • Morphemic analysis • Semantic feature analysis • Use of dictionary and thesaurus • Word play • Computer-assisted learning	Chapter 1: The Reading Act Chapter 2: Assessment and Intervention Chapter 3: Emergent and Developing Literacy Chapter 4: Overview of Word-Recognition Approaches Chapter 6: Meaning Vocabulary Chapter 12: Reading in the Content Areas Chapter 13: Use of Technology for Literacy Learning

Instructional Need	Assessment Strategy	Intervention Strategy	Text References
Phonics analysis	• Observation • Checklist or rating scales • Informal Reading Inventory (IRI) • Running record • *Concepts About Print* by M. Clay	• Making words • Multisensory approaches • Word sorts • Using generalizations (inductive and deductive) • Analytic approach • Synthetic approach • Onsets and rimes • Games • Combining with context and structural analysis • Key words • Use of predictable books	Chapter 2: Assessment and Intervention Chapter 3: Emergent and Developing Literacy Chapter 5: Phonics for Word Recognition
Literal comprehension	• Retellings • Questioning techniques • Whole-class responses • ReQuest • Summary writing • Informal Reading Inventory (IRI)	• K-W-L technique • Think-aloud procedure • Concept mapping • Graphic organizers • Discussions in literature circles • Reading aloud evidence for answers to questions • Question-answer relationship (QAR) • Predictions • Context clues • Purpose setting • Study guides	Chapter 2: Assessment and Intervention Chapter 6: Meaning Vocabulary Chapter 8: Comprehension: Part 2 Chapter 9: Major Approaches and Materials for Reading Instruction Chapter 10: Language and Literature Chapter 12: Reading in the Content Areas

(Continued)

Instructional Need	Assessment Strategy	Intervention Strategy	Text References
Higher-order comprehension	• ReQuest • Journal writing • Summary writing • Informal Reading Inventory (IRI)	• K-W-L • Question-answer relationship (QAR) • Concept building • Reciprocal Teaching • Think-aloud procedure • Discussion in literature circles • Purpose setting • Predictions about consequences • Reading aloud to confirm predictions • Story mapping • Propaganda techniques • Simulations • Creative drama • Study guides • Story grammar activities • Anaphora recognition • Critical evaluation • Visualization • Computer-assisted instruction	Chapter 2: Assessment and Intervention Chapter 7: Comprehension: Part 1 Chapter 8: Comprehension: Part 2 Chapter 9: Major Approaches and Materials for Reading Instruction Chapter 10: Language and Literature Chapter 12: Reading in the Content Areas Chapter 13: Use of Technology for Literacy Learning
Structural analysis	• Checklist or rating scale • Informal Reading Inventory (IRI)	• Making words • Onsets and rimes activities • Generalizations about syllabication and accent • Prefixes, suffixes, and root words • Using the dictionary	Chapter 2: Assessment and Intervention Chapter 4: Overview of Word-Recognition Approaches Chapter 5: Phonics for Word Recognition

Instructional Need	Assessment Strategy	Intervention Strategy	Text References
Context clues	• Cloze procedure • Informal Reading Inventory (IRI)	• Cloze procedure • Think-aloud • Discussion in literature circles • Learning types of clues	Chapter 2: Assessment and Intervention Chapter 3: Emergent and Developing Literacy Chapter 4: Overview of Word-Recognition Approaches Chapter 6: Meaning Vocabulary
Fluency	• Checklist or rating scale • Informal Reading Inventory (IRI) • Self-assessment of recorded readings	• Chunking • Guided reading • Language experience approach (LEA) • Repeated readings • Readers' theater • Reading aloud • Recorded books • Rhythm walks	Chapter 1: The Reading Act Chapter 2: Assessment and Intervention Chapter 3: Emergent and Developing Literacy Chapter 9: Major Approaches and Materials for Reading Instruction Chapter 13: Use of Technology for Literacy Learning
Reading rate	• Checklist or rating scale • Informal Reading Inventory (IRI)	• Readers' theater • Repeated readings • Flexibility training • Traffic-light reading • Skimming • Scanning • Timed readings with comprehension checks	Chapter 2: Assessment and Intervention Chapter 3: Emergent and Developing Literacy Chapter 11: Reading/ Study Techniques
Locating information	• Self-assessment • Checklist or rating scale • Observations	• SQ3R • Multimedia presentations • WebQuests	Chapter 2: Assessment and Intervention Chapter 11: Reading/ Study Techniques

(Continued)

Instructional Need	Assessment Strategy	Intervention Strategy	Text References
		• Inquiry project-based learning activities • Using the library • Using tables of contents and indexes • Using dictionaries, thesauruses, and encyclopedias • Internet search strategies	Chapter 12: Reading in the Content Areas Chapter 13: Use of Technology for Literacy Learning
English for English-language learners	• Interviews • Discussions • Observation • Informal Reading Inventory	• Concept development • Conversations • Reading aloud • Language experience approach (LEA) • Translations • Bilingual trade books • Creative dramatics • Picture dictionaries • Instruction on letter sounds • Multisensory instruction • Common root words • Essential words • Academic vocabulary • Cognates • Pronoun antecedents • English syntax • Interactive books • Bilingual dictionaries • Word Walls • Sentence frames	Chapter 1: The Reading Act Chapter 4: Overview of Word-Recognition Approaches Chapter 5: Phonics for Word Recognition Chapter 6: Meaning Vocabulary Chapter 7: Comprehension: Part 1 Chapter 8: Comprehension: Part 2 Chapter 9: Major Approaches and Materials to Reading Instruction Chapter 11: Reading/Study Techniques Chapter 12: Reading in the Content Areas Chapter 13: Use of Technology for Literacy Learning

Glossary

adequate yearly progress (AYP)   A component of the ESEA legislation that requires states and school systems to collect annual data that represents the progress of students in meeting established assessment goals or progress in key subject areas.

affective   Relating to attitudes, interests, values, appreciations, and opinions.

allusion   An indirect reference to a person, place, thing, or event considered to be known to the reader.

alphabetic principle   The concept that letters represent speech sounds.

alternative assessment   All types of assessment other than standardized tests.

analogies   Comparisons of two similar relationships, stated in the form of the following example: *Author* is to *book* as *artist* is to *painting*.

analytic approach to phonics instruction   Teaching the sounds of letters in already known words. Sight words are taught first and letter sounds second, in context.

anaphora   Use of a word as a substitute for another word or group of words.

anecdotal record   A written account of a specific incident or behavior in the classroom.

anticipation guides   Sets of declarative statements related to materials about to be read that are designed to stimulate thinking and discussion.

antonyms   A pair of words that have opposite meanings.

appositive   A word or a phrase placed beside another word or phrase as a restatement.

assessment   The collection of data, such as test scores and informal records, to measure student achievement.

auditory acuity   Sharpness of hearing.

auditory discrimination   The ability to differentiate among sounds.

authentic assessment   A measurement of a student's performance on activities that reflect real-world learning experiences.

automaticity   The ability to carry out a task without having to give it much attention.

AYP   *See* **adequate yearly progress.**

balanced approach to reading instruction   An approach in which teachers concentrate on providing both word recognition and comprehension strategy and skill instruction along with ample opportunities to read complete works of literature, to use reading materials to solve problems, and to explore nonfiction and fiction material.

bar graphs   Graphs that use vertical or horizontal bars to compare quantities.

big book   A large, over-sized book that the whole class can share together, often characterized by predictability, repetition, and rhyme.

blogs   Web logs, or web-based journals, that allow the author to add audio or video clips and links to other websites.

bottom-up processing   Processing printed text by examining the printed symbols, with little input being required from the reader.

CAI   *See* **computer-assisted instruction.**

Caldecott Award   An annual award for excellence in illustration.

categorization   Classification into related groups.

circle or pie graphs   Graphs that show relationships of individual parts to a whole circle.

cloze procedure   A technique in which the teacher deletes words or other structures from a passage and leaves blanks in their places. The students then fill in the blanks by using the surrounding context to determine the missing material. It can be used as a method of instruction, a means of testing for comprehension, or a method of estimating reading difficulty.

CMI   *See* **computer-managed instruction.**

cognitive development   The development of the ability to think and reason.

computer-assisted instruction (CAI)   Instruction that makes use of a computer to administer a programmed instructional sequence or other educational experience.

computer-managed instruction (CMI)   Using the computer for such tasks as record keeping, diagnosis, and prescription of individualized assignments.

consonant blend   Two or more adjacent consonant letters whose sounds are blended together, with each individual sound retaining its identity.

consonant digraph   Two adjacent consonant letters that represent a single speech sound.

content-area textbooks   Textbooks in areas of information, such as English, social studies, science, and mathematics.

context clues   Clues to word meanings or pronunciations found in the surrounding words or sentences.

creative dramatics   Acting out stories spontaneously, without a script.

creative reading   Reading beyond the lines.

criterion-referenced test   A test designed to yield measurements interpretable in terms of specific performance standards.

critical reading   Reading for evaluation.

cumulative tales   Traditional tales displaying rhythm and a pattern with a repetitive sequence of events or refrain.

curriculum standards   Statements or descriptions of expectations outlining what students should know and be able to do at particular grade levels and in specific content areas.

database   An organized body of information that can be sorted and searched electronically.

desktop-publishing program   Computer software that combines text and graphics for classroom publishing.

developing literacy   A stage of literacy development where children begin to read and write by decoding and recognizing high-frequency vocabulary words.

developmentally appropriate practice   A framework or an approach for working with young children in which the teacher considers each child's competencies and adjusts instruction accordingly.

dialect   Regional or social adaptations of a language; distinguishing features may include pronunciation, vocabulary, and syntax.

digital literacy   A type of media literacy that includes skills in viewing and visually representing.

diphthong   Vowel sounds that are so closely blended that they can be treated as single vowel units for the purposes of word identification.

direct instruction   Teacher control of the learning environment through structured lessons, goal setting, choice of activities, and feedback.

directed reading activity (DRA)   A strategy in which detailed lesson plans are followed to teach the reading of stories or nonfiction selections.

directed reading-thinking activity (DRTA)   A general plan for directing the reading of content-area reading selections or basal reader stories and for encouraging children to think as they read, to predict, and to check their predictions.

disaggregated data   Scores that show the progress of subgroups of students, including racial/ethnic groups, economically disadvantaged students, students with disabilities, and students with limited English proficiency.

DRA   *See* **directed reading activity.**

dramatic play   Simulating real-life or authentic experiences, such as playing a cashier at a grocery store or server at a restaurant.

DRTA   *See* **directed reading-thinking activity.**

eclectic approaches   Approaches that combine desirable aspects of a number of different major approaches.

electronic bulletin boards   Network locations to which messages are posted so that readers interested in the topic can read the messages electronically. Sometimes referred to as newsgroups.

electronic discussion groups   Network locations to which messages are posted so that readers interested in the topic can participate in electronic discussion by reading and responding to messages.

electronic mailing list   Electronic distributor of messages on a particular topic to a group of readers who have "subscribed" to the list.

ellipsis   The omission of a word or group of words that are to be "understood" by the reader.

e-mail (electronic mail)   Messages sent electronically from one computer user to another.

emergent literacy   A developing awareness of the interrelatedness of oral and written language.

environmental print   Words that children frequently see in the world around them.

etymology   The origin and history of words.

euphemism   The substitution of a less offensive word or phrase for an unpleasant term or expression.

experience chart   A written account about common experiences, dictated by the student(s) and recorded by the teacher.

expository (style)   A precise, factual writing style.

fables   Brief moral tales in which animals or inanimate objects speak.

fantasy   A genre of literature including highly imaginative, fictional stories, with fanciful or supernatural elements.

fiction   Stories that are not true, written in a narrative style, for the purpose of entertainment.

figurative language   Nonliteral language.

fluency   The ability to read with automaticity, appropriate rate, good expression, and good comprehension.

formal assessment   The use of a testing instrument based on extensive normative data and for which reliability and validity can be verified.

formative assessment   Ongoing assessment designed to offer feedback on progress for both the teacher and the learner.

frustration level   A level of reading difficulty with which a reader is unable to cope; when reading material is on this level, on an IRI, the reader usually recognizes less than 90 percent of the words that he or she reads or comprehends less than 50 percent of what he or she reads.

genre   A type of classification of literature, such as historical fiction, biography, or folktales.

grapheme   A written symbol that represents a phoneme.

graphic aids   Maps, graphs, tables, and illustrations that provide information in nonfiction materials.

graphic organizers   Visual depictions of text material, such as webs.

graphophonic clues (or cues)   Clues from associating phonemes with graphemes.

guide words   Words used in dictionaries, encyclopedias, and other reference books to aid users in finding entries. The first guide word names the first entry on the page; the second guide word names the final entry on the page.

guided reading   An instructional model of delivery that provides structure and purpose for reading.

homographs   Words that have identical spellings but sound different and have different meanings.

homonyms   Pairs or groups of words that are spelled differently but are pronounced alike; homophones.

homophones   *See* **homonyms.**

hyperbole   An extreme exaggeration.

hypermedia   Text, sound, or pictures (still or animated) linked in a nonsequential manner, allowing access to the material in an order chosen by the user.

hypertext   Information that is linked in a nonsequential manner, allowing students to choose the paths that they will take through the information.

idiom   A group of words that, taken as a whole, has a meaning different from that of the sum of the meanings of the individual words.

independent reading level   A level of reading difficulty low enough that the reader can progress without noticeable hindrance; on an IRI, the reader can ordinarily recognize at least 99 percent of the words and comprehend at least 90 percent of what he or she reads.

individualized reading approach   An approach to reading instruction that is characterized by students' self-selection of reading materials, self-pacing, and student-teacher conferences.

inflectional endings   Endings that when added to nouns change the number, case, or gender; when added to verbs change the tense or person; and when added to adjectives change the degree.

informal reading inventory (IRI)   An informal instrument designed to help the teacher determine a child's independent, instructional, frustration, and capacity levels.

InQuest   *See* **Investigative Questioning Procedure.**

instructional level   A level of difficulty at which the reader can read with understanding with teacher assistance; on an IRI, the reader can ordinarily recognize at least 95 percent of the words in a selection and comprehend at least 75 percent of what he or she reads.

interactive theory of reading   A theory that depicts reading as a combination of reader-based and text-based processing.

Internet   International "network of networks" that links a multitude of computers.

interpretive reading   Reading between the lines.

invented spelling   Temporary unconventional spelling resulting from children's attempts to associate sounds with letters.

Investigative Questioning Procedure (InQuest)   A comprehension strategy that combines student questioning with creative drama.

IRI   *See* **informal reading inventory.**

journal   Written record of reflections, events, and ideas.

kinesthetic   Pertaining to body movement and muscle feelings.

knowledge-based processing   Bringing one's prior world knowledge and background of experiences to the interpretation of the text.

K-W-L teaching model   A teaching model for expository text; stands for What I *Know,* What I *Want* to Learn, What I *Learned.*

language arts   Listening, speaking, reading, writing, viewing, and visually representing.

language experience approach (LEA)   An approach in which reading and the other language arts are interrelated in the instructional program and the experiences of children are used as the basis for reading materials.

LEA   *See* **language experience approach.**

legend (of a map)   The map's key to symbols used.

legends   Unverified historical stories that originated orally.

line graphs   Graphs that show changes in amounts by connecting with line segments points representing the amounts.

linguistics   The scientific study of human speech.

listening comprehension level   A potential reading level or the level at which a student can comprehend what is read to him or her.

literal comprehension   Understanding ideas that are directly stated.

literature circles   Groups established to allow students to exchange ideas about books that they are reading.

literature-based approaches   Approaches that use high-quality literature as a basis for reading instruction.

meaning vocabulary   Words for which meanings are understood.

media literacy   The ability to understand and evaluate information that is viewed and read.

metacognition   A person's knowledge of the functioning of his or her own mind and his or her conscious efforts to monitor or control this functioning.

metacognitive strategies   Techniques for thinking about and monitoring one's own thought processes.

metaphor   A direct comparison not using the word *like* or *as.*

minimally contrasting spelling patterns   Words that vary in spellings by only a single letter.

miscue   An unexpected oral-reading response that deviates from the text.

modality   A sensory system for receiving and processing information (visual, auditory, kinesthetic, tactile).

morphemes   The smallest units of meaning in a language.

motivation   Incentive to act.

multimedia   The use of a number of different media (for example, graphics, text, moving images, and sound effects) in the same application.

multiple intelligences   Several distinct areas of potential that readers possess to different degrees.

myths   Traditional literature selections that feature characters such as gods, heroes, or supernatural beings.

narrative (style)   Storylike presentation.

Newbery Award   An annual award for the most distinguished contribution to American literature for children.

nonfiction   True stories designed to inform or instruct.

norm-referenced test   A test designed to yield results interpretable in terms of a norm, the average or mean results of a sample population.

onsets and rimes   Word parts; onsets are the consonants or consonant clusters at the beginning of a syllable and rimes are the vowels, or vowel combinations and any consonants that follow.

perception   The interpretation of sensory impressions.

performance-based assessment   A measurement of a student's ability to create an assigned response or product to demonstrate her or his level of competence.

personification   Giving the attributes of a person to an inanimate object or abstract idea.

phoneme   The smallest unit of sound in a language.

phonemic awareness   An understanding that speech consists of a series of small units of sound, or phonemes.

phonics   The association of speech sounds with printed symbols.

phonological awareness The awareness of sound patterns in words, such as phonemes, onsets and rimes, and syllables.

picture graphs Graphs that express quantities with pictures.

podcasts Audio files delivered via the Internet, for users to listen to with a computer or other device that can play the files.

portfolio A collection of work or artifacts gathered over a period of time.

pourquoi tales Traditional literature selections that often explain "why."

predictable book A book that is written with repetitive and rhythmic language patterns, often featuring familiar concepts.

print conventions The language rules that involve location, punctuation, and capitalization when reading and writing.

programmed instruction A method of presenting instructional material in small, sequential steps; active involvement of the learner, immediate reinforcement, and self-pacing are emphasized.

propaganda techniques Techniques of writing used to influence people's thinking and actions, including bandwagon technique, card stacking, glittering generalities, name calling, plain-folks talk, testimonials, and transfer techniques.

prosody The rhythmic patterns of oral language or speech.

readability An objective measure of the difficulty of written material.

readers' theater Reading aloud from scripts in a dramatic style.

reading and writing workshops Instructional procedure consisting of a minilesson, a status-of-the-class report, reading or writing, and sharing.

reading miscue inventory (RMI) An informal instrument that considers both the quality and the quantity of miscues made by the reader.

reading rate Speed of reading, often reported in words per minute.

reading/study techniques Techniques designed to enhance comprehension and retention of written material.

reciprocal teaching A technique to develop comprehension and metacognition in which the teacher and students take turns being "teacher." They predict, generate questions, summarize, and clarify ideas.

relative clauses Clauses that refer to an antecedent (may be restrictive or nonrestrictive).

Response to Intervention (RTI) A framework of tiered academic intervention designed to provide early assistance to students who experience difficulty learning.

retelling A student's recounting of a story or other material that he or she has read or heard.

rimes See **onsets and rimes.**

RMI See **reading miscue inventory.**

RTI See **Response to Intervention.**

rubric A set of criteria used to describe and evaluate a student's level of proficiency in a particular subject area.

running record A strategy for recording miscues during a student's oral reading.

scaffolding Providing support through modeling or feedback and then withdrawing support gradually as the learner gains competence.

scale (of a map) The part of a map showing the relationship of a given distance on a map to the same distance on the area represented.

scanning Moving the eyes rapidly over the selection to locate a specific bit of information, such as a name or a date.

schema (pl., **schemata**) A preexisting knowledge structure (cluster of information) developed about a thing, place, or idea.

schemata See **schema.**

self-concept Opinion of oneself.

semantic clue (or cue) A meaning clue.

semantic feature analysis A technique in which the presence or absence of particular features in the meaning of a word is indicated through symbols on a chart, making it possible to compare word meanings.

semantic maps Graphic representations of relationships among words and phrases in written material.

semantic webbing Making a graphic representation of relationships in written material through the use of a core question, strands (answers), strand supports (facts and inferences from the story), and strand ties (relationships of the strands to each other).

shared-book experience Reading and rereading books in a group activity for understanding and enjoyment.

sight words Words that are recognized immediately, without having to resort to analysis.

simile A comparison using *like* or *as*.

skimming Reading selectively to pick up main ideas and general impressions about the material.

SQ3R A study method consisting of five steps: Survey, Question, Read, Recite, Review.

SQRQCQ A study method consisting of six steps: Survey, Question, Read, Question, Compute, Question.

standardized test A norm-referenced published test that has been constructed by experts in the field and is administered, scored, and interpreted according to specific criteria.

story grammar A set of rules that define story structures.

story mapping Making graphic representations of stories that make clear the specific relationships of story elements.

structural analysis Analysis of words by identifying prefixes, suffixes, root words, inflectional endings, contractions, word combinations forming compound words, and syllabication.

study guides Duplicated sheets prepared by the teacher and distributed to students to help guide reading in content fields and alleviate some difficulties that interfere with understanding.

subskill theory of reading A theory that depicts reading as a set of subskills that children must master and integrate.

summative assessment An assessment administered at the end of an instructional unit or time period; often used to summarize progress of students as they complete their involvement in the learning task.

synonyms Groups of words that have the same, or very similar, meanings.

syntactic clue (or cue) A clue derived from the word order in sentences.

synthetic approach to phonics instruction Teaching pupils to blend together individual known letter sounds in order to decode written words. Letter sounds are taught first; then they are blended into words.

tactile Pertaining to the sense of touch.

technological literacy The ability to use various technological resources (for example, computers, CDs, and DVDs) for learning and completing various types of projects, such as writing research papers and doing multimedia presentations.

text leveling A process that organizes texts according to a defined continuum of characteristics so that students may be matched with appropriate materials.

text-based processing Trying to extract the information that resides in the text.

thematic literature unit An integrated learning experience that is structured around a theme, based on a topic such as homes, families, survival, taking care of our earth, wild animals, pets, a specific geographic region (for example, South America), or a specific group of people (for example, Japanese); a genre, such as biography, science fiction, or folktales; an author, such as Cynthia Voigt, Judith Viorst, or Maurice Sendak; or a single book.

think-alouds Verbalizing aloud the thought processes present as one reads a selection orally.

top-down model of reading A model that depicts reading as beginning with the generation of hypotheses, or predictions, about the material by the reader.

topic sentence A sentence that sets forth the central thought of the paragraph in which it occurs.

trade book A book for sale to the general public.

traditional literature A literary genre of stories, without identified authors, which are passed from generation to generation through oral narration.

transactive theory of reading A theory based on Rosenblatt's idea that every reading act is a transaction that involves a reader and a text and occurs at a particular time in a specific context, with meaning coming into being during the transaction between the reader and the text.

vicarious experience An indirect experience.

videoconferencing The holding of conferences over the Internet with others who can be seen on their computer monitors and heard through the speakers.

viewing Receiving and deriving information from visual images, sometimes accompanied by sound, as in viewing of television, videos, or live performances.

visual acuity   Sharpness of vision.

visual discrimination   Ability to differentiate between different shapes.

visual literacy   The ability to derive meaning from still pictures, animations, and images in the context of video presentations, as well as the ability to visually represent meaning through them.

visualization   Picturing events, places, and people described by an author.

visually representing   Presenting information through use of still pictures, animations, and videos.

vowel digraph   Two adjacent vowel letters that represent a single speech sound.

WebQuests   Inquiry projects in which students make use of links to online resources.

wikis   Websites that let users edit content.

word bank   A collection of sight words that have been mastered by an individual student, usually recorded on index cards.

word consciousness   Having awareness of and interest in words and word meanings.

word sorts   Categorization activities that involve classifying words into categories.

word webs   Graphic representations of the relationships among words that are constructed by connecting the related terms with lines.

word-processing software   Computer software designed to allow entry, manipulation, and storage of text (and sometimes images).

World Wide Web (WWW)   A part of the Internet that allows users to choose special words or symbols with a mouse click or keyboard stroke and be automatically connected to related web locations.

writing process   A student-centered procedure for writing consisting of prewriting, drafting, revising, editing, and publishing.

writing workshop   A framework or model for teaching writing that includes a minilesson designed to improve specific skills, a writing time when students are engaged in authentic writing, a conference time when students meet with the teacher individually, and a sharing time when students read or listen to the sharing of a student's written selection.

WWW   *See* **World Wide Web.**

zone of proximal development   The span between a child's actual skill level and potential level; a period when assistance should be provided.

References

Adams, Marilyn Jager. *Beginning to Read: Thinking and Learning About Print.* Cambridge, Mass.: MIT Press, 1990.

Adams, Marilyn Jager. "Modeling the Connections Between Word Recognition and Reading." In *Theoretical Models and Processes of Reading*, 5th ed., edited by Robert B. Ruddell and Norman J. Unrau. Newark, Del.: International Reading Association, 2004, 1182–1243.

Adams, Marilyn Jager, Diane Ravitch, Nancy Neil, E. D. Hirsch, Jr., Wiley Blevins, and Linda Bath. "*Beginning to Read*: A Critique by Literacy Professionals and a Response by Marilyn Jager Adams." *The Reading Teacher* 44 (February 1991): 370–395.

Afflerbach, Peter, P. David Pearson, and Scott G. Paris. "Clarifying Differences Between Reading Skills and Reading Strategies." *The Reading Teacher* 61 (February 2008): 364–373.

Aiken, Adel G., and Lisa Bayer. "They Love Words." *The Reading Teacher* 56 (September 2002): 68–74.

Ainslie, Dodie. "Word Detectives." *The Reading Teacher* 54 (December 2000/January 2001): 360–364.

Airasian, Peter W., and Mary E. Walsh. "Constructivist Cautions." *Phi Delta Kappa* 78 (February 1997): 444–449.

Allen, Linda. "An Integrated Strategies Approach: Making Word Identification Instruction Work for Beginning Readers." *The Reading Teacher* 52 (November 1998): 254–268.

Allington, Richard L. "What I've Learned About Effective Reading Instruction from a Decade of Studying Exemplary Elementary Classroom Teachers." *Phi Delta Kappan* 83 (June 2002): 740–747.

Ambe, Elizabeth BiFuh. "Inviting Reluctant Adolescent Readers into the Literacy Club: Some Comprehension Strategies to Tutor Individuals or Small Groups of Reluctant Readers." *Journal of Adolescent & Adult Literacy* 50 (May 2007): 632–639.

Anderson, Rebecca, Michael Grant, and Bruce Speck. *Technology to Teach Literacy: A Resource for K–8 Teachers.* Upper Saddle River, N.J.: Pearson, 2008.

Anderson, Richard C., Elfrieda H. Hiebert, Judith A. Scott, and Ian A. G. Wilkinson. *Becoming a Nation of Readers: The Report of the Commission on Reading.* Washington, D.C.: National Institute of Education, 1985.

Anderson, Richard C., J. Mason, and L. Shirey. *The Reading Group: An Experimental Investigation of a Labyrinth.* Technical Report No. 271. Urbana–Champaign: Center for the Study of Reading, University of Illinois, 1983.

Anderson, Richard C., and William E. Nagy. "Word Meanings." In *Handbook of Reading Research*, Vol. 2, edited by Rebecca Barr, Michael L. Kamil, Peter Mosenthal, and P. David Pearson. New York: Longman, 1991, 690–724.

Andrade, Heidi G. "Using Rubrics to Promote Thinking and Learning." *Educational Leadership* 57, no. 5 (February 2000): 13–18.

Applegate, Mary Dekonty, Kathleen Benson Quinn, and Anthony J. Applegate. "Profiles in Comprehension." *The Reading Teacher* 60 (September 2006): 48–57.

Armbruster, Bonnie B. "On Answering Questions." *The Reading Teacher* 45 (May 1992): 724–725.

Armbruster, Bonnie, Fran Lehr, and Jean Osborn. *Put Reading First: The Research Building Blocks for Teaching Children to Read.* Jessup, Md.: National Institute for Literacy at ED Pubs, September 2001.

Armbruster, Bonnie B., and William E. Nagy. "Vocabulary in Content Area Lessons." *The Reading Teacher* 45 (March 1992): 550–551.

Armstrong, Thomas. *Multiple Intelligences in the Classroom.* Alexandria, Va.: Association for Supervision and Curriculum Development, 1994.

Arya, Poonam, Prisca Martens, G. Pat Wilson, Bess Altwerger, Lijun Jin, Barbara Laster, and Debora Lang. "Reclaiming Literacy Instruction: Evidence in Support of Literature-Based Programs." *Language Arts* 83 (September 2005): 63–72.

Ashton-Warner, Sylvia. *Teacher.* New York: Simon & Schuster, 1963.

Assaf, Lori, and Rubén Garza. "Making Magazine Covers That Visually Count: Learning to Summarize with Technology." *The Reading Teacher* 60 (April 2007): 678–680.

"A Talk with Marilyn Adams." *Language Arts* 68 (March 1991): 206–212.

Atwell, Nancie. *In the Middle: Writing, Reading, and Learning with Adolescents.* Upper Montclair, N.J.: Boynton/Cook, 1987.

Atwell, Nancie. *In the Middle: New Understandings About Writing, Reading, and Learning*, 2nd ed., Portsmouth, N.H.: Heinemann, 1998.

Au, Kathryn H. "An Overview of New Concepts of Assessment: Impact on Decision Making and Instruction." Paper presented at the International Reading Association Convention, Atlanta, May 6, 1990.

Au, Kathryn H. "Constructing the Theme of a Story." *Language Arts* 69 (February 1992): 106–111.

August, Diane, María Carlo, Cheryl Dressler, and Catherine Snow. "The Critical Role of Vocabulary Development for English Language Learners." *Learning Disabilities Research and Practice* 20 (2005): 50–57.

August, Diane, and Timothy Shanahan, eds. *Developing Literacy in Second-Language Learners: Report of the National Literacy Panel on Language-Minority Children and Youth.* Mahwah, N.J.: Erlbaum, 2006.

Avalos, Mary A., Alina Plasencia, Celina Chavez, and Josefa Rascón. "Modified Guided Reading: Gateway to English as a Second Language and Literacy Learning." *The Reading Teacher* 61 (December 2007/January 2008): 318–329.

Avery, Charles W., and Beth Faris Avery. "Merging Reading and Cooperative Strategies Through Graphic Organizers." *Journal of Reading* 37 (May 1994): 689–690.

Babbs, Patricia J., and Alden J. Moe. "Metacognition: A Key for Independent Learning from Text." *The Reading Teacher* 36 (January 1983): 422–426.

Bailey, Mildred Hart. "The Utility of Phonic Generalizations in Grades One Through Six." *The Reading Teacher* 20 (February 1967): 413–418.

Ball, E. W., and B. A. Blachman. "Does Phoneme Awareness Training in Kindergarten Make a Difference in Early Word Recognition and Developmental Spelling?" *Reading Research Quarterly* 26, no. 1 (1991): 49–66.

Barger, Jeff. "Building Word Consciousness." *The Reading Teacher* 60 (November 2006): 279–281.

Barnitz, John G. "Developing Sentence Comprehension in Reading." *Language Arts* 56 (November/December 1979): 902–908, 958.

Baroni, Dick. "Have Primary Children Draw to Expand Vocabulary." *The Reading Teacher* 40 (April 1987): 819–820.

Barta, Jim, and Martha Crouthers Grindler. "Exploring Bias Using Multicultural Literature for Children." *The Reading Teacher* 50 (November 1996): 269–270.

Barton, James. "Interpreting Character Emotions for Literature Comprehension." *Journal of Adolescent and Adult Literacy* 40 (September 1996): 22–28.

Barton, Jim, Donna Sawyer, and Cindy Swanson. "They Want to Learn How to Think: Using Art to Enhance Comprehension." *Language Arts* 85 (November 2007): 125–133.

Barton, Keith C., and Lynne A. Smith. "Themes or Motifs? Aiming for Coherence Through Interdisciplinary Outlines." *The Reading Teacher* 54 (September 2000): 54–63.

Basden, Jonathan C. "Authentic Tasks as the Basis for Multimedia Design Curriculum." *T•H•E Journal* 29 (November 2001): 16–21.

Baumann, James F., Helene Hooten, and Patricia White. "Teaching Comprehension Through Literature: A Teacher-Research Project to Develop Fifth Graders' Reading Strategies and Motivation." *The Reading Teacher* 53 (September 1999): 38–51.

Baumann, James F., Leah A. Jones, and Nancy Seifert-Kessell. "Using Think-Alouds to Enhance Children's Comprehension Monitoring Abilities." *The Reading Teacher* 47 (November 1993): 184–193.

Baumann, James F., and Maribeth C. Schmitt. "The What, Why, How, and When of Comprehension Instruction." *The Reading Teacher* 39 (March 1986): 640–646.

Baumann, James F., Donna Ware, and Elizabeth Carr Edwards. "'Bumping into Spicy, Tasty Words That Catch Your Tongue': A Formative Experiment on Vocabulary Instruction." *The Reading Teacher* 61 (October 2007): 108–122.

Beck, Isabel, and Connie Juel. "The Role of Decoding in Learning to Read." *American Educator* 8 (Summer 1995): 8–23.

Beck, Isabel L., and Margaret G. McKeown. "Learning Words Well—A Program to Enhance Vocabulary and Comprehension." *The Reading Teacher* 36 (March 1983): 622–625.

Beck, Isabel, and Margaret McKeown. "Conditions of Vocabulary Acquisition." In *Handbook of Reading Research*, Vol. 2, edited by Rebecca Barr, Michael L. Kamil, Peter Mosenthal, and P. David Pearson. New York: Longman, 1991, 789–814.

Beck, Isabel, Margaret McKeown, and Linda Kucan. *Bringing Words to Life: Robust Vocabulary Instruction.* New York: Guilford Press, 2002.

Bell, Sherry Mee, and Steve McCallum. *Handbook of Reading Assessment.* Boston: Pearson, 2008.

Bellows, Barbara Plotkin. "Running Shoes Are to Jogging as Analogies Are to Creative/Critical Thinking." *Journal of Reading* 23 (March 1980): 507–511.

Berger, Linda R. "Reader Response Journals: You Make the Meaning . . . and How." *Journal of Adolescent & Adult Literacy* 39 (February 1996): 380–385.

Bergeron, Bette S. "Seeking Authenticity: What Is 'Real' About Thematic Literacy Instruction." *The Reading Teacher* 49 (April 1996): 544–551.

Bertrand, John. "Children at Risk of School Failure." In *Empowering Children at Risk of School Failure: A Better Way*, edited by John Bertrand and Carole Stice. Norwood, Mass.: Christopher-Gordon, 1995, 1–15.

"Best of Blogs." *eSchool News* 8 (August 2005): 8.

Bidwell, Sandra M. "Ideas for Using Drama to Enhance Reading Instruction." *The Reading Teacher* 45 (April 1992): 653–654.

Bintz, William P., and Karen S. Shelton. "Using Written Conversation in Middle School: Lessons from a Teacher Researcher Project." *Journal of Adolescent & Adult Literacy* 47 (March 2004): 482–507.

Bishop, Penny A., Cynthia Reyes, and Susanna W. Pflaum. "Read Smarter, Not Harder: Global Reading Comprehension Strategies." *The Reading Teacher* 60 (September 2006): 66–69.

Blachowicz, Camille L. Z. "Making Connections: Alternatives to the Vocabulary Notebook." *Journal of Reading* 29 (April 1986): 643–649.

Blachowicz, Camille L. Z., and Peter Fisher. "Vocabulary Instruction." In *Handbook of Reading Research*, Vol. 3, edited by Michael L. Kamil, Peter B. Mosenthal, P. David Pearson, and Rebecca Barr. Mahwah, N.J.: Erlbaum, 2000, 503–523.

Blachowicz, Camille L. Z., and Peter Fisher. "Keep the 'Fun' in Fundamental: Encouraging Words Awareness and Incidental Word Learning in the Classroom Through Word Play." In *Vocabulary Instruction: Research to Practice*, edited by James F. Baumann and Edward J. Kame'enui. New York: Guilford Press, 2004, 218–237.

Blachowicz, Camille L. Z, and Peter J. Fisher. *Teaching Vocabulary in All Classrooms.* Upper Saddle River, N.J.: Pearson Education, 2006.

Blachowicz, Camille L. Z., and John J. Lee. "Vocabulary Development in the Whole Literacy Classroom." *The Reading Teacher* 45 (November 1991): 188–195.

Blachowicz, Camille L. Z., and Connie Obrochta. "Vocabulary Visits: Virtual Field Trips for Content Vocabulary Development." *The Reading Teacher* 59 (November 2005): 262–268.

Blair, Timothy R., William H. Rupley, and William Dee Nichols. "The Effective Teacher of Reading: Considering the 'What' and 'How' of Instruction." *The Reading Teacher* 60 (February 2007): 432–438.

Blanton, William E., Karen D. Wood, and Gary B. Moorman. "The Role of Purpose in Reading Instruction." *The Reading Teacher* 43 (March 1990): 486–493.

Bluestein, N. Alexandra. "Comprehension Through Characterization: Enabling Readers to Make Personal Connections with Literature." *The Reading Teacher* 55 (February 2002): 431–434.

Boling, Erica. "Classroom Blogging." In Erica Boling, Jill Castek, Lisa Zawilinski, Karen Barton, and Theresa Nierlich, "Collaborative Literacy: Blogs and Internet Projects." *The Reading Teacher* 61 (March 2008): 504–505.

Boodt, Gloria M. "Critical Listeners Become Critical Readers in Remedial Reading Class." *The Reading Teacher* 37 (January 1984): 390–394.

Booth, David. *Classroom Voices.* Toronto: Harcourt Brace, 1994.

Borkowski, J. G., and B. E. Kurtz. "Metacognition and Executive Control." In *Cognition in Special Children: Comparative Approaches to Retardation, Learning Disabilities, and Giftedness*, edited by J. G. Borkowski and J. D. Day. Norwood, N.J.: Ablex, 1987, 123–152.

Bormuth, J. R. "The Cloze Readability Procedure." In *Readability in 1968*, edited by J. R. Bormuth. Champaign, Ill.: National Council of Teachers of English, 1968.

Boulware-Gooden, Regina, Suzanne Carreker, Ann Thornhill, and R. Malatesha Joshi. "Instruction of Metacognitive Strategies Enhances Reading Comprehension and Vocabulary Achievement of Third Grade Students." *The Reading Teacher* 61 (September 2007): 70–77.

Brabham, Edna Greene, and Susan Kidd Villaume. "Continuing Conversations About Literature Circles." *The Reading Teacher* 54 (November 2000): 278–280.

Brabham, Edna Greene, and Susan Kidd Villaume. "Vocabulary Instruction: Concerns and Visions." *The Reading Teacher* 56 (November 2002): 264–268.

Bransford, John D. "Schema Activation and Schema Acquisition: Comments on Richard C. Anderson's Remarks." In *Theoretical Models and Processes of Reading*, 5th ed., edited by Robert B. Ruddell and Norman J. Unrau. Newark, Del.: International Reading Association, 2004, 607–619.

Braselton, Stephania, and Barbara C. Decker. "Using Graphic Organizers to Improve the Reading of Mathematics." *The Reading Teacher* 48 (November 1994): 276–281.

Breen, Leonard. "Connotations." *Journal of Reading* 32 (February 1989): 461.

Brimijoin, Kay, Ede Marquissee, and Carol Ann Tomlinson. "Using Data to Differentiate Instruction." *Educational Leadership* 60, no. 5 (February 2003): 70–72.

Bristow, Page Simpson. "Are Poor Readers Passive Readers? Some Evidence, Possible Explanations, and Potential Solutions." *The Reading Teacher* 39 (December 1985): 318–325.

Broemmel, Amy D., and Kristin T. Rearden. "Should Teachers Use Teachers' Choices Books in Science Classes?" *The Reading Teacher* 60 (November 2006): 254–265.

Bromley, Karen. "Nine Things Every Teacher Should Know About Words and Vocabulary Instruction." *Journal of Adolescent and Adult Literacy* 50 (April 2007): 528–537.

Brown, A. L., and J. D. Day. "Macrorules for Summarizing Texts: The Development of Expertise." *Journal of Verbal Learning and Verbal Behavior* 22, no. 1 (1983): 1–14.

Brown, A. L., J. D. Day, and R. Jones. "The Development of Plans for Summarizing Texts." *Child Development* 54 (1983): 968–979.

Brown, Kathleen. "What Kind of Text—For Whom and When? Textual Scaffolding for Beginning Readers." *The Reading Teacher* 53 (December 1999/January 2000): 292–307.

Bruck, Maggie, and Rebecca Treiman. "Learning to Pronounce Words: The Limitations of Analogies." *Reading Research Quarterly* 27, no. 4 (1992): 374–388.

Brunner, Cornelia. "Judging Student Multimedia." *Electronic Learning* 15 (May/June 1996): 14–15.

Burchers, Sam, Max Burchers, and Bryan Burchers. *Vocabulary Cartoons: Kids Learn a Word a Minute and Never Forget It.* Punta Gorda, Fla.: New Monic Books, 1998.

Burmeister, Lou E. "Usefulness of Phonic Generalizations." *The Reading Teacher* 21 (January 1968): 349–356, 360.

Burns, M. K. "Empirical Analysis of Drill Ratio Research: Refining the Instructional Level for Drill Tasks." *Remedial and Special Education* 25 (May 2004): 167–173.

Busching, Beverly A., and Betty Ann Slesinger. "Authentic Questions: What Do They Look Like? Where Do They Lead?" *Language Arts* 72 (September 1995): 341–351.

Buss, Kathleen, and Lee Karnowski. *Reading and Writing Literacy Genres.* Newark, Del: International Reading Association, 2000.

Butler, Andrea, and Jan Turbill. *Towards a Reading-Writing Classroom.* Portsmouth, N.H.: Heinemann, 1987.

Butler-Pascoe, Mary Ellen, and Karin M. Wiburg. *Technology and Teaching English Language Learners.* Boston: Allyn & Bacon, 2003.

Cadiero-Kaplan, Karen. "Literacy Ideologies; Critically Engaging the Language Arts Curriculum." *Language Arts* 79 (May 2002): 372–381.

Cai, Mingshui. "Transactional Theory and the Study of Multicultural Literature." *Language Arts* 85 (January 2008): 212–220.

California State Board of Education. *Content Standards.* Sacramento: California State Board of Education, 2004. Retrieved from http://www.cde.ca.gov/be/st/ss/enggrade1.asp.

Calkins, Lucy. *The Art of Teaching Writing*, 2nd ed., Portsmouth, N.H.: Heinemann, 1994.

Cambourne, Brian. "Why Do Some Students Fail to Learn to Read? Ockham's Razor and the Conditions of Learning." *The Reading Teacher* 54 (May 2001): 784–786.

Camp, Deanne. "It Takes Two: Teaching with Twin Texts of Fact and Fiction." *The Reading Teacher* 53 (February 2000): 400–408.

Campbell, Linda. *Mindful Learning: 101 Proven Strategies for Student and Teacher Success.* Thousand Oaks, Calif.: Corwin Press, 2003.

Carlo, María S., Diane August, Barry McLaughlin, Catherine E. Snow, Cheryl Dressler, David N. Lippman, Teresa J. Lively, and Claire E. White. "Closing the Gap: Addressing the Vocabulary Needs of English-Language Learners in Bilingual and Mainstream Classrooms." *Reading Research Quarterly* 39 (April/May/June 2004): 188–215.

Carney, J. J., D. Anderson, C. Blackburn, and D. Blessing. "Pre-teaching Vocabulary and the Comprehension of Social Studies Materials by Elementary School Children." *Social Education* 48 (1984): 71–75.

Carnine, Douglas W. "Phonics Versus Look-Say: Transfer to New Words." *The Reading Teacher* 30 (March 1977): 636–640.

Carpenter, Marilyn. "Children's Books That Focus on the Meaning of Citizenship." *Language Arts* 82 (September 2004): 64.

Carr, Kathryn S., Dawna L. Buchanan, Joanna B. Wentz, Mary L. Weiss, and Kitty J. Brant. "Not Just for the Primary Grades: A Bibliography of Picture Books for Secondary Content Teachers." *Journal of Adolescent and Adult Literacy* 45 (October 2001), 146–153.

Carrier, Karen A., and Alfred W. Tatum. "Creating Sentence Walls to Help English-Language Learners Develop Content Literacy." *The Reading Teacher* 60 (November 2006): 285–288.

Carroll, John B., Peter Davies, and Barry Richman. *The American Heritage Word Frequency Book.* Boston: Houghton Mifflin, 1971.

Cartwright, Kelly B. "Fostering Flexibility and Comprehension in Elementary Students." *The Reading Teacher* 59 (April 2006): 628–634.

Casteel, Carolyn P., and Bess A. Isom. "Reciprocal Processes in Science and Literacy Learning." *The Reading Teacher* 47 (April 1994): 538–545.

Castek, Jill, Jessica Bevans-Mangelson, and Bette Goldstone. "Reading Adventures Online: Five Ways to Introduce the New Literacies of the Internet Through Children's Literature." *The Reading Teacher* 59 (April 2006): 714–728.

Castek, Jill, Lisa Zawilinski, Karen Barton, and Theresa Nierlich. "Collaborative Internet Projects." In Erica Boling, Jill Castek, Lisa Zawilinski, Karen Barton, and Theresa Nierlich, "Collaborative Literacy: Blogs and Internet Projects." *The Reading Teacher* 61 (March 2008): 505–506.

Ceprano, Maria A. "A Review of Selected Research on Methods of Teaching Sight Words." *The Reading Teacher* 35 (December 1981): 314–322.

Chall, Jeanne S., and Vicki A. Jacobs. "Poor Children's Fourth-Grade Slump." *American Educator* 27, no. 1 (2003): 14–15.

Chamberlain, Julia, and Dorothy Leal. "Caldecott Medal Books and Readability Levels: Not Just 'Picture' Books." *The Reading Teacher* 52 (May 1999): 898–902.

Chapman, Carolyn, and Rita King. *Differentiated Instructional Strategies for Reading in the Content Areas.* Thousand Oaks, Calif.: Corwin Press, 2003.

Chappuis, Stephen, and Jan Chappuis. "The Best Value in Formative Assessment." *Educational Leadership* 65 (December 2007/January 2008): 14–18.

Charron, Nancy Necora. "'I Learned That There's a State Called Victoria and He has Six Blue-Tongued Lizards!'" *The Reading Teacher* 60 (May 2007): 762–769.

Cheng, Pui-wan. "Metacognition and Giftedness: The State of the Relationship." *Gifted Child Quarterly* 37 (Summer 1993): 105–112.

Chiappe, P., and L. Siegel. "A Longitudinal Study of Reading Development of Canadian Children from Diverse Linguistic Backgrounds." *The Elementary School Journal* 107 (2006): 135–152.

Church, Susan M. "Is Whole Language Warm and Fuzzy?" *The Reading Teacher* 47 (February 1994): 362–370.

Clark, Eve V. *The Lexicon in Acquisition.* Cambridge: Cambridge University Press, 1993.

Clark, Kathleen F. "What Can I Say Besides 'Sound It Out'? Coaching Word Recognition in Beginning Reading." *The Reading Teacher* 57 (February 2004): 440–449.

Clausen-Grace, Nicki, and Michelle Kelley. "You Can't Hide in R⁵: Restructuring Independent Reading to Be More Strategic and Engaging." *Voices from the Middle* 14 (March 2007): 38–49.

Clay, Marie. *The Early Detection of Reading Difficulties.* Auckland, New Zealand: Heinemann, 1979.

Clay, Marie M. *The Early Detection of Reading Difficulties,* 3rd ed. Auckland, New Zealand: Heinemann, 1993.

Clay, Marie. *An Observation of Early Literacy Achievement.* Portsmouth, N.H.: Heinemann, 2006.

Clymer, Theodore. "The Utility of Phonic Generalizations in the Primary Grades." *The Reading Teacher* 50 (November 1996): 182–187.

Coiro, Julie. "Reading Comprehension on the Internet: Expanding Our Understanding of Reading Comprehension to Encompass New Literacies." *The Reading Teacher* 56 (February 2003): 458–464.

Coiro, Julie, and Elizabeth Dobler. "Exploring the Online Reading Comprehension Strategies Used by Sixth-Grade Skilled Readers to Search for and Locate Information on the Internet." *Reading Research Quarterly* 42 (April/May/June 2007): 214–250.

Cole, Ardith Davis. "Beginner-Oriented Texts in Literature-Based Classrooms: The Segue for a Few Struggling Readers." *The Reading Teacher* 51 (March 1998): 488–501.

Come, Barbara, and Anthony Fredericks. "Family Literacy in Urban Schools: Meeting the Needs of At-Risk Children." *The Reading Teacher* 48 (April 1995): 566–570.

Commeyras, Michelle. "Using Literature to Teach Critical Thinking." *Journal of Reading* 32 (May 1989): 703–707.

Compton-Lilly, Catherine. "'Sounding Out': A Pervasive Cultural Model of Reading." *Language Arts* 82 (July 2005): 441–451.

Cox, Carole. "Literature-Based Teaching: A Student Response-Centered Curriculum." In *Reader Response in Elementary Classrooms*, edited by Nicholas Karolides. Mahwah, N.J.: Erlbaum, 1997.

Cunningham, James W., and Lisa K. Wall. "Teaching Good Readers to Comprehend Better." *Journal of Reading* 37 (March 1994): 480–486.

Cunningham, Patricia M. "Decoding Polysyllabic Words: An Alternative Strategy." *The Reading Teacher* 31 (April 1978): 608–614.

Cunningham, Patricia M. "A Compare/Contrast Theory of Mediated Word Identification." *The Reading Teacher* 32 (April 1979): 774–778.

Cunningham, Patricia M. *Phonics They Use: Words for Reading and Writing.* New York: HarperCollins, 1991.

Cunningham, Patricia, and Richard Allington. *Classrooms That Work: They Can All Read and Write*, 2nd ed. New York: HarperCollins, 1999.

Cunningham, Patricia M., and James W. Cunningham. "Making Words: Enhancing the Invented Spelling-Decoding Connection." *The Reading Teacher* 46 (October 1992): 106–115.

Dahl, Karin L., and Patricia L. Scharer. "Phonics Teaching and Learning in Whole Language Classrooms: New Evidence from Research." *The Reading Teacher* 53 (April 2000): 584–594.

Dailey, Kathleen, and Kimberly Owen. "Dramatic Play and Literacy Development." Presentation at International Reading Association Convention, Toronto, Canada, May 1994.

Dale, Edgar, and Jeanne S. Chall. "A Formula for Predicting Readability." *Educational Research Bulletin* 27 (January 21, 1948): 11–20, 28; (February 18, 1948): 37–54.

Damico, James, with Ruthie Riddle. "Exploring Freedom and Leaving a Legacy: Enacting New Literacies with Digital Texts in the Elementary Classroom." *Language Arts* 84 (September 2006): 34–44.

Daneman, Meredyth. "Individual Differences in Reading Skills." In *Handbook of Reading Research*, Vol. 2, edited by Rebecca Barr, Michael L. Kamil, Peter Mosenthal, and P. David Pearson. New York: Longman, 1991, 512–538.

Daniels, Harvey. *Literature Circles: Voice and Choice in Book Clubs & Reading Groups.* Portland, Maine: Stenhouse, 2002.

Danielson, Charlotte, and Leslye Abrutyn. *An Introduction to Using Portfolios in the Classroom.* Alexandria, Va.: Association for Supervision and Curriculum Development, 1997.

Davis, Anita P., and Thomas R. McDaniel. "An Essential Vocabulary: An Update." *The Reading Teacher* 52 (November 1998): 308–309.

Davis, Zephaniah T., and Michael D. McPherson. "Story Map Instruction: A Road Map for Reading Comprehension." *The Reading Teacher* 43 (December 1989): 232–240.

DeBenedictis, Deb. "Sustained Silent Reading: Making Adaptations." *Voices from the Middle* 14 (March 2007): 29–37.

DeSerres, Barbara. "Putting Vocabulary in Context." *The Reading Teacher* 43 (April 1990): 612–613.

Deubel, Patricia. "Podcasts: Where's the Learning?" *T·H·E Journal*, (June 2007). Retrieved from http://www.thejournal .com/articles/20764 on June 11, 2007.

Devaney, Laura. "Study: eBooks Could Spark Interest in Reading." *eSchool News Online* (August 2, 2007). Retrieved from http://www .eschoolnews.com/news/PFshowstory.cfm?ArticleID+7294 on August 31, 2007.

Dever, Christine T. "Press Conference: A Strategy for Integrating Reading with Writing." *The Reading Teacher* 46 (September 1992): 72–73.

Dickerson, Dolores Pawley. "A Study of Use of Games to Reinforce Sight Vocabulary." *The Reading Teacher* 36 (October 1982): 46–49.

Digital Girls Project. *Overall View of the Digital Girls Project*, 2005. Retrieved from www.digitalgirls.org/txp on August 29, 2007.

Dixon-Krauss, Lisbeth. "Using Literature as a Context for Teaching Vocabulary." *Journal of Adolescent & Adult Literacy* 45 (December 2001/January 2002): 310–318.

Dixon-Krauss, Lisbeth. *Vygotsky in the Classroom.* White Plains, N.Y.: Longman, 1996.

Dlott, Ann Marie. "A (Pod)Cast of Thousands." *Educational Leadership* 64, no. 7 (2007): 80–82.

Dlugosz, D. W. "Rethinking the Role of Reading in Teaching a Foreign Language to Young Learners." *ELT Journal* 54 (2000): 284–291.

Dodge, Bernie. WebQuest.Org, 2007. http://webquest.org/index .php. Retrieved August 25, 2007.

Donovan, Carol, and Laura Smolkin. "Children's Genre Knowledge: An Examination of K–5 Students' Performance on Multiple Tasks Providing Differing Levels of Scaffolding." *Reading Research Quarterly* 37 (October/November/December 2002): 428–465.

Dorr, Roberta E. "Something Old Is New Again: Revisiting Language Experience." *The Reading Teacher* 60 (October 2006): 138–146.

Dowhower, S. I. "Speaking of Prosody: Fluency's Unattended Bedfellow." *Theory into Practice* 30 (1991): 165–173.

Dowhower, Sarah L. "Supporting a Strategic Stance in the Classroom: A Comprehension Framework for Helping Teachers Help Students to Be Strategic." *The Reading Teacher* 52 (April 1999): 672–688.

Downing, John. "How Children Think About Reading." In *Psychological Factors in the Teaching of Reading*, compiled by Eldon E. Ekwall. Columbus, Ohio: Merrill, 1973.

Downing, John. "Reading—Skill or Skills?" *The Reading Teacher* 35 (February 1982): 534–537.

Dreher, Mariam Jean. "Motivating Children to Read More Nonfiction." *The Reading Teacher* 52 (December 1998/January 1999): 414–416.

Dreher, Mariam Jean, and Harry Singer. "Story Grammar Instruction Unnecessary for Intermediate Grade Students." *The Reading Teacher* 34 (December 1980): 261–268.

Drucker, Mary J. "What Reading Teachers Should Know About ESL Learners." *The Reading Teacher* 57 (September 2003): 22–29.

Duffelmeyer, Frederick A. "The Influence of Experience-Based Vocabulary Instruction on Learning Word Meanings." *Journal of Reading* 24 (October 1980): 35–40.

Duffy, Gerald G., and James V. Hoffman. "In Pursuit of an Illusion: The Flawed Search for a Perfect Method." *The Reading Teacher* 53 (September 1999): 10–16.

Duffy, Gerald G., Laura R. Roehler, and Beth Ann Herrmann. "Modeling Mental Processes Helps Poor Readers Become Strategic Readers." *The Reading Teacher* 41 (April 1988): 762–767.

Dugan, Jo Ann. "Transactional Literature Discussions: Engaging Students in the Appreciation and Understanding of Literature." *The Reading Teacher* 51 (October 1997): 86–96.

Duke, Nell K. "Content-Rich Comprehension Instruction." Presentation at the International Reading Association Convention, Toronto, Canada, 2007.

Duke, Nell K., and P. David Pearson. "Effective Practices for Developing Reading Comprehension." In *What Research Has to Say About Reading Instruction*, edited by Alan E. Farstrup and S. Jay Samuels. Newark, Del.: International Reading Association, 2002, 205–242.

Duncan, Patricia H. "I Liked the Book Better: Comparing Film and Text to Build Critical Comprehension." *The Reading Teacher* 46 (May 1993): 720–725.

Durkin, Dolores. "What Is the Value of the New Interest in Reading Comprehension?" *Language Arts* 58 (January 1981): 23–43.

Dwyer, Edward J. "Solving Verbal Analogies." *Journal of Reading* 32 (October 1988): 73–75.

Dymock, Susan. "Teaching Expository Text Structure Awareness." *The Reading Teacher* 59 (October 2005): 177–182.

Dymock, Susan. "Comprehension Strategy Instruction: Teaching Narrative Text Structure Awareness." *The Reading Teacher* 61 (October 2007): 161–167.

Ebbers, Margaretha. "Science Text Sets: Using Various Genres to Promote Literacy and Inquiry." *Language Arts* 80 (September 2002): 40–50.

Echevarria, Jana, and Deborah J. Short. "The Sheltered Instruction Observation Protocol (SIOP)." n.d. Retrieved from www.siopinstitute.net/pdf/sioppaper.pdf on January 23, 2008.

Echevarria, Jana, M. E. Vogt, and Deborah Short. Making Content Comprehensible for English Language Learners: The SIOP Model. Needham Heights, Mass.: Allyn & Bacon, 2004.

Edinger, Monica. "Empowering Young Writers with Technology." *Educational Leadership* 51 (April 1994): 58–60.

Edwards, Elizabeth Carr, George Font, James F. Baumann, and Eileen Boland. "Unlocking Word Meanings: Strategies and Guidelines for Teaching Morphemic and Contextual Analysis." In *Vocabulary Instruction: Research to Practice*, edited by James F. Baumann and Edward J. Kame'enui. New York: Guilford Press, 2004, 159–176.

Ehri, L. C., and C. Robbins. "Beginners Need Some Decoding Skill to Read Words by Analogy." *Reading Research Quarterly* 27, no. 1 (1992): 13–26.

El-Hindi, Amelia E. "Beyond Classroom Boundaries: Constructionist Teaching with the Internet." *The Reading Teacher* 51 (May 1998): 694–700.

El-Hindi, Amelia E. "Integrating Literacy and Science in the Classroom: From Ecomysteries to Readers' Theatre." *The Reading Teacher* 56 (March 2003): 536–538.

Emans, Robert. "The Usefulness of Phonic Generalizations Above the Primary Grades." *The Reading Teacher* 20 (February 1967): 419–425.

Emery, Donna W. "Helping Readers Comprehend Stories from the Characters' Perspectives." *The Reading Teacher* 49 (April 1996): 534–541.

Englot-Mash, Christine. "Tying Together Reading Strategies." *Journal of Reading* 35 (October 1991): 150–151.

Enz, Billie, ed. "Strategies for Promoting Parental Support for Emergent Literacy Programs." *The Reading Teacher* 49 (October 1995): 168–170.

Evans, Carol. "*Monstruos, Pesadillas*, and Other Frights: A Thematic Unit." *The Reading Teacher* 47 (February 1994): 428–430.

Faber, Sharon. How to Teach Reading When You're Not a Reading Teacher. Nashville: Incentive Publications, 2006.

Fallon, Irmie, and JoBeth Allen. "Where the Deer and the Cantaloupe Play." *The Reading Teacher* 47 (April 1994): 546–551.

Farr, Roger, and Nancy Roser. Teaching a Child to Read. New York: Harcourt Brace Jovanovich, 1979.

Fawson, Parker C., and D. Ray Reutzel. "But I Only Have a Basal: Implementing Guided Reading in the Early Grades." *The Reading Teacher* 54 (September 2000): 84–97.

Fay, Leo. "Reading Study Skills: Math and Science." In *Reading and Inquiry*, edited by J. Allen Figurel. Newark, Del.: International Reading Association, 1965.

Felber, Sheila. "Story Mapping for Primary Students." *The Reading Teacher* 43 (October 1989): 90–91.

Fiene, Judy, and Susan McMahon. "Assessing Comprehension: A Classroom-Based Process." *The Reading Teacher* 60 (February 2007): 406–417.

Fisette, Dolores. "Practical Authentic Assessment: Good Kid Watchers Know What to Teach Next." *The California Reader* 26 (Summer 1993): 4–7.

Fisher, Bobbi. "The Environment Reflects the Program." *Teaching K–8* 20 (August/September 1989): 82, 84, 86.

Fisher, Bobbi. Joyful Learning. Portsmouth, N.H.: Heinemann, 1991.

Fisher, Douglas. "Side Trip: Letting Students 'Just Read'?" *Voices from the Middle* 14 (March 2007): 32.

Fitzgerald, Jill. "Helping Readers Gain Self-Control over Reading Comprehension." *The Reading Teacher* 37 (December 1983): 249–253.

Fitzgerald, Jill. "Enhancing Two Related Thought Processes: Revision in Writing and Critical Reading." *The Reading Teacher* 43 (October 1989): 42–48.

Flanigan, Kevin, and Scott C. Greenwood. "Effective Content Vocabulary Instruction in the Middle: Matching Students, Purposes, Words, and Strategies." *Journal of Adolescent & Adult Literacy* 51 (November 2007): 226–238.

Flitterman-King, Sharon. "The Role of the Response Journal in Active Reading." *The Quarterly of the National Writing Project and the Center for the Study of Writing* 10, no. 3 (1988): 4–11.

Flood, James, and Diane Lapp. "Reading and Writing Relations: Assumptions and Directions." In *The Dynamics of Language Learning*, edited by James R. Squire. Urbana, Ill.: ERIC Clearinghouse on Reading and Communication Skills, 1987.

Flynn, Linda L. "Developing Critical Reading Skills Through Cooperative Problem Solving." *The Reading Teacher* 42 (May 1989): 664–668.

Flynn, Rosalind M. "Curriculum-Based Readers Theatre: Setting the Stage for Reading and Retention." *The Reading Teacher* 58 (December 2004/January 2005): 360–365.

Flynn, Rosalind M., and Gail A. Carr. "Exploring Classroom Literature Through Drama: A Specialist and a Teacher Collaborate." *Language Arts* 71 (January 1994): 38–43.

Flynt, E. Sutton, and William G. Brozo. "Developing Academic Language: Got Words?" *The Reading Teacher* 61 (March 2008): 500–502.

Forbes, Leighann S. "Using Web-Based Bookmarks in K–8 Settings: Linking the Internet to Instruction." *The Reading Teacher* 58 (October 2004): 148–153.

Forcier, Richard C., and Don E. Descy. *The Computer as an Educational Tool*. Upper Saddle River, N.J.: Pearson Education, 2008.

Forell, Elizabeth. "The Case for Conservative Reader Placement." *The Reading Teacher* 38 (May 1985): 857–862.

Fortescue, Chelsea M. "Using Oral and Written Language to Increase Understanding of Math Concepts." *Language Arts* 71 (December 1994): 576–580.

Fortson, Laura, and Judith Reiff. *Early Childhood Curriculum*. Boston: Allyn & Bacon, 1995.

Foss, Abigail. "Peeling the Onion: Teaching Critical Literacy with Students of Privilege." *Language Arts* 79 (May 2002): 393–403.

Fountas, Irene C., and Gay S. Pinnell. *Guided Reading: Good First Reading for All Children*. Portsmouth, N.H.: Heinemann, 1996.

Fountas, Irene C., and Gay Su Pinnell. *Matching Books to Readers: Using Leveled Books in Guided Reading, K–3*. Portsmouth, N.H.: Heinemann, 1999.

Fournier, David N. E., and Michael F. Graves. "Scaffolding Adolescents' Comprehension of Short Stories." *Journal of Adolescent & Adult Literacy* 46 (September 2002): 30–39.

Fowler, Gerald. "Developing Comprehension Skills in Primary Students Through the Use of Story Frames." *The Reading Teacher* 36 (November 1982): 176–179.

Fox, Barbara J. *Word Recognition Activities: Patterns and Strategies for Developing Fluency*. Upper Saddle River, N.J.: Merrill/Prentice Hall, 2003.

Frager, Alan M. "Affective Dimensions of Content Area Reading." *Journal of Reading* 36 (May 1993): 616–622.

Fredericks, Anthony D. "Mental Imagery Activities to Improve Comprehension." *The Reading Teacher* 40 (October 1986): 78–81.

Freedman, Glenn, and Elizabeth G. Reynolds. "Enriching Basal Reader Lessons with Semantic Webbing." *The Reading Teacher* 33 (March 1980): 667–684.

Freedman, Lauren, and Cynthia Carver. "Preservice Teacher Understandings of Adolescent Literacy Development: Naïve Wonder to Dawning Realization to Intellectual Rigor." *Journal of Adolescent and Adult Literacy* 50 (May 2007): 654–665.

French, Joyce, Nancy Ellsworth, and Marie Amoruso. *Reading and Learning Disabilities: Research and Practice*. New York: Garland, 1995.

Fresch, Mary Jo. "Self-Selection of Early Literacy Learners." *The Reading Teacher* 49 (November 1995): 220–227.

Fry, Edward. *Elementary Reading Instruction*. New York: McGraw-Hill, 1977a.

Fry, Edward. "Fry's Readability Graph: Clarifications, Validity, and Extension to Level 17." *Journal of Reading* 21 (December 1977b): 249.

Fry, Edward. "The Most Common Phonograms." *The Reading Teacher* 51 (April 1998): 620–622.

Fry, Edward. "Readability Versus Text Leveling." *The Reading Teacher* 56 (November 2002): 286–291.

Fuhler, Carol J. "Response Journals: Just One More Time with Feeling." *Journal of Reading* 37 (February 1994): 400–405.

Galda, Lee, Emily Carr, and Susan Cox. "The Plot Thickens." *The Reading Teacher* 43 (November 1989): 160–166.

Gale, David. "Why Word Play?" *The Reading Teacher* 36 (November 1982): 220–222.

Gallagher, Janice Mori. "Pairing Adolescent Fiction with Books from the Canon." *Journal of Adolescent & Adult Literacy* 39 (September 1995): 8–14.

Gallagher, William J. "The Contradictory Nature of Professional Teaching Standards." *Phi Delta Kappan* 87 (October 2005): 112–115.

Galley, M. "Court Blocks School Ban on Weapons Images." *Education Week* 23 (2004): 6.

Gambrell, Linda. "Creating Classroom Cultures That Foster Reading Motivation." *The Reading Teacher* 50 (September 1996): 14–25.

Gambrell, Linda B. "Shifts in the Conversation: Teacher-Led, Peer-Led, and Computer-Mediated Discussions." *The Reading Teacher* 58 (October 2004): 212–215.

Ganske, Kathy, James K. Monroe, and Dorothy S. Strickland. "Questions Teachers Ask About Struggling Readers and Writers." *The Reading Teacher* 57 (October 2003): 118–128.

Gardner, Howard. "Reflections on Multiple Intelligences: Myths and Messages." *Phi Delta Kappan* 77 (November 1995): 200–209.

Gardner, Michael K., and Martha M. Smith. "Does Perspective Taking Ability Contribute to Reading Comprehension?" *Journal of Reading* 30 (January 1987): 333–336.

Gaskins, Irene West, Linnea C. Ehri, Cheryl Cress, Colleen O'Hara, and Katherine Donnelly. "Procedures for Word Learning: Making Discoveries About Words." *The Reading Teacher* 50 (December 1996/January 1997): 312–327.

Gaskins, Irene West, Linnea C. Ehri, Cheryl Cress, Colleen O'Hara, and Katherine Donnelly. "Analyzing Words and Making Discoveries About the Alphabetic System: Activities for Beginning Readers." *Language Arts* 74 (March 1997): 172–184.

Gaskins, Irene West, Eric Satlow, Daniel Hyson, Joyce Ostertag, and Linda Six. "Classroom Talk About Text: Learning in Science Class." *Journal of Reading* 37 (April 1994): 558–565.

Gaskins, Robert W., Jennifer C. Gaskins, and Irene W. Gaskins. "A Decoding Program for Poor Readers—And the Rest of the Class, Too!" *Language Arts* 68 (March 1991): 213–225.

Gestwicki, Carol. *Developmentally Appropriate Practice.* Albany, N.Y.: Delmar, 1995.

Gibson, Karen Sue. "Students' Favorite Prereading Activities, K–5." Unpublished doctoral dissertation. Houston, Tex.: University of Houston, 2004.

Giles, Vickey. "Students' Favorite Prereading Activities, 6–12." Unpublished doctoral dissertation. Houston, Tex.: University of Houston, 2005.

Gill, J. Thomas, Jr. "Development of Word Knowledge as It Relates to Reading, Spelling, and Instruction." *Language Arts* 69 (October 1992): 444–453.

Gill, Sharon Ruth. "Reading with Amy: Teaching and Learning Through Reading Conferences." *The Reading Teacher* 53 (March 2000): 500–509.

Gill, Sharon Ruth. "Teaching Rimes with Shared Reading." *The Reading Teacher* 60 (October 2006): 191–193.

Gill, Sharon Ruth. "Learning About Word Parts with Kidspiration." *The Reading Teacher* 61 (September 2007): 79–84.

Gillet, Jean Wallace, and J. Richard Gentry. "Bridges Between Nonstandard and Standard English with Extensions of Dictated Stories." *The Reading Teacher* 36 (January 1983): 360–365.

Gipe, Joan P. "Use of a Relevant Context Helps Kids Learn New Word Meanings." *The Reading Teacher* 33 (January 1980): 398–402.

Glass, Gerald G. "The Strange World of Syllabication." *The Elementary School Journal* 67 (May 1967): 403–405.

Glynn, Shawn. "Teaching with Analogies: Building on the Science Textbook." *The Reading Teacher* 49 (March 1996): 490–492.

Golden, Joanne M. "Children's Concept of Story in Reading and Writing." *The Reading Teacher* 37 (March 1984): 578–584.

Golden, Joanne M., Annyce Meiners, and Stanley Lewis. "The Growth of Story Meaning." *Language Arts* 69 (January 1992): 22–27.

Goldenberg, Claude. "Instructional Conversations: Promoting Comprehension Through Discussion." *The Reading Teacher* 46 (December 1992/January 1993): 316–326.

Goldstone, Bette. "Children's Books That Mirror Techno Texts." *The Reading Teacher* 59 (April 2006): 725–726.

Goodman, Kenneth S. "Reading: A Psycholinguistic Guessing Game." In *Perspectives on Elementary Reading*, edited by Robert Karlin. New York: Harcourt Brace Jovanovich, 1973.

Goodman, Kenneth S. "Unity in Reading." In *Theoretical Models and Processes of Reading*, 3rd ed., edited by Harry Singer and Robert B. Ruddell. Newark, Del.: International Reading Association, 1985.

Goodman, Kenneth S. *What's Whole in Whole Language?* Portsmouth, N.H.: Heinemann, 1986.

Goodman, Kenneth S. "Why Whole Language Is Today's Agenda in Education." *Language Arts* 69 (September 1992): 354–363.

Goodman, Kenneth S. "Reading, Writing, and Written Texts: A Transactional Sociopsycholinguistic View." In *Theoretical Models and Processes of Reading*, 4th ed., edited by Robert B. Ruddell, Martha Rapp Ruddell, and Harry Singer. Newark, Del.: International Reading Association, 1994, 1093–1130.

Goodman, Kenneth S., and Catherine Buck. "Dialect Barriers to Reading Comprehension Revisited." *The Reading Teacher* 50 (March 1997): 454–459.

Goodman, Yetta. "Miscue Analysis for Classroom Teachers: Some History and Some Procedures." *Primary Voices K–6* 3 (November 1995): 2–9.

Gordon, Christine, and P. David Pearson. *Effects of Instruction in Metacomprehension and Inferencing on Students' Comprehension Abilities* (Technical Report No. 269). Urbana-Champaign, Ill.: University of Illinois, Center for the Study of Reading, 1983.

Gough, Philip B. "Word Recognition." In *Handbook of Reading Research*, edited by P. David Pearson et al. New York: Longman, 1984.

Gove, Mary. "Clarifying Teachers' Beliefs About Reading." *The Reading Teacher* 37 (December 1983): 261–268.

Grabe, Mark, and Cindy Grabe. *Integrating Technology for Meaningful Learning.* Boston: Houghton Mifflin, 2007.

Graves, Donald. *A Fresh Look at Writing.* Portsmouth, N.H.: Heinemann, 1994.

Graves, Michael F. *The Vocabulary Book: Learning and Instruction.* Urbana, Ill.: National Council of Teachers of English, 2006.

Graves, Michael F., and Maureen C. Prenn. "Costs and Benefits of Various Methods of Teaching Vocabulary." *Journal of Reading* 29 (April 1986): 596–602.

Graves, Michael F., and Susan M. Watts-Taffe. "The Place of Word Consciousness in a Research-Based Vocabulary Program." In *What Research Has to Say About Reading Instruction*, edited by Alan E. Farstrup and S. Jay Samuels. Newark, Del.: International Reading Association, 2002.

Greenewald, M. Jane, and Rosalind L. Rossing. "Short-Term and Long-Term Effects of Story Grammar and Self-Monitoring Training on Children's Story Comprehension." In *Solving Problems in*

Literacy: Learners, Teachers, and Researchers, edited by Jerome A. Niles and Rosary V. Lalik. Rochester, N.Y.: National Reading Conference, 1986.

Greenwood, Scott C., and Kevin Flanigan. "Overlapping Vocabulary and Comprehension: Context Clues Complement Semantic Gradients." *The Reading Teacher* 61 (November 2007): 249–254.

Gregg, Madeleine, and Diane Carver Sekeres. "Supporting Children's Reading of Expository Text in the Geography Classroom." *The Reading Teacher* 60 (October 2006): 102–110.

Griffith, Priscilla, and Mary Olson. "Phonemic Awareness Helps Beginning Readers Break the Code." *The Reading Teacher* 45 (March 1992): 516–523.

Grisham, Dana L., and Thomas D. Wolsey. "Recentering the Middle School Classroom as a Vibrant Learning Community: Students, Literacy, and Technology Intersect." *Journal of Adolescent & Adult Literacy* 49 (May 2006): 648–660.

Groff, Patrick. "The Maturing of Phonics Instruction." *The Reading Teacher* 39 (May 1986): 919–923.

Groff, Patrick. "Where's the Phonics? Making a Case for Its Direct and Systematic Instruction." *The Reading Teacher* 52 (October 1998): 138–141.

Guilfoyle, Christy. "NCLB: Is There Life Beyond Testing?" *Educational Leadership* 64 (November 2006): 8–13.

Guillaume, Andrea M. "Learning with Text in the Primary Grades." *The Reading Teacher* 51 (March 1998): 476–486.

Guinee, Kathleen, and Maya B. Eagleton. "Spinning Straw into Gold: Transforming Information into Knowledge During Web-Based Research." *English Journal* 95 (March 2006): 46–52.

Gunderson, Lee. "Voices of the Teenage Diasporas." *Journal of Adolescent and Adult Literacy* 43 (May 2000): 692–706.

Gunning, Thomas G. "Word Building: A Strategic Approach to the Teaching of Phonics." *The Reading Teacher* 48 (March 1995): 484–488.

Guskey, Thomas. "The Rest of the Story." *Educational Leadership* 65 (December 2007/January 2008): 28–35.

Guthrie, John T. "Models of Reading and Reading Disability." *Journal of Educational Psychology* 65 (1973): 9–18.

Guzzetti, Barbara J., Barbara J. Kowalinski, and Tom McGowan. "Using a Literature-Based Approach to Teaching Social Studies." *Journal of Reading* 36 (October 1992): 114–122.

Haager, Diane, Janette Klingner, and Sharon Vaughn. *Evidence-Based Reading Practices for Response to Intervention.* Baltimore: Brooks, 2007.

Hacker, Charles J. "From Schema Theory to Classroom Practice." *Language Arts* 57 (November/December 1980): 866–871.

Hadaway, Nancy L., and Terrell A. Young. "Content Literacy and Language Learning: Instructional Decisions." *The Reading Teacher* 47 (April 1994): 522–527.

Hamann, Lori S., Loree Schultz, Michael W. Smith, and Brian White. "Making Connections: The Power of Autobiographical Writing Before Reading." *Journal of Reading* 35 (September 1991): 24–28.

Hancock, Marjorie R. "Character Journals: Initiating Involvement and Identification Through Literature." *Journal of Reading* 37 (September 1993): 42–50.

Hare, Victoria Chou. "What's in a Word? A Review of Young Children's Difficulties with the Construct 'Word.'" *The Reading Teacher* 37 (January 1984): 360–364.

Harmon, Janis M. "Vocabulary Teaching and Learning in a Seventh-Grade Literature-Based Classroom." *Journal of Adolescent & Adult Literacy* 41 (1998): 518–529.

Harmon, Janis M., and Wenda B. Hedrick. "Zooming In and Zooming Out: Enhancing Vocabulary and Conceptual Learning in Social Studies." *The Reading Teacher* 54 (October 2000): 155–159.

Harp, Bill. "When the Principal Asks: 'Why Are You Doing Piagetian Task Testing When You Have Given Basal Placement Tests?'" *The Reading Teacher* 41 (November 1987): 212–214.

Harp, Bill. "When the Principal Asks, 'Why Are You Doing Guided Imagery During Reading Time?'" *The Reading Teacher* 41 (February 1988): 588–590.

Harp, Bill. "When the Principal Asks: 'Why Aren't You Using the Phonics Workbooks?'" *The Reading Teacher* 42 (January 1989): 326–327.

Harris, Albert J., and Edward R. Sipay. *How to Increase Reading Ability*, 8th ed. New York: Longman, 1985.

Harris, Sandra. "Bringing About Change in Reading Instruction." *The Reading Teacher* 49 (May 1996): 612–618.

Harris, Theodore L., and Richard E. Hodges, eds. *The Literacy Dictionary: The Vocabulary of Reading and Writing.* Newark, Del.: International Reading Association, 1995.

Harvey, Stephanie. "Nonfiction Inquiry: Using Real Reading and Writing to Explore the World." *Language Arts* 80 (September 2002): 12–22.

Haycock, Kati. "No More Invisible Kids." *Educational Leadership* 64 (November 2006): 38–42.

Heald-Taylor, B. Gail. "Three Paradigms for Literature Instruction in Grades 3 to 6." *The Reading Teacher* 49 (March 1996): 456–466.

Heilman, Arthur W. *Phonics in Proper Perspective.* Upper Saddle River, N.J.: Prentice Hall, 2002.

Heller, Mary F. "Comprehending and Composing Through Language Experience." *The Reading Teacher* 42 (November 1988): 130–135.

Helman, Lori A. "Building on the Sound System of Spanish: Insights from the Alphabetic Spellings of English-Language Learners." *The Reading Teacher* 57 (February 2004): 452–460.

Henry, Laurie A. "SEARCHing for an Answer: The Critical Role of New Literacies While Reading on the Internet." *The Reading Teacher* 59 (April 2006): 614–627.

Herrell, Adrienne L. *Fifty Strategies for Teaching English Learners.* Columbus, Ohio: Merrill, 2000.

Herrmann, Beth Ann. "Two Approaches for Helping Poor Readers Become More Strategic." *The Reading Teacher* 42 (October 1988): 24–28.

Hess, Mary Lou. "Understanding Nonfiction: Purpose, Classification, Response." *Language Arts* 68 (March 1991): 228–232.

Heward, W. *Exceptional Children.* Upper Saddle River, N.J.: Merrill/Prentice Hall, 2006.

Hiebert, Elfrieda H., and Jacalyn Colt. "Patterns of Literature-Based Reading Instruction." *The Reading Teacher* 43 (October 1989): 14–20.

Hill, Sharon. "Our Visions of Possibility for Literacy: Keeping the Passion: What Really Matters." *Language Arts* 83 (May 2006): 392–394.

Hoffman, James V. "Critical Reading/Thinking Across the Curriculum: Using I-Charts to Support Learning." *Language Arts* 69 (February 1992): 121–127.

Holdaway, Don. *The Foundations of Literacy.* Portsmouth, N.H.: Heinemann, 1979.

Holloway, John H. "A Value-Added View of Pupil Performance." *Educational Leadership* 57 (February 2000): 84–85.

Hopkins, J. "All Students Being Equal." *Technology & Learning* 26 (2006): 26–28.

Huck, Charlotte S., Susan Hepler, and Janet Hickman. *Children's Literature in the Elementary School,* 6th ed. Fort Worth: Harcourt Brace, 1997.

Huff-Benkoski, Kelly Ann, and Scott C. Greenwood. "The Use of Word Analogy Instruction with Developing Readers." *The Reading Teacher* 48 (February 1995): 446–447.

Hughes, Sandra M. "Impact of Whole Language on Four Elementary School Libraries." *Language Arts* 70 (September 1993): 393–399.

Hunter-Grundin, Elizabeth. "Spoken Language in Emergent Literacy Learning." *Reading Today* 7 (February/March 1990): 22.

Ikpeze, Chinwe H., and Fenice B. Boyd. "Web-Based Inquiry Learning: Facilitating Thoughtful Literacy with WebQuests." *The Reading Teacher* 60 (April 2007): 644–654.

International Reading Association & National Council of Teachers of English. *Standards for the English Language Arts: A Project of National Council of Teachers of English and International Reading Association.* Newark, Del.: International Reading Association; Urbana, Ill.: National Council of Teachers of English, 1996.

International Visual Literacy Association. *Frequently Asked Questions: What Is Visual Literacy?* 1998. Retrieved from http://www.ivla.org/organization/whatis.htm.

Irwin, Judith Westphal. *Teaching Reading Comprehension Processes,* 2nd ed. Englewood Cliffs, N.J.: Prentice-Hall, 1991.

Ivey, Gay, and Douglas Fisher. *Creating Literacy-Rich Schools for Adolescents.* Alexandria, Va.: Association for Supervision and Curriculum, 2006.

Iwicki, Ann L. "Vocabulary Connections." *The Reading Teacher* 45 (May 1992): 736.

Jaeger, Elizabeth. "Literacy, Logic, and Intuition." *Language Arts* 84 (May 2007): 441–449.

Jasmine, Julia. *Addressing Diversity in the Classroom.* Westminster, Calif.: Teacher Created Materials, 1995.

Jenkins, Joseph R., Patricia F. Vadasy, Julia A. Peyton, and Elizabeth A. Sanders. "Decodable Text—Where to Find It." *The Reading Teacher* 57 (October 2003): 185–189.

Jennings, Jack, and Diane Stark Rentner. "Ten Big Effects of the No Child Left Behind Act on Public Schools." *Phi Delta Kappan* 88 (October 2006): 110–113.

Jensen, Eric. *Teaching with the Brain in Mind.* Alexandria, Va.: Association for Supervision and Curriculum Development, 2005.

Johnson, Dale D., and James F. Baumann. "Word Identification." In *Handbook of Reading Research,* edited by P. David Pearson et al. New York: Longman, 1984.

Johnson, Dale D., and P. David Pearson. *Teaching Reading Vocabulary,* 2nd ed. New York: Holt, 1984.

Johnson, Dale D., Susan D. Pittelman, and Joan E. Heimlich. "Semantic Mapping." *The Reading Teacher* 39 (April 1986): 778–783.

Johnson, Nancy M., and M. Jane Ebert. "Time Travel Is Possible: Historical Fiction and Biography—Passport to the Past." *The Reading Teacher* 45 (March 1992): 488–495.

Johnson, Terry D., and Daphne R. Louis. *Literacy Through Literature.* Portsmouth, N.H.: Heinemann, 1987.

Johnston, Francine R. "The Reader, the Text, and the Task: Learning Words in First Grade." *The Reading Teacher,* 51 (May 1998): 666–675.

Johnston, Francine R. "The Timing and Teaching of Word Families." *The Reading Teacher* 53 (September 1999): 64–75.

Jones, Jill A. "Student-Involved Classroom Libraries." *The Reading Teacher* 59 (March 2006): 576–580.

Jones, Linda L. "An Interactive View of Reading: Implications for the Classroom." *The Reading Teacher* 35 (April 1982): 772–777.

Jones, Margaret B., and Denise D. Nessel. "Enhancing the Curriculum with Experience Stories." *The Reading Teacher* 39 (October 1985): 18–22.

Joseph, Laurice M. "Incremental Rehearsal: A Flashcard Drill Technique for Increasing Retention of Reading Words." *The Reading Teacher* 59 (May 2006): 803–807.

Juel, Connie. "Beginning Reading." In *Handbook of Reading Research,* Vol. 2, edited by Rebecca Barr, Michael L. Kamil, Peter Mosenthal, and P. David Pearson. New York: Longman, 1991, 759–787.

Juel, Connie. "Learning to Read and Write: A Longitudinal Study of Fifty-Four Children from First Through Fourth Grade." *Journal of Educational Psychology* 80 (1988): 437–447.

Kachuck, Beatrice. "Relative Clauses May Cause Confusion for Young Readers." *The Reading Teacher* 34 (January 1981): 372–377.

Kamil, Michael I. "Vocabulary and Comprehension Instruction: Summary and Implications of the National Reading Panel Findings." In *The Voice of Evidence in Reading Research,* edited by P. McCardle and V. Chhabra. Baltimore: Brookes, 2004, 213–234.

Kane, Sharon. "Teaching Decoding Strategies Without Destroying Story." *The Reading Teacher* 52 (April 1999): 770–772.

Kara-Soteriou, Julia, Lisa Zawilinski, and Laurie A. Henry. "Children's Books and Technology in the Classroom: A Dynamic Combo for Supporting the Writing Workshop." *The Reading Teacher* 60 (April 2007): 698–707.

Karnowski, Lee. "Using LEA with Process Writing." *The Reading Teacher* 42 (March 1989): 462–465.

Kauchak, Donald, and Paul Eggen. *Introduction to Teaching: Becoming a Professional.* Upper Saddle River, N.J.: Pearson/Merrill/Prentice Hall, 2008.

Keene, Ellin, and Susan Zimmerman. *Mosaic of Thought: Teaching Comprehension in a Reader's Workshop.* Portsmouth, N.H.: Heinemann, 1997.

Kelley, Michelle, and Nicki Clausen-Grace. "R5: The Sustained Silent Reading Makeover That Transformed Readers." *The Reading Teacher* 60 (October 2006): 148–156.

Kiefer, Barbara Z., Detra Price-Dennis, and Caitlin L. Ryan. "Children's Books in a Multimodal Age." *Language Arts* 84 (September 2006): 92–99.

Kieffer, Michael J., and Nonie K. Lesaux. "Breaking Down Words to Build Meaning: Morphology, Vocabulary, and Reading Comprehension in the Urban Classroom." *The Reading Teacher* 61 (October 2007): 134–144.

Klein, Perry D., and David R. Olson. "Texts, Technology, and Thinking: Lessons from the Great Divide." *Language Arts* 78 (January 2001): 227–236.

Knobel, Michele, and Colin Lankshear. "Discussing New Literacies." *Language Arts* 84 (September 2006): 78–86.

Kolb, Gayla. "Read with a Beat: Developing Literacy Through Music and Song." *The Reading Teacher* 50 (September 1996): 76–77.

Kornfeld, John, and Georgia Leyden. "Acting Out: Literature, Drama, and Connecting with History." *The Reading Teacher* 59 (November 2005): 230–238.

Kragler, Sherry, Carolyn A. Walker, and Linda E. Martin. "Strategy Instruction in Primary Content Textbooks." *The Reading Teacher* 59 (November 2005): 254–261.

Kraus, Jo Anne. "Playing the Play: What the Children Want." *Language Arts* 83 (May 2006): 413–421.

Krieger, Evelyn. "Developing Comprehension Through Author Awareness." *Journal of Reading* 33 (May 1990): 618–619.

Kristo, Janice V., and Rosemary A. Bamford. *Nonfiction in Focus.* New York: Scholastic, 2004.

Kupiter, Karen, and Patricia Wilson. "Updating Poetry Preferences: A Look at the Poetry Children Really Like." *The Reading Teacher* 47 (September 1993): 28–35.

Kymes, Angel. "Teaching Online Comprehension Strategies Using Think-Alouds." *Journal of Adolescent & Adult Literacy* 48 (March 2005): 492–500.

Labbo, Linda D. "12 Things Young Children Can Do with a Talking Book in a Classroom Computer Center." *The Reading Teacher* 53 (April 2000): 542–546.

Labbo, Linda D. "Books and Computer Response Activities That Support Literacy Development." *The Reading Teacher* 59 (November 2005): 288–292.

Labbo, Linda D. "Five Internet Sites Too Good to Miss." *The Reading Teacher* 59 (May 2006): 810–812.

LaBerge, David, and S. Jay Samuels. "Toward a Theory of Automatic Information Processing in Reading." In *Theoretical Models and Processes of Reading*, 3rd ed., edited by Harry Singer and Robert B. Ruddell. Newark, Del.: International Reading Association, 1985.

Lancia, Peter. "Literary Borrowing: The Effects of Literature on Children's Writing." *The Reading Teacher* 50 (March 1997): 470–475.

Lane, Holly, and Tyran Wright. "Maximizing the Effectiveness of Reading Aloud." *The Reading Teacher* 60 (April 2007): 668–675.

Leal, Dorothy J., and Julia Chamberlain-Solecki. "A Newbery Medal-Winning Combination: High Student Interest Plus Appropriate Readability Levels." *The Reading Teacher* 51 (May 1998): 712–714.

Lee, Gretchen. "Technology in the Language Arts Classroom: Is It Worth the Trouble?" *Voices from the Middle* 7 (March 2000): 24–32.

Lefever-Davis, Shirley, and Cathy Pearman. "Early Readers and Electronic Texts: CD-ROM Storybook Features That Influence Reading Behaviors." *The Reading Teacher* 58 (February 2005): 446–454.

Leland, Christine H., and Jerome C. Harste, with Kimberly R. Huber. "Out of the Box: Critical Literacy in a First-Grade Classroom." *Language Arts* 82 (March 2005): 257–268.

Lemke, J. L. "Multiplying Meaning: Visual and Verbal Semiotics in Scientific Text." In *Reading Science*, edited by J. R. Martin and R. Veel. London: Routledge, 1998, 87–113.

Lenters, Kimberly. "No Half Measures: Reading Instruction for Young Second-Language Learners." *The Reading Teacher* 58 (December 2004/January 2005): 328–336.

Lesaux, N., and L. Siegel. "The Development of Reading in Children Who Speak English as a Second Language (ESL)." *Developmental Psychology* 39 (2003): 1005–1019.

Lesesne, Teri. *Naked Reading: Uncovering What Tweens Need to Become Lifelong Readers.* Portland, Maine: Stenhouse, 2006.

Leu, Donald J., Jr. "Internet Workshop: Making Time for Literacy." *The Reading Teacher* 55 (February 2002): 466–472.

Leu, Donald J., Jr., Jill Castek, Laurie A. Henry, Julie Coiro, and Melissa McMullan. "The Lessons That Children Teach Us: Integrating Children's Literature and the New Literacies of the Internet." *The Reading Teacher* 57 (February 2004): 496–503.

Leu, Donald J., Jr., Charles K. Kinzer, Julie L. Coiro, and Dana W. Cammack. "Toward a Theory of New Literacies Emerging from the Internet and Other Information and Communication Technologies." In *Theoretical Models and Processes of Reading*, edited by Robert B. Ruddell and Norman J. Unrau. Newark, Del.: International Reading Association, 2004, 1570–1613.

Lever-Duffy, Judy, and Jean B. McDonald. *Teaching and Learning with Technology.* Boston: Pearson Education/Allyn & Bacon, 2008.

Lewis, Jill, and Gary Moorman, eds. *Adolescent Literacy Instruction Policies and Promising Practices.* Newark, Del.: International Reading Association, 2007.

Lewis, Maureen, David Wray, and Patricia Rospigliosi. " . . . And I Want It in Your Own Words." *The Reading Teacher* 47 (April 1994): 528–536.

Lightbrown, Patsy A., and Nina Spada. *How Languages Are Learned.* Oxford, England: Oxford University Press, 1999.

Lipman, Doug. *Improving Your Storytelling: Beyond the Basics for All Who Tell Stories in Work or Play.* Little Rock, Ark.: August House, 1999.

Lipson, Marjorie Y., Sheila W. Valencia, Karen K. Wixson, and Charles W. Peters. "Integration and Thematic Teaching: Integration to Improve Teaching and Learning." *Language Arts* 70 (April 1993): 252–263.

Lipson, Marjorie, and Karen Wixson. *Assessment and Instruction of Reading and Writing Disability,* 2nd ed. New York: Longman, 1997.

Littrell, Annette. " 'My Space': Using Blogs as Literature Journals with Adolescents." Dissertation. Cookeville: Tennessee Technological University, 2005.

Livingston, Nancy, and Catherine Kurkjian. "Fun Summer Books (Summer Reading, and Some'r Not!)." *The Reading Teacher* 59 (May 2006): 818–824.

Livingston, Nancy, and Catherine Kurkjian. "Summer Reading: Books Too Good To Miss." *The Reading Teacher* 60 (May 2007): 794–801.

Lohr, Linda L. *Creating Graphics for Learning and Performance.* Upper Saddle River, N.J.: Pearson/Merrill/Prentice Hall, 2008.

Long, Emily S. "Using Acrostic Poems for Research Reporting." *The Reading Teacher* 46 (February 1993): 447–448.

Louie, Belinda Y. "Guiding Principles for Teaching Multicultural Literature." *The Reading Teacher* 59 (February 2006): 438–448.

Lubliner, Shira. "Help for Struggling Upper-Grade Elementary Readers." *The Reading Teacher* 57 (February 2004): 430–438.

Lundberg, I., J. Frost, and O. Peterson. "Effects of an Extensive Program for Stimulating Phonological Awareness in Preschool Children." *Reading Research Quarterly* 23 (1988): 263–284.

Lyon, G. Reid. *Research in Learning Disabilities: Research Directions* (Technical Report). Bethesda, Md.: National Institutes of Child Health and Human Development, 1991.

Maeroff, G. "The Virtual School House." *Education Week* 22, no. 24 (2003): 40, 28.

Mandler, J. M. *Stories, Scripts, and Scenes: Aspects of Schema Theory.* Hillsdale, N.J.: Erlbaum, 1984.

Manyak, Patrick. "Character Trait Vocabulary: A Schoolwide Approach." *The Reading Teacher* 60 (March 2007): 574–577.

Manyak, Patrick C. "What's Your News? Portraits of a Rich Language and Literacy Activity for English-Language Learners." *The Reading Teacher* 61 (March 2008): 450–458.

Manyak, Patrick C., and Eurydice B. Bauer. "English Learners: Explicit Code and Comprehension Instruction for English Learners." *The Reading Teacher* 61 (February 2008): 432–434.

Manzo, Anthony, Ula Manzo, and Julie Jackson Albee. "iReap: Improving Reading, Writing, and Thinking in the Wired Classroom." *Journal of Adolescent & Adult Literacy* 46 (September 2002): 42–47.

Marcell, Barclay. "Teaching Tips Traffic Light Reading: Fostering the Independent Usage of Comprehension Strategies with Informational Text." *The Reading Teacher* 60 (May 2007): 778–781.

Martinez, Miriam. "Motivating Dramatic Story Reenactments." *The Reading Teacher* 46 (May 1993): 682–688.

Martinez-Roldán, Carmen M. "The Inquiry Acts of Bilingual Children in Literature Discussions." *Language Arts* 83 (September 2005): 22–32.

Martinez-Roldán, Carmen M., and Julia M. Lopez-Robertson. "Initiating Literature Circles in a First-Grade Bilingual Classroom." *The Reading Teacher* 53 (December 1999/January 2000): 270–281.

Marzano, Robert J. "A Cluster Approach to Vocabulary Instruction: A New Direction from the Research Literature." *The Reading Teacher* 38 (November 1984): 168–173.

Mason, George. "The Word Processor and Teaching Reading." *The Reading Teacher* 37 (February 1984): 552–553.

Massey, Dixie D. " 'The Discovery Channel Said So' and Other Barriers to Comprehension." *The Reading Teacher* 60 (April 2007): 656–666.

Mather, Nancy, Janice Sammons, and Jonathan Schwartz. "Adaptations of the Names Test: Easy-to-Use Phonics Assessments." *The Reading Teacher* 60 (October 2006): 114–122.

Mathison, Carla. "Activating Student Interest in Content Area Reading." *Journal of Reading* 33 (December 1989): 170–176.

Mayher, John S. "Frank Smith: A Compass for My Mind." *Language Arts* 83 (May 2006): 464–467.

McCabe, Patrick. "Enhancing Self-Efficacy for High-Stakes Reading Tests." *The Reading Teacher* 57 (September 2003): 12–20.

McClure, Amy A., and Connie S. Zitlow. "Not Just the Facts: Aesthetic Response in Elementary Content Area Studies." *Language Arts* 68 (January 1991): 27–33.

McConaughy, Stephanie H. "Word Recognition and Word Meaning in the Total Reading Process." *Language Arts* 55 (November/December 1978): 946–956, 1003.

McDaniel, Cynthia. "Critical Literacy: A Questioning Stance and the Possibility for Change." *The Reading Teacher* 57 (February 2004): 472–481.

McDonald, Jacqueline. "Graphs and Prediction: Helping Children Connect Mathematics and Literature." *The Reading Teacher* 53 (September 1999): 25–29.

McGee, Lea, and Judith A. Schickedanz. "Repeated Interactive Read-Alouds in Preschool and Kindergarten." *The Reading Teacher* 60 (May 2007): 742–751.

McGee, Lea M., and Gail E. Tompkins. "The Videotape Answer to Independent Reading Comprehension Activities." *The Reading Teacher* 34 (January 1981): 427–433.

McGill-Franzen, Anne. "'I Could Read the Words!' Selecting Good Books for Inexperienced Readers." *The Reading Teacher* 46 (February 1993): 424–426.

McIntyre, Ellen. "Story Discussion in the Primary Grades: Balancing Authenticity and Explicit Teaching." *The Reading Teacher* 60 (April 2007): 610–620.

McKeon, Christine A. "The Nature of Children's E-Mail in One Classroom." *The Reading Teacher* 52 (April 1999): 698–706.

McKeown, Margaret G., Isabel L. Beck, Richard C. Omanson, and Charles A. Perfetti. "The Effects of Long-Term Vocabulary Instruction on Reading Comprehension: A Replication." *Journal of Reading Behavior* 15 (1983): 3–18.

McMackin, Mary C., and Nancy L. Witherell. "Different Routes to the Same Destination: Drawing Conclusions with Tiered Graphic Organizers." *The Reading Teacher* 59 (November 2005): 242–252.

McMillan, Merna M., and Lance M. Gentile. "Children's Literature: Teaching Critical Thinking and Ethics." *The Reading Teacher* 41 (May 1988): 876–878.

McWhirter, Anna M. "Whole Language in the Middle School." *The Reading Teacher* 43 (April 1990): 562–565.

Meltzer, Nancy S., and Robert Herse. "The Boundaries of Written Words as Seen by First Graders." *Journal of Reading Behavior* 1 (Summer 1969): 3–14.

Menke, Deborah J., and Michael Pressley. "Elaborative Interrogation: Using 'Why' Questions to Enhance the Learning from Text." *Journal of Reading* 37 (May 1994): 642–645.

Merkley, Donna J. "Modified Anticipation Guide." *The Reading Teacher* 50 (December 1996/January 1997): 365–368.

Merkley, Donna M., and Debra Jefferies. "Guidelines for Implementing a Graphic Organizer." *The Reading Teacher* 54 (December 2000/January 2001): 350–357.

Mesmer, Heidi Anne E. "Scaffolding a Crucial Transition Using Text with Some Decodability." *The Reading Teacher* 53 (October 1999): 130–142.

Mesmer, Heidi Anne E., and Priscilla L. Griffith. "Everybody's Selling It—But Just What Is Explicit, Systematic Phonics Instruction?" *The Reading Teacher* 59 (December 2005/January 2006): 366–376.

Mesmer, Heidi Anne E., and Elizabeth Hutchins. "Using QARs with Charts and Graphs." *The Reading Teacher* 56 (September 2002): 21–27.

Miller, Etta, Luther B. Clegg, and Bill Vanderhoff. "Creating Postcards from the Famous for Social Studies Class." *Journal of Reading* 36 (October 1992): 134–135.

Miller, Sam, and Gerry Duffy. "Are We Crazy to Keep Doing This?" *Reading Today* 24 (December 2006/January 2007): 18.

Mills, Heidi, Diane Stephens, Timothy O'Keefe, Julie Riley Waugh. "Theory in Practice: The Legacy of Louise Rosenblatt." *Language Arts* 82 (September 2004): 47–55.

Moats, Louisa C. *Speech to Print: Language Essentials for Teachers.* Baltimore: Brookes, 2001.

Mohr, Kathleen, and Eric Mohr. "Extending English-Language Learners Classroom Interactions Using the Response Protocol." *The Reading Teacher* 60 (February 2007): 440–450.

Moldofsky, Penny Baum. "Teaching Students to Determine the Central Story Problem: A Practical Application of Schema Theory." *The Reading Teacher* 36 (April 1983): 740–745.

Monke, L. "The Overdominance of Computers." *Educational Leadership* 63 (December 2005/January 2006): 20–23.

Moore, Margaret. "Electronic Dialoguing: An Avenue to Literacy." *The Reading Teacher* 45 (December 1991): 280–286.

Moore-Hart, Margaret. "A Writers Camp in Action: A Community of Readers and Writers." *The Reading Teacher* 59 (December 2005/January 2006): 326–338.

Morrow, Lesley Mandel. "Using Story Retelling to Develop Comprehension." In *Children's Comprehension of Text: Research into Practice*, edited by K. Denise Muth. Newark, Del.: International Reading Association, 1989.

Morrow, Lesley, and Linda Gambrell. "Literature-Based Instruction in the Early Years." In *Handbook of Early Literacy Research*, edited by S. B. Newman and D. K. Dickinson. New York: Guilford Press, 2002.

Morrow, Lesley Mandel, and Susan B. Neuman. "Introduction: Family Literacy." *The Reading Teacher* 48 (April 1995): 550–551.

Mosenthal P., and T. J. Na. "Quality of Text Recall as a Function of Children's Classroom Competence." *Journal of Experimental Child Psychology* 30 (1980): 1–21.

Moss Barbara. "Teaching Expository Text Structures Through Information Trade Book Retellings." *The Reading Teacher* 57 (May 2004): 710–718.

Moss, Barbara, and Harry Noden. "Pointers for Putting Whole Language into Practice." *The Reading Teacher* 47 (December 1993/January 1994): 342–344.

Moss, Barbara, and Judith Hendershot. "Exploring Sixth Graders' Selection of Nonfiction Trade Books." *The Reading Teacher* 56 (September 2002): 6–17.

Mountain, Lee. "Flip-a-Chip to Build Vocabulary." *Journal of Adolescent & Adult Literacy* 48 (September 2002): 62–68.

Mountain, Lee. "ROOTing Out Meaning: More Morphemic Analysis for Primary Pupils." *The Reading Teacher* 58 (May 2005): 742–748.

Mountain, Lee. "Synonym Success—Thanks to the Thesaurus." *Journal of Adolescent & Adult Literacy* 51 (December 2007/January 2008): 318–324.

Moustafa, Margaret. "Comprehensible Input PLUS the Language Experience Approach: A Longterm Perspective." *The Reading Teacher* 41 (December 1987): 276–286.

Moustafa, Margaret, and Elba Maldonado-Colon. "Whole-to-Parts Phonics Instruction: Building on What Children Know to Help Them Know More." *The Reading Teacher* 52 (February 1999): 448–458.

Mueller, Jon. *The Authentic Assessment Toolbox: Enhancing Student Learning Through Online Faculty Development.* [On-line journal], Merlot, 2005.

Munson, Jennie Livingston. "Story and Poetry Maps." *The Reading Teacher* 42 (May 1989): 736–737.

Nagel, David. "Research: Students Actually Use the Internet for Education." *T•H•E Journal* (August 2007). Retrieved from http://www.thejournal.com/the/printarticle??id+21116 on September 3, 2007.

Nagel, David. "LeapFrog Intros Handheld Early Literacy Device." *T•H•E Journal.* Retrieved from http://www.thejournal.com/articles/22471 on April 18, 2008.

Nagy, William E. *Teaching Vocabulary to Improve Reading Comprehension.* Urbana, Ill.: National Council of Teachers of English, 1988.

Nagy, William E., and Richard C. Anderson. "How Many Words Are There in Printed School English?" *Reading Research Quarterly* 19, no. 3 (1984): 304–330.

Nagy, William E., Patricia A. Herman, and Richard C. Anderson. "Learning Words from Context." *Reading Research Quarterly* 20, no. 2 (1985): 233–253.

Nagy, William E., and Judith A. Scott. "Vocabulary Processes." In *Handbook of Reading Research*, Vol. 3, edited by Michael L. Kamil, Peter B. Mosenthal, P. David Pearson, and Rebecca Barr. Mahwah, N.J.: Erlbaum, 2000, 269–284.

Nathan, R. G., and Keith E. Stanovich. "The Causes and Consequences of Differences in Reading Fluency." *Theory into Practice* 30 (1991): 176–184.

National Reading Panel. *Teaching Children to Read: An Evidence-Based Assessment of the Scientific Research Literature on Reading and Its Implications for Reading Instruction.* Washington, D.C.: National Institute of Child Health and Human Development, 2000.

Nelson-Herber, Joan. "Expanding and Defining Vocabulary in Content Areas." *Journal of Reading* 29 (April 1986): 626–633.

Nessel, Denise D. "Storytelling in the Reading Program." *The Reading Teacher* 38 (January 1985): 378–381.

Neufeld, Paul. "Comprehension Instruction in Content Area Classes." *The Reading Teacher* 59 (December 2005/January 2006): 302–312.

Newman, Gayle. "Comprehension Strategy Gloves." *The Reading Teacher* 55 (December 2001/January 2002): 329–332.

Nicholson, Tom. "The Flashcard Strikes Back." *The Reading Teacher* 52 (October 1998): 188–192.

Niday, Donna, and Mark Campbell. "You've Got Mail: 'Near-Peer' Relationships in the Middle." *Voices from the Middle* 7 (March 2000): 55–61.

Nilsen, Alleen Pace, and Don L. F. Nilsen. "A New Spin on Teaching Vocabulary: A Source-Based Approach." *The Reading Teacher* 56 (February 2003): 436–439.

Nistler, Robert J., and Angela Maiers. "Stopping the Silence: Hearing Parents' Voices in an Urban First-Grade Family Literacy Program." *The Reading Teacher* 53 (May 2000): 670–680.

Nolan, Thomas E. "Self-Questioning and Prediction: Combining Metacognitive Strategies." *Journal of Reading* 35 (October 1991): 132–138.

Nolte, Ruth Yopp, and Harry Singer. "Active Comprehension: Teaching a Process of Reading Comprehension and Its Effects on Reading Achievement." *The Reading Teacher* 39 (October 1985): 24–31.

Norman, Kimberly A., and Robert C. Calfee. "Tile Test: A Hands-On Approach for Assessing Phonics in the Early Grades." *The Reading Teacher* 58 (September 2004): 42–52.

Norton, Donna E. "Modeling Inferencing of Characterization." *The Reading Teacher* 46 (September 1992a): 64–67.

Norton, Donna E. "Understanding Plot Structures." *The Reading Teacher* 46 (November 1992b): 254–258.

Norton, Donna E. "Circa 1942 and the Integration of Literature, Reading, and Geography." *The Reading Teacher* 46 (April 1993): 610–614.

Norton, Donna E. *Through the Eyes of a Child: An Introduction to Children's Literature.* Upper Saddle River, N.J.: Merrill, 2003.

Ogle, Donna M. "K-W-L: A Teaching Model That Develops Active Reading of Expository Text." *The Reading Teacher* 39 (February 1986): 564–570.

Ogle, Donna M. "The Know, Want to Know, Learn Strategy." In *Children's Comprehension of Text: Research into Practice*, edited by K. Denise Muth. Newark, Del.: International Reading Association, 1989.

Oja, Leslie Anne. "Using Story Frames to Develop Reading Comprehension." *Journal of Adolescent and Adult Literacy* 40 (October 1996): 129–130.

Oleneski, Sue. "Using Jump Rope Rhymes to Teach Reading Skills." *The Reading Teacher* 46 (October 1992): 173–175.

Ollila, Lloyd O., and Margie I. Mayfield. *Emerging Literacy: Preschool, Kindergarten, and Primary Grades.* Boston: Allyn & Bacon, 1992, 166–195.

Ollmann, Hilda E. "Integrating Content Area Skills with Fiction Favorites." *Journal of Reading* 34 (February 1991): 398–399.

Olness, Rebecca. *Using Literature to Enhance Writing Instruction: A Guide for K–5 Teachers.* Newark, Del.: International Reading Association, 2005.

Onofrey, Karen A., and Joan Leikam Theurer. "What's a Teacher to Do: Suggestions for Comprehension Strategy Instruction." *The Reading Teacher* 60 (April 2007): 681–684.

Orellana, Marjorie Faulstich, and Arcelia Hernández. "Talking the Walk: Children Reading Urban Environmental Print." In *Promising Practices for Urban Reading Instruction*, edited by Pamela A. Mason and Jeanne Shay Schumm. Newark, Del.: International Reading Association, 2005.

Orellana, Marjorie Faulstich, and Ernest Morrell. "Professional Resources for Teaching Multimodal Literacies." *Language Arts* 84 (September 2006): 87–91.

Oster, Lester. "Using the Think-Aloud for Reading Instruction." *The Reading Teacher* 55 (September 2001): 64–69.

Owens, Roxanne Farwick, Jennifer L. Hester, and William H. Teale. "Where Do You Want to Go Today? Inquiry-Based Learning and Technology Integration." *The Reading Teacher* 55 (April 2002): 616–625.

oz-Teachernet. "Book Raps." Retrieved from http://www.oz-teachernet .edu.au/projects/br on February 2008. Last modified August 2007.

Palincsar, Annemarie Sullivan, and Ann L. Brown. "Interactive Teaching to Promote Independent Learning from Text." *The Reading Teacher* 39 (April 1986): 771–777.

Palmer, Barbara. "Dolch List Still Useful." *The Reading Teacher* 38 (March 1985): 708–709.

Palmer, Barbara C., Vikki S. Shackelford, Sharmane C. Miller, and Judith T. Leclere. "Bridging Two Worlds: Reading Comprehension, Figurative Language Instruction, and the English-Language Learner." *Journal of Adolescent & Adult Literacy* 50 (December 2006/January 2007): 258–267.

Palmer, Rosemary G., and Roger A. Stewart. "Nonfiction Trade Book Use in Primary Grades." *The Reading Teacher* 57 (September 2003): 38–48.

Palmer, Rosemary G., and Roger A. Stewart. "Models for Using Nonfiction in the Primary Grades." *The Reading Teacher* 58 (February 2005): 426–434.

Parsons, Linda T. "Visualizing Worlds from Words on a Page." *Language Arts* 83 (July 2006): 492–500.

Paugh, Patricia, Jane Carey, Valerie King-Jackson, and Shelley Russell. "Negotiating the Literacy Block: Constructing Spaces for Critical Literacy in a High-Stakes Setting." *Language Arts* 85 (September 2007): 31–42.

Paul, Dierdre Glenn. "The Train Has Left: The No Child Left Behind Act Leaves Black and Latino Literacy Learners Waiting at the Station." *Journal of Adolescent & Adult Literacy* 47 (May 2004): 648–656.

Pavonetti, Linda M. "Joan Lowery Nixon: The Grande Dame of Young Adult Mystery." *Journal of Adolescent & Adult Literacy* 39 (March 1996): 454–461.

Pavonetti, Linda M., Kathryn M. Brimmer, and James F. Cipielewski. "Accelerated Reader: What Are the Lasting Effects on the Reading Habits of Middle School Students Exposed to Accelerated Reader in the Elementary Grades?" *Journal of Adolescent & Adult Literacy* 46 (December 2002/January 2003): 300–311.

Pearson, P. David. "Changing the Face of Comprehension Instruction." *The Reading Teacher* 38 (April 1985): 724–738.

Pearson, P. David. "Focus on Research: Teaching and Learning Reading: A Research Perspective." *Language Arts* 70 (October 1993): 502–511.

Pearson, P. David, et al. *The Effect of Background Knowledge on Young Children's Comprehension of Explicit and Implicit Information.* Urbana–Champaign, Ill.: University of Illinois, Center for the Study of Reading, 1979.

Pearson, P. David, and Nell K. Duke. "Effective Practices for Developing Reading Comprehension." In *What Research Has to Say About Reading Instruction*, edited by Alan E. Farstrup and S. J. Samuels. Newark, Del.: International Reading Association, 2002.

Pearson, P. David, and Linda Fielding. "Comprehension Instruction." In *Handbook of Reading Research*, Vol. 2, edited by Rebecca Barr, Michael L. Kamil, Peter Mosenthal, and P. David Pearson. New York: Longman, 1991, 815–860.

Pearson, P. David, Elfrieda H. Hiebert, and Michael L. Kamil. "Vocabulary Assessment: What We Know and What We Need to Learn." *Reading Research Quarterly* 42 (2007): 282–296.

Pearson, P. David, and Dale D. Johnson. *Teaching Reading Comprehension.* New York: Holt, Rinehart and Winston, 1978.

Peebles, Jodi L. "Incorporating Movement with Fluency Instruction: A Motivation for Struggling Readers." *The Reading Teacher* 60 (March 2007): 578–581.

Pellegrino, James, Naomi Chudowski, and Robert Glaser. *Knowing What Students Know: The Science and Design of Educational Assessment.* Washington, D.C.: National Academy Press, 2001.

Perkins-Gough, Deborah, reviewer. "Special Report: RAND Report on Reading Comprehension." *Educational Leadership* 60 (November 2002): 92.

Peterson, B. "Selecting Books for Beginning Readers." In *Bridges to Literacy: Learning from Reading Recovery*, edited by D. Deford, C. Lyons, and G. S. Pinnell. Portsmouth, N.H.: Heinemann, 1991, 119–147.

Pettersen, Nancy-Laurel. "Grate/Great Homonym Hunt." *Journal of Reading* 31 (January 1988): 374–375.

Pigg, John R. "The Effects of a Storytelling/Storyreading Program on the Language Skills of Rural Primary Students." Unpublished paper. Cookeville: Tennessee Technological University, 1986.

Pikulski, John J. "Questions and Answers." *The Reading Teacher* 42 (April 1989): 637.

Pilgreen, Janice. "Teaching the Language of School to Secondary English Learners." In *Adolescent Literacy Instruction: Policies and Promising Practices*, edited by Jill Lewis and Gary Moorman. Newark, Del.: International Reading Association, 2007.

Popham, W. James. "Phony Formative Assessments: Buyer Beware!" *Educational Leadership* 64 (November 2006): 86–87.

Popp, Marcia. *Learning Journals in the K–8 Classroom.* Mahwah, N.J.: Erlbaum, 1997.

Pressley, Michael. *Advanced Educational Psychology.* New York: HarperCollins, 1995.

Pressley, Michael. "Comprehension Instruction: What Makes Sense Now, What Might Make Sense Soon." *Reading Online* 5

(September 2001). Retrieved from http://www.readingonline.org/articles/art_indes.asp?HREF–articles/handbook/pressley/index.html.

Pressley, Michael. "Metacognition and Self-Regulated Comprehension." In *What Research Has to Say About Reading Instruction*, edited by Alan E. Farstrup and S. Jay Samuels. Newark, Del.: International Reading Association, 2002, 291–309.

Quiocho, Alice. "The Quest to Comprehend Expository Test: Applied Classroom Research." *Journal of Adolescent & Adult Literacy* 40 (March 1997): 450–455.

Rand, Muriel K. "Story Schema: Theory, Research and Practice." *The Reading Teacher* 37 (January 1984): 377–382.

Ranker, Jason. " 'There's Fire Magic, Electric Magic, Ice Magic, or Poison Magic': The World of Video Games and Adrian's Compositions About Gauntlet Legends." *Language Arts* 84 (September 2006): 21–33.

Raphael, Taffy E. "Question-Answering Strategies for Children." *The Reading Teacher* 36 (November 1982): 186–190.

Raphael, Taffy E. "Teaching Learners About Sources of Information for Answering Comprehension Questions." *Journal of Reading* 27 (January 1984): 303–311.

Raphael, Taffy E. "Teaching Question-Answer Relationships, Revisited." *The Reading Teacher* 39 (February 1986): 516–522.

Raphael, Taffy, et al. "Research Directions: Literature and Discussion in the Reading Program." *Language Arts* 69 (January 1992): 54–61.

Raphael, Taffy E., and Kathryn H. Au. "QAR: Enhancing Comprehension and Test Taking Across Grades and Content Areas." *The Reading Teacher* 59 (November 2005): 206–221.

Raphael, Taffy E., and P. David Pearson. "Increasing Students' Awareness of Sources of Information for Answering Questions." *American Educational Research Journal* 22 (1985): 217–236.

Raphael, Taffy E., and J. McKinney. "An Examination of 5th and 8th Grade Children's Question Answering Behavior: An Instructional Study in Metacognition." *Journal of Reading Behavior* 15 (1983): 67–86.

Raphael, Taffy E., and C. A. Wonnacott. "Heightening Fourth-Grade Students' Sensitivity to Sources of Information for Answering Comprehension Questions." *Reading Research Quarterly* 20 (1985): 282–296.

Rasinski, Timothy V. "Speed Does Matter in Reading." *The Reading Teacher* 54 (October 2000): 146–151.

Rasinski, Timothy V. "The Role of Interest, Purpose, and Choice in Early Literacy." *The Reading Teacher* 41 (January 1988): 396–400.

Readence, John E., R. Scott Baldwin, and Martha H. Head. "Direct Instruction in Processing Metaphors." *Journal of Reading Behavior* 18, no. 4 (1986): 325–339.

Readence, John E., R. Scott Baldwin, and Martha H. Head. "Teaching Young Readers to Interpret Metaphors." *The Reading Teacher* 40 (January 1987): 439–443.

Renaissance Learning. *Accelerated Reader: Understanding Reliability and Validity*. Wisconsin Rapids, Wis.: Renaissance Learning, 2006.

Rhoder, Carol. "Mindful Reading: Strategy Training That Facilitates Transfer." *Journal of Adolescent & Adult Literacy* 45 (March 2002): 498–512.

Rhoder, Carol, and Patricia Huerster. "Use Dictionaries for Word Learning with Caution." *Journal of Adolescent & Adult Literacy* 45 (May 2002): 730–735.

Rhodes, Joan A., and Tammy M. Milby. "Teacher-Created Electronic Books: Integrating Technology to Support Readers with Disabilities." *The Reading Teacher* 61 (November 2007): 255–259.

Rich, Dorothy. "What Educators Need to Explain to the Public." *Phi Delta Kappan* 87 (October 2005): 154–158.

Richards, Meribethe. "Be a Good Detective: Solve the Case of Oral Reading Fluency." *The Reading Teacher* 53 (April 2000): 534–539.

Richek, Margaret Ann. "Words Are Wonderful: Interactive, Time-Efficient Strategies to Teach Meaning Vocabulary." *The Reading Teacher* 58 (February 2005): 414–423.

Richey, David D., and John Wheeler. *Inclusive Early Childhood Education: Merging Positive Behavioral Supports, Activity-Based Interventions, and Developmentally Appropriate Practice*. Albany, N.Y.: Delmar Thomson Learning, 2000.

Richgels, Donald, Karla Poremba, and Lea M. McGee. "Kindergartners Talk About Print: Phonemic Awareness in Meaningful Contexts." *The Reading Teacher* 49 (May 1996): 632–642.

Richler, Howard. "Word Play: You're Likely to Be Clipped." *Notes Plus* (March 1996): 11–12.

Robinson, Francis P. *Effective Study*, rev. ed. New York: Harper & Row, 1961.

Robinson, H. Alan, Vincent Faraone, Daniel R. Hittleman, and Elizabeth Unruh. *Reading Comprehension Instruction, 1783–1987*. Newark, Del.: International Reading Association, 1990.

Roblyer, M. *Integrating Educational Technology into Teaching*. Upper Saddle River, N.J.: Merrill/Prentice Hall, 2006.

Roe, Betty D. *Use of Storytelling / Storyreading in Conjunction with Follow-up Language Activities to Improve Oral Communication of Rural First Grade Students: Phase I*. Cookeville, Tenn.: Rural Education Consortium, 1985.

Roe, Betty D. *Use of Storytelling / Storyreading in Conjunction with Follow-up Language Activities to Improve Oral Communication of Rural Primary Grade Students: Phase II*. Cookeville, Tenn.: Rural Education Consortium, 1986.

Roe, Betty D. *Report on Non-Instructional Assignment*. Cookeville: Tennessee Technological University, 1990.

Roe, Betty D. "Using Technology for Content Area Literacy." In *Linking Literacy and Technology: A Guide for K–8 Classrooms*, edited by Shelley B. Wepner, William J. Valmont, and Richard Thurlow. Newark, Del.: International Reading Association, 2000.

Roe, Betty D., and Elinor P. Ross. *Integrating Language Arts Through Literature & Thematic Units*. Boston: Pearson Allyn & Bacon, 2006.

Roe, Betty D., Suellen Alfred, and Sandy H. Smith. *Teaching Through Stories: Yours, Mine, and Theirs.* Norwood, Mass.: Christopher-Gordon, 1998.

Roe, Betty D., and Sandy H. Smith. "University/Public Schools Keypals Project: A Collaborative Effort for Electronic Literature Conversations." In *Rethinking Teaching and Learning Through Technology.* Proceedings of the Mid-South Instructional Technology Conference, Murfreesboro, Tenn., 1997.

Rog, Lori Jamison, and Wilfred Burton. "Matching Texts and Readers: Leveling Early Reading Materials for Assessment and Instruction." *The Reading Teacher* 55 (December 2001/January 2002): 348–356.

Roney, R. Craig. "Background Experience Is the Foundation of Success in Learning to Read." *The Reading Teacher* 38 (November 1984): 196–199.

Rosenbaum, Catherine. "A Word Map for Middle School: A Tool for Effective Vocabulary Instruction." *Journal of Adolescent and Adult Literacy* 45 (September 2001): 44–49.

Rosenblatt, Louise M. "Literature—S.O.S!" *Language Arts* 68 (1991), 444–448.

Rosenblatt, Louise M. *The Reader, the Text, and the Poem: The Transactional Theory of the Literary Work.* Carbondale: Southern Illinois University Press, 1978.

Rosenblatt, Louise M. *Literature as Exploration,* 5th ed. New York: Modern Language Association of America, 1995.

Rosenblatt, Louise M. "The Transactional Theory of Reading and Writing." In *Theoretical Models and Processes of Reading,* 5th ed., edited by Robert B. Ruddell and Norman J. Unrau. Newark, Del.: International Reading Association, 2004, 1363–1398.

Rosenblatt, Louise. *Making Meaning with Texts: Selected Essays.* Portsmouth, N.H.: Heinemann, 2005.

Roser, Nancy, and Connie Juel. "Effects of Vocabulary and Instruction on Reading Comprehension." In *New Inquiries in Reading Research and Instruction,* Thirty-First Yearbook of the National Reading Conference, edited by J. A. Niles and L. A. Harris. Rochester, N.Y.: National Reading Conference, 1982.

Ross, Elinor. *The Workshop Approach: A Framework for Literacy.* Norwood, Mass.: Christopher-Gordon, 1996.

Rosso, Barbara Rak, and Robert Emans. "Children's Use of Phonic Generalizations." *The Reading Teacher* 34 (March 1981): 653–657.

Roth, Froma P., Deborah Speece, and David Cooper. "A Longitudinal Analysis of the Connection Between Oral Language and Early Literacy." *Journal of Educational Research* 95 (May 2002): 259–274.

Rubinstein-Avila, Eliane. "Conversing with Miguel: An Adolescent English Language Learner Struggling with Later Literacy Development." *Journal of Adolescent & Adult Literacy* 47 (December 2003/January 2004): 290–301.

Ruddell, Martha Rapp, and Brenda A. Shearer. "'Extraordinary,' 'Tremendous,' 'Exhilarating,' 'Magnificent': Middle School At-Risk Students Become Avid Word Learners with the Vocabulary Self-Collection Strategy (VSS)." *Journal of Adolescent & Adult Literacy* 45 (February 2002): 352–363.

Rumelhart, David E. "Schemata: The Building Blocks of Cognition." In *Comprehension and Teaching: Research Reviews,* edited by John T. Guthrie. Newark, Del.: International Reading Association, 1981.

Rumelhart, David E. "Toward an Interactive Model of Reading." In *Theoretical Models and Processes of Reading,* 5th ed., edited by Robert B. Ruddell and Norman J. Unrau. Newark, Del.: International Reading Association, 2004, 1149–1179.

Rupley, William H., John W. Logan, and William D. Nichols. "Vocabulary Instruction in a Balanced Reading Program." *The Reading Teacher* 52 (December 1998/January 1999): 336–356.

Saccardi, Marianne. "Predictable Books: Gateways to a Lifetime of Reading." *The Reading Teacher* 49 (April 1996a): 588–590.

Saccardi, Marrianne C. "Preditable Books: Gateways to a Lifetime of Reading." *The Reading Teacher* 49 (May 1996b): 632–642.

Saddler, Bruce, and Heidi Andrade. "The Writing Rubric." *Educational Leadership* 62 (October 2004): 48–52.

Sadow, Marilyn W. "The Use of Story Grammar in the Design of Questions." *The Reading Teacher* 35 (February 1982): 518–522.

Salinger, Terry S. *Literacy for Young Children,* 2nd ed. Englewood Cliffs, N.J.: Merrill, 1996.

Saltpeter, J., "Telling Tales with Technology." *Technology & Learning* 25 (2005): 18–24.

Sameroff, Arnold, and Susan McDonough. "Educational Implications of Developmental Transitions: The 5- to 7-Year Shift." In *Early Childhood Education 96/97,* edited by Karen Paciorek and Joyce Munro. Guilford, Conn.: Dushkin, 1996–1997, 40–44.

Samuels, S. Jay. "Decoding and Automaticity: Helping Poor Readers Become Automatic at Word Recognition." *The Reading Teacher* 41 (April 1988): 756–760.

Samuels, S. Jay. "Toward a Theory of Automatic Information Processing in Reading, Revisited." In *Theoretical Models and Processes of Reading,* 5th ed., edited by Robert B. Ruddell and Norman J. Unrau. Newark, Del.: International Reading Association, 2004, 1127–1147.

Samuels, S. Jay. "Toward a Model of Reading Fluency." In *What Research Has to Say About Fluency Instruction.* Newark, Del.: International Reading Association, 2006, 24–46.

Samuels, S. Jay, and Sumner W. Schachter. "Controversial Issues in Beginning Reading Instruction: Meaning Versus Subskill Emphasis." In *Readings on Reading Instruction,* edited by Albert J. Harris and Edward R. Sipay. New York: Longman, 1984.

Santman, Donna. "The Values of Literacy." *Language Arts* 83 (May 2006): 389–390.

Santoro, Lana Edwards, David J. Chard, Lisa Howard, and Scott K. Baker. "Making the Most of Classroom Read-Alouds to Promote Comprehension and Vocabulary." *The Reading Teacher* 61 (February 2008): 396–408.

Sawyer, John Michael. "Using Media Knowledge to Enhance the Literary Schema of Literarily Impoverished Students." *Journal of Reading* 37 (May 1994): 683–684.

Scharer, Patricia L., and Deana B. Detwiler. "Changing as Teachers: Perils and Possibilities of Literature-Based Language Arts Instruction." *Language Arts* 69 (March 1992): 186–192.

Scharrer, Erica. "Making a Case for Media Literacy in the Curriculum: Outcomes and Assessment," *Journal of Adolescent & Adult Literacy* 46 (December 2002/January 2003): 354–358.

Schmidt, Patricia Ruggiano. "KWLQ: Inquiry and Literacy Learning in Science." *The Reading Teacher* 52 (April 1999): 789–792.

Schmoker, Mike. *Results Now: How We Can Achieve Unprecedented Improvements in Teaching and Learning.* Alexandria, Va.: Association for Supervision and Curriculum Development, 2006.

Schwartz, Robert M. "Decisions, Decisions: Responding to Primary Students During Guided Reading." *The Reading Teacher* 58 (February 2005): 436–443.

Schwartz, Robert M. "Learning to Learn Vocabulary in Content Area Textbooks." *Journal of Reading* 32 (November 1988): 108–118.

Schwartz, Robert M. "Self-Monitoring in Beginning Reading." *The Reading Teacher* 51 (September 1997): 40–48.

Schwartz, Robert M., and Taffy E. Raphael. "Concept of Definition: A Key to Improving Students' Vocabulary." *The Reading Teacher* 39 (November 1985): 198–205.

Schwarzer, David, Alexia Haywood, and Charla Lorenzen. "Fostering Multiliteracy in a Linguistically Diverse Classroom." *Language Arts* 80 (July 2003): 453–460.

Sears, Sue, Cathy Carpenter, and Nancy Burstein. "Meaningful Reading Instruction for Learners with Special Needs." *The Reading Teacher* 47 (May 1994): 632–638.

Sebesta, Sam Leaton, James William Calder, and Lynne Nelson Cleland. "A Story Grammar for the Classroom." *The Reading Teacher* 36 (November 1982): 180–184.

Sensenbaugh, Roger. "Reading Recovery." *ERIC Digest.* Bloomington: Indiana University Press, September 1995.

Serafini, Frank, and Cyndy Giorgis. *Reading Aloud and Beyond: Fostering the Intellectual Life with Older Readers.* Portsmouth, N.H.: Heinemann, 2003.

Serim, Ferdi, and Melissa Koch. *Netlearning: Why Teachers Use the Internet.* Sebastopol, Calif.: Songline Studios and O'Reilly & Associates, 1996.

Shamir, Adina, and Ofra Korat. "How to Select CD-ROM Storybooks for Young Children: The Teacher's Role." *The Reading Teacher* 59 (March 2006): 532–543.

Shanahan, Timothy. "Reading-Writing Relationships, Thematic Units, Inquiry Learning . . . In Pursuit of Effective Integrated Literacy Instruction." *The Reading Teacher* 51 (September 1997): 12–19.

Shanahan, T., and S. Neuman. "Conversations: Literacy Research That Makes a Difference." *Reading Research Quarterly* 32 (1997): 202–211.

Shanahan, Timothy, Bonita Robinson, and Mary Schneider. "Integrating Curriculum: Avoiding Some of the Pitfalls of Thematic Units." *The Reading Teacher* 48 (May 1995): 718–719.

Shanklin, Nancy L., and Lynn K. Rhodes. "Comprehension Instruction as Sharing and Extending." *The Reading Teacher* 42 (March 1989): 496–500.

Shaw, Evelyn. "A Novel Journal." *The Reading Teacher* 41 (January 1988): 489.

Shiflett, Anne Chalfield. "Marketing Literature: Variations on the Book Talk Theme." *Journal of Adolescent & Adult Literature* 41 (April 1998): 568–570.

Shoop, Mary. "InQuest: A Listening and Reading Comprehension Strategy." *The Reading Teacher* 39 (March 1986): 670–674.

Siegel, Marjorie. "Rereading the Signs: Multimodal Transformations in the Field of Literacy Education." *Language Arts* 84 (September 2006): 65–77.

Silver-Pacuilla, H., and S. Fleischman. "Technology to Help Struggling Students." *Educational Leadership* 63 (2006): 84–85.

Singer, Harry, John D. McNeil, and Lory L. Furse. "Relationship Between Curriculum Scope and Reading Achievement in Elementary Schools." *The Reading Teacher* 37 (March 1984): 608–612.

Sippola, Arne E. "What to Teach for Reading Readiness—A Research Review and Materials Inventory." *The Reading Teacher* 39 (November 1985): 162–167.

Sippola, Arne E. "K-W-L-S." *The Reading Teacher* 48 (March 1995): 542–543.

Skillings, Mary Jo, and Robbin Ferrell. "Student-Generated Rubrics: Bringing Students into the Assessment Process." *The Reading Teacher* 53 (March 2000): 452–455.

Slavin, Robert E., Nancy A. Madden, Nancy L. Karweit, Lawrence J. Dolan, and Barbara A. Wasik. "Success for All: Getting Reading Right the First Time." In *Getting Reading Right from the Start*, edited by Elfrieda H. Hiebert and Barbara M. Taylor. Boston: Allyn & Bacon, 1994, 125–147.

Smith, Carl B. "Prompting Critical Thinking." *The Reading Teacher* 42 (February 1989): 424.

Smith, Frank. "Twelve Easy Ways of Making Learning to Read Difficult and One Difficult Way to Make It Easy." *Psycholinguistics and Reading* (1973): 183–196.

Smith, Frank. *Unspeakable Acts, Unnatural Practices: Flaws and Fallacies in 'Scientific' Reading Instruction.* Portsmouth, N.H.: Heinemann, 2003.

Smith, Lynn Alleen. "Think-Aloud Mysteries: Using Structured, Sentence-by-Sentence Text Passages to Teach Comprehension Strategies." *The Reading Teacher* 59 (May 2006): 764–773.

Smith, Marilyn, and Thomas W. Bean. "Four Strategies That Develop Children's Story Comprehension and Writing." *The Reading Teacher* 37 (December 1983): 295–301.

Smith, Michael, and Jeffrey D. Wilhelm. "'I Just Like Being Good at It': The Importance of Competence in the Literate Lives of Young Men." *Journal of Adolescent & Adult Literacy* 47 (March 2004): 454–461.

Smolen, Lynn Atkinson, and Victoria Ortiz-Castro. "Dissolving Borders and Broadening Perspectives Through Latino Traditional Literature." *The Reading Teacher* 53 (April 2000): 566–578.

Smolin, Louanne Ione, and Kimberly A. Lawless. "Becoming Literate in the Technological Age: New Responsibilities and Tools for Teachers." *The Reading Teacher* 56 (March 2003): 570–577.

Smolkin, Laura B., and Carol A. Donovan. "Looking Closely at the Science Trade Book: Gail Gibbons and Multimodal Literacy." *Language Arts* 83 (September 2005): 52–62.

Smolkin, Laura, and David Yaden, Jr. "*O* Is for Mouse: First Encounters with the Alphabet Book." *Language Arts* 69 (October 1992): 432–441.

Snow, Catherine, M. Susan Burns, and Peg Griffin, eds. *Preventing Reading Difficulties in Young Children.* Washington, D.C.: National Academy Press, 1998.

Solvie, Pamela A. "The Digital Whiteboard: A Tool in Early Literacy Instruction." *The Reading Teacher* 57 (February 2004): 484–487.

Sousa, David A. *How the Brain Learns to Read.* Thousand Oaks, Calif.: Corwin Press, 2005.

Spache, George D. *Good Reading for Poor Readers*, 6th ed. Champaign, Ill.: Garrard Press, 1966.

Spencer, Brenda H., and Andrea M. Guillaume. "Integrating Curriculum Through the Learning Cycle: Content-Based Reading and Vocabulary Instruction." *The Reading Teacher* 60 (November 2006): 206–219.

Spiegel, Dixie Lee. "Comprehension Materials: Quality of Directions and Instructional Language." *The Reading Teacher* 43 (March 1990a): 502–504.

Spiegel, Dixie Lee. "Reinforcement in Phonics Materials." *The Reading Teacher* 43 (January 1990b): 328–329.

Spiegel, Dixie Lee. "The Role of Trust in Reader-Response Groups." *Language Arts* 73 (September 1996): 332–339.

Spiegel, Dixie Lee, and Jill Fitzgerald. "Improving Reading Comprehension Through Instruction About Story Parts." *The Reading Teacher* 39 (March 1986): 676–682.

Spiro, Rand J. *Etiology of Comprehension Style.* Urbana–Champaign: Center for the Study of Reading, University of Illinois, 1979.

Sprenger, M. *Memory 101 for Educators.* Thousand Oaks, Calif.: Corwin Press, 2007.

Staal, Laura A. "The Story Face: An Adaptation of Story Mapping That Incorporates Visualization and Discovery Learning to Enhance Reading and Writing." *The Reading Teacher* 54 (September 2000): 26–31.

Stahl, Steven A. "Saying the 'P' Word: Nine Guidelines for Exemplary Phonics Instruction." *The Reading Teacher* 45 (April 1992): 618–625.

Stahl, Steven A. "Separating the Rhetoric from the Effects: Whole Language in Kindergarten and First Grade." In *Reading, Language, and Literacy: Instruction for the Twenty-First Century*, edited by F. Lehr and J. Osborn. Hillsdale, N.J.: Erlbaum, 1994, 101–114.

Stahl, Steven A. "Instructional Models in Reading: An Introduction." In *Instructional Models in Reading*, edited by Steven A. Stahl and David A. Hayes. Mahwah, N.J.: Erlbaum, 1997, 1–29.

Stahl, Steven A., Jean Osborn, and Fran Lehr. *Beginning to Read: Thinking and Learning About Print—A Summary.* Champaign: Center for the Study of Reading, University of Illinois, 1990.

Stahl, Steven A., and Sandra J. Vancil. "Discussion Is What Makes Semantic Maps Work in Vocabulary Instruction." *The Reading Teacher* 40 (October 1986): 62–67.

Standards for the Assessment of Reading and Writing. Prepared by the IRA/NCATE Joint Task Force on Assessment. Newark, Del.: International Reading Association, 1996.

Stanovich, Keith. "Romance and Reality." *The Reading Teacher* 47 (December 1993/January 1994): 280–291.

Stauffer, Russell G. "Reading as a Cognitive Process." *Elementary English* 44 (April 1968): 348.

Stauffer, Russell G. *Teaching Reading as a Thinking Process.* New York: Harper & Row, 1969.

Stevens, Kathleen C. "Can We Improve Reading by Teaching Background Information?" *Journal of Reading* 25 (January 1982): 326–329.

Stewart, Roger A., Edward E. Paradis, Bonita D. Ross, and Mary Jane Lewis. "Student Voices: What Works in Literature-Based Developmental Reading." *Journal of Adolescent & Adult Literacy* 39 (March 1996): 468–478.

Stiggins, R. J. *Student-Involved Classroom Assessment for Learning.* Upper Saddle River, N.J.: Pearson/Merrill/Prentice Hall, 2005.

Stivers, Jan. "The Writing Partners Project." *Phi Delta Kappan* 77 (June 1996): 694–695.

Strassman, Barbara K., and Trisha O'Connell. "Authoring with Video." *The Reading Teacher* 61 (December 2007/January 2008): 330–333.

Strickland, Dorothy. "Some Tips for Using Big Books." *The Reading Teacher* 41 (May 1988): 966–968.

Strickland, Dorothy, and Lesley Morrow. "Creating a Print-Rich Environment." *The Reading Teacher* 42 (November 1988): 156–157.

Strickland, Dorothy, and Lesley Morrow. "Family Literacy: Sharing Good Books." *The Reading Teacher* 43 (March 1990): 518–519.

Struggling Readers, Day 1: Closing the Decoding Crack. Bothell, Wash.: The Wright Group, 2000.

Sullivan, Jane. "The Electronic Journal: Combining Literacy and Technology." *The Reading Teacher* 52 (September 1998): 90–92.

Sulzby, Elizabeth. "I Can Write! Encouraging Emergent Writers." In *Early Childhood Education 94/95*, 15th ed., edited by Karen M. Paciorek and Joyce H. Munro. Guilford, Conn.: Dushkin, 1994, 204–207.

Sulzby, Elizabeth, William H. Teale, and George Kamberelis. "Emergent Writing in the Classroom: Home and School Connections." In *Emerging Literacy: Young Children Learn to Read and Write*, edited by Dorothy Strickland and Lesley Morrow. Newark, Del.: International Reading Association, 1989.

Sumida, Anna Y., and Meleanna A Meyer. "T⁴ = Teaching to the Fourth Power: Transformative Inquiry and the Stirring of Cultural Waters." *Language Arts* 83 (May 2006): 437–449.

Sweet, Anne, and Catherine Snow. *Rethinking Reading Comprehension.* New York: Guilford Press, 2003.

Swindall, Vickie, and R. Jeffrey Cantrell. "Character Interviews Help Bring Literature to Life." *The Reading Teacher* 53 (September 1999): 23–25.

Tate, Marcia. *Reading and Language Arts Worksheets Don't Grow Dendrites: 20 Literacy Strategies That Engage the Brain.* Thousand Oaks, Calif.: Corwin Press, 2005.

Taylor, Barbara, D. Peterson, P. David Pearson, and Michael Rodriguez. "Looking Inside Classrooms: Reflecting on the 'How' as Well as the 'What' in Effective Reading Instruction." *The Reading Teacher* 56 (December 2002): 270–279.

Teale, William H., and Linda B. Gambrell. "Raising Urban Students' Literacy Achievement by Engaging in Authentic, Challenging Work." *The Reading Teacher* 60 (May 2007): 728–739.

Teale, William, and Elizabeth Sulzby. "Emergent Literacy: New Perspectives." In *Emerging Literacy: Young Children Learn to Read and Write*, edited by Dorothy Strickland and Lesley Morrow. Newark, Del.: International Reading Association, 1989.

Thelen, Judith N. "Vocabulary Instruction and Meaningful Learning." *Journal of Reading* 29 (April 1986): 603–609.

Thornburg, David. *The New Basics: Education and the Future of Work in the Telematic Age.* Alexandria, Va.: Association for Supervision and Curriculum Development, 2002.

Tierney, Robert J., and James W. Cunningham. "Research on Teaching Reading Comprehension." In *Handbook of Reading Research*, edited by P. David Pearson et al. New York: Longman, 1984.

Tomlinson, Carol Ann. *Fulfilling the Promise of the Differentiated Classroom: Strategies and Tools for Responsive Teaching.* Alexandria, Va.: Association for Supervision and Curriculum Development, 2003.

Tomlinson, Carol Ann. "Learning to Love Assessment," *Educational Leadership* 65 (December 2007/January 2008): 8–13.

Tovani, Cris. *I Read It, But I Don't Get It: Comprehension Strategies for Adolescent Readers.* Portland, Maine: Stenhouse, 2000.

Tovey, Duane R. "Children's Grasp of Phonics Terms vs. Sound-Symbol Relationships." *The Reading Teacher* 33 (January 1980): 431–437.

Tower, Cathy. "Questions That Matter: Preparing Elementary Students for the Inquiry Process." *The Reading Teacher* 53 (April 2000): 550–557.

Trachtenburg, Phyllis. "Using Children's Literature to Enhance Phonics Instruction." *The Reading Teacher* 43 (May 1990): 648–654.

Trelease, Jim. *The Read-Aloud Handbook*, 6th ed. New York: Viking Penguin, 2006.

Tunnell, Michael, and James Jacobs. *Children's Literature, Briefly.* Upper Saddle River, N.J.: Pearson, 2008.

Tyner, Beverly, and Sharon Green. *Small-Group Reading Instruction: A Differentiated Teaching Model for Intermediate Readers, Grades 3–8.* Newark, Del.: International Reading Association, 2005.

Tyson, Eleanore S., and Lee Mountain. "A Riddle or Pun Makes Learning Words Fun." *The Reading Teacher* 36 (November 1982): 170–173.

U.S. Department of Education. *President Clinton's Call to Action for American Education in the 21st Century: Technological Literacy*, 1997. Retrieved from http://www.ed.gov/updates/PresEdPlan/part11.html.

Valenza, Joyce Kasman. "Library as Multimedia Studio." *Electronic Learning* 16 (November/December 1996): 56–57.

Valmont, William J. "Cloze Deletion Patterns: How Deletions Are Made Makes a Big Difference." *The Reading Teacher* 37 (November 1983): 172–175.

Valmont, William J. *Technology for Literacy Teaching and Learning.* Boston: Houghton Mifflin, 2003.

Van Horn, Leigh. "The Character Within Us: Readers Connect with Characters to Create Meaning and Understanding." *Journal of Adolescent & Adult Literacy* 40 (February 1997): 342–347.

Van Leeuwen, Charlene, and Martha Gabriel. "Beginning to Write with a Word Processor: Integrating Writing Process and Technology in a Primary Classroom." *The Reading Teacher* 60 (February 2007): 420–429.

Vardell, Sylvia M., Nancy L. Hadaway, and Terrell A. Young. "Matching Books and Readers: Selecting Literature for English Learners." *The Reading Teacher* 59 (May 2006): 734–741.

Vaughn, S., P. Mathes, S. Linan-Thompson, and D. Francis. "Teaching English Language Learners at Risk for Reading Disabilities to Read in English or Spanish: Putting Research into Practice." *Learning Disabilities Research and Practice* 20 (2005): 58–67.

Veatch, Jeanette. "From the Vantage of Retirement." *The Reading Teacher* 49 (1996): 510–516.

Villaume, Susan Kidd, and Edna Greene Brabham. "Comprehension Instruction: Beyond Strategies." *The Reading Teacher* 55 (April 2002): 672–675.

Villaume, Susan Kidd, and Edna Green Brabham. "Questions and Answers." *The Reading Teacher* 56 (February 2003): 478–482.

Vygotsky, Lev. *Thought and Language*, rev. ed., edited by Alex Kozulin. Cambridge, Mass.: MIT Press, 1986.

Wade, Anne, Phillip Abrami, and Jennifer Sclater. "An Electronic Portfolio to Support Learning," *Canadian Journal of Learning and Technology* 31 (Fall 2005). Retrieved from http://www.cjlt.ca/content/vol31.3/wade.html.

Wade, S. E., and J. R. Fauske. "Dialogue Online: Prospective Teachers' Discourse Strategies in Computer-Mediated Discussions." *Reading Research Quarterly* 39 (April/May/June 2004): 134–160.

Wagstaff, Janiel M. "Building Practical Knowledge of Letter-Sound Correspondences: A Beginner's Word Wall and Beyond." *The Reading Teacher* 51 (December 1997/January 1998): 298–304.

Walberg, Herbert J., Victoria Chou Hare, and Cynthia A. Pulliam. "Social-Psychological Perceptions and Reading Comprehension." In *Comprehension and Teaching: Research Reviews*, edited by John T. Guthrie. Newark, Del.: International Reading Association, 1981, 140–159.

Walker, Barbara. *Diagnostic Teaching of Reading: Techniques for Instruction and Assessment.* Upper Saddle River, N.J.: Prentice Hall, 2000.

Walker, Barbara. *Diagnostic Teaching of Reading: Techniques for Instruction and Assessment.* Upper Saddle River, N.J.: Prentice-Hall, 2005.

Walker, Barbara. *Diagnostic Teaching of Reading: Techniques for Instruction and Assessment.* Upper Saddle River, N.J.: Pearson/Prentice Hall, 2008.

Walker-Dalhouse, Doris, A. Derick Dalhouse, and Dennis Mitchell. "Development of a Literature-Based Middle School Reading Program: Insights Gained." *Journal of Adolescent & Adult Literacy* 40 (February 1997): 362–370.

Waller, T. Gary. *Think First, Read Later! Piagetian Prerequisites for Reading.* Newark, Del.: International Reading Association, 1977.

Walmsley, Sean A. "Getting the Big Idea: A Neglected Goal for Reading Comprehension." *The Reading Teacher* 60 (November 2006): 281–285.

Walshe, R. D. "Donald Graves in Australia." In *Donald Graves in Australia—"Children Want to Write . . . ,"* edited by R. D. Walshe. Rozelle, NSW, Australia: Primary English Teaching Association, 1986.

Ware, Paige D. "From Sharing Time to Showtime! Valuing Diverse Venues for Storytelling in Technology-Rich Classrooms." *Language Arts* 84 (September 2006): 45–54.

Watson, Dorothy J. "Whole Language: Why Bother?" *The Reading Teacher* 47 (May 1994): 600–607.

Watson, Jerry J. "An Integral Setting Tells More Than When and Where." *The Reading Teacher* 44 (May 1991): 638–646.

Waugh, Joyce Clark. "Using LEA in Diagnosis." *Journal of Reading* 37 (September 1993): 56–57.

Weaver, Phyllis, and Fredi Shonhoff. "Subskill and Holistic Approaches to Reading Instruction." In *Readings on Reading Instruction*, edited by Albert J. Harris and Edward R. Sipay. New York: Longman, 1984.

Weeg, Patti. "See What's Going On . . ." Retrieved from http://www.globalclassroom.org on September 16, 2007. The page was last updated on July 13, 2006.

Weissman, Kathleen E. "Using Paragraph Frames to Complete a K-W-L." *The Reading Teacher* 50 (November 1996): 271–272.

Wendt, Jeremy, and Jason Beach. "Educational Technology." Presentation at Tennessee Technological University, Cookeville, August 14, 2007.

Wepner, Shelley B., and Lucinda C. Ray. "Using Technology for Reading Development." In *Linking Literacy and Technology; A Guide for K–8 Classrooms*, edited by Shelley B. Wepner, William J. Valmont, and Richard Thurlow. Newark, Del.: International Reading Association, 2000, 76–105.

Wertheim, Judy. "Teaching Guides for Novels." *The Reading Teacher* 42 (December 1988): 262.

Whaley, Jill Fitzgerald. "Story Grammars and Reading Instruction." *The Reading Teacher* 34 (April 1981): 762–771.

White, Thomas G., Joanne Sowell, and Alice Yanagihara. "Teaching Elementary Students to Use Word-Part Clues." *The Reading Teacher* 42 (January 1989): 302–308.

Whitin, Phyllis. "Leading into Literature Circles Through the Sketch-to-Sketch Strategy." *The Reading Teacher* 55 (February 2002): 444–450.

Whitin, Phyllis E., and David J. Whitin. "The Numbers and Beyond: Language Lessons for the Mathematics Classroom." *Language Arts* 74 (February 1997): 108–115.

Wiggins, Grant, and Jay McTighe. *Understanding by Design.* Alexandria, Va.: Association for Supervision and Curriculum Development, 1998.

Wiggins, Robert A. "Large Group Lesson/Small Group Follow-Up: Flexible Grouping in a Basal Reading Program." *The Reading Teacher* 47 (March 1994): 450–460.

Wikipedia. "Wiki." Last modified July 23, 2006. Retrieved from http://en.wikipedia.org/wiki/Wiki on August 29, 2007.

Wilhelm, Jeff. "Literacy by Design: Why Is All This Technology So Important?" *Voices from the Middle* 7 (March 2000): 4–14.

Williams, Bronwyn T. "Girl Power in a Digital World: Considering the Complexity of Gender, Literacy, and Technology." *Journal of Adolescent & Adult Literacy* 50 (December 2006/January 2007): 300–307.

Williams, Cheri, and Ruth P. Lundstrom. "Strategy Instruction During Word Study and Interactive Writing Activities." *The Reading Teacher* 61 (November 2007): 204–212.

Williams, Joanna P. "Reading Comprehension Strategies and Teacher Preparation." In *What Research Has to Say About Reading Instruction*, edited by Alan E. Farstrup and S. Jay Samuels. Newark, Del.: International Reading Association, 2002, 243–260.

Williams, T. Lee. "'Reading' the Painting: Exploring Visual Literacy in the Primary Grades." *The Reading Teacher* 60 (April 2007): 636–642.

Wiseman, Donna L. "Helping Children Take Early Steps Toward Reading and Writing." *The Reading Teacher* 37 (January 1984): 340–344.

Wixson, Karen K. "Questions About a Text: What You Ask About Is What Children Learn." *The Reading Teacher* 37 (December 1983): 287–293.

Wolfe, Patricia, and Pamela Nevills. *Building the Reading Brain, PreK-3.* Thousand Oaks, Calif.: Corwin Press, 2004.

Wolk, Steven. "Using Picture Books to Teach for Democracy." *Language Arts* 82 (September 2004): 26–35.

Wood, Delores, and Joanne Nurss. "Print Rich Classrooms Support the Development of Print Awareness." *Georgia Journal of Reading* 14 (Fall/Winter 1988): 21–23.

Wortham, Sue. *The Integrated Classroom.* Englewood Cliffs, N.J.: Merrill, 1996.

Worthing, Bernadette, and Barbara Laster. "Strategy Access Rods: A Hands-On Approach." *The Reading Teacher* 56 (October 2002): 122–123.

Worthy, Jo. "A Matter of Interest: Literature That Hooks Reluctant Readers and Keeps Them Reading." *The Reading Teacher* 50 (November 1996): 204–212.

Yatvin, Joanne, Constance Weaver, and Elaine Garan. "Reading First: Cautions and Recommendations." *Language Arts* 81 (September 2003): 28–33.

Yopp, Hallie Kay. "Developing Phonemic Awareness in Young Children." *The Reading Teacher* 45 (May 1992): 696–703.

Yopp, Hallie. "Read-Aloud Books for Developing Phonemic Awareness: An Annotated Bibliography." *The Reading Teacher* 48 (March 1995a): 538–542.

Yopp, Hallie Kay. "A Test for Assessing Phonemic Awareness in Young Children." *The Reading Teacher* 49 (September 1995b): 20–29.

Yopp, Ruth Helen, and Hallie Kay Yopp. "Sharing Informational Text with Young Children." *The Reading Teacher* 53 (February 2000): 410–423.

Yopp, Ruth Helen, and Hallie Kay Yopp. "Ten Important Words Plus: A Strategy for Building Word Knowledge." *The Reading Teacher* 61 (October 2007): 157–160.

Zarillo, James. "Teachers' Interpretations of Literature-Based Reading." *The Reading Teacher* 43 (October 1989): 22–28.

Zarillo, James, and Carole Cox. "Efferent and Aesthetic Teaching." In *Stance and Literary Understanding: Exploring the Theories, Research, and Practice,* edited by Joyce Many and Carole Cox. Norwood, N.J.: Ablex, 1992.

Zolt, Nina. "Urban Mythbusters: Rethinking Some Things We 'Know' about Urban Schools." *Education Week* 24, no. 18 (2005): 31.

Zucker, Carol. "Using Whole Language with Students Who Have Language and Learning Disabilities." *The Reading Teacher* 46 (May 1993): 660–670.

Zumwalt, Marcus. "Words of Fortune." *The Reading Teacher* 56 (February 2003): 439–441.

Zutell, J., and Timothy V. Rasinski. "Training Teachers to Attend to Their Students' Oral Reading Fluency." *Theory into Practice* 30 (1991): 211–217.

Zygouris-Coe, Vicky, Matthew Wiggins, and Lourdes Smith. "Engaging Students with Text: The 3-2-1 Strategy." *The Reading Teacher* 58 (December 2004/January 2005): 381–384.

Name Index

Subject Index

A

Abbreviation expansion application, 478

Accelerated Reader (AR) program, 509–510

Accents (accentuation), 132, 135, 138, 156–157

Achievement tests. *See* Formal assessment

Adequate yearly progress (AYP), 38

Adverb referents, 268

Aesop's fables, 271

Aesthetic stance by reader, 22–23

Affective aspects of reading, 15–18
  aesthetic stance, 22–23
  defined, 6, 15
  in fluency development, 16–17
  interests, 17
  internal versus external motivation, 15–16
  negative attitudes, changing, 17, 18
  positive attitudes, nurturing, 15
  positive reinforcement, 15
  self-concepts, 17–18

Affixes. *See* Prefixes; Suffixes

Allusion, 204

Alphabet books, 152, 496

Alphabetic principle, 81, 149, 153

Alphabetical order, 444
  card catalog, 406
  dictionaries, 387, 401, 403
  indexes, 398–399
  reference books, 401
  word cards, 346

Alternative and authentic assessments, 43–61
  bias issues, 60
  conferences and interviews, 48–49
  defined, 43
  informal tests, 56–60, 61
  literary interests appraisal, 55, 56
  observation, 43–47
  portfolio, 49, 51–52, 53
  retellings, 49, 50
  rubrics, 48, 50
  self-appraisal, 52–55

Analogies, 194–195

Analogy approach to phonics instruction, 163–165

Analytic approach to phonics instruction, 158–160

Anaphora, 267–268, 269

Anecdotal records of observations, 44, 45

Anticipation guides
  as comprehension aids, 233–235
  as content-area study guides, 436

Anticipation/reaction guides
  as comprehension aids, 236–238
  as content-area study guides, 436
  for this book, 2, 36, 72, 110, 142, 174, 217, 260, 308, 356, 388, 425, 472

Antonyms, 213

Appendices in books, 400

Application (comprehension strategy), 246

Appositives, 187

Approaches to reading instruction
  anticipation/reaction guide, 308
  basal reading programs, 310–322
  computer use, 351
  directed reading activity (DRA), 315–316, 317–319
  directed reading-thinking activity (DRTA), 320–322
  eclectic approaches, 351–353
  guided reading, 88, 316, 320
  individualized reading approach, 334, 336–340, 352
  language experience approach (LEA), 117, 343–350, 352
  literature circles, 47, 55, 328, 330–331
  literature-based, 322–343
  phonics instruction, 307
  programmed instruction, 351
  thematic literature units, 331–334, 335, 352
  whole-class reading of core book, 325–328, 329, 352

AR (Accelerated Reader) program, 509–510

Art, as response to literature, 383

Assessments, 35–70. *See also* Formal assessment
  adequate yearly progress, 38
  alternative and authentic, 43–61
  anticipation/reaction guide, 36
  audio recordings for, 513
  basal publisher offerings, 310, 311
  of comprehension, 225–226, 227, 416
  with computer-managed instruction, 509
  conferences and interviews, 48–49
  content-area reading, 424
  as continuous process, 35–36
  current trends, 37–39
  curriculum standards, 37–39
  defined, 35
  difficulty of materials, 65–68, 227–228, 428
  with directed reading-thinking activities, 322
  disaggregated data for subgroups, 38, 39
  for early intervention, 105–106
  e-book recall lists for, 488
  of emergent literacy, 61–62, 105–106
  formal, 35, 40–43
  formative, 35
  in individualized reading approach, 336, 337, 338–339
  informal tests, 56–60, 61
  intervention guided by, 35–36, 62–68
  with language experience approach, 345
  literary interests appraisal, 55, 56
  literature log for, 330
  literature-based instruction and, 323
  observation, 43–47, 322, 345
  oral-reading skills, 382
  performance-based, 48
  portfolio, 49, 51–52, 53
  questions for, 295, 299, 300–301
  of reading interests, 378
  reference guide, 517–521
  retellings, 49, 50, 246
  rubrics, 48, 50